T0142057

Lecture Notes of the Institute for Computer Sciences, Social Informatics and Telecommunications Engineering 442

More information about this series at https://link.springer.com/bookseries/8197

Sara Paiva · Xuejun Li · Sérgio Ivan Lopes ·
Nishu Gupta · Danda B. Rawat · Asma Patel ·
Hamid Reza Karimi (Eds.)

Science and Technologies for Smart Cities

7th EAI International Conference, SmartCity360°
Virtual Event, December 2–4, 2021
Proceedings

Springer

Editors
Sara Paiva (iD)
Instituto Politécnico de Viana do Castelo
Viana do Castelo, Portugal

Sérgio Ivan Lopes (iD)
Instituto Politécnico de Viana do Castelo
Viana do Castelo, Portugal

Danda B. Rawat
Howard University
Washington, DC, USA

Hamid Reza Karimi
Politecnico di Milano
Milan, Italy

Xuejun Li
Auckland University of Technology
Auckland, New Zealand

Nishu Gupta (iD)
SRM Institute of Science and Technology
Chennai, India

Asma Patel
Staffordshire University
Stoke-on-Trent, UK

ISSN 1867-8211   ISSN 1867-822X (electronic)
Lecture Notes of the Institute for Computer Sciences, Social Informatics
and Telecommunications Engineering
ISBN 978-3-031-06370-1   ISBN 978-3-031-06371-8 (eBook)
https://doi.org/10.1007/978-3-031-06371-8

This Springer imprint is published by the registered company Springer Nature Switzerland AG
The registered company address is: Gewerbestrasse 11, 6330 Cham, Switzerland

Preface

We are delighted to introduce the proceedings of the 7th edition of the EAI SmartCity360°
International Convention (SmartCity360° 2021) which, due to the safety concerns and
travel restrictions caused by the COVID-19 pandemic, took place online, for the second
consecutive year, in a live stream performed via the Zoom platform. Considering the
commitment of the entire team involved in this event, the technical and scientific quality
was not affected in any way by the restrictions that this year still imposed.

This volume of proceedings refers to six of the conferences co-located at the convention, in distinct areas of the smart cities field, which brought together researchers,
developers, and practitioners from all around the world. The program of SmartCity360°
2021 consisted of 45 papers selected from 109 submissions in a single-blind review
process.

EdgeIoT 2021 (the 2nd International Conference on Intelligent Edge Processing
in the IoT Era) aimed at addressing the decentralization of contemporary processing
paradigms, notably edge processing, focusing on the increasing demand for intelligent
processing at the edge of the network, which is paving the way to the intelligent IoT era,
and it featured ten contributions.

IC4S 2021 (the 2nd International Conference on Cognitive Computing and Cyber
Physical Systems) received seven contributions that presented fundamental principles
emphasizing the integration of cyber and physical elements, addressing infrastructure
for building cyber physical systems (CPS), and highlighting the design, implementation,
and investigation of CPS applications.

S-Cube 2021 (the 12th International Conference on Sensor Systems and Software)
featured six contributions that focused on the state-of-the-art in the broad area of system
development and software support for wireless sensors networks (WSN).

SmartGov 2021 (the 3rd International Conference on Smart Governance for Sustainable Smart Cities) featured seven contributions that addressed mainly the rapid change
in the ways that cities and settlements have to be managed and also how emerging digital technologies offer new ways for local government to understand and monitor the
dynamics of the city.

SmartGift 2021 (the 6th International Conference on Smart Grid and Innovative
Frontiers in Telecommunications) featured five contributions that addressed connections
and interactions between networked entities to allow the seamless provision of a wide
variety of new services that provide a way of life that is secure, convenient, comfortable,
and sustainable in future smart cities.

Finally, PFSM 2021 (the 1st International Conference on Privacy and Forensics in
Smart Mobility) featured ten contributions focused on the areas of privacy-preserving
and digital forensics for the emerging smart mobility systems and the wider field of
smart cities.

The coordination between all members of the team was fundamental to the success of
SmartCity360° 2021. A word of appreciation to the President of the European Alliance
for Innovation, Imrich Chlamtac, to the Convention Manager, Elena Davydova, to the

Conference Team Supervisor, Karolina Marcinova, and to all of the Conference Managers who impeccably supported all the logistics of each of the conferences involved in the convention. A word of appreciation also to all Conference Chairs and Organizing Committee members who professionally contributed to the success and scientific quality of the papers that are part of this volume. To the reviewers, also a word of appreciation for the time they dedicated to making their precious contributions to further raise the scientific quality of the final versions of the papers.

Finally, a special mention to the authors who submitted their work to the 7th edition of the EAI SmartCity360° International Convention. We believe that this convention constituted, and will continue to constitute, an excellent forum to discuss science and technology aspects relevant to smart cities.

March 2022   Sara Paiva

Organization

SmartGift 2021

Advisory Committee

Imrich Chlamtac   University of Trento, Italy

Steering Committee

Imrich Chlamtac   University of Trento, Italy
Kun Yang   University of Essex, UK
Victor C. M. Leung   University of British Columbia, Canada

Organizing Committee

Convention Co-chairs

Sara Paiva   Instituto Politécnico de Viana do Castelo, Portugal
Henrique Santos   University of Minho, Portugal

Convention Manager

Elena Davydova   European Alliance for Innovation, Slovakia

General Chairs

Peter Chong   Auckland University of Technology, New Zealand
Jack Xuejun Li   Auckland University of Technology, New Zealand

Technical Program Committee Chair

Saeed Rehman   Flinders University, Australia

Sponsorship and Exhibit Chair

Hakilo Sabit   Auckland University of Technology, New Zealand

Local Chair

Minh Nguyen   Auckland University of Technology, New Zealand

Workshops Chair

Arun Kumar   National Institute of Technology, India

Publicity and Social Media Chair

Boon-Chong Seet   Auckland University of Technology, New Zealand

Publications Chair

G. G. Md. Nawaz Ali   University of Charleston, USA

Web Chair

Minglong Zhang   Auckland University of Technology, New Zealand

Technical Program Committee

James Cercone	University of Charleston, USA
Ferdous Wahid Khan	Airbus, Germany
Craig Baguley	Auckland University of Technology, New Zealand
Ramon Zamora	Auckland University of Technology, New Zealand
Shafiqur Tito	Manukau Institute of Technology, New Zealand
Xiaoyou Lin	University of Auckland, New Zealand
Asim Anwar	University of Lahore, Pakistan
Paul Gardner-Stephen	Flinders University, Australia
Ishtiaq Ahmad	University of South Australia
Fakhrul Alam	Massey University, New Zealand
Sayan Kumar Ray	Manukau Institute of Technology, New Zealand
Aziz Ahmad	University of New South Wales, Australia
Salman Naseer	University of the Punjab, Pakistan
Shafiq Alam	Whitireia Institute of Technology, New Zealand
Md. Noor-A-Rahim	University College Cork, Ireland
Mohammad Khyam	Central Queensland University, Australia
Md. Amjad Hossain	Shepherd University, USA
Jim Samuel	University of Charleston, USA
Ek Esawi James	Madison University, USA
Yiyang Pei	Singapore Institute of Technology, Singapore
Shiying Han	Nankai University, China
Haibo Zhang	University of Otago, New Zealand
Pushpendu Kar	University of Nottingham Ningbo China, China
Shahinoor Rahman	New Jersey City University, USA
Sira Yongchareon	Auckland University of Technology, New Zealand
Peter Chong	Auckland University of Technology, New Zealand
Xuejun Li	Auckland University of Technology, New Zealand

Boon-Chong Seet	Auckland University of Technology, New Zealand
Saeed Rehman	Flinders University, Australia
Minglong Zhang	Auckland University of Technology, New Zealand
Arun Kumar	National Institute of Technology, India
Hakilo Sabit	Auckland University of Technology, New Zealand
G. G. Md. Nawaz Ali	University of Charleston, USA
Minh Nguyen	Auckland University of Technology, New Zealand
Jing Ma	Auckland University of Technology, New Zealand
Hui Li	Peking University, China
Hanxu Hou	Dongguan University of Technology, China
Huayu Zhang	Purple Mountain Laboratories, China
Lu Lu	University of Chinese Academy of Sciences, China
Sanjib Kumar Panda	National University of Singapore, Singapore
Ashok Kumar Turuk	NIT Rourkela, India

Edge-IoT 2021

Steering Committee

Imrich Chlamtac	University of Trento, Italy
Sérgio Ivan Lopes	Instituto Politécnico de Viana do Castelo, Portugal

Organizing Committee

General Chair

Sérgio Ivan Lopes	Instituto Politécnico de Viana do Castelo, Portugal

General Co-chairs

Mauro Migliardi	University of Padua, Italy
Pedro Santos	Instituto Politécnico do Porto, Portugal

Technical Program Committee Co-chairs

Paula Fraga-Lamas	Universidade da Coruña, Spain
Tiago M. Fernández-Caramés	Universidade da Coruña, Spain

Workshops Chair

António Moreira	Instituto Politécnico do Cávado e do Ave, Portugal

Posters Track Chair

José Lima   Instituto Politécnico de Bragança, Portugal

Publicity and Social Media Chair

Pedro Pinto   Instituto Politécnico de Viana do Castelo, Portugal

Publications Chairs

Alessio Merlo   University of Genoa, Italy
Luca Verderame   University of Genoa, Italy

Web Chair

Silvestre Malta   Instituto Politécnico de Viana do Castelo, Portugal

Technical Program Committee

Cezary Orłowski   WSB University in Gdańsk, Poland
Catarina Silva   Universidade de Coimbra, Portugal
Paula María Castro Castro   Universidade da Coruña, Spain
Dixys Leonardo Hernández Rojas   Technical University of Machala, Ecuador
Chi-Hua Chen   Fuzhou University, China
Luca Bianconi   Gruppo Sigla s.r.l., Italy
Pedro Miguel Moreira   Instituto Politécnico de Viana do Castelo, Portugal
Teodoro Aguilera Benítez   University of Extremadura, Spain
Paulo Leitão   Instituto Politécnico de Bragança, Portugal
Josu Bilbao   IKERLAN Technology Center, Spain
Felix Freitag   Technical University of Catalonia, Spain
Fernando J. Álvarez Franco   Universidad de Extremadura, Spain
Daniel Albuquerque   Instituto Politécnico de Viseu, Portugal
Luís Ferreira   Instituto Politécnico do Cavado e do Ave, Portugal
António M. R. Cruz   Instituto Politécnico de Viana do Castelo, Portugal
Paulo Pedreiras   Universidade de Aveiro, Portugal
Alberto Sillitti   Innopolis University, Russia
Luigi Benedicenti   University of New Brunswick, Canada
Ilsun You   Soonchunhyang University, South Korea
Fang-Ye Leu   Tunghai University, Taiwan
Kangbin Yim   Soonchunhyang University, South Korea
Carlo Ferrari   Universita' degli Studi di Padova, Italy
Francesco Palmieri   Universita' degli Studi di Salerno, Italy
Riccardo Pecori   Università del Sannio, Italy
Valentina Casola   Università "Federico II" di Napoli, Italy
Alessandra De Benedictis   Università "Federico II" di Napoli, Italy

Massimiliano Rak	Università della Campania Luigi Vanvitelli, Italy
Alexandre Meslin	Pontifical Catholic University of Rio de Janeiro, Brazil
Luís Barreto	Instituto Politécnico de Viana do Castelo, Portugal
Ahmad Keshavarz	Persian Gulf University, Iran
Habib Rostami	Persian Gulf University, Iran

IC4S 2021

Steering Committee

Imrich Chlamtac	University of Trento, Italy

Organizing Committee

General Chair

Nishu Gupta	SRM Institute of Science and Technology, India

Technical Program Committee Chair

Manuel J. Cabral S. Reis	University of Trás-os-Montes and Alto Douro, Portugal

Panels Chair

Isha Bharti	Capgemini America, Inc., India

Web Chair

Ahmad Hoirul Basori	King Abdulaziz University, Saudi Arabia

Publicity and Social Media Chair

Pascal Lorenz	University of Haute-Alsace, France

Publicity and Social Media Co-chair

Rani Deepika Balavendran Joseph	University of North Texas, USA

Workshops Chair

Hendra Yufit Riskiawan	State Polytechnic of Jember, Indonesia

Posters Track Chair

Parvesh Kumar   Vaagdevi College of Engineering, India

Sponsorship and Exhibits Chair

Srinivasa Kiran Gottapu   University of North Texas, USA

Publications Chair

Prakash Pareek   Vishnu Institute of Technology, India

Technical Program Committee

Sumathi Lakshmiranganatha   Los Alamos National Laboratory, USA
Mukesh Prasad   University of Technology Sydney, Australia
Pranjal Vyas   Nanyang Technological University, Singapore
Daniele Riboni   University of Cagliari, Italy
Ayantika Chatterjee   IIT Kharagpur, India
William Hurst   Wageningen University and Research,
                                         The Netherlands
Anuj Abraham   A*STAR, Singapore
Felix Härer   University of Fribourg, Switzerland
Justin Dauwels   Delft University of Technology, The Netherlands
Nguyen Tan Luy   Industrial University of Ho Chi Minh City,
                                         Vietnam
Palak Talwar   Lyft, USA
Teresa Guarda   Universidad Estatal Península de Santa Elena,
                                         Ecuador
Ariel Teles   University of Maranhão, Brazil
Raluca Maria Aileni   University Politehnica of Bucharest, Romania
Raghavendra Pal   NIT Surat, India
Anil Kumar Gupta   C-DAC, Pune, India
Dwi Putro Sarwo Setyohadi   State Polytechnic of Jember, Indonesia
Athanasios Kakarountas   University of Thessaly, Greece

SmartGov 2021

Steering Committee

Imrich Chlamtac   University of Trento, Italy

Organizing Committee

General Chair

Danda B. Rawat   Howard University, USA

Technical Program Committee Chairs

Yun Lin   Harbin Engineering University, China
Wenjia Li   New York Institute of Technology, USA
Varun Menon   SCMS School of Engineering and Technology,
                                            India

Web Chair

Babu Ram Dawadi   Tribhuvan University, Nepal

Publicity and Social Media Chair

Al-Sakib Khan Pathan   Independent University, Bangladesh

Workshops Chair

Kayhan Zrar Ghafoor   Knowledge University, Iraq

Publications Chairs

Linwei Niu   Howard University, USA
Danda B. Rawat   Howard University, USA

Posters Track Chairs

Linwei Niu   Howard University, USA
Sumarga Kumar Sah Tyagi   Zhongyuan University of Technology, China

Technical Program Committee

Tamanna Dalwai   Muscat College, Oman
Adriana Reveiu   Bucharest University of Economic Studies,
                                            Romania
Ralf-Martin Soe   Tallin University of Technology, Estonia
Teresa Pereira   Polytechnic Institute of Viana do Castelo,
                                            Portugal
Guan Gui   Nanjing University of Posts and
                                            Telecommunications, China
Lei Chen   Georgia Southern University, USA
Ruolin Zhou   University of Massachusetts Dartmouth, USA

Chao Li	RIKEN-AIP, Japan
Sai Huang	Beijing University of Posts and Telecommunications, China
Jianhua Tang	Seoul National University, South Korea
Jian Wang	Fudan University, China
Aman Shakya	Tribhuvan University, Nepal
Rajeeb Kumar Kanth	University of Turku, Finland
Pradeep Kumar Paudyal	Nepal Telecommunications Authority, Nepal
Basanta Joshi	Tribhuvan University, Nepal
Sandeep Verma	National Institute of Technology, Jalandhar, India
Nawab Muhammad Faseeh	Qureshi Sungkyunkwan University, South Korea
Bijoy Antony Jose	Cochin University of Science and Technology, India
M. V. Rajesh Maliyeckal	Model Engineering College, India
Shynu P. G.	Vellore Institute of Technology, Chennai, India
Ragesh Warrier	Adi Shankara Institute of Engineering & Technology, India
Xingwang Li	Henan Polytechnic University, China

PFSM 2021

Steering Committee

| Imrich Chlamtac | University of Trento, Italy |

Organizing Committee

General Chair

| Asma Patel | Staffordshire University, UK |

General Co-chair

| Esther Palomar | University of Alcala, Spain, and Birmingham City University, UK |

Technical Program Committee Chairs

| Rakan Aldmour | Staffordshire University, UK |
| Mostafa Tajdini | Staffordshire University, UK |

Web Chair

| Salameh Abu Rmeileh | Birmingham City University, UK |

Publicity and Social Media Chairs

Rakan Aldmour   Staffordshire University, UK
Salameh Abu Rmeileh   Birmingham City University, UK

Workshops Chair

Hoshang Kolivand   Liverpool John Moores University, UK

Sponsorship and Exhibits Chair

Asma Patel   Staffordshire University, UK

Publications Chair

Asma Patel   Staffordshire University, UK

Local Chair

Sara Paiva   Instituto Politécnico de Viana do Castelo, Portugal

Technical Program Committee

Shiva Asadianfam	Islamic Azad University, Qom, Iran
Zahra Rezaei	University of Lethbridge, Canada
Hossein Ahmadi	University of Birmingham, UK
Ataolalah Zarei	University of Windsor, Canada
Amjad Khan Rahman	Prince Sultan University, Saudi Arabia
Itimad Raheem Ali	UOITC, Iraq
Faris Amin M. Abuhashish	University of Petra, Jordan
Abdolvahab Ehsani Rad	Azad University, Iran
William Hurst	Wageningen University and Research, The Netherlands
Tansila Saba	Prince Sultan University, Saudi Arabia
Hasan Chizari	University of Gloucestershire, UK
Parvane Esmaeili	Girne American University, Cyprus
Gabor Kecskemeti	Liverpool John Moores University, UK
Anwar Yahya Ibrahim	Babylon University, Iraq
Saba Jodaki	Azad University, Iran
Alireza Norouzi	Azad University, Iran
Thar Baker Shamsa	University of Sharjah, UAE
Majid Harouni	CMPLab, Iran
Fares Yousefi	Liverpool John Moores University, UK
Hamid Rastgari	Azad University, Iran
Zorica Bogdanović	University of Belgrade, Serbia

Nicolas Sklavos	University of Patras, Greece
Anastasius Moumtzoglou	Aglaia Kyriakou Children's Hospital, Greece
Aliyi Lawal	Leeds Trinity University, UK
Ahmed Al-Masri	American University in the Emirates, UAE
Mamoun Alazab	Charles Darwin University, Australia
Thar M. S. Baker Shamsa	University of Sharjah, UAE

S-CUBE 2021

Steering Committee

| Imrich Chlamtac | University of Trento, Italy |
| Henrique Santos | University of Minho, Portugal |

Organizing Committee

General Chair

| Hamid Reza Karimi | Politecnico di Milano, Italy |

Technical Program Committee Chair

| Ahmet Enis Cetin | University of Illinois at Chicago, USA |

Posters and PhD Track Chair

| Dongsheng Yang | Northeastern University, USA |

Publicity and Social Media Chair

| Len Gelman | University of Huddersfield, UK |

Workshops Chair

| Ali Zemouche | Université de Lorraine, France |

Publications Chairs

| Josep M. Rossell | Universitat Politècnica de Catalunya, Spain |
| Defeng Wu | Jimei University, China |

Technical Program Committee

Gholamreza Anbarjafari (Shahab)	University of Tartu, Estonia
Ömer Nezih Gerek	Eskisehir Technical University, Turkey
Yusuf Ozturk	San Diego State University, USA

Xiao-Zhi Gao	University of Eastern Finland, Finland
Liu Jun	Singapore University of Technology and Design, Singapore
Zhengtian Wu	Suzhou University of Science and Technology, China
Kalyana Veluvolu	Kyungpook National University, South Korea
Sendren Xu	National Taiwan University of Science and Technology, Taiwan
B. D. Parameshachari	GSSS Institute of Engineering and Technology for Women, India
Jing Jin	East China University of Science and Technology, China
Gisela Pujol	Universitat Politècnica de Catalunya, Spain
Ning Wang	Harbin Engineering University, China
Hang Su	Politecnico di Milano, Italy

Contents

Cognitive Computing and Cyber Physical Systems

Sensor Systems and Software

Smart Grid and Innovative Frontiers in Telecommunications

Raspberry Pi-Based Intelligent Cyber Defense Systems for SMEs: An Exploratory Study

Sreenivas Sremath Tirumala[1]($\boxtimes$), Narayan Nepal[2], and Sayan Kumar Ray[1]

[1] School of Digital Technologies, Manukau Institute of Technology, Auckland, New Zealand
{sreenivas.tirumala,sayan.ray}@manukau.ac.nz

[2] Technology and Innovation Research Group, School of Information Technology, Whitecliffe, Christchurch, New Zealand
narayann@whitecliffe.ac.nz

Abstract. Ongoing ransomware attacks have forced business to think about security of their resources. Recently, small-to-medium enterprises (SMEs) have become easy targets for attackers since they don't have cyber defense mechanism in place other than simple firewall systems which are quite vulnerable. Cyber defense systems are costly and often not within the budget of SMEs which inspired to think about low cost yet highly efficient cyber defense solutions. This research explores the prospects of implementing a Raspberry Pi (Raspberry Pi)-based intelligent cyber-defense system (iCDS) for SME networks and Smart-homes to filter malicious contents from incoming traffic. Primarily, the work presented in this paper tries to evaluate the hardware capability of network interfaces (both internal, and attached) of Raspberry Pi for handle high volumes of incoming traffic. For this, we measure the network performance of the Raspberry Pi using the speed test software. The results show that the built in Ethernet interface outperforms the built in WiFi and external attached USB to Ethernet Adapter in terms of latency, download and upload throughput.

Keywords: Cyber defense · Raspberry-Pi · Intelligent cyber-defense system

1 Introduction

The internet revolution had notable impact on day-to-day activities of small-to-medium enterprises (SMEs). The cloudification (moving the software and other operations services to cloud) of SMEs partially impacted the dependence on local hardware and networking configurations. In recent times high speed internet has become a mandatory requirement for SMEs since majority of services are operated through cloud. This reliance on internet made SMEs exposed to the rest of the world, particularly for hackers as soft targets for exploitation particularly through ransomware attacks. The operational implications of providing a secure environment for SMEs is costly due to demanding resource requirements like manpower and technology. With limited operational budget, majority of SMEs rely on internet service providers (ISPs) and local firewall or antivirus software for providing IT security. In countries like New Zealand, where majority of the

S. Paiva et al. (Eds.): SmartCity360° 2021, LNICST 442, pp. 3–14, 2022.
https://doi.org/10.1007/978-3-031-06371-8_1

business are SMEs, impose budget and resource constraints and are not be able to afford operational costs for providing cyber defense systems. According to a survey conducted by InternetNZ, about 48% of computers in SMEs are used by hackers for testing new malware and/or as bots to simulate Denial of Service (DoS) attacks. Also, considering the recent events where gaming devices are usd for mining bitcoins, there is a high chance for Smart-Homes being easy targets by hackers. Hence, the internal networks of SMEs (and Smart-Homes) have to be secured enough to prevent such external attacks.

Simple rule-based firewalls (i.e., based on administrator defined policies) of SMEs have failed to prevent attacks from random malware. Rule-based intruder detection systems (IDS) have managed to counter the attacks to some extent but not fully capable to provide complete security to the organization's network. The rule-based systems simply monitor and filter incoming network traffic based on set of predefined rules (malware signatures) stored in the repository. From the literature and implementation documents [1] it can be concluded that highly efficient IDS is more powerful and assertive in identifying malicious packets entering a network. However, traditional IDS requires special equipment and manpower and thus are resource savvy and costly to install and maintain. Also, it requires regular upgrades to identify and respond to new threats. Thus, majority of the SMEs with limited budget find it difficult to implement and maintain an effective IDS. Implementing low cost IDS solution that can operate as Security as a Service (SECaaS) and can be offered as subscription-based service, is another option for SMEs to consider. However, SECaaS still relies on rule-based systems and incurs all drawbacks of cloud-based and other remote service offerings. Moreover, the fact that SECaaS is expensive, a major concern for SMEs and are not effective for networks with IoT based devices [2, 3]. With the rapid integration of IoT with traditional networks, SECaaS may become a burden as the subscriptions needs to be paid in spite of them being used few times, purging less resources or bandwidth.

Formerly, computer networks are protected by firewall from the external attacks which is not different ffor SMEs. However, the usage of algorithms to create malware with no standard structure or pattern challenged the capabilities of simple rule-based firewalls and IDS. Majority of the firewall systems as well as IDS are based on administrator defined policies, or in simple terms, rule based. At present, the traffic is monitored and 'filtered' based on a set of rules (malware signatures) present in the repository. The limitations of firewalls, IDS and SECaaS discussed above, indicate an immediate necessity of introducing a low-cost, low-resourced yet advanced network security solution for SMEs particularly for stopping, as much as possible, the malicious network traffic from entering the SME networks.

This inspired to undertake an exploratory study on designing an intelligent intruder detection systems (iids) that can be implemented on a low-cost device to provide a small budget solution to SMEs and smart-homes. There has been some background work on non-rule based (pattern recognition based) solution for detecting malware [4]. This paper explores the prospects of implementing a low-cost intelligent cyber defense system (iCDS), in form of a filtering device, to protect the SMEs from malicious traffic. The proposal considers the plausibility of using Raspberry Pi device as a commercial IDS with the purpose of filtering malicious network traffic from entering SME networks. Primarily, through a systematic experimental evaluation this work tries to explore the capability of network interfaces of Raspberry Pi device to understand their competence in handling high volumes of incoming traffic similar to commercial IDS systems. A comparative study of the performance of the inbuilt network interfaces, namely Ethernet (wired) and WiFi on the Raspberry Pi device, as well as an externally connected USB adapter interface (USB to Ethernet interface) are carried out in context to network parameters like latency, download throughput and upload throughput.

The remainder of the paper is structured as follows. Section 2 provides a review of the different filtering approaches and an introduction of the usage of Raspberry Pi-based IDS. While, Sect. 3 explores the prospects of using Raspberry Pi device as an iCDS, Sect. 4 discusses the evaluation results and Sect. 5 concludes the paper.

2 Review of Traditional IDS and Raspberry Pi-Based IDS

Traditional firewalls and IDSs use packet inspection for filtering traffic based on malware impressions [5, 6], and [7]. The workable solution proposed in [6] used a conceptual 'trust' based filtering that only allowed 'useful' packets to pass through. False positive results are often produced by the trust-based approach (similar to traditional fuzzy rule-based approach) and hence it was inconsistent in nature [6]. However, the proposed approach was successful in detecting malicious contents resulting from insider attacks in an organization. Since, iCDS mostly deals with identifying and filtering malicious contents from external network traffic trying to penetrate inside an SME network, insider attacks at this stage of the research is not considered. The filtering approach presented in [5] consisted of a restriction and access policy working as a traditional gateway. However, no evidence of experimental evaluation of the approach is proposed. An interesting machine learning based filtering model using Support Vector Machines (SVM) and Naïve Bayes is presented in [7], which also provides a good practical implementation scenario. However, due to its resource heavy and computationally complex nature, this proposed approach is unsuitable for SMEs. All these discussed research work provide an overview of important methods proposed for malicious network traffic filtering based on purpose and relevance. However, these implementations are generic in nature, not cost effective, and demand high configuration hardware for implementation. The next subsection discusses the implementation of Raspberry Pi-based low-cost IDS systems.

2.1 Background Study of Raspberry Pi-Based IDS

There is a lack of systematic literature review on implementing low cost IDS solutions for SMEs. Furthermore, very few research projects have been done on the feasibility of implementing Raspberry Pi (or a similar device)-based low-cost IDS for SMEs. This research gap provides an immediate necessity of such a research study to start with. A standard case of identifying low cost IDS solution for SME networks (containing different IoT devices), particularly using Raspberry Pi-based implementation, is relevant to the current research. IoT-based IDS implementations proposed by the research fraternity are mostly for non-commercial purpose and are either policy-based or graph-based. Policy-based approaches [8, 9] depend on a fixed predefined policy based on a specific domain or problem-based scenario similar to traditional network traffic packet

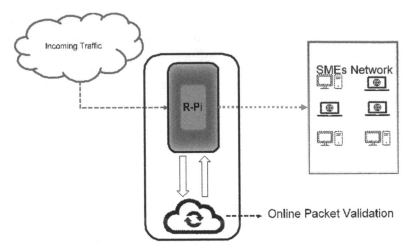

Fig. 1. The block diagram of iCDS representing various components

filtering approaches. The graph-based approaches [10] implement polices stored in a repository, which can be updated periodically (follows a dynamic rule). Such updates, however, lead to latency. A Raspberry Pi based firewall proposed by [11] to secure home networks, uses a remote cloud database with set of predefined rules. It uses on-board Ethernet interface for incoming network traffic and WiFi for outgoing traffic. The proposed approach is prone to delays and when applied for SME networks may incur significant latency. Another non-commercial implementation named as Pi- IDS is a Raspberry Pi 2.0-based standalone firewall implemented to filter websites in a school network. Although, an interesting concept, it has significant limitations in context to operation time and network traffic filtering capability.

Few research also proposed installing open source IDSs on Raspberry Pi so that it can replace a regular computer and can operate as a complete IDS of its own. For example, NetGaurd, proposed for traffic monitoring to track man-in-the-middle attacks, installs an open VPN and IDS software on Raspberry Pi to implement a complete IDS [12]. However, NetGaurd is nothing different to a traditional IDS and just provides privacy by hiding the IP of the monitoring source, as an extra feature. There are few other similar implementations like [3, 14]. The mere purpose of these implementation is to install and test IDS software on Raspberry Pi for various purposes. Two other research proposed by [15] and [16], used classification techniques for detection malicious contents in incoming network traffic. However, not only these two proposals lacked the technical details of hardware and software limitations of Raspberry Pi when experimenting it as an IDS, but also, they considered limited traffic with known malicious variants during the experiments. So, previous research mostly focused on studying how Raspberry Pi-based IDS can be implemented and if it can replace the traditional rule-based IDS implemented on normal computers. These implementations, knowingly or unknowingly overlooked the different challenges, including hardware limitations, to make Raspberry Pi operate as a fully commercial and real-world implementation of IDS. Furthermore, such implementations are vertically divided into cloud based and non-cloud based and do not emphasize the need of a mixed model or fail- over model.

2.2 Key Challenges to Consider in Raspberry Pi-Based IDS

On a practical note, the following challenges need to be considered if implementing a Raspberry Pi- based iCDS for filtering malicious network traffic contents from entering SME networks.

Handling High Volumes of Traffic: Raspberry Pi has one on-board Ethernet port, which limits and delays the flow of incoming (from the internet) and outgoing traffic (after filtering). How to handle such latency? If external Ethernet adapter is used, what are its implications in terms of power, cost and heat?

Processing Capabilities: Rasberry Pi, being an embedded system has a low end processer and its processing capabilities may create some issue while handling the traffic and may effect a significant increase in processing and serialization delay too.

Heat and Power Source: Is the hardware of Raspberry Pi capable enough to run continuously and uninterrupted for a week?

Storage and Real-Time Updates of Repository: Efficient mechanism to store and update the repository (for rule based, signature based or any other approach).

Hardware Capability for Storage and Execution of Algorithms: There is a need for AI-based IDS for packet level monitoring of network traffic to filter malicious content. Therefore, is it possible to store and efficiently execute powerful AI algorithms on Raspberry Pi?

The overall research consists of various plausibility studies for hardware, software and algorithms. The AI-based algorithmic evaluation is been initiated and published [4]. This systematic experimental evaluation presented in this paper is confined to understand the capability of input network interface(s) of Raspberry-Pi.

3 Raspberry Pi as an iCDS: From Perspective of Hardware Capability

This current research explores the prospects of implementing a Raspberry Pi (Raspberry Pi)-based low cost and intelligent cyber-defense system (iCDS) for SME networks, the architecture of which is presented in Fig. 1. In the iCDS, all incoming traffic to the network of the SME will go through the Raspberry Pi device that will scan the traffic for any malicious contents. The traffic will be monitored and filtered through a cloud-based filtering system and all malicious traffic will be quarantined for further actions by the SME. A deep learning-based signature verification system will be used for filtering the traffic in the next phase of this work. The primary focus of the work presented in this paper is to explore (a) the feasibility of using Raspberry Pi device to develop an iCDS, and (b) if the hardware components present in the latest Raspberry Pi devices are capable and compatible enough to support the use of Raspberry Pi-based iCDS for commercial SME networks. Use of Raspberry Pi as a low-cost device is becoming common in various IoT-based systems due to its simple operation, cost effective usage and support of open source software and operating systems. From the literature study presented in Sect. 2, it can be concluded that, although, research has shown the effectiveness of using Raspberry Pi-based commercial IDSs, previous work done on this aspect (i.e., use of Raspberry Pi as a commercial IDS) have not evaluated the efficiency and capabilities of the hardware components, especially, the Ethernet and WiFi modules on the Raspberry Pi board when handling input and output traffic. Also, typically, a commercially available IDS/Firewall will need gigabyte Ethernet-based connections for its input and output interfaces depending on the network requirements but each iCDS, on the other hand, need to have at least two physical interfaces with high end throughput to segregate the internal and external network traffic from each other. Thus, to explore whether it is possible to develop a Raspberry Pi-based iCDS, monitoring the performance of the different hardware interfaces on the Pi device when handling high volume of real traffic, is necessary. The following sub-sections will discuss these in detail.

3.1 Use of Raspberry Pi as an iCDS

Raspberry Pi is a low-cost computer that is commonly finding its usage in IoT and cyber-physical systems. Currently, Raspberry Pi 4 is the latest version and it has built in Ethernet interface and WiFi module. Owing to its tiny size, negligible power consumption and low cost, Raspberry Pi 4 can ideally be used as a commercial iCDS for filtering of malicious traffic entering the SME networks. However, traffic filtering using Raspberry Pi device will not be a straight forward process since Raspberry Pi can use only one network interface at any given time even if it may have multiple network interface connections (i.e., internet traffic only goes through the particular interface connection). For traffic filtering purpose an IDS needs at least two network interfaces, one for incoming traffic and the other for outgoing traffic. When connected to an external network, incoming and outgoing internet traffic to and from the network only flows through the particular interface of the Raspberry Pi that is directly connected to the external network, be it the Ethernet interface or the WiFi interface. Even if multiple USB adapters are connected to the different available ports in the Raspberry Pi device, internet traffic from the external network will only flow through one of these connections and that is an issue with the use of Raspberry Pi as an iCDS.

Using some channel bonding technology, however, it is possible to channelize the network traffic to flow through two separate network interface connections, one for incoming traffic entering the Raspberry Pi device from external network and the other for outgoing traffic from the Raspberry Pi device. This will need two network interface connections (e.g., network adaptors or network interface cards) in the Raspberry Pi 4.0 board and such connections can be in any form, like, the on-board Ethernet interface, on-board WiFi interface, USB Ethernet, and USB WiFi. For traffic filtering purpose, the Raspberry Pi device connected to a SME network, will require incoming and outgoing network traffic flowing through any of the two separate network interfaces. Based on such flow of network traffic, the following combinations are possible:

Option1: Network traffic entering the Raspberry Pi device through the on-board Ethernet interface and flowing out through the on-board WiFi interface.

Option 2: Network traffic entering the Raspberry Pi device through the on-board Ethernet interface and flowing out through USB Ethernet interface.

Option 3: Network traffic entering the Raspberry Pi device through the on-board WiFi interface and flowing out through the USB WiFi interface.

Option 4: Network traffic entering the Raspberry Pi device through the on-board WiFi interface and flowing out through the USB Ethernet interface.

There are, however, few issues with the selection of the different interfaces on the Raspberry Pi 4.0 board for incoming and outgoing network traffic unless proper channel bonding is used. One such issue, for example, when choosing option 1 (on-board Ethernet interface for incoming traffic and WiFi interface for outgoing traffic), the configuration will face an issue with the assigned IP addresses for the two interfaces. Generally, individual IP addresses will be assigned to the Ethernet interface and WiFi interface, respectively, for incoming packets entering the Raspberry Pi board to identify the particular entry interface's IP address and filtered outgoing packets (i.e., network traffic packets leaving the Raspberry Pi board to enter the SME network gateway) to identify the exit interface's IP address. Since, network traffic flows through only one connection (at a time) on the Raspberry Pi board, in absence of channel bonding technique, all traffic will just identify the Ethernet interface's IP address and flow through that, whereas, the other WiFi interface connection will remain unnoticed. This implies, that traffic will not enter the gateway of the SME network. Also, in case of option 3, when choosing two WiFi interfaces for incoming and outgoing traffic there can be an issue with the Raspberry Pi board not properly identifying the particular WiFi interface after every reboot operation (i.e., which interface is for incoming and which one is for outgoing traffic). There is a possibility that Raspberry Pi may not identify the WiFi interfaces correctly when rebooted and that may lead to incorrect communication of the network traffic. Thus, from these discussions it can be concluded that it is feasible to use Raspberry Pi device to develop an iCDS but proper channel bonding needs to be used for tracking the network traffic entering and exiting the different interfaces on board. In the following sections we study the performance of different interfaces on the Raspberry Pi device in handling high volume of real traffic entering the device.

3.2 Proposed Testbed for the Experiments

Figure 2 shows the proposed system model for using Raspberry Pi 4 as the iCDS in order to filter malicious packets from entering SME networks. Ideally, Raspberry Pi 4.0 device with 4 GB of RAM and 1.5 GHz 64-bit quad-core Arm Cortex-A72 processor will be used. It has built in Ethernet and WiFi interfaces. The Gigabit Ethernet interface in Raspberry Pi 4.0 can reduce communication latency and provide faster network connectivity. The device also has USB 3.0 and 2.0 ports. USB 3.0 ports can enable transfer of data up to ten times faster than USB 2.0. Based on the discussion provided in the previous sub-section, the proposed model will likely opt for option 2, where the on-board Ethernet interface will be used for incoming network traffic from external networks trying to enter the SME network through the Raspberry Pi 4-based iCDS and an USB Ethernet interface (in form of an adaptor) will be used as the exit for the filtered outgoing traffic from the Raspberry Pi device to the gateway of the connected SME network (refer to Fig. 2). There is also an issue with choosing USB Ethernet for communication (option 2) as it may slow down the transfer of outgoing network traffic from the Raspberry Pi device to the gateway of the SME network, however, with the choice of proper USB Ethernet adaptor this shortcoming can be overcome. USBs are rated at speeds different to Ethernet, for instance, USB 3.0 is rated at 5 gigabits per second whereas USB 2.0 is rated at 54 megabits per second. For our proposed experimental testbed in this research, a Raspberry Pi 4.0 device is used that has a Gigabit Ethernet interface. Also, to ensure that the network communication on the Raspberry Pi 4.0 board does not slow down, a USB 3.0 Gigabit Ethernet interface (adaptor) is used so that communication between the two Gigabit Ethernet interfaces (the on-board one and the USB one) can happen. All the incoming internet traffic meant for the SME network will first enter the Raspberry Pi based iCDS acting as a protective shield for the SME network.

This entire research work will be carried out in two phases. In the first phase, as mentioned before, the aim is to study the feasibility of using Raspberry device to develop the iCDS and to explore if hardware interfaces on the Pi device are capable of handling high volume of real traffic to support its usage as a commercial iCDS, which is what this paper will discuss. In the following phase, the incoming traffic on the Raspberry Pi device will be sent through a cloud-based validation system where the signatures of the packets will be thoroughly checked to identify malicious contents (e.g., malwares). Such checking will be done at the signature-based detection online module (shown as cloud) of the proposed model where a lightweight AI-based pattern recognition and deep learning algorithm will inspect every packet to filter the malicious contents before letting the outgoing packets pass through the exit USB Ethernet interface to safely enter the SME network's gateway. These second phase activities are kept for future work and hence are not discussed in this paper. An important point that needs mentioning here is how the Raspberry Pi device can capture and track the network traffic flowing between its incoming and outgoing interfaces. This can be done in the following way. On starting, the Raspberry Pi device will load two scripts, the first of which is a shell script that will set up a software bridge connection between the incoming and outgoing interfaces. The bridge interface will have its own unique IP address assigned and will allow for network connectivity. The second Python script will tcpdump the network packets (flowing between the input and output interfaces) on the Raspberry Pi 4.0 device so that they can be captured and assessed.

4   Performance of the Raspberry Pi Interfaces

4.1   Measurement of Latency

Latency is a significant aspect in determining the efficiency of any network interface. In the experiments conducted, latency of each interface on the Pi board (i.e., Ethernet, WiFi, and USB interfaces) is measured individually based on the incoming unfiltered real network traffic entering each interface separately over a time interval of t to t + 1. Figure 3 depicts the latency comparison of the three interfaces on the Raspberry Pi 4.0 device based on separate measurements of the incoming network traffic.

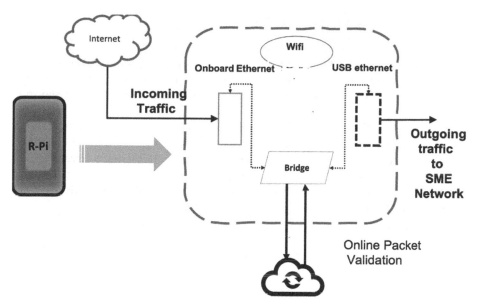

Fig. 2. The hardware architecture for the proposed Raspberry Pi-based iCDS

As can be seen in Fig. 3, the latency of the built-in WiFi interface on the Raspberry Pi device is considerably high in comparison to the latencies of the built-in Ethernet and USB Adapter interfaces. Apart from the fact that Ethernet (wired) connections usually offers better network speed and significantly lower latency compared to WiFi (wireless) connections, the other reason can be that the built-in WiFi on the Pi device has a single antenna and not a MIMO, so lower speed and more latency anyway. On the other hand, the Ethernet interface also offers lower latency than the USB adapter interface.

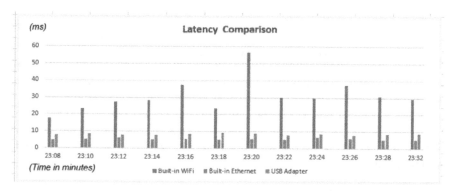

Fig. 3. Latency comparison of Raspberry-pi interfaces when handling external traffic

4.2   Measurement of Download Traffic Throughput

Similar to latency, download and upload throughput of network traffic are other important aspects of determining the efficiency of a communication interface. The download
traffic for each interface on the Raspberry Pi 4.0 device is measured separately over the
t to t + 1 time interval and the comparison results for the three interfaces are shown in
Fig. 4.

From the given figure, it is evident that the throughput of the built-in Ethernet interface on the Pi device is significantly higher than the throughput of the WiFi and USB
Adapter interfaces. Again, this can be related to the fact that Ethernet connections generally offer better network speed and thus better (download) throughout in comparison
to WiFi and the USB connections. Performance of the in-built WiFi and USB interfaces
look somewhat similar.

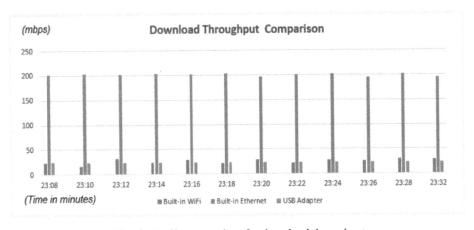

Fig. 4. Traffic comparison for download throughput

4.3   Measurement of Upload Traffic Throughput

Figure 5 compares the throughput of the upload traffic for the three network interfaces on
the Raspberry Pi 4.0 device. The upload throughout performance of the built-in Ethernet
interface has somewhat outperformed the other two interfaces. The USB Adapter on the
Pi 4.0 device, unlike the Ethernet, shares a common bus and hence its bandwidth is also
distributed among other ports, which is why it experiences some internal delays and has
a low throughput.

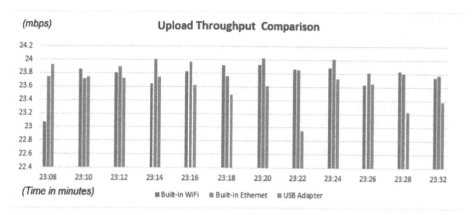

Fig. 5. Traffic comparison for upload throughput

5 Conclusions and Future Work

Primarily, the work presented in this paper has a two-fold focus: (a) to explore the feasibility of using Raspberry Pi device to develop a low-cost intelligent cyber-defense system or iCDS for commercial SME networks, and (b) to study if the hardware components present in the latest Raspberry Pi devices are capable and compatible enough to support the use of Raspberry Pi-based iCDS for SMEs. Based on the detailed discussions presented in the paper, it can be concluded that it is feasible to use Raspberry Pi device to develop a low-cost iCDS as an alternative to the traditional rule-based IDSs in use. Moreover, from the experimental results as discussed in Sect. 4, it is evident that the different interfaces on the Raspberry Pi 4.0 device, e.g., built-in Ethernet (wired) connection, WiFi and the external USB Adapter, studied in this research are capable of handling high volumes of traffic entering the Raspberry Pi device from outside networks. The evaluations also showed that in terms of network performance comparison carried out based on parameters, like, latency, downward traffic throughout and upward traffic throughput, the built-in Ethernet network interface has outperformed the other two interfaces and thus can be an ideal choice to use for handling external traffic.

While, this paper explains the first phase of the research work on this topic, as mentioned in Subsect. 3.2, further work (second phase) will be focused on the following:

Incoming traffic on the Raspberry Pi device will be sent through a cloud-based validation system where the signatures of the packets will be thoroughly checked to identify malicious contents (e.g., malwares).

A lightweight AI-based pattern recognition and deep learning algorithm will be prepared to inspect the packets and filter out malicious contents before the packets can safely enter the SME networks.

A functional prototype of this low-cost iCDS will be developed, which will use the deep-learning based signature verification model for filtering malicious contents from incoming network traffic.

References

1. Khraisat, A., Gondal, I., Vamplew, P., Kamruzzaman, J.: Survey of intrusion detection systems: techniques, datasets and challenges. Cybersecurity **2**(1), 1–22 (2019)
2. Ali, B., Awad, A.I.: Cyber and Physical Security Vulnerability Assessment for iot-Based Smart Homes. Multidisciplinary Digital Publishing Institute (2018)
3. Granjal, J., Monteiro, E., Silva, J.S.: Security for the internet of things: a survey of existing protocols and open research issues. IEEE Commun. Surveys Tutorials **17**(3), 1294–1312 (2015)
4. Tirumala, S.S., Valluri, M.R., Nanadigam, D.: Evaluation of feature and signature based training approaches for malware classification using autoencoders. In: 2020 International Conference on COMmunication Systems & NETworkS (COMSNETS), pp. 1–5. IEEE (2020)
5. Malikovich, K.M., Rajaboevich, G.S., Karamatovich, Y.B.: Method of constucting packet filtering rules. In: International Conference On Information Science and Communications Technologies (icisct), IEEE (2017)
6. Meng, W., Li, W., Kwok, L.F.: Towards effective trust-based packet filtering in collaborative network environments. IEEE Trans. Netw. Serv. Manage. **14**(1), 233–245 (2017)
7. Serdechnyi, V., Barkovska, O., Rosinskiy, D., Axak, N., Korablyov, M.: Model of the internet traffic filtering system to ensure safe web surfing. In: International Scientific Conference "Intellectual Systems of Decision Making and Problem of Computational Intelligence" Springer, Cham (2019)
8. Kolias, C., Kambourakis, G., Stavrou, A., Voas, J.: DDoS in the IoT: Mirai and other botnets. IEEE Comput. **50**(7), 80–84 (2017)
9. Lu, D., Huang, D., Walenstein, A., Medhi, D.: A secure microservice framework for iot. In: Symposium on Service-Oriented System Engineering (SOSE), IEEE (2017)
10. Pahl, M.O., Aubet, F.X., Liebald, S.: Graph-based IoT microservice security. In: Network Operations and Management Symposium, (NOMS), IEEE (2018)
11. Gupta, N., Naik, V., Sengupta, S.: A firewall for internet of things. In: 9th International Conference on Communication Systems and Networks (COMSNETS), IEEE (2017)
12. Taib, A.M., Zabri, M.T., Radzi, N.A.M., Kadir, E.A.: NetGuard: Securing Network Environment Using Integrated OpenVPN, Pi-Hole, and IDS on Raspberry Pi. In: Charting the Sustainable Future of ASEAN in Science and Technology Springer, Singapore (2020)
13. Jesús, R.L.J., Cristhian, P.V.O., René, R.G.M., Heberto, F.M.: How to Improve the IoT Security Implementing IDS/IPS Tool using Raspberry Pi 3B. In: Editorial Preface from the Desk of Managing Editor (2019)
14. Tripathi, S., Kumar, R.: Raspberry pi as an intrusion detection system, a honeypot and a packet analyzer. In: International Conference on Computational Techniques, Electronics and Mechanical Systems (CTEMS) IEEE (2018)
15. Soe, Y.N., Feng, Y., Santosa, P.I., Hartanto, R., Sakurai, K.: Implementing lightweight iot-ids on raspberry pi using correlation-based feature selection and its performance evaluation. In: International Conference on Advanced Information Networking and Applications, Springer, Cham (2019)
16. Sumanth, R., Bhanu, K.N.: Raspberry Pi based intrusion detection system using k-means clustering algorithm. In: Second International Conference on Inventive Research in Computing Applications (ICIRCA), IEEE (2020)

Inter-satellite Optical Analog Network Coding Using Modulated Retro Reflectors

Jia Yanmei[1,2] , Lyu Congmin[1,2], Shen Pengfei[1,2], and Lu Lu[1,2(✉)]

[1] University of Chinese Academy of Sciences, Beijing 100049, China
lulu@csu.ac.cn
[2] Technology and Engineering Center for Space Utilization,
Chinese Academy of Sciences, Beijing 100094, China

Abstract. Information sharing, real-time data exchange, and low SWaP (Size, Weight and Power) inter-satellite communication are the key technologies for cooperative satellite. In order to build a high-throughput inter-satellite optical communication network suitable for micro-satellites, an analog network coding (ANC) system based on modulated retro reflectors (MRR) was designed for two way relay channel (TWRC). Different from traditional-scheduling (TS) based TWRC, MRR ANC saves two sets of pointing, acquisition and tracking (PAT) devices at the end terminals. Specifically, our proposed MRR ANC system is suitable for small satellites with tight SWaP constrains. In this paper, we solve the power allocation problem of MRR ANC using Lagrange multiplier method under sum rate maximization criteria. We evaluated the system throughput and bit error rate (BER) performances using numerical simulations. The results show that both sum rate and BER performances of MRR ANC are improved using our proposed method compared with conventional uniform power allocation scheme. When each bidirectional link distance is 200 km, the non-channel-coded BER of each terminal is 10^{-5} using on-off keying (OOK) modulation. Compared with traditional scheduling, the system throughput of MRR ANC was improved by 1.8 times.

Keywords: Modulated retro reflector · Analog network coding · Power allocation · Throughput

1 Introduction

With the development of space technology, the amount of information exchange and the data transmission rate between applied satellite systems is increasing. The demand for inter-satellite network is increasingly urgent. Small satellites have the characteristics of low cost, dynamic and flexible reconstruction, so it

This work was supported in part by the Key Research Program of the Chinese Academy of Sciences, under Grant ZDRW-KT-2019-1-0103.

has become a trend to use small satellites to form a space-based integrated information network, information fusion and interconnection. Compared with radio frequency (RF) systems, free space optical communication (FSOC) has lower size, weight, and power (SWaP) advantages in addition to higher data rates, spectrum competition, and security [1]. FSOC is the best means to realize large-capacity and high-speed network [2]. Inter-satellite FSOC network has become a major development direction [3–6].

It is difficult to form a high-speed, real-time and high-throughput FSOC network with low SWaP value for traditional "point-to-point" FSOC [7,8]. Agile laser beams with fast steering and tracking will be required for FSOC network with low SWaP value. The cost and the complexity are other important issues. Modulated retro reflector (MRR) only needs Pointing, Acquisition and Tracking (PAT) at one end, and a corner reflector or a "cat's eye" onboarded at the other end [9,10]. MRR is usually a few kilograms, and its power consumption is a few watts [11], which meets the requirements of low SWaP value of micro satellites. At present, most of the research focuses on the application of MRR in point-to-point communication scenarios [12]. Using the MRR Array, "point-to-multipoints" laser communication can be realized. For example, the all-sky coverage inter-satellite omnidirectional optical communication (ISOC) based on MEMS modulation reflector is being developed by the Jet Propulsion Laboratory [13].

Due to the short insight time of inter-satellite laser communication, satellite networking requires relay satellites to increase the data transmission time and communication range. Two Way Relay Channel (TWRC) is a basic unit in FSOC network. In order to further improve the real-time performance and throughput of FSOC networks, this paper proposes an inter-satellite ANC scheme based on MRR (MRR ANC), which is used to meet the demand of real-time and high-throughput information sharing and exchange for FSOC network of micro satellites. MRR ANC system model is established, and the power allocation, system throughput and average BER of MRR ANC system are simulated and analyzed, and the feasibility of MRR ANC system is evaluated. The results show that MRR ANC system can improve the system throughput with low SWaP value. MRR ANC system rate and BER performances can be improved by using power allocation.

The remainder of this paper is organized as follows: Sect. 2 presents MRR ANC system design. Section 3 gives the system model for MRR ANC. Section 4 proposes optimal power allocation for MRR ANC. Section 5 calculates the throughput for MRR ANC. Section 6 presents our simulation analyses and discussion. Finally, Sect. 7 concludes this paper.

2   MRR ANC System Design

The communication process of traditional point-to-point FSOC in TWRC channel is shown in Fig. 1. To complete the optical relay communication, the system requires at least three PATs and four time slots for the TWRC information exchange. Taking the PAT used on the NASA LLCD (Lunar Laser Communications Demonstration) [1] as an example, each terminal will require a weight resource of about 30.7 kg, power consumption of about 90 W, and volume of 315 mm × 261 mm × 185 mm. Due to the small divergence angle and precise pointing of the laser beam, PAT has certain requirements on the attitude and stability of the satellite platform.

MRR as FSOC terminal can realize "point-to-multipoints" communication, can save the PAT on the satellites, so it is suitable for inter-satellite FSOC of micro satellites. The working principle of MRR and the TWRC channel information exchange process are shown in Fig. 2 and Fig. 3.

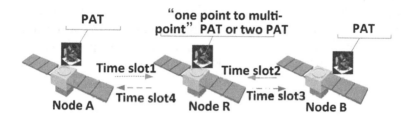

Fig. 1. Schematic diagram of traditional point-to-point laser communication terminal information exchange in TWRC

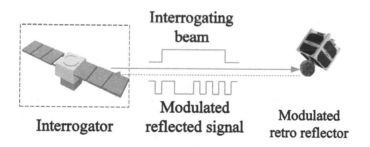

Fig. 2. MRR system architecture diagram

This paper proposes MRR ANC system as shown in the Fig. 4. The satellite FSOC network based on MRR takes the main satellite as the network node, the "one-point-to-multipoint" PAT is installed on the main satellite, and MRR array is installed on the sub-satellite. The main satellite is the interrogator and the sub-satellite is the passive end. The main satellite sends the interrogating beam to the sub-satellite, and the sub-satellite modulates the information on the interrogating beam to complete the inter-satellite bidirectional communication. The network structure can be rapidly and dynamically reconstructed to adapt

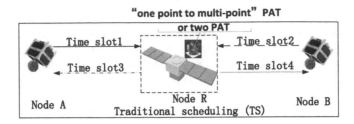

Fig. 3. Information exchange between MRR terminals on the help of relay

the rapidly changing space situation and mission. Compared with the ANC system implemented by the traditional FSOC terminal, the MRR ANC system can save the PATs on subsatellites. By using ANC, the packet exchange between two end nodes can be completed in two time slots with the help of relay node, and the throughput can be increased by two times theoretically.

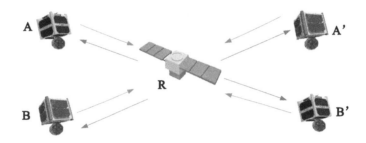

Fig. 4. MRR ANC system architecture diagram

Comparison of transmission time slots between ANC and traditional scheme is shown in the Fig. 5. The traditional scheduling needs 4 time slots to complete the information exchange between subsatellite A and B. The MRR ANC system can complete the information exchange in 2 time slots. This system can be used as the basic unit of FSOC network.

3   System Model

The transmission equation of conventional FSOC can be expressed as [14]

$$P_{\mathrm{STS}} = P_{\mathrm{Las}}G_{\mathrm{T}}L_{\mathrm{T}}L_{\mathrm{R}}T_{\mathrm{atm}}G_{\mathrm{rec}}L_{\mathrm{rec}}L_{PE}. \tag{1}$$

For a given modulation reflector antenna gain and modulation efficiency, the MRR transmission equation can be expressed as:

$$P_{\mathrm{SMRR}} = P_{\mathrm{Las}}G_{\mathrm{T}}L_{\mathrm{T}}L_{\mathrm{R}}T_{\mathrm{atm}}G_{\mathrm{MRR}}L_{\mathrm{MRR}}ML_{\mathrm{R}}T_{\mathrm{atm}}G_{\mathrm{rec}}L_{\mathrm{rec}}L_{PE}. \tag{2}$$

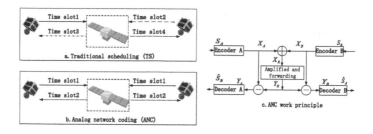

Fig. 5. MRR ANC work principle diagram

In Eqs. 1 and 2, P_{STS} denotes the optical signal received by the receiver, P_{SMRR} is the power of the MRR signal received by the main satellite, P_{Las} is the emitted power, G_T is the transmitter antenna gain at the interrogator, L_T is the transmitting antenna loss, L_R is the loss of free space, T_{atm} is the atmospheric transmission loss, G_{MRR} is the optical gain of the MRR, L_{MRR} is the optical loss of the MRR, M is the modulation coefficient of the MRR, G_{rec} is the optical antenna gain of the interrogator, L_{rec} is the optical loss of the receiver. Atmospheric losses are not considered because we tend to establish inter-satellite link.

The MRR antenna gain, optical loss, modulation efficiency are increased based on the transmitter and receiver related terms. Compared with the traditional laser communication link, the MRR link has higher distance loss, attenuates as $1/R^4$ not $1/R^2$. On-off Keying (OOK) modulation format and intensity modulation with direct detection (IM/DD) are used. The signal reception model can be expressed as $y = \eta hx + n$, where y is the received signal, η is the photoelectric conversion efficiency of the receiver, h represents channel state, $x \in \{0, 1\}$ denotes binary signal, n is white Gaussian noise.

For MRR ANC system, the two subsatellites A and B modulate signals on top of the interrogating beam and reflect back to the main satellite R simultaneously in the first time slot. The main satellite receives the imposed signals $y_R = h_{A1}\sqrt{P_A}(X_A + z_{RA}) + h_{B1}\sqrt{P_B}(X_B + z_{RB}) + z_R$, where P_A and P_B represent the power of the main satellite to subsatellites A and B, respectively. h_{A1} and h_{B1} are respectively the channel gain between A and R, B and R. z_{RA}, z_{RB} and z_R are Gaussian white noises with zero mean and σ_n^2 variance. h_{A1} and h_{B1} include channel attenuation from the interrogating beam emitted by the main satellite to the sub-satellite, channel attenuation from the signal light reflected by the sub-satellite, and random channel attenuation due to pointing error of the main satellite.

The main satellite R amplifies and forwards the received signal Y_R with the gain β in the second time slot. Assume that the channel state is known, the received signal of subsatellite A and B can be denoted by $y_A = \beta h_{A2}y_R + z_A$ and $y_B = \beta h_{B2}y_R + z_B$ respectively. z_A and z_B are Gaussian white noise with zero mean, the variance of σ_n^2. h_{A2} and h_{B2} include the inherent channel attenuation between the satellite and the main satellite and random channel attenuation due to pointing error. Y_R is estimated based on Linear Minimum Mean Square Error (LMMSE), the amplification factor β can be expressed as [15].

$$\beta = \sqrt{P_R \Big/ \left(|h_{A1}|^2 P_A + |h_{B1}|^2 P_B + \left(|h_{A1}|^2 P_A + |h_{B1}|^2 P_B + 1 \right) \sigma_n^2 \right)}. \quad (3)$$

Assuming that the subsatellite A and B can accurately predict the channel state, the opposite signal can be obtained by subtracting its own signal from the received signals. The opposite signal can be denoted as $y'_A = \beta \sqrt{P_B} h_{A2} h_{B1} X_B + \beta h_{A2} z_R + z'_A$, $y'_B = \beta \sqrt{P_A} h_{A1} h_{B2} X_A + \beta h_{B2} z_R + z'_B$, where z'_A and z'_B are sum of $|h_{A1}|^2 P_A \sigma_n^2$ and σ_n^2, sum of $|h_{B1}|^2 P_B \sigma_n^2$ and σ_n^2 respectively. The signal-to-noise ratio of the signals received by subsatellites A and B can be expressed as [16,17]:

$$\gamma_A = \beta^2 |h_{A2}|^2 |h_{B1}|^2 P_B \Big/ \left(\left(\beta^2 |h_{A2}|^2 + |h_{A1}|^2 P_A + 1 \right) \sigma_n^2 \right). \quad (4)$$

$$\gamma_B = \beta^2 |h_{A1}|^2 |h_{B2}|^2 P_A \Big/ \left(\left(\beta^2 |h_{B2}|^2 + |h_{B1}|^2 P_B + 1 \right) \sigma_n^2 \right). \quad (5)$$

The achieved rate of half duplex TWRC system using MRR ANC based on γ_A and γ_B is [16,17]

$$R_{\text{sum}} = \tfrac{1}{2} \log \left(1 + \gamma_A \right) + \tfrac{1}{2} \log \left(1 + \gamma_B \right)$$
$$= \tfrac{1}{2} \log \left(1 + \gamma_A \right) \left(1 + \gamma_B \right) \quad (6)$$

4   Optimal Power Allocation

In MRR ANC system, in order to minimize the outage probability and maximize the total amount of system information exchange, power allocation is needed. The goal of power allocation can be to achieve the maximum system rate, the minimum outage probability, the best signal-to-noise ratio or the best bit error rate. In this paper, the optimal power allocation target is to maximize sum rate of MRR ANC system in TWRC channel.

The problem can be equivalent to maximizing the sum rate on the constraint of $P_A + P_B + P_R = P_T$:

$$(P_A P_B P_R) = \max_{P_A P_B P_R} R_{\text{sum}}(R) \, P_A + P_B + P_R = P_T \quad (7)$$

According to Eq. 6, Eq. 7 is equivalent to

$$(P_A P_B P_R) = \max_{P_A P_B P_R} (1 + \gamma_A)(1 + \gamma_B) \, P_A + P_B + P_R = P_T \quad (8)$$

Since $(1 + \gamma_A)(1 + \gamma_B) = 1 + \gamma_A + \gamma_B + \gamma_A \gamma_B \le (1 + (\gamma_A + \gamma_B)/2)^2$, only when $\gamma_A = \gamma_B$, $(1 + \gamma_A)(1 + \gamma_B)$ can reach the upper limit, and if $\gamma_A + \gamma_B$ achieves the maximum value, the upper limit will reache the maximum. Because $\frac{1}{\gamma_A} + \frac{1}{\gamma_B} = \frac{\gamma_A + \gamma_B}{\gamma_A \gamma_B} \ge \frac{4}{\gamma_A + \gamma_B}$, if and only if $\gamma_A = \gamma_B$, $\frac{1}{\gamma_A} + \frac{1}{\gamma_B}$ reaches the lower limit and if $\gamma_A + \gamma_B$ achieves the maximum, the lower limit will be minimum. Hence, if $\frac{1}{\gamma_A} + \frac{1}{\gamma_B}$ reaches the lower limit, $(1 + \gamma_A)(1 + \gamma_B)$ will be the maximum. By substituting Eqs. 4 and 5, we will get

$$\frac{1}{\gamma_A} + \frac{1}{\gamma_B} = \frac{\left(\left(\beta^2|h_{A2}|^2 + |h_{A1}|^2 P_A + 1\right)\sigma_n^2\right)}{\beta^2|h_{A2}|^2|h_{B1}|^2 P_B} + \frac{\left(\left(\beta^2|h_{B2}|^2 + |h_{B1}|^2 P_B + 1\right)\sigma_n^2\right)}{\beta^2|h_{A1}|^2|h_{B2}|^2 P_A}$$

(9)

Substituting Eq. 3 into Eq. 9, we will get

$$\frac{1}{\gamma_A} + \frac{1}{\gamma_B} = \frac{P_R|h_{A2}|^2\sigma_n^2 + (P_A|h_{A1}|^2\sigma_n^2 + \sigma_n^2)[P_A|h_{A1}|^2 + P_B|h_{B1}|^2 + (P_A|h_{A1}|^2 + P_B|h_{B1}|^2 + 1)\sigma_n^2]}{|h_{A2}|^2|h_{D1}|^2 P_R P_B} + \frac{P_R|h_{B2}|^2\sigma_n^2 + (P_B|h_{B1}|^2\sigma_n^2 + \sigma_n^2)[P_A|h_{A1}|^2 + P_B|h_{B1}|^2 + (P_A|h_{A1}|^2 + P_B|h_{B1}|^2 + 1)\sigma_n^2]}{|h_{A1}|^2|h_{B2}|^2 P_A P_R}$$

(10)

Using Lagrangian least multiplier method to find the minimum value of Eq. 10 on the constrains of $P_A + P_B + P_R = P_T$, the optimal power allocation can be obtained. In order to simplify the problem, it is assumed that the power of the continuous optical signal transmitted by the relay node is large enough and the Gaussian white noise carried by the continuous optical signal is ignored [18]. Consider power allocation of the power reflected back by MRR and the power of the relay node $(P_{MRRA}, P_{MRRB}, P_R)$, on the constraint of $P_{MRRA} + P_{MRRB} + P_R = P'_T$. The channel attenuation coefficients of the signals reflected from the sub satellite MRR of A and B are the same as that of h_{A2} and h_{B2}. Formula 10 can be simplified as

$$\frac{1}{\gamma_A} + \frac{1}{\gamma_B} = \frac{\left(|h_{A2}|^2 P'_T\sigma_n^2 + \sigma_n^4\right)P_{MRRA} + \left(|h_{B2}|^2 P'_T\sigma_n^2 + \sigma_n^4\right)P_{MRRB}}{|h_{A2}|^2|h_{B2}|^2 P_{MRRA} P_{MRRB} P_R}$$

(11)

Using Lagrange multiplier method, the optimal power allocation can be obtained as follows [15]

$$P_R = \frac{1}{2}P'_T$$

(12)

$$P_{MRRA} = \frac{1}{2 + 2\sqrt{\dfrac{|h_{A2}|^2 P'_T\sigma_n^2 + \sigma_n^4}{|h_{B2}|^2 P'_T\sigma_n^2 + \sigma_n^4}}} P'_T$$

(13)

$$P_{MRRB} = \frac{1}{2 + 2\sqrt{\dfrac{|h_{B2}|^2 P'_T\sigma_n^2 + 1\sigma_n^4}{|h_{A2}|^2 P'_T\sigma_n^2 + 1\sigma_n^4}}} P'_T$$

(14)

5   Throughput

The upper and lower limits of channel capacity can be calculated. The throughput is compared by calculating the upper bound of traditional scheduling method and the lower bound of channel capacity of MRR ANC system. Suppose that the channels between A and R, B and R are independent and obey Gaussian white noise distribution, and all nodes have the same transmit power. According to [19], the theoretical upper limit of channel capacity of traditional scheduling method is

$$C_{\text{traditional}} = \alpha \left(\log \left(1 + 2R_{\text{SN}} \right) + \log \left(1 + R_{\text{SN}} \right) \right) \qquad (15)$$

The theoretical lower limit of the channel capacity of the ANC system is

$$C_{\text{ANC}} = 4\alpha \log \left(1 + \frac{R_{\text{SN}}^2}{3R_{SN} + 1} \right) \qquad (16)$$

6   Simulation Results Analysis and Discussion

In this section, we perform numerical simulation on sum rage, BER and capacity of MRR ANC. It is assumed that the positional relationship between the relay node and the nodes at both ends is a straight line, and the relay node is located between the two end nodes. See Table 1 for the parameters used.

Performance of optimal power allocation and the unified power allocation (the reflected power of the two endpoints and the transmission power of the relay node are the same, respectively are $1/3$ of the total power) are compared with the achievable sum rates, BER and capacity.

Table 1. Parameters for simulations

Term	Parameter	Formula	Value
Tx power	$\leq 5\,\text{W}$	Measured	$37\,\text{dBm}$
Transmitter loss	–	Measured	$-1.0\,\text{dB}$
Tx antenna gain	Full angle e^{-2} divergence	$32/\theta_{div}, \theta_{div} = 30\mu rad$	$105.5\,\text{dB}$
Interrogator range loss	$R = 200\,\text{km}, \lambda = 850\,\text{nm}$	$(\lambda/4\pi R)^2$	$-294.4\,\text{dB}$
Electro-optic modulator	Insert loss	measured	$-4\,\text{dB}$
MRR T/R Antenna gain	$D_{retro} = 5\,\text{cm}, S = 0.4$	$(\pi D_{retro}/\lambda)^4 S$	$213.8\,\text{dB}$
Range loss(retro return)	$R = 200\,\text{km}, \lambda = 850\,\text{nm}$	$(\lambda/4\pi R)^2$	$-249.4\,\text{dB}$
Receiver antenna gain	$D_{rec} = 20\,\text{cm}$	$(\pi D_{rec}/\lambda)^2$	$117.4\,\text{dB}$
Receiver loss	Fiber coupling loss	–	$-1\,\text{dB}$
Receiver sensitivity	S_v	$(BER = 10^{-10})$	$-38\,\text{dB}$
Predicted receiver power	–	–	$-35\,\text{dB}$
Noise standard deviation	σ_n	–	$10^{-7}\text{A}/\sqrt{Hz}$
Pointing error loss	L_{PE}	–	$-1\,\text{dB}$

Regardless of whether the distances between the nodes A and B and the relay node are the same or different, the sum rate that can be achieved by the optimal power allocation scheme is better than the unified power allocation scheme as shown in Fig. 6 and Fig. 7. When the distance between the end node and the relay node is the same, the achievable rate is higher. When the distance between the end node and the relay node is different, the sum rate achieved by the Lagrange multiplier power allocation scheme is more different than the unified power allocation scheme.

When the two end nodes A and B are at the same distance from the relay node, the BER performance of the end nodes is compared. Figure 8 shows that the BER performance that can be achieved by the optimal power allocation scheme is better than that of the unified power allocation scheme.

Figure 9 and Fig. 10 shows that, with the increase of the signal-to-noise ratio, the throughput of ANC are both 1.81 times of the traditional scheduling (the signal-to-noise ratio of 65 dB), no matter ignoring the noise carried by the interrogating beam or considering the noise. The result is consistent with the theoretical derivation of [19]. It can be proved that the simplified method of power allocation in this paper is reasonable.

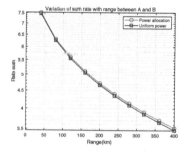

Fig. 6. The distance from node A or B to relay node is the same

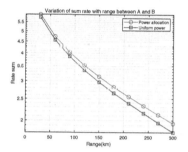

Fig. 7. The distance from node A or B to relay node is different

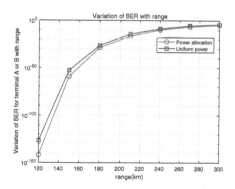

Fig. 8. Variation of BER with distance in MRR ANC systems

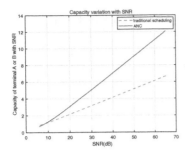

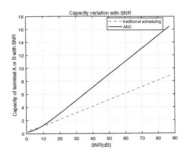

Fig. 9. Capacity bounds as functions of SNR, ignoring noise of interrogating laser

Fig. 10. Capacity bounds as functions of SNR, considering noise of interrogating laser

7 Conclusion

In this paper, an MRR ANC system is designed in TWRC to meet the needs of real-time, high throughput data exchange and low SWaP value of micro-satellite space FSOC network. The model of MRR ANC system is established. In order to achieve the best quality of communication service, the power allocation scheme of MRR ANC system is proposed with the goal of maximum sum rate.

We believe that MRR ANC's low SWaP value, suitable for small satellite platforms, and "point to point" characteristics will make small satellite inter-satellite laser communication network a reality. The limitations of MRR ANC lies in its communication distance. The difficulty with ANC implementation is to improve the performance of the modulated reflector under low SWaP conditions.

Simulation results show that the sum rate of the system is better than that of the unified power allocation scheme after the optimal power allocation, and the BER performance of the power allocation scheme with the target of maximum sum rate is also better than that of the unified power allocation scheme under the same communication distance. By comparing the communication capacity of MRR ANC with that of traditional scheduling, it can be concluded that the throughput of MRR ANC is 1.8 times of that of traditional scheduling when the signal-to-noise ratio is 65 dB. The simulation results show that MRR ANC system is feasible, which provides a new method for small satellite laser communication network.

In the future, we can further consider the research of power allocation with the minimum outage probability and the best bit error rate performance as the optimization objectives. At the same time, the optimization scheme of power allocation can also be applied to physical layer network coding (PNC).

References

1. Boroson, D.M., Robinson, B.S.: The lunar laser communication demonstration: NASA's first step toward very high data rate support of science and exploration missions. In: Elphic, R.C., Russell, C.T. (eds.) The Lunar Atmosphere and Dust Environment Explorer Mission (LADEE), pp. 115–128. Springer, Cham (2015). https://doi.org/10.1007/978-3-319-18717-4_6

2. Chang, C.W., Cheng, L.Y., Luo, D., et al.: Progress of space laser communication and conception of its application in space based networks. J. Spacecr. TT C Technol. **34**(2), 176–183 (2015)

3. Pulliam, J., et al.: TSAT network architecture. In: MILCOM 2008–2008 IEEE Military Communications Conference, pp. 115–128. IEEE (2008). https://doi.org/10.1109/MILCOM.2008.4753508

4. Thomas, S., Andreas, H., et al.: ESA long-term monitoring of space debris in GEO, GTO and first surveys of MEO. In: 28th Inter-Agency Debris Coordination Committee (IADC) Meeting, International Association of Drilling Contractors IADC (2010)

5. Cao, D.R., Li, T.L., Sun, Y., et al.: Latest developments and trends of space laser communication. Chin. Opt. **11**(6), 901–913 (2018)

6. Jiang, H.L., Fu, Q., Zhao, Y.W., et al.: Development status and trend of space information network and laser communication. Chin. J. Internet Things **3**(2), 1–8 (2019)

7. Shubert, P., Cline, A., McNally, J., Pierson, R.: Design of low SWaP optical terminals for free space optical communications. In: Free-Space Laser Communication and Atmospheric Propagation XXIX, vol. 10096 (2017)

8. Radhakrishnan, R., Edmonson, W.W.: Survey of inter-satellite communication for small satellite systems: physical layer to network layer view. IEEE Commun. Surv. Tutor. **18**(4), 2442–2473 (2016)

9. Arnon, S., Barry, J., Karagiannidis, G., et al.: Advanced optical wireless communication systems. Hybrid RF/FSO Commun. (11), 273–302 (2012)

10. Li, X.: Research on the performance of the Modulating Retro-reflector free Space Optical Communications over Atmospheric Turbulence. Jilin Province (2020)

11. Goetz, P.G., et al.: Modulating retro-reflector lasercom systems for small unmanned vehicles. IEEE J. Sel. Areas Commun. **30**(5), 986–992 (2012)

12. Hu, J., Wang, J., Wang, K., et al.: The research on aperture averaging of modulating retro-reflector optical communication. In: 2020 International Conference on Wireless Communications and Signal Processing (WCSP) (2020)

13. Velazco, J.E., Griffin, J., Wernicke, D., et al.: High data rate inter-satellite omnidirectional optical communicator. In: 2019 IEEE Aerospace Conference (2019)

14. Liu, D.X., Zeng, J., Sun, S.F., et al.: Performance budget of space optical communication in atmospheric channel. Radio Commun. **536**(10), 68–72 (2020)

15. Xu, K., Zhang, D., Xu, Y., Ma, W.: On the equivalence of two optimal power-allocation schemes for A-TWRC. IEEE Trans. Veh. Technol. **63**(4), 1970–1976 (2014)

16. Rankov, B., Wittneben, A.: Spectral efficient protocols for halfduplex fading relay channels. IEEE J. Sel. Areas Commun. **25**(2), 379–389 (2007)

17. Katti, S.R.: Network Coded Wireless Architecture. Massachusetts Institute of Technology (2009)

18. Li, X., Zhao, X., Zhang, P., et al.: Probability density function of turbulence fading in MRR free space optical link and its applications in MRR free space optical communications. IET Commun. **11**(16), 2476–2481 (2017)
19. Katti, S., Gollakota, S., Katabi, D.: Embracing wireless interference: analog network coding. ACM SIGCOMM Comput. Commun. Rev. **9**(4), 1–14 (2007)

3-Dimensional Reconstruction of a Highly Specular or Transparent Cylinder from a Single Image

Arpita Dawda[1(✉)], Akash Varasada[2], and Minh Nguyen[1]

[1] Auckland University of Technology, Auckland, New Zealand
arpidawda@gmail.com
[2] Adani Power Mundra Limited, Shiracha, India

Abstract. In production lines, high-speed inspection and quality control are necessary to maintain the quality of a product. Automation in quality checking saves time, reduces manual work, and increases the accuracy of the output. Machine Vision is one of the keys to automation. The inspection of highly specular or transparent surface of the object in ambient lighting conditions is the limitation of traditional machine vision concepts. Some applications do not require to inspect all the features of a product in detail. To overcome time constraints, only essential parameters of the manufactured object are measured during the inspection. For symmetric 3D geometric shape objects, only their perimeter and height are measured. In this paper, a simple approach is proposed to reconstruct the 3-dimensional model of a highly specular or transparent cylinder from a single image captured in a calibrated environment. The paper informs about experiments using the proposed technique; heights and the diameters are measured accurately for three different size cylinders. Two of them are made of stainless steel, and one of them is transparent. All experiments are performed in ambient lighting conditions. The cylinders are translated in X and Y directions with respect to the camera. The dimensions of the cylinders are calculated and compared for five different poses to check the effects of camera position on the accuracy of the results. In the end, the results are compared with the actual dimensions to check the accuracy of the system.

Keywords: 3D reconstruction · Highly specular surface · Transparent object · Metric measurements · Single camera · Single image · Inspection

1 Introduction

In high-speed production lines as seen in Fig. 1, automatic inspection and quality control are necessary to identify faulty and maintain the quality of a product. Machine Vision used to reconstruct 3D information, is one of the keys to

Facteon Intelligent Technology Ltd.

© ICST Institute for Computer Sciences, Social Informatics and Telecommunications Engineering 2022
Published by Springer Nature Switzerland AG 2022. All Rights Reserved
S. Paiva et al. (Eds.): SmartCity360° 2021, LNICST 442, pp. 27–40, 2022.
https://doi.org/10.1007/978-3-031-06371-8_3

such automation. In the last few decades, a significant number of techniques for 3-dimensional (3D) shape measurements have been proposed. These 3D measurement techniques can be classified into two categories: surface contact and surface non-contact techniques [5]. A mechanical probe-based *coordinate measuring machine* (CMM) is one of the examples of surface contact techniques. However, CMM only measures a limited number of points on the surface, and it is relatively slow compared to surface non-contact methods. Also, the surface contact method increases the chances of damage to the object.

For high-speed 3D inspection of objects, surface non-contact techniques are preferred. Time-of-flight, stereo vision, laser range scanning and structured lighting are some of the surface non-contact techniques [2].

Computer stereo vision system uses the same principle by replacing eyes with two CCD or CMOS cameras. They are displaced horizontally to obtain two different views. A disparity map is obtained by finding corresponding points in two slightly different images [22]. The disparity map is used to perform 3D shape measurement.

Among surface non-contact techniques, structured lighting is a widely used 3D shape measurement technique for reflective surfaces. It is used to perform a full-field inspection with high resolution and accuracy. A projector projects a sequence of coded patterns onto object surfaces, and the camera captures images of the reflected pattern. The object surface deforms the reflected patterns. The height information of the object surface is embedded in the phase distribution of the reflected pattern. The calibration is performed to understand the correspondences between the camera and the projector. The 3D coordinates of the object surfaces can be calculated by using phase to height mapping in calibrated environments [2,5]. However, there are many drawbacks of using the above mentioned traditional methods which are explained briefly in next section.

In some applications, it is not essential to reconstruct the detailed 3D model of the object. Only the overall shape of the object and some necessary measurements are sufficient. For example, the diameter and height are the essential

Fig. 1. An automotive stainless steel wheel production line

measurements for a cylindric object. This paper focuses on cylindrical objects. Here, we present a simple approach to reconstruct the overall shape of the highly specular cylinder from a single image captured by a single camera. The same approach could also be applied to calculate the dimensions of other solid shapes such as cubes, cuboids, or prisms. However, one important condition is that the border of the bottom part of the object has to be visible in the image.

The remainder of this paper is structured as follows: Sect. 2 briefly describes all steps of methodology such as calibration of a single camera and ellipse fitting. Section 3 explains all the steps of our technique to measure the height and the diameter of the cylinder in detail. Section 4 shows results for two different cylinders for different poses, compared with actual ground truth. Section 5 concludes.

2   Methodology

Generally, a 3D object is reconstructed using multiple cameras or laser by using the concepts of stereo vision or laser triangulation, respectively [18]. However, both concepts have their own sets of difficulties. To understand the difficulties, we assume that the cylinder is in a vertical position. In stereo vision, two slightly different images of the cylinder are captured in a calibrated environment. Stereo matching is performed on these two images to generate the disparity map [4]. However, it is difficult to find corresponding points for highly specular or transparent objects. The ambient lighting of working environment increases the difficulties for inspection. Also, only the front half of the cylinder would be reconstructed in one go from the disparity map. Moreover, to reconstruct the whole cylinder, we need to rotate the cylinder by 180 °C. The same process of stereo matching is repeated to reconstruct the other half of the cylinder. In the end, both halves are merged. However, it is challenging to merge both halves of the cylinder accurately.

Another option is to use the concept of laser triangulation. Here, a thin luminous straight laser line is projected on to the surface of the cylinder. The camera captures images of the projected line." To reconstruct the whole surface of an object, the object must be moved relative to the measurement system, i.e., the unit built by the laser line projector and the camera [18]." In our case, the cylinder is rotated at regular intervals for reconstruction. However, it is very challenging to calibrate a laser and a camera with respect to a rotating positioning system. If we use a linear positioning system, then we can reconstruct only half of the cylinder in one scan. Therefore, the same problem arises like the one in stereo of merging two halves of the cylinder accurately. Also, if the surface of the cylinder is reflective, the optical signal cannot be correctly retrieved. Therefore, it is usually challenging for any optical method to accurately measure shiny objects or objects with a broad range of reflectivity variation across the surface.

In industrial inspection, we have time constraints which do not allow us to use the expensive process of finding corresponding points such as stereo vision or to do laser triangulation [18]. The flow chart in Fig. 2 represents our suggested approach for the 3D reconstruction of a cylinder using a single camera.

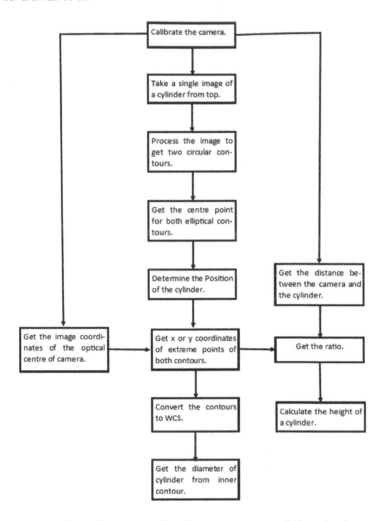

Fig. 2. Overall approach for 3D reconstruction of the cylinder.

2.1 Single Camera Calibration

To perform metric measurements accurately in the world coordinate system (WCS), the only prerequisite is that the camera has been calibrated. The camera is calibrated for a specific plane in WCS for which measurements are obtained. In our case, the calibration plate is placed on besides the cylinder to define the measurement plane. We use calibration plate with hexagonally arranged marks. It contains five finder pattern and atleast one of them should be completely visible in the image for estimating the pose of the relative camera.

Generally, multiple images are captured of a calibration plate in different poses in a specified plane. Here, the specified plane is the measurement plane, which is defined as the plane $Z = 0$ of the WCS. These images, along with the internal camera parameters and the description of calibration plate, work as inputs for calibration. The output comprises the internal and external camera parameters. To determine external parameters, the pose of the calibration plate which is placed directly on the measurement plane is calculated. The external camera parameters describe the relationship between the measurement plane and the camera [18].

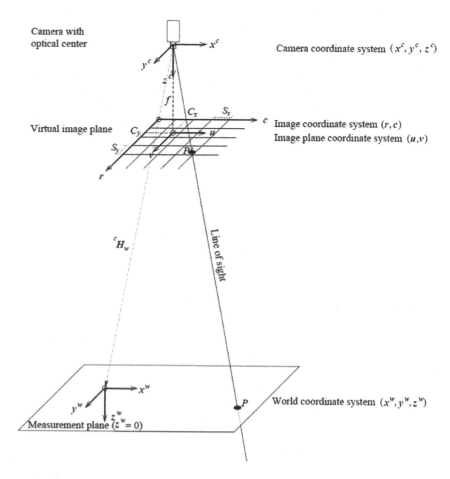

Fig. 3. Transformation of image points in WCS [18].

Figure 3 shows how an image point is transformed into world coordinates. "Given the image coordinates of one point, the goal is to determine the world coordinates of the corresponding point in the measurement plane. For this, the line of sight, i.e., a straight line from the optical centre of the camera through the given point in the image plane, must be intersected with the measurement plane. [18]" The image coordinates are transformed into camera coordinates first and finally into world coordinates using the calibration data.

2.2 Ellipse Fitting

Ellipse extraction is an important task in vision based application as this geometric shape occurs frequently [6,7]. For highly specular or transparent objects, accurate ellipse extraction is difficult. Because low contrast affects accurate extraction of edge contours [8]. "There are three main categories of ellipse extraction methods:Fitting algorithms, Hough-transform techniques, and edge contour following methods [9]." In the first category, an ellipse equation is fitted to a sequence of points. The second category performs ellipse extraction by considering it as a peak-seeking problem in parameter space. Arc-segments are extracted and grouped into an elliptic hypothesis in the last category [9].

In this research, we use Fitting-based edge extraction method as it is proven to be the most accurate among other available methods [10–13]. This method fits an ellipse equation to a sequence of points and tries to minimise the error between the given data and an ellipse equation [14–17]. "There are two types of ellipse-fitting algorithms, algebraic fitting which solves the minimisation problem by exploring the algebraic equation, or geometric fitting which minimises geometric distances of given points to the fitted elliptic curve [9]."

For this research, we use Fitzgibbon's approach for ellipse fitting. This method incorporates the ellipticity constraint into the normalization factor by minimizing the algebric distance. The benefit of using this approach is that it provides useful results under all different noise and occlusion conditions. Also, this direct least-squares fitting method is specifically designed for ellipses. It guarantees that the output will be an ellipse [3].

3 Outline of Our Technique

To reconstruct the cylinder, we need two dimensions, diameter and height of the cylinder. The process of measuring dimensions accurately using a calibrated camera is described below.

3.1 Measurement of the Diameter of a Cylinder

In our approach, the camera is looking at the cylinder from the top instead of the front like conventional 3D reconstruction techniques typically do. After calibrating the camera, a single image of the cylinder is taken from the top. Figure 4 shows an example of the image of the cylinder used for 3D reconstruction. The cylinder shown in image is the largest one among the three cylinders used for this research. This right circular cylinder is made of stainless steel which makes its surface highly reflective. Here, the cylinder is positioned in a way that the bottom and the top of the cylinder is perpendicular to the optical axis of the camera. We can noticeably see two elliptical contours in the image. The camera is calibrated for the bottom plane. Therefore, the edge of the inner ellipse is extracted to measure the diameter of the cylinder. Figure 4 shows the image of the cylinder with detected elliptical contours. It is essential to extract the edges

Fig. 4. An image of the cylinder from top with extracted edges (Courtesy of BLINDED).

of elliptical contours accurately. We need to make sure that the reflection caused by ambient lighting does not affect the accuracy of edge extraction.

Now, we fit an ellipse through the inner contour, which gives us the diameter of the cylinder in the image coordinate system. As stated before, the Fitzgibbon et al. approach is used for ellipse fitting [3]. This extracted inner contour is projected in WCS to get the diameter in metric units. The world coordinates are determined for each point of the detected elliptical contour in the measurement plane. A circular contour will be formed in the measurement plane. We fit a circle through this circular contour using an algebaric approach. This approach minimises the algebraic distance between the contour points and the resulting circle [20]. The diameter of this circular contour in plane $Z = 0$ corresponds to the diameter of the cylinder. The diameter is calculated in metric units using the calibration data.

3.2   Measurement of the Height of a Cylinder

Now, the method to measure the height of the cylinder is described in detail. The setup to measure the height is the same as before. First, the image of the cylinder is processed to accurately extract the edges of two ellipses, which represents the top and the bottom of the cylinder. After extracting the edges, we fit an ellipse through these contours using fitzgibbon approach [19]. Figure 4 shows the image of the cylinder with two extracted edges of elliptical contours. Now, there are three possible cases: (1) The projection centre of the camera and the cylinder's centre line are collinear. (2) The cylinder is horizontally shifted. (3) The cylinder is vertically shifted.

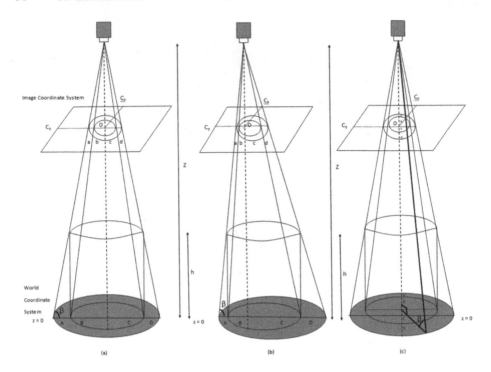

Fig. 5. Three different cases for height measurement.

Figure 5, (a), (b) and (c) illustrate Case 1, Case 2 and Case 3, respectively. As we can see in Fig. 5 (a), we get two concentric elliptical contours in the image plane for Case 1. The second case is shown in Fig. 5 (b). Here, the centre of the camera is not collinear with the centre line of the cylinder. Therefore, we get two elliptical contours which are not concentric. However, the centres of these two elliptical contours share same horizontal axis. Figure 5 (c) shows the third case where the cylinder is vertically displaced. In this case also, the centre of the camera is not collinear with the centre of the cylinder and we get two non-concentric elliptical contours. Instead of horizontal axis, the centres of these two elliptical contours share same vertical axis. Now, our method to measure the height of the cylinder is described in detail below.

To calculate the height, it is essential to find the ratio of $a : b : c : d$ (See Fig. 5). Here, a and d are the distance in pixels between the left extreme points and the right extreme points of both contours, respectively. In case 1 and 2, b and c are the distance between the optical centre and the left and the right extreme points of the internal elliptical contours, respectively. In case 3, b and c are the distance between the optical centre and the top and the bottom extreme points of the internal elliptical contours, respectively. Also, a and d are the distance in pixels between the top extreme points and the bottom extreme points of both contours, respectively. To find this ratio for case 1 and 2, we need to know the X-coordinates of the horizontal extreme points of the contours and also of the optical centre of the camera in the image plane. In case of vertical displacement, we need to know Y- coordinates of the vertical extreme points of the contours and also of the optical centre of the camera in the image plane. The image coordinates of the optical centre of the camera are calculated during the calibration. We can get this parameter by extracting the intrinsic parameters of the camera. After obtaining all the image coordinates the ratio $a : b : c : d$ is calculated. Now, this ratio will correspond to the ratio of $A : B : C : D$ in world coordinate system. A and D represents the height of the cylinder in measurement plane.

We already know that,

$$B + C = D_1 \tag{1}$$

where D_1 is the diameter of the cylinder which is calculated before.

From Fig. 5,

$$A = ax, \; B = bx, \; C = cx, \; D = dx \tag{2}$$

Substituting in Eq. (1),

$$bx + cx = D_1 \tag{3}$$

Here, x is an unknown factor which converts from image coordinate system to world coordinate system:

$$(b + c)x = D_1 \tag{4}$$

$$x = D_1/(b + c) \tag{5}$$

A, B, C and D are calculated by substituting the value of x in Eq. (2). To calculate the height, we also need to know the distance between the camera and the measurement plane. While calibrating the camera, we place the calibration plate directly onto the measurement plane. Therefore, we can determine the distance between the camera and the measurement plane by determining the pose of the calibration plate. The pose of the calibration plate is obtained during the calibration process. By accessing the external parameters of the camera, we can get the distance between the camera and the measurement plane denoted as Z.

Now,

$$\tan \beta = Z/(A + B) = h/A, \tan \beta = Z/(C + D) = h/D \tag{6}$$

In Fig. 5 (c), the angle β is shown slightly to the right for better understanding of the image. In real, the angle β is the angle of the right triangle formed by the camera, the bottom extreme point of outer ellipse and the projection of the centre of the camera in measurement plane.

$$h = (A/(A + B)) \cdot Z, h = (D/(C + D)) \cdot Z \tag{7}$$

Here, h is the height of the cylinder. We can cross-check the results by using the $D/(C + D)$ ratio for height calculation. By measuring the height and the diameter of the cylinder, we can accurately reconstruct the cylinder from a single image.

4   Experiments and Results

Fig. 6. Setup for experiment.

In this experiment, we are using Genie Nano M4020 monochrome camera, which has $4,112 \times 3,008$ resolution. HALCON software is used to perform image processing tasks. The first step of the experiment is to calibrate the camera. The HALCON calibration plate with hexagonally arranged marks is used to calibrate the camera. The calibration plate is placed besides the cylinder (See Fig. 6). This specifies the bottom of the cylinder as the measurement plane. For large objects, we can also place the calibration board inside the cylinder. The camera is mounted at a distance Z from the top of the cylinder. To test this concept, we used three cylinders of different dimensions. Among them, two cylinders are made of stainless steel and one is made of transparent plastic material. Here, a can and a washing machine drum is used to study the case of highly specular surfaces. Figure 7 shows the images of three cylinders used for this research. All experiments are performed in ambient lighting condition of working environment. A single image of the cylinder with the calibration board is captured from the top. The camera is calibrated by using the image of the calibration board as a reference. Now, the cylinder is translated in X and Y directions with respect to the camera. The dimensions of the cylinder are calculated for five different positions.

(a) Transparent Cylinder.   (b) Can.   (c) Drum.

Fig. 7. Cylinders.

Figure 8 shows the input images of the objects used for this research. Figure 8a shows the case when transparent Cylinder 1 is in leftmost position with respect to the camera. Figure 8b represents the top-most position of Cylinder 2 (a can) with respect to the camera. Figure 8c depicts the collinear axes case for Cylinder 3 (a drum).

(a) Cylinder 1 in left-most (b) Cylinder 2 in top-most (c) Cylinder 3 in centre
position.   position.   position.

Fig. 8. Cylinders with extracted elliptical contours.

The edges of the two elliptical contours are extracted by applying thresholding and edge detection algorithms. After extracting the edges, fitzgibbon approach is applied to fit an ellipse through these contours [19]. The image coordinates of the extreme points of the two elliptical contours are obtained from elliptical contours. Also, the projection of the optical centre of the camera in the image coordinate system is obtained as a result of calibration. The diameter of the inner ellipse in the world coordinate system depicts the diameter of the cylinder. In Fig. 8, the diameter of all three cylinders for the given case are mentioned.

Now, the distance between the camera and the measurement plane and the image coordinates of the optical centre of the camera are two crucial parameters for height calculation. Both of them are obtained as a result of calibration. Here, the distance between the camera and the measurement plane is 35.194 cm for Cylinder 1 and 2 and 106.062 cm for Cylinder 3.

Now, the height of the cylinder is measured using the method defined above. Table 1 compares the results for five different positions of the cylinders in either X or Y direction with the actual parameters for Cylinder 1, 2 and 3. The accuracy of the output is also calculated in the table. Moreover, the accuracy of the output predominantly depends on the accuracy of the calibration. Another critical factor is the edge detection and ellipse fitting step for the two elliptical contours.

Table 1. Comparison of output dimensions.

Objects	Cylinder 1			Cylinder 2			Cylinder 3		
Dimensions	Height (cm)	Diameter (cm)	Accuracy (%)	Height (cm)	Diameter (cm)	Accuracy (%)	Height (cm)	Diameter (cm)	Accuracy (%)
Actual Dimensions	3	3	-	12.5	7.3	-	37	49.5	-
Left-most Position	2.79	2.8	94	11.58	7.22	94.94	36.71	49.26	99.39
Right-most Position	2.87	3	97.83	12.38	7.21	98.93	36.85	48.98	99.22
Centre Position	2.89	3	98.16	12.43	7.22	99.24	36.92	49.17	99.53
Top-most Position	2.69	2.9	96.83	12.49	7.22	99.54	35.74	48.79	97.72
Bottom-most Position	2.75	2.9	95.5	12.37	7.22	98.93	36.98	49.24	99.67

5 Conclusion

To conclude, this research provides a simple, fast, cost-effective and feasible approach for the 3D reconstruction of even a highly specular or transparent cylinder from a single image. The main advantage of this method is that it overcomes the limitation of traditional machine vision methods and solves the problem of inspecting highly specular or transparent objects even in ambient lighting conditions. To do so, the only prerequisite is that the top and the bottom of the cylinder are perpendicular to the optical axes of the camera. Also, it is necessary that we can accurately extract the two elliptical contours which represent the top and the bottom of the cylinder. Another crucial parameter of this research is the calibration of the camera as all important parameters required for measurements are obtained from the output of the calibration. The accuracy of output is inversely proportional to the calibration error. For small calibration error, we can achieve the highest accuracy. By analysing the results, the accuracy of the output does not depend on the position of the cylinder with respect to the camera or on the size of the cylinder.

Moreover, this research could also be used for calculating the dimensions of other types of solid shapes such as cube, cuboids or prisms. Also, we can calculate the volume and the surface area of the product from measured dimensions. Due to the time efficiency of the designed solution, the method is applicable in the industrial production and inspection process.

Acknowledgement. Supported by Facteon Intelligent Technology Ltd.

References

1. Asoudegi, E., Pan, Z.: Computer vision for quality control in automated manufacturing systems. Comput. Ind. Eng. **21**(1–4), 141–145 (1991)
2. Chen, F., Brown, G., Song, M.: Overview of three-dimensional shape measurement using optical methods. Opt. Eng. **39**(1), 10–22 (2000)
3. Fitzgibbon, A., Pilu, M., Fisher, R.B.: Direct least square fitting of ellipses. IEEE Trans. Pattern Anal. Mach. Intell. **21**(5), 476–480 (1999)
4. Klette, R.: Concise Computer Vision. Springer, London (2014). https://doi.org/10.1007/978-1-4471-6320-6
5. Lin, H., Gao, J., Zhang, G., Chen, X., He, Y., Liu, Y.: Review and comparison of high-dynamic range three-dimensional shape measurement techniques. J. Sensors (2017)
6. Pătrăucean, V., Gurdjos, P., Gioi, V.: Joint a contrario ellipse and line detection. IEEE Trans. Pattern Anal. Mach. Intell. **39**, 788–802 (2017)
7. Ren, J., Owais, H.M., Song, T., Lin, D.: Towards fast and accurate ellipse and semi-ellipse detection. In: Proceedings of IEEE International Conference on Image Processing, pp. 743–747 (2018)
8. Ouellet, J.N., H'ebert, P.: Precise ellipse estimation without contour point extraction. Mach. Vis. Appl. **21**, 59–67 (2010)
9. Xu, Z., Xu, S., Qian, C., Klette, R.: Ellipse extraction in low-quality images. In: 2019 16th International Conference on Machine Vision Applications (MVA), pp. 1–5. IEEE (2019)
10. Kanatani, K., Sugaya, Y., Kanazawa, Y.: Ellipse fitting. In: Guide to 3D Vision Computation, pp. 11–32 (2016)
11. Kanatani, K., Sugaya, Y., Kanazawa, Y.: Ellipse Fitting for Computer Vision: Implementation and Applications. Morgan and Claypool, Williston (2016)
12. Kovalevsky, V.: Modern Algorithms for Image Processing. Apress, Springer, Delware (2019). https://doi.org/10.1007/978-1-4842-4237-7
13. Masuzaki, T., Sugaya, Y., Kanatani, K.: High accuracy ellipse-specific fitting. In: Klette, R., Rivera, M., Satoh, S. (eds.) PSIVT 2013. LNCS, vol. 8333, pp. 314–324. Springer, Heidelberg (2014). https://doi.org/10.1007/978-3-642-53842-1_27
14. Prasad, D.K., Leung, M.K., Quek, C.: ElliFit: an unconstrained, noniterative, least squares based geometric ellipse fitting method. Pattern Recogn. **46**, 1449–1465 (2013)
15. Wang, Y., He, Z., Liu, X., Tang, Z., Li, L.: A fast and robust ellipse detector based on top-down least-square fitting. In: Proceedings of British Machine Vision Conference, pp. 156.1–156.12 (2015)
16. Mulleti, S., Seelamantula, C.S.: Ellipse fitting using the finite rate of innovation sampling principle. IEEE Trans. Image Process. **25**, 1451–1464 (2016)

17. Chojnacki, W., Brooks, M.J., Hengel, A.V.D., Gawley, D.: On the fitting of surfaces to data with covariances. IEEE Trans. Pattern Anal. Mach. Intell. **22**, 1294–1303 (2000)
18. Solution Guide III-C 3D Vision, Machine Vision in 3D World Coordinates, Version 18.05, MVTec Software GmbH, München (2018)

Websites

19. fit_ellipse_contour_xld (2019). www.mvtec.com/doc/halcon/12/en/fit_ellipse_contour_xld.html
20. fit_circle_contour_xld (2019). www.mvtec.com/doc/halcon/12/en/fit_circle_contour_xld.html
21. Machine Vision 2019. https://en.wikipedia.org/wiki/Machine_vision. Accessed 10 July 2019
22. Stereo Vision 2017, The MathWorks Inc. http://au.mathworks.com/discovery/stereo-vision.html. Accessed 13 July 2019

Temporal Colour-Coded Facial-Expression Recognition Using Convolutional Neural Network

Minh Nguyen[✉] and Wei Qi Yan

School of Engineering, Computer and Mathematical Sciences,
Auckland University of Technology, Auckland, New Zealand
minh.nguyen@aut.ac.nz

Abstract. This research primarily aims to solve the problem of the high suicide rate in NZ; in this project, we plan to implement an AI-based recognition system for the long-term mental health issue for discovering potential suicidal population in NZ society. Visual data (CCTV video footages) possesses affluent and bountiful information; however, the amount of data grows explosively; thus we often fail to capture the patterns and extract meaningful featured data for any reliable analysis. Moreover, AI-detected human facial microexpressions are usually ambiguous and return with various uncertain patterns. It is extremely tough to identify and verify the emotions of somebody in the last few minutes, hours, days, weeks, or months. In a nutshell, it is very challenging to assess the depression so as to predict their suicidal probability. Pertaining to solve this problem, we will design a novel temporal expression recognition system based on the accumulation of seven colour-coded human emotional expressions, namely, anger, disgust, fear, happiness, sadness, surprise, and neutral. We propose to use various colour dots (rain-drops) to replace the feelings of people. We assume that, just like the colour, people have three primitive emotions: joy (green), sadness (blue), and anger (red). The mixture of these will lead to other feelings: anger + joy = surprise (yellow), anger + sad = scare (purple), joy + sad = disgust (cyan), and when these three primitive feelings are additive, we get a neutral state (white). Long-term feelings are emotions accumulated overtime, digitally presented by using any drops of colours on to a white canvas. Each canvas can be the feeling of someone in a predefined period (the last five minute, for instance). By implementing this, the emotions of target persons over the previous one month could be effectively packed down into a movie of approx. 2 h (60 Hz). At any time, such a video could be assessed by using AI algorithms for stress level assessment (in the last one month) so as to decide the requirements of mental treatment.

Keywords: Computer vision · Object detection · Deep learning · Facial expression recognition

© ICST Institute for Computer Sciences, Social Informatics and Telecommunications Engineering 2022
Published by Springer Nature Switzerland AG 2022. All Rights Reserved
S. Paiva et al. (Eds.): SmartCity360° 2021, LNICST 442, pp. 41–54, 2022.
https://doi.org/10.1007/978-3-031-06371-8_4

1 Introduction

1.1 Research Background and Significance

New Zealand has one of the highest teenage suicide rate in the developed world [1]. While the numbers are staggering, they are nothing new. Now, scientists believe there is a significant link between mental health and suicide risk [2]. That is, if a person has a mental health problem, they are more likely to commit suicide. At the same time, poverty, domestic violence, drug or alcohol abuse and despair are also objective factors that affect mental health (increase of depression).

Almost one-third of New Zealanders own personal experience of mental distress; Māori and young adults aged 18 to 24 years have higher rates of mental distress. Patients with depression have suicidal thoughts, and suicide is the most dangerous symptoms of depression. Hence, suicide is a severe mental problem in New Zealand. We have one of the highest teenage suicide rates among 41 OECD and EU countries. Even though there are a plethora of youth support centres and counselling services all over the country; many are ashamed to seek assistance. It could be more effective if we would like to accurately and automatically sense who are currently vulnerable to suffering this problem and necessitate to accommodate support.

Patient with depression have suicidal thoughts, and suicide is the most dangerous symptoms of depression. People with depression are depressed and pessimistic. It is easy to have suicidal thoughts when it is serious. They often feel lack interest, lack of mental and physical strength, and then their eyes are always with tears; they think that life is worse than death.

At present, the key to the check of suicide risk is to rely on people's mental health risk assessment [3], such as the existence of hidden psychological dangers, psychological crisis emergency assessment and so on. The presence or absence of hidden psychological trouble is a test to evaluate whether the individual has hidden psychological disorder and the severity of its existence.

Judgmental assessment of the emergency degree of psychological crisis mainly focuses on the judgment and its harm to oneself and others:

1. Whether he/she will commit suicide, self-harm, attack others or other dangerous behaviours.
2. Whether there are serious risks and hidden dangers of psychological problems that may break out at any time.

Thus it can be seen that the current assessment of the severity of mental health problems of suicides is subjective. It may be that the depressed person does not get the attention and intervention in the first place due to deliberate cover-up during testing or the inexperience of the psychologist. It is also possible that because people around do not care enough about the person concerned, they do not find the hidden psychological problems, so they do not control the risk factors in the first time and carry out effective psychological intervention and treatment.

Deep learning methods, especially in the field of image classification and recognition, have achieved fruitful results in recent years [5], the technique of extracting image features by training facial expression recognition (some are seen in Fig. 1) has attracted

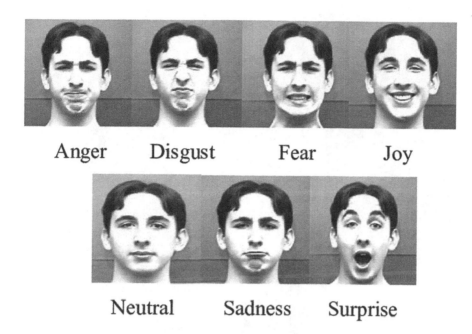

Fig. 1. Some examples of seven basic human emotions [4]

great attention [6–8]. Among many deep learning algorithms, convolution neural network (CNN) technique is more effective in learning the most effective deep features of images [9]. Because CNN has the advantages of autonomous learning of graphic components, compared with other visual-based methods, it can detect people's current psychological state in the first time. The question is "can CNN help efficiently detect depression by finding the presents of negative facial expression?"

The goal is to identify the vulnerable population better and provide a good foundation for follow-up psychological counselling work. This transformative research explores a unique theory of the feasibility of converting a massive fuzzy quantity of temporal emotions (individuals or a community) into a more manageable, intuitive, visual representation of mental health status. Today, Artificial Intelligence (AI) benefits us to recognise micro-expression via cameras or CCTV (i.e., closed-circuit television) systems, e.g., smile detection. However, these expressions are captured in a sequence of video frames, or in a fraction of a second (most cameras nowadays acquire 30–60 frames per second). In contrast, depression is a long-term feeling; negative emotions must be accumulated over a long time (namely, weeks, months, or even years). It sluggishly drains the optimism, energy, and drive; and produces suicidal thoughts bit by bit. Therefore, we will have to care for someone for an extended period to identify for any those at risk.

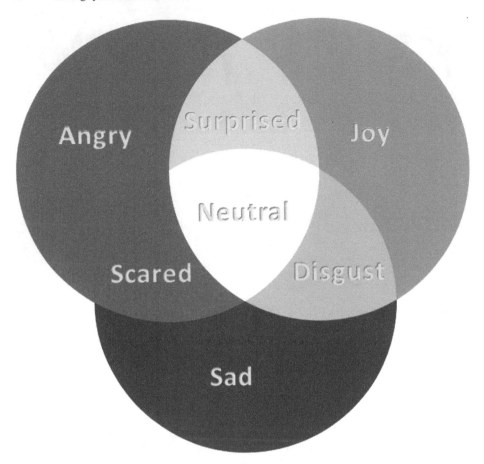

Fig. 2. Proposed colours of seven emotions

1.2   Research Objective and Plan

This paper aims to use image processing and CNN; to recognise long-term negative facial expressions, and thus, help estimate the likelihood of someone who may commit suicide (after months of depression). We hope that it could be used to help reducing the suicide rate in New Zealand and even internationally.

However, it is only easy for computer vision to recognise micro-expression, e.g. expression (smile detection, for instance) presented only in a fraction of a second (30–60 frames per second). After a long period, the data collected could be accumulated and become extremely large for any reliable analysis. Moreover, micro-expressions are often returned with various uncertainties. It is hard for it to know the true feeling (could be up and down) of someone in the last few minutes, hours, days, weeks, or months. In short, it is very challenging to assess the stress level of someone to conclude for the sucidural probability.

We propose to use various colour dots to replace feelings of people. We assume that just like colour space, people have three primitive feelings: joy, sadness, and anger. The mix of these feelings will create other feelings: anger + joy = surprise, anger + sad = scare, joy + sad = disgust, and when these three primitive feelings are added together, we get neutral feeling. To simplify it, we create a colour additive table as shown in Fig. 2.

Long-term feelings are emotions accumulated overtime, presented by painting many colour dots on to a white canvas. Each canvas can be the feeling of someone in a pre-defined period (the last five minute, for instance). By doing this, the emotional feelings of target persons during the previous one month could be effectively compressed into a movie of approx. 2 h (60 Hz). At any time, such a film could be assessed by AI for stress levels changed to make some decisions for the requirement of mental treatments. The details of designs, implementations, and testing results will be further discussed in the next few sections.

The idea of converting complex human emotions into colours is unique. We have a goal to extend it into a commercial product - an anger management IoT device. There are several research impacts on NZ:

- The IoT device could help reduce the depression, stress levels, and the suicide rate in NZ; we would like to offer the use of this on vulnerable individuals who are currently receiving mental health services through their GP or family doctor.
- The research helps create a more healthy working/teaching/learning environment (e.g. classroom, office, etc.). The device displays the average feeling (negative/positive) of a room/office/lab for an extended period; this helps management to think of applying necessary actions (e.g. team-building activities) to raise the healthy working environment for NZers. We will meet and talk to these clients about the pros.; we will offer the use of the devices in classrooms and offices.

2   Backgrounds and Related Works

2.1   Basic Emotions of Human Beings

In 1971, psychologists Ekman and Friesen put forward six basic emotions of human beings [10], namely Surprise, Sadness, Anger, Fear, Disgust and Happiness. In order to describe facial expressions, different methods of facial expressions were born. Facial action coding system (FACS) was proposed [11], which can distinguish different facial expressions according to the movements of facial muscles and muscle groups. Facial animation parameters (FAPS) is another expression encoding method [12], which describes facial expressions according to the movement of facial features.

Usually, people's emotion is expressed through the combination of changes in each part of the facial muscles. However, people will hide real disguise emotions in particular circumstances, such as lying or negotiations. The consequent facial expressions do not reflect the true inner feelings; the study found that the facial will reveal a small, local, duration within half a second of facial expression [13]. Unlike regular facial expressions, the micro facial expression is entirely spontaneous, unable to forge or suppressed, can reflect the real emotion. According to the research of the Ekman et al. [14], this micro-expression can be divided into six basic categories: happiness, sadness, anger, surprise, disgust and fear.

2.2 Available Facial Expression Database

Many have constructed models of CNN by training and learning fatigue expressions from expression databases. CNN generally requires a large number of sample data; however, due to identity protection, not many available fatigue expression databases could be found easily. Some are listed below, and they are widely used at present.

CK+ Expression Database. The CK+ emoji database is an extension of the Cohn-Kanade database and was released in 2010 [15]. The CK+ database includes 123 subfolders, with a total of 593 emoji images. The information on each picture contains the classification label. In this total of 593 photos, 327 of them are with the expression classification label, including the depressed expression and non-depressed expression.

Fer2013 Facial Expression Database. This facial expression database is composed of 35,886 face images; among them, the training image 28708, available test and private test are 3589 pieces. Each image is fixed by the size of 48×48 of a grey image, labelled with different kinds of expressions.

Colorferet Database. It contains more than 10,000 pictures of more than 1,000 people, each with different expressions, lighting, poses and ages. Also, this paper also took photos of fatigue expression to enrich the sample data. The images obtained through the above three methods included 10,000 face images, among which about 2,000 were fatigue expression images.

2.3 Existing Suicide Prevention Programs

In early 2018, the Public Health Agency of Canada announced a pilot program for a suicide prevention program [16] developed by the Canadian government in collaboration with Ottawa-based artificial intelligence company Advanced Symbolics. The pilot project will study and predict regional suicide rates by monitoring posts from Canadian social media accounts, including anything related to suicide. Throughout the trial, the researchers will analyze 160,000 social media accounts to identify a possible rise in community suicide rates across Canada. Government health authorities will be notified when AI technology predicts that suicide rates are likely to rise in certain areas. If the project is successful, AI could help Canadian health authorities indicate where the next suicide spike will occur, allowing interventions to be launched months in advance.

Back in 2011, Facebook developed an artificial suicide reporting system. Users can upload screenshots of suicide content posted by others for audit. Vetted, Facebook sends emails to suicidal users; they could chat online with a crisis intervention representative from the National Suicide Prevention Lifeline by clicking a link in the email, new ways to help those who are unwilling to call [17]. In 2015, the system allowed users to "tag" suicide-related content, allowing Facebook employees to speed up the review of posts and respond appropriately. In 2017, Facebook tried again to use the new "active detection" AI technology. The technology scans all posts for potential suicide attempts and, if necessary, sends mental health resources to users at risk of suicide or their friends, or to contact a local emergency hotline, without waiting for a user to report, to maximize help. The system has been successfully tested in the United States and plans to expand to more countries. For now, the assessment and management of suicide risk remain highly subjective, despite many attempts and efforts by researchers to use artificial intelligence to prevent suicide.

3 Design, Implementation, and Results

As said in the Introduction section, we plan to use three primary colours: red, blue, green, and their blending colours: yellow, cyan, magenta, and white; to present seven emotions. They are (1) anger; (2) disgust; (3) fear; (4) joy/happy; (5) sadness (6) surprise; (7) neutral. Therefore, the first step we need to do is to build a system that could classify these emotions. Using CNN, we need to build Emotional Expression Data-set with the seven classes as mentioned above.

3.1 Build of Emotional Expression Database via Web Crawler

In addition to the available database, we could extend the dataset by searching and downloading the Internet for emotional facial images through the Web crawler [18]. We crawl the web pages and download photos in batches while restricting the grasping content.

The crawling process is as follows:

- We simulate the browser to make a request: enter the URL to complete the request of the server and get the header information about the type, cookie, browser type and others.
- We get the server page response. If the server is running normally, we will receive real-time feedback, including data in binary format such as HTML, JSON string, picture, video.
- We analyse and store the content. If it is a picture, it is saved for further processing.

The emotional recognition based on micro-expressions consists of three steps, namely image pre-processing, feature extraction and emotion classification.

3.2 Image Pre-processing

In the practical engineering application, the source image data is broad in quantity and high in dimension. It is likely to contain a lot of noise interference information that is meaningless to the research. Therefore, it is necessary to pre-process the source image before model training to remove redundant noise, focus on crucial information, and compensate or recover some lost knowledge. Follows are some of our pre-processing steps.

Image Normalisation. The image normalisation step makes the face photos acquired under different directions and lighting conditions have consistency. Generally, the face images after face detection and alignment cannot be extracted directly for features. Scale normalisation is also needed to remove redundant information so that the image size is the same, and grey normalisation reduces the influence of light. The normalised operation can transform all images into a unified form, which is conducive to subsequent batch processing.

Scale Normalization. The size of face images after scale normalized face detection and alignment is different. Most machine learning algorithms require input is a fixed size. We apply scale normalization: images are extracted from the target face regions and cropping for the same size. We set the distance between the pupils of both eyes as d, take the midpoint of connection between the two pupils as the origin, take d in the horizontal direction, $0.7d$ in the vertical direction upward, and $1.7d$ in the downward direction, and then uniformly normalize it to 224×224 after shearing.

Grayscale of the Normalized Image. To reduce the calculation cost, we convert the colour images into gray-scale images. Grey image is a unique colour image where three-channel components are the same. Gray-scale image can effectively reduce the subsequent computation burden compared to coloured ones. According to the characteristic that the human eye has the highest sensitivity to green and the lowest sensitivity to blue, the value of each component weight and the transformation formula is shown:

$$Grey(i,j) = 0.3R(i,j) + 0.59G(i,j) + 0.11B(i,j) \tag{1}$$

Histogram Equalization. Finally, we apply histogram equalization to transforms the histogram of the original image into uniform distribution for image grey level normalization. This action makes image grey level clearer, improve the overall contrast, and weaken the influence of light on image analysis. In our system, histogram equalization improves not only the image contrast but also transforms it into a uniform distribution of pixel values.

3.3 ADA Boost for Face Detection

Among many machine learning methods, Ada Boost algorithm [19] is one of the most widely used face detections. Ada Boost algorithm learns the training samples repeatedly, weights the weak classifier with the lowest classification error rate obtained from each training, and then receive a classifier with better effect. Ada Boost classification detection algorithm for face detection does not rely on subjective prior knowledge and model construction, only extracts objective face image features, and realizes real-time detection with high timeliness according to the feedback results of feature classifier. Boosting is a method to enhance the accuracy of a weak classifier into a robust classifier after multiple classifications.

3.4   Model Trained and Deployment

After pre-processing and face detection, the facial features of depression can be trained and learned through Xception network [20]. Xception is an improvement on the Inception V3 model by Google. It replaces the convolution in Inception V3 with the deep separable convolution so that the convergence speed and recognition accuracy can be improved.

3.5   Temporal Colour-Coded Facial Expression Recognition

Assume that we have a reliable face recognition and emotion detection, which could return a result like such: Emotion = [anger: 10%; disgust: 5%; fear: 15%; joy/happy: 50%; sadness: 1%; surprise: 15%; neutral: 4%]. We could run an algorithm to paint the emotion onto our emotional canvas, as described in Algorithm 1.

Algorithm 1: Emotional canvas creation

initialization;
while *there is a frame from video/webcam* **do**
    face-detection();
    for *each face* **do**
        emotion-detection();
        for *each emotion* **do**
            | fill-random-circle(emotion-colour, radius=certainty)
        end
    end
    save-canvas-as-a-frame();
end
Result: Write output as a video for further analysis

The colour dots are dropping down on the canvas at random locations, just like raindrops, with seven colours, as indicated in Fig. 2. Basically, the algorithm helps reduce the dimension of the temporal emotional expression of one-to-many people in a video footage down to only one 2D colour picture/video. It also eliminates the effect of storing all historical data, e.g. emotion detected too long ago will be filed away (by other more recent ones). Figure 3 displays two emotional canvas created from two video sequences, one with a lot of sadness moments (left figure), and the other one with loads of laughter (right figure). It is easy to notice the majority of blue dots in the sadness sample, while, the happy one contains significantly more green drops.

Fig. 3. Two samples of emotion canvas: a sad output (left) and a happy output (tight)

4   Results and Analysis

4.1   Accuracy of Emotional Facial Expression on Still Images

In the experiment, the cross verification method was adopted. The facial expression images of nine people were randomly selected as the training set and the facial expression images of the remaining one person as the test set so that each person's facial expression images were taken as a test sample. The experiment was conducted for ten times, and the average recognition rate of the ten experiments was finally accepted as the experimental result. We acquire photos with seven kinds of expression: Angry (AN), Neutral (NE), Disgust (DI), Feared (FE) Happy (HA), Sad (SA), Surprised (SU). The recognition rate of individual expressions and the overall recognition are recorded. Happy face returned with the highest accuracy (approx. 90%), while fear expression has the lowest detection rate (approx. 40–50%) (Table 1).

Table 1. Results for emotional detection

	True positive	True negative	False pos	False neg
Accuracy	81.82%	76.92%	18.18%	23.08%

4.2 Accuracy on Video Footages

It is challenging to quantify the accuracy of any emotional detection for an extended period or long video sequences. Therefore, we will not be able to conclude the accuracy in percentages. Instead, we try to run the system on various Youtube video footages, some are positive, with happy talks/comedies, some are negative, with cries and tears. After testing, we found out that the classification of the positive and negative primary trend is relatively robust. All positive video footages return a majority of green canvas; while negative video footages produce mostly blue and red dots.

To present the outcome, we have uploaded on Youtube two sample output:

- A happy video at https://www.youtube.com/watch?v=KQuXGXkLwyg
- A sad video at https://www.youtube.com/watch?v=Y-Bul6oA5IY

Figure 4 displays screenshots of these two outputs. We recommend reviewers to access the Youtube links, to visualise the contribution of this paper. The left canvas is the live drops of emotional colour drops; the right is footage with face and emotional expression detection. The bottom part displays the expression trends using just three primary feelings, namely, happiness (green), anger (red), and sadness (blue).

Besides the three main lines, there are ten other background lines, which colour is the mix of these three main lines (quantitatively):

$$Line(R, G, B) = (Anger, Happiness, Sadness)$$

By that, this single colour represents the average emotion at each moment of the video sequence. Thanks to it, we have successfully reduced the temporal emotional expression of a video sequence during any particular period down to only one single colour. If we want to quantify the emotion, we could just pick the Hue value, and the mixed feeling could expressively be represented.

(a) A happy video at https://www.youtube.com/watch?v=KQuXGXkLwyg

(b) A sad video at https://www.youtube.com/watch?v=Y-Bul6oA5IY

Fig. 4. Two samples of emotion canvas (Color figure online)

5 Conclusion, Limitations and Future Work

5.1 Conclusion

Aiming at the problem of high suicide rate, this project investigated the suicide situation both internationally and in New Zealand, and designed and implemented a suicide expression recognition system for suicidal people in the society. The aim is to identify the potential suicide population better and provide a good foundation for follow-up psychological counselling work. To quantify the mental health issues or likelihood of someone might commit suicide, we develop an algorithm that is capable to represent the complex temporal emotional expression of somebody down to just one single video sequence using colour raindrops.

The experimental results show that the recognition effect of the deep learning algorithm CNN is suitable to detect the seven selected types of expressions. Several video sequences and experiments are carried out to make the foundation for the feasibility of the project. Predictably, if the system can be successfully developed further, it will effectively quantify/detect a part of the suicide population, and thus reduce the suicide rate.

5.2 Limitations

Although this project uses cutting-edge modelling techniques, there are still many areas for improvement.

- Image preprocessing: Limited by hardware resources, the acquired expression image in this project is processed into a greyscale image of 48×48, and the parts outside the range are discarded. However, the retained image range will affect the features learned by CNN algorithm. To put it simply, the larger the enclosed image range is, the more features CNN can learn. Therefore, the accuracy of the model can be improved by increasing the capacity of retained images. Typical resolutions are 64×64 and 128×128.
- Data set expansion: CNN algorithm needs a large amount of data to learn the features in the data. In the case of less data, it isn't easy to get a good recognition effect. Therefore, the expansion of different types of emoticons, predominantly negative emoticons, is significant.

5.3 Future Works

This project design a system for negative expression recognition. With the assistance of other functions, the system can better achieve the goal of reducing the suicide rate.

- Questionnaire function: As a matter of fact, some potential suicide patients will not show evident expression. This phenomenon will limit the recognition effect of the system. But suicidal tendencies don't just affect the target's facial expression. They also affect the target's movement to answer specific questions. Therefore, combining some auxiliary functions, such as filling out questionnaires, and connecting the judgment results of other additional operations based on image recognition results, can effectively improve the recognition accuracy of the system.
- Image acquisition: Predictably, most people will not make blatant suicidal expressions when the system collects images. These predisposed emoticons are often inadvertently displayed to the outside world. In the future, the link of image acquisition can be optimized to contain users' expressions in certain activities.

References

1. Roh, B.-R., Jung, E.H., Hong, H.J.: A comparative study of suicide rates among 10–19-year-olds in 29 OECD countries. Psychiatry Investig. **15**(4), 376 (2018)
2. Keyes, C.L., Lopez, S.J.: Toward a science of mental health. In: Oxford Handbook of Positive Psychology, pp. 89–95 (2009)
3. Godin, P.: 'you don't tick boxes on a form': a study of how community mental health nurses assess and manage risk. Health Risk Soc. **6**(4), 347–360 (2004)
4. Kwong, J.C.T., Garcia, F.C.C., Abu, P.A.R., Reyes, R.S.: Emotion recognition via facial expression: utilization of numerous feature descriptors in different machine learning algorithms. In: TENCON 2018–2018 IEEE Region 10 Conference, pp. 2045–2049. IEEE (2018)
5. Al-Saffar, A.A.M., Tao, H., Talab, M.A.: Review of deep convolution neural network in image classification. In: 2017 International Conference on Radar, Antenna, Microwave, Electronics, and Telecommunications (ICRAMET), pp. 26–31. IEEE (2017)
6. Zhao, X., Shi, X., Zhang, S.: Facial expression recognition via deep learning. IETE Tech. Rev. **32**(5), 347–355 (2015)
7. Lv, Y., Feng, Z., Xu, C.: Facial expression recognition via deep learning. In: 2014 International Conference on Smart Computing, pp. 303–308. IEEE (2014)
8. Liu, P., Han, S., Meng, Z., Tong, Y.: Facial expression recognition via a boosted deep belief network. In: Proceedings of the IEEE Conference on Computer Vision and Pattern Recognition, pp. 1805–1812 (2014)
9. Vyas, A.S., Prajapati, H.B., Dabhi, V.K.: Survey on face expression recognition using CNN. In: 2019 5th International Conference on Advanced Computing & Communication Systems (ICACCS), pp. 102–106. IEEE (2019)
10. Kätsyri, J., Sams, M.: The effect of dynamics on identifying basic emotions from synthetic and natural faces. Int. J. Hum. Comput. Stud. **66**(4), 233–242 (2008)
11. Ekman, R.: What the Face Reveals: Basic and Applied Studies of Spontaneous Expression Using the Facial Action Coding System (FACS). Oxford University Press, Oxford (1997)
12. Pardàs, M., Bonafonte, A.: Facial animation parameters extraction and expression recognition using hidden Markov models. Signal Process. Image Commun. **17**(9), 675–688 (2002)
13. Le Ngo, A.C., Oh, Y.-H., Phan, R.C.-W., See, J.: Eulerian emotion magnification for subtle expression recognition. In: 2016 IEEE International Conference on Acoustics, Speech and Signal Processing (ICASSP), pp. 1243–1247. IEEE (2016)
14. Ekman, P., Friesen, W.V.: Constants across cultures in the face and emotion. J. Pers. Soc. Psychol. **17**(2), 124 (1971)
15. Lucey, P., Cohn, J.F., Kanade, T., Saragih, J., Ambadar, Z., Matthews, I.: A complete dataset for action unit and emotion-specified expression. In: 2010 IEEE Computer Society Conference on Computer Vision and Pattern Recognition Workshops (CVPRW), pp. 94–101 (2010)
16. Dick, K.: Artificial intelligence and mental illness. Health Sci. Inquiry **9**(1), 5 (2018)
17. Robinson, J., Rodrigues, M., Fisher, S., Herrman, H.: Suicide and social media. Melbourne, Australia: Young and Well Cooperative Research Centre (2014)
18. Yang, D.-Z., Zhao, G., Wang, T.: Application of webcrawler in information search and data mining. Comput. Eng. Des. **30**(24), 5658–5662 (2009)
19. Ma, S., Du, T.: Improved adaboost face detection. In: 2010 International Conference on Measuring Technology and Mechatronics Automation, vol. 2, pp. 434–437. IEEE (2010)
20. Chollet, F.: Xception: deep learning with depthwise separable convolutions. In: Proceedings of the IEEE Conference on Computer Vision and Pattern Recognition, pp. 1251–1258 (2017)

Why Dealing with Electrical Faults for Smart Microgrid is not Enough?

Pragya Kirti Gupta[1], Sai Shibu Narayanan Babu[2],
Anjana Mohandas Sheeladevi[2], and Venkatesh Pampana[1(✉)]

[1] fortiss GmbH, Munich, Germany
{gupta,pampana}@fortiss.org
[2] Center for Wireless Networks and Applications, Amrita Vishwa Vidyapeetham,
Amritapuri, India
{saishibunb,anjanams}@am.amrita.edu

Abstract. With increasing use of Information and Communication Technologies (ICT) in smart grids, the need to study the faults induced by software and communication systems is important towards realizing stable operation of microgrids. Since the effect of faults in the electrical, communication and software systems is different, the impact of these faults in each other system, the knowledge of their effects and causes is necessary to design appropriate recovery actions. In this paper, we study the faults and their impact on the microgrids. We emphasize on the necessity of software and communication fault handling in order to create resilient microgrids. This paper highlights the effects of software and communication faults on electrical system and vice-versa. A detailed study of the commonly occurring faults in a microgrid and their cascading effects is presented. Towards this a cause-and-effect analysis of the commonly occurring faults on the performance of the microgrid is carried out. Finally, we identify potential research areas where the fault handling approaches can be included and improved to make the microgrid more resilient.

Keywords: Faults · Failures · Microgrid challenges · Cause-effect analysis · Fishbone analysis · Cascading faults · Resilience · Self-healing

1   Introduction

The 2019 massive power outage in Latin American countries affecting Argentina, Uruguay, Paraguay, Chile and Brazil is the perfect example of a fault occurring in one part of the distribution system and cascading to the extent of a partial power outage in these five countries [1]. As the cause of the outage is still being investigated, it illustrates the failure of the automatic protection system of the grid. In this instance, a well-planned automatic protection system that could either isolate the fault or switch to backup power resources was already operational. However, the protection system failed to control the power fluctuation leading to further power outage and damage to the devices. This example illustrates that the failure (observed as the power outage) could have been caused

S. Paiva et al. (Eds.): SmartCity360° 2021, LNICST 442, pp. 55–74, 2022.
https://doi.org/10.1007/978-3-031-06371-8_5

by multiple faults (physical damage to the grid lines or cyber-attack). Once the failure of power supply occurred, it further induced faults (short-circuits) that led to the breakdown of the electrical system for 24 h affecting millions of people. Even though the use of automatic switches to isolate the faults are installed, their synchronized operation needs coordination.

Towards the automation of complex decisions and to operate complex microgrid systems, fault handling is a crucial aspect that engineers, designers and researchers need to deal with. In fact, a significant feature of microgrids is its ability to automatically handle faults, which is often referred to as self-healing. In general, self-healing systems include two aspects: self and healing. The term 'self' refers to the system's ability to observe its own behavior. In the context of faults and failures, this information also includes the knowledge of abnormal behavior that is specifically identified as faults. The healing actions are the recovery measures designed to counter the effects of the faults. Towards the objective of defining and designing healing actions, knowledge about the faults and failures is necessary. However, there are several questions surrounding faults and fault handling in a microgrid that need to be investigated. The bigger research question that should be investigated is *why dealing with electrical faults for smart microgrids is not enough?* To answer this, we focus on the following questions in this paper: - RQ1: *What are the effects of electrical faults on the ICT system and viceversa?* Faults from the electrical systems may cause either power disruptions or power disturbances. However, the effect of software and communication faults and their impact on the electrical distribution system are still unclear. - RQ2: *What are the commonly occurring faults in a microgrid and their impact?* Not all faults can be observed and handled by the microgrid controller. Therefore, an estimation of the fault space and the scope of faults for designing recovery actions are necessary. This estimation helps in identifying the appropriate recovery mechanisms for self-healing microgrids.

This paper is organized into six sections. In the Sect. 2, the concept of microgrid is discussed along with the basic concept and layout of an islanded microgrid. In the Sect. 3, some of the scenarios are presented to highlight the effect of faults on each other leading to cascading effects. Section 4 describes various faults and fault handling techniques, highlighting the gap in the on-going research for resilient microgrid. Section 5 deals with the commonly occurring faults in a microgrid and their impact. Finally, in the Sect. 6, we highlight some of the emerging solutions and future trends in fault handling.

2   Concept of Microgrid

In 2017, IEEE encompassed the vision for microgrids and provided a specific definition of microgrid in the IEEE Standard for Microgrid Controllers [2]. *A microgrid is a group of interconnected loads and distributed energy resources with clearly defined electrical boundaries that acts as a single controllable entity with respect to the grid and can connect and disconnect from the grid to enable it to operate in both grid-connected or island mode.* A typical microgrid is composed of three systems: electrical, software and communication. This standard essentially provides three distinct characteristics for microgrids, namely *a) clearly defined electrical boundaries, b) a control system to manage and dispatch resources as a single controllable entity and c) installed generation capacity that exceeds the critical load; this allows the microgrid to be disconnected from the main grid, i.e., to operate as an entity in islanded mode, and supply local loads.* The conceptual model of the microgrid considered in this work is shown in Fig. 1. Conceptually a microgrid is comprised of three individual domains: electrical, software and communication. A typical microgrid has: 1) consumers, which are the energy consumption units, 2) generators, which are the renewable energy sources, 3) storage units such as batteries, 4) controller, which is the energy management system and 5) grid connectors, which provide the ability to connect or disconnect from the grid. The power distribution and communication distribution in the microgrid are also shown in Fig. 1. Power supply from the grid is distributed to the consumers (including controller) and storage units. Power supply from the generators is supplied to consumers, storage unit or fed into the grid. Communication distribution is further shown in terms of the data generated by each component.

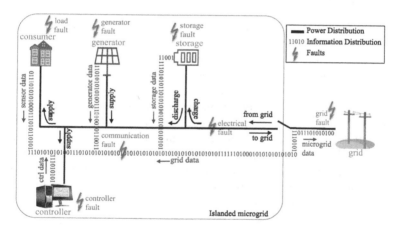

Fig. 1. Microgrid with components, faults, power and information flow.

Smartness in the microgrid is not limited to load balancing or meeting the demand. It also includes the ability to detect and recover from the faults and failures, which may arise due to factors such as environmental changes, weather or climatic conditions and hardware malfunctions. This aspect of faults originating in different parts in the microgrid is also shown in Fig. 1. Faults that affect the device operations at consumer level are shown as load faults. These faults can also be induced by generators or storage units. Faults in the generators are labeled as generator faults. Similarly, the storage units faults are mentioned as storage faults. A microgrid can be affected by grid faults and faults in the power distribution infrastructure like wires and relays. These are labeled as electrical faults. In a microgrid, faults are not limited to devices or electrical infrastructure. Software faults in the controller also affect microgrid performance, which are referred here as controller faults. Therefore, microgrids should be resilient towards the disturbances in power supply, communication channel and software faults using various fault handling approaches.

3   Effect of Faults

In this section, we investigate the RQ1 on the effects of faults originating in one system and their effect on the other parts of the microgrid. In the existing microgrids, fault handling techniques are designed considering the other systems as a black-box [3]. There are many fault handling techniques in the individual systems. This narrow approach of dealing with faults in individual systems is not sufficient to introduce self-healing in the microgrid. A complete microgridcentric approach to fault handling should encompass not only individual faults, but also their effect on the other compositional systems. For the above mentioned reasons, a self-healing microgrid should be able to detect and recover from the following classes of faults:

1. Errors and failures occurring in any of electrical, software or communication systems. Here, the electrical system includes power system components, smart devices (Photovoltaic, batteries, sensors, actuators etc.). Software includes the microgrid controller and communication includes all types of communication channels relevant to the microgrid.
2. Faults that have a cascading effect on other systems. For example, a software fault leading to incorrect commands can induce short-circuit faults [4].
3. Faults that have similar symptoms, but have different effects. For example, according to Table A.20 in IEEE Guide to Classification for Software Anomalies [5], a wrong input accepted by the software could lead to wrong decision-making, whereas the wrong input accepted as command/signal by the hardware can lead to incorrect actuation of the hardware. The same input problem leads to logical fault in software and wrong controlling in the hardware.

Table 1 shows fault sources and their effects in the originating system and in other compositional systems. Here $\bigcirc$ denotes the effect of the fault affecting only the individual system, while × denote faults in one individual system cascading into other systems. There are faults that occur within the individual system, but do not affect other systems. Although such faults are observable by other systems, they affect only the system in which they occur. For example, voltage fluctuations occurring while transitioning from island mode to grid-connected mode is observable by the controller, but does not impact the functioning of the controller. These faults are generally accounted for while designing the microgrid and are shown as *circles* in Table 1. On the other hand, there are faults which occur in one system, but can induce faults in other systems. For example, high voltage spike due to environmental factors can affect the functioning of the

Table 1. Fault affecting an individual system and their cascading effects

	Software	Electrical	Communication
Software	O	X	X
Electrical	X	O	X
Communication	X	X	O

sensors connected with the power network. The wrong values from the sensors can induce software faults (out of range or garbage values). Such faults are shown with a *cross* symbol in Table 1. The cascading effect is discussed only for faults that are observable and not hidden. The occurrence of fault in one system adversely affects another system in the following ways:

1. *Software faults inducing fault in electrical system:* A fault in the microgrid controller leads to failure/fault in the electrical system. For example, logical faults in the software lead to wrong commands, which result in short circuit faults in the electrical network. The outcome of the short circuit fault could be power outage or further damaging the devices connected with the network.
2. *Software faults inducing fault in communication system:* Software faults can also flood the network traffic to an extent that the communication system either crashes or stops responding. For example, errors messages from the software application can clog the communication network resulting in the denial-of-service.
3. *Electrical faults inducing software failure:* Any fault in the electrical system can lead to disruption of software application. For example, an unbalanced network or frequent power spikes in the electrical network can cause long disruptions in power supply. This power outage can affect the hardware platform on which software is running resulting in crash of the software.
4. *Electrical faults inducing communication failure:* Similar to the previous case, electrical faults may not directly affect the communication, but they can break down the hardware (router, switch) resulting in network crash. It should be noted that in case of Power Line Communication (PLC), harmonic distortions directly affect the communication network as well.
5. *Communication faults inducing software failure:* In complex systems like microgrids, the software system depends heavily on the communication system. Interactions with other software and hardware entities depend on a robust communication channel. A heavy data rate and loss of data in an unstable communication network result in wrong inputs to the software. This results in either software crash or wrong computation in decision-making.
6. *Communication faults inducing electrical failure:* A highly robust communication system aids in the reliable data sharing that in turn helps in smart operations. The faults induced due to the lack of communication can lead to cascading effect. The dependency of loss of communication and power loss are also topics of research [6]. For example, the power outage in September 2011 in US (Arizona, Southern California, and Baja California, Mexico) started

with the tripping of a single power line and led to cascading blackout in the neighboring regions. Since the grid operators of the affected regions were unaware of the power outage, any coordination or controlling of the outage at the initial stage could not be carried out [7].

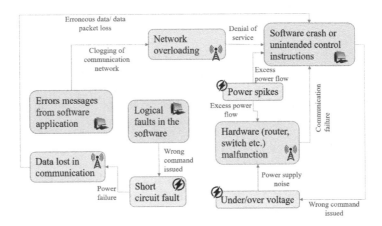

Fig. 2. Fault effecting an individual system and cascading into other systems.

In Fig. 2 specific fault cases are shown, where faults originating in an individual system lead to cascading effect in other systems. One of the fault case shown in Fig. 2 is the software crash. Software crashes at the controller leads to unintended control instructions issued to the switches. Wrong control of the switches may lead to under- or over-voltage situations that leads to hardware damage. Hardware damage can further lead to power spikes in the overall distribution grid. Another fault case shown is the logical fault in the controller where the incorrect analysis is carried out. Due to the logical mistake, more than one switch is open or closed simultaneously leading to short circuit faults. This can also lead to loss in the communication network, ultimately resulting in the loss of data at the controller. Existing fault handling approaches in the microgrids do not focus on the cascading effects of faults, especially the faults from the microgrid controller affecting the protection system. These specific fault cases are foreseeable and counter actions can be included at the design and planning stage. These specific fault cases conclude that the system experts from multiple domains should be involved in design phase, standards from different domain must be referred to develop system specifications and testing strategies for system conformance should also be established.

4   Faults and Fault Handling: A Survey

In Fig. 3 a generic understanding of faults, errors and failures is presented. Faults are the adjudged or hypothesized cause of an error [8]. In other words, fault causes error, which is observed when the system exhibits failure. Error is that part of the system state that may cause a subsequent failure [8]. Failures are the indicators of fault, without knowing the cause. A failure occurs when an error reaches the service interface and alters the service. A failure is a transition from correct service to incorrect service, where correctness of a service is described as the service performing the intended system functions [8].

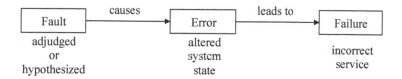

Fig. 3. Generic understanding of fault, error and failure.

4.1 Faults in a Microgrid

We now discuss faults in the compositional system of microgrid, namely faults in electrical, communication and software control system.

Faults in Electrical Systems in Microgrids. Faults in the electrical system can be caused due to several factors such as varying environment, operation or aging of infrastructure. In the electrical system, the classical fault categories are shown in Fig. 4. An electrical fault occurring in a circuit or device causes deviation in the voltage and current values from their nominal ranges. This deviation may result in over-current, under-voltage, unbalance of the phases, reversed power or high voltage surges. As a result, the normal operation of the network is interrupted, equipment failure or fire in the electrical connection occurs. Electrical system faults shown in Fig. 4 are mainly classified into two types, namely open and short circuit faults. Short-circuit faults can be further categorized as symmetrical or unsymmetrical faults. A considerable part of fault detection and identification is towards handling short-circuit or open-circuit faults. Fault location detection in electrical systems is a well-established research area, which focuses on the localization and identification. To handle the electrical system faults within a microgrid, major focus is on the power supply stabilization and grid protection. Since the inception of the microgrid concept, one particular fault scenario that remains the focus of researchers is the intentional switching to island mode operations to protect the grid from any damage caused by the electrical faults. Most research work follows the vision of Lasseter [9] to protect the grid by considering the basic structure of the microgrid as having local microsource controllers, system optimizer and distributed protection. He defined the protection process as *when the fault is on the utility grid, the desired response may be to isolate the microgrid from the main utility as quickly as possible to protect the microgrid loads. In case the fault is within the microgrid, the protection coordinator must isolate the smallest possible section of the radial feeder to* *eliminate the fault.* He did not mention the kind of faults that must be handled, but only used electrical system faults that the microgrid controller must handle. High Voltage DC (HVDC) grid is becoming popular especially in transportation sector and microgrids. Yi Wang and his team investigated pole to ground faults in HVDC transmission lines [10]. They simulated HVDC system to study the system behaviour in case of fault. Their results show that during a pole to ground fault, the system can be under damped condition when the impedance between the ground and the line is small. If the impedance is large, the system is in a over damped condition. Investigation on the existing approaches for faults in microgrids shows that faults are mainly restricted to the following categories; balanced, unbalanced, line-to-line, single-line to ground, double-line to ground and three-phase faults [11–15]. Most of the fault detection techniques are focused on detecting the maximum and minimum deviation values of current and voltage.

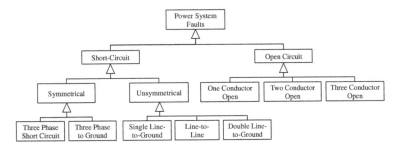

Fig. 4. Overview of the electrical system faults.

Faults in Communication Systems in Microgrids. The increased use of communication technologies in the microgrid also mean that the faults from communication system can affect the functioning of the electrical system. Faults in the communication channels can lead to the erroneous controlling of electrical infrastructure. Since the use of wireless communication network is foreseeable in the future, a quick overview of faults in communication network will help in understanding the need for handling communication faults to increase the resilience of the microgrids. Krings and Ma [16] studied the faults in the wireless communication network based on the earlier work by Thambidurai and Park [17]. They classified faults into several categories like benign and malicious, as shown in Fig. 5.

1. Transmissive symmetric: a single erroneous message is delivered to all receiving nodes. The messages, even faulty, are all identical. This indicates that the error has occurred due to the fault in the sender. Therefore the node can be identified

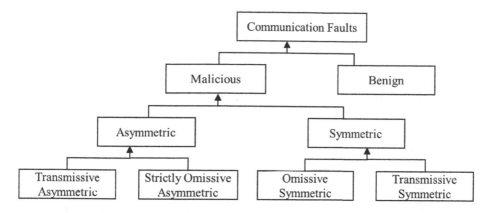

Fig. 5. Classification of the communication faults as proposed by Thambidurai and Park [17].

2. Omissive symmetric: no message is delivered to any receiving node. As before, all nodes are affected the same, however, the omissive behavior results in the destination nodes to most likely take different action as if the message had been received.
3. Transmissive asymmetric: this fault can exhibit any form of arbitrary asymmetric behavior, capable of delivering different erroneous messages to different receivers. This fault will need special attention to find which node has failed, whether it is the receiver or sender or in the communication link.
4. Strictly omissive asymmetric: a correct message is delivered to some nodes and no message is received by other nodes. Here, the omissions have the capability of affecting the system in an asymmetric way, since those nodes which have not received the message, will most likely react differently. In this case the sender or the receiver or some of the communication links get failed.

In addition to the faults, the communication system faces threats from cyber-attacks and malicious data injection due to the insecure networking. Peter Eder-Neuhauser [18] describes about the smart grid attack model, smart grid security model and the classification of existing malware types. Bo Chen [19] also discussed about different cyber-security issues in smart grids and conducted a study on modification of cyber-attacks, providing transient stability to the smart grids with voltage support devices. For a wide area monitoring, Shang Li [20] developed a distributed sequential cyber-attack detector using an adaptive sampling technique, to detect the false data injection. These works gave insight into the importance of addressing cyber-attack along with the communication faults in smart grids.

Faults in Software Systems in Microgrids. Microgrid Controller monitors and controls the electrical infrastructure within a microgrid can also encounter

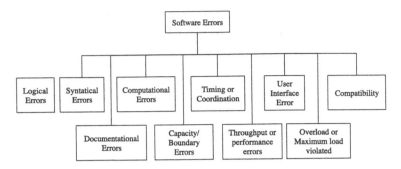

Fig. 6. Overview of software errors as proposed by Sommervile [21].

faults. The cause of the faults may vary from design time to run time. Few software faults are shown in Fig. 6. Some of the causes are described below:

1. Incomplete requirements: Many times the requirement elicitation for the target system is inconsistent, wrong or missing.
2. Incomplete communication: The lack of communication between the clients, designers and the software developers lead to a wrong interpretation of the requirements.
3. Incomplete documentation: Important documents like user manuals, operator manuals and design documents are written at different stages of the development. When these documents are not well written, incomplete or consistent, then the probability of faults increases.
4. Logical design flaws: These include incorrect computations, process definitions and unclear boundary conditions.
5. Weak testing: Once the coding is complete, incomplete test plans and insufficient error detection during software testing can also lead to fault during runtime.

Above mentioned causes can induce software faults, which can lead to the adverse effect on the operations of the microgrid. Authors found very limited focus on the effects of software faults in the microgrid fault handling research. In most cases, it is assumed that the microgrid controller follows prescribed safety standards and use standard protocols like SCADA etc.

From the above review of the existing literature, it can be concluded that the faults and their causes exist in each of the individual compositional system, but not in coordination (when coupled together).

4.2   Fault Handling Approaches in Microgrid

In this section, we review the widely used fault handling approaches in three different areas i.e. electrical, communication and software system.

Electrical Faults Handling: In a conventional grid, fault location, identification and restoration are carried out manually as they are time consuming. In the event of power outage, the rescue team has to manually travel throughout the transmission line path and check the condition at every pole. The operation turns out worse at night or during rainy season. The modern electrical fault handling techniques are listed below:

- The arc fault detection device [22] designed for household protection is a circuit breaker that isolates the power terminals when it detects an arc fault. This will prevent the house from catching fire. Surge protection devices protect the electrical and electronics equipment from lightning strike [23]. Residual Current Devices protect people from electric shock by isolating the power supply when earth leakage is detected [24].
- At substation level, air circuit breakers and vacuum circuit breakers are employed to isolate high voltage supplies. They provide protection against short circuit and over current and couples feeders within the distribution network [25]. Automatic Voltage Regulators (AVR) provide protection against burnouts and over-voltage in small factories and residential loads. AVR conditions the incoming power supply by using power electronic devices to protect devices against over voltage, harmonics, and surge [26].
- Khandare et al. [27] explored the possibilities of using numerical relay in microgrids to detect faulty lines, isolate the fault line and protect electronic loads. They designed the numerical relay and simulated it in different fault conditions to validate the design. Their findings concluded that in addition to primary fault protection devices like numerical relays, a secondary system is mandatory for added protection.
- Pilaquinga et al. [28] proposed a protection scheme for a 3-bus radial microgrid with a static compensator and storage system. They developed a bidirectional over-current relay as a primary protection system and frequency relays as secondary protection system. The proposed system was capable of detecting most of faults occurring in the microgrid during grid connected mode as well as islanded mode.
- On-line and off-line fault detection techniques for inverter based islanded microgrid proposed by Kuthsav Thattai, et al. [29] used Park's Vector Trajectory (PVT) and Hilbert-Huang Transform (HHT) and analyzed transient faults in load current at the point of common coupling (PCC).

Communication Faults Handling: Communication faults affect the performance of the system. A fault is detected when there is a delay or loss of information in the network. Time out and frequent monitoring processes can help to detect the faults. The two methods of handling these types of faults are fate sharing and the principle of optimality. The fate sharing principle [30] states that it is fine to lose the information from a node if the node itself is down at the same time. A node is a data point from where data is being transmitted. It can be a single sensor point or an aggregated point in which multiple sensor data are aggregated. The principle of optimality states [31] that network protocol should be designed to operate in two different modes: failure free mode and failure mode. The cause of communication faults can be a communication link failure, node failure etc. The protocols to handle such failures depend on the number of nodes, network topology and geographical placement of node. Towards fault management by the microgrid controller, cyber-attacks resulting in denial-of-service (DoS) [32] have been looked into. Danzi et al. looked into the software-defined microgrid control model, where data exchange and control information are shared over the power-line communication.

Software Fault Handling: Increased synergy between electrical grid and ICT in a microgrid has resulted in additional complexity of fault detection and identification techniques. A fault could manifest itself differently in the system. For example, faults in ICT may lead to faults in electrical system, or multiple faults may have the same effect on the system due to the dynamic nature of the grid. The challenge is in the identification of faults accurately. In the survey conducted by Medeiros et al. [33], they emphasized that 48% failures occur in the middleware and 43% in the microgrid application. They also highlighted that the software faults are still harder to deal with due to several reasons like unknown failure semantics, use of proprietary applications etc. Fault handling approaches for software systems holds unique importance in the functioning of microgrid control system. In software systems, the topic of fault handling is studied as one of the aspects of ensuring dependability [8]. Fault handling in software systems is defined as the process that prevents faults from being activated again. It involves four steps: fault diagnosis, fault isolation, system reconfiguration and system re-initialization. Two popular fault handling approaches are by designing fail-safe or fail-operational systems. Fail-safe system are the ones that switch to a safe mode when failure is encountered. Fail-operational systems can still operate after a failure, with a reduced functionality.

Another fault handling approach fitting into the vision of future grids is *self-healing* capability. Self-healing properties have often been described as one of the core properties of autonomic computing. In the technology and automation context, the essence of autonomic computing [34, 35] lies in the self-management of the system, which includes self-configuration, self-optimization, self-healing and self-protection.

Research towards making fault-tolerant systems exist in abundance [36–39]. Various fault analysis techniques and dependability issues in the software systems have also been studied [8, 40]. Specifically with respect to smartgrids, advanced fault detection and handling techniques in electrical network [41–43], in software systems [44, 45] and in the communication networks [46, 47] are already in use.

From the above review of the existing fault handling literature, it can be concluded that there is hardly any focus on the faults induced by the software in distribution network. Study on the impact of software bug in the microgrid controller leading to errors and impacting the operations of microgrids is largely missing.

5 Fault Classification

In this section we investigate the commonly occurring faults in a microgrid and their impact. To investigate and systematically analyze potential causes of faults that lead to microgrid not performing any of its prescribed functions, a cause and effect analysis is carried out. A problem-solving tool also known as *fishbone analysis* is used. The benefit of doing the cause and benefit analysis of faults is that it helps in the deciding the scope of fault handling. Based on such analysis the microgrid controller can be designed in such a manner that the fault handling mechanisms are put in place at the design stage. The possibility of handling specific faults can also be extended during the operational stage. The fishbone diagram shown in Fig. 7, also known as Ishikawa model, is an effective tool to identify and classify the cause of faults that lead to lower performance situation in the microgrid. Ishikawa proposed generic categories for causes of fault as: environment, materials, machine, measurement, man, and method [48]. The low performance could be power outage situation, software error or communication network problem. The cause of the lower performance can originate from: i)instrumentation and control ii) communication network iii) electrical network iv) user v) environments and vi) microgrid control system. In this work, these categories are modified. For instance, the *machine* refers to the *instrumentation and control* category that helps in capturing the measurable values of the environment. The *measurement* refers to the power supply indicators listed under the *electrical* category. The *man* is indicated by the user/people interacting with the system. The *method* is the way data is collected, manipulated and analyzed, which are listed in the *communication and microgrid control system* categories. Finally, the *environment* category represents the impact of the climate on the microgrid.

A detailed description of each category is as following:

- Faults in *instrumentation and control* category are the faults in the hardware devices, including smart sensors that capture the observable parameters from the environment like temperature, humidity, movement etc. Small power generation units like Photovoltaic and smart power backups like smart batteries. These devices provide data to build intelligence in the microgrid. For example, energy efficient consumption, optimized use of local power generation etc. These smart devices could also fail. This may lead to sensors sending incorrect values, which results in wrong decisions. Other kind of hardware damages include relay malfunctions that lead to recording noises and incorrect data reading.
- Faults in the *communication* category relate to the faults in the communication distribution. The primary objective of the communication network is message forwarding. If the data that is transmitted doesn't reach the receiver's end in a certain specified format, the primary objective is not fulfilled. Faults in the communication network are diverse and are discussed in Sect. 4. Network coverage issues, varying bandwidth, data losses, unsecured data transfer and time synchronization issues are few issues that an unstable communication network might experience. Clock synchronization issues

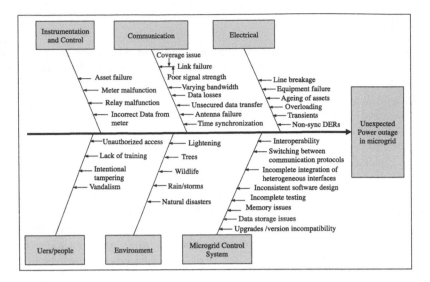

Fig. 7. Fishbone analysis of faults and failures from various sources in a microgrid, which are a mix up of design and runtime faults.

between the distributed entities may lead to a delay in controlling the switches in the specified order, which can generate unbalanced power supply in the electrical network, leading to power outage situation. Faults in the communication network vary from no data transmission to wrong response received as acknowledgment.

- Faults in the *electrical* category are the faults that affect power supply in the microgrid. Line breakages could be due to adverse conditions such as tree felling(in case of overhead lines) or erroneous digging of the ground (in case of underground lines). Extreme changes in weather such as floods, heavy rain, increased thunderstorms, could lead to heating up of wires, melting of fuses, short-circuiting etc. Loose connections of the electrical wires and connected peripherals can cause fire or could lead to sudden voltage variations. Transient currents due to sudden release or withdrawal of power can result in instabilities in the distribution network. With increased inclusion of renewable energy generators into the microgrid this situation is expected to occur frequently. The overload situations, where several high energy consumption devices are simultaneously connected, leading to a sudden deficit of power could also induce instabilities.

- Faults can also be introduced by humans. The *Users/people* category deals with faults occurring due to human interaction. Users interacting with microgrids range from common household habitants to the system operator. Various roles are defined for users based on the extent of their interaction with the microgrid. Faults could be caused due to lack of training amongst the users. There could be unauthorized users who access microgrid information in order to shut down the system or steal sensitive data. Intentional tempering of smart meters and sensors could also lead to faults. Other issues include vandalism with the intention to break or interrupt smart monitoring and control processes.

– *Environment* category represents the surroundings in which the system under the observation operates. Weather conditions play a big role in the functioning of devices and communication. During peak summers, sensors are prone to burn or melt due to high heat. During storms, communication network often fails to function as desired.

– Faults in the *microgrid control system* category deal with the faults in the controller. These faults may emerge during the operational stage due to various reasons such as insufficient requirements, design defects, and errors in coding, testing and maintenance. Insufficiency in requirements could be due to incomplete and inconsistent description of the target system. Design defects arise due to the incorrect design specifications or the inconsistent translation of requirements etc. The choice of programming paradigm used for the implementation and implementation of logic for the software controllers may also lead to wrong control actions. Some other examples of coding errors include incorrect configurations, uninitialized variables, invalid file path, wrong interface specification, version issues with standard libraries etc. During testing and maintenance phases, if the software is either not tested thoroughly or changes in the software are not tracked and maintained, then the microgrid controller will not be able to monitor and control as required.

The faults in the microgrid are also context-specific, based on the geographical setting, devices in use, etc. However, fishbone analysis reveals the enormity of the fault in microgrid environment. It emphasises that focusing on the faults and failures from the electrical domain is not sufficient to create a resilient microgrid, as there are multiple systems operating simultaneously. This fishbone analysis helps the developers and designers of microgrid to plan recovery and observe the effects of the faults. Such analysis of commonly occurring faults helps in identifying the dependencies at the design stage.

6   Promising Solutions and Future Directions

With the fault cases and survey presented in the previous sections, it is clear that fault detection and recovery in the microgrids are highly desirable. The existing methods that exist individually in electrical, software and communication system must be brought together in the microgrid. As much as data capturing and analysis is required, the design of the application and platform to handle enormous data is equally important. A generic fault handler should be part of each microgrid controller, so that the cascading effects of faults can be observed. The underlying architecture of the microgrid controller has to be generic to include fault profiles and fault detection based on the domain-specific models and data analytics. A generic fault handler and the design helps in the recovery related decisions. Data analytics based fault handling provides capabilities such as anomaly detection and predictive maintenance. During the survey conducted, we found some of the promising solutions used for fault detection and recovery, resulting in improved resilience of the microgrid. Following are the few of the approaches:

- **Multi-Agent System (MAS):** Application of MAS in the electrical engineering for design and distributed controls is explored by many researchers [49,50]. Autonomous independent agents interact and coordinate with each other to fulfil both individual and system goals. Howell et al. [51] argued that in the smart grid system each individual microgrid can be considered as an autonomous agent such that the intelligence and decision making can be distributed among agents. Plenty of research articles exist on the local and global goals of agents such as storage management within a microgrid and local balancing by the negotiating agents [52,53].

- **Architectures:** In the conventional grid, power flow is in one direction only, hence the system architecture is also layered with decisions executed in a top-down manner. In microgrids, distributed decision and coordination require system architectures to also be distributed. Existing approaches of Service-Oriented Architecture (SOA), MAS and Holonic Systems provide distributed decision and definition of different levels of automation [51]. Hybrid approaches also exist that combine these system architectures for fine-grained control within a microgrid and better coordination among each other [54,55]. An Agent based architecture is proposed and demonstrated for fault location isolation and supply restoration (FLISR) application in electrical system automation by Zhabelova et al. [56]. A survey on software architectures by Ramesh et al. [57] provides an overview of the use of software technologies in the legacy systems like power grids. They have also presented the list of existing reference architectures for smartgrids.
  Towards fault-tolerance embedded in the design, agent based systems are used [58,59], where the model-based approach is used to define the communication between agents to define the internal behaviour of agents and resolve conflicts among agents in the electrical grid.

- **Data Analytics based fault handling:** In the last five years, there has been an exponential growth of Artificial Intelligence (AI) based approaches from anomaly detection to power stabilization. In case of reconfiguration of the electrical network to stabilize voltage in the network, approaches like genetic algorithm [60,61], reinforcement learning [62] and deep reinforcement learning [63] are widely popular. Apart from this, anomaly detection, uncertainty quantification and predictive maintenance are some of the areas where data analytics is being used to handle faults at the operational stage.

7   Conclusion

In this paper, we explained faults and failures from different compositional systems and then presented the fault scope in a microgrid. With the help of fault cases and their cause-effect analysis, the cascading effect of faults was analyzed. The categories considered in the analysis were: electrical system, smart devices, communication network, data handling, users, microgrid control system. We found that not just the electrical faults, but faults occurring in the software and the communication systems affect the microgrid operations. We further studied the cascading effects of faults in the microgrid, which highlights the need for including fault detection and diagnosis in the design of the microgrid control system. By reviewing the existing fault handling strategies, we found that interdependency and cascading effects of faults require further research. Authors suggested some areas of research, where fault handling methods can be combined with the existing methods such as architecture designing, agent based systems and data analytics. In conclusion, authors emphasize that to make grid resilient and stable, approaches of design(architectures) should be combined with the faults handling using data analytics.

Acknowledgement. The authors would like to thank Dr. Markus Duchon, Dr. Maneesha V Ramesh, Dr. Aryadevi R D, Mr. Sudharsan V C and Shri Mata Amritanandamayi Devi for supporting the research work. This work was partly done under the Project "Smart Services and Optimization for Microgrids (SSOM)" in the scheme of Project-based Personnel Exchange Program with Indo-German (DST-DAAD) Joint Research Collaboration.

References

1. Guardian, T.: Millions across South America hit by massive power cut (2019). https://www.theguardian.com/world/2019/jun/16/millions-across-south-america-hit-by-massive-power-cut-argentina-uruguay-paraguay-brazil
2. IEEE Power and Energy Society. IEEE Standard for the Specification of Microgrid Controllers, IEEE STD 2030.7-2017. IEEE (2017)
3. Dinkel, M., Stesny, S., Baumgarten, U.: Interactive self-healing for black-box components in distributed embedded environments. In: 2007 ITG-GI Conference on Communication in Distributed Systems (KiVS), pp. 1–12 (2007)
4. Friedman, A.: Diagnosis of short-circuit faults in combinational circuits. IEEE Trans. Comput. **100**, 746–752 (1974)
5. Zubrow, D., Baldwin, M.: IEEE Guide to Classification for Software Anomalies. IEEE STD 1044.1-1995, p. i (1996)
6. Parandehgheibi, M., Turitsyn, K., Modiano, E.: Modeling the impact of communication loss on the power grid under emergency control. In: 2015 IEEE International Conference on Smart Grid Communications (SmartGridComm), pp. 356–361 (2015)
7. Ferc, N.: Arizona-southern California outages on 8 September 2011: causes and recommendations. FERC and NERC (2012)
8. Avizienis, A., Laprie, J., Randell, B.: Fundamental concepts of dependability. University of Newcastle upon Tyne, Computing Science (2001)
9. Lasseter, R.: Microgrids. In: 2002 IEEE Power Engineering Society Winter Meeting. Conference Proceedings (Cat. No. 02CH37309), vol. 1, pp. 305–308 (2002)
10. Wang, Y., Zhang, Z., Fu, Y., Hei, Y., Zhang, X.: Pole-to-ground fault analysis in transmission line of DC grids based on VSC. In: 2016 IEEE 8th International Power Electronics and Motion Control Conference (IPEMC-ECCE Asia), pp. 2028–2032 (2016)

11. Laaksonen, H., Kauhaniemi, K.: Fault type and location detection in islanded microgrid with different control methods based converters. In: 19th International Conference on Electricity Distribution (CIRED), Vienna, Austria (2007)
12. Nikkhajoei, H., Lasseter, R.: Microgrid fault protection based on symmetrical and differential current components. In: Power System Engineering Research Center, pp. 71–74 (2006)
13. Zhou, Y., Xu, G., Chen, Y.: Fault location in power electrical traction line system. Energies 5, 5002–5018 (2012)
14. Hong, Y., Wei, Y., Chang, Y., Lee, Y., Liu, P.: Fault detection and location by static switches in microgrids using wavelet transform and adaptive network-based fuzzy inference system. Energies 7, 2658–2675 (2014)
15. Sadeghkhani, I., Golshan, M., Guerrero, J., Mehrizi-Sani, A.: A current limiting strategy to improve fault ride-through of inverter interfaced autonomous microgrids. IEEE Trans. Smart Grid 8, 2138–2148 (2017)
16. Krings, A., Ma, Z.: Fault-models in wireless communication: towards survivable ad hoc networks. In: MILCOM 2006–2006 IEEE Military Communications Conference, pp. 1–7 (2006)
17. Thambidurai, P., Park, Y.: Interactive consistency with multiple failure modes. In: Proceedings [1988] Seventh Symposium on Reliable Distributed Systems, pp. 93–100 (1988)
18. Eder-Neuhauser, P., Zseby, T., Fabini, J., Vormayr, G.: Cyber attack models for smart grid environments. Sustain. Energy Grids Netw. 12, 10–29 (2017)
19. Chen, B., Mashayekh, S., Butler-Purry, K., Kundur, D.: Impact of cyber attacks on transient stability of smart grids with voltage support devices. In: 2013 IEEE Power and Energy Society General Meeting, pp. 1–5 (2013)
20. Li, S., Yılmaz, Y., Wang, X.: Quickest detection of false data injection attack in wide-area smart grids. IEEE Trans. Smart Grid 6, 2725–2735 (2014)
21. Sommerville, I.: Software Engineering. Addison-Wesley, New York (2010)
22. Electrical Safety. Arc Fault Detection Devices reduce the risk of electrical fire (2019). https://www.se.com/in/en/home/renovation/home-protection.jsp
23. Electrical Safety. Surge protection devices: your best defence (2019). https://www.se.com/in/en/home/renovation/electronic-equipment-protection.jsp
24. Electrical Safety. Protect your family with Residual Current Devices (2019). https://www.se.com/in/en/home/renovation/people-protection.jsp
25. Electrical Safety. Circuit Breakers and Switches (2019). https://www.se.com/ww/en/product-category/4200-circuit-breakers-and-switches/
26. Generator System. Working Principle of Automatic Voltage Regulator (2019). https://medium.com/@dieselgenerator/working-principle-of-automatic-voltage-regulator-1ff1275f5495
27. Khandare, P., Deokar, S., Dixit, A.: Advanced technique in micro grid protection for various fault by using numerical relay. In: 2017 2nd International Conference for Convergence in Technology (I2CT), pp. 803–807 (2017)
28. Pilaquinga, D., Pozo, M.: Novel protection schema for a radial microgrid system. In: 2017 IEEE PES Innovative Smart Grid Technologies Conference - Latin America (ISGT Latin America), pp. 1–6 (2017)
29. Thattai, K., Sahoo, A., Ravishankar, J.: On-line and off-line fault detection techniques for inverter based islanded microgrid. In: 2018 IEEE 12th International Conference on Compatibility, Power Electronics and Power Engineering (CPE-POWERENG 2018), pp. 1–6 (2018)
30. Clark, D.: The design philosophy of the DARPA Internet protocols. In: Symposium Proceedings on Communications Architectures and Protocols, pp. 106–114 (1988)

31. Gupta, A., Rothermel, K.: Fault handling for multi-party real-time communication. In: ICSI (1995)
32. Danzi, P., Angjelichinoski, M., Stefanović, Č, Dragičević, T., Popovski, P.: Software-defined microgrid control for resilience against denial-of-service attacks. IEEE Trans. Smart Grid **10**, 5258–5268 (2018)
33. Medeiros, R., Cirne, W., Brasileiro, F., Sauvé, J.: Faults in grids: why are they so bad and what can be done about it? In: Proceedings. First Latin American Web Congress, pp. 18–24 (2003)
34. Kephart, J., Chess, D.: The vision of autonomic computing. Computer **36**, 41–50 (2003)
35. Laster, S., Olatunji, A.: Autonomic computing: towards a self-healing system. In: Proceedings of the Spring, pp. 62–78 (2007)
36. Nelson, V.: Fault-tolerant computing: fundamental concepts. Computer **23**, 19–25 (1990)
37. Ericson, C., et al.: Hazard Analysis Techniques for System Safety. Wiley, Hoboken (2015)
38. Koren, I., Krishna, C.: Fault-Tolerant Systems. Morgan Kaufmann, Burlington (2010)
39. Lyu, M., et al.: Handbook of Software Reliability Engineering. IEEE Computer Society Press, California (1996)
40. Avižienis, A., Laprie, J.-C., Randell, B.: Dependability and its threats: a taxonomy. In: Jacquart, R. (ed.) Building the Information Society. IIFIP, vol. 156, pp. 91–120. Springer, Boston, MA (2004). https://doi.org/10.1007/978-1-4020-8157-6_13
41. Hwang, I., Kim, S., Kim, Y., Seah, C.: A survey of fault detection, isolation, and reconfiguration methods. IEEE Trans. Control Syst. Technol. **18**, 636–653 (2010)
42. Alwash, S., Ramachandaramurthy, V.: Novel fault-location method for overhead electrical distribution systems. IEEJ Trans. Electr. Electron. Eng. **8**, S13–S19 (2013)
43. Kezunovic, M.: Smart fault location for smart grids. IEEE Trans. Smart Grid **2**, 11–22 (2011)
44. Paradkar, A.: Case studies on fault detection effectiveness of model based test generation techniques. ACM SIGSOFT Softw. Eng. Notes **30**, 1–7 (2005)
45. Hall, T., Beecham, S., Bowes, D., Gray, D., Counsell, S.: A systematic literature review on fault prediction performance in software engineering. IEEE Trans. Software Eng. **38**, 1276–1304 (2012)
46. Pereira, E., Pereira, R.: Fault monitoring and detection of distributed services over local and wide area networks. In: 12th International Conference on Parallel and Distributed Systems, ICPADS 2006, vol. 2 (2006)
47. Krings, A., Ma, Z.: Fault-models in wireless communication: towards survivable ad hoc networks. In: Military Communications Conference, MILCOM 2006, pp. 1–7. IEEE (2006)
48. Ishikawa, K., Ishikawa, K.: Guide to quality control. Asian Productivity Organization Tokyo (1982)
49. McArthur, S., et al.: Multi-agent systems for power engineering applications-Part I: concepts, approaches, and technical challenges. IEEE Trans. Power Syst. **22**, 1743–1752 (2007)
50. Zhabelova, G.: Software architecture and design methodology for distributed agent-based automation of smart grid. University of Auckland (2014)
51. Howell, S., Rezgui, Y., Hippolyte, J., Jayan, B., Li, H.: Towards the next generation of smart grids: semantic and holonic multi-agent management of distributed energy resources. Renew. Sustain. Energy Rev. **77**, 193–214 (2017)

52. Brazier, F., et al.: Agents negotiating for load balancing of electricity use. In: Proceedings. 18th International Conference on Distributed Computing Systems (Cat. No. 98CB36183), pp. 622–629 (1998)
53. Vytelingum, P., Voice, T., Ramchurn, S., Rogers, A., Jennings, N.: Agent-based micro-storage management for the smart grid (2010)
54. Gupta, P., Gibtner, A., Duchon, M., Koss, D., Schätz, B.: Using knowledge discovery for autonomous decision making in smart grid nodes. In: 2015 IEEE International Conference on Industrial Technology (ICIT), pp. 3134–3139 (2015)
55. Gupta, P., Duchon, M.: Developing self-similar hybrid control architecture based on SGAM-based methodology for distributed microgrids. Designs 2, 41 (2018)
56. Zhabelova, G., Vyatkin, V., Dubinin, V.: Toward industrially usable agent technology for smart grid automation. IEEE Trans. Industr. Electron. 62, 2629–2641 (2014)
57. Ramesh, A., Karthikeyan, P., Padmanaban, S., Balasubramanian, S., Guerrero, J.: A Bibliographical Survey on Software Architectures for Smart Grid System. Preprints (2018)
58. Haqiq, A., Bounabat, B.: Towards integration of fault tolerance in agent-based systems. Procedia Comput. Sci. 127, 264–273 (2018)
59. Haegg, S.: A sentinel approach to fault handling in multi-agent systems. In: Australian Workshop on Distributed Artificial Intelligence, pp. 181–195 (1996)
60. Tomoiagă, B., Chindriş, M., Sumper, A., Sudria-Andreu, A., Villafafila-Robles, R.: Pareto optimal reconfiguration of power distribution systems using a genetic algorithm based on NSGA-II. Energies 6, 1439–1455 (2013)
61. Ebrahimi Moghadam, M., Falaghi, H., Farhadi, M.: A novel method of optimal capacitor placement in the presence of harmonics for power distribution network using NSGA-II multi-objective genetic optimization algorithm. Math. Comput. Appl. 25, 17 (2020)
62. Gao, Y., Shi, J., Wang, W., Yu, N.: Dynamic distribution network reconfiguration using reinforcement learning. In: 2019 IEEE International Conference on Communications, Control, and Computing Technologies for Smart Grids (SmartGridComm), pp. 1–7 (2019)
63. Yang, Q., Wang, G., Sadeghi, A., Giannakis, G., Sun, J.: Two-timescale voltage control in distribution grids using deep reinforcement learning. IEEE Trans. Smart Grid 11, 2313–2323 (2019)

Intelligent Edge Processing in the IoT Era

Energy and Load Aware Fog Node Placement for Smart Farming

Jagruti Sahoo[✉]

Department of Computer Science and Mathematics, South Carolina State University,
Orangeburg, USA
jagrutisahoo@ieee.org

Abstract. Smart farming has enabled farmers to reduce cost, improve agricultural yield, and make better decisions using Internet of Things (IoT) technology. IoT nodes such as soil sensors and pH probes provide farmers with a real-time update on the farm. Traditionally, the farm data sensed by IoT nodes are processed by a cloud data center. However, it results in a higher delay in sending results to the farmer. Fog computing is a recent paradigm that reduces the delay by deploying fog nodes on the farm to process the farm data. However, the fog nodes need to be placed in proper locations as it will impact the energy consumption of IoT nodes in transmitting data to the fog node. Moreover, the placement must ensure a fair distribution of load among the fog nodes to ensure effective resource utilization. Therefore, it is critical to determine the optimal location of fog nodes to minimize the energy consumption of IoT nodes and balance load among the fog nodes. We ensure load balancing by minimizing the maximum load. In this paper, we model the fog node placement as an optimization problem and present an Integer Programming Formulation (ILP) formulation of the same. We also propose a placement algorithm designed based on k-means clustering. Our simulation results show that the proposed algorithm performs close to the optimal placement in terms of energy consumption and load distribution.

Keywords: Cloud computing · Fog computing · Internet of Things

1 Introduction

Agricultural production will need to increase by 60% to meet the food demand of the growing population in 2050. However, with diminishing natural resources, unpredictable weather conditions, and shrinking arable land, it is a significant challenge to increase the yield to meet future food demand [1]. Smart farming is an emerging technique that can improve agricultural yield by using IoT nodes (e.g., sensors, robots, and GPS) and advanced information and communication technologies [2]. With smart farming, the farm processes can be made smarter, automated, and data-driven, enabling the farmers to make informed decisions, reduce agricultural efforts, and minimize costs.

Typically, a smart farming system uses a remote cloud server for storage and computation. While a cloud server is needed to support compute-intensive applications, it

© ICST Institute for Computer Sciences, Social Informatics and Telecommunications Engineering 2022
Published by Springer Nature Switzerland AG 2022. All Rights Reserved
S. Paiva et al. (Eds.): SmartCity360° 2021, LNICST 442, pp. 77–91, 2022.
https://doi.org/10.1007/978-3-031-06371-8_6

does not meet the real-time requirement of latency-sensitive agricultural applications such as soil and water quality monitoring [3], intelligent greenhouses [3], disease and pest monitoring [3]. Fog computing is an effective paradigm that has emerged recently to allow the execution of latency-sensitive applications at the network edge, thereby reducing the latency [4, 5]. A fog infrastructure consists of edge devices such as gateways and mobile devices that can provide computational and storage resources for IoT applications. Those edge devices, also known as fog nodes, receive farm variables from the IoT nodes and execute tasks with varying resource requirements. Figure 1 shows the high-level view of a smart farming system.

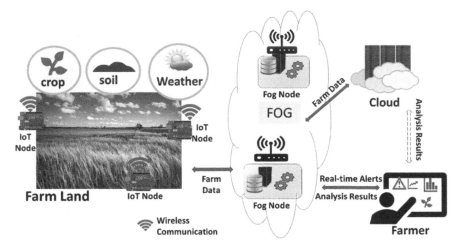

Fig. 1. Smart farming system

The IoT nodes used in smart farming are mostly battery-operated devices. As the nodes are deployed in remote locations, it is a tedious task to replace their batteries. IoT nodes need to conserve their energy to continue sensing the farm and sending the sensed measurement to the fog. However, the locations of fog nodes affect the energy consumption. Therefore, the fog nodes must be deployed in proper locations that minimize the energy consumption of the IoT nodes. Since fog nodes have limited processing capacity and IoT nodes generate workload with varying resource requirements, it is imperative that IoT nodes' workload need to be distributed as evenly as possible among the deployed fog nodes to ensure effective utilization of fog resources. The load balancing can be achieved by minimizing the maximum load on fog nodes.

In this paper, we address the problem of finding the optimal location of fog nodes, referred to as fog node placement. It entails two objectives: minimizing the energy consumption and minimizing the maximum load. We consider that the placement must meet a given budget, and we represent it in terms of the number of fog nodes that need to be deployed. Clearly, the fog node placement problem is a variation of the k-median problem that finds k centers for a given number of facilities to minimize the communication cost between the centers and the facilities [6].

The optimal placement of fog nodes for various IoT domains has been addressed in the literature [7–15]. However, there has been a handful of papers that solve the fog node placement for smart farming. Moreover, there are limited efforts on addressing the placement that ensures the energy-efficiency of IoT nodes.

In this paper, we present an ILP model of the fog node placement problem. We propose a placement algorithm, referred to as the k-fog node placement (k-FNP), to find the appropriate location of fog nodes. The k-FNP algorithm is designed based on k-means clustering [16]. In k-FNP, the IoT nodes are grouped into k clusters, and cluster centers represent the fog node location. In k-means clustering, IoT nodes are assigned to their nearest cluster, i.e., cluster that offers the smallest distance between the IoT nodes and the cluster centers. However, k-FNP uses a composite metric consisting of energy consumption and load within a cluster for the cluster selection process, where an IoT node selects the cluster with the smallest value of the composite metric.

The remainder of the paper is organized as follows. Section 2 discusses the related works. The fog node placement problem and the proposed algorithm are presented in Sect. 3. Section 4 presents the simulation results. Section 5 provides the conclusion.

2 Related Works

Yuan et al. [7] proposed a search and clustering algorithm to decide the fog node position based on sensor node peak density. Their algorithm is a modification of the k-means algorithm. In addition, an integrated optimization model is proposed to deal with all the resource constraints and delay. Density-based clustering algorithms perform well when the fog node has very high resource availability. However, in energy crunch situations, some fog nodes drain out all their energies very fast.

Jiang et al. [8] proposed an architecture for smart manufacturing. Also, they proposed a k-means based clustering algorithm and validated it through a prototype model. Three kinds of deployment, i) random deployment, ii) k-means clustering, and iii) improved k-means clustering, are considered. The SDN-based clustering is implemented on the fly based on available resources. A flow conservation-based optimization model is proposed to balance resource constraints and deal with the network delay and computing cost. The SDN-based algorithms are very effective for real-time decision-making. However, fog node placement is an infrequent activity, and usually, it is carried out when existing hardware infrastructure fails to handle growing resource needs. For each decision, fog nodes have to depend on SDN controllers/servers, which introduces an additional resource burden. As this method is implemented in a resource-rich scenario, it may not be suitable for other areas such as smart farming, connected drone coalition, and underwater sensor networks.

Manogaran & Rawal [9] proposed an optimal node placement and resource allocation algorithm to deal with communication delays for the Internet of Everything (IoE) environment. A profit function is defined to deal with resource allocation problem. The proposed RA-Fog algorithm decides the fog node placement based on latency, cost, and resource utilization. A novel fog-cloud architecture is proposed to minimize service delays. Considering the complex IoT/IoE environment scenario, only resource allocation consideration does not always find an optimal fog topology. Though resource allocation is an essential factor, the energy constraints of IoT nodes and the cost of implanting suggested fog topology are equally vital for a robust architecture. The RA-Fog algorithm will suffer heavily in energy crunch situations.

It is evident that in large-scale IoT environments, fog nodes work as a smooth transit point for heavy delay-sensitive applications. [10] proposes an edge node (EN) deployment architecture to be implemented in an airport to deal with traffic diversity and wireless diversity. In this deployment strategy, the ENs collect data from the candidate IoT nodes and sends maintenance instructions to designated IoT nodes. The throughput is the prime factor in this heavy data traffic scenario. Though node and network diversity are considered here, minimizing the number of edge nodes may lead to infrastructure fatality.

Lin et al. [11] addressed the optimal deployment of smart gateways for smart home environments. The deployment is modeled as a binary integer programming. The goal is to minimize the deployment cost while ensuring that the gateways cover all service areas in a smart home. To find the candidate gateway locations, the house floor plan is transformed into a new plan consisting of multiple nodes based on the coverage required for the service areas in the house. Although the deployment provides the required communication infrastructure for smart home IoT services, the model does not consider either energy consumption or IoT workload in choosing the gateway location.

Zhang et al. [12] addressed the edge server placement problem in smart farming that involves minimizing the data transmission delay between the sensors and edge servers and the energy cost of edge servers. Moreover, the load is balanced among the edge servers. However, the energy consumption of sensors is not considered in finding the edge server locations.

3   Optimal Fog Node Placement

3.1   Problem Description

The fog node placement problem involves finding the optimal location of fog nodes and assigning IoT nodes to appropriate fog nodes to minimize the energy consumption of IoT nodes and ensure load balancing. Load balancing can be achieved by minimizing the maximum load.

3.2   ILP Formulation

Minimize

$$\sum_{i \in F} \sum_{j \in S} E_{ij} x_{ij} + \lambda \tag{1}$$

Subject to

$$\sum_{i \in F} y_i \leq K \tag{2}$$

$$\sum_{i \in F} x_{ij} = 1 \quad \forall j \in S \tag{3}$$

$$x_{ij} \leq y_i \ \forall i \in F, j \in S \tag{4}$$

$$x_{ij}d_{ij} \leq R \tag{5}$$

$$\sum_{j \in S} \sum_{k \in A_j} x_{ij}L_{jk} \leq \lambda, \forall i \in F \tag{6}$$

$$0 \leq \lambda \leq P \tag{7}$$

The first term in (1) represents the energy consumption objective. We used the energy model proposed in [17] to compute the energy consumption of IoT nodes. As the receiving energy of IoT nodes is negligible, the energy consumption includes the transmission energy only. Given a fog node location i, the transmission energy of an IoT node i in transmitting b_j bits to the location i is computed as follows:

$$E_{ij} = E_{elec} * b_j + \varepsilon_{amp} * b_j * d_{ij}^2 \tag{8}$$

where E_{elec} is the electronic energy required for coding, modulation, filtering, etc., ε_{amp} is the amplification energy, and d_{ij} is the distance between the IoT node j and the fog node location i. The second term in (1) represents the objective for load balancing. The decision variable λ represents the maximum load on a fog node that needs to be minimized (Table 1 and 2).

Table 1. ILP notations

Notation	Meaning
F	Set of candidate fog node locations
S	Set of IoT nodes
A_j	Set of tasks generated by an IoT node j
C_{ij}	Energy cost between location i and IoT node j
d_{ij}	Distance between location i and IoT node j
b_j	Size of data generated by IoT node j
L_{jk}	Size of task k requested by IoT node j
R	Transmission Range of IoT Node
P	Processing Capacity of a Fog node

Table 2. Decision variables

Notation	Meaning
x_{ij}	1 if IoT node j is served by a fog node deployed in location i and 0 otherwise
y_i	1 if location i is chosen to deploy a fog node 0 otherwise
λ	Maximum load among the fog nodes

Constraint (2) ensures that the number of fog nodes must be limited to k. It represents the maximum budget for deploying fog nodes. Constraint (3) ensures that an IoT node j is assigned to exactly one of the fog nodes. Constraint (4) indicates that an IoT node j is assigned to location i only if a location has been selected to deploy a fog node. Since the IoT nodes have a limited transmission range, we introduce a distance constraint (5). It ensures that the distance between an IoT node and the location to which it is assigned must not exceed the transmission range of the IoT node. Constraint (6) ensures that the total load on any fog node is limited by the selected maximum load. As fog nodes have limited processing capacity, constraint (7) ensures that the maximum load must not exceed that fog capacity.

3.3 *K*-means Based Fog Node Placement (k-FNP) Algorithm

The fog node placement problem can be solved using the clustering concept, where the IoT nodes are grouped to form a given number of clusters and the cluster center provide the location for deploying fog nodes. We design our algorithm based on k-means clustering which is an effective way to cluster a set of given data points into k distinct clusters. In k-means clustering, the Euclidean Distance between the data point and the centroid of a cluster is used in the cluster selection procedure, where the data point selects the cluster with the smallest distance.

	Algorithm 1: k-FNP
Input	A set of IoT nodes, $S=\{ s_1, s_2, \ldots s_m \}$
	k: Number of clusters
Output	Cluster centers, $C=\{ c_1, c_2, \ldots c_k \}$
1.	Select k random initial cluster centers
2	$itr=1$
3.	while $itr <= MaxItr$ // Stopping condition
4.	do
5.	for $j=1,2,\ldots.m$ do //Cluster Selection
6.	$Z_j = \emptyset$ // Set of Candidate Clusters for IoT node s_j
7.	for $i=1,2,\ldots.k$ do
8.	//Check Distance 'd' and Capacity Constraints
9.	//G_i: Current load of cluster c_i, w_j: load of IoT Node s_j, P: fog capacity
10.	if $d(s_j, c_i) <= R$ and $G_i + w_j <= P$
11.	$Z_j = Z_j \cup \{c_i\}$
12.	//h_j Index of cluster selected for IoT node s_j
13.	$h_j = \underset{c_i \epsilon Z_j}{argmin} \ M(s_j, c_i)$ // Cluster Selection Metric
14.	$G_{h_j} = G_{h_j} + w_j$ //Update Cluster Load
15.	for $i=1,2,\ldots.k$ do //Update Centroid
16.	//$Loc(s_j)$: Location of IoT node s_j
17.	$c_i = mean (\{Loc(s_j), s_j \epsilon S \mid h_j = i\}$
18.	$itr= itr+1$

However, we design a composite metric consisting of two parameters: 1) the energy consumption of IoT node incurred by transmitting data to the centroid, 2) the current load of the cluster. The current load of a cluster is considered so that IoT nodes will be assigned to a cluster with a minimum load, minimizing the maximum load. Since our goal is to minimize the energy consumption and balance the load among the fog nodes, we sort the clusters using the composite metric and assign an IoT node to the cluster with the smallest value of the metric.

Since the composite metric components are in different units, they are normalized by converting each parameter into a range (0,1). The cluster selection metric for an IoT node s_j and cluster c_i is computed as follows:

$$M (s_j, c_i) = \alpha E_{ij} + \beta L_{ij} \tag{9}$$

where E denotes the transmission energy consumed by IoT node s_j if it is assigned to cluster c_i. L denotes the total load (including the workload of IoT node s_j) of cluster c_i. α and β denote the parameters that control the importance of energy efficiency and load balancing, respectively on the cluster selection metric. These parameters can be selected by the network designer during the deployment phase depending on whether the parameters are given equal or difference preference. For example, if more preference is given for energy efficiency, then α should be set to a value higher than β.

A pseudo-code of k-FNP is shown in Algorithm 1. The algorithm starts by selecting k random centroids from IoT node locations which are considered as candidate locations for fog nodes. As shown in the ILP, the distance between an IoT node and the centroid of its cluster must be limited to one hop. Moreover, the total load in a cluster must not exceed the processing capacity of a fog node. Thus, in our algorithm, for each IoT node, clusters that meet the distance and capacity requirements are selected. The clusters are then sorted using the composite metric given by (9). The IoT node is assigned to the cluster with the smallest value of the composite metric. After all the IoT nodes are assigned to one of the k clusters, the center of each cluster is updated as the mean of locations of IoT nodes that belong to the cluster. The algorithm repeats until a certain number of iterations, *MaxItr* is reached.

4   Performance Evaluation

4.1   Simulation Setup

We used IBM Cplex optimization studio [18] to implement the proposed ILP model. We compared the optimal solution with the proposed k-FNP algorithm under a small-scale scenario that consists of 4 to 10 IoT nodes randomly deployed in an area of 100 m × 100 m. The placement algorithm is executed offline prior to deploying the fog infrastructure. We considered two configurations of the small-scale scenario: 1) small-scale scenario-I that has variable number of IoT nodes, and 2) small-scale scenario-II that has fixed number (i.e., 10) of IoT nodes. We consider fog nodes with a capacity of 15000 MIPS. We consider a transmission range of 60 m for the IoT nodes. We consider that each IoT node generates a number of tasks with varying resource requirements. Each task will execute on a fog node and process the data received from the IoT nodes.

We also consider a large-scale scenario consisting of 50 to 200 nodes deployed in an area of 300 m × 300 m. The large-scale scenario is used to compare the k-FNP algorithm with a random placement algorithm. The random placement algorithm randomly selects k fog nodes that satisfy the distance and capacity constraints. Both k-FNP and the random placement algorithms are implemented using Python. In our large-scale scenario, the capacity of fog nodes is set to 40000 MIPS. The transmission range of IoT nodes is set to 125 m. We set the parameter k to 50% and 20% of the number of IoT nodes in small-scale and large-scale scenarios, respectively. The simulation parameters are listed in Table 3.

4.2   Performance Metrics

We consider the following metrics to evaluate the effectiveness of the proposed algorithm.

1) *Energy Consumption*: It is given by the sum of energy consumed by IoT nodes in transmitting data to the fog node that execute their tasks.
2) *Standard Deviation of load*: We use standard deviation to measure the distribution of load among the deployed fog nodes.

3) *Maximum Load*: It is the maximum load (in MIPS) that a fog node can host. This metric is also used to evaluate the load balancing performance of the proposed algorithm.

Table 3. Simulation parameters

Notation	Meaning
Number of IoT Nodes	4–10, 50–200
CPU Capacity of Fog Node	15000 MIPS, 40000 MIPS
Data Size of IoT Node	1 Mbps-4 Mbps
Number of Tasks	5–10
Task Size	500 MIPS-1000 MIPS
Transmission Range	60 m, 125 m
E_{elec} (nJ/bit)	50
$\mathcal{E}_{amp}$ (pj/bit/m^2)	100

4.3   Results and Discussions

Figure 3 shows the energy consumption of IoT nodes for small-scale scenario-I. The energy consumption of k-FNP remains close to that of ILP. Both ILP and k-FNP show consistent energy performance irrespective of the number of IoT nodes. An increase in the number of IoT nodes results in more clusters as k increases proportionally to

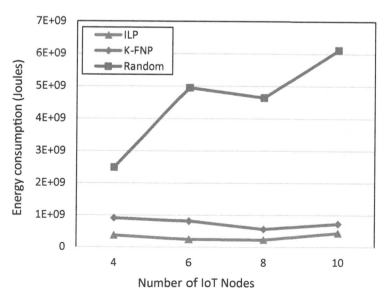

Fig. 2. Energy consumption (Small-Scale Scenario-I)

the number of nodes. With more clusters, the distance between nodes and their cluster center decreases, and the total energy remains the same compared to when there are fewer nodes. On the other hand, the energy consumption of random placement is significantly higher than that of ILP and k-FNP. This is because, random placement does not aim to optimize the energy efficiency of IoT nodes (Fig. 2).

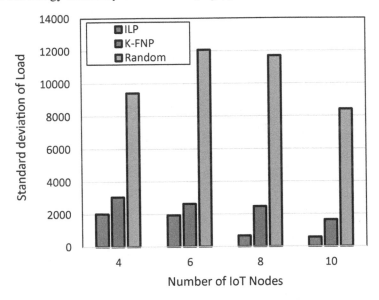

Fig. 3. Standard deviation (Small-Scale Scenario-I)

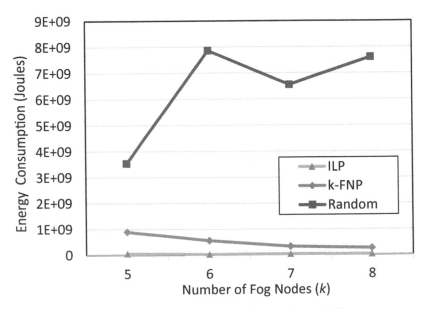

Fig. 4. Energy consumption (Small-Scale Scenario-II)

Figure 4 shows the standard deviation of load in all three schemes. We observe that k-FNP performs close to the ILP in terms of balancing the load. It outperforms random placement for any number of IoT nodes. This is because, random placement considers neither the cluster load nor the fog capacity in selecting a cluster for an IoT node. We observe that ILP and k-FNP experience a reduction in standard deviation as the number of nodes increases. Since increase in number of nodes results in more clusters and as a result, allows for efficient distribution load among the clusters.

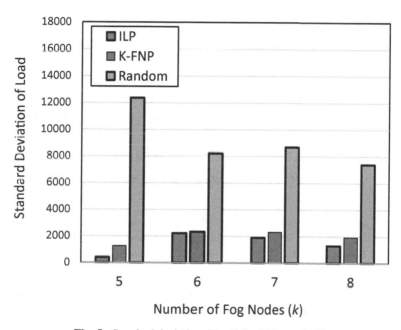

Fig. 5. Standard deviation (Small-Scale Scenario-II)

Figure 5 shows the energy efficiency performance for small-scale scenario-II with respect to the number of fog nodes (i.e., k). We observe a considerable gap between the random placement and k-FNP. Both ILP and k-FNP show a decrease in energy consumption with increase in k. This is because higher values of k lead to more clusters, decreasing the distance between IoT nodes and their selected clusters, eventually decreasing the energy requirement of IoT nodes. The performance of k-FNP is slightly lower than that of ILP, which leads to the conclusion that k-FNP can yield placements close to the optimal solutions.

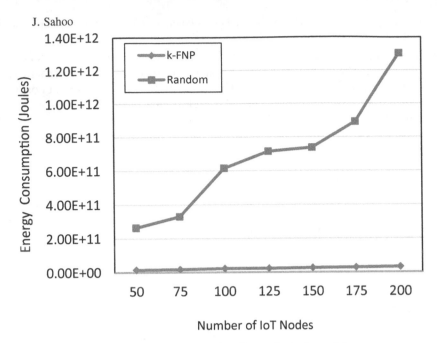

Fig. 6. Energy consumption (Large-Scale Scenario)

Figure 6 shows the standard deviation of load for small-scale scenario-II. It shows that k-FNP performs close to ILP, whereas random placement exhibits drastically poor performance across all nodes.

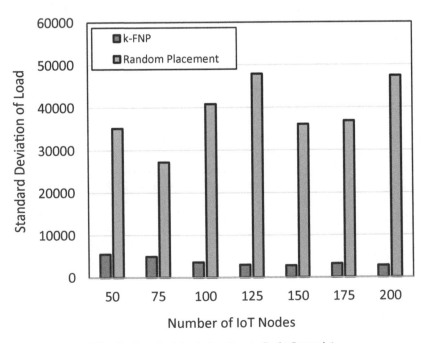

Fig. 7. Standard deviation (Large-Scale Scenario)

Figure 7 and Fig. 8 show the energy consumption and standard deviation obtained with k-FNP and random placement under a large-scale scenario. In Fig. 7, we observe an increase in energy consumption for random placement as the number of nodes increases. As k is set to only 20% of the number of IoT nodes, some fog nodes are still farther from the IoT nodes compared to when k is set to 50%, resulting in higher energy consumption. The growth in energy consumption of k-FNP is significantly low than that of the random placement, confirming the suitability of k-FNP in finding appropriate fog nodes.

In Fig. 8, we observe a considerable performance gap between k-FNP and random placement. Although the random placement considers the transmission range and fog capacity constraint in selecting clusters, it does not consider the load of IoT nodes, thereby resulting in a non-uniform distribution of load among the fog nodes.

Table 4. Maximum load (MIPS) (Small Scale Scenario-I)

Number of IoT Nodes	ILP	k-FNP	Random Placement
4	13392	13500	18000
6	13498.5	13800	24700
8	11606	13400	25800
10	11262.5	12700	21700

Table 5. Maximum load (MIPS) (Small Scale Scenario-II)

Number of Fog Nodes	ILP	k-FNP	Random Placement
5	11262.5	12238.7	21566.3
6	10934.5	11636.45	21218.05
7	9954	11062.35	22306
8	8882.5	10143.45	19316.9

Table 4 shows the maximum load for small-scale scenario-I. Both ILP and k-FNP experience a slight variation maximum load with an increase in the number of IoT nodes. k-FNP shows a maximum load close to optimal placement, thereby confirming its ability to minimize the maximum load. Moreover, on average, k-FNP yields 69% better performance than random placement.

Table. 5 shows the maximum load on a fog node with respect to the number of fog nodes for small-scale scenario-II. As the number of fog nodes increases, the maximum load decreases slightly for both ILP and k-FNP. As the IoT tasks have heterogeneous computational requirements, with higher value of k, the fog load can be balanced more effectively than with a lower value of k. We observe that random placement yields significantly higher maximum load irrespective of the number of IoT nodes. On average,

Random placement results in a maximum load that is twice as much as the maximum load of the optimal placement obtained by the ILP. On the other hand, k-FNP remains close to ILP for any number of fog nodes.

Table 6. Maximum load (MIPS) (Large Scale Scenario)

Number of IoT Nodes	k-FNP	Random Placement
50	35415.4	79717
75	34356	76616.85714
100	31414.6	101471.2
125	31044	127496
150	33034.2	83322
175	34041.4	99661.8
200	33690	148673.3

The maximum load for the large-scale scenario is shown in Table. 6. k-FNP shows consistent performance in balancing load even in the presence of many IoT nodes. On the contrary, random placement shows significant variation in maximum load. Moreover, the maximum load in random placement peaks at 148673 MIPS for 200 nodes, which is 4.4 times higher than that of k-FNP.

5 Conclusion

In this paper, we address the fog node placement problem that entails finding appropriate fog nodes to minimize the energy consumption of IoT nodes and minimize the maximum load to ensure an even distribution of IoT workload among fog nodes. First, we present an ILP formulation of the fog node placement problem. Then, we propose a placement algorithm that is based on k-means clustering. A composite metric consisting of two parameters: energy consumption and cluster load, is designed to address the two objectives: minimization of energy consumption and load balancing. Our simulation results show that the proposed algorithm performs close to the ILP in terms of both objectives and hence can produce good quality solutions. In the future, we would like to address the placement issue considering complex scenarios that involve heterogeneous fog nodes that vary in terms of resource and security requirements.

Acknowledgment. This work is supported by the National Institute of Food and Agriculture, United States Department of Agriculture, Evans-Allen project number SCX-314–02-19.

References

1. Elijah, O., Rahman, T.A., Orikumhi, I., Leow, C.Y., Hindia, M.N.: An overview of Internet of Things (IoT) and data analytics in agriculture: benefits and challenges. IEEE Internet Things J. **5**(5), 3758–3773 (2018)
2. Ivanov, S., Bhargava, K., Donnelly, W.: Precision farming: sensor analytics. IEEE Intell. Syst. **30**(4), 76–80 (2015)
3. Ahmed, N., De, D., Hussain, I.: Internet of Things (IoT) for smart precision agriculture and farming in rural areas. IEEE Internet Things J. **5**(6), 4890–4899 (2018)
4. Naha, R.K., et al.: Fog computing: survey of trends, architectures, requirements, and research directions. IEEE Access **6**, 47980–48009 (2018)
5. Mouradian, C., Naboulsi, D., Yangui, S., Glitho, R.H., Morrow, M.J., Polakos, P.A.: A comprehensive survey on fog computing: state-ofthe-art and research challenges. IEEE Commun. Surveys Tutorials **20**(1), 416–464 (2018)
6. Xia, X., et al.: Budgeted data caching based on k-median in mobile edge computing. In: IEEE International Conference on Web Services (ICWS), pp. 197–206 (2020)
7. Yuan, X., He, Y., Fang, Q., Tong, X., Du, C., Ding, Y.: An improved fast search and find of density peaks-based fog node location of fog computing system. In: IEEE International Conference on Internet of Things (iThings) and IEEE Green Computing and Communications (GreenCom) and IEEE Cyber, Physical and Social Computing (CPSCom) and IEEE Smart Data (SmartData), pp. 635–642 (2017)
8. Jiang, C., Wan, J., Abbas, H.: An edge computing node deployment method based on improved k-means clustering algorithm for smart manufacturing. IEEE Syst. J. **15**(2), 2230–2240 (2021)
9. Manogaran, G., Rawal, B.S.: An efficient resource allocation scheme with optimal node placement in iot-fog-cloud architecture. IEEE Sensors J. **21**(22), 25106–25113 (2021)
10. Zhao, Z., Min, G., Gao, W., Wu, Y., Duan, H., Ni, Q.: Deploying edge computing nodes for large-scale iot: a diversity aware approach. IEEE Internet Things J. **5**(5), 3606–3614 (2018)
11. Lin, P.: Optimal smart gateway deployment for the Internet of Things in smart home environments. In: IEEE 4th Global Conference on Consumer Electronics (GCCE), pp. 273–274 (2015)
12. Zhang, J., Li, X., Zhang, X., Xue, Y., Srivastava, G., Dou, W.: Service offloading oriented edge server placement in smart farming. Softw Pract Exper. 1– 18, (2020)
13. Gravalos, I., Makris, P., Christodoulopoulos, K., Varvarigos, E.A.: Efficient gateways placement for internet of things with QoS constraints. In: IEEE Global Communications Conference (GLOBECOM), pp. 1–6 (2016)
14. Lee, J.-H., Chung, S.-H., Kim, W.-S.: Fog server deployment technique: an approach based on computing resource usage. Int. J. Distrib. Sensor Netw. **15**(1), 1550147718823994 (2019)
15. da Silva, R.A.C., da Fonseca, N.L.S.: On the Location of Fog Nodes in Fog-Cloud Infrastructures. Sensors **19**(11), 2445 (2019)
16. Guo, X., Lin, H., Wu, Y., Peng, M.: A new data clustering strategy for enhancing mutual privacy in healthcare IoT systems. Futur. Gener. Comput. Syst. **113**, 407–417 (2020)
17. Heinzelman, W.R., Chandrakasan, A., Balakrishnan, H.: Energy-efficient communication protocol for wireless microsensor networks. In: The 33rd Annual Hawaii International Conference on System Sciences, vol. 2, p. 10 (2000)
18. IBM CPLEX Optimizer [Online] Available: https://www.ibm.com/analytics/cplex-optimizer

Identification and Classification of Human Body Parts for Contactless Screening Systems: An Edge-AI Approach

Diogo Rocha[1], Pedro Rocha[1], Jorge Ribeiro[1], and Sérgio Ivan Lopes[1,2](✉)

[1] ADiT-LAB, Instituto Politécnico de Viana do Castelo, Rua Escola Industrial
e Comercial Nun'Álvares, 4900-347 Viana do Castelo, Portugal
`sil@estg.ipvc.pt`
[2] IT - Instituto de Telecomunicações, Campus de Santiago,
3810-193 Aveiro, Portugal

Abstract. Continuous monitoring of vital signs like body temperature and cardio-pulmonary rates can be critical in the early prediction and diagnosis of illnesses. Optical-based methods, i.e., RGB cameras and thermal imaging systems, have been used with relative success for performing contactless vital signs monitoring, which is of great value for pandemic scenarios, such as COVID-19. However, to increase the performance of such systems, the precise identification and classification of the human body parts under screening can help to increase accuracy, based on the prior identification of the Regions of Interest (RoIs) of the human body. Recently, in the field of Artificial Intelligence, Machine Learning and Deep Learning techniques have also gained popularity due to the power of Convolutional Neural Networks (CNNs) for object recognition and classification. The main focus of this work is to detect human body parts, in a specific position that is lying on a bed, through RGB and Thermal images. The proposed methodology focuses on the identification and classification of human body parts (head, torso, and arms) from both RGB and Thermal images using a CNN based on an open-source implementation. The method uses a supervised learning model that can run in edge devices, e.g. Raspberry Pi 4, and results have shown that, under normal operating conditions, an accuracy in the detection of the head of 98.97% (98.4% confidence) was achieved for RGB images and 96.70% (95.18% confidence) for thermal images. Moreover, the overall performance of the thermal model was lower when compared with the RGB model.

Keywords: Edge-AI · Identification · Classification · Validation · Thermal · RGB

© ICST Institute for Computer Sciences, Social Informatics and Telecommunications Engineering 2022
Published by Springer Nature Switzerland AG 2022. All Rights Reserved
S. Paiva et al. (Eds.): SmartCity360° 2021, LNICST 442, pp. 92–103, 2022.
https://doi.org/10.1007/978-3-031-06371-8_7

1   Introduction

Due to the recent COVID-19 outbreak, new problems emerged in the way that our health professionals work. COVID-19 is known for its high transmission rate through the air, being its progression typically controlled in three stages [1]: 1) social distancing; 2) quarantine suspects and 3) isolate infected. Statistics point to approximately 80% of infected individuals develop light symptoms as low fever, headache, or myalgia, although there are other 15% that can have the low symptoms and as well pneumonia or breathing problems. The remaining 5%, besides the previous symptoms, are likely to develop skeptic shock, respiratory failure, or multi-organ failure and need additional attention by healthcare professionals and increased contact with the patients, which may be a source of additional infection [2]. Therefore, continuous contactless vital signs screening has a huge potential for reducing the physical contact between patients and healthcare professionals.

This work was developed under the R&D project CoViS[1], whose aim is to design and develop a real-time contactless health monitoring system, that uses a multimodal approach based on Doppler radar techniques [3] to measure the cardiorespiratory rates, and thermography images based on infrared to assess the human body temperature. Therefore, to improve the system performance, the prior identification of the Regions-of-Interest (RoIs)—head, torso, arms—of the individual under screening is of major importance. In that context, with the images captured by the cameras, the software must be capable to identify and classify the individual body parts, lying and stand or even in other perspectives, and perform the screening task properly contextualized, accordingly.

We investigated the use of Convolutional Neural Network (CNN) in an open-source implementation using small electronic devices to the classification of human body parts, in particular when a human is lying for example in a bed. The main focus of this work is to detect parts of the body in a specific position through RGB and Thermal images, and not detect the segmentation or pose estimation of the human body. In this sense, the work is based on the data gathering from a thermal camera and the position of the human body in the context of a healthcare environment (ex. a person lying in bed). To create the prediction model we used a specific camera in different positions to obtain the images (RGB and Thermal) for the dataset. Thus, the previous processing task was analyzing the images and execute the interpolation in order to adapt the size of the images to be used with the CNN implementation. The method uses a supervised learning model that can run in edge devices, e.g. Raspberry Pi 4,

This paper will be organized in sections, starting with Sect. 2 called Related Work, which will showcase projects that use technologies necessary for the future implementation of this project. Section 3 called Adopted Methodology will contain our data set preparation and the AI algorithm selection that we developed

---

[1] *CoViS—Contactless Vital Signs Monitoring in Nursing Homes using a Multimodal Approach*, Project website: https://covis.wavecom.pt/.

throw this project. Section 4 will be the results of our AI algorithm. Finally, Sect. 5, where the conclusions are taken and the future work is defined.

2   Related Work

Due to the success of the applicability of Artificial Intelligence techniques in computer vision, in the last years have been presented some other approaches using Camera Pose Estimation with Deep Learning [4], in particular for image classification, image segmentation, object detection, and many more image characteristics. Using the basis of Convolutional Neural Networks, different approaches have been presented for example using the idea for regressing the absolute camera pose from an RGB image or thermal/heat image use. Besides the promising results, in general, the resulting accuracy was sub-optimal, compared to classic feature-based solutions in particular in a particular position of the body in the camera field. This led to a surge of learning-based pose estimation methods that can complement the approach of classifying human body parts in a specific position. In the future we intend to explore and complement this work and their context applicability using other Deep Learning Approaches as PoseNet [5], LSTM-Pose, Bayesian and Support Vetor Machine Pose Net [6], and 3D human pose estimation classification and recognition [7–9] with different encoders (GoogleNet, densenet, for example) and with different opensource language/frameworks implementations (tensorflow posenet (1), MediaPipe (2), for example). On another end, in the last years, different opensource implementations have been presented to classify or recognize characteristics in images. In the last years a huge number of works have been exploring CNN implementation, mainly using opensource approaches, for example, the Tensorflow [12], Pytorch [10], Keras [11] or other implementations in Java, C++, and python, to present a few. In this work we followed the exploration of the Tensorflow lite implementation [12,13], by the fact of the promising results for identifying and classify characteristics in images as well as the ability and capacity to run in edge devices, e.g. Raspberry Pi 4. In the future, we intend to explore other implementations or even improve some in order to better accurate the results of the models and other specificities of Convolutional Neural Networks.

Plagemann et al. [14] propose a point detector particularly designed for analyzing the human shape. The interest points, which are based on identifying geodesic extreme points, coincide with salient points of the body, which can be classified as, e.g., hand, foot or head using local shape descriptors. According to the authors, their approach provides a natural way of estimating a 3D orientation vector for a certain interest point, that can be used to simplify the classification problem as well as estimate the orientation of the body parts in space. The training set consists of 789 recorded frames from a different sequence, resulting in 6312 patches extracted at interest point locations. They evaluated the classifier in the test set and it proved to be almost perfect with 98% accuracy for the patches containing the head. The respective numbers for hands and feet were 82% and 79%. This method presents an increase in performance over the state-of-the-art alternatives.

In [15], Romero et al. present a method for estimating 2D human pose from video using only optical flow. Their method, called *FlowCap* method uses a Kalman filter to propagate body part positions and velocities over time and a regression method to predict 2D body pose from part centers. No range sensor is required and FlowCap estimates 2D human pose from monocular video sources containing human motion. Such sources include hand-held phone cameras and archival television videos. The authors, also demonstrate 2D body pose estimation in a range of scenarios and show that the method works with real-time optical flow. The method was trained using the HumanEva training set [16], composed of approximate 7000 training images of the full-body, and the authors generated two generic datasets: The upper body dataset is composed of approximately 7, 000 training examples, while the full-body dataset has approximately 14, 000. The results suggest that the training data generated [15] could be used to directly train a CNN to estimate pose from flow (and image data).

Cao et al. [17], propose to efficiently detect the 2D pose of multiple people in an image. The approach uses a nonparametric representation, which refers to Part Affinity Fields (PAFs), to learn to associate body parts with individuals in the image. The architecture encodes global context, allowing a greedy bottom-up parsing step that maintains high accuracy while achieving real-time performance, irrespective of the number of people in the image. The architecture is designed to jointly learn part locations and their association via two branches of the same sequential prediction process. In this paper, the authors presented an explicit non-parametric representation of the key-points association that encodes both position and orientation of human limbs. Second, they designed an architecture for jointly learning parts detection and parts association. Third, they demonstrate that a greedy parsing algorithm is sufficient to produce high-quality parses of body poses, that maintain efficiency even as the number of people in the image increases. They showed representative failure cases as well.

3 Adopted Methodology

Figure 1 illustrates the adopted methodology, which consists of four distinct steps:

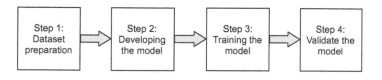

Fig. 1. Adopted methodology.

The first step consisted of the dataset preparation. All the images were obtained with the FLIR E54 [18] camera. The FLIR E54 thermal camera has two built-in cameras, one based on a CMOS RGB sensor, and the other based on a thermal imaging sensor. The thermal imaging sensor has a resolution of 320×240 pixels and operates in the interval from -20 to $120\,°C$, with a temperature accuracy of $\pm0.3\,°C$. On the other hand, the RGB chipset has a resolution of 1280×960 pixels. The camera has built-in Wi-Fi connectivity and is also capable of performing live-streaming. The second step focused on developing the model that will enable the identification and the classification of human body parts, more specifically the head, torso, and arms, which has been done by manually evaluating the pictures taken in the previous step. The third step consists of training the model, which also included the model tuning iterations. Lastly, the final step consisted of the model validation with new images representing the practical application case under study.

3.1 Dataset Preparation

The dataset was obtained during three weeks, where several subjects have participated in different poses to simulate the application case under study. Figure 2 depicts the experimental apparatus used to obtain the dataset, where three camera positions have been considered. The images were obtained using the thermal camera FLIR E54, being that we obtained 876 images, 438 thermal and 438 RGB, of which 42 correspond to Setup 1, and have been taken from a low tripod with about 1.2 m in height and a distance from the subject of 1.50 m. Setup 2 was obtained using the tripod at approximately 0.70 m height, which resulted in a distance to the subject of 2.1 m. In Setup 3, 279 pictures have been acquired using a giraffe tripod at 2 m height and a distance to the subject of 2.50 m.

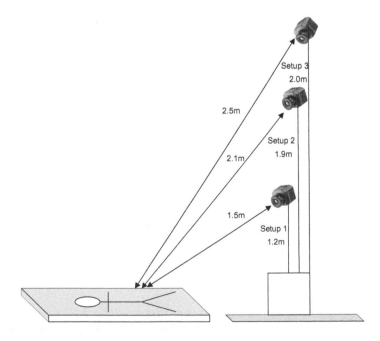

Fig. 2. Image acquisition procedure with the three setups evaluated.

Figure 3 illustrates two example images obtained with the FLIR E54 camera, RGB and Thermal, respectively, with all relevant Regions of Interest (RoI) identified before labeling.

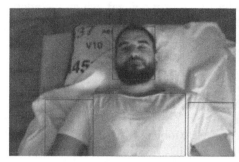

Fig. 3. Regions of Interest (RoI) definition. Example of images (RGB+Thermal) obtained with the FLIR E54 camera.

3.2 Model Definition

Our model was conceptualized firstly with a focus on the head, torso, and arms. However, the detection of the head and torso have been prioritized due to its applicability for contactless vital signs monitoring applications. In different environments, several scenarios have been portrayed for distinct patient's positions at a nursing room bed, in a way to make the experiment as close as possible to a real situation. We used FLIR E54 to capture the RGB and Thermal datasets, which have been captured at the same time instant.

Contactless vital signs monitoring techniques rely on different technologies that need to be optimally calibrated and aligned for increased accuracy. In that sense, the need for detecting different parts of the body—in both RGB and thermal images—is of great value to increase the accuracy of such methods. This way, the proposed model for detection and identification has been prioritized by the relevance of the body parts: 1) head, 2) torso, and 3) arms. The body parts detection will be performed and evaluated using both types of images for all the datasets produced.

All the acquired RGB images that are part of the three produced datasets have been labeled accordingly to the model previously defined. Regarding the thermal images, we opted to ignore the arms part because, in the context of the application we are targeting, only the head and torso are being considered, which simplifies the model and facilitates its deployment in resource-constrained edge devices, since fewer resources will be needed, leading to the improvement of the overall model efficiency.

3.3 Model Training

The two types of images captured (RGB and Thermal) have been then used to spot the differences in the detection and identification of body parts. The training process was performed using the GPU (Graphical Processing Unit) NVIDIA GeForce GTX 1650 With Max-Q Design, 4 GB GDDR5 and both CUDA and CUDNN extensions have been enabled to speed up processing.

First, the RGB images subset has been trained with 479 images, that have been labeled based on the body parts model previously defined, which included the head, torso, and arms. Then, the SSD MobileNet V2 FPNLite model [13,20, 21] was used with a resolution of 640 × 640 in every image to initialize the train of the RGB model. The train was performed during 2.000 iterations and, in the end, a tune has been performed, we altered the iterations number, which resulted in more than 50.000 iterations. The total duration of the train was approximately 48 h. Secondly, the subset of the thermal images (also 479 images), has been trained and labeled based on the body parts model previously defined, but which included only the head and torso. Then, the SSD MobileNet V2 FPNLite model [13,20,21] was used with a resolution of 320 × 320 in every image. The train was performed during 1.000 iterations and, in the end, a tune has been performed, we altered the iterations number, which resulted in more than 50.000 iterations. The total duration of the train was approximately 38 h. The technique used for validation was the train/test split.

- After acquiring the images, they were converted from resolution 1280 × 960 to 640 × 640 in the RGB dataset, and from the resolution 320 × 240 to 320 × 320 for the thermal images. This step has been carried out to achieve optimal performance with the pre-trained CNN implementation. In this case, each image was associated with specific ground-truth labeling and the classification categories (Head, Torso, Arms).
- Then the dataset was split into two subsets, i.e., training and validation sets. The training set consists of 115 images randomly selected from all the dataset, and the validation set consists of 341 images that remained and that makes 456 images. The 456 images in total, trained and validated are still less than the 479 that we total captured, that's because we decided to exclude some images in order to get better results, i.e., lack of light or blurred images. That resulted in excluding 41 RGB images and 23 thermal images, that lead 438 RGB images and 456 thermal images in total.

Typically, during a CNN evaluation some specific metrics based on False Positives, False Negatives, True Positives, True Negatives (presented as the confusion matrix), model accuracy, precision, root-mean-square error, F1-score, as well as some CPU and GPU performance processing metrics, such as the mean Average Precision (mAP) and the Intersection over Union (IoU)—which determines how many objects were detected correctly and how many false positives were generated.

To evaluate the robustness of the MobileNet V2 FPNLite model [13,20,21], real images without ideal conditions from outside our dataset, have also been used. Moreover, a conventional webcam has also been used to evaluate in a live stream the quality of the obtained data. Both MobileNet models were trained and evaluated with an Open Source TensorFlow Object, in particular, the detection accuracy (DA) and confidence level (CL), described in the next section. Figure 4 depicts the implemented MobileNet V2 SSD architecture.

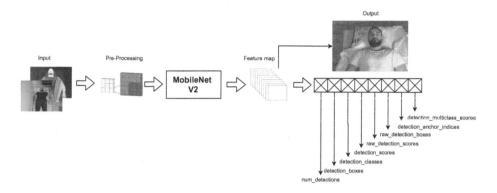

Fig. 4. MobileNet V2 SSD architecture.

4 Results and Discussion

The results obtained with the RGB dataset, varied depending on the setup used, cf. Fig. 2, we evaluated them in detection accuracy (DA) and confidence level (CL) which was computed based on the percentage of cases with confidence above 90%. In general, head detection produced the best results. The torso generated pretty satisfactory results, although not as good as the head detection. Lastly, the arms, which gave us subpar results compared to the other body parts. The results obtained are compiled in Table 1.

Still, in the RGB dataset, the first setup produced an head DA of 95.51% with a CL of 95.23%, and torso DA of 90.50% with a CL of 83.33%. The arms had a DA of 38.87% and CL of 22.62%. These results were obtained from 42 images with the conditions described in Sect. 3.1. On the second setup, the DA of the head is 97.82% with an LoC of 95.76%, with the torso DA being 77.19% and CL of 61.86%. The arms produced a DA of 46.41% and a CL of 19.49%. To obtain these results, 118 images were tested. And in the third and last one, the DA of the head is 99.97% with a CL of 100.00%, the torso DA 94.45% with a CL of 92.45%, and the arms DA 63.27% with a CL of 52.35%. These results refer to 278 images.

With all this, the general results for all the RGB datasets were 98.97% regarding the head DA with a CL of 98.40%, 89.42% regarding the torso DA with a CL of 83.33% and a DA of 56.39% for the arms with a CL of 40.87%.

Regarding the thermal dataset, we had the same three setups, but we opted to not label the arms. With this in mind, the first setup gave us a head DA of 90.69% with a CL of 88.89% and a torso DA of 46.99% with a CL of 37.78%. These results came from 45 images with the conditions described in Sect. 3.1. On the second one, the DA of the head is 97.78% with a CL of 96.88%, with the

Table 1. Results summary for the three evaluated setups.

	Setup 1		Setup 2		Setup 3		Total	
	RGB	Thermal	RGB	Thermal	RGB	Thermal	RGB	Thermal
Accuracy								
Head	95.51%	90.69%	97.82%	97.78%	99.97%	96.93%	98.97%	96.70%
Torso	90.50%	46.99%	77.19%	41.54%	94.45%	42.10%	89.42%	42.64%
Arms	38.87%	–	46.41%	–	63.27%	–	56.39%	–
Confidence								
Head	95.23%	88.89%	95.76%	96.88%	100.00%	95.05%	98.40%	95.18%
Torso	83.33%	37.78%	61.86%	33.59%	92.45%	31.45%	83.33%	32.89%
Arms	22.62%	–	19.49%	–	52.34%	–	40.87%	–
Number of images	42	45	118	128	278	283	438	456

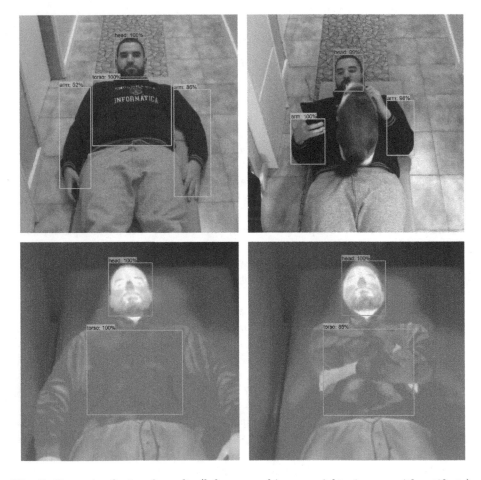

Fig. 5. Example of setup 3 results (left - normal images, right - images with artifacts).

torso DA being 41.54% and CL of 33.59%. To obtain these results, 128 images were analyzed. Finally, in the last one, the DA of the head is 96.93% with a CL of 95.05% and the torso DA 42.10% with a CL of 31.45%. These results came from 283 images. These results gave the thermal model an overall DA for the head of 96.70% with a CL of 95.18% and a torso DA of 42.64% with a CL of 32.89%, with a total of 456 images tested.

To visualize the models processing the test images, we used the plugin TensorBoard from TensorFlow. As presented in Fig. 5, the results on the left show the analysis of a normal image that was submitted for classification with both RGB and Thermal models, respectively, where the identification box and its CL are presented. Additionally, in Fig. 5, the images on the right show the results after processing images with artifacts (cat and arms crossed), which shows the results of both models operating in abnormal conditions and illustrate the models' resilience to artifacts.

In this work, we used the Tensorflow lite implementation [12] by the capacity to run in edge devices, e.g. Raspberry Pi 4. In the future, we intend to explore other implementations or even improve some in order to better accurate the results of the models and other specificities of Convolutional Neural Networks, for example, works like [22] or other recent improvements using feature pyramid architecture for object detection or other new approaches for the applicability context of this work, as the architectures Resnet, R-NN-Regions with CNN features, Recurrent Convolutional Neural Network, ExtremeNet or other.

5   Conclusions and Future Work

This work is centered on the study and exploration of the complementarity of Artificial Intelligence, Machine Learning, Deep Learning, Computer Vision approaches for the identification and classification of human body parts for contactless screening systems. The main focus is to detect parts of the body in a specific position through RGB and Thermal images and not detect the segmentation or pose estimation of the human body. The proposed methodology focuses on the detection and classification of human body parts (head, torso, and arms) from both RGB and Thermal images using an implementation of the Convolutional Neural Networks through an open-source approach. The method uses a supervised learning model that can run in edge devices, e.g. Raspberry Pi 4. Using and opensource implementation and following the general methods and metrics for the model creation and validation, based on the obtained results we can conclude that the best setup for the RGB results, with the aim of the project in mind, was the third one. Because was almost infallible on the detection of the head, the torso part, compared with the other two setups, showed significantly better results and the arms part was as well above the others. We also decided to remove the arms label from the thermal dataset to preserve the general accuracy of our model. Furthermore, we also realized that the results for the thermal dataset were worse than for the RGB one, this is given the fact that the RGB was trained with superior image size. We also observed that the placing of the camera and the distance to the actor, are fundamentals variables to obtain a good result since we had promising results with the third setup in the RGB dataset and good results in the thermal dataset. Due to the promising results achieved, we are able in the future to extend the work with the complementary approaches of human body pose estimation to improve the training strategy and network architectures on prediction accuracy using Artificial Intelligence/Machine Learning potentialities for the identification and classification of human body parts for contactless screening systems.

Acknowledgments. This work is a result of the project CoViS - Contactless Vital Signs Monitoring in Nursing Homes using a Multimodal Approach, with reference POCI-01-02B7-FEDER-070090, under the PORTUGAL 2020 Partnership Agreement, funded through the European Regional Development Fund (ERDF).

References

1. Rohmetra, H., Raghunath, N., Narang, P., et al.: AI-enabled remote monitoring of vital signs for COVID-19: methods, prospects and challenges. Computing (2021). https://doi.org/10.1007/s00607-021-00937-7
2. Vital Surveillances: The Epidemiological Characteristics of an Outbreak of 2019 Novel Coronavirus Diseases (COVID-19) - China (2020). http://weekly.chinacdc.cn/en/article/id/e53946e2-c6c4-41e9-9a9b-fea8db1a8f51. Accessed 11 Jul 2021
3. Silva, F., Almeida, R., Pinho, P., Marques, P., Lopes, S.I.: Evaluation of a low-cost COTS bio radar for vital signs monitoring. In: 2021 IEEE International Smart Cities Conference (ISC2), Virtual Conference (2021)
4. Shavit, Y., Ferens, R.: Introduction to Camera Pose Estimation with Deep Learning. arXiv arXiv:abs/1907.05272 (2019)
5. Kendall, A., Grimes, M., Cipolla, R.: PoseNet: a convolutional network for real-time 6-DOF camera relocalization. In Proceedings of the IEEE International Conference on Computer Vision, pp. 2938–2946 (2015). https://github.com/alexgkendall/caffe-posenet
6. Walch, F., Hazirbas, C., Leal-Taixe, L., Sattler, T., Hilsenbeck, S., Cremers, D.: Image-based localization using LSTMs for structured feature correlation. In Proceedings of the IEEE International Conference on Computer Vision, pp. 627–637 (2017)
7. Fürst, M., Gupta, S., Schuster, R., Wasenmüller, O., Stricker, D.: HPERL: 3D Human Pose Estimation from RGB and LiDAR (2020). https://arxiv.org/pdf/2010.08221.pdf
8. Sárándi, I., Linder, T., Arras, K., Leibe, B.: MeTRAbs: metric-scale truncation-robust heatmaps for absolute 3D human pose estimation (2020). https://arxiv.org/abs/2007.07227
9. Véges, M., Lőrincz, A.: Absolute human pose estimation with depth prediction network. In: 2019 International Joint Conference on Neural Networks (IJCNN), pp. 1–7 (2019). https://arxiv.org/abs/1904.05947
10. Image Classification using Pytorch. https://pytorch.org/. Accessed 9 Jul 2021
11. Image Classification using Keras. https://keras.io/examples/vision/image_classification_from_scratch/. Accessed 9 Jul 2021
12. Google Tensorflow Lite webpage. https://www.tensorflow.org/lite. Accessed on 28 Jul 2021

13. Tensorflow MobileNet V2 FPNLite - Feature Pyramid Network. https://www.tensorflow.org/lite/guide/hosted_models. Accessed 13 Jul 2021
14. Plagemann, C., Ganapathi, V., Koller, D., Thrun, S.: Real-time identification and localization of body parts from depth images. In 2010 IEEE International Conference on Robotics and Automation, pp. 3108–3113. IEEE (2010)
15. Romero, J., Loper, M., Black, M.J.: FlowCap: 2D human pose from optical flow. In: Gall, J., Gehler, P., Leibe, B. (eds.) GCPR 2015. LNCS, vol. 9358, pp. 412–423. Springer, Cham (2015). https://doi.org/10.1007/978-3-319-24947-6_34
16. Sigal, L., Balan, A.O., Black, M.J.: HumanEva: synchronized video and motion capture dataset and baseline algorithm for evaluation of articulated human motion. Int. J. Comput. Vis. **87**(1–2), 4 (2010)
17. Cao, Z., Simon, T., Wei, S.E., Sheikh, Y.: Realtime multi-person 2d pose estimation using part affinity fields. In: Proceedings of the IEEE Conference on Computer Vision and Pattern Recognition, pp. 7291–7299 (2017)
18. FLIR E54, Advanced Thermal Imaging Camera. https://www.flir.com/products/e54/. Accessed 15 Jul 2021
19. Juang, C.F., Chang, C.M.: Human body posture classification by a neural fuzzy network and home care system application. IEEE Trans. Syst. Man Cybern. Part A Syst. Hum. **37**(6), 984–994 (2007)
20. Howard, A.G., et al.: MobileNets: efficient convolutional neural networks for mobile vision applications. arXiv arXiv:abs/1704.04861 (2017)
21. Sandler, M., Howard, A., Zhu, M., Zhmoginov, A., Chen, L.: MobileNetV2: inverted residuals and linear bottlenecks, pp. 4510–4520 (2018). https://doi.org/10.1109/CVPR.2018.00474
22. Ghiasi, G., Lin, T.-Y., Le, Q.: NAS-FPN: learning scalable feature pyramid architecture for object detection, pp. 7029–7038 (2019). https://doi.org/10.1109/CVPR.2019.00720
23. TensorFlow Object Detection API. https://github.com/tensorflow/models/tree/master/research/object_detection. Accessed 16 Jul 2021

A Collaborative Industrial Augmented Reality Digital Twin: Developing the Future of Shipyard 4.0

Aida Vidal-Balea[1,2]([mail]) [iD], Oscar Blanco-Novoa[1,2] [iD], Paula Fraga-Lamas[1,2] [iD], Miguel Vilar-Montesinos[3] [iD], and Tiago M. Fernández-Caramés[1,2] [iD]

[1] Faculty of Computer Science, Department of Computer Engineering, Universidade da Coruña, 15071 A Coruña, Spain
aida.vidal@udc.es
[2] Centro de Investigación CITIC, Universidade da Coruña, 15071 A Coruña, Spain
[3] Navantia S.A., Astillero de Ferrol, 15403 Ferrol, Spain

Abstract. Training of workshop operators and maintenance of industrial machinery is a major expense in large companies, since the lack of this process or its poor execution increase the cost and risks associated with the operation and handling of sensitive and/or hazardous machinery. Augmented Reality (AR), specifically Industrial Augmented Reality (IAR), can be useful in such a context, since it is a key technology in the Industry 4.0 paradigm that can enhance worker performance, reduce risks and improve production processes. This article proposes an IAR digital twin system that provides a dynamic way for industrial companies to perform operator training with a full-size model of the real equipment and to carry out a step-by-step in-situ guidance by adding contextual information and alerts so that maintenance processes are performed more safely and efficiently even by operators with a low level of training. The proposed system also allows several users to use devices simultaneously, providing a new way of collaborative interaction, thus facilitating communications and awareness of the environment. In addition, an Industrial Internet of Things (IIoT) system was successfully integrated with the developed system, enabling real-time interaction with the environment. Since one of the aims of the developed system was to provide a smooth user experience, performance tests were carried out with several simultaneous users by measuring their response latency as the number of connected users increased. As a result, it has been identified the IAR layer of the proposed architecture as the bottleneck of the system, as it has to deal with rendering delays.

This work was supported by the Plant Information and Augmented Reality research line of the Navantia-UDC Joint Research Unit (IN853B-2018/02). This work has also been funded by the Xunta de Galicia (by grant ED431C 2020/15, and grant ED431G 2019/01 to support the Centro de Investigación de Galicia "CITIC", the Agencia Estatal de Investigación of Spain (by grants RED2018-102668-T and PID2019-104958RB-C42) and ERDF funds of the EU (FEDER Galicia 2014-2020 & AEI/FEDER Programs, UE).

S. Paiva et al. (Eds.): SmartCity360° 2021, LNICST 442, pp. 104–120, 2022.
https://doi.org/10.1007/978-3-031-06371-8_8

Keywords: Industry 4.0 · Augmented Reality · Industrial Augmented Reality · Digital twin · Maintenance · Training · Microsoft HoloLens · Collaborative application

1   Introduction

In recent years there has been a significant growth in what is called Industry 4.0, also known as the Fourth Industrial Revolution. This term was firstly used by the German government in 2011 [1,2]. Collecting as much information as possible from business processes and obtaining intelligence to fuel smart manufacturing is one of the pillars of Industry 4.0. Another goal is to achieve physical and digital world convergence through technologies such as cyber-physical systems or digital twins [3]. A digital twin is a virtual replica of a physical entity that allows real-time monitoring and actuation during operation using data and simulations [4].

Among these new industrial developments, the shipbuilding industry is being constantly updated and is incorporating new technologies into its working processes under the Industry 4.0 paradigm. One of the most attractive technologies for the so-called Shipyard 4.0 [5] is Augmented Reality (AR) (specifically Industrial Augmented Reality (IAR)), as well as Mixed Reality (MR), which provide a wide range of capabilities that can be leveraged in order to construct strong and effective solutions able to integrate virtual components in real-world scenarios.

The aim of this article is to study and test the capabilities that Augmented and Mixed Reality (AR/MR) and the Internet of Things (IoT) (and more specifically the Industrial Internet of Things (IIoT)), can provide in order to ease and optimize production and maintenance tasks in an industrial environment while showing real-time information on top of real objects, leading to the idea of creating a virtual digital twin of a ship or of one of its components. To validate this objective, a demo application for Microsoft HoloLens 2 smartglasses [6] was developed. This application allows for training the workshop operators and to provide a dynamic way of guiding them during the building and maintenance processes of the vessels. In addition, the developed collaborative framework allows workshop operators to learn and share their knowledge in an interactive way.

The rest of this paper is structured as follows. Section 2 reviews the latest AR/MR systems for training and assistance, as well as other proposed digital twin projects. Section 3 presents the design requirements, the communications architecture of the proposed system and relevant details of its implementation. Section 4 describes the performed experiments and validation tests, analyzing the key findings. Finally, Sect. 5 is devoted to the conclusions.

2   Related Work

The digital twin is one of the key technologies for Industry 4.0 together with AR/MR and IIoT, since they provide valuable tools for manufacturing, training, healthcare and smart city environments. As of writing, no mature developments that study and integrate these three technologies have been found in the literature. The following cited works are some of the few examples that have been found regarding the integration of these three technologies.

The authors of [7] present a Proof-of-Concept (PoC) of a smart shelf with a system of QR codes that, when scanned, display on F4 smart glasses a remote Matlab simulation of stress analysis using a network of strain gauges. In [8], the authors define an AR framework as a visualization interface for an IoT infrastructure. Such a solution makes use of standard network localization techniques to find near-by device positions, which are sent to the AR devices for tracking them.

The developments previously described, despite integrating AR/MR and IoT partially, are mostly PoCs and do not use sophisticated tracking and interaction systems such as those offered by the Microsoft Hololens glasses. For instance, HoloLens glasses are used in [9], where the authors propose the integration of MR devices with the Mobius platform, one of the open source OneM2M IoT platforms. However, the development is tightly coupled with OneM2M applications and the authors considered that future work will be required to fulfill the requirements of OneM2M.

With respect to collaborative working environments, only a couple of recent preliminary works on collaborative AR/MR applications have been published in the literature. For example, Chusetthagarn et al. [10] demonstrated a PoC for visualizing sensor data in disaster management systems. HoloLens spatial anchors are used in this project via a built-in sharing prefab offered by Holo-Toolkit, a Unity package for creating a collaborative AR/MR environment. Regrettably, such an implementation is now deemed deprecated. However, it is important to remember that Microsoft has been working on a Microsoft HoloLens sharing system, which includes, among other features, a UDP-based discovery procedure. Nonetheless, despite the fact that the described Microsoft development is, to the authors' knowledge, the most promising collaborative framework option at the time of writing, it is yet undocumented and still not available after the release of HoloLens 2 [11].

Regarding the application of IAR to industrial scenarios, two of the most frequent applications are training and assistance. For example, operators and supervisors can also use assistance systems to get the visual or acoustic information they need to complete a task [12]. This type of information is sent in a ubiquitous and seamless manner, allowing it to be viewed in a context-aware manner.

It is known that well-trained operators have a major impact on productivity. In this scenario, IAR can assist with training by giving contextual knowledge and step-by-step guidance for completing specified operations. In addition, IAR systems can assist in monitoring the trainees' performance after they have completed a task. When training workers to operate machinery like the one used for line assembly, such support and feedback are critical, because they reduce the time and effort spent checking documentation [13] while also improving the accuracy (e.g., by lowering the error rate in assembly tasks [14]) and efficiency of the completed operation. As a result, IAR can shorten new employee training time and reduce skill needs by substantially reducing the influence of prior experience on the learning process. Furthermore, the presented instructions may be tailored to the workers' past experience. IAR emerges as a human-centered tool in this regard, assisting non-expert and less experienced operators in accomplishing new tasks.

IAR has already been shown to be beneficial in a variety of prior aid tasks, such as robot interaction and guiding systems. For example, while directing a telepresence robot, the authors of [15] employ AR as an improved user interface that uses visual cues to improve users' spatial awareness and give more precise dimensions and distances. AR-based methods for directing robot motions have also been described in other recent studies [16], while [17] provides a comprehensive overview of AR-based remote guiding systems.

IAR systems may also provide rapid access to documents such as manuals, 3D models, and historical data [18]. Moreover, IAR aids decision-making in real-world scenarios by integrating physical experience with displayed data that are retrieved in real-time [19].

More complex methods have been recently presented. For example, an olfactory-based AR system was proposed to assist in the detection of maintenance difficulties [20]. In addition, the authors of [21] want to improve a simulation-based support application by integrating contextual awareness using sensors. Another paper that incorporates IoT interactions is [22], which describes a framework for Microsoft HoloLens smart glasses that simplifies AR and IoT device integration. Additionally, by modeling logical items within a virtualized realm and then connecting such a logic with physical realities, IAR can make a significant contribution towards the definition of the characteristics of a digital twin [23].

In [24] authors develop a tool for Unity to create 3D manuals based on traditional paper manuals used in manufacturing industries. They conducted a study when training operators with different techniques: paper, 3D and AR. They concluded that operators who do not use paper are able to get the right training twice as fast in comparison to traditional approaches. It is important to note that, in such a paper, all tests related to AR were performed with projections on screens instead of with Head Mounted Display (HMD) devices like Microsoft HoloLens smart glasses.

A digital twin environment allows for rapid analysis and real-time decisions made through accurate analytics. Initially the term Digital Twin was first used in the aerospace industry [25], but it quickly spread to other areas. In [26] the authors review the academic literature on digital twins since 2003, showing a rapid growth and evolution both in the definitions and technologies used. Bevilacqua et al. [27] describe the development of a theoretical reference model to create a digital twin for risk management in work environments. It is based on a model that integrates data obtained from sensors, experts and historical data. It aims to improve the safety level of operators in the work environment. In [28] a digital twin for an industrial ice-cream machine is proposed. The system is able to use real data obtained from sensors inside the real machine while it is working, or it can be fed by simulated data for fault monitoring and performance assessment.

Regarding systems that integrate AR/MR within a digital twin system, it is important to indicate that AR/MR is commonly used to optimize the integration of the information provided by the digital twin with the real environment. Just a few articles have been found in literature on this topic: among them, the only one that stands out was written by Aschenbrenner et al. [29], who describe the development of digital twins of robotic arms whose visualization is performed with AR devices.

3   Analysis and Design of the AR/MR System

The main goal of the proposed system is to ease and optimize the maintenance and repair tasks of complex machinery in industrial environments by using the advantages offered by AR/MR technologies. Specifically, the developed system is oriented to enable people with a lower technical level to properly perform complex tasks and in a safer way in a shipyard or a vessel, where the availability of highly qualified personnel may involve high transport costs or important delays.

The AR/MR system can guide step by step the person performing the tasks through visual indications and 3D models in order to accomplish them successfully and with less risk.

The use of 3D visual animations improves and speeds up the understanding of the required steps compared to traditional paper manuals or blueprints and, therefore, allows for optimizing the process and increases the guarantees and lowers the risks for the worker and the equipment.

In addition, a digital twin experience was included on the system, making use of the IIoT to integrate real-time information and interactions between the virtual and real models.

The AR/MR system also has the capability of sharing the experience among multiple users, allowing them to interact and see the same pieces and animations at the same time.

3.1   Design Requirements

There are several requirements and features that are desirable for the proposed system and which are mainly related to 3D modeling and the IIoT subsystem, since they are key components of the digital twin experience:

3D Model Requirements

- Visualize 3D models aligned with the real world using the Microsoft HoloLens Smartglasses.
- Seamless user interaction with the virtual environment using the hands to make gestures and manipulate the objects.

- Visualization of 3D animations illustrating different steps of the process.
- Text information and warnings about important or dangerous steps.
- Option to scale and move the object from the original position.
- Menu that follows the user around.

IIoT Requirements

- Get real time data and parameters from the real machine.
- Show visual labels with the data from the IIoT system.
- Allow interaction with the real world through the IIoT system when something changes in the virtual environment.

Shared Experience Requirements

- Allow several users to use the same experience at the same time.
- Align virtual object between the different AR/MR devices and keep them in sync when they are moved, rotated or scaled.
- Keep the status of all the virtual elements synchronized across all the connected devices.

Figure 1 shows the different modules of the designed system as well as the communications architecture. The IIoT layer is composed of the different sensors and actuators that comprise an IIoT network. It can be physically located in the same area where the AR/MR visualization application is running, or it can even be in a different location.

The service layer is in charge of coordinating all the processes as well as managing the different protocols used by the heterogeneous devices. It consists of three subsystems:

- IIoT Service: it is in charge of the communications and management with the IIoT layer. It makes use of the MQTT API through an MQTT broker called Mosquitto [30]. It handles requests related to IIoT data and commands coming from AR/MR devices through the HTTP API. If it is necessary to forward the request to the IIoT layer, it is also in charge of the translation and adaptation of the requests between the AR/MR layer and the IIoT layer. It also takes care of the persistence of the sensor data thanks to a MongoDB database.
- Anchor Sharing Service: this is the service that manages shared AR/MR experiences, ensuring that all devices use the same environment tracking information. To do this, it is necessary to share some data packets called anchors among the devices. These packets are generated at an end device and contain the spatial information necessary for any other device to be able to recognize the environment and to position itself in the same spatial reference system. The Anchor Sharing Service also manages the persistence of the anchors and the distribution of each one to the corresponding devices through the REST API.

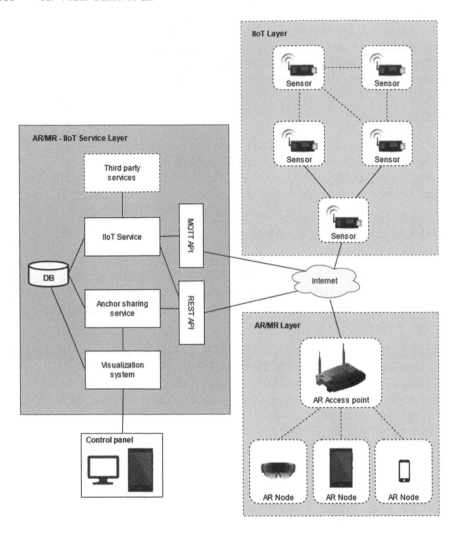

Fig. 1. Architecture of the proposed system.

– Visualization System: this system consists of a control panel that allows the user to visualize the status of the system and the active anchors and sessions at any given moment in time.

The AR/MR layer is composed of the end AR/MR devices (smart glasses or tablets) that users utilize to visualize the 3D information and animations, and to interact with the additional information provided by the IIoT system.

3.2   AR/MR Development

In order to show the capabilities of the proposed system, an application was developed for Microsoft HoloLens smart glasses that allows for visualizing the

3D model of a cooler. The developed solution was aimed at creation of a digital twin that will provide indications on repair and maintenance processes, and will show operation parameters that are measured in real time by hardware sensors embedded on the cooling unit.

The development was carried out using Unity [31]. All models were exported from the source CAD programs and then manipulated and optimized for the augmented reality experience using Blender.

The development was structured in different stages. First, the models were exported and polished in order to optimize them for running on AR/MR devices. In general, CAD models are designed parametrically and contain a very high level of detail. Due to the characteristics of the real-time rendering engines used by AR devices and the limited computational capabilities of embedded devices, a geometry cleaning process is required, which in many cases cannot be fully automated. An example of optimization of one of the parts of the 3D model is shown in Fig. 2, where the original and final models are compared.

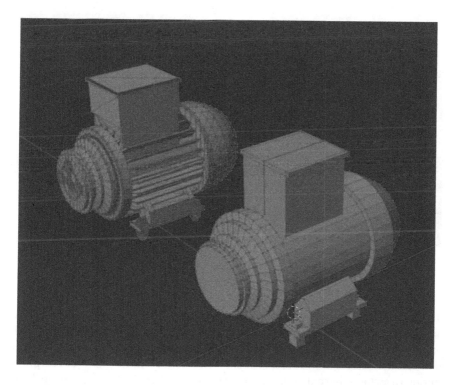

Fig. 2. Optimization example of one of the parts of the 3D model.

In a second stage the model was integrated into Unity and a user interface was developed to manipulate the 3D model and interact with the scene. For such a purpose, the design and interaction recommendations of the HoloLens framework [32] were implemented, thus making the panel follow the user and face him/her.

In a third stage the animations and contextual information for each step were added, including alerts and interaction with the user during the included maintenance or repair processes.

Finally, the sharing system was introduced, allowing several users in the same location to interact with the application at the same time (this collaboration is illustrated in a real scenario in Fig. 3 during the system tests). All users share the same spatial reference system, so that all virtual 3D objects are aligned with reality and, at the same time, they are synchronized among the different devices in such a way that if one user moves the 3D model, it will be moved instantaneously in all the devices that share the same experience. In the same way, the interactions of a user with the model have an effect on the instances of the model in the rest of the devices, favoring communications and collaboration between users.

Fig. 3. Collaborative interaction with the 3D model of the cooler.

To implement the sharing system, a framework to facilitate the communications among the different devices is needed. Unity provides a framework called UNet [33] that allows for creating different virtual elements and for keeping their movements synchronized, providing a set of tools for online game development. Its major drawback is that it is deprecated since 2018 and will soon no longer be available in Unity. As an alternative, there is an open source framework called Mirror [34], which enables collaborative games in Unity, allowing communications between two nodes in a local or remote network. Mirror provides an abstraction layer that allows for synchronizing different parts of the virtual environment in a relatively simple way, removing the complexity associated with handling network operations as discussed in [35]. Due to the previous reasons, and since the programming interface is compatible with Unet and due to the large number of users currently using it, Mirror was the framework selected for the development of the proposed application. In addition, since Mirror is open source, the code will be always available and can be modified in case any change is needed to fulfill the development requirements.

3.3 IIoT Integration

The IIoT Layer is responsible for interconnecting the AR smart glasses and IIoT devices. In order to be compatible with other applications and sensor networks, the use of a secure communications system based on HTTPS is proposed. The HTTP protocol is natively implemented in most AR/MR development environments and facilitates its integration with existing system components. The use of other IIoT-oriented protocols could be tempting, but it is not always straightforward to implement such protocols in the development environments available for AR/MR frameworks, as it is explained in [36]. Moreover, HTTP is not appropriate for sending the large amounts of data that are often needed in 3D AR and MR environments.

The IIoT service can be deployed in the cloud or using cloudlets (i.e., powerful local computers that act as Edge Computing devices). This helps by reducing latency times as the services can be placed closer to the client and, in scenarios with a large number of connected devices, it helps to reduce the amount of traffic generated to the cloud server as data can be preprocessed or aggregated by cloudlets before is sent to the cloud. Specifically, the IIoT services were implemented on top of NodeRed [37], which allows for an easy integration of the different technologies involved. As it can be seen in the architecture diagram (Fig. 5), IIoT devices communicate with the service using an MQTT network, since it is currently one of the most popular technologies for integrating IIoT sensors and actuators. Such an integration makes it compatible with many existent solutions. On the other end, the AR/MR devices communicate with the service by using a REST API via HTTPS for compatibility reasons, as discussed before. The NodeRed service is in charge of keeping the state of the system, converting between protocols and acting as an interface that connects with the persistence layer or database.

As an example, Fig. 4 shows the implemented virtual panels that display real-time information from the IIoT sensors located on the real cooler.

4   Experiments

In order to determine the performance of the proposed system, a testbed was designed using a pair of HoloLens 2 glasses and a desktop computer to determine how a large number of users impacts the latency of the system.

The Mirror framework used to implement the AR communications can be used to develop both desktop and embedded applications. Thus, the resulting communications system is interoperable between heterogeneous devices. This

Fig. 4. Virtual panels where the information about a valve is displayed.

allows for developing a graphical desktop application that emulates the communications of a device. Launching several instances of such an application causes the load to increase progressively, in the same way to what would happen if more AR/MR devices were connected to the system and moved around the virtual environment.

Regarding IIoT communications, they are composed of an MQTT part (in the IIoT device layer) and an HTTP part (in the AR/MR device layer). In order to find the most restrictive component of the system, the same previous setup was used (Hololens 2 and a desktop computer). A set of benchmarks was executed in order to determine independently the performance of the MQTT broker (Mosquitto) and the HTTP server (NodeRed) and to obtain the average latencies as the request demand increases. Since the number of requests grows with the number of users, the performed tests can give an idea of the scalability of the whole system.

The technical characteristics of the devices used for testing are the following:

- Desktop computer: Intel Core i7-7700 3.6 GHz (8 cores) CPU, 16 GB RAM and an NVIDIA GFORCE GTX 660 with 2 GB of DDR RAM.
- Router: Sagemcom F@ST 5366S 5G Gigabit (IEEE 802.11 a/b/g/n/ac).
- AR glasses: Microsoft HoloLens 2 (Qualcomm Snapdragon 850, Wi-Fi (IEEE 802.11 ac (2×2)), 4 GB of LPDDR DRAM).

In Fig. 5, the architecture of the designed experimental setup is depicted. At the top are all the emulated clients, which store their measurement records into a database where they will be processed and analyzed.

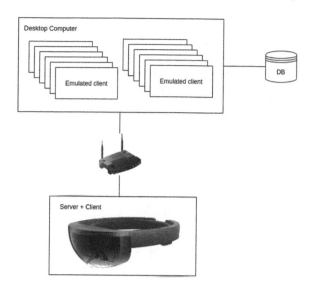

Fig. 5. Diagram of the setup for the experiments.

4.1   AR/MR Layer Experiments

This first set of tests were devised to determine how the developed system behaves depending on the number of contacted users. For such a purpose, the average latency of all connected clients was recorded for different scenarios (5, 10, 15 and 20 simultaneous users). Moreover, a 5 GHz and a 2.4 GHz WiFi network was used for each of the scenarios in order to compare the performance between both of them.

The simulation environment also emulates the 3D model rendering process in order to perform the measurements when considering all the delays that a user would experience during the execution of the application. This means that there is a limit when adding more users, as the computational load of the test computer increases gradually until it reaches a point where the high computational load might compromise the results.

It should also be noted that the evaluation testbed measures the latency since the packet is encapsulated on the source device, until it is processed on the target device and its contents are rendered on the screen. This means that the latency times shown on the results do not include only network latency, but also rendering times and, in many cases, waiting times related to the refresh rate of the device screen. This ensures a more accurate measurement of the response times that a real user would perceive when using the application.

Tables 1 and 2 show the latency measurements taken for both 2.4 and 5 GHz, respectively. On both cases average latency increases as more clients are added to the same shared experience and, as it can be expected, 5 GHz latency is lower. On the other hand, the standard deviation is almost the same on both scenarios and variance is small, which implies that there is a good and stable connection between the smart glasses.

Table 1. Latency experimented by a user on a 2.4 GHz network (ms).

Clients	Average	Standard dev	Variance
5	25.6712	13.4464	0.24392
10	43.9239	20.4037	0.50026
15	64.1954	28.2183	0.87689
20	89.7708	34.7472	1.36900

Table 2. Latency experimented by a user on a 5 GHz network (ms).

Clients	Average	Standard dev	Variance
5	22.4897	13.5303	0.25951
10	37.6301	21.4463	0.562
15	58.6853	32.2307	1.17312
20	82.4164	41.6821	1.86244

4.2   IIoT Layer Experiments

The second set of experiments was devised to be less restrictive than the ones related to the AR/MR communication due to the nature of IIoT data, since IIoT payload are usually light and spaced in time at regular intervals. In order to determine the capacity of the system, two mock endpoints were designed for MQTT and HTTP, and a script was used to simulate the existence of several clients simultaneously. In order to simulate the worst-case scenario, each client launches consecutive requests concurrently and independently of the others without waiting times.

In Fig. 6 it can be clearly seen that MQTT outperforms HTTP. This is expected, since MQTT is a lighter protocol and more suitable for the type of data handled in the IIoT layer. It can be observed that Mosquitto is able to handle more than 200,000 packets before it starts losing some of them. In contrast, NodeRed was able to handle a maximum of 1,500 requests per second.

These results show that MQTT is not going to be the limiting factor in the system. Nonetheless, it should be noted that the capacity of handling 1,500 requests per second is more than enough for most industrial scenarios.

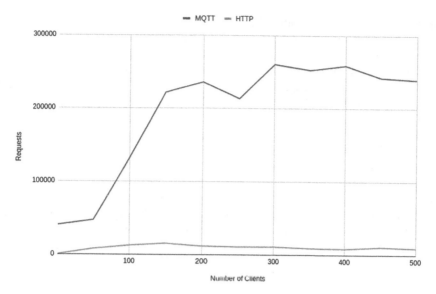

Fig. 6. Linear representation of the number of attended by the system according to the number of concurrent users.

4.3   Results

The obtained results show that slightly better times were obtained in the 5 GHz band, as expected due to the characteristics of such a band and the lower saturation of its spectrum. In any case, it can be observed that all latencies in the AR layer are below 100 ms. It is important to note that these times not only include the network latency but also add rendering times, so these times will be close to the real delays a user will experience when using the developed application.

It has also been determined that the response delay limiting factor is located in the AR layer, as it works with large amounts of data and includes processing times that are almost negligible for the IIoT layer. However, it is important to note that these results are only representative for the described setup. It is viable to vertically scale the system, adding more computational capacity, as well as horizontally, scaling by distributing the load among different devices. Specifically, in the AR/MR layer, the proximity characteristics of the generated and consumed data allow for moving the computation load closer to the end user by using cloudlets, which would greatly improve performance and further reduce the latency experienced by the user [38].

5   Conclusion

The use of IAR along IIoT and digital twin technologies can become an important part of Industry 4.0 factories but, as of writing, the literature includes a small number of systems that make use of such technologies when focusing on maintenance, training and assistance processes. To tackle the previously mentioned issues, a collaborative IAR system for training and guidance in assembly processes was created specifically for this article. After describing the proposed communications architecture, the implementation based on Microsoft HoloLens smart glasses was detailed, including the IIoT integration that led to the development of the digital twin system. The IAR digital twin system was evaluated to determine its limitation capacities. The limiting aspect has been identified as within the IAR layer, which deals with bigger volumes of data and involves rendering delays that are nearly non-existent in the IIoT layer. As a conclusion, some best practices and lessons learned are outlined to guide future IAR developers.

Regarding future work, it will be focused on improving the interaction with the IoT system from the AR application. In addition, some experiments in terms of usability and user performance in industrial scenarios will be carried out, as well as security and network performance of the different protocols used on the system.

References

1. Announcement of the Industrie 4.0 project in the 2011 Hannover fair. https://www.vdi-nachrichten.com/Technik-Gesellschaft/Industrie-40-Mit-Internet-Dinge-Weg-4-industriellen-Revolution. Accessed 28 Jul 2021
2. Industrie 4.0 (February 2019). https://www.bmbf.de/de/zukunftsprojekt-industrie-4-0-848.html. Accessed 28 Jul 2021
3. Qi, Q., Tao, F.: Digital twin and big data towards smart manufacturing and industry 4.0: 360 degree comparison. IEEE Access **6**, 3585–3593 (2018)
4. Rasheed, A., San, O., Kvamsdal, T.: Digital twin: values, challenges and enablers from a modeling perspective. IEEE Access **8**, 21980–22012 (2020)
5. Fraga-Lamas, P., Fernández-Caramés, T.M., Blanco-Novoa, Ó, Vilar-Montesinos, M.A.: A review on industrial augmented reality systems for the industry 4.0 shipyard. IEEE Access **6**, 13358–13375 (2018)
6. Microsoft HoloLens official web page. https://www.microsoft.com/en-us/hololens. Accessed 28 Jul 2021
7. Revetria, R., Tonelli, F., Damiani, L., Demartini, M., Bisio, F., Peruzzo, N.: A real-time mechanical structures monitoring system based on digital twin, Iot and augmented reality. In: Proceedings of the 2019 Spring Simulation Conference (SpringSim), Tucson, pp. 1–10 (2019)
8. Jo, D., Kim, G.J.: ARIoT: scalable augmented reality framework for interacting with Internet of Things appliances everywhere. IEEE Trans. Consum. Electron. **62**(3), 334–340 (2016)
9. Lee, S., Lee, G., Choi, G., Roh, B., Kang, J.: Integration of OneM2M-based IoT service platform and mixed reality device. In: Proceedings of the 2019 IEEE International Conference on Consumer Electronics (ICCE), Las Vegas, pp. 1–4 (2019)
10. Chusetthagarn, D., Visoottiviseth, V., Haga, J.: A prototype of collaborative augment reality environment for HoloLens. In: Proceedings of the 2018 22nd International Computer Science and Engineering Conference (ICSEC), Thailand, pp. 1–5 (2018)

11. GitHub: "MixedReality Sharing". https://github.com/microsoft/MixedReality-Sharing. Accessed 28 Jul 2021
12. Alesky, M., Vartiainen, E., Domova, V., Naedele, M.: Augmented reality for improved service delivery. In: Proceedings of the IEEE 28th International Conference on Advanced Information Networking and Applications, Canada, pp. 382–389. IEEE (2014)
13. Hořejší, P.: Augmented reality system for virtual training of parts assembly. In: Proceedings of the 25th DAAAM International Symposium on Intelligent Manufacturing and Automation (DAAAM), Vienna, pp. 699–706. Procedia Engineering (2015)
14. Tang, A., Owen, C., Biocca, F., Mou, W.: Comparative effectiveness of augmented reality in object assembly. In: 2003 Proceedings of the SIGCHI Conference on Human Factors in Computing Systems (CHI), Florida, pp. 73–80 (2003)
15. Mosiello, G., Kiselev, A., Loutfi, A.: Using augmented reality to improve usability of the user interface for driving a telepresence robot. Paladyn J. Behav. Robot. 4(3), 174–181 (2013)
16. Herrera, K.A., Rocha, J.A., Silva, F.M., Andaluz, V.H.: Training systems for control of mobile manipulator robots in augmented reality. In: Proceedings of the 2020 15th Iberian Conference on Information Systems and Technologies (CISTI), Sevilla, pp. 1–7. IEEE (2020)
17. Lapointe, J.-F., Molyneaux, H., Allili, M.S.: A literature review of AR-based remote guidance tasks with user studies. In: Chen, J.Y.C., Fragomeni, G. (eds.) HCII 2020. LNCS, vol. 12191, pp. 111–120. Springer, Cham (2020). https://doi.org/10.1007/978-3-030-49698-2_8
18. Zollmann, S., Hoppe, C., Kluckner, S., Poglitsch, C., Bischof, H., Reitmayr, G.: Augmented reality for construction site monitoring and documentation. Proc. IEEE 102(2), 137–154 (2014)
19. Moloney, J.: Augmented reality visualisation of the built environment to support design decision making. In: Proceedings of the 10th International Conference on Information Visualisation, IV 2006, London, pp. 687–692. IEEE (2006)
20. Erkoyuncu, J., Khan, S.: Olfactory-based augmented reality support for industrial maintenance. IEEE Access 8, 30306–30321 (2020)
21. Lampen, E., Lehwald, J., Pfeiffer, T.: A context-aware assistance framework for implicit interaction with an augmented human. In: Chen, J.Y.C., Fragomeni, G. (eds.) HCII 2020. LNCS, vol. 12191, pp. 91–110. Springer, Cham (2020). https://doi.org/10.1007/978-3-030-49698-2_7
22. Blanco-Novoa, Ó., Fraga-Lamas, P., Vilar-Montesinos, M.A., Fernández-Caramés, T.M.: Creating the internet of augmented things: an open-source framework to make IoT devices and augmented and mixed reality systems talk to each other. Sensors 20(11), 3328 (2020)
23. Minerva, R., Lee, G.M., Crespi, N.: Digital twin in the IoT context: a survey on technical features, scenarios, and architectural models. IEEE 108(10), 1785–1824 (2020)
24. Hořejší, P., Novikov, K., Šimon, M.: A smart factory in a Smart City: virtual and augmented reality in a smart assembly line. IEEE Access 8, 94330–94340 (2020)
25. Shafto, M., Conroy, M., Doyle, R., Glaessgen, E., Kemp, C., LeMoigne, J., et al.: DRAFT modeling, simulation, information technology & processing roadmap. Technology Area 11, NASA - National Aeronautics and Space Administration (2010)
26. Liu, M., Fang, S., Dong, H., Xu, C.: Review of digital twin about concepts, technologies, and industrial applications. Manuf. Syst. 58, 346–361 (2021)

27. Bevilacqua, M., et al.: Digital twin reference model development to prevent operators' risk in process plants. Sustainability **12**(3), 1088 (2020)
28. Karadeniz, A.M., Arif, İ., Kanak, A., Ergün, S.: Digital twin of eGastronomic things: a case study for ice cream machines. In: 2019 IEEE International Symposium on Circuits and Systems (ISCAS), Sapporo, Japan, pp. 1–4. IEEE (2019)
29. Aschenbrenner, D., et al.: Mirrorlabs - creating accessible Digital Twins of robotic production environment with Mixed Reality. In: IEEE International Conference on Artificial Intelligence and Virtual Reality (AIVR), pp. 43–48 (2020)
30. Eclipse Mosquitto official web page. https://mosquitto.org/. Accessed 22 Jul 2021
31. Unity 3D development platform official web page. https://unity.com/. Accessed 22 Jul 2021
32. Microsoft HoloToolkit official web page. https://github.com/microsoft/MixedRealityToolkit. Accessed 22 Jul 2021
33. UNet official web page. https://docs.unity3d.com/Manual/UNet.html. Accessed 29 Jul 2021
34. Mirror Networking official web page. https://mirror-networking.com/. Accessed 22 Jul 2021
35. Vidal-Balea, A., Blanco-Novoa, O., Fraga-Lamas, P., Fernández-Caramés, T.M.: Developing the next generation of augmented reality games for pediatric healthcare: an open-source collaborative framework based on ARCore for implementing teaching, training and monitoring applications. Sensors **21**, 1865 (2021)
36. Blanco-Novoa, O., Fraga-Lamas, P., Vilar-Montesinos, M., Fernández-Caramés, T.M.: Creating the internet of augmented things: an open-source framework to make IIoT devices and augmented and mixed reality systems talk to each other. Sensors **20**(11), 3328 (2020)
37. Node-RED official web page. https://nodered.org/. Accessed 22 Jul 2021
38. Vidal-Balea, A., et al.: Analysis, design and practical validation of an augmented reality teaching system based on Microsoft HoloLens 2 and Edge Computing. Eng. Proc. **2**, 52 (2020)

Edge and Fog Computing for IoT: A Case Study for Citizen Well-Being

Luca Bianconi[1], Yuri Lechiara[1], Luca Bixio[2], Roberto Palermo[2], Sara Pensieri[3]([✉]) [iD],
Federica Viti[4] [iD], and Roberto Bozzano[3] [iD]

[1] Gruppo Sigla S.R.L, via Finocchiaro Aprile 31/5a, 16129 Genoa, Italy
{luca.bianconi,yuri.lechiara}@grupposigla.it
[2] FlairBit S.R.L, via Maragliano 6/5, 16121 Genoa, Italy
{luca.bixio,roberto.palermo}@flairbit.io
[3] National Research Council of Italy - Institute for the Study of the Anthropic Impacts and the
sustainability of the Marine Environment (CNR-IAS), via de Marini 16, 16149 Genoa, Italy
{sara.pensieri,roberto.bozzano}@cnr.it
[4] National Research Council of Italy - Institute of Biophysics (CNR-IBF), via de Marini 16,
16149 Genoa, Italy
federica.viti@cnr.it

Abstract. Citizen well-being during indoor and outdoor activities is a prerogative in the paradigm of smart city. Air quality, together with thermo-hygrometric, light and noise comfort are some of the most relevant parameters that affect the perception of the state of well-being. An internet of things (IoT) network based on LoRaWAN end-nodes has been set up with the aim to provide an approach to improve the well-being of citizens living in an urban district in Savona (Liguria region, Italy) under the umbrella of the PickUP project. The main focus of the project was the design of innovative methods and tools for energy and environmental management and the reduction of consumption in heterogeneous districts. The proposed IoT architecture comprises a Fog node constituted of a Raspberry Pi 4 to analyze in near-real-time the heterogeneous data and to provide feedback to the proper actuators in case of need of changes in the ventilation and heating of the occupied room. Moreover, the infrastructure provides insights about the air quality in outdoor areas to local authorities, in order to implement mitigation action or strategies. Results demonstrate the usefulness of the proposed architecture with a precise focus on social impact, but also reveal economic implications linked to an intelligent use of energy resources and to the development of energy efficiency strategies.

Keywords: Edge and fog node · LoRaWAN · Citizen well-being · Energy efficiency · Air quality

1 Introduction

The quality of both indoor and outdoor environments is fundamental to guarantee and evaluate citizen well-being because it is nowadays assessed that quality of indoor environment affects human health [1] as well as exposure to pollutant air, posing severe risk for morbidity and mortality [2].

S. Paiva et al. (Eds.): SmartCity360° 2021, LNICST 442, pp. 121–139, 2022.
https://doi.org/10.1007/978-3-031-06371-8_9

In working places, physical environmental conditions contribute to guarantee a comfortable and productive space [3, 4]. At home, where people usually spend more than 60% of their life, the overall quality of life and health strongly depends on indoor environmental quality (IEQ) parameters, such as indoor air quality (IAQ) (e.g., airborne contaminants), aesthetics, potable water surveillance, ergonomics, acoustics, lighting and electromagnetic frequency levels [5]. The same features are considered for assessing the value of a property [6].

All the aforementioned issues trigger a growing and permanent interest towards safety, health, well-being, and sustainability in working, public and private indoor environments, contributing to define the Quality of Life of an area.

Some IEQ parameters are related to the energy efficiency and management of indoor environments [5, 7], which need to be monitored in order to assess the level of comfort. In most cases, structural and functional changes for improving life inside the buildings are devoted to optimize the management of energy production and demand [8]. However, retrofitting existing structures must consider the benefits both on IEQ and energy saving [9]. Furthermore, indoor sensors in public buildings must comply with local regulations, be compact, positioned in safe positions, not accessible to unauthorized people, autonomous and capable of guaranteeing continuous and long-term monitoring [10, 11].

In working spaces, the goal of reducing energy consumption is usually achieved by limiting air circulation or by using regulated forced ventilation, creating an airtight space, unsafe for people's health. A typical example of this condition is the increase in carbon dioxide (CO_2) levels due to human respiration, which causes fatigue and reduced productivity [12]. Volatile organic compounds (VOCs) that arise from a wide spectrum of sources, such as building materials, furniture, detergents and even human activities (such as sweat), could be responsible for the so-called Sick Building Syndrome [13–16].

Within the urban districts, a significant share of consumption is due to buildings. Statistics estimate that buildings in Europe are responsible for the majority (40%) of final energy consumption, with 14% of the overall share being ascribable to non-residential buildings. For example, the reduction in energy consumption and in the consequent emission of greenhouse gases have a valuable economic and environmental impact [17]. Analogous considerations are especially valid for ancient buildings, neglecting modern concepts of energy efficiency.

Outdoor air quality is often controlled by local stakeholders interested in development or application of mitigation strategies to improve citizen's well-being. Monitoring is often performed through networks of sensors installed, in most cases, in the busiest streets of downtown.

To evaluate the conditions of well-being in relation to buildings and urban districts, it is essential to implement autonomous and smart sensor networks capable of continuously monitoring the most important IEQ parameters, to balance the minimization of energy consumption and the improvement of air quality (indoor and outdoor).

This was the main driver for the realization of the PickUP project (www.pickup-energy.it), whose general objective was to develop a tool to evaluate (i) the energy exploitation and environmental quality of heterogeneous urban districts, in order to reduce consumption and its impact on the environment, and (ii) the comfort of internal public spaces. The demonstration phase took place in the urban area of the city of

Savona (Liguria, Italy) and the test bench was represented by two sites: the headquarters of the Municipal Police "Clelia Corradini" and a large U-shaped building that houses the "Colombo-Pertini" primary and intermediate schools.

The developed IoT network was established to assess the internal energy efficiency of the Municipal Police station and the well-being of its workers, and to monitor the outdoor air quality in the vicinity of the primary and intermediate school.

Specifically, indoor well-being monitoring was performed through a network of smart sensors, able to acquire air temperature, humidity, concentration of CO_2 and VOC, light and noise levels. This choice was based on the fact that although the most relevant parameters are those related to the volatile chemical compounds in the air, other factors can also affect the comfort and health, including temperature, humidity, light and noise levels, particles, pollen or mold spores. Temperature and CO_2 are also fundamental from energetic point of view, since the most impacting equipment is related to air conditioning and ventilation, whose proper functioning is strictly related to temperature and CO_2.

Outdoor well-being was evaluated in the open spaces of the school and in the nearby streets, monitoring air particle matter and pollution (e.g., PM1, PM2.5, PM10) other than environmental ancillary parameter such as air temperature, humidity and atmospheric pressure.

2 Low Power Wide Area Networks

IoT enabled technologies allow the creation and adaptation of "smart buildings", conceived as sensor networks distributed in several areas throughout the whole building, in a relatively affordable way. Wireless sensors are particularly suitable to this aim, since they avoid heavy infrastructural operations [18, 19].

Low Power Wide Area Networks (LPWAN) identify a class of low-power-consumption wireless technologies designed for use in Wide Area Networks (WAN), presenting different technical characteristics (concerning communication frequencies and standards of adopted protocol) and licensing models. This class of networks, explicitly created to implement machine-to-machine (M2M) communication, allows obtaining greater efficiency compared to common mobile networks. It also provides a significantly reduced cost (in energetic and economic terms), and the ability to natively allow a higher number of nodes connected to the infrastructure. Depending on the specific technology used, LPWAN can support data packages up to some kilobytes long, with a transfer rate of a few hundreds of Kbps, guaranteeing a range of action of several kilometers. In LPWAN, the sensors represent nodes, which are usually compact, autonomous in data acquisition, powered for years through small batteries, and easy to configure and operate. Such nodes are generally versatile and do not require infrastructural interventions for their installations, also in ancient or not-cabled buildings. The use of autonomous nodes allows extending the monitoring network outdoors, integrating them into mobile platforms.

Among the others LPWAN, Long Range Wide-Area Network (LoRaWAN), which relies on Long Range (LoRa) radio modulation scheme, allows the creation of private networks. LoRa is a proprietary spread spectrum modulation derived by Chirp Spread Spectrum (CSS) technique with integrated Forward Error Correction (FEC) developed by Semtech. This technology enables long-range data transmission and operates in the unlicensed Industrial, Scientific and Medical (ISM) frequency bands (868 MHz and 433 MHz in Europe, 915 MHz and 433 MHz in USA). Using 125 kHz, 250 kHz and 500 kHz of bandwidth, smaller payloads of a maximum of 250 bytes can be transmitted over a distance of tens of kilometers also in urban environments. Battery-powered devices equipped with LoRa radio transceivers usually have several years of lifetime. LoRaWAN networks are assembled in a star-of-stars network topology, where several end-nodes are linked to one or more gateways which route the packets through a back-end communication channel, such as Ethernet [20, 21].

All aforementioned features make LoRa technology an optimal solution for the implementation of energy and comfort monitoring systems of buildings or for acquisition of environmental parameters.

3   Architectural Design and Implementation of the Communication Infrastructure

A monitoring infrastructure based on LPWAN technologies has been designed, implemented and installed on the test sites selected within the project PickUP. Such infrastructure aimed at fulfilling two complementary objectives. Firstly, to integrate the elements producing/collecting the data (i.e., sensors) and, secondly, to create the telecommunications backbone of data between the sensors and the remote nodes (i.e., cloud servers), delivering the information elaboration logics and hosting the PickUP platform. This infrastructure has been designed considering the need for allowing the remote control and monitoring of the state of individual installed units. This functionality resulted to be specifically useful in the context of the current SARS-COVID-19 pandemic. Most of the PickUP experimental activities were performed during 2020 restrictions and emergency status.

Following the architectural models proposed by the Open Fog Consortium in 2017 [22], the developed architecture consists in a communication and integration layer structured on three levels, characterized by different devices and protocols according to their role within this infrastructure. The three levels are labelled as: "Edge", "Fog" and "Cloud" (Fig. 1).

The main goal of this communication and integration architecture is to enable the efficient data collection from sensors, and their secure transfer to the remote elaboration components. This architecture also implements bidirectional communications Cloud-Edge to enable simple actuation functionalities.

Specifically, the Edge level is composed of sensors monitoring environmental parameters (e.g. temperature, humidity, CO_2, VOC, PM concentration, noise, lighting) suitable for both the indoor and outdoor scenarios. All installed sensors are based on LoRa technology for implementing the physical layer, and LoRaWAN protocol for the communication layer.

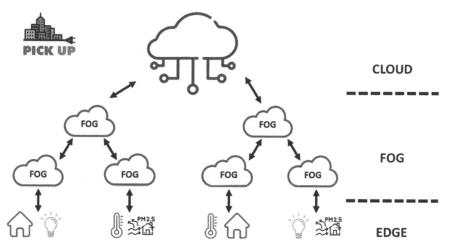

Fig. 1. Architectural model used for the experimentation (inspired to Open Fog Architecture).

Sensors-gateway communication is based on LoRaWAN protocol. Data transfer from each gateway to the cloud relies on TCP/IP protocol, adopting RESTful HTTP calls of information encoded according to LoRaWAN specifications. Each gateway is coupled with a Raspberry Pi 4 and an LTE router, composing the Fog node.

The adoption of Fog level does not require a continuous Ethernet connection: the services can run independently from the availability of Ethernet connection and can send the update to the Cloud only in case of availability. The use of smaller and less power demanding devices (i.e. switches, gateway, access point) installed close to the Edge level minimizes the latency needed to retrieve the data and processed them, since it is not needed the transfer of the data to the Cloud for processing. In fact, the Fog level has the objectives to guarantee data transfer from LoRaWAN gateways to the PickUP cloud, and to perform early elaborations and real-time data processing (i.e., data treatment and intelligence features) avoiding the latencies commonly experimented when relying on traditional cloud-based data processing.

The Raspberry Pi 4 was used for implementing the remote management features needed to monitor and maintain the nodes and the data collection state, whereas the router was needed for providing the internet connectivity to the Fog node by an LTE link. The Fog node is strongly based on the computational power provided by the Raspberry Pi 4, in charge of performing real-time analysis and of applying intelligent functionalities at node-level (e.g., those based on Artificial Intelligence/Machine Learning models). Fog node is designed to move computational tasks closer to where data is produced (i.e., from cloud towards sensors) in order to minimize latencies generated by the traditional approach and to tackle security leaks. Considering these objectives, the open source Eclipse ioFog was installed into the Raspberry Pi 4 to create a distributed Edge Compute Network (ECN), to run any microservice on it dynamically, securely, and remotely. Thus, the Raspberry Pi 4 implements some key functionalities: the first task is the local storage of the information collected, since the data acquired by sensors are stored locally, processed and then sent, from time to time, to the cloud for long-term storage and more refined processing. The others tasks consist in the information redundancy, since stored data are kept locally until the server receives them and in the system monitoring, since it is possible to connect to the node for checking whether the node features are working correctly and if data are flowing regularly from the edge layer. Furthermore, the Fog level has been used to implement, experiment and validate the application of collaboration features among end-nodes (e.g., nodes mutual recognition, node health state awareness and sharing of resources).

Cloud represents the third level of the infrastructure. It mostly consists of a so-called LoRa Server, that is a remote application hosted on cloud servers and implementing Gateway Bridge, Network Server and Application Server features needed to complete an overall LoRaWAN communication infrastructure. The LoRa Server is based on the open-source project called ChirpStack, and it was configured and customized according to the project's architecture peculiarities. It acts as proxy for all the messages coming from the hardware LoRaWAN gateway as the result of the collection performed by all the individual LoRaWAN sensors installed on the pilot sites.

The LoRa Server decodes in readable JSON format and forwards the information to other PickUP architecture elements to create the data lake and prepare the data for data analysis and prediction functionalities (Fig. 2).

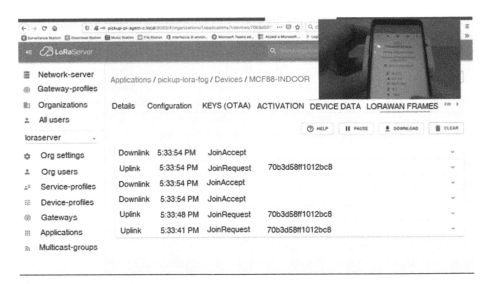

Fig. 2. Dashboard of the ChirpStack LoRaWAN server.

Data from the Edge sensors are collected by the gateways on the Fog level and then sent through the Internet to the Gateway Bridge using the UDP protocol. Network Server manages the state of the LoRaWAN network, administers and monitors the activation of LoRaWAN sensors and manages inbound and outbound messages flows. Finally, the Application Server provides WEB and API interfaces to manage applications, gateways and devices registration, thus enabling advanced configurations and facilitating mainte-nance operations for the system administrators team. It can also process uplink data and forward them to one or multiple configured integrations. The software platform Senseioty was used to provide a cloud dashboard for the visualization of both the last available measurement and the time-series. Figure 3 shows an example of the user-interface.

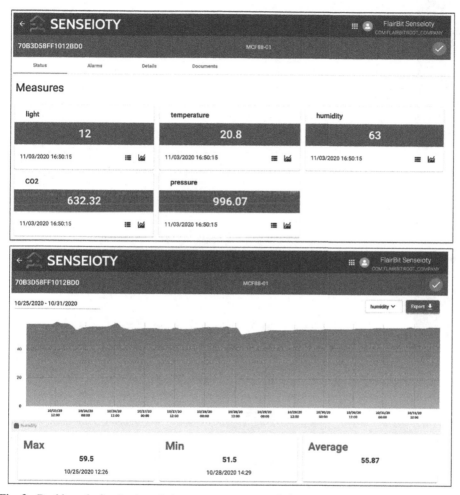

Fig. 3. Dashboards for (top) real time measurement and (bottom) time-series as provided by Senseioty platform.

In this way, it is possible to integrate the LoRa Server with external applications to build added-value business services. For example, as part of the PickUP project, some mobile applications have been developed to allow users of the police station and the school to monitor the comfort of their rooms by viewing the data processed on dedicated management and analysis dashboards (Fig. 4), and to provide feedback on their well-being (Fig. 5). The availability of these feedbacks represented a key requirement for implementing Demand-Response algorithms based on Artificial Intelligence, which

were developed as additional service within the project and the details of which can be
found in Bianco et al. [23].

Fig. 4. Screenshots of the (top) real-time and (bottom) historical dashboards developed for the
end-users.

Fig. 5. Snapshot of the interface of the mobile application to retrieve feedbacks from end-users.

The dashboards were implemented to provide a graphical interface to visualize collected data enabling both historical and real-time analysis. These dashboards are user-dedicated tools providing access to different types information. They are made available through the use of two different technologies according to their scope: for real-time analysis they are based on Angular JS, whereas for historical time-series they are based on Power BI.

The end-nodes used to monitor air quality are on the shelf, and they have been chosen to answer the need of the network to be fully operational on the long-term basis and to guarantee efficient and effective LoRaWAN communication. The selected end-nodes for internal well-being monitoring were powered by a 3.6 V lithium battery assuring an annual lifetime, whereas end-nodes for outdoor environment were powered by embedded solar power. The proposed architecture based on LoraWAN allows the use of multiple end-nodes with one gateway, does not require cabled infrastructure and only a TCP/IP connection is needed to connect gateway and server. The low-cost of each device contributes to keeping the capital cost for the overall architecture under control and distributed throughout a multiannual temporal scale.

Moreover, the use of commercial devices allows the reusability and replicability of the proposed solution in other different sites. The adoption of open hardware (and open source) solutions has been evaluated and adopted for trials in a controlled environment as in the case of Arduino-based sensors as well as Raspberry PI-based LoRaWAN gateways that have been approached even though they are not presented.

3.1 Police Station Building Setup

An experimental activity was carried out inside the building of the Clelia Corradini police headquarters in Savona (PS, hereafter) focused on the usage of LoRaWAN technologies for monitoring indoor well-being. Considering the overall architecture described above, the following levels have been adopted for this site: i) for the Edge layer, six internal sensors have been installed (three ERS-sound devices by ELSYS (Elektroniksystem i Umeå AB), and three MCF-LW12VOC devices by Enginko srl) for monitoring level of light, air temperature, relative humidity, noise level, motion detection, atmospheric pressure, CO_2 and VOC.

The six end nodes were installed in meaningful places of the building, taking into consideration police station's daily activities; ii) the Fog layer integrated an indoor LoRaWAN gateway (Conduit MTCDT series by Multi-Tech Systems, Inc.) with a Raspberry Pi 4 and a Router 3/4G model RUT955 by Teltonika Networks (Fig. 6).The end nodes were set up to provide a data stream every 10–30 min (the former for ELSYS sensors, the latter for MCF88 sensors), compliant with the European constraints of duty-cycle to be applied to LPWAN transmission [24]. All nodes used the Over the Air Activation (OTAA) method for joining the network.

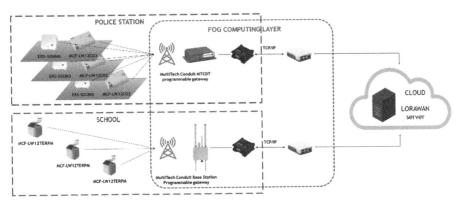

Fig. 6. Schematic diagram of the IoT network implemented for the (top left) Clelia Corradini police station and the (bottom left) Colombo-Pertini school.

3.2 School Building Setup

At the school's building Colombo-Pertini of Savona (SC, hereafter) an experiment focused on outdoor air quality monitoring has been performed. LoRaWAN technology was exploited to implement an infrastructure for outdoor environmental monitoring. Taking into consideration the presented architecture, the levels involved into this pilot site consist of: i) for the Edge, three MCF-LW12TERPM devices by Enginko srl, were installed for outdoor air quality monitoring, specifically consisting in observations of air temperature, relative humidity, atmospheric pressure and concentration of PM1, PM10 and PM25; ii) regarding the Fog, an outdoor LoRaWAN gateway (Conduit IP67 base station by Multi-Tech Systems, Inc.) integrated with a Raspberry Pi 4 and a Router 3/4G model RUT955 by Teltonika Networks were exploited (Fig. 6). The sampling time of the end-nodes was set to 30 min, to satisfy the constraints of the European duty cycle for LPWAN [24]. OTAA method was used by the end nodes to join the network also in this case.

An end-node and the Fog node were installed on the roof of the school Colombo-Pertini (A letter in Fig. 7) whereas the other two end-nodes were positioned in via Caboto (B letter in Fig. 7) and in via Manzoni (C letter in Fig. 7) at an aerial distance of 52.9 m and of 133 m from the Fog node, respectively.

Fig. 7. Map of the end-nodes and Fog node installation on the roof of school Colombo-Pertini (A letter) and the end nodes of via Caboto (B letter) and via Manzoni (C letter).

4 Results and Discussion

Diagnostic services and identification of anomalies are key factors to determine the well-being of people both for indoor and outdoor application, as the case of thermo-hygrometric comfort for public buildings or the anomalous concentration of air particulate matter in an urban district. Pandemic status has also clearly enlightened the need to closely monitor indoor occupancy.

To this aim, a continuous monitoring of the variables of interest has been set-up in both scenarios and the capability of the Fog node to analyze the observation in near-real-time was exploited to generate alarm in case of observed anomalies (i.e., values exceeding thresholds) or sensor's fault and to provide feedback to actuators, when available. The proposed IoT infrastructure has the role to provide real-time data from heterogenous sensors that constituted the backbone of a more complex architecture constituted of a prevision module and an action module. The prevision module uses the acquired data to forecast power consumption and perceived comfort exploiting the use of Neural Network algorithm, whilst the action module is responsible for acting on available heat pumps or for tuning of thermostatic valves and air conditioning system. Once an issue is detected, such as temperature over or below thresholds depending on the season in a room, an alarm is issued via TCP/IP and/or Wifi to the monitoring dashboard. If the problem persists for more than 30 min, automatically the action module will act on the thermostatic valves to increase or decrease the temperature interfacing with the existing respective control units or remote terminal units (RTU). In case of failure, a fault alert is issued via TCP/IP and/or Wifi to the monitoring dashboard and an e-mail and a SMS are sent to the persons in charge of control.

The same procedures have been set-up in case of CO_2 or VOC values exceeding the thresholds, in this case the system will automatically act on the heating, ventilation and air conditioning system (HVAC) to ventilate the room.

Table 1 summarizes the thresholds used to generate alarm for each monitored parameter on the basis of legislation in force.

Table 1. Threshold used to generate alarm for each monitored parameter on the basis of legislation in force.

Parameter	Threshold	Legislation
Room temperature in summer	26 °C	American Society of Heating, Refrigerating and Air-Conditioning Engineers, (ASHRAE) Standard 55–2017
Room temperature in winter	20 °C	American Society of Heating, Refrigerating and Air-Conditioning Engineers, (ASHRAE) Standard 55–2017
Indoor carbon dioxide	1000 ppm	National Institute for Occupational Safety and Health (NIOSH) Recommendation
Indoor volatile organic compound	500 ppb	U.S. Environmental Protection Agency recommendation
Daily outdoor PM10	50 μg m^{-3}	2008/50/CE directive
Daily outdoor PM25	20 μg m^{-3}	2008/50/CE directive
Indoor light	500 lx	UNI EN 12464–1 2011
Average sound	80 dB	Italian legislation number D.Lgs.81/2008
Average peak	140 dB	Italian legislation number D.Lgs.81/2008

4.1 Evaluation of the LoRaWAN Network

For each aforementioned scenario and for each IoT packet received by the implemented Fog node, all the parameters related to the quality of the radio transmission were stored. Specifically, the strength of the received signal (RSSI), the signal-to-noise ratio (SNR) as well as the information content of the node (payload) and date and time of receipt of the packets were stored.

The implemented network envisaged the use of the Adaptive Data Rate algorithm, which automatically allows to maximize communication efficiency by reducing the energy consumption of the nodes. As performance metrics, packet delivery ratio (PDR),

RSSI and SNR were used, acquired during three months of continuous monitoring (from January to April 2021). RSSI and SNR values were directly provided by the gateway as metadata for each received message, whereas PDR is defined as the ratio between the number of packets received and the number of packets transmitted. Table 2 summarizes the results in terms of PDR and highlights how the developed network was effective for a continuous monitoring of citizen well-being in both indoor and outdoor scenarios.

Table 2. Packet delivery ratio during three months of continuous monitoring.

Sensor type	Position	Packet received	Packets transmitted	PDR [%]
MCF88 indoor	PS control room	4147	4202	98.69
MCF88 indoor	PS meeting room	4132	4136	99.90
MCF88 indoor	PS entrance	3973	4019	98.85
ELSYS	PS meeting room	11752	11969	98.18
ELSYS	PS control room	11974	12159	98.48
ELSYS	PS entrance	7811	7962	98.10
MCF88 outdoor	SC via Caboto	4079	4226	96.52
MCF88 outdoor	SC roof	4123	4245	97.12
MCF88 outdoor	SC via Manzoni	4133	4225	97.82

RSSI values provided as metadata by the gateway for each transmission and for each end-node for the PS site, showed, as expected, better results for the end-node located in the proximity of the Fog node (i.e., the devices installed at the second floor in the meeting room), with respect to the end-nodes installed at the entrance or in the control room at the second floor. RSSI values ranging between -30 dBm and -40 dBm were observed for the end-nodes closest to the Fog node, and a drop in the received power down to -70 dBm and -120 dBm was observed for the other nodes. This behavior is clearly ascribable to the presence of obstacles, especially the walls in the building which are responsible for a not negligible contribution to the path loss.

RSSI values measured by the gateway collocated on the roof of the school showed better performance for nearby nodes with respect to those installed in the neighboring streets of via Manzoni and via Caboto, due to the proximity between node and gateway, obtaining comparable values for the other two neighboring stations.

Measured SNR values showed, on average, positive values for all indoor nodes, ranging from 5 dB to 10 dB, although an increase of negative values were observed during the last weeks of monitoring for both devices installed in the control room, maybe due to variations in room usage in relation to the evolving pandemic scenario.

On the other hand, SNR values provided by the gateway installed on the school demonstrated that the chosen locations are suitable for monitoring the air quality of the area, since positive values were obtained, in the range between 0 dB and 10 dB considered as optimal for LoRaWAN transmission [25].

4.2 Evaluation of Indoor Occupancy

The implemented network allowed the provision as a service information about the occupancy for the rooms in which the end-nodes were installed at PS, at the entrance, in the meeting room and in the control room located at the second floor of the building.

The monitoring of the estimated occupancy in those rooms was strategic, especially in the pandemic situation, since it allowed to organize spaces according to their use and in a future perspective has provided fruitful insight for potential building renovation. Occupancy assessment is a key element for both the implementation of energy efficiency strategies and the correct evaluation of the occupants' comfort conditions [26, 27]. Indeed, data acquired during the experimentation can be used to further reduce the consumption of energy by air conditioners, lighting systems, IT infrastructures and other systems inside the PS. The data ensure suitable conditions of comfort when users actually occupy the premises in accordance with their specific needs and the type of activity they are carrying out.

Sound measurements provided by the end-nodes were used to infer about the occupancy of the chosen rooms. The time series of sound pressure levels provided by the end-node installed at the entrance of the PS during three months of continuous monitoring evidenced a clear pattern with low values (below 50 dB) during nighttime (between 01 am and 07 am) and high values (up to 60 dB) during the day. A clear cycle on daily and weekly basis can be also observed in the time-series of the sound pressure levels acquired by the end-node installed in the control-room from November 2020 and April

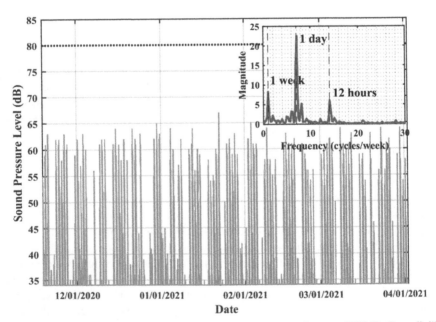

Fig. 8. Time series of sound pressure levels acquired in the control room of "Clelia Corradini" PS between November 2020 and April 2021. The upper right box in the figure shows the result of the spectral analysis performed on the overall time series. Horizontal dotted line marks the threshold used to generate the alarm.

2021, as evidenced by the spectral analysis performed on the time series (Fig. 8). Very low values, close to the instrumental limit, were observed during night (between 7 pm and 7 am) and during Friday evening, Saturday and Sundays with very few exceptions (Fig. 8).

4.3 Evaluation of Thermo-hygrometric and Light Comfort

Indoor comfort is strictly linked to the psychophysical conditions of individuals, but the analysis of thermo-hygrometric and light status of the room can provide additional insights for implementing optimization policies.

While the thermo-hygrometric comfort is ruled by the standard ISO 7730 dealing with the ergonomics of thermal environments, the analytical determination and interpretation of thermal well-being by calculating indices and local thermal well-being criteria, visual comfort is not quantitatively measurable. It may depend on the color rendering of the light sources and the balance in the distribution of luminance.

End-nodes able to measure pressure, atmospheric temperature, relative humidity and light level were installed in some selected rooms of police station, namely the entrance, the meeting room and the control room. The aim was to provide a tool for improving the level of comfort to the people occupying the room in an automatic way by acting on the existing heating and illumination remote control units.

The time series of air temperature presented well marked diurnal cycles and clearly allowed the identification of issues related to the air-conditioning or heating of the rooms. For instance, the Fog node reported strong anomalies in the meeting room between late June and September 2020, when temperature exceeded 30 °C, and several alerts were reported in the first two weeks of December 2020, when less than 15 °C were recorded (Fig. 9a). Relative humidity values during the whole period of monitoring (December 2019-April 2021) spanned from 10% to 80%, thus no alert messages were issued for humidity.

Light observations followed the diurnal cycle. During winter months values close to 0 between 7 pm and 8 am were collected for the meeting room (Fig. 9b) and the same trend was observed for the control room, whereas in the main entrance darkness was observed only for three hours between 4 am and 7 am. During summer, the hours of light increased and darkness was observed between 10 pm and 6 am of the following day in the meeting room (Fig. 9b). The different day-length throughout the season is also clearly evidenced by the spectral analysis performed for winter and summer months (upper right box in Fig. 9b).

Light levels in the main entrance and in the control-room show more variability with darkness only between 5 am and 6 am.

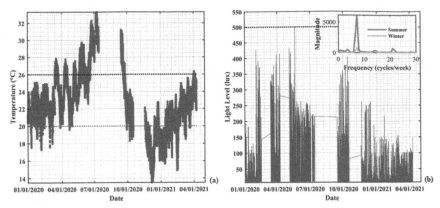

Fig. 9. Time series of (a) air temperature acquired in the meeting room of "Clelia Corradini" police station with horizontal black and red dotted line showing the thresholds used for summer and winter, respectively, and (b) light level acquired in the meeting room of "Clelia Corradini" police station with the upper right box showing the result of the spectral analysis performed on the timeseries of winter and summer months with black horizontal dotted line showing the used threshold.

4.4 Evaluation of Air Quality

The multiple sources of indoor air pollution are typically divided, based on their nature, into chemical, physical and biological pollutants; they come partly from the outside (outdoor air pollution, pollen), but many are produced from internal sources. The main internal sources of pollution are represented by: occupants, presence of dust, existing structures, building materials and systems like air conditioners, humidifiers and plumbing systems, among others.

CO_2 and VOC measurements were considered as indicators for indoor air quality evaluation since carbon dioxide concentration increases as the number of people present in a confined space increases and in the absence of adequate ventilation.

To evaluate the outdoor air quality the chosen parameters were PM1, PM10, and PM25 since they are air pollutants and their levels are strictly linked with fossil fuels for automotive and heating.

Real-time analysis of CO_2 and VOC concentrations in the selected rooms, allowed to quickly intervene in case of malfunctioning or need of tuning of the air ventilation control system of the room when VOC values were over 500 ppb and/or CO_2 exceeded the threshold of 1000 ppm, that is commonly considered the limit over which people begin to get headache. In the three months of monitoring, no anomalies were detected and the dynamic of CO_2 concentration was very similar for the entrance and the meeting room and followed a diurnal cycle with values between 350 ppm and 650 ppm. In the control room the values are generally lower than 300 ppm with peaks up to 650 ppm in agreement with an irregular occupancy of the room. On the contrary VOC data were greater in the control room than in the entrance and in the meeting room. In the control room values varied between 400 and 500 ppb, with several episodes over 800 ppb detected by the Fog node. In the other two rooms VOC spanned between 400 and 500 ppb, and only in few episodes, the exceeding of the limit of 500 ppb occurred at the entrance and in the meeting rooms in winter months and were suddenly detected by the Fog node (Fig. 10a).

The analysis of the particulate evidence similarities among the three sites, with a clear monthly periodicity and a less evident cycle of 24 h due to the dynamic of urban traffic (Fig. 10b). PM1 values reached up to about 85 μg m^{-3}, PM10 values were commonly less than 200 μg m-3 and PM25 less than 100 μg m^{-3} but both PM10 and PM25 showed some peaks up to 350 μg m-3 and 120 μg m^{-3}, respectively, in December 2020 and in late February 2021 presumably linked with the Christmas holidays and the easing of anti-pandemic restrictions, respectively (Fig. 10c).

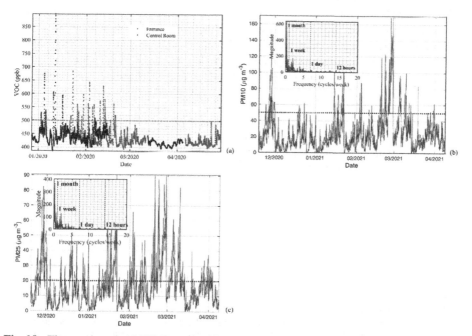

Fig. 10. Time series of: (a) VOC acquired in the control room of the "Clelia Corradini" police station with horizontal red dotted line showing the used threshold; (b) PM10 and (c) PM25 acquired in the streets adjacent to the "Colombo-Pertini" school with horizontal black dotted line showing the used threshold.

5 Conclusions

Comfort can be defined as a sensation perceived by a user within a given domestic or working environment as well as during outdoor activities, which states the perceived level of well-being. Environmental well-being may concern three different sensory domains: the thermo-hygrometric, the visual, and the acoustic comfort. Furthermore, in addition to the assessment of comfort in a strict sense, it is important to evaluate the well-being of the citizens in terms of air quality-related parameters being directly correlated to respiratory-olfactory well-being.

To this aim, an IoT network has been designed and operated in the framework of the regional project PickUP in the premises of the Clelia Corradini police station and of the Colombo-Pertini school in Savona.

Edge node was constituted of environmental sensors with LoRaWAN capability and all acquired data were managed by a Fog node aiming at monitoring and improving the perceived comfort of people living in the urban district of the police station and the school. Specifically, the availability of a Fog node based on Raspberry Pi 4 allowed the detection in near real time of anomalies and issues related to air-conditioning, heating or a lack of proper ventilation of the rooms as well as the exceeding of thresholds in case of poor air quality both indoor and outdoor.

Results evidence the capability of the proposed network to monitor in the long-term citizen well-being and to quickly activate the proper actuators in case of need, if available. The presented infrastructure is easily replicable in any urban district, since it employs low-power and low-cost Edge and Fog nodes, and it is scalable, thus it is easy to integrate new sensors. Also, the related dashboard and services provided as monitoring tools can be easily adapted.

Acknowledgement. This work is a result of the PickUP project (Piattaforma di integrazione sensori Iot per Controllo Kpi energetici in ambito Urbano per la Pianificazione interventi) grant Programma Operativo Regionale del Fondo Europeo di Sviluppo Regionale 2014–2020 (POR FESR 2014–2020) of the Ligurian Region, Italy.

References

1. Cincinelli, A., Martellini, T.: Indoor air quality and health. IJERPH **14**(11), 1286 (2017). https://doi.org/10.3390/ijerph14111286
2. Manisalidis, I., Stavropoulou, E., Stavropoulos, A., Bezirtzoglou, E.: Environmental and health impacts of air pollution: a review. Front. Public Health. **8**, 14 (2020). https://doi.org/10.3389/fpubh.2020.00014
3. Danna, K., Griffin, R.W.: Health and well-being in the workplace: a review and synthesis of the literature. J. Manag. **25**, 357–384 (1999). https://doi.org/10.1177/014920639902500305
4. Šujanová, P., Rychtáriková, M., Sotto Mayor, T., Hyder, A.: A healthy, energy-efficient and comfortable indoor environment, a review. Energies **12**, 1414 (2019). https://doi.org/10.3390/en12081414
5. Al horr, Y., Arif, M., Katafygiotou, M., Mazroei, A., Kaushik, A., Elsarrag, E.: Impact of indoor environmental quality on occupant well-being and comfort: A review of the literature. Int. J. Sustain. Built Environ. **5**(1), 1–11 (2016). https://doi.org/10.1016/j.ijsbe.2016.03.006
6. Potrč Obrecht, T., Kunič, R., Jordan, S., Dovjak, M.: Comparison of health and well-being aspects in building certification schemes. Sustainability **11**, 2616 (2019). https://doi.org/10.3390/su11092616
7. Prochorskaitė, A., Malienė, V.: Health, well-being and sustainable housing. Int. J. Strateg. Prop. Manag. **17**(1), 44–57 (2013). https://doi.org/10.3846/1648715X.2012.762949
8. Lim, J., Kim, J.J., Kim, S.: A holistic review of building energy efficiency and reduction based on big data. Sustainability **13**(4), 2273 (2021). https://doi.org/10.3390/su13042273
9. Ortiz, M., Itard, L., Bluyssen, P.M.: Indoor environmental quality related risk factors with energy-efficient retrofitting of housing: a literature review. Energy and Buildings **221**, 110102 (2020). https://doi.org/10.1016/j.enbuild.2020.110102

10. van Kemenade, P.L.W., Loomans, M.G.L.C., Opschoor, S., Hensen, J.L.M.: Building comfort performance assessment using a monitoring tool. In: Proceedings of the 13th International Conference on Indoor Air Quality and Climate, pp. 1–7, Hongkong, China (2014)
11. Molina, F., Yaguana, D.: Indoor environmental quality of urban residential buildings in cuenca—ecuador: comfort standard. Buildings **8**, 90 (2018). https://doi.org/10.3390/buildi ngs8070090
12. Erdmann, C.A., Steiner, K.C., Apte, M.G.: Indoor carbon dioxide concentrations and sick building syndrome symptoms in the building assessment survey and evaluation study revisited. In: Proceedings of Indoor Air 2002, pp. 443–448. EPA (2002)
13. Sabah A. Abdul-Wahab, (ed.): Sick Building Syndrome. Springer Berlin Heidelberg, Berlin, Heidelberg (2011). https://doi.org/10.1007/978-3-642-17919-8
14. Guo, P., et al.: Sick building syndrome by indoor air pollution in dalian. China. IJERPH. **10**, 1489–1504 (2013). https://doi.org/10.3390/ijerph10041489
15. Ghaffarianhoseini, A., et al.: Sick building syndrome: are we doing enough? Archit. Sci. Rev. **61**, 99–121 (2018). https://doi.org/10.1080/00038628.2018.1461060
16. Hoang Quoc, C., Vu Huong, G., Nguyen Duc, H.: Working conditions and sick building syndrome among health care workers in Vietnam. IJERPH. **17**, 3635 (2020). https://doi.org/ 10.3390/ijerph17103635
17. Ahmed Ali, K., Ahmad, M.I., Yusup, Y.: Issues, impacts, and mitigations of carbon dioxide emissions in the building sector. Sustainability **12**, 7427 (2020). https://doi.org/10.3390/su1 2187427
18. Ghayvat, H., Mukhopadhyay, S., Gui, X., Suryadevara, N.: WSN- and IOT-based smart homes and their extension to smart buildings. Sensors **15**, 10350–10379 (2015). https://doi.org/10. 3390/s150510350
19. Xia, M., Song, D.: Application of wireless sensor network in smart buildings. In: Gu, X., Liu, G., Li, Bo. (eds.) MLICOM 2017. LNICSSITE, vol. 226, pp. 315–325. Springer, Cham (2018). https://doi.org/10.1007/978-3-319-73564-1_31
20. Nanni, S., Benetti, E., Mazzini, G.: Indoor monitoring in Public Buildings: workplace well-being and energy consumptions. An example of IoT for smart cities application. Adv. Sci. Technol. Eng. Syst. **2**(3), 884–890 (2017). https://doi.org/10.25046/aj0203110
21. Petäjäjärvi, J., Mikhaylov, K., Yasmin, R., Hämäläinen, M., Iinatti, J.: Evaluation of LoRa LPWAN technology for indoor remote health and wellbeing monitoring. Int. J. Wireless Inf. Networks **24**(2), 153–165 (2017). https://doi.org/10.1007/s10776-017-0341-8
22. IEEE Standard for Adoption of OpenFog Reference Architecture for Fog Computing. IEEE. https://doi.org/10.1109/IEEESTD.2018.8423800
23. Bianco, G., Bracco, S., Delfino, F., Ferro, G., Parodi, L., Robba, M., Rossi, M.: A Demand Response Energy Management System (DR-EMS) for sustainable district. In: 2020 7th International Conference on Control, Decision and Information Technologies (CoDIT), pp. 551–556. IEEE, Prague, Czech Republic (2020). https://doi.org/10.1109/CoDIT49905.2020.926 3796
24. Saelens, M., Hoebeke, J., Shahid, A., Poorter, E.D.: Impact of EU duty cycle and transmission power limitations for sub-GHz LPWAN SRDs: an overview and future challenges. EURASIP J. Wirel. Commun. Netw. **2019**(1), 1–32 (2019). https://doi.org/10.1186/s13638-019-1502-5
25. Eric B.: LoRa Documentation, (2019) https://buildmedia.readthedocs.org/media/pdf/lora/lat est/lora.pdf
26. Garg, V., Bansal, N.K.: Smart occupancy sensors to reduce energy consumption. Energy and Buildings **32**, 81–87 (2000). https://doi.org/10.1016/S0378-7788(99)00040-7
27. Duarte, C., Van Den Wymelenberg, K., Rieger, C.: Revealing occupancy patterns in an office building through the use of occupancy sensor data. Energy and Buildings **67**, 587–595 (2013). https://doi.org/10.1016/j.enbuild.2013.08.062

Improvement of RSSI-Based LoRaWAN Localization Using Edge-AI

Azin Moradbeikie[1,2](✉), Ahmad Keshavarz[1], Habib Rostami[1], Sara Paiva[2], and Sérgio Ivan Lopes[2,3]

[1] PGU—Persian Gulf University, Bandar Bushehr, Iran
{amoradbeiki,a.keshavarz,habib}@pgu.ac.ir

[2] ADiT-Lab—Instituto Politécnico de Viana do Castelo, Rua Escola Industrial e Comercial Nun'Álvares, 4900-347 Viana do Castelo, Portugal
{spaiva,sil}@estg.ipvc.pt

[3] IT—Instituto de Telecomunicações, 3810-193 Aveiro, Portugal

Abstract. Localization is an essential element of the Internet of Things (IoT) leading to meaningful data and more effective services. Long-Range Wide Area Network (LoRaWAN) is a low-power communications protocol specifically designed for the IoT ecosystem. In this protocol, the RF signals used to communicate between IoT end devices and a LoRaWAN gateway (GW) can be used for communication and localization simultaneously, using distinct approaches, such as Received Signal Strength Indicator (RSSI) or Time Difference of Arrival (TDoA). Typically, in a LoRaWAN network, different GWs are deployed in a wide area at distinct locations, contributing to different error sources as they experience a specific network geometry and particular environmental effects. Therefore, to improve the location estimation accuracy, the weather effect on each GW can be learned and evaluated separately to improve RSSI-based distance and location estimation. This work proposes an RSSI-based LoRaWAN location estimation method based on Edge-AI techniques, namely an Artificial Neural Network (ANN) that will be running at each GW to learn and reduce weather effects on estimated distance. Results have shown that the proposed method can effectively improve the RSSI-based distance estimation accuracy between 6% and 49%, and therefore reduce the impact of the environmental changes in different GWs. This leads to a location estimation improvement of approximately 101 m.

Keywords: IoT · RSSI · LoRaWAN · Localization · Edge-AI

1 Introduction

Shortly, the Internet of Things (IoT) will be the main part of many industrial and non-industrial systems [1]. The basic and essential required technology for the proper adoption of IoT is spatial data gathering. Therefore, localization techniques are an important feature for the next generation of IoT systems.

© ICST Institute for Computer Sciences, Social Informatics and Telecommunications Engineering 2022
Published by Springer Nature Switzerland AG 2022. All Rights Reserved
S. Paiva et al. (Eds.): SmartCity360° 2021, LNICST 442, pp. 140–154, 2022.
https://doi.org/10.1007/978-3-031-06371-8_10

The most commonly used approach for outdoor localization is based on Global Navigation Satellite Systems (GNSS). Global Positioning System (GPS) is one of the GNSS methods and provides a typical location estimation accuracy between 10 and 100 m [2].

Other outdoor localization methods designed for IoT-based systems should be according to their fundamental limitations. Important limitations of these systems include low power consumption and low cost [3]. These criteria are not fulfilled by GNNS systems—such as GPS, GLONASS, or GALILEO—because its chips are rather expensive and power-hungry, not addressing the cost and autonomy key criteria that IoT-based systems demand. As a result, IoT end devices should consume additional power to send their location information to a cloud-based server using an additional communication radio that also demands additional power to communicate. According to mentioned GNNS drawbacks, it is not a favorable solution for the localization of IoT-based systems.

Wireless-based technologies can also be used for localization [4]. In this approach, location estimation is determined by using different features of the wireless signals transmitted by the IoT end devices, such as Received Signal Strength (RSS) or Time Difference of Arrival (TDoA), among others. In this case, wireless signals can be used for both positioning and communication at the same time. However, the performance of these different techniques in Wireless-based localization is highly related to signal availability (coverage) and network geometry (DoP - dilution of precision).

IoT systems can be deployed over a wide area and the communication range between devices and network elements should be extended to guarantee high availability. Long-range communication technologies are composed of cellular technologies (5G, 4G/LTE) and Low-Power Wide-Area Network (LPWAN) technologies. As major disadvantages, cellular technologies present a higher operational cost, due to more complex hardware and the use of licensed spectrum, which also compromises its ecosystem development [5].

On the other hand, LPWAN provides long-range communication among IoT end nodes and servers with low cost and low power consumption. LPWAN is the best option to provide high geometry communication ability for IoT systems. There are three main LPWAN technologies: NB-IoT, Sigfox, and LoRaWAN. NB-IoT works in licensed spectrum and Sigfox coverage is provided by member companies. So, NB-IoT and Sigfox do not provide the ability to create private networks for customized deployment. Despite NB-IoT and Sigfox, LoRaWAN works in a license-free spectrum and it provides the possibility to establish a private network for IoT systems [6].

The star topology of LoRaWAN network architecture is shown in Fig. 1, where IoT end devices communicate throw LoRaWAN Gateways (GWs). LoRaWAN GWs gather the transmitted IoT end node packets and their RF signal features (RSS, SNR, SF, etc.), which may be used for Quality-of-Service (QoS) assessment and other third-party applications, such as for end-device localization. Next, LoRaWAN GWs sent the collected data to the LoRaWAN network server. The LoRaWAN network server receives the RF signal features of each end device transmitted through different GWs and sends them to the LoRaWAN application server. Finally, the application server estimates the end device localization by using the estimated distances. Range estimation is determined by the received signal features obtained from distinct GWs.

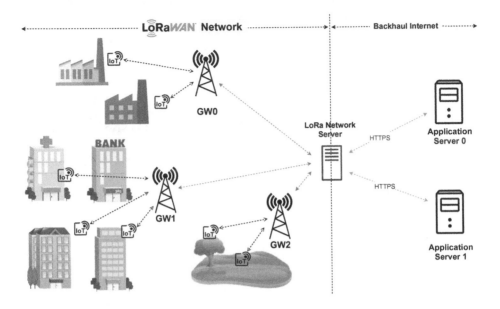

Fig. 1. LoRa network architecture.

As shown in Fig. 1, different LoRa GWs are placed in different locations. Different locations lead to different error sources since the GWs are affected by their surrounding environment. Therefore, to improve the location estimation accuracy, the environmental conditions that impact the distance estimation accuracy at each GW should be learned and evaluated separately. However, generating and sending information about each GW condition to the LoRaWAN network server can lead to a localization delay and consume a huge amount of bandwidth and energy from the network. To solve this problem, we propose a method to improve the RSSI-based LoRaWAN ranging estimation accuracy using edge computing. Edge computing follows a decentralized architecture [8], providing computation capabilities at the network edge. So, it leads to real-time data analysis, low operational cost, high scalability, reduced latency, and QoS improvement.

In this paper, we focus on the RSS-based localization principle. RSS-based localization methods are well-known, but when used in a changing environment, they can lead to poor estimation accuracies. These environmental-induced errors include multipath, non-line of sight (NLoS), wide-area effects, multi-floor effects, human-body effects, weather effects, and signal variations [7]. To improve localization accuracy, it is important to improve the distance estimation errors, which may be done by mitigating the environmental changing effects and its related errors in the ranging estimation stage, by introducing an Edge-AI learning stage to increase the accuracy in the distance estimation between IoT end devices and LoRaWAN GWs. Thus, the proposed method focus on the improvement of the ranging estimation based RSSI and an ANN algorithm to learn different weather situations on the received signal by different GWs. We evaluate the accuracy of this algorithm for large real-world areas.

The remainder of this document is organized as follows: Sect. 2 presents the related works; Sect. 3 introduces the proposed method for improving RSSI-based LoRaWAN localization; Sect. 4 describes the evaluation of the proposed method and puts forward a discussion around the results achieved. Lastly, in Sect. 5 the main conclusions are undertaken, and future work guidelines are presented.

2   Related Works

The localization problem has a long history in different application domains and several works have been put forward to achieve increased accuracy in low-cost GNSS-free positioning systems. In [7], Li et al. demonstrate the evolution of location-based services. GNSS-based systems are the most common for outdoor localization [9], but they are not a suitable solution for IoT applications due to higher cost, higher power consumption, and consequently low autonomy. On the other hand, LoRaWAN based localization methods are becoming popular for low-cost outdoor localization in the IoT ecosystem. They can be divided into three categories: 1) time-based, 2) path-loss and RSSI-based, and 3) fingerprint-based localization methods [10]. In this section, a brief overview of the workflow of LoRaWAN localization methods is provided.

Time of Arrival (ToA), Time Difference of Arrival (TDoA), and Round-Trip Time of Flight (RToF) are three time-based localization methods [11]. In ToA-based localization, the signal propagation time is used for distance estimation. TDoA determines the IoT end node distance by measuring the time difference at the arrival of signals. RToF measures the signal propagation round-trip time to estimate the distance between GW and IoT devices. Legacy localization methods use triangulation for location estimation and need precise synchronization between the network elements (ToA-based) or at least between the GWs (TDoA-based) and the accuracy of estimated location is highly dependent on it. So, time-based methods can lead to more complex hardware which impacts not only the end-device cost but also its autonomy [12].

RSSI and path-loss modeling is a commonly used method in LoRaWAN localization. In this approach, the received signal strength is collected and the path loss is computed in the GW, being used for the distance estimation between the IoT end device and the GW. RSSI lacks high accuracy duo to signal multipath and fading. To overcome these problems, a high number of RSSI readings is needed [13]. There are many different methods in this category [14–16]. In [14,15], authors used RSSI for location estimation in which assumes a well-known and measured path loss of the area. In [16], authors adopt LoRaWAN for Search and

Rescue operations. They have first characterized the LoRa path loss in three mountain scenarios. Then, they developed a localization algorithm that can be applied to estimate the position of injured persons by using known path loss and received RSSI. Authors in [14,17] realized that location estimation error rapidly increased because of the GWs noise. So, they propose GWs selection strategies for RSSI-based outdoor localization.

Fingerprint-based localization can be described in two stages: 1) learning stage (offline) and 2) localization stage (online). In the learning stage, various signal features in different places of area are collected and stored as a dataset. In the localization stage, the location estimation is performed by using a stored dataset. There are three different categories in the Fingerprint-based localization method: Visual Fingerprint, Motion Fingerprint, and Signal Fingerprint [18]. In [19], authors aims to provide accurate localisation in an urban LoRa network, using an ANN-based fingerprinting approach. In [20], authors studied various regression and machine learning models on received RSSI to accommodate the variability of factors for ranging estimation by using fingerprint. Authors in [21] mentioned it is not feasible work only with labelled samples in an outdoor environment. So, they proposed a semi supervised deep neural network for location estimation in LoRa. In [10], the authors proposed a LoRa signal-based positioning method that uses a fingerprint algorithm. They estimated the locations using probabilistic means based on three different algorithms that use interpolated fingerprint RSSI maps.

The weather condition is an environment error source that leads to location estimation error. Several works have evaluated the impact of meteorological conditions on packet reception, including the impact of weather conditions, and humidity [22]. In [23], authors analyze different weather situations on received signal strength. They mentioned that the RSS is strong during the day when the solar radiation is high.

Different GWs in LoRaWAN can settle in various places. Various places in a large area can experience distinct weather situations at the same time. Therefore, different GWs should evaluate the received signals based on their specific condition. For this purpose, Edge-AI can provide the required facilities and effectively improve the range measurements. Moreover, by taking advantage of edge computing we are bringing computation and storage to the edge of the network, near to where the data originates yielding reduced network load and better performance of services [24]. In this paper, the advantages of using Edge-AI for range estimation improvement in LoRaWAN are evaluated.

3   Proposed Method

In this section, a short overview of the basic principles for distance prediction based on RSSI is put forward, followed by the description of the proposed method for the improvement of RSSI-based ranging using Edge-AI and environmental data for distance estimation.

3.1 RSSI-Based Distance-Loss Modeling

RSSI-based distance-loss modeling is the simplest and widely used method for distance prediction. Typically, these methods take advantage of simple and well-known path-loss modeling, where each receiver (LoRa GW) measures the received signal strength of a pre-determined transmitted power from a sender (IoT end device). The RSSI value at each GW can then be used to estimate the distance between the GW and IoT device using the path-loss model equation, which enables us to estimate the distance between transmitter and receiver, as presented by the Eq. 1:

$$RSSI = -10n log_{10}(d) + A \tag{1}$$

where n is the path-loss exponent of the communication channel which varies depending on specific environmental conditions, and A is the RSSI value at a reference distance from the receiver. In this case, both n and A are environmental-dependent and can change during time, as outdoor atmospheric conditions modify. In addition, the measured RSSI is prone to noise and interference, which can lead to large errors in distance estimation. Typically, the strength of the received signal has three main contributions. The first and main contribution is the sender signal power that can follow different path loss models. The second part is large-scale fading caused by shadowing and the last part is small-scale fading caused by different copies of the transmitted signal. Several environmental factors, contribute as error sources in the propagation of the signal between the transmitter and the receiver. The path-loss model previously introduced averages these contributions in a rough approach and does not consider any dynamic changes in the environmental conditions. Moreover, GWs are installed in various and environmentally distinct places, on top of a building, near a river, with distinct heights. These particular setup conditions are known to affect the distance-loss model and lead to transient changes in the propagated signal which impact the distance estimation process due to the omnipresence of these environmental-related error sources.

In the next subsection, the proposed method for weather effect reduction in RSSI-based distance estimation is proposed.

3.2 Distance Estimation Improvement Method

To improve distance estimation, the inclusion of the weather conditions will be considered and an ANN algorithm is adopted. ANN is an information processing system that mimics the human brain. It consists of many interconnected processing nodes (neurons) collaborating to solve a specific task. ANN is composed of three basic blocks: i) ANN is feed by input data as vector data; ii) ANN generates data and compares the generated data with the desired output; and iii) ANN alters the weights of neural network connections for a better approximation of the output.

The proposed method consists of three main steps: data gathering, system training, and system test. In the first step, data gathering, each GW is equipped with two sensors: a temperature sensor and a relative humidity sensor. In addition, the GWs receive other relevant weather information from the LoRaWAN network server periodically. When the GW receives data from the IoT end devices, it collects and registers RSSI and the weather information for each received signal. These values are fed as an input vector into the ANN. In the second step, the ANN obtains the best weights for the neural network connections to improve the approximation of the output. In this step, the real distance between the IoT end devices and GW is fed as an expected output to the ANN. In our system, four different types of ANN have been considered: a) Multilayer Perception (MLP) with one hidden layer; b) MLP with two hidden layers; c) Feed-Forward Artificial Neural Networks; and d) Radial Basis Function (RBF) network. The number of MLP neurons is considered equal to 20. MLP and Feed-Forward with two layers have 15 and 8 neurons, respectively. MLP with two hidden layers and Feed-Forward are both shown in Fig. 2.

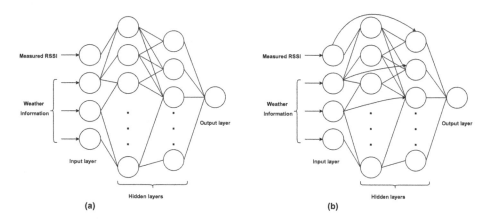

Fig. 2. ANN structure: a) MLP with two hidden layers, b) Feed-Forward neural network with two hidden layers.

In the last step, the GWs send the estimated distance to the LoRaWAN network server—which merges all the estimated distances coming from all the GWs—and sends them to the LoRaWAN application server to compute the IoT end devices localization [25].

4   Method Evaluation

In this section, the effect of weather changes on the accuracy of the predicted distance by the GWs and predicted location by LoRa application server is evaluated. To this purpose, we first overview and describe the used datasets in the evaluation of the proposed approach, followed by the presentation and discussion of final the evaluation results.

4.1 LoRaWAN Dataset

Two publicly available datasets have been used to create the dataset used in the final evaluation. The first is LoRaWAN dataset provided by [26]. This LoRaWAN dataset aims to provide the global research community with a benchmark tool to evaluate fingerprint localization algorithms in large outdoor environments with various properties. It is a large dataset of LoRaWAN messages obtained in the city center of Antwerp together with network information, such as the receiving time of the message, base station IDs', and RSSI. The collection methodology is presented in detail in [26]. A total of 20 cars of the Belgian postal services were equipped with low-power devices communicating via LoRaWAN with a central server. At the same time, the location of the car, as estimated by a GPS device, was also reported. In this dataset, the GPS estimates are considered as the spatial ground truth. For the evaluation of our method, LoRaWAN messages transmitted during four days in January 2019 have been adopted (14th, 15th, 17th, and 18th). This period contains 10423 messages that have been received by different gateways. The GWs position in Antwerp is shown in Fig. 3, being the GWs evaluated identified in red.

The second one is the weather information dataset provided by [27]. This dataset provides different weather information about different cities including temperature, relative humidity, wind speed, etc. To evaluate the proposed method, the weather information of the city of Antwerp has been included in the LoRaWAN dataset. The included weather information comprises temperature, relative humidity, and weather condition. Different weather conditions (fogy, rainy, passing clouds, etc.) are denoted and added to the dataset by a specific integer number, raising from 1 to 8, respectively.

4.2 Distance Estimation Results

As mentioned, GWs in different places have distinct environment error sources and each one of these error sources has a specific influence on distance estimation accuracy. To illustrate this issue, three GWs (i.e. GW2, GW193, and GW223) in diverse places were considered and distance prediction accuracy assessment has been provided in two distinct scenarios: 1) using only RSSI data; and 2) using RSSI and outdoor environmental data (i.e. humidity, temperature, and weather condition). GW2 is surrounded by buildings, GW 193 is near the lake, and GW223 is near a park. As mentioned, four types of neural networks are considered (MLP with one hidden layer, MLP with two hidden layers, Feed-Forward artificial neural networks, and RBF network) for distance prediction, and the model with less distance prediction error is then adopted. To make a reliable evaluation, k-fold cross-validation (k is equal to 10) was applied during the simulation. Then, the average distance prediction error is reported.

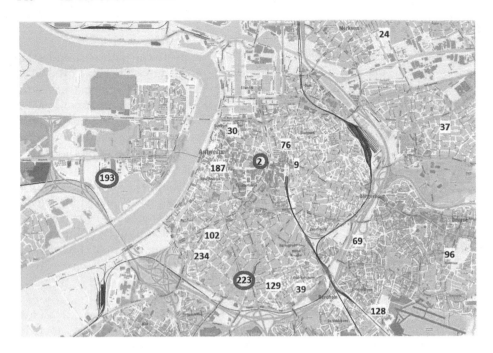

Fig. 3. LoRa gateways positions in Antwerp. (Color figure online)

The simulation is performed on a laptop simulating an edge device. The laptop has a Core-i3 processor with CPU and RAM equal to 2.4 GHz and 4 GB respectively and the clock Precision is equal to 1.0e−03. The simulation is done using Matlab and the relative computational cost has been evaluated.

The results obtained for GW2, GW193, and GW223, are presented for both scenarios in Figs. 4, 5, and 6, respectively.

As shown in Fig. 4, the distance prediction accuracy of GW2 by using only RSSI data is less than 400 m for 52% of the cases. To evaluate the weather effect on distance prediction accuracy of GW2, we used a Feed-Forward neural network that leads to better performance (Levenberg-Marquardt as training algorithm). By considering the weather factor, the distance prediction accuracy increases to 68% in 52% of the cases. Therefore, the weather consideration in this gateway leads to a 16% accuracy increment. In addition, by including the weather conditions, a distance prediction error of more than 600 m has decreased 10% (from 27% to 17%).

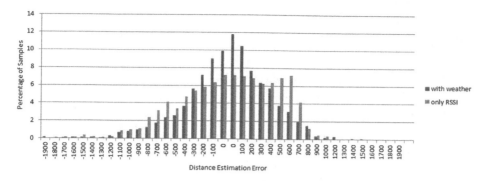

Fig. 4. Distance Prediction Error of LoRa GW2.

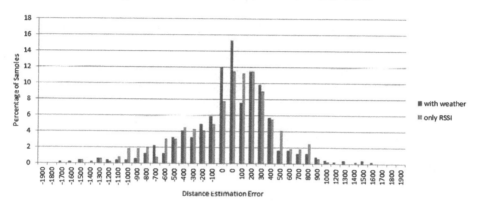

Fig. 5. Distance prediction error of LoRa GW193.

As depicted in Fig. 5, the distance prediction accuracy of GW193 by using only RSSI is less than 400 m for 64% of data. To evaluate the weather effect on RSSI, MLP with one hidden layer has better performance (Levenberg-Marquardt as training algorithm). By considering the weather effect, the distance prediction accuracy increases to 70%. Hence, the weather error in this gateway leads to a decrease in accuracy of 6%. In addition, by including the weather conditions, a distance prediction error of more than 600 m has reduced 4% (from 19% to 15%).

As illustrated in Fig. 6, the distance prediction accuracy of GW223 by using RSSI is less than 400 m for 14% of the data. By considering the weather effect, the distance prediction accuracy increases to 63%. Therefore, the weather error in this gateway leads to an accuracy reduction of 49%. In addition, by including the weather conditions, a distance prediction error of more than 600 m reduced 20% (from 47% to 27%). Training and validation curves of GWs are shown in Fig. 7.

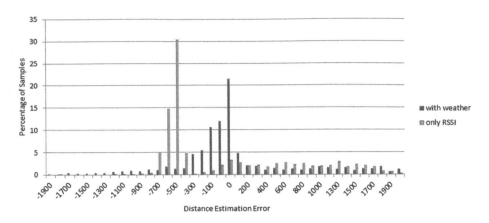

Fig. 6. Distance prediction error of LoRa GW223.

By results observation, by considering the weather situation the RSSI-based distance prediction improves but the improvement rate varies for different GWs. In addition, the distance prediction error of more than 800 m means an environment error source existence that should be considered for the improvement of distance prediction accuracy.

4.3   Localization Estimation Results

To evaluate the location estimation accuracy, two scenarios for 32 different messages of objects, received by all three gateway, are investigated. In the first scenario, each gateway sends the measured RSSI of the sender to the LoRa network server. Then, the LoRa network server merges the received measured RSSI from the different gateway and sends it to the LoRa application server to compute the location of the objects. In the second scenario, each gateway computes the distance of the objects based on the measured RSSI after weather effect mitigation. Then, the LoRa gateway sends the computed distance to the LoRa network server. LoRa network server merges and sends them to the LoRa application server. LoRa application server computes the object location based on the computed distance. The location estimation error of these two scenarios is shown in Fig. 8. The first scenario has a mean error of 624 m and the second scenario has a mean error of 522 m. So, The proposed method (second scenario) leads to a location estimation improvement of approximately 101 m.

4.4   Edge-AI Deployment

Based on expressed results, the weather situation has a distinct effect and a considerable impact on the GWs, based on their locations. For applying these effects, there are two different methods. First, each GW can be equipped with various sensors to determine their environmental condition followed by transmission to the LoRaWAN application server throw the LoRaWAN network server.

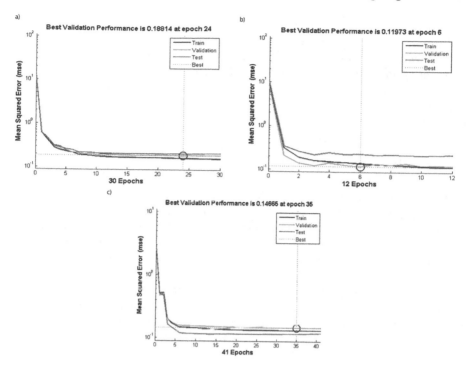

Fig. 7. Training and validation curves of GWs: a) GW2, b) GW193, and c) GW223.

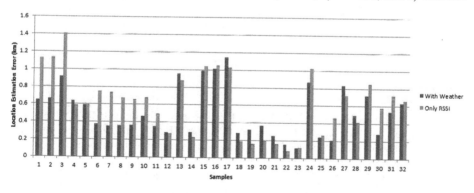

Fig. 8. Location estimation error.

The LoRaWAN application server determines IoT end device distances from GWs by the received information. By increasing the number of IoT end devices, this method fails in fulfilling latency requirements due to long response times. In addition, network data usage will increase with the increase of IoT end devices.

Second, different GWs compute the IoT end device distance by using measured RSSI and their environmental condition. This method can be implemented by including Edge-AI at the GWs. Edge-AI provides computational capabilities at the LoRaWAN GWs, which are physically close to the end devices. This can lead to low latency results and ranging estimation improvement.

The computational cost of the second method can be expressed in two ways. First, the training step and test are provided in the edge device. In this case, it is composed of 413 structs. Second, the training step is done in the server and the learned net is transferred to the edge for evaluation. In this case, it is composed of 108 struts.

5 Conclusion and Future Work

Various environment error sources affect distance estimation. As GWs are placed in distinct places, they are impacted by their environmental surroundings differently. In this paper, we studied the problem of various effects of weather situations on different GWs in a LoRaWAN network. The problem was defined to improve RSSI-based distance estimation in LoRaWAN networks. For this purpose, we proposed an RSSI-based method to improve range estimation in LoRaWAN networks using Edge-AI. The proposed method improved the estimated distance by adopting ANN for weather effect learning in each GW. Numerical results demonstrated the distance improvement performance of our proposed scheme over the basic method based on RSSI. Our proposed method leads to decrements between 4% and 20% of the distance prediction error of more than 600 m and increment between 6% to 49% of the distance prediction error of less than 400 m. This improved estimated distance leads to a location estimation improvement of approximately 101 m. For future work, we are going to investigate the weather effect on other signal features and evaluate its impact on location estimation.

References

1. Mekki, K., Bajic, E., Chaxel, F., Meyer, F.: Overview of cellular LPWAN technologies for IoT deployment: Sigfox, LoRaWAN, and NB-IoT. In: 2018 IEEE International Conference on Pervasive Computing and Communications Workshops (percom Workshops), pp. 197–202 (2018)
2. Fernandes, C.D., et al.: Hybrid indoor and outdoor localization for elderly care applications with LoRaWAN. In: 2020 IEEE International Symposium on Medical Measurements and Applications (MeMeA), pp. 1–6 (2020)
3. Pereira, F., Correia, R., Pinho, P., Lopes, S.I., Carvalho, N.B.: Challenges in resource-constrained IoT devices: energy and communication as critical success factors for future IoT deployment. Sensors 20, 6420 (2020). https://doi.org/10.3390/s20226420
4. Zafari, F., Gkelias, A., Leung, K.: A survey of indoor localization systems and technologies. IEEE Commun. Surv. Tutorials 21(3), 2568–2599 (2019)
5. Lopes, S.I., Pereira, F., Vieira, J.M.N., Carvalho, N.B., Curado, A.: Design of compact LoRa devices for smart building applications. In: Afonso, J.L., Monteiro, V., Pinto, J.G. (eds.) GreeNets 2018. LNICST, vol. 269, pp. 142–153. Springer, Cham (2019). https://doi.org/10.1007/978-3-030-12950-7_12

6. Erturk, M., Aydın, M., Buyukakkalar, M.T., Evirgen, H.: A survey on LoRaWAN architecture, protocol and technologies. Future Internet 11(10), 216 (2019)
7. Li, Y., et al.: Location-enabled IoT (LE-IoT): a survey of positioning techniques, error sources, and mitigation. arXiv preprint arXiv:2004.03738 (2020)
8. El-Sayed, H., et al.: Edge of things: the big picture on the integration of edge, IoT and the cloud in a distributed computing environment. IEEE Access 6, 1706–1717 (2017)
9. Gao, Z., Li, Y., Zhuang, Y., Yang, H., Pan, Y., Zhang, H.: Robust Kalman Filter aided GEO/IGSO/GPS raw-PPP/INS tight integration. Sensors 2019(19), 1–17 (2019)
10. Choi, W., Chang, Y., Jung, Y., Song, J.: Low-Power LoRa signal-based outdoor positioning using fingerprint algorithm. ISPRS Int. J. Geo-Inf. 7(11), 440 (2018)
11. Aernouts, M., BniLam, N., Berkvens, R., Weyn, M.: TDAoA: a combination of TDoA and AoA localization with LoRaWAN. Internet Things 11, 100236 (2020)
12. Pospisil, J., Fujdiak, R., Mikhaylov, K.: Investigation of the performance of TDoA-based localization over LoRaWAN in theory and practice. Sensors 20(19), 5464 (2020)
13. Kwasme, H., Sabit, E.: RSSI-based localization using LoRaWAN technology. IEEE Access 7, 99856–99866 (2019)
14. Lam, K.H., Cheung, C., Lee, W.: New RSSI-based LoRa localization algorithms for very noisy outdoor environment. In: 2018 IEEE 42nd Annual Computer Software and Applications Conference (COMPSAC), vol. 2, pp. 794–799 (2018)
15. Savazzi, P., Goldoni, E., Vizziello, A., Favalli, L., Gamba, P.: A Wiener-based RSSI localization algorithm exploiting modulation diversity in LoRa networks. IEEE Sens. J. 19(24), 12381–12388 (2019)
16. Bianco, G.M., Giuliano, R., Marrocco, G., Mazzenga, F., Mejia-Aguilar, A.: LoRa system for search and rescue: path-loss models and procedures in mountain scenarios. IEEE Internet Things J. 8(3), 1985–1999 (2020)
17. Lam, K.H., Cheung, C., Lee, W.: LoRa-based localization systems for noisy outdoor environment. In: IEEE 13th International Conference on Wireless and Mobile Computing, Networking and Communications (WiMob) 2017, pp. 278–284 (2017)
18. Vo, Q.D., De, P.: A survey of fingerprint-based outdoor localization. IEEE Commun. Surv. Tutorials 18(1), 491–506 (2015)
19. Nguyen, T.A.: LoRa localisation in cities with neural networks (2019)
20. Mahnoor, A., Khan, M.A., Hassan, S.A., Mahmood, A., Qureshi, H.K., Gidlund, M.: RSSI fingerprinting-based localization using machine learning in LoRa networks. IEEE Internet Things Mag. 3(4), 53–59 (2020)
21. Shyan, C.Y., Hsu, C.S., Huang, C.Y.: A semi-supervised transfer learning with grid segmentation for outdoor localization over LoRaWans. Sensors 21(8), 2640 (2021)
22. Cattani, M., Boano, C.A., Römer, K.: An experimental evaluation of the reliability of LoRa long-range low-power wireless communication. J. Sens. Actuator Netw. 6(2), 7 (2017)
23. Elijah, O., et al.: Effect of weather condition on LoRa IoT communication technology in a tropical region: Malaysia. IEEE Access 9, 72835–72843 (2021)
24. Sarker, V.K., Queralta, J.P., Gia, T.N., Tenhunen, H., Westerlund, T.: A survey on LoRa for IoT: integrating edge computing. In: Fourth International Conference on Fog and Mobile Edge Computing (FMEC), pp. 295–300. IEEE (2019)
25. Chen, Y., Francisco, J.A., Trappe, W., Martin, R.P.: A practical approach to landmark deployment for indoor localization. In: 2006 3rd Annual IEEE Communications Society on Sensor and Ad Hoc Communications and Networks, vol. 1, pp. 365–373. IEEE (2006)

26. Aernouts, M., Berkvens, R., Van Vlaenderen, K., Weyn, M.: Sigfox and LoRaWAN datasets for fingerprint localization in large urban and rural areas. Data **3**(2), 13 (2018)
27. Antwerp Homepage, January 2019. https://www.timeanddate.com/weather/belgium/antwerp

Large-Scale Video Analytics Through Object-Level Consolidation

Daniel Rivas[1,2]($\boxtimes$), Francesc Guim[3], Jordà Polo[1], Josep Ll. Berral[1], and David Carrera[1]

[1] Barcelona Supercomputing Center (BSC), Barcelona, Spain
{daniel.rivas,jorda.polo,josep.berral,david.carrera}@bsc.es
[2] Universitat Politècnica de Catalunya, Barcelona, Spain
[3] Intel Iberia, Barcelona, Spain
francesc.guim@intel.com

Abstract. As the number of installed cameras grows, so do the compute resources required to process and analyze all the images captured by these cameras. Video analytics enables new use cases, such as smart cities or autonomous driving. At the same time, it urges service providers to install additional compute resources to cope with the demand while the strict latency requirements push compute towards the end of the network, forming a geographically distributed and heterogeneous set of compute locations, shared and resource-constrained. Such landscape (shared and distributed locations) forces us to design new techniques that can optimize and distribute work among all available locations and, ideally, make compute requirements grow sublinearly with respect to the number of cameras installed. In this paper, we present FoMO (*Focus on Moving Objects*). This method effectively optimizes multi-camera deployments by preprocessing images for scenes, filtering the empty regions out, and composing regions of interest from multiple cameras into a single image that serves as input for a pre-trained object detection model. Results show that overall system performance can be increased by 8x while accuracy improves 40% as a by-product of the methodology, all using an *off-the-shelf* pre-trained model with no additional training or fine-tuning.

Keywords: Video analytics · DNN · Inference · Background substraction · Motion detection

1 Introduction

Rapid advances in the field of deep learning have led to an equally rapid and unprecedented increase in interest in video analytics applications. Smart cities or autonomous driving are just two examples of use cases that require an automatic analysis of video feeds to trigger different actions. However, video feeds are commonly processed individually, and, at the same time, the execution of neural networks is a computationally expensive task. This leads to the cost of video

S. Paiva et al. (Eds.): SmartCity360° 2021, LNICST 442, pp. 155–171, 2022.
https://doi.org/10.1007/978-3-031-06371-8_11

analytics systems growing linearly with the number of cameras being deployed. We believe there is a window of opportunity to optimize video analytics systems by combining mechanisms that reduce the search space within an image, thanks to our knowledge of how neural networks look for objects within the input image.

Neural networks can learn to find objects anywhere on an image, even when these objects represent a small fraction of the input and the rest of the image is of no interest. To make this possible, neural networks classify many regions (in the order of thousands) proposed at an earlier stage of the network. This implies that neural networks end up looking at regions that are empty of objects of interest. We could argue that this is what makes neural networks so powerful (especially convolutional neural networks for image analysis), as it means they can focus attention without developers or users needing to hint them where to look in the image. However, it also implies that most of the work will yield no meaningful results with an increased chance of wrong results (any positive detection on an *empty* region is a false positive). Moreover, neural networks have a *hard time* detecting small objects [3]. However, some of the smaller objects are captured at an even higher resolution than that used by the network's input layer, but once the captured image is resized to feed the neural network, these objects become just a few indistinguishable pixels. For example, an 8 MP camera (4K UHD resolution, or 3840×2160 pixels) captures an object at 20 m with a pixel density of over 100 px/m, enough to get a sharp image of a license plate. Nonetheless, if the image gets resized to standard definition (640×480 pixels), density drops below 20 px/m (calculated for a camera with 3 mm focal length placed 4 m height), which is unsuited for most detection tasks. For reference, 320×320 pixels is a common input size for *edge* detection models.

We make the following key observation: scenes captured by static cameras do not move; objects of interest do. We do not need to check the entire scene, just whatever is new in it. By focusing on footage from static cameras, we can extract the regions of the scene that contain *objects of interest* (i.e., objects not yet classified) and filter the rest of the image out. For this task, we have multiple techniques at our disposal that we can apply to identify and extract such regions of interest, like motion detection or background subtraction. This step alone lets the object detection model analyze objects at a higher resolution and, potentially, increase its accuracy. At the same time, we can optimize the analysis of multiple scenes by merging regions from different cameras into a composite frame that can be passed to the model as a single input. Therefore, we can effectively exploit the intrinsic parallelism of neural networks and work on multiple video streams simultaneously, reducing the total number of inferences required by the system.

In this paper, we present FoMO (*Focus on Moving Objects*). A method to optimize video analytics by removing the analysis of *uninteresting* parts of the scene, distributing the work, and consolidating information from multiple cameras to reduce the compute requirements of the analysis. Moreover, as a by-product, neural networks can analyze objects from the scenes at a higher resolution, which results have shown to improve the accuracy of the models tested by several fold.

The paper is organized as follows: in Sect. 2, we introduce some of the concepts of computer vision and video analytics from which we base our work. Then, we present and describe FoMO in Sect. 3. In Sect. 4, we detail the experimental setup and the methodology followed during the evaluation. In Sect. 5, we presents the results of FoMO's evaluation. The literature review and previous work is presented in Sect. 6. Finally, Sect. 7 concludes the paper.

2   Background and Considerations

In this section, we revise several considerations made in this paper and the concepts behind each one.

2.1   Video Analytics Systems

Video analytics applications can be divided into *online* and *offline* video analytics, depending on *when* the information extracted from the frames is needed. On the one hand, online video analytics requires images to be processed in real-time, as actions are triggered by the analysis of what is in front of the camera when images are captured. An ALPR (Automatic License Plate Recognition) system controlling a barrier to entry a given facility would fall under this category, as well as an autonomous car detecting obstacles to avoid them. At the same time, past information is no longer useful for online systems. Consequently, such systems are subject to strict latency constraints and are typically evaluated by the single inference latency. Therefore, they are unable to fully exploit parallelism due to the *hazards* of request consolidation under strict deadlines.

On the other hand, offline video analytics processes images captured in the past. For example, a system to query the contents of recorded footage to obtain the fragments or timestamps that contain the queried objects [8] falls under this category. These systems analyze images in bulk and are commonly evaluated based on the turnaround latency of the queries (i.e., total system throughput). Therefore, they can prioritize resource utilization over single inference latency.

Online and offline video analytics are two categories with very distinct requirements. In this paper, we focus on online video analytics for two reasons. First, they show subpar scalability as the set of available optimizations while scheduling requests or orchestrating available resources is limited. Second, offline video analytics can also benefit from an online analysis to pre-process images and reduce the search space of queries [7].

2.2   Selection Region of Interest

Object detection is, in fact, a combination of region proposal and image classification problems. Region proposal techniques suggest a set of regions in the input image that might contain objects of interest (i.e., objects the neural network was trained to detect). These regions are then processed as independent images and are classified based on their contents. The region is considered a positive example if the highest-scoring classification is above a user-defined threshold. Intuitively, the quality of the region proposal mechanisms has a high impact on the quality of the detection results. There are several methods available, such as Selective Search or Focal Pyramid Networks (FPN) [9].

Neural networks that differentiate region proposal and classification in two stages are called *Two-Shot* detection models. On the contrary, *Single-Shot* detection models skip the region proposal stage and yield localization and class predictions all at once. Regardless of the number of shots, all object detection models predict bounding boxes and classes using a single input layer of a fixed size decided during training. Larger input layers potentially yield more accurate predictions, as more pixels (i.e., information) are taken into account. This is especially true for smaller objects that are more difficult to detect correctly. However, any increment in the input layer's size is followed by an increment in the compute requirements that is not always matched with an equal increment in accuracy.

2.3 Moving/Foreground/Salient Object Detection

FoMO relies on background subtraction (BGS) methods that can detect and extract objects of interest. Such methods allow us to differentiate between *background* and *foreground* objects. However, which objects compose the background and foreground is not always clear and is subject to interpretation. For example, in most scenarios, a car would be considered part of the foreground, as cars come and go from the field of view of the camera and are often an object of interest to identify or detect (e.g., autonomous driving or smart cities). However, a broken car in a scrapyard will probably remain where it is for as long as other objects that are typically considered background objects (e.g., traffic lights or buildings). Once that car is correctly identified, there is no need to process it on successive frames repeatedly. Therefore, we make the following assumption: *foreground* objects move, *background* objects are stationary.

As for the set of techniques that can leverage the extraction of foreground objects, we have mainly considered traditional computer vision techniques that deliver *relatively* good results at a small compute overhead. Newer and more accurate methods make use of neural networks to provide high-quality results [11], but their compute requirements are higher than that of many neural networks, which significantly reduces the room for improving the system performance. Moreover, it is important to note that, while an accurate algorithm to detect salient objects is desirable, background subtraction methods that offer more modest results *usually* increase the number of false positives instead of false negatives. That is, more or larger regions are flagged as foreground/moving than those that actually changed, which can be caused due to camera jitter, changes in the lighting conditions, or other phenomenons causing unwanted frame-to-frame variations. However, false positives increase the amount of work but do not necessarily translate into false positives being predicted by the detection model. Ultimately, the selection of a more or less accurate BGS method will depend on the compute capabilities available at the edge locations (cameras or compute next to the cameras).

3   Focus on Moving Objects

In this paper, we present FoMO (Focus on Moving Objects), a novel method to optimize and distribute video analytics workloads in Edge locations. FoMO has been conceived with static cameras in mind, and its goal is to maximize the *pixel-to-object ratio* that is processed at each inference, i.e., it aims to maximize the number of pixels processed by the neural network that belong to actual objects of interest instead of the background. Towards this goal, each frame is preprocessed to extract the regions of interest that have a higher chance of containing objects of interest. Working with static cameras, we can safely assume that such regions of interest intersect with regions whose content has changed over time.

Figure 1 depicts the main steps involved in FoMO. First, a set of static cameras (either in a single location or geographically distributed) periodically capture images from the scenes. Then, each scene is processed individually, and background subtraction is computed to extract moving objects (i.e., regions of the image where movement has been detected). Depending on the compute and network bandwidth available at the Edge, video scenes can be processed locally or sent to a central location. In both cases, a single entity, known as *composer*, is in charge of receiving the objects from all the scenes and consolidating objects into a single RGB matrix known as *composite frame*. This step is called *frame composition*.

During frame composition, each object is treated as an independent unit of work that can be allocated separately or jointly from other objects from the same or other scenes. Objects are selected based on a pre-defined composition policy that determines the order and rate at which objects are composed and processed. The selected objects are placed together at each composition interval, forming a mosaic of objects (i.e., the composite frame). A few-pixels wide border is added to mark frontiers between objects. Next, the composite frame is used as input for the object detection model. Finally, the predicted coordinates of the detected objects are translated back to the original coordinates of the corresponding scene.

3.1   Extraction of Objects of Interest

Frame decoding results in a 3-D matrix containing the RGB color of every pixel in the scene captured by the camera. When cameras capturing the scene are static, consecutive RGB matrices will often have little to no pixel-to-pixel variation. At a higher level of abstraction, this correlation among frames means that nothing is moving in the scene (or the camera lens could not capture it). Consequently, whenever an object is moving in the scene, only some subregions are affected. This is the basis for *motion detection* algorithms, which are extensively used to trigger the analysis of a given frame to save computation on frames that do not contain anything new. In this paper, however, we extend this idea and consider

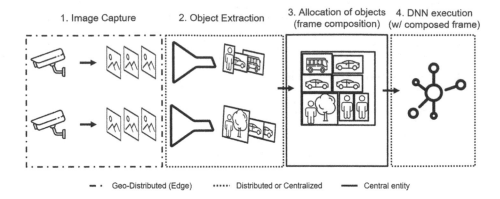

Fig. 1. Main steps involved in the process of FoMO.

that moving objects, not whole frames, are of interest. The rationale is that for an object to trigger an action, it has to either enter, leave or interact with the scene (i.e., moving in the scene). Thus, we can focus on the regions that contain change and discard the rest. As these subregions are usually a tiny fraction of the whole frame, we can combine several subregions from different cameras into a composed frame. This frame can be processed by a neural network the same way it would process an entire frame.

Motion detection involves many challenges (e.g., camera jitter or variations in lighting, among others), and there is no single nor standard method that can handle all of them robustly. Moreover, it usually relies on background initialization algorithms to model the background without foreground objects. Among all available methods, we prioritized simplicity (i.e., speed) over accuracy for two reasons. First, the method must run in resource-constrained (Edge) nodes and do it faster than it would take to process the whole frame by the neural network. Second, the accuracy of these methods is usually evaluated by error metrics that compare the modeled background to the ground-truth background at the pixel level. However, artifacts and other inconsistencies in the generated background do not necessarily translate into a lower recall of objects of interest or a lower accuracy of the object detection model.

We have evaluated FoMO using three different BGS methods to extract objects of interest from a scene. These methods differ by the way they model the background and, second, by how they identify foreground objects. The three BGS methods are:

– **PtP Mean** (Moving Average Pixel-to-Pixel): The background corresponds to the moving average of n frames (not necessarily consecutive) at pixel level. Objects are extracted by applying first a Gaussian blur to the background model and the current frame to reduce noise. Then, the absolute difference between both frames is computed before a binary threshold decides which level of difference constitutes change and which does not.

- **MOG2** (Mixture of Gaussians): Each pixel is modeled as a distribution over several Gaussians, instead of being a single RGB color. This method is better than the moving average at preserving the edges and is already implemented in OpenCV.
- **Hybrid**: The background is modeled as a Mixture of Gaussians (MOG2), but objects are extracted applying the same operations as in the PtP Mean to detect differences between the background and the current frame.

As output, all three methods provide a black and white mask of the same dimensions as the frames. From the mask, the bounding boxes of the objects moving are easily extracted by detecting adjacent pixels. Bounding boxes of an area smaller than a pre-defined minimum are discarded. This threshold helps to filter minor variations out. However, it also defines the method's sensitivity, and the optimal value will vary from scene to scene depending on the minimum size of objects (in pixels) to detect.

All three methods can run in the order of milliseconds in resource-constrained nodes. Performance and accuracy of these methods are analyzed in Sect. 5, where we explore their impact on the final results. In short, a more sensitive motion detector will generate false positives (i.e., non-interesting objects being extracted, like a tree with moving leaves) and, therefore, introduce more or larger regions than necessary to be composed in the following step.

Effectively, the breakdown of the scene into objects opens the door to two major optimizations. On the one hand, we can decide which regions should be processed and which can be omitted. Potentially, this reduces the amount of data moved around and processed by the detection model. Consequently, it increases the pixel-to-object ratio, as we achieve the same results while processing only those pixels that we have considered of interest. On the other hand, video analytics can now be distributed while consuming less network bandwidth, as, potentially, only a fraction of the scene must be sent over the network.

3.2 Composition Policies

After moving objects have been extracted from the frames, the composer has a pool of them in the form of cropped images, each with a different size and aspect ratio. At each composition interval, the composer decides what objects are to be allocated in the resulting composite frame. Currently, objects are selected in a purely first-come, first-serve manner. However, not all objects can be allocated during the subsequent allocation cycle, as there is a limit to the number of objects composed in one frame. The threshold is not a fixed value and is set upon one of two pre-defined composition policies.

To the composer, objects become the minimum unit of work to be allocated into composite frames. Therefore, we could argue that the composer treats composite frames as a type of resource, a resource that can be shared among requests (i.e., objects). At the same time, the composite frame can be considered elastic, as it can be overprovisioned by simply adding more objects to it. Nonetheless, as in any other type of shared resource, there is a point at which a higher degree of overprovisioning degrades the overall performance. Object detection models can locate and classify multiple objects within an input image and do it with a single forward pass over the network. However, there is a minimum number of pixels required for the model to successfully detect an object (closely related to the focal view and input size of the network). Similarly, the larger an object is, the better can a model detect it accurately.

During composition, the composer and the composition policy must consider the trade-off between the resource savings from consolidating more objects into a single composite frame and the accuracy drop involved. After a frame is composed, the resulting frame is resized to match the neural network's input size regardless of its original size. At the same time, adding one more object to the composition could potentially result in a larger frame, depending on whether the new object can be allocated without increasing the dimensions of the composite frame with all previous objects. The larger the resulting composite frame, the smaller its objects become after the frame is resized to feed the neural network. Consequently, the more objects allocated in a composite frame, the higher the amount of computation saved (i.e., fewer inferences per camera), but also the higher the impact on the accuracy of the model. Unfortunately, there is no known mechanism to determine beforehand where the limit is or even where the sweet spot is.

FoMO implements two policies that limit the number of objects allocated in a single composite frame, albeit the exact number differs from composition to composition. The first policy, namely *downscale limit policy*, limits the downscaling factor to which objects will be subjected after the composite frame is resized to feed the neural network's input. This is equivalent to setting an upper limit to the dimensions of the resulting composite frame. This policy prioritizes the quality of the detection results over the system's performance. The second policy, namely *elastic policy*, does not set a hard limit but a limit on the number of camera frames to consider on each composition. That is, the dimensions of the composite frame can be arbitrarily large but the objects allocated belong to, at most, n camera frames, being n user-defined. Effectively, this policy prioritizes system's performance over quality of the detection results.

3.3 Allocation Heuristic

Composing objects into a composite frame can be seen as allocating 2D images into a larger 2D canvas. For the sake of simplicity, we consider objects to be 2-D during allocation, as the third dimension is always of size 3 in RGB images. The allocation can be mapped to the *bin packing problem*. Bin packing is an optimization problem that tries to pack (allocate) items (objects) of different volumes into bins of a fixed volume (composite frame) while minimizing the number of bins used (blank spaces in the composite node). This problem is, unfortunately, known to be an NP-hard problem. Therefore, FoMO approximates a solution using a *first-fit* heuristic, where objects are first sorted into decreasing width (arbitrary) order. For this task, a sub-optimal solution results in a composite frame with more blank spaces than needed. Blank spaces reduce the density of meaningful pixels (i.e., pixels that are part of an object of interest) and, ultimately, reduce the number of objects that a single composed frame can fit.

4 Experimental Setup

In this section, we provide the specific experimental setup used throughout the evaluation presented in Sect. 5.

4.1 Dataset

For the evaluation, we have used the VIRAT dataset [10]. VIRAT contains footage captured with static cameras from 11 different outdoor scenes.

Dataset Curation. VIRAT contains frame-by-frame annotations for all objects in the scene, with bounding box and label (classes person, car, vehicle, bike, and object). However, annotations include both static and moving objects. We evaluate FoMO by its capability to detect moving objects. Therefore, we have curated the dataset to remove all annotations from static objects and avoid these objects artificially lowering the final accuracy. Thus, we consider objects static if their coordinates in a given frame do not change to 10 frames prior (10 has been arbitrarily chosen and corresponds to the frame skipping we used during the evaluation). Nonetheless, cameras often suffer from a slight jitter, mainly due to wind. Whenever that happens, the bounding boxes of a given object on consecutive frames may not perfectly match, even if the object has not moved. To avoid false positives in such cases, we still consider an object static when its coordinates remained static for at least 90% of the frames.

Figure 2 shows the percentage of area occupied by objects in each scene of the VIRAT dataset. Results show that scenes are mostly *empty* and objects represent as little as 2% of the scene and no more than a quarter of the scene. Moreover, some scenes appear to be *quiet*, i.e., only a tiny fraction of objects in the scene are moving. When considering moving objects only, the average area taken by these objects fluctuates between 1% and 8% of the scenes. These results highlight the potential benefits that can be achieved by removing all the empty regions.

Moreover, we have made the following considerations during the evaluation:

- Only sequences with at least 1000 frames have been considered.
- Discarded the first 250 frames (approx. 10 s) to give a time window to initialize the background modeling of some methods.
- Frame skipping of 10 frames.

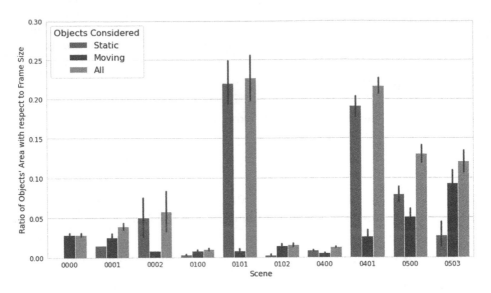

Fig. 2. Percentage of area that represent objects in each scene, according to ground-truth annotations.

4.2   Object Detection Models

All experiments have been carried out using pre-trained object detection models that are publicly and freely available in the TensorFlow Model Zoo [1]. We decided upon the use of pre-trained models instead of training or fine-tuning the models on our data to remove training as a variable on which to focus, which is an important one nonetheless.

The following are the three DNN models used throughout the evaluation:

- SSD + MobileNet V2 with an input layer of $320 \times 320 \times 3$ pixels.
- Same as previous with an additional FPN (Feature Pyramid Network) that improves the quality of predictions [9].
- Same as previous with an input layer of $640 \times 640 \times 3$ pixels to improve the quality of predictions.

4.3   Background Subtraction Mechanisms

Background subtraction (BGS) algorithms, albeit not directly part of our contributions, are key to extracting the set of objects that will constitute the system's workload. At the same time, they have an undeniable impact on the quality of the region proposal. An accurate BGS algorithm will extract all or most objects of interest and nothing else (i.e., discard all regions that do not contain objects of interest). However, to have a complete overview of how FoMO performs, we must break the accuracy of these methods down into *precision* and *recall*, as each one will have a different impact on the overall performance.

Precision is defined as the ratio of *True Positives* (TP) with respect to the sum of TP and *False Positives* (FP), i.e., what proportion of predictions are correct. In the context of *object extraction*, we can see precision at the pixel level and define it as the proportion of extracted area (i.e., number of pixels) that does belong to objects of interest with respect to the total extracted area (including that without objects of interest). *Recall* is defined as the ratio of TP with respect to the total number of positive examples (TP + FN), i.e. what proportion of positive examples are correctly detected. In the context of *object extraction*, we define recall as the proportion of extracted area that does belongs to objects of interest with respect to the total area of the objects of interest in the scene (including the area of the objects not extracted). Thus, low precision BGS mechanisms will cause *uninteresting* regions to occupy space in the composed frame, potentially shrinking other regions or leaving them out of the composition (hence, delaying their processing). Low recall mechanisms will cause FoMO to directly miss predictions as entire objects were not extracted and will, therefore, not make it into the neural network's input. On the contrary, a high precision and high recall BGS mechanism will maximize FoMO's efficiency, while accuracy will be made to only depend on the neural network model chosen.

The experiments aim to quantify the impact that different methods for BGS, with more or less accuracy on the extraction of objects, have on the system's resource usage and the quality of the detections.

The configuration of the three BGS methods is, for all experiments, as follows:

- PtP Mean: The moving average is computed over the last 20 frames with a frame skipping of 10 (i.e., spanning over 200 consecutive frames in total).
- MOG: Computed every frame. Implementation from OpenCV.
- Hybrid: MOG background model is updated once every 50 frames (2 s). The difference with the current frame to extract objects is computed with respect to the latest background model available.

4.4   Metrics of Interest

In video analytics, the two main metrics of interest are inference accuracy and cost. For the cost, we use latency as a proxy. For the inference accuracy, we use the average precision as used in the PASCAL Visual Object Classes (VOC) Challenge [6]. To consider a detection as either positive or negative, we use a value of 0.3 for the Intersection over Union (IoU) between the predicted and the ground-truth bounding boxes. The IoU is a matric that measures the overlap between two bounding boxes.

5   Results

The following experiments evaluate the potential of our method by analyzing upper and lower-bound scenarios. Therefore, we have replicated the same stream whenever more than one stream is used unless otherwise stated. By replicating the stream, we avoid potential variability introduced by different load distributions across streams that is difficult to quantify. Consequently, if one object is captured at the *i-th* frame of a stream, the same object will be captured in the same *i-th* frame in all other streams. However, each frame's decoding and preprocessing (i.e., background subtraction, motion detection, and cropping) is computed for each stream individually to obtain an accurate and realistic performance evaluation.

5.1   Accuracy Boost vs Resource Savings

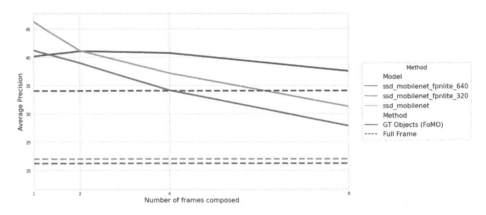

Fig. 3. Mean Average Precision (mAP) by scene for three different DNNs with an increasing number of frames composed into a single inference. The reduction in number of inferences is equivalent to the number of frames composed.

Figure 3 shows the mAP averaged for all scenes of the dataset for the three different pre-trained models. Each model is evaluated using the full frame as input compared to using a composed frame with objects from 1, 2, 4, and 8 parallel streams. The objects in each frame are extracted based on the ground truth annotations from the curated dataset, i.e., without background subtraction. Therefore, these results represent an upper bound precision for FoMO. It is important to understand why the mean average precision appears especially low for the baseline method (*Full Frame*) during inference for the two smaller models. As mentioned in Sect. 4 (and, more specifically, as shown in Fig. 2), moving objects are, on average, a tiny fraction of the frame's area. Hence, once the frame gets downscaled to the neural network's input size, objects become too small to be detected accurately. This is why the bigger model, with an input twice as large as the other two models (640×640 pixels compared to 320×320 pixels), gets around 50% improvement in accuracy over them.

From the mAP results of the models using FoMO, we extract two key observations. On the one hand, results show that a larger model does not necessarily translate into a higher mAP when inferencing over composite frames, as it happens with the baseline. The larger model is up to 10% below the smaller models when the composite frame contains objects from only one camera frame. When the number of objects to compose is small (as it is expected when only a single camera frame is considered), the composition may result in a composite frame smaller than the model's input size. Consequently, the frame must be enlarged to the appropriate dimensions expected by the neural network. Thus, these results indicate that accuracy is also impacted negatively when objects are zoomed in. On the other hand, as already discussed, accuracy takes a hit when more frames (hence, more objects too) are considered during the composition, as objects become smaller. However, results show that a larger input size seems to mitigate this impact. The largest model still achieves 10% higher accuracy composing frames eight cameras compared to the full-frame inference using the same model.

5.2   Impact of BGS Techniques

There are multiple available techniques to compute background subtraction to detect and extract moving objects in a scene. Each technique provides a different trade-off in terms of latency (or required resources) and quality of the solution. The quality of these techniques, however, can be measured through different metrics. We are interested in detecting moving objects but not *everything* that is moving (e.g., leaves or camera jitter). Some methods are more sensitive to minor variations than others, and the level of sensitivity will impact what is considered actual movement and what is just background noise. Therefore, a higher sensitivity potentially results in a higher rate of false positives (i.e., lower precision) and a lower rate of false negatives (i.e., higher recall), as more objects will get extracted.

Figure 4 shows the recall, precision, and average precision of the three object detection models using the four BGS methods considered plus the baseline (*Full Frame*, i.e., no object extraction). On the one hand, results show how FoMO performs compared to the baseline method. The upper bound for FoMO can be defined by the ground-truth annotations (*GT Objects*), as no object is missed during the extraction. GT Objects consistently outperforms the baseline by a considerable margin on every metric and model, except one case. For example, GT Objects achieves twice the AP of the baseline for the two smaller models, although this margin reduces to 30% when the larger model processes the objects. However, baseline surpasses FoMO's upper bound recall by a 10% when using the largest model. This seems to be related to what results in Sect. 5.1 showed when composition considers objects from only one frame, i.e., the resulting composite frame is smaller than the neural network's input, and objects must be enlarged. Nonetheless, a baseline's precision half of FoMO's mitigates this issue.

On the other hand, results show what can be expected from using a more or less accurate BGS method. MOG and Hybrid are close on all metrics. Again, precision is where FoMO seems to provide larger benefits, especially for small input sizes. Both MOG and Hybrid outperform baseline's precision by a factor of 2 using the smaller models and close to 50% for the larger model. However, all BGS methods seem to miss objects during extraction, and recall takes a hit. Nevertheless, the AP of both methods still outperforms the baseline by a 60% and 30% when using the two smaller models, while baseline outperforms the other two by 12% in AP using the larger model. Finally, PtP Mean lacks far behind on the recall, which hits its average precision. Nevertheless, results show that FoMO consistently increases precision regardless of the BGS method, while the accuracy of the selected method will mainly impact its recall.

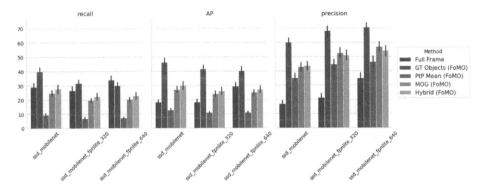

Fig. 4. Recall, Precision, and Average Precision of three SSD MobileNet V2 pre-trained models after using the different methods to create the input for the model. *Full Frame* uses the frame as captured by the camera; GT Objects: objects are cropped from the ground truth annotations; MOG: Mixture of Gaussians; PtP Mean: Pixel-to-Pixel Mean; Hybrid: MOG for background modeling and then pixel-to-pixel difference with respect the current frame.

5.3   Performance and Resource Usage

FoMO's main goal is to improve the overall system performance. This is achieved by reducing the amount of computing required to process a single frame. After decoding, each frame undergoes three consecutive steps: 1. object extraction, 2. frame composition, 3. inference. We now evaluate the first two, as the third will be determined by the neural network used.

Table 1 shows the average latency to extract objects of interest for each of the three methods considered in the experiments. These results were obtained using a single core on an Intel Xeon 4114. Pixel-to-Pixel mean is, on average, eight times slower than MOG2 and almost six times slower than the Hybrid method. The table does not show timings for the executions that use ground truth annotations as those are synthetic executions that do not require any background subtraction to get the objects' bounding boxes.

Table 1. Average latency (milliseconds) to extract objects using the three methods considered in the experiments

Method	Latency (millisec)
PtP Mean	22.0
MOG2	2.7
Hybrid	3.8

The next step is the composition of objects into the composite frame. Potentially, the composition is performed once for multiple scenes. Figure 5 shows the time required to compose a frame with respect to the number of objects to compose and the width of the resulting composite frames (and height, as these are always 1:1). Results show how the latency increases with the number of objects to compose. The number of camera frames considered within a composition interval indirectly impacts the latency, as the more frames are considered, the more objects we can expect to be available for composition (although not necessarily always true). The increasing dimensions of the resulting composite frames highlight this relationship. The frame is enlarged to try to fit a larger number of objects. Nonetheless, we can expect the detection models to yield worse accuracy when processing the larger composite frames, as objects will appear smaller once shrunk to the model's input size. Therefore, datapoints with composition latency in hundreds of milliseconds are too large to be reliably used unless the detection model has an appropriately sized input layer. In that case, inference cost will also be higher, and, therefore, the cost of composing many objects can be hidden.

6   Related Work

Given the amount of data and compute required to train neural networks, the training step has garnered most of the attention from both academia and industry. However, as neural networks start being widely deployed for production use cases, optimizing inference is gaining interest from the industry. Most of the previous works has focused on the optimization of either the neural network architecture itself (using techniques to prune layers [8] or reduce weight precision through quantization) or on the optimization of the application's pipeline (using cascade classifiers [7,8] or reducing the number of frames to process [4]). In the context of video analytics systems, there are two main directions: reducing the amount of work [4] and optimizing the inference pipeline [8].

Regarding what impacts the quality of the predictions of a neural network, the work in [3] argues that, in general, a detector can only provide high quality predictions if presented with high quality [region] proposals. Similarly, authors in [5] demonstrate how deep neural networks have difficulties to accurately detect smaller objects by design.

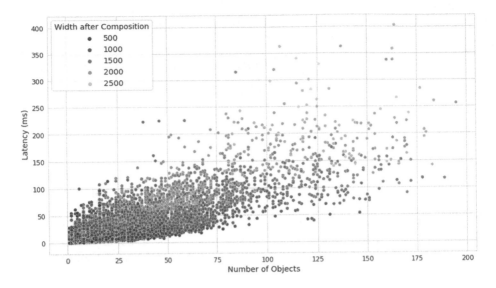

Fig. 5. Time to compose a frame, i.e. latency, in milliseconds (Y-Axis) with respect to the number of objects to compose (X-Axis). The color palette shows the width of the resulting composite frame. Each dot is a composition with objects from up to eight parallel streams.

Regarding the usage of traditional computer vision techniques, authors in Authors in [2] provide a taxonomy and evaluation (in terms of accuracy and performance) of scene background initialization algorithms, which helped us decide what were the most sensible methods to implement in FoMO.

Previous methods have focused on optimizing the different transformations applied to the input image. However, all these methods still devote a significant amount of computation to decide whether a certain region contains true positives or not (region proposal) when, in practice, most will not. Our method aims to reduce the amount of work wasted on this purpose. Moreover, this allows us to stack regions of different cameras to reduce the total computation of the system and increase the overall system throughput. At the same time, our results have shown that by increasing the quality of proposals, accuracy increases considerably as a *side effect*.

To the best of our knowledge, no previous work proposes and evaluates a method combining traditional computer vision techniques to quantize and distribute portions of scene, consolidate multiple scenes into one, and process them with a single inference.

7   Conclusions

In this paper, we have presented FoMO, a method that distributes the load of video analytics and, at the same time, reduces the compute requirements of video analytics and improves the accuracy of the neural network models used for object detection. Results have shown how FoMO is able to scale the number of cameras being processed with a sub-linear increment in the amount of resources required while still improving accuracy with respect to the baseline. Results have shown that the number of inferences can be reduced by 8 while still achieving between 10% and 40% higher mean average precision with the same model. Moreover, the methodology used shows how video analytics can be effectively deployed in resource-constrained edge locations by tackling its optimization from a different perspective that opens a new line of research.

References

1. TensorFlow 2 Detection Model Zoo. https://github.com/tensorflow/models/blob/master/research/object_detection/g3doc/tf2_detection_zoo.md (2021). Accessed 25 June 2021
2. Bouwmans, T., Maddalena, L., Petrosino, A.: Scene background initialization: a taxonomy. Pattern Recogn. Lett. **96**, 3–11 (2017)
3. Cai, Z., Vasconcelos, N.: Cascade R-CNN: delving into high quality object detection. In: Proceedings of the IEEE Conference on Computer Vision and Pattern Recognition, pp. 6154–6162 (2018)
4. Canel, C., et al.: Scaling video analytics on constrained edge nodes. arXiv preprint arXiv:1905.13536 (2019)
5. Eggert, C., Brehm, S., Winschel, A., Zecha, D., Lienhart, R.: A closer look: small object detection in faster R-CNN. In: 2017 IEEE International Conference on Multimedia and Expo (ICME), pp. 421–426. IEEE (2017)
6. Everingham, M., Van Gool, L., Williams, C.K., Winn, J., Zisserman, A.: The pascal visual object classes (VOC) challenge. Int. J. Comput. Vis. **88**(2), 303–338 (2010)
7. Hsieh, K., et al.: Focus: querying large video datasets with low latency and low cost. In: 13th {USENIX} Symposium on Operating Systems Design and Implementation ({OSDI} 2018), pp. 269–286 (2018)
8. Kang, D., Emmons, J., Abuzaid, F., Bailis, P., Zaharia, M.: NoScope: optimizing neural network queries over video at scale. arXiv preprint arXiv:1703.02529 (2017)
9. Lin, T.Y., Dollár, P., Girshick, R., He, K., Hariharan, B., Belongie, S.: Feature pyramid networks for object detection. In: Proceedings of the IEEE Conference on Computer Vision and Pattern Recognition, pp. 2117–2125 (2017)
10. Oh, S., et al.: A large-scale benchmark dataset for event recognition in surveillance video. In: CVPR 2011, pp. 3153–3160. IEEE (2011)
11. Zeng, D., Zhu, M., Kuijper, A.: Combining background subtraction algorithms with convolutional neural network. J. Electron. Imaging **28**(1), 013011 (2019)

Edge AI System Using a Thermal Camera for Industrial Anomaly Detection

Vítor M. Oliveira🆔 and António H. J. Moreira$^{(\boxtimes)}$ 🆔

2Ai – School of Technology, IPCA, Barcelos, Portugal
`a13062@alunos.ipca.pt, amoreira@ipca.pt`

Abstract. Predictive maintenance plays an important role in reducing long-term maintenance costs, unplanned downtime, and improving the lifetime of industrial machines. A common trait of machines is that they produce heat while working, resulting in a temperature pattern. Temperature can be a key parameter for monitoring the condition of machines, further aiding the diagnostics of problems. This paper presents an Internet of Things (IoT) system that monitors and detects thermal anomalies in industrial machines using deep neural networks (DNNs). The proposed system enables the DNN to run and make predictions inside a microcontroller, reducing the amount of data that needs to be transmitted to any external server. Furthermore, this system uses a platform that centralizes multiple sensors with the option of communicating with a server that runs two additional neural networks that are specialized in highlighting zones of interest in the thermal image and monitoring the temperature behavior over time. The system was tested in a laboratory and two industrial environments. Overall, the system performed well and can detect machine anomalies while also drastically reducing the amount of data needed to be transmitted. The system also presented high adaptability to different environments.

Keywords: Edge AI · Anomaly detection · Deep neural networks · Thermal camera · Industrial IoT

1 Introduction

Predictive maintenance (PdM) is used to prevent and delay industrial equipment failure. In many industrial areas, it is not economical to shut down machines for maintenance during production, since such interruption will waste time, money, and often the resources being processed [1].

One popular method of PdM is monitoring machines using infrared thermography (IRT) technology. IRT is based on measuring the distribution of radiant thermal energy (heat) emitted from a target surface and converting this to a surface temperature map or thermogram. Thermal energy is present with the operation of all machines. It can be in the form of friction losses, energy losses, or any combination thereof. IRT enables early

© ICST Institute for Computer Sciences, Social Informatics and Telecommunications Engineering 2022
Published by Springer Nature Switzerland AG 2022. All Rights Reserved
S. Paiva et al. (Eds.): SmartCity360° 2021, LNICST 442, pp. 172–187, 2022.
https://doi.org/10.1007/978-3-031-06371-8_12

detection of equipment flaws and faulty industrial processes under normal operating conditions, thereby reducing system downtime, catastrophic breakdown, and maintenance costs [2].

Many companies talk about the Industrial Internet of Things (IIoT) and the potential of connecting multiple physical assets to the Internet. However, expanding the number of sensors means larger amounts of data, and data will be useless unless there is someone or something to interpret it. With near real-time data streaming in, it is very difficult for a person to visualize small changes in images or graphs that may indicate the beginning of anomalies. Machine Learning helps to pinpoint areas for someone to focus their time on. The computer deals with the monitoring and warns the analyst, so he can focus on meaningful anomalies.

The main strategies of PdM are based on three techniques: 1) Regression Models that predict the machine's remaining useful time (RUL); 2) Flagging Anomalous Behaviour; 3) Classification Models to predict failure in a time frame. The description of these techniques is very related to the workflow of popular machine learning methods, and in fact, modern implementations of PdM are focused on using machine learning models like: ARIMA [3], Random Forests [4] or CNN's [5].

The trend towards combining machine learning with PdM raises the question of whether machine failures can be easily predicted. Although technological developments have improved the possibilities for companies to cope with machine breakdowns, their practical application is still a challenging task for many reasons [6].

This paper proposes a small and low-cost device that can silently monitor a machine and send data to the server only when it detects an anomaly. Specifically, it runs a convolutional neural network (CNN) inside an ESP32 microcontroller to detect anomalous patterns in thermal images. When moving large amounts of data across the wide-area network (WAN), monetary costs, transmission delays, and privacy leakage can become a major concern as more devices are added to a company's network. The alternative is using edge devices that process all data locally and extract specific insights, transmitting only the necessary information to the end-user. This reduces the bandwidth consumption, allowing the expansion of IoT devices without the need to exponentially expand the company's resources [7]. The system developed also runs two deep neural networks on a server with the purpose of reinforcing anomaly detection and improving user decision-making.

2 Related Work

The compression of complex mathematical models such as neural networks to fit smaller embedded systems is becoming a field of interest for IoT since it enables these systems to become intelligent and make decisions without user intervention.

F. Funk et al. [8] introduced a system that utilizes a neural network inside a microcontroller to automatically control the speed of a DC motor. The algorithm runs on an Arm Cortex-Mo microcontroller with only 4 kB of RAM and can adapt the motor's desired speed to changes in motor characteristics, e.g., heating or wear-out.

P. Andrade et al. [9] implemented an unsupervised TinyML solution based on the TEDA algorithm inside an Arduino Nano 33 IoT to detect road anomalies and changes using the accelerometer sensor data embedded in a vehicle. The authors concluded that the experiments could detect potholes, bumps, and obstacles.

Also, G. Cerutti et al. [10] used a CNN model in an ARM-Cortex-M4 based microcontroller to detect people's presence with a low-resolution thermal image acquired by the 8x8 infrared sensor Grid-EYE. The system required minimal power to continuously classify images using only 6kB of RAM.

M. Kraft et al. [11] described a system to estimate the density of people in a space, facilitating energy savings in buildings. It uses a U-Net model inside a Raspberry Pi 4 that gathers thermal images using the infrared sensor MLX90640.

Although solutions on the edge are growing, to the best of the author's knowledge, there are still few designed to tackle the recent problems in the industry as discussed earlier.

The rest of this paper will be divided into four sections. Sect. 2 will describe the methods used to develop the system. Sect. 3 will discuss the experiments made in a laboratory setup and in two industrial environments. Sect. 4 will discuss the results obtained for each experiment. The paper ends in Sect. 5 by drawing the conclusions and discussing the implications and future work of this project.

3   Methodology

3.1   System Overview and Prototype

The overall system (Fig. 1) is divided into three parts. The main part represented in Fig. 1 (a), shows the edge system which gathers a thermal image and predicts anomalies inside the microcontroller. The second part defined in Section (b) of Fig. 1 is the communication bridge between the device and the user dashboard. The last part described in Fig. 1 (c). is a server that runs two complex neural network models to give more information to the user. The dashboard and neural networks server were tested on an Intel Core i7-7500U 2.70GHz 12GB RAM laptop.

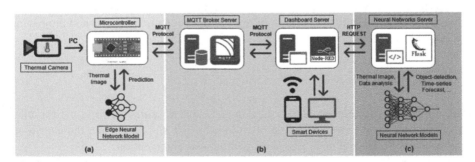

Fig. 1. Overview of the system, (a) Edge System, (b) Dashboard, (c) Neural Networks Server.

3.2 Acquisition Hardware

Thermal Imaging. The system uses the low-cost thermal infrared sensor MLX90640 with 32×24 pixels produced by Melexis. Although it presents a low resolution, it has already been utilized in security smart systems for human localization and action recognition [12], so it has the potential to gather the characteristics of industrial machines. The module can also measure object temperatures between –40 °C to 300 °C which is enough range for testing the system in various industrial machines (e.g., many motors or hydraulic presses overheat below 200 °C).

Edge Processing Unit. The processing unit is the ESP-WROOM-32. This module was selected among other Microcontroller Units (MCUs) for being a cheap and low-power system, having a dual-core microprocessor, and for the built-in Wi-Fi antenna. It also has 520 KB of on-chip SRAM, which is enough memory to gather the thermal sensor data and process it with a quantized feed-forward deep convolutional neural network (CNN). The MCU also includes a 4 MiB flash memory that can store the CNN model architecture and weights [13].

3.3 Software Solution

ThermalCheck Device. As shown in Fig. 1 (a), the system uses the IR camera to collect images. The images are transmitted to the microcontroller via the I^2C protocol and then are sent to an embedded convolutional neural network (CNN) that classifies the thermal images. The predictions are sent to an external server using the MQTT protocol. This protocol is optimized for sending lightweight messages over high-latency or unreliable networks, which is well-suited for IoT devices [14].

Tiny ML Implementation. The CNN running on the edge device was trained on a computer using the Keras (2.2.4) library in Python (3.6.7). First, the images, which are in a float array of 768 positions, are sent to the computer via Wi-Fi or USB port. Then, the array is converted to an image and manually labelled with the corresponding class. In the model's training phase, data augmentation was used to increase the size and variability of the dataset, which overall improves the training process [15]. The model was then exported to the MCU if it performed well on new images.

Using the tinymlgen library from EloquentArduino[1], the finished model is converted to a C file byte array optimized so it can fit on the microcontroller [16]. The model is stored in the flash memory of the microcontroller. The MCU uses the TensorFlow Lite Micro library to read the converted model and make predictions. This library is prepared to receive as input the 768-pixel array directly from the camera.

Back Office. The back office (BO) converts the information processed by the microcontroller to visual feedback for the user. The BO is split into two servers: the first receives the data and presents the information to the user, and the second processes the data further using two neural networks to give more insight to the user. This second server is designed to be mostly inactive and turn on only at a specific time to target a specific machine and help the operator decide if, in fact, it has a fault.

---

[1] https://github.com/eloquentarduino/tinymlgen.

Dashboard Server. In Fig. 1 (b), the link between the edge system and the interface is an MQTT Broker, which routes all messages from one client to another. The system used both a local broker installed on a laptop, and a public Eclipse Mosquitto broker to transmit data over the Internet. The dashboard was made in Node-RED, which is a flow-based platform to connect hardware devices with online services.

The MQTT topics transmitted from Node-Red to the MCU are string sequences that control the microcontroller behavior. Conversely, the MCU transmits the thermal image and the predictions as float arrays and the interface extracts and displays relevant information for the user, e.g., the ratio of anomalies for all predictions and temperature statistics (average, maximum and minimum values).

Since some images received on the dashboard had imperfections related to interferences, a function was developed to ignore images with unrealistic temperature values. This function was implemented to compute the average temperature of any location in the image and is defined by the following equation:

$$t_c = \frac{\sum\limits_{i=a-k}^{a+k}\sum\limits_{j=b-k}^{b+k} p_{i,j}}{(k*2+1)^2} \tag{1}$$

where a, b is the image starting position at the central pixel of the kernel, k is the width of the kernel in relation to the central pixel, and $p_{i,j}$ is the pixel value at position i, j. This function is also useful to monitor areas of interest in the thermal image.

Neural Networks Server. The neural networks server shown in Fig. 1 (c) is made using FLASK, which is a Python framework to build web applications. It receives the thermal image and temperature statistics from Node-RED via an HTTP Request and uses them as input to a temporal anomaly detection model and a pattern detection model. The output of these networks is then sent back to Node-RED. The time of prediction for these models is dependent on the delay placed on the MCU image gathering process, which by default is 5 s.

1. Temporal Anomaly Detection
   The first server-based model is based on temporal anomaly detection. Whenever a temperature pattern changes in a working industrial machine, it may be a sign that the machine may soon come to a fault. It was studied two different approaches to analyze the temperature of these machines over time.

   The first was using a neural network model approach with a Long-Short Term Memory (LSTM). LSTMs are useful for learning sequences containing longer-term patterns of unknown length, due to their ability to maintain long-term memory [17].

   The LSTM will predict the next temperature value and the standard deviation according to the previous values seen. The standard deviation will act as the confidence level of the model. If there is an unexpected pattern, then the real value will be outside the range of the predicted value deviation, resulting in an anomaly.

   There were four different LSTM methods considered and are explained below:
   - LSTM_2MODELS: This configuration uses one LSTM to predict the next temperature value and another LSTM to predict the next standard deviation.

- LSTM_2OUTS: This configuration only has one LSTM to forecast both temperature and standard deviation values.
- LSTM_DROPOUT: The model uses dropout layers to make the output always different. The standard deviation is calculated with multiple predictions on the same temperature forecast [18].
- LSTM_ROLLING_AFTER: This model predicts only the next temperature value. It then uses a rolling window function which will be detailed in Sect. 4.1 to calculate the deviation using the predicted temperatures

  The second approach was using the seasonal stochastic model SARIMA. This model uses autoregression and moving windows to forecast the next value and the confidence intervals. It needs cyclical data arranged in seasonal patterns [19].

  After analysing the two approaches, it was found that SARIMA had better performance with a small dataset, but it failed to fit a larger dataset with increased pattern variation resulting in unstable predictions. On the contrary, this does not occur with LSTMs, which train better and overfit less with bigger datasets and variation [20]. For this reason, it was chosen to focus on LSTMs for temporal anomaly detection.

2. Pattern Detection

  The second server-based model locates and classifies anomalous patterns in thermal images. Currently, the YOLO network is one of the most used models for predictions on thermal images. According to M. Kristo et al. [21], using the YOLOv3 model achieved excellent results in person detection in difficult weather conditions for a sophisticated video vigilance system. It was compared to other modern models and achieved similar results while being faster. Also, A. Banuls et al. [22] utilized the YOLOv3 architecture for detecting objects in search and rescue scenes and reported a good performance of the model in both RGB and thermal images.

  The YOLOv3 model is made for complex object detection tasks (e.g., human tracking, vehicle detection). Since the thermal camera resolution is very low, the level of detail and variation is also lacking, which makes training with the standard model inefficient since most of the layers are not necessary since deeper convolutions try to find details in images. Instead, it was used the YOLOv3-Tiny which is a smaller version using only a 24 layers model compared to the standard, which has 106 layers. The tiny version has increased detection speed and works well in smaller datasets while ensuring good detection accuracy [23].

4 Experiments

The validation of the system was split into two phases: first, a laboratory test to check the performance of the system; and second, deploying the system in an industrial environment to validate it with working machinery as seen in Fig. 2.

4.1 Laboratory Setup

The laboratory experiment seen in Fig. 2 (a), uses a controlled setup that can be manipulated to test many aspects of the system's capabilities.

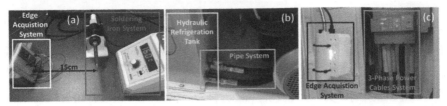

Fig. 2. Experiments Overview: (a) Laboratorial Setup, (b) Hydraulic Refrigeration Setup, (c) 3-Phase Power Cable Setup.

Hardware Setup. The setup consisted of a soldering iron with an adjusted temperature. The iron's normal operation was set to 160 °C. It was placed in the center of the thermal camera lens from 15 cm to 25 cm. The close-up images are shown in Fig. 3.

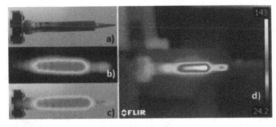

Fig. 3. Laboratorial Experiment: (a) soldering iron, (b) thermal image, (c) merge between image (a) and (b), (d) Ground-Truth thermal image using the FLIR C3 thermal camera.

Edge Neural Network. For the edge model, the dataset was split in four classes of 500 images each. The classes are: "Initial" (iron is at 40 °C–100 °C), "Nominal" (iron is at 100°–160 °C), "Nothing" (iron is at 35°C or less.), and "Anomaly". In the Anomaly class, the images were created synthetically by obstructing the iron with different objects changing the thermal pattern. Although, this class does not represent a scenario of a real fault in a soldering iron, it could show if the model is able to distinguish patterns changes on a low-res thermal image.

The dataset was split into an 80/20 ratio in a train and validation set since it is one of the most common ratios with good results for learning [24]. The data passes through an augmentation function which randomly tweaks the images with horizontal flips, rotations of 0–10°, width/height shifts of 0–10%, axis shears and zooms of 0–10%. The data was also normalized by dividing all pixels by 300 °C (Sect. 3.2).

The CNN model was trained for 300 epochs with a batch-size of 32 samples and using the Adam optimizer with a learning rate of 1e-03.

After optimizing the network to a C file, the model size was 761 KB. Keeping in mind that the model needs to fit into a microcontroller with limited resources, the network has 30.484 parameters with the following architecture (Table 1):

Table 1. Edge CNN model.

Layer	Filters / Neurons	Kernel Size	Activation Function
Convolution 2D	4	3×3	RELU
Max Pooling 2D	–	2×2	–
Convolution 2D	6	3×3	RELU
Convolution 2D	6	3×3	RELU
Flatten	–		
Dense	64		RELU
Dense	4		SOFTMAX

Temporal Anomaly Detection. The temperature forecast dataset was created using a 5 V relay module controlled by an Arduino that switched on and off the soldering iron with a two-minute delay in between. Using (1) on the iron core, the images collected are converted in a time-scries format by calculating the average temperature of the iron with a kernel of 5×5 pixels.

The standard deviation dataset was created by passing the temperature dataset through a moving standard deviation function defined as:

$$z_k = \sqrt{\frac{\sum_{i=k-m+1}^{k} (y_i - \overline{y})^2}{m-1}} \quad \forall k = 1, \ldots, n \tag{2}$$

where m is the window size, n is the number of metric values, y_i is the metric value at the element i^{th}, and $\overline{y}$ is the average of the metric.

After testing multiple windows, the best fit was using the five previous samples.

Both datasets have 464 samples split in a 70/30 ratio between the train and validation sets and normalized by 300 °C. To choose the best LSTM configuration, the four models were trained for 300 epochs with a batch-size of 8, using the Adam optimizer (learning rate of 1e-03) and with mean squared error as the loss function.

The architecture was equal for all configurations using two LSTM layers with 50 neurons each followed by a dense layer with one neuron. In the network with dropout, those layers were added after each LSTM layer and the scenario with the least error found was using 10% dropout. They were evaluated using the following four metrics and the results are presented in Table 2:

- Loss: the minimum loss value of the model.
- Test RMSE: the root mean squared error (RMSE) of the temperature predictions compared to the validation data.
- Deviation RMSE: The RMSE of the predicted standard deviation compared to the validated standard deviation created using (2).
- Processing Time: The average model processing time based on 100 predictions.

Table 2. LSTM configuration results. Test and Deviation RMSE are in Celsius (°C).

	Loss	Test RMSE	Deviation RMSE	Processing time (s)
LSTM_2MODELS	2e-05^2, 0.0678^3	1.8689	**1.5003**	0.0868
LSTM_2OUTS	0.0323	*2.7110*	1.7115	0.0570
LSTM_DROPOUT	2.1e-05	1.6993	1.6035	*1.1114*
LSTM_ROLLING_AFTER	1.9e-05	1.5953	1.8702	**0.0457**

Based on the table, the model selected was the first configuration which had the lowest total RMSE. The second configuration had the worst Test RMSE, and the third had a very slow processing time. The fourth configuration's drawback, albeit displaying good results, is that the standard deviation is fully dependent on the predicted temperature, which always comes with an error. A visual representation of the selected configuration can be seen in Fig. 4.

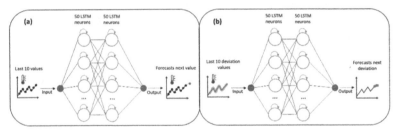

Fig. 4. LSTM_2MODELS configuration. (a) LSTM for temperature forecast. (b) LSTM for temperature deviation forecast.

The best parameters for the temperature forecast model were two LSTM layers with 127 and 24 neurons each, the learning rate was 0.0133, and the best optimizer was Adam. As for the standard deviation forecast, the best model was three LSTM layers with 47, 39, and 63 neurons, the learning rate of 9.09e-04, and the Adam optimizer. To decrease the false anomalies detected, the standard deviation was multiplied by three (3-sigma deviation) to increase the tolerance of the model.

Pattern Detection. The dataset for the pattern detection model is made of images from the anomaly class of the edge model. Since the images acquired have small resolution, they are first pre-processed by increasing the resolution ten-fold and passing a median filter to remove noise while preserving sharp edges. This makes the zones of interest in the image stand out, which can facilitate the model learning process.

---

^{2} LSTM for temperature forecast.
^{3} LSTM for standard deviation forecast.

The dataset was created by manually drawing bounding boxes on the gaps made by obstructions on the laboratory iron. The TinyYOLO model was then trained for 100 epochs with 500 images in an 80/20 split.

4.2 Industrial Environment

The system was then tested in a real scenario with a hydraulic refrigeration system and a 3-Phase cable system (Fig. 5).

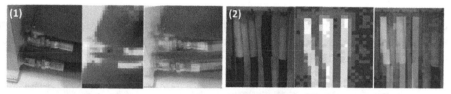

Fig. 5. On the left (1) is the Hydraulic Refrigeration system, the thermal image captured by the MLX90640 sensor, and the merge between images. On the right (2) is the 3-Phase Power Cable system, the thermal image, and the merge between images.

Hydraulic Refrigeration System. The first experiment is monitoring a refrigeration system for a hydraulic press. The setup is shown in Fig. 2 (b) and the close-up in Fig. 5 (1). This system has a refrigeration tank and two pipes. The edge device gathered images every five seconds for four days. It was extracted from every image the mean temperature of the tank and the two pipes using a 3×3 kernel using (1).

The dataset was split into four classes like the previous experiment. To train the edge model, it was necessary to create anomalies synthetically, since in the limited time that the camera gathered images, there were no reports of them. The anomalies were created by changing the pixels of the thermal images from 10–20 °C specifically on the tank and the two pipes. The model architecture was changed to meet the pattern complexity by adding a Max Pooling Layer 2D with a kernel of 2×2 between the last two convolution layers and increasing those layer's filters to 8. The model was trained in an 80/20 split with 1000 images in each class for 100 epochs with the rest of the parameters equal to the previous experiment.

For the Temporal Anomaly Detection, the model was trained to forecast the temperature of the refrigeration tank in the same way as in the laboratory experiment with the difference of using a batch-size of 32 to meet a larger dataset of 7714 samples.

The pattern detection model was not evaluated due to the limited time of the experiment. However, the model would be useful to extract the positions of the tank and pipes to calculate more accurate temperatures of the refrigeration components and use that data in the Temporal Anomaly Detection model.

3-Phase Power Cable. The final experiment was monitoring a 3-phase power cable as shown in Fig. 2 (c). The camera was focused on the electric board, which had four cables seen on Fig. 5 (2). The images were gathered every five seconds for two days. The same logic from the previous experiment was also applied for this one. The edge model dataset had 900 images for each of the four classes. As for the Temporal Anomaly Detection, the model was trained with samples of the red wire. The dataset had a total of 5882 samples.

5   Results

The main goal of this work was to evaluate the viability of the edge system The system was tested in a laboratory, and it was further validated in two industrial environments. The implementation of the three models in the interface is displayed in Fig. 6.

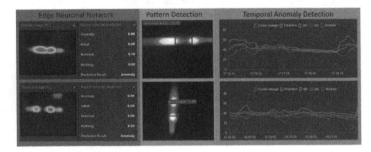

Fig. 6. Interface Models Result. In the graphs the x-axis is time and y-axis is in degrees (°C).

5.1   Laboratory Evaluation

The edge model predicted most images correctly having a validation accuracy of 94.37% with a f1-score of 92.25%. In Fig. 7 (a), are displayed five predictions of this model for all classes.

As for the Temporal Anomaly Detection (Fig. 8 (a)), the model did not correctly fit some parts of the dataset, resulting in false anomalies. The main reason for this is that the training samples were too low for the model to learn the pattern correctly.

Despite that, the model predicted the rest of the dataset correctly, having a Test RMSE of 1.4931 °C and a Deviation RMSE of 0.3535 °C.

The pattern detection model had problems fitting the data, resulting in underwhelming results. Even though the model predicted some of the anomalies, the score was always less than 70%. The model validation loss was 4.11.

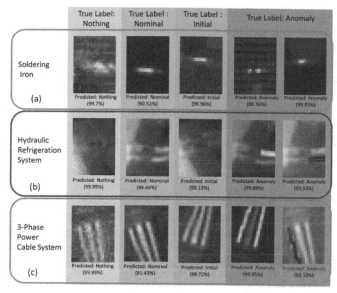

Fig. 7. Edge Neural Network Model Predictions. (a) Soldering Iron, (b) Hydraulic Refrigeration System and (c) 3-Phase Power Cable System.

5.2   Industrial Evaluation

In the industrial environment, the evaluations were focused on the Edge Neural Network and the Temporal Anomaly Detection. These models performed better than the previous results, mainly because the dataset had more samples.

The edge model in the hydraulic refrigeration system, as seen in Fig. 7 (b), performed well with a validation accuracy of 99.73% and an f1-score of 99.5%. The model identified all the anomalies, having only a small difficulty distinguishing the "Initial" from the "Nominal" class. The Temporal Anomaly Detection model identified an abnormal peak in the dataset (Fig. 8 (b)). This peak could have happened because of transmission errors, interferences, or obstructions between the camera and the tank, but although this was not a real anomaly, the potential of the network can be seen. The model had a Test RMSE of 0.182 °C, and a Deviation RMSE of 0.07 °C.

As for the 3-phase power cable system, the edge model had a validation accuracy of 98.95% and an f1-score of 98.5%. The predictions are seen in Fig. 7 (c).

The Temporal Anomaly Detection model had a Test RMSE of 0.258 °C and a Deviation RMSE of 0.04 °C. A small part of the test dataset had missing data due to connection issues, which resulted in a strong transition of temperature values which the model picked up as an anomaly (Fig. 8 (c)).

In all experiments, the edge model performed well, with an overall accuracy above 90%, which means that this approach can in fact help companies detect machine anomalies while also cutting the data transmission to minimal levels. The temporal anomaly detection model served as a good support model that could help in identifying different types of anomalies that may escape the edge model. The only step back is that it requires a considerable amount of data to be useful. The pattern detection model did not perform well in finding the anomalies in the dataset, which, for the most part, is due to the smaller resolution of the thermal camera and the quality of the dataset acquired. This model, however, still presents great potential for improving the accuracy of the temporal anomaly detection model.

6 Conclusions

This work presented the design and evaluation of a low-cost edge system that monitors thermal patterns of industrial machines and detects anomalies. The proposed system presented good results and showed high adaptability to different setups.

Overall, the edge system took less than a second to gather and process the thermal image, feed it to the CNN and have a prediction ready to send to the external server. This system can send the predictions and the thermal image to the server if there needs to be a deeper analysis on the machine, but the major benefit is that it can process everything inside and only when an anomaly occurs, transmit data to the server.

As for future work, further investigation of the pattern detection model is needed by testing other pre-processing options, improving the dataset quality, and verifying if it improves the detection score. It is also considered a strong option to test and compare it with other state-of-the-art object detection models.

Acknowledgment. This project was funded by national funds (PIDDAC), through the FCT – Fundação para a Ciência e Tecnologia and FCT/MCTES under the scope of the project UIDB/05549/2020 and through the special FCT program "Verão Com Ciência" with the project 2Ai Summer School (process 77, 20/229). Moreover, it was also funded by SmartHealth "NORTE-01-0145-FEDER-000045", supported by Northern Portugal Regional Operational Programme (Norte2020), under the Portugal 2020 Partnership Agreement, through the European Regional Development Fund (FEDER).

Appendix

Temporal Anomaly Detection Results

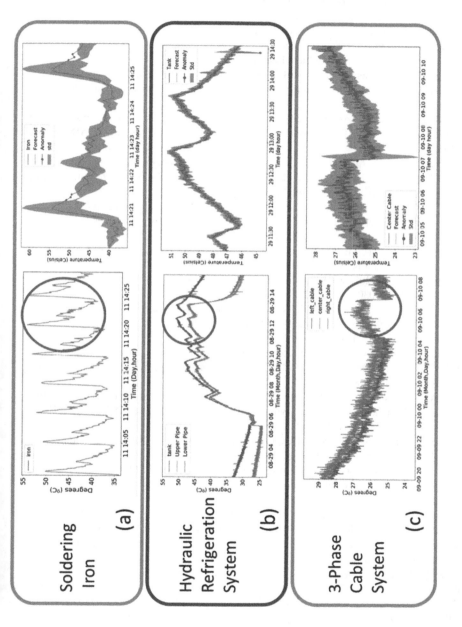

Fig. 8. Temporal Anomaly Detection Model results. (a) Soldering Iron, (b) Hydraulic Refrigeration System and (c) 3-Phase Power Cable System.

References

1. Zhu, Z., et al.: Preventive maintenance subject to equipment unavailability. IEEE Trans. Reliab. (2019). https://doi.org/10.1109/tr.2019.2913331
2. Bagavathiappan, S., Lahiri, B.B., Saravanan, T., Philip, J., Jayakumar, T.: Infrared thermography for condition monitoring - a review, Infrared Phys. Technol. **60**, 35-55 (2013) https://doi.org/10.1016/j.infrared.2013.03.006
3. Kanawaday, A., Sane, A.: Machine Learning for Predictive Maintenance of Industrial Machines using IoT Sensor Data (2018) https://doi.org/10.1109/ICSESS.2017.8342870
4. Paolanti, M., et al.: Machine Learning approach for Predictive Maintenance in Industry 4.0. (2018) https://doi.org/10.1109/MESA.2018.8449150
5. Sun, W., Liu, J., Yue, Y.: AI-enhanced offloading in edge computing: when machine learning meets industrial IoT. IEEE Netw. **33**(5), 68–74 (2019). https://doi.org/10.1109/MNET.001.1800510
6. Kammerer, K., et al.: Anomaly detections for manufacturing systems based on sensor data—insights into two challenging real-world production settings. Sensors (Switzerland) **19**(24), 5370 (2019). https://doi.org/10.3390/s19245370
7. Zhou, Z., Chen, X., Li, E., Zeng, L., Luo, K., Zhang, J.: Edge intelligence: paving the last mile of artificial intelligence with edge computing. Proc. IEEE **107**(8), 1738–1762 (2019). https://doi.org/10.1109/JPROC.2019.2918951
8. Funk, F., Bucksch, T., Mueller-Gritschneder, D.: ML training on a tiny microcontroller for a self-adaptive neural network-based DC motor speed controller. In: Gama, J., et al. (eds.) ITEM/IoT Streams -2020. CCIS, vol. 1325, pp. 268–279. Springer, Cham (2020). https://doi.org/10.1007/978-3-030-66770-2_20
9. Andrade, P., et al.: An Unsupervised TinyML Approach Applied for Pavement Anomalies Detection Under the Internet of Intelligent Vehicles (2021) https://doi.org/10.1109/MetroInd4.0IoT51437.2021.9488546
10. Cerutti, G., Prasad, R., Farella, E.: Convolutional Neural Network on Embedded Platform for People Presence Detection in Low Resolution Thermal Images (2019) https://doi.org/10.1109/ICASSP.2019.8682998
11. Kraft, M., Aszkowski, P., Pieczyński, D., Fularz, M.: Low-cost thermal camera-based counting occupancy meter facilitating energy saving in smart buildings. Energies **14**(15), 4542 (2021). https://doi.org/10.3390/en14154542
12. Spasov, G., et al.: Using IR Array MLX90640 to Build an IoT Solution for ALL and Security Smart Systems. (2019) https://doi.org/10.1109/ET.2019.8878637
13. Maier, A., Sharp, A., Vagapov, Y.: Comparative analysis and practical implementation of the ESP32 microcontroller module for the internet of things. (2017) https://doi.org/10.1109/ITECHA.2017.8101926
14. Masdani, M.V., Darlis, D.: A Comprehensive Study on MQTT as a Low Power Protocol for Internet of Things Application. (2018) https://doi.org/10.1088/1757-899X/434/1/012274
15. Mikołajczyk, A., Grochowski, M.: Data augmentation for improving deep learning in image classification problem. (2018) https://doi.org/10.1109/IIPHDW.2018.8388338
16. Dokic, K.: Microcontrollers on the edge – is ESP32 with camera ready for machine learning? In: El Moataz, A., Mammass, D., Mansouri, A., Nouboud, F. (eds.) ICISP 2020. LNCS, vol. 12119, pp. 213–220. Springer, Cham (2020). https://doi.org/10.1007/978-3-030-51935-3_23
17. Malhotra, P., Vig, L., Shroff, G., Agarwal, P.: Long Short Term Memory Networks for Anomaly Detection in Time Series. (2015)
18. Gal, Y., Ghahramani, Z.: Dropout as a Bayesian approximation: Representing model uncertainty in deep learning. (2016)

19. Chen, P., et al.: Time Series Forecasting of Temperatures using SARIMA: An Example from Nanjing. (2018) https://doi.org/10.1088/1757-899X/394/5/052024
20. Ying, X.: An Overview of Overfitting and its Solutions. (2019) https://doi.org/10.1088/1742-6596/1168/2/022022
21. Kristo, M., et al.: Thermal object detection in difficult weather conditions using YOLO. IEEE Access**8**, 125459-125476 (2020), https://doi.org/10.1109/ACCESS.2020.3007481
22. Banuls, A., et al.: Object Detection from Thermal Infrared and Visible Light Cameras in Search and Rescue Scenes. (2020) https://doi.org/10.1109/SSRR50563.2020.9292593
23. Adarsh, P., Rathi, P., Kumar, M.: YOLO v3-Tiny: Object Detection and Recognition using one stage improved model. (2020) https://doi.org/10.1109/ICACCS48705.2020.9074315
24. Gholamy, A., Kreinovich, V., Kosheleva, O.: Why 70/30 or 80/20 relation between training and testing sets : a pedagogical explanation. Dep. Tech. Reports (2018)
25. Huda, A.S.N., Taib, S.: Application of infrared thermography for predictive/preventive maintenance of thermal defect in electrical equipment. Appl. Therm. Eng. **61**(2), 220–227 (2013). https://doi.org/10.1016/j.applthermaleng.2013.07.028

Power Consumption Analysis for the Development of Energy Efficient Bluetooth 5 Based Real-Time Industrial IoT Systems

Iván Froiz-Míguez$^{(\boxtimes)}$ (iD), Paula Fraga-Lamas (iD),
and Tiago M. Fernández-Caramés (iD)

Department of Computer Engineering, Centro de Investigación CITIC, Universidade
da Coruña, 15071 A Coruña, Spain
{ivan.froiz,paula.fraga,tiago.fernandez}@udc.es

Abstract. Recent improvements in embedded device hardware have led
to increased performance and energy-efficiency, enabling the development
of new low-power Industrial IoT (IIoT) solutions. When it comes to the
development of energy efficient industrial systems, the most commonly
used options are Low Power Wide Area Networks (LPWAN) technologies. However, these sub-Gigahertz technologies are often limited in terms
of transmission due to duty cycle, so they are not a viable option when it
comes to sending constant data flows in real time. The 2.4 GHz band is
an option for these cases and, for power-constrained devices, Bluetooth is
a reference technology in terms of low power consumption. Nevertheless,
communications have frequently a short range, so it is usually difficult to
use it in IIoT harsh scenarios. To tackle these issues, the new Bluetooth
5 standard introduces a new transmission mode (Bluetooth 5 LE Coded)
that allows a longer range, thus improving the link budget and providing
an increase of the sensitivity. In this paper, we analyze the power consumption, transmission times and range of a real-time IIoT system developed on Bluetooth 5, comparing its results with the Bluetooth Legacy
version. For this purpose, several tests were carried out with different
configuration parameters and in different transmission modes. The performed experiments allow for concluding that LE Coded offers significant
advantages respect to Legacy with similar power consumption.

Keywords: Bluetooth 5 · Power consumption · Energy efficiency ·
Real-time · Coverage · IIoT

1 Introduction

The latest advances in the technologies involved in the IoT paradigm have progressed significantly, and more and more solutions are being offered by the manufacturers to improve diverse features. One of such features, which is common
to the developers of most IoT technologies, is power consumption, since devices

S. Paiva et al. (Eds.): SmartCity360° 2021, LNICST 442, pp. 188–206, 2022.
https://doi.org/10.1007/978-3-031-06371-8_13

are becoming more efficient in terms of energy, which makes it possible to use alternative power supply mechanisms like energy harvesting.

Another aspect in which there is a variety of alternatives is the communications between the devices, which can be deployed conforming different topologies, such as stars, mesh networks, rings or trees. The technology of the communications link can also vary: while some technologies are designed for long range and low-frequency data transmission, others have been devised for short range and more frequent transmissions. For instance, the most popular Low-Power Wide-Area Network (LPWAN) technologies make use of star topologies and have been devised for long range communications. To achieve such long ranges, sub-1 GHz bands are used, whose use may involve certain data transmission restrictions, like the existence of duty cycles for technologies that operate in license-exempt bands (e.g., LoRaWAN) to avoid excessive channel occupancy.

A frequency band that is widely used by IoT technologies is the 2.4 GHz Industrial, Scientific and Medical (ISM) band. There is a significant number of technologies that use this band for IoT applications, including ZigBee, Bluetooth, WiFi (i.e., IEEE 802.11 b/g/n/ac) or Thread. The devices that make use of such technologies tend to operate in the opposite way to the ones that make use of LPWAN technologies, as there are no duty-cycle restrictions for sending data, but they can use low transmit power levels if they are operating on constrained power sources.

Bluetooth is an example of a widely used communications technology for low-power short-range devices like wearables or real-time monitoring sensors [1]. The latest version of Bluetooth (Bluetooth 5) has improved numerous aspects of the protocol, providing more bandwidth and better response times, as well as increased range and less power consumption [2]. This paper presents a development based on such a new Bluetooth standard, which was used by the authors through the Joint Research Unit between UDC and Navantia [3] for creating a sensor to monitor oxygen concentration levels. The main objective of the developed system is to provide oxygen level measurements and display alarms in confined spaces, where oxygen concentration levels may vary due to certain tasks performed by industrial operators (e.g., argon welding). Specifically, such oxygen concentration levels can be displayed in real time and alarms are triggered when the oxygen level drops below a certain level or when the Bluetooth connection is lost.

The system presented in this paper is intended for being used in industrial environments, where, due to electromagnetic interference and shielding from metal objects, it is particularly challenging to achieve stable real-time communications. This can be accomplished thanks to the use of the Bluetooth LE Coded mode, which reduces the data rate to 125 Kb/s and adds more data to the frame to make use of error correction, which enables to decode the frame up to 4 times farther without increasing the transmission power. This provides extra sensitivity and improves the link budget, which is important in industrial environments. However, it should be noted that, although the use of LE Coded does not imply an increase in transmission power, sending longer frames involves longer transmission times (up to 8 times longer), which increases energy consumption and is not valid for all situations (as it will be discussed later in Sect. 4).

The rest of this article is structured as follows. After reviewing the background knowledge in Sect. 2 and describing the developed system in Sects. 3, 4 and 5 analyze the key aspects that impact the energy consumption of Bluetooth 5 in the developed system. Finally, Sect. 6 is devoted to the conclusions.

2   Background

2.1   Wireless Low-Power Communications: Bluetooth Versus ZigBee

The IIoT system proposed in this paper was designed to make use of the 2.4 GHz band to take advantage of time-unrestricted transmissions. In such a band, there are several wireless technologies that provide low power features, being ZigBee, which is based on the IEEE 802.15.4 standard, one of the most popular.

Bluetooth is another low-power technology that has evolved remarkably in the last years. In fact, there are already in the market Bluetooth 5 commercial System-on-Chips (SoCs), like nrf52840 and nrf52833 from Nordic Semiconductor, which are able to act as Bluetooth, ANT, ZigBee 3.0 or Thread 1.1 transceivers. This kind of modules enables the creation of hybrid systems, which can make use of, for example, ZigBee and Bluetooth. However, it must be considered that two radio modules that operate in the same frequency band with different protocols can cause interference and channel saturation problems, especially when there are continuous transmissions, as it was previously analyzed in [4] and [5] (such paper show how interference affects ZigBee when it is used simultaneously with another wireless protocol).

With respect to ZigBee modules, the DigiXbee EFR32MG SoC is widely used. The datasheet provided by the manufacturer specifies an indoor range of 60 m and outdoor range of 1,2 km with a power of 8 dBm [6]. There is also an XBee 3 Pro version that triples the previously mentioned range values of the Digi XBee 3 board, but it makes use of 19 dBm of transmit power, which cannot be supplied in a continuous way by most battery-powered devices.

Dementyev et al. [7] carried out a study that compared Bluetooth Low Energy (BLE) and Zigbee, concluding that BLE was able to achieve a lower consumption than ZigBee. In fact, the results show that, theoretically, BLE has a better ratio between data transfer and consumption, while IEEE 802.15.4 has more coverage range due to better sensitivity. However, the new LE Coded PHY of Bluetooth 5 adds more sensitivity while reducing the bitrate.

Due to the previously mentioned studies, it can be stated that ZigBee does not provide any improvement in sensitivity and range with respect to Bluetooth LE Coded so, the system presented in this paper is based exclusively on Bluetooth.

2.2   Bluetooth Performance

Since Bluetooth have a centimeter wavelength, it is interesting to see how its LE Coded (Long Range) mode works indoors, where there are no Line of Sight

(LoS) communications, as different materials and obstacles will affect the propagation of the signal. For example, Zhan et al. [8] measured the throughput at different indoor distances with all the different Bluetooth 5 PHYs as well as the reception sensitivity. The authors concluded that with the LE Coded PHY (S = 8, 125 Kb/s), it can be obtained the same range and a transmission power of 8 dBm less than the one needed for the Legacy version. Nonetheless, it should be noted that throughput is not a determining factor for most IIoT systems, being more important the reception signal quality.

Another important aspect to analyze is Bluetooth power consumption, since one of the goals of most IIoT developments is to minimize the consumed energy to extend the life of battery-powered devices. In the literature there is a lack of papers on the analysis of Bluetooth 5 energy consumption. One of the exceptions is [9], where the authors analyzed the energy consumption for different connection parameters for Bluetooth 5. In such a paper, the authors showed that, although Bluetooth 5 requires more power than BLE, transmission time is shorter, therefore the overall power consumption of Bluetooth 5 for sending data is lower than for BLE.

In contrast to such a publication, this paper is focused on the LE Coded mode, comparing its impact with the Legacy version and analyzing consumption, transmission times and range. In general, LE Coded mode is used to send periodical data over long distances with the highest power level (similarly to LPWAN technologies). In such a mode, Nordic Semiconductor achieved a range of 1.3 km with Line-of-Sight (LoS) when using two development kits (nRF52840-DK [10]) with a transmission power of 0 dBm [11].

In the case of confined spaces monitoring, a transmission power of 0 dBm, even though it cannot be considered as a high transmit power, it ends up consuming quite a lot of energy if frequent transmissions are performed, so it becomes a problem when operating with a constrained power source. In addition, it is worth considering that the use of the 2.4 GHz ISM band derives into using a centimeter wave that does not have a large penetration factor and, in a closed environment like a confined space, it can become completely blocked in certain areas made of certain materials (e.g., metallic surfaces) and when there is significant electromagnetic noise in the environment. In such circumstances is where the use of the LE Coded mode becomes important.

Finally, the fact that there are actually billions of interconnected IoT devices is a challenge for communications, there are currently numerous mechanisms to manage this growing number of devices connected to the Internet, IPv6 is the main alternative, although its implementation is not being as fast as expected, there are transition mechanisms that allow coexistence. In this aspect 6LoWPAN (IPv6 over Low-Power Wireless Personal Area Networks) offers a very attractive alternative to manage this problem, since it allows Bluetooth devices to connect automatically to the Internet. For instance, R. Amornpornwiwat et al. [12] present a comparison of 6LoWPAN with BLE versus WiFi and Ethernet over IP, being the first one the most energy efficient.

3   Developed System

The developed IIoT system is based on a node that carries a 650 mA LiPo battery, an Arduino Nano 33 BLE (which is based on the nrf52840 SoC) [13], a KE-25 fast-response oxygen sensor [14] and a DHT-22 temperature and humidity sensor. The IIoT node sensor data are collected by mobile devices (e.g., smartphones, tablets) carried by the industrial operators which have to support Bluetooth 5 (for the experiments documented in this paper, a OnePlus 8T smartphone was used). For such a mobile device, an Android application was developed. Figures 1 and 2 show, respectively, the electronic schematic of the IIoT node and the main screen of the developed Android app.

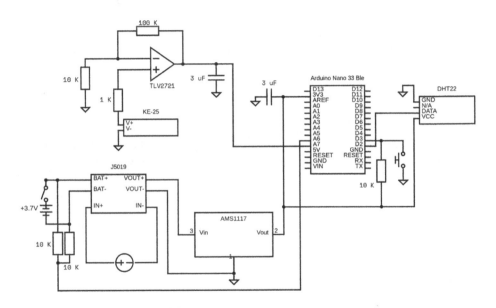

Fig. 1. IIoT node circuit schematic.

For testing and prototyping purposes, Nordic Development Kits were used (in particular, nrf52840-DK [15] and nrf52833-DK [16]). Energy consumption measurements were performed via an oscilloscope (Hanmatek DOS1102) with 110 MHz of bandwidth, 1 GS/s, ±100 ppm of sample rate and a sensitivity of 5 mV/div. Measurements were collected by using a Shunt resistor of 10 Ω. It is important to note that the hardware used for the energy consumption measurements is practical, but it does not provide the best accuracy for measuring low currents in idle or sleep states due to the scale difference. For such a reason, this paper focuses only on the events that consume the most, which are to processing and to the use of the radio module. As a consequence, energy consumption is not measured when the module is in idle or sleep, since it is too low to be quantified accurately with the selected measurement setup.

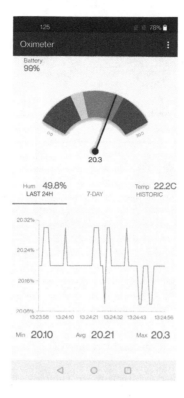

Fig. 2. Main screen of the developed Android application.

Since the developed system needs to be scalable, the energy consumption was tested with different topologies:

- A daisy-chain linear topology, where the nodes can act as sensors and relays, with two Bluetooth interfaces per node (one works as a peripheral GATT and the other one as a central GATT, using the first node as an entry-point for the Bluetooth device.
- Mesh topology. Such a type of topology is more robust, since any node can act as entry point and, being totally decentralized, nodes are able to scan for other nodes in range to retransmit data.

Figures 3(a) and 3(b) show the structure of the two topologies used in the tests.

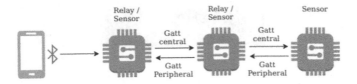

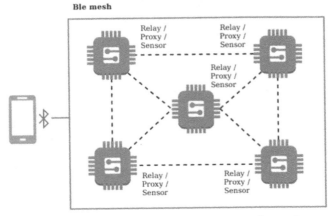

(a) Communications architecture for the daisy-chain linear topology.

(b) Communications architecture of the mesh topology.

Fig. 3. Communications architecture for the daisy-chain linear topology.

4   Experiments and Results

Several tests were performed in order to compare energy consumption and signal coverage when transmitting in different transmission modes. Thus, the objective is to determine the optimal mode for the proposed use case that gives the best balance between consumption, coverage and deployment needs.

4.1   Energy Consumption Tests

The developed prototype described in Sect. 3 was analyzed in terms of consumption. Specifically, consumption tests were performed only for the nrf52833 module. The module internal circuitry allows to measure only the consumption of the SoC, thus isolating the rest of the components. Such an approach provides more fairness when judging the results, since it will only depend on the SoC hardware and on the firmware implemented for each test.

The passive components of the hardware prototype (i.e., power boost, voltage regulator, operational amplifier and voltage divider) consume an average of 10.4 mA.

With respect to the two used sensors, the KE-25 does not consume current: it is based on a galvanic cell that generates an output voltage depending on the oxygen levels. In the case of DHT-22, it performs measurements every 20 s and it has a consumption of 0.3 mA when measuring and 60 μA in standby. Note that, in the tested use cases, temperature and humidity do not fluctuate, so it is usually only necessary to make use of an internal thermistor to correct the calculation of the oxygen levels depending on the ambient temperature.

For the performed tests, a specific firmware was developed for each scenario. For the daisy-chain linear topology, energy consumption was measured for the two operating modes on a Generic Attribute Profile (GATT) connection: data transmission (when there is an established connection) and advertisement mode (when no connections are performed).

The parameters used in the GATT are the following:

- Advertisement time: 120 ms.
- Minimum acceptable connection interval: 20 ms.
- Maximum acceptable connection interval: 75 ms.
- Transfer time: 500 ms.

For the mesh topology, the proxy events (GATT Bearer advertisement and GATT Bearer transmission) and the mesh events (data publish event) were analyzed when using the next parameters:

- GATT Bearer advertisement time: 200 ms.
- Publish time: 500 ms.

Figure 4 shows the power consumption of the main GATT peripheral operation over time. Such a Figure shows a period of 240 ms that allows for observing how energy consumption varies over time: the first area includes two peaks that are related to advertisement events when no devices are connected (during 'LE Coded Advertising'), then a second area ('establish connection') is associated with connection establishment and includes a sequence of 9 peaks. It is important to note that the length of this area depends on the client Received Signal Strength Indicator (RSSI). The third area represents the data sending process, once the device is connected: it includes a peak due to a GATT request, while the next peak is associated with a GATT reply. Finally, the last peak is related to an additional GATT request.

To reduce power consumption, it was first decreased the transmission power. It is worth mentioning that Nordic Semiconductor provides an online tool that allows for estimating power consumption based on various Bluetooth parameters [17]. In particular, the used Bluetooth hardware allows for transmitting at −40 dBm, −30 dBm, −20 dBm, −16 dBm, −12 dBm, −8 dBm, −4 dBm and 0 dBm. Figures 5 and 6 show how energy consumption differs for the advertisement and data sending events when transmitting at −40 dBm, −20 dbm, −8 dBm and 0 dBm, respectively.

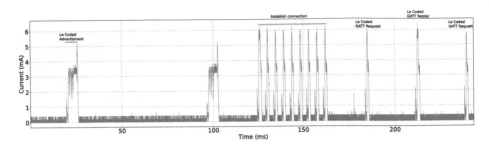

Fig. 4. Energy consumption of the main functionality of the GATT peripheral.

As it can be observed, energy savings for the analyzed Bluetooth events are not especially significant when lowering the transmission power: they go from an average of 4.77 mA in advertising and 3.09 mA in data transmission at 0 dBm, to 2.74 mA and 2.42 mA, respectively, at −40 dBm. The average consumption for each transmit power can be seen in Table 1. Although the consumption is not reduced significantly, the Bluetooth communications range drops dramatically when lowering the power levels, as it will be discussed later on in Sect. 4.3.

Table 1. Average consumption at different power levels for LE Coded mode.

Bluetooth event	−40 dBm	−30 dBm	−20 dBm	−16 dBm	−8 dBm	−4 dBm	0 dBm
Average Advertisement Current (mA)	2.74	2.86	3.12	3.37	3.56	4.06	4.77
Advertisement Energy Consumption (μA h)	138.9	144.9	157.9	170.4	179.9	204.9	240.4
Average Data Transmission Current (mA)	2.42	2.50	2.61	2.69	2.77	2.91	3.09
Data Transmission Energy Consumption (μA h)	5.2	5.3	5.4	5.5	5.6	5.8	6.1

Thus, reducing transmit power lowers power consumption, existing the largest difference when broadcasting advertisements. This is due to the fact that the duration of the advertisements is longer than data payload transmissions, so the average consumption of the peaks for the advertisements is more impacted by changes in transmit power than in the case of data transmission events.

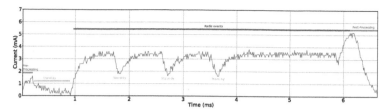

(a) Current consumed during advertising event when transmitting at -40 dBm.

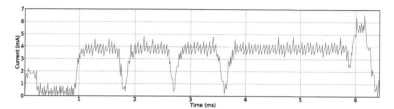

(b) Current consumed during advertising event when transmitting at -20 dBm.

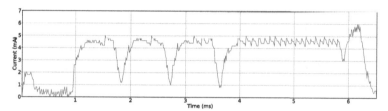

(c) Current consumed during advertising event when transmitting at -8 dBm.

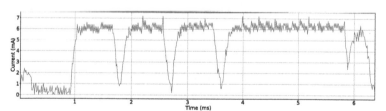

(d) Current consumed during advertising event when transmitting at 0 dBm.

Fig. 5. Power consumption for advertisements transmitted at different power levels.

Another important point to consider is the consumption when using LE Coded mode. This mode allows for improving the communications range up to 4 times the values achieved in Bluetooth Legacy mode (physical layer used on the Bluetooth 4.x standard) when transmitting at the same transmission power. However, LE Coded mode requires more time on air for the transmissions, which implies that is necessary to turn on the radio module more time, deriving into a

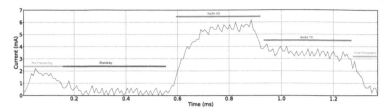

(a) Current consumed during data sending when transmitting at -40 dBm.

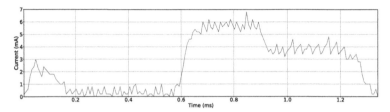

(b) Current consumed during data sending when transmitting at -20 dBm.

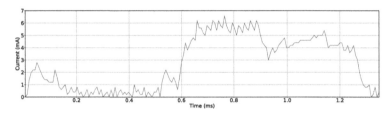

(c) Current consumed during data sending when transmitting at -8 dBm.

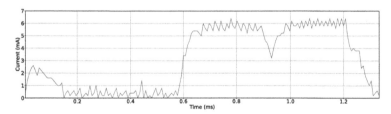

(d) Current consumed during data sending when transmitting at 0 dBm.

Fig. 6. Power consumption comparison when sending data at different power levels.

higher energy consumption. Figure 7 shows the energy consumption of an advertisement and data transmission event when transmitting at −40 dBm in Legacy mode. Such a figure can be compared with the results shown in Figs. 5a and 6a. It can be concluded that the peak values are quite similar but the amplitude of the events is significantly higher in LE Coded, especially in advertising events.

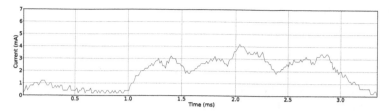

(a) Power consumption of a Legacy advertisement when transmitting at -40 dBm.

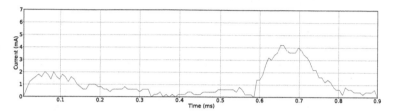

(b) Power consumption of Legacy data sending when transmitting at -40 dBm.

Fig. 7. Legacy events at the same transmission power level.

Table 2 compares the average current and event duration values for Legacy and LE Coded modes when transmitting -40 dBm. As it can be observed in the table, both data transmission and advertisement events in Legacy mode are more energy efficient than in LE Coded mode: they consume on average 1.31 mA less in the case of data transmissions and 0.89 mA less during advertisements. Moreover, the results indicate that advertisements can definitely drain more power, especially in LE Coded mode, since their duration is 3.03 ms longer than in Legacy mode. Nonetheless, it must be noted that, when using GATT peripheral, advertisements are only used when no devices are connected, so an overall lower advertisement time allows for saving energy at the expense of making device reconnections slower. In the case of data transmission events, they last only 0.43 ms more in LE Coded.

Table 2. Power consumption and duration of Bluetooth events in Legacy and LE Coded modes when transmitting at -40 dBm.

Bluetooth event	Avg. current (mA)	Duration (ms)
Data Tx (Legacy mode)	1.11	0.9
Advertisement (Legacy mode)	1.85	3.35
Data Tx (LE Coded mode)	2.42	1.33
Advertisement (LE Coded mode)	2.74	6.38

4.2   Mesh Mode

The GATT client-server mode evaluated in the previous subsection has an important limitation in operation: in a multi-node scenario it is only possible to connect to a single GATT peripheral at the same time. Therefore, when using GATT client-server mode, in order to collect information from a specific node, it is necessary to be physically in the range of such a node, requiring to disconnect from any other node.

In the mentioned multi-node scenario, a more efficient communications alternative consists in conforming a BLE mesh. The mesh is able to create a distributed network where nodes can relay information from others in range and any of them can serve as an entry point to access the network data, thus overcoming the limitation in range derived from the use of centimeter bands. However, the use of a Bluetooth mesh involves three important considerations:

- BLE Mesh is a broadcast-based network protocol, where every device in the network sends and receives all messages to and from all devices within the radio range, which implies that the radio transceiver is running constantly. As a consequence, the power consumption of a regular mesh node should be almost the same as the RX current of the radio. The reason is that the radio has to scan the radio channel continuously for packets, which involves to draw a significant amount of current. However, there is a mesh mode for low consumption: a mesh with Low Power Nodes (LPN) that allows IoT nodes to send data periodically and sleep the rest of time, thus decreasing energy consumption considerably. For instance, Mahdi et al. [18] analyzed the power consumption of an LPN node within a Bluetooth 4.x mesh: with a 235 mA battery and publishing messages every 10 s they achieved a lifetime up to 15.6 months.
- Regarding the previous point, an LPN node is not able to participate actively in the mesh on its own. Such a kind of nodes are used in certain scenarios where battery-operated devices that send periodic data need to be deployed. In such cases, the node may not be able to scan continuously, but still would want to participate in the mesh network to control and communicate with other mesh nodes [19]. The LPN makes use of a special node (Friend node) to participate in the mesh network with significantly shorter scanning duty cycle. Friend nodes can communicate and relay data through other nodes, by re-broadcasting received mesh messages. Since such an operation would require a significant amount of power, nodes need to be typically wall-powered or working with another type of continuous energy source.
- The BLE mesh mode is actually a Bluetooth 4.x standard, so using LE Coded is not supported officially. It is possible to implement a mesh that communicates using LE Coded mode, but it is necessary to consider the longer processing time and preambles of this mode by adjusting times and buffer sizes in the timeslot Application Programming Interface (API) to compensate for the longer on-air packets.

In order to evaluate the consumption performance in mesh mode, an LPN node was tested. Figure 8a shows the power consumption for a data publishing event on an LPN node with -40 dBm of power transmission. Although the showed functionality falls more on the Friend node, it is also possible for an LPN node to function as a proxy, allowing it to be used as an entry point. This functionality is not particularly costly from a usage point of view, since it only has to send advertisements when there is no device connected to the node and use GATT transmissions when it is connected.

Figures 8b and 8c illustrate the energy consumption of the advertisement and GATT transmission events of a proxy LPN node, respectively. It is necessary to take into account that these events are in Legacy mode, as opposed to the LE Coded used in the publication event (Fig. 8a). This is due to the fact that Mesh mode has different layers used by the Bearer (the communications system that is used to transport data). Bluetooth mesh may be used over either of these two bearers: the Advertising Bearer or the GATT Bearer [20].

The Advertising Bearer is used to receive messages and broadcast messages from/to other nodes, while the GATT Bearer allows a device to communicate indirectly with nodes of a mesh network using a protocol known as the Proxy Protocol (which also implies that the mesh node implements the proxy role).

As it was previously mentioned, the mesh mode is a Bluetooth 4.x standard, so, by default, there is no implementation of the LE Coded physical layer. Nevertheless, part of the standard was implemented to make use of the PHY LE Coded. The internal communications of the mesh nodes (GATT Advertisement) was successfully implemented and properly working with this mode. The proxy protocol, in charge of using the nodes as entry point for Bluetooth devices (GATT Bearer), remained in Legacy mode.

It is possible to see the remarkable difference in the event duration between GATT client-server and mesh mode through Figs. 7, 8b and 8c. Both the advertising and the transmission event are much shorter in mesh mode than in GATT client-server mode, due to the fact that the information sent in the events is much smaller.

To further reduce consumption, there are two parameters directly involved, Poll Timeout and Receive Window that can be adjusted. These parameters affect directly the communications between the LPN and the associated Friend node. The LPN wakes up periodically and polls the Friend node for any new messages. The Friend node then delivers associated mesh messages to the LPN. Longer Poll Timeouts mean more time in sleep by the LPN. For longer Poll Timeouts, Receive Window becomes irrelevant [18]. However, for this particular case, since data transfer is fast (set to 500 ms), it is also possible to decrease the Receive Window, which means the radio interface needs to remain less time in receive mode.

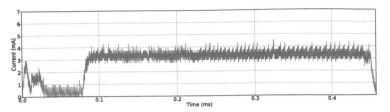

(a) Power consumption for data publishing event on a LPN.

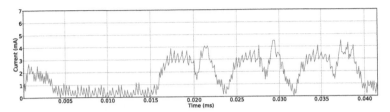

(b) Power consumption for GATT Bearer Advertising event on a LPN.

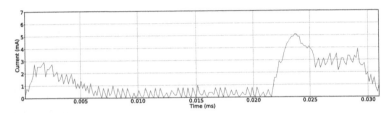

(c) Power consumption for GATT Bearer data transmission event on a LPN.

Fig. 8. Power consumption on a LPN.

4.3 LE Coded Vs Legacy Mode Range

This subsection analyzes the reception quality at different points when making use either of Legacy or LE Coded mode. Figure 9 shows a map of the indoor scenario in which the tests were carried out. Such Figure represents the location of the deployed nodes, as well as their antenna orientation. In this case, two independent tests were carried out: one between spots A and B with the transmission powers indicated in Table 3, and another one between locations C and D with the transmission power showed in Table 4. The mentioned tables show the RSSI values and error rates in reception obtained for each scenario.

The experimental results shown in Tables 3 and 4 indicate that reception is more stable when using LE Coded due to its higher RSSI values (up to -96 dBm in Legacy and -103 dBm in LE Coded, according to the manufacturer datasheet). In addition, the fact that LE Coded mode allows for decoding with a lower RSSI than in Legacy mode, provides an extra sensitivity for packet decoding, which is particularly interesting at points where there is low connection quality.

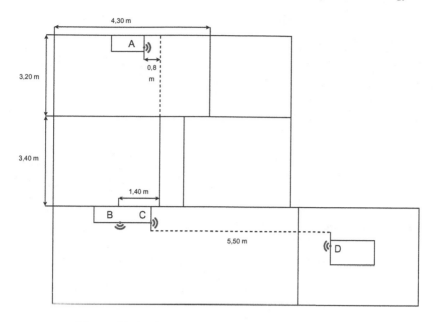

Fig. 9. Nodes layout in the indoor test environment.

At points C and D (Table 4), it can be observed that when transmitting at −40 and −30 dBm, there is a significant impact on the transmission range, losing between 70% and 67% of the packets, respectively, with LE Coded, and every packet in Legacy mode. In contrast, with a power level of −20 dBm there was no loss in both modes. In case of points A and B (Table 3), transmission power values were higher, and a more linear error rate can be observed, but a clear improvement in signal strength is obtained when using LE Coded mode instead of Legacy mode.

Table 3. Coverage results at points A and B

Power level (dBm)	Mode	Error rate (%)	Min. RSSI (dBm)	Max. RSII (dBm)	Avg. RSSI (dBm)
−16	LE Coded	17	−91	−87	−88.4
	Legacy	99	−87	−87	−87
−12	LE Coded	0	−91	−81	−84.7
	Legacy	57	−86	−81	−82.7
−8	LE Coded	0	−90	−79	−83.4
	Legacy	15	−86	−80	−82.4

Table 4. Coverage results at points C and D

Power level (dBm)	Mode	Error rate (%)	Min. RSSI (dBm)	Max. RSSI (dBm)	Avg. RSSI (dBm)
−40	LE Coded	70	−92	−89	−88.9
	Legacy	100	N/A	N/A	N/A
−30	LE Coded	67	−91	−88	−88.4
	Legacy	100	N/A	N/A	N/A
−20	LE Coded	0	−88	−78	−85.4
	Legacy	0	−87	−78	−86.1

5 Key Findings

From all the tests carried out, the following conclusions were obtained:

- There are no considerable savings in power consumption by lowering the transmitter power to the lowest levels. For instance, from −8 dBm to −20 dBm there is difference of only 0.44 mA and 0.16 mA for advertising and transmission events, respectively. The main difference is in airtime, specially in advertisements since make more use of the radio module than transmission events. In LE Coded this is much more noticeable, for instance the data transmission event last 0.43 ms more in LE Coded while the advertisement event takes 3.03 ms more.
- The GATT client/server mode is more energy efficient than the mesh mode. Nevertheless, it is a fairly simple communications mechanism and has limitations in multi-node networks. The mesh mode provides full redundant communications, but this also implies higher energy consumption. In the evaluated use case, where the frequency of data update is too high, even when using LPN nodes. Thus, the time LPN nodes remain in sleep mode is reduced and they present a considerable consumption. Taking into consideration less frequent update times, a better balance between consumption and network redundancy could be obtained.
- At the light of the obtained results, probably the best solution for the deployment of this particular case is an hybrid approach. The multi-link mode allows several GATT peripherals to connect to one central device. Then, the integration of several central devices will provide more redundancy to connectivity.
- With respect to coverage, the use of LE Coded allows for making more stable communications or even deploy less nodes. The advertisement mode in LE Coded mode consumes significantly more than legacy, since it needs to use the radio module more. It also has more time on the air and, since Bluetooth only has 3 channels for advertisement, there is a risk of saturating the band. In connection mode there is less difference between LE Coded and legacy modes.

– The LE Coded mode can definitely help low-power BLE solutions to improve the range for legacy devices that typically provide a short range of a few meters when operating at their lowest transmission levels. Although it is not widely used in these cases due to the longer duration of the frames and consequently higher consumption, the obtained times do not present significant differences among the different connection modes, especially when a payload has a reduced size and it can offer an improvement in the link budget in noise environments. With power levels of -16 dBm and -12 dBm, LE Coded outperformed Legacy mode reception rate by 82% and 57%, respectively. In addition, when transmitting at -40 dBm, the energy consumption remained stable with a slight increase in LE Coded mode (1.32 mA more) and with an event duration of just 0.43 ms longer than in Legacy mode.

6   Conclusions

The aim of this work was to perform a power consumption analysis of Bluetooth 5 LE Coded PHY and Legacy modes to develop next-generation energy efficient Bluetooth 5 real-time IIoT applications. After analyzing all the tests carried out, it can be concluded that no significant savings were obtained by lowering transmit power. In addition, the main difference between LE Coded and Legacy was in transmission time, especially for advertisement events. With respect to the different topologies evaluated, GATT client/server mode is more energy efficient that the mesh mode even when using LPN nodes. The obtained results also emphasize the importance of hybrid approaches for deployment, especially when mixing both topologies. When it comes to coverage, the use of LE Coded allows for making more stable communications. Despite its longer frame duration, which implies higher energy consumption, the obtained times do not present significant differences among the different connection modes, especially when a payload has a small size. To sum up, LE Coded can offer significant advantages in the link budget in harsh industrial environments.

Acknowledgment. This work has been funded by the Xunta de Galicia (by grant ED431C 2020/15, and grant ED431G2019/01 to support the Centro de Investigación de Galicia "CITIC"), the Agencia Estatal de Investigación of Spain (by grants RED2018-102668-T and PID2019-104958RB-C42) and ERDF funds of the EU (FEDER Galicia 2014–2020 & AEI/FEDER Programs, UE).

References

1. Fraga-Lamas, P., et al.: Design and empirical validation of a Bluetooth 5 Fog computing based industrial cps architecture for intelligent industry 4.0 shipyard workshops. IEEE Access **8**, 45496–45511 (2020)
2. Woolley, M.: Bluetooth Core Specification v5.1: Feature Overview. https://www.bluetooth.com/bluetooth-resources/bluetooth-core-specification-v5-1-feature-overview/. Accessed 1 July 2021

3. Froiz-Míguez, I., Fraga-Lamas, P., Varela-Barbeito, J., Fernández-Caramés, T.M.: LoRaWAN and Blockchain based safety and health monitoring system for industry 4.0 operators. In: Proceedings of the 6th International Electronic Conference on Sensors and Applications, vol. 42(1), Article no. 77 (2019)

4. Siekkinen, M., Hiienkari, M., Nurminen, J.K., Nieminen, J.: How low energy is Bluetooth low energy? Comparative measurements with ZigBee/802.15.4. In: 2012 IEEE Wireless Communications and Networking Conference Workshops (WCNCW)

5. Froiz-Míguez, I., Fernández-Caramés, T.M., Fraga-Lamas, P., Castedo, L.: Design, implementation and practical evaluation of an IoT home automation system for fog computing applications based on MQTT and ZigBee-WiFi sensor nodes. Sensors **18**(8), 2660 (2018)

6. Digi XBee 3, Specifications. https://www.digi.com/products/embedded-systems/ digi-xbee/rf-modules/2-4-ghz-rf-modules/xbee3-zigbee-3#specifications. Accessed 21 July 2021

7. Dementyev, A., Hodges, S., Taylor, S., Smith, J.: Power consumption analysis of bluetooth low energy, ZigBee and ANT sensor nodes in a cyclic sleep scenario. In: 2013 IEEE International Wireless Symposium (IWS) (2013)

8. Zhang, C., Yan, Y.: Experimental performance evaluation of Bluetooth 5 for in-building networks. In: Proceedings of the 11th International Conference on Network of the Future, pp. 115–119 (2020)

9. Bulić, P., Kojek, G., Biasizzo, A.: Data transmission efficiency in bluetooth low energy versions. Sensors **19**(17), 3746 (2019)

10. Nordic nRF52840-DK, Datasheet. https://infocenter.nordicsemi.com/pdf/ nRF52840_OPS_v0.5.pdf. Accessed 21 July 2021

11. Nordic Semiconductor. Tested by Nordic: Bluetooth Long Range. https://blog. nordicsemi.com/getconnected/tested-by-nordic-bluetooth-long-range. Accessed 6 June 2021

12. Amornpornwiwat, R., Piyachat, P., Chawathaworncharoen, V., Visoottiviseth, V., Takano, R.: MATEMA6: machine tele-monitoring assistance with 6LoWPAN. In: ICT International Student Project Conference (ICT-ISPC), pp. 49–52 (2016)

13. Nordic nRF52840 SoC. https://www.nordicsemi.com/Products/nRF52840. Accessed 21 July 2021

14. Figaro, Maxell Oxygen Sensors KE-25. https://www.figarosensor.com/product/ entry/ke-25.html. Accessed 21 July 2021

15. Nordic nRF52840 Development Kit. https://www.nordicsemi.com/Products/ Development-hardware/nRF52840-DK. Accessed 7 July 2021

16. Nordic nRF52833 Development Kit. https://www.nordicsemi.com/Products/ Development-hardware/nRF52833-DK. Accessed 7 July 2021

17. Online Power Profiler for BLE. https://devzone.nordicsemi.com/nordic/power/w/ opp/2/online-power-profiler-for-ble. Accessed 1 July 2021

18. Darroudi, S.M., Caldera-Sànchez, R., Gomez, C.: Bluetooth mesh energy consumption: a model. Sensors **19**(5), 1238 (2019)

19. Bluetooth Mesh Networking: Friendship. https://www.bluetooth.com/blog/ bluetooth-mesh-networking-series-friendship. Accessed 21 July 2021

20. Bluetooth Mesh, API Reference. https://infocenter.nordicsemi.com/index.jsp? topic=%2Fcom.nordic.infocenter.meshsdk.v5.0.0%2Fmodules.html. Accessed 21 July 2021

Towards Orchestration of Cloud-Edge Architectures with Kubernetes

Sebastian Böhm[(✉)] and Guido Wirtz

Distributed Systems Group, University of Bamberg, Bamberg, Germany
{sebastian.boehm,guido.wirtz}@uni-bamberg.de

Abstract. Edge computing brings computational resources, reliable network infrastructure, and real-time capabilities closer to devices. Providing resources and workloads at the edge is mainly realized with container technology. The appropriate placement in terms of when, where, and how to provide containerized workloads is still an ongoing problem domain. Kubernetes is nowadays the state-of-the-art platform for containerized service orchestration to tackle these issues. Although Kubernetes misses capabilities like using real-time network metrics for scheduling and topology awareness, it is still used for realizing cloud-edge architectures. In this paper, we analyze current cloud-edge architectures implemented with Kubernetes and how they solve general requirements of edge computing and orchestration. Furthermore, we identify shortcomings in these implementations based on the fundamental requirements of edge computing and orchestration. Even if issues like obtaining network-related metrics and implementing topology awareness are solved well, other requirements like real-time processing of metrics, fault-tolerance, and the placement of container registries are in early stages.

Keywords: Edge computing · Edge orchestration · Cloud computing · Container orchestration · Kubernetes

1 Introduction

In recent years, edge computing has evolved as a supplementary layer to cloud computing where computational resources, so-called edge nodes, are placed close to data-generating entities, often Internet of Things (IoT) devices. The number of IoT devices is still growing and will exceed 30 billion by 2025.[1] In consequence, it is necessary to re-think the current concentration on cloud computing. The primary driver of edge computing is the need to provide location-aware resource and service provisioning because typical use cases like autonomous driving, smart traffic control systems, and other real-time services require low response times (<20 ms) [5]. Edge computing aims to achieve low latency, higher network

---

All links were last followed on June, 26, 2021.

[1] https://www.statista.com/statistics/1101442/iot-number-of-connected-devices-worldwide/.

© ICST Institute for Computer Sciences, Social Informatics and Telecommunications Engineering 2022
Published by Springer Nature Switzerland AG 2022. All Rights Reserved
S. Paiva et al. (Eds.): SmartCity360° 2021, LNICST 442, pp. 207–230, 2022.
https://doi.org/10.1007/978-3-031-06371-8_14

reliability, and enhanced privacy. The data is processed close to data-generating devices and not necessarily uploaded to the cloud [35]. However, the assignment of workloads to heterogeneous edge nodes, often low-end devices, requires real-time monitoring of available and demanded resources and is a fairly complex task. An efficient and sophisticated management is inevitable [37]. The workloads are usually handled by the usage of container technology. Compared to full-blown Virtual Machines (VMs), this lightweight way of virtualization, meanwhile seen as a de facto standard in edge computing, facilitates providing workloads on cloud and edge [24,29]. Containers are small in size, share the same kernel of an operating system, and are executed on a container runtime (e.g., Docker) that is available for a large number of platforms and architectures [4]. In particular, the process of container orchestration comprises the dynamic assignment of containerized workloads to the cloud or edge nodes based on available and demanded resources. Further, orchestration must provide a certain quality of service, e.g., in terms of realized latency or response time [7].

Nowadays, Kubernetes (K8s) is the state-of-the-art container orchestration platform and used in many application areas to achieve highly available, scalable, and fault-tolerant clusters.[2] Nevertheless, considering, using, and evaluating K8s for the implementation of cloud-edge architectures is still an ongoing process in research. In this paper, we want to discuss the current state-of-the-art K8s-based cloud-edge implementations. At this, we analyze essential requirements of cloud-edge architectures especially w.r.t. their orchestration. In addition, we identify existing architectural and conceptual proposals for edge and fog orchestration that are using K8s as a platform to realize orchestration following the essential requirements of edge computing. Furthermore, we examine potential weaknesses in already existing implementations with K8s and propose a set of architectural and conceptual improvements that are compliant with the claims of cloud-edge orchestration. This enables us to evaluate the fit of K8s as a single, uniform, and easy-to-use orchestration platform, which offers the possibility to manage large cloud-edge systems. Our research questions are as follows:

RQ1: What essential requirements of cloud-edge orchestration do exist, are covered by K8s, and what are the arising shortcomings?

RQ2: What are the potential benefits and drawbacks of already established K8s-based cloud-edge environments?

RQ3: Are the potential drawbacks of the established cloud-edge environments using K8s solvable without breaking the fundamental concepts of edge computing and architectural design of K8s?

To answer these research questions, we perform a literature review and obtain the most critical characteristics, requirements, and challenges regarding orchestration of cloud-edge environments. This helps us to evaluate the capabilities of K8s and contributes to RQ1. Targeting RQ2, we review the most popular architectures using K8s to analyze the state-of-the-art. In the next step, we map the obtained requirements running a cloud-edge system to the already established cloud-edge implementations with K8s and identify potential strengths and weak-

---

[2] https://kubernetes.io/.

nesses. Lastly, we evaluate conceptually, based on the considered studies, if the obtained K8s-based drawbacks are solvable and if it is realizable and compliant with cloud-edge architectures to answer RQ3.

The remainder of the paper is structured as follows: Sect. 2 presents a short introduction on edge computing, orchestration, and K8s in general. Section 3 discusses the related work evaluating edge (orchestration) solutions. In Sect. 4, we analyze K8s-based orchestration architectures, limitations, and potential solutions for K8s in cloud-edge environments. Limitations of the considered solutions will be part of Sect. 5. We critically discuss our findings and outline the limitations of our study in Sect. 6. We conclude our work with a summary and what we plan to do in the future (Sect. 7).

2 Conceptual Foundations

This chapter describes the conceptual foundations of edge computing and orchestration of cloud-edge architectures. Furthermore, a basic understanding of K8s as orchestration platform will be provided to support answering RQ1.

2.1 Edge Computing

Edge computing is a new paradigm where computational resources are placed close to data-generating devices. This placement strategy aims to increase the bandwidth and reduce latency [6]. In comparison to cloud computing, where all data is stored and processed in a centralized manner, edge computing acts as an additional decentralized layer to support and take load from the cloud [37]. Especially resource-constrained IoT devices can benefit from the increased bandwidth and ultra-low response times (<20 ms) because they are often performing real-time analytics or video surveillance activities with a large amount of traffic. In addition, IoT environments usually work in a geographically distributed way that suffers from unstable network connections [30]. Long distances coupled with many hops to the data-receiving and data-processing endpoints (i.e., servers in the cloud) intensify breaking the core requirement of low latency for critical applications. The higher the physical distance to the processing endpoints, the higher the transmission latency [35]. Edge computing can be classified into different technologies. The most frequent types, also called edge technologies, are Cloudlet, Mobile Edge Computing (MEC), Micro Data Center (MDC) [23], and Fog [8] (Fig. 1). All of them offer provision models to interact with the cloud. MEC has been introduced by Nokia in 2014 and provides computing, network, and storage resources, predominantly near mobile base stations. Following the general objectives of the edge computing paradigm, MEC aims to enable billion of resource-constraint devices with network capabilities low-latency access to process compute-intensive tasks, like real-time analytics [13]. Usually, MEC resources are placed next to mobile Radio Access Network (RAN) stations, where a high bandwidth enables fast and dynamic deployment of applications that are processing requests with real-time needs. This reduces the amount of data that

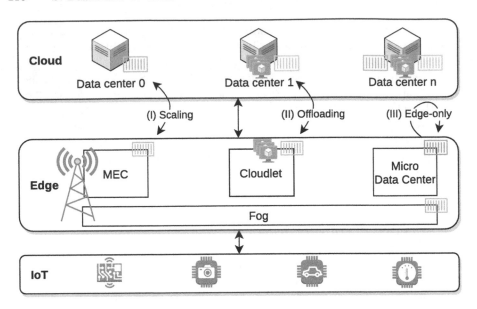

Fig. 1. Cloud-edge architecture with provision models and edge technologies.

is uploaded to the cloud considerably and mitigates network congestion. However, it is not clearly defined whether MEC layers should replace the cloud layer completely. Data may or may not be still forwarded to the cloud [2,8].

A cloudlet is a decentralized set of devices that form a virtualized cluster for running low-latency applications. Cloudlets are self-managing, easy-to-deploy by local maintainers, and bring the cloud one step closer to the edge. They require a reliable, high bandwidth internet connection because workloads are transmitted as VM overlays that are executed on top of an already installed base image. In addition, it is one core requirement to shift those VM overlays rapidly if served devices change their physical location, like vehicles in smart traffic control systems. Originally, cloudlets are supposed to run VM overlays to serve requesting devices [34]. However, [3] considered containers for application migration in cloudlets and [31,32] linux containers as lightweight alternative.

Micro Data Centers (mDCs) are similar to cloudlets because they want to achieve low-response times by extending the cloud layer. In contrast to cloudlets that are set up in a decentralized manner maintained by independent owners, mDCs run in one single, isolated, and secured unit. This comprises protection in terms of physical as well as software-related access control because multi-tenancy is an essential requirement of mDCs. They usually have a reliable, fast, and persistent connection to the cloud to enable data exchange.[3]

---

[3] https://www.networkworld.com/article/2979570/microsoft-researcher-why-micro-datacenters-really-matter-to-mobiles-future.html.

Lastly, the fog paradigm, which is often interpreted as synonym to edge computing [30,37,41], can reduce the latency between cloud and IoT devices. In contrast to the presented edge technologies in the former paragraph, the fog computing layer is one step closer to the service requesting devices and is designed in a decentralized manner. A large number of heterogeneous fog devices is required to manage, cooperate, and communicate to achieve the objective of low-latency [9,40]. It is still an open question if there is a fundamental difference between edge and fog computing. However, both technologies are sharing a common set of services (e.g., computation, storage, and networking) in a similar way as an intermediate layer between the cloud and IoT layer. We treat edge and fog as similar and related technologies and do not introduce a further differentiation, as many other authors [9,30,37,41].

As indicated in Fig. 1, applications with low-latency requirements can be deployed in different ways. The three most frequent so-called provision models are (I) scaling, (II) offloading, and (III) edge-only deployments, even if the edge layer is not supposed to replace the cloud completely [2,8]. (I) Scaling to the edge, also called distributed offloading, keeps the application running in the cloud and edge layer simultaneously. This provision model applies especially if the cloud and edge layer need to work together because both are running out of resources. For example, the edge node may reach the available amount of storage and the cloud may violate the latency requirement [1]. (II) Offloading from cloud to edge and vice versa is the most frequently discussed and used approach. Applications and tasks are moved to the edge layer to achieve better response times, e.g., due to periodic high load. Equally, applications may be shifted to the cloud when the load decreases [18]. (III) Edge-only deployments are also possible, where the applications are placed only on the edge layer and moved across different edge nodes, to fulfill the needed latency. Offloading is not necessarily destined for this way of placement. However, many solutions perform a mixed approach even if they focus on edge placement in specific [36].

2.2   Orchestration of Cloud-Edge Architectures

Cloud-edge environments introduce new complexities that arise when new layers with different provision models are added to the cloud. Cloud-Edge orchestration comprises all activities to distribute a set of applications to the cloud, edge, and IoT layer given a set of objectives. There are multiple objectives involved to run this architecture efficiently (Sect. 2.1).

The essential parts are performance-related aspects like the optimal placement of applications dependent on the real-time latency and bandwidth of devices in the architecture to the origin of potential requests. Complex optimization and scheduling models are required to distribute applications according to resource demand and supply of CPU, memory, disk, and network utilization [37]. In addition, cloud-edge architectures must be fault-tolerant and resilient if some nodes in the network become unavailable [42]. The decentralized, distributed, and large-scale nature of edge layers intensifies the complexity because often edge resources are equipped with low-power devices [18,19]. Associated with

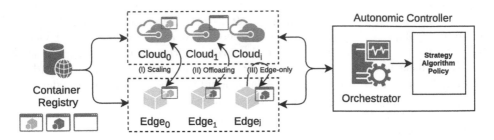

Fig. 2. Generic orchestration architecture, based on [10].

large-scale deployments, orchestration must provide extensibility to dynamically scale up and scale down the number of available nodes [28]. Security is also an important part of cloud-edge environments because edge technologies like cloudlets and mDCs are shared across different tenants (Sect. 2.1). In addition, they may be publicly accessible [41]. Hence, concepts like authentication, authorization, and user access control are inevitable running cloud-edge systems [42].

All types of provision models require a fast and efficient way of moving applications through the different layers. For this, container virtualization can be seen as the de facto standard to run applications in this regards. Containers include the application, all necessary libraries, and the runtime environment. They run on top of a so-called container engines, like Docker, and share the same kernel of an operating system. During runtime, the containers are isolated and can only use a previously defined amount of resources, such as CPU or memory. Running applications in this way involves several advantages: Containers are small in size and provide fast startup times [4]. Especially the portability of containers has led to wide acceptance in edge computing [24,29].

Figure 2 shows a generic container orchestration architecture based on [10]. Applications are provided by a container registry and executed on cloud and/or edge nodes. The autonomic controller consists of an orchestrator that implements an orchestration strategy, algorithm, or policy responsible for assigning those applications on different nodes. At this, different provision models can be realized, as explained in the former section.

2.3   Kubernetes

K8s can be used to run workloads on a set of nodes and to implement the described generic orchestration architecture from the last chapter. We present a minimal working cluster in Fig. 3. It consists of at least one master node, also called control plane, that carries all system-related services to run the cluster. Further, at least one worker node is needed to run the assigned workloads.[4]

The master node contains a set of services to manage the set of worker nodes. All system-related services are running as containers and can be distributed

---

[4] It is even possible to run single-node clusters by attaching workloads to the master node; however, this should not be done in production environments.

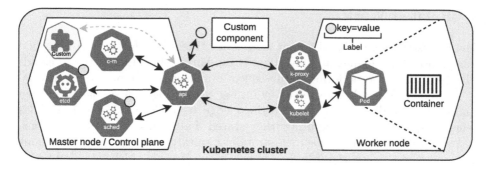

Fig. 3. General Kubernetes architecture.

among different nodes to achieve high availability. The controller-manager (*c-m*) observes all nodes running in the cluster and keeps track of the current state. For instance, as part of the controller manager, the replication manager can restart pods on other nodes in case of failing nodes. The Kube Scheduler (KS), in Fig. 3 named *sched*, assigns containerized workloads that are running in pods to worker nodes based on filtering and scoring to find the most appropriate node for deployment. For example, previously defined constraints and available resources on nodes are taken into consideration. K8s holds the cluster data in a strongly consistent distributed key-value store *etcd*, for example, currently running assignments. All data will automatically be distributed across all running etcd instances to achieve redundancy. The *api* component is used to interact with all system-related components, exposed as REST API. Not shown as optional component in Fig. 2 is the Horizontal Pod Autoscaler (HPA) that can dynamically increase and decrease the number of pods based on CPU and memory utilization.[5] All worker nodes run a so-called *kubelet* that interacts with the controller manager on the master node. This component manages the lifecycle of pods based on the commands from the controller manager. Furthermore, this component transmits the current node status to the control plane. Lastly, the kube-proxy (*k-proxy*) is used to make workloads available via the network in the form of services by opening ports and forwarding traffic.[6]

As annotated in Fig. 3, K8s allows to replace and modify several components. The scheduling component can be modified or replaced entirely. Custom labels can be assigned to nodes, for example, to enrich the information basis for the scheduling process. Possible for a customized scheduling and scaling are also external applications that are interacting with the api or containerized components that can even be deployed as control plane components, for example, if the scheduler is supposed to be replaced.[7]

---

[5] https://kubernetes.io/docs/tasks/run-application/horizontal-pod-autoscale/.
[6] https://kubernetes.io/docs/concepts/overview/components/.
[7] https://kubernetes.io/docs/concepts/extend-kubernetes/.

3   Related Work

The works that are related to our survey are three-fold. Firstly, we identified those works that defined and investigated fundamental characteristics of cloud-edge computing and performed a subsequent evaluation based on a set of criteria.

[45] conducted a literature survey on fog computing and similar or related computing paradigms, like the described edge technologies in Fig. 1. Besides general aspects of fog computing, they stated limitations, research directions, and potential solutions for fog orchestration. Limitations and research directions were mapped to potential solutions from various authors. Although cloud-edge orchestration was not the focus of this work in specific, many useful aspects were included for future research. In [39], a comprehensive literature survey was performed to obtain the state-of-the-art orchestration challenges, also for edge and fog computing. The authors also presented a mapping between these challenges and provided a list of corresponding potential solutions as described in different studies. [26] followed this qualitative approach and investigated several requirements, like infrastructural-, platform-, and application-related criteria. These criteria were used to evaluate established fog architectures and use cases. In terms of orchestration, the authors collected a comprehensive set of resource allocation and scheduling algorithms as a discipline of orchestration. Again, these obtained criteria were used to evaluate a selected set of solutions that tackle this problem domain. In [41], the motivation, challenges, and opportunities in edge computing were discussed. The authors provided a reasonable set of aspects that must be handled, especially in regards to orchestration-related activities.

Secondly, the works that evaluate edge (orchestration) architectures are related to our study. Whereas the studies in the former paragraph explicitly evaluate general challenges in edge and fog computing, the following studies target cloud-edge or edge orchestration in specific. For example, [19] defined several requirements for orchestration in terms of node-handling capabilities (e.g., joining/leaving the cluster, scheduling, and device mapping to containers). They evaluated container orchestration tools like Mesos, Kubernetes, and Docker Swarm. Although they do not compare different cloud-edge architectures implemented with these tools, their defined requirements contribute to the collection of features an orchestration system should comply with. Similar to the studies in the first part, [42] analyzed the state-of-the-art of fog orchestration. Their study provides a detailed overview of requirements and what orchestration must fulfill. Based on these obtained criteria, they evaluated well-established and standardized fog orchestration architectures. They conclude that most of these cloud-edge architectures can deal with the challenges in fog computing. However, there was no practical implementation covered.

Thirdly, those evaluations that focus only on one certain aspect of cloud-edge orchestration are further in relation to our work: General architectural and algorithmic challenges, for example, for resource provisioning and scheduling, were part of [25]. The qualitative literature review leads to a comprehensive set of limitations that are mapped to potential solutions. In addition, starting points were added to support further investigations. [1] also provided a comprehensive survey in a subarea of cloud-edge orchestration. They analyze offloading strategies based on a set of criteria that was theoretically derived. A similar approach was made by [43]. They analyzed several offloading algorithms based on a previously set of criteria and presented an overview.

Although many of the approaches investigated several challenges, research directions, and potential solutions for issues in cloud-edge orchestration, there is no comprehensive overview of K8s-based cloud-edge and edge architectures in specific. Therefore, we provide a comprehensive evaluation of those modifications according to the requirements of cloud-edge architectures.

4   Kubernetes as Edge Orchestration Platform

To get an overview of the current state-of-the-art of cloud-edge orchestration with K8s, we analyzed 18 research papers. We obtained these papers from different databases like IEEE Explore, SpringerLink, and ArXiv. We used the term Kubernetes ∧ (edge ∨ fog) ∧ (computing ∨ orchestration)

Finally, we only considered those papers which identified potential shortcomings of K8s and provided a set of solutions by retaining K8s. In total, seven out of 18 publications were excluded. Besides a short introduction on the considered solutions, this chapter also discusses limitations of K8s for edge orchestration and presents potential solutions stated in the literature to answer RQ2.

4.1   Kubernetes-Based Edge Orchestration Architectures

The set of K8s-based edge orchestration systems can be basically separated into three parts, namely (open-source) frameworks and solutions that are tackling essential orchestration activities in edge computing, solutions that applied custom modifications and extensions to K8s for cloud-edge orchestration, and finally those solutions that orchestrate only the edge-layer with a modified K8s. This chapter shortly outlines the general approach of these platforms and solutions.

Platform-Based Solutions. The first part comprises frameworks like KubeEdge (KE)[8], Baetyl[9], OpenYurt (OY)[10], or ioFog[11]. These frameworks often use K8s as an underlying platform without any modifications to run the required system-related services and the target applications as containerized workloads. These platforms usually provide a mechanism to enable an easy setup of cloud-edge architectures. They provide routines to deploy infrastructure components like virtual networks, additional middleware like message brokers, preconfigured service- or event bus endpoints, and management capabilities. Users can easily connect devices to the architecture and monitor their current

---

[8] https://kubeedge.io/en/.
[9] https://baetyl.io/en.
[10] https://github.com/openyurtio/openyurt.
[11] https://iofog.org/.

state. Platforms like KE advertise resource optimization to enable the usage of the platform with low-end devices, which are very common in the field of edge computing. The primary lack of those platforms is the missing dynamic workload allocation capability. Those platforms are not able to perform intelligent placement decisions based on the current resource utilization on edge devices, offloading of containerized workloads from cloud to edge and vice versa, and finally scaling out to the edge [17]. In consequence, some authors used the modifiability and extensibility of K8s (Sect. 2.3) to implement custom cloud-edge and edge architectures, which are described in the following paragraphs.

Custom Cloud-Edge Architectures. Secondly, we present architectures using cloud and edge layers in collaboration to provide orchestrations.

[17] propose *KaiS*. This scheduling framework dispatches requests decentralized at the edge and cooperates with the cloud to improve the long-term rate of request processing and system overhead. Furthermore, they used centralized service orchestration in the cloud to assign containerized workloads to edge nodes. The architecture made usage of learning dispatching and orchestration techniques. The authors obtained that *KaiS* can distinctly reduce the throughput rate and scheduling costs compared to K8s or other greedy approaches. A scalable and custom solution was described in [21] as a multi-objective optimization problem to minimize interference and energy consumption of deployments. They deployed custom containers on all nodes in the cluster to meet the requirements of co-allocation of dependent workloads on a single node to reduce the carbon footprint of the entire cloud-edge orchestration. Compared to a First Come First Serve algorithm, *KEIDS* and the introduced optimizations on *KEIDS* led to different improvements in reducing carbon footprint, performance, and energy minimization. The solution, named *Swirly*, presented in [15], aims to fulfill several requirements of cloud-edge orchestration. *Swirly* is a scheduler running in the cloud and creates service topology to support scheduling. It supports large-scale and topology-aware deployments with a minimal number of container instances by taking real-time resource utilization (e.g., CPU, memory, and latency) into consideration. They deployed a custom container on all nodes to achieve the previously mentioned goals. As a benchmarking result, they concluded that the proposed solution is able to manage up to 300000 devices. [33] proposed a cloud-edge architecture with network-aware scheduling for an air monitoring service. They implemented several extensions, like custom schedulers, and applied modifications to K8s to support location-aware scheduling. As a result, they compared their network-aware scheduler with the default KS and other approaches based on integer linear programming. They showed that their proposed architecture with the modified scheduler leads to a noticeable reduction in network latency. A further notable example of K8s-based implementations is the work of [16]. The proposed architecture aims to get K8s ready for the orchestration of geographically distributed clusters. They placed additional components, e.g., for measuring network latency on each node, and proposed a custom scheduler for scheduling activities. This solution targets the cloud and edge layer for placing workloads and performs periodic latency probes to determine optimized latency-

aware deployments. An evaluation has shown that the architecture can adjust the deployment based on real-time conditions. [20] designed an architecture with the focus on fault-tolerance by defining application isolation, data transport, and multi-cluster management. They deployed fault-tolerant Kafka clusters in cloud and edge to achieve a reliable storage layer. In addition, they deployed master nodes on the cloud in high availability mode. Finally, they evaluated that a two-node failure does not mitigate the operational state of the cluster. Lastly, the solution of [44] is worth mentioning. They propose *Fogernetes*, a fog computing platform, which is based on a labeling system to achieve network-aware and resource-oriented deployments. The deployments are based on assigning a set of key-value pairs to nodes and adding those to the deployment file as well. As a case study, they deployed a video streaming architecture with a camera, client, middleware, and central processing unit in the cloud and showed that K8s followed a location-aware deployment based on the defined mappings.

Custom Edge Architectures. Thirdly, we give a short conceptual overview of solutions that considered only the edge layer for orchestration activities.

[22] propose a fog architecture based on K8s that aims to deploy multi-container applications on resource-limited fog devices. They introduced several plugins to the default KS to achieve more efficient and location-aware distribution of containers, for example, by distributing multi-container deployment on neighboring nodes. As a result, they conclude that the service quality was not mitigated and the procedure might evolve as common practice to utilize fog architectures. In [12], a decoupled and native modification was executed on K8s to achieve location-aware, latency-aware, and fault-tolerant deployments. Based on a decoupled architecture, deployments are calculated by the usage of an external component. This component passes the created deployment to an unmodified K8s cluster architecture. The native modification runs on K8s as an additional component and interacts directly via API calls to achieve a more robust integration into K8s. Finally, the authors performed several experiments on allocation costs and failover time to evaluate the proposed modifications. [27] proposes an edge solution for industrial IoT to reduce the scheduling time by applying single-step scheduling, especially in the field of 5G. The implemented custom scheduler achieves latency-aware deployments and optimizes the deployment time and temperature of all nodes in the cluster. As a result, they reduced the scheduling time and considered additional metrics, like latency, jitter, and packet loss in the scheduling process. In [11], the inherent issues in the scheduling process were addressed by implementing an agent-based approach to reduce the load on the master node while scheduling. The scheduler runs instead of the default scheduler and addresses only the fog layer. The authors followed an agent-based approach that shifts selected scheduling tasks of K8s, like node filtering and scoring, to agents, which are placed on nodes in the architecture. An evaluation has shown that the agentified scheduler significantly needed less time for deployments with a small number (<10) of replicas.

4.2   General Limitations of K8s for Edge Orchestration

We distinguished the general limitations of K8s as an orchestration platform in resource awareness and architectural shortcomings. These categories exhibit substantial obstacles running K8s in production for cloud-edge architectures.

Resource Awareness. Dealing with real-time resource demands and supplies in terms of the current CPU, memory, storage, and network utilization can be seen as a major challenge in orchestrating cloud-edge architectures. Since conditions are dynamically changing and shifting actions must be initiated in an appropriate amount of time, K8s shows several limitations in this regard. Frequently mentioned are the limited capabilities of the default K8s scheduler to deal with other resources like CPU and memory utilization. Especially for small edge and IoT devices other resource types are also essential, e.g., the current quality of the network connection [12,21,22,27,33]. Other authors using K8s as platform for orchestration mention that the missing capabilities taking the resource consumption for shifting applications or tasks from cloud to edge as further scheduling metric is a major drawback. Considering energy efficiency might be important for mitigating unnecessary offloading actions and reducing carbon footprint [21,33].

Cloud-edge deployments benefit from latency- and bandwidth-aware orchestrations. That means it is desirable to place multi-component applications close to each other in order to reduce the communication cost [22,33]. Following the main objective of edge computing, applications must be placed close to requesting devices. Therefore, latency is one of the most important measurements that should play an essential role in scheduling container workloads to edge devices. K8s does not provide a built-in mechanism to run deployments based on bandwidth and latency that might limit the application in cloud-edge environments [12,16,21,22,33].

Lastly, the KS shows several obstacles for the usage of K8s in edge computing. As pointed out in Sect. 2.3, the KS assigns workloads in the form of pods to nodes based on filtering and scoring by node priority calculation. K8s takes the workloads to be scheduled one-by-one at a time and does not preferentially consider assigned priorities to pods to a set of available nodes [17,22,27,33]. Furthermore, developers are allowed to define the resource requests of pods statically. If those definitions are far away from the actual resource usage, nodes might be underutilized. The scheduling algorithm might lead to unassigned pods if no resources are left on nodes, even if the containers in the pods to be scheduled could be distributed among different nodes [22,33]. The missing understanding of the network topology is one further downside. K8s interprets the set of worker nodes as homogeneous with similar capabilities, although cloud-edge architectures usually consists of heterogeneous nodes in a geographical distributed architecture [12,14,16,17,21,22,33,44]. Without a topology, K8s can not realize location-aware deployments that are required for the different provision models and edge technologies (Sect. 2.2).

Architectural Shortcomings. Besides the resource-related shortcomings of K8s, there are also architectural issues that are part of related works (Sect. 3). By definition, the decentralized organization is an essential characteristic of edge computing (Sect. 2.1). However, K8s exhibits a centrally organized control plane that manages the lifecycle of a large set of nodes and applications running on them. Even though the control plane can run in a high availability manner [20], this architecture violates the decentralized notion [11,17,22]. In addition and solid relation to the topology criteria in the former chapter, the distributed nature of edge-computing is degraded because K8s does not hold a network topology to model geographically distributed and independent cloud-edge clusters [17]. Lastly, one single K8s cluster can at most handle 5000 nodes with 150000 pods and 300000 containers in total.[12] A very large edge cluster requires additional coupling, e.g., by the usage of cluster federation [14,15].

4.3 Potential Solutions for K8s as Edge Orchestration Platform

This section provides a short overview of potential solutions to overcome the most critical challenges in edge computing, according to the former section.

Providing Resource Awareness. The missing capability of dealing with other resources like CPU and memory was the most frequently mentioned downside taking K8s as an orchestration system, especially in regards to latency, bandwidth, energy consumption, and costs to determine future scheduling activities. Some authors implemented a custom way to collect additional metrics, like bandwidth and latency, with containerized applications and agents that are running alongside the K8s components. These metrics are further analyzed by custom schedulers that are running as normal containers alongside the default KS to alter deployments [11,15–17,21,27]. K8s also offers to implement custom and native schedulers that can also run together with or without the default K8s scheduler.[13] Furthermore, there are already implementations that are using the default KS with scheduler extenders that allow to alter scheduling decisions of the filtering and scoring step of the default KS [22,33]. As pointed out in Sect. 2.3, the default KS starts with filtering and prioritizing nodes based on predicates. The priority step can be revised and added to the default KS by recompilation, for example, as performed by [22]. Lastly, creating new deployment manifests based on custom containers was already done by researchers to modify the orchestration [12,44]. Finally, the issue of potentially unscheduled pods must be addressed, for example, by splitting up deployments and distribute them to different nodes [22]. Moving already running pods to different nodes might also be an option [16]. This solution, however, does not address the issue of static resource assignments to pods and potential under- and over-utilization of the infrastructure. According to the investigated solutions, real-time data analysis

---

[12] https://kubernetes.io/docs/setup/best-practices/cluster-large/.
[13] https://kubernetes.io/docs/tasks/extend-kubernetes/configure-multiple-schedulers/.

is desired, respectively, must be regularly revised to avoid not properly chosen resource assignments.

Implementing Cloud-Edge Architectures. The orchestration of cloud-edge architectures should follow a decentralized organization and should not rely on a master node as it is the case with K8s. However, this requirement can be relaxed because it is common practice to introduce centralized schedulers for the edge, as shown by several examples [16,17,44]. Agent-based and other decentralized approaches together with centralized components have already been realized with K8s, even specific for edge-computing [11,17]. The missing awareness of network topology can be seen as a major drawback, perhaps the most serious. As explained in Sect. 2.2, edge orchestration is supposed to implement various provision models. For example, to perform (II) edge offloading from cloud to edge or vice versa requires knowledge about the position and assignment of nodes to layers (Fig. 1). Therefore, K8s must provide a way to define a network topology in order to orchestrate cloud-edge environments with different edge technologies. As indicated in Sect. 2.3, labels can be assigned to nodes in order to implement a network topology. Based on so-called affinities and anti-affinities, the set of usable nodes for pod deployment can be limited in a reasonable way. The investigated solutions commonly used affinities to express the corresponding layer (i.e., cloud, edge, or IoT) a node is assigned to and additional context-related information, like the target location [12,16,22,44] or the device type [33].

5   Limitations of the Proposed Solutions

Although the proposals based on K8s provided contributions to get K8s ready for the edge, there are still some issues that must be considered running cloud-edge environments in production. In this chapter, we present an overview of the investigated solutions and the identified drawbacks. Again, we distinguished the limitations in resource-related and architectural shortcomings.

5.1   Resource-Related Solutions

Table 1 shows an overview of which requirements in terms of resource-awareness are supported (●), partially supported (○), or not supported (*no circle*). Also, we mention where no details could be found (✽).

First, most of the proposals modifying K8s for edge environments considered the *cloud* and the *edge* layer. Architectures where the cloud holds the K8s master node with control planes or custom scheduler components and the edge layer, consisting of a set of worker nodes, are a frequent architectural design. However, some solutions only consider the edge layer, which runs all necessary components. In regards to the scheduling process, most of the authors used *custom* containerized schedulers that are replacing the *native* default scheduler in K8s completely. [12,33] used an unmodified version of the *native* scheduler (○) in collaboration with a *custom* scheduler [12] or an *extender* [33]. In addition,

Table 1. Comparison of resource-awareness in different Kubernetes implementations for cloud-edge architectures.

Authors	Year	Cloud	Edge	IoT	Recompiled	Native	Extender	Custom	CPU	Memory	Disk	Energy	Latency	Bandwidth	K8s API	Custom
		Layer			Scheduler				Resources				Network		Metrics	
[17] Han	2021	●	●						●	●	●		●			●
[22] Kayal	2020		●			●			○	○	○		○		○	
[21] Kaur	2020	●	●						●	●	●	●	●			✻
[12] Eidenbenz	2020		●				○		●	○	○	○	●		●	
[15] Goethals	2020	●	●						●	○	○	○	●		○	●
[27] Ogbuachi	2020		●						●	●	●	●	●			●
[33] Santos	2019	●	●		○	●	●		○	○	○		○	○	○	
[11] Casquero	2019		●						●	○	○	○			○	
[16] Haja	2019	●	●						●	○	○	○	●		○	●
[20] Javed	2018	●	●			○			○	○	○				○	
[44] Wöbker	2018	●	●			○			○	○	○				○	

●=fully supported; ○=partially supported; *no circle* = not supported; ✻ = n/a

there are proposals that do not include customization of the scheduler and work with implicit scheduling [20] respectively affinities and anti-affinities to implement scheduling to the cloud and edge layer [44]. In general, all solutions are aware of *CPU, memory,* and *disk* resources. However, most of the solutions take the static resource assignments (○) for scheduling decisions. Only a few approaches scheduled based on dynamic real-time metrics (●). One approach considers the *energy* consumption, which might be important for devices running on battery [21]. Latency-aware deployments are crucial in edge-deployments. Some authors achieved those deployments by periodically measuring the network latency (●) between nodes. Other solutions only consider predefined and static assignments (○). The currently available bandwidth is rarely considered in the investigated solutions. There are predefined static (○) definitions of bandwidth [33] as well as periodic (●) checks [21]. The *K8s API* is used to measure the current CPU and memory utilization to support the scheduling and scaling decisions. As clarified in Sect. 4.2, the set of considered metrics must be extended. Some solutions make usage of the unmodified K8s API (○) without any modification or extensions. Also, we investigated solutions that deploy *custom* (●) containers in addition to the native metrics components [15,16]. However, there is one solution [12] that is replacing the metrics server compatible with the K8s API (●) to gather latency between nodes. Missing explanations and definitions were also the case (✻).

5.2   Architectural Solutions

After highlighting the resource-related shortcomings, we will review the architectural implementations according to the obtained requirements. Topology plays a major role because edge-cloud orchestrators must be aware of the network they orchestrate to support all provision models and edge technologies.

A few authors allow explicit addressing (●) of *cloud* and *edge* layers for deployment or scheduling workloads. Other solutions [20,21] take the cloud and edge layer as a single system running orchestration and workloads. Often, only the edge layer is in the focus of orchestration activities, as shown in Table 2. Workloads are not supposed to be moved through the different layers. Some solutions, like [17,33,44] facilitate the *scaling* model, where applications can run on cloud and edge in a replicated manner (●). Due to the implemented scheduler algorithms, [20] and [21] support scaling to edge only implicitly (○). Explicit *offloading* (●) from cloud to edge is rarely supported because most works take the cloud as a control layer, which is not supposed to run workloads. Implicit *offloading* (○) might occur when nodes are failing and K8s resiliency feature is shifting and restarting the workload on another node. However, this is only possible for architectures where workloads can be assigned to the cloud. Nearly all works also enable *edge-only* deployments, where workloads are executed and

Table 2. Comparison of architectural capabilities in different kubernetes implementations for cloud-edge architectures.

Authors	Year	Topology			Provision model			Fault-tolerance			Container registry		
		Cloud	*Edge*	*IoT*	*Scaling*	*Offloading*	*Edge-only*	*Cluster*	*Control plane*	*Cluster storage*	*Cloud*	*Edge*	*Replicated*
[17] Han	2021	●	●		●	●	●	●			●		
[22] Kayal	2020		●				●		●		●		
[21] Kaur	2020	○	○		○	○	●	●				✱	
[12] Eidenbenz	2020		●				●					✱	
[15] Goethals	2020		●				●					✱	
[27] Ogbuachi	2020		●				●				●		
[33] Santos	2019	●	●		●	○	●				●	●	●
[11] Casquero	2019		●				●				●		
[16] Haja	2019	●	●				●	●				✱	
[20] Javed	2018	○	○		○	○	○		●	○		✱	
[44] Wöbker	2018	●	●		●	○	●				●		

●=fully supported; ○=partially supported; *no circle* = not supported; ✱ = n/a moved across the edge layer to achieve fast response times (●). Partial *edge-only* means that workloads are implicitly scaled-out (○) by K8s, for example, if only edge nodes are available for deployment and users or the HPA increase the number of replicas. The investigated solutions poorly cover fault-tolerance. For our analysis, we only consider the fault-tolerance concerning the architecture of K8s itself, not the fault-tolerance of the deployed applications.

This follows our objective to identify architectural shortcomings. Even if most of the deployments offer high availability, a crashing master node that is running the *control plane* stops scheduling, scaling, monitoring, and the resiliency features in K8s and is not acceptable if these solutions operate in critical areas. [17,21] introduce geographically independent (●) K8s *clusters* to provide fault-tolerance. However, the *control plane* is not replicated according to the recommendation deploying at least three master nodes (●) for production environments.[14] Only [20] implemented a fault-tolerant K8s architecture by considering three master nodes that are also running the distributed key-value store *etcd* as *cluster storage* (○). Nevertheless, it might be worth considering to decouple etcd from the master nodes running the control plane components by deploying an external etcd cluster, which is interacting with the master nodes. Compared to the stacked cluster storage setup (○), where etcd is distributed on the master nodes, an external storage cluster would achieve a higher degree of resiliency and reduce the load on the master nodes (●). This is especially recommended for setups that need to handle a large number of nodes.[15] Container registries are mainly provided by the cloud in a non-geographically *replicated* manner. The position of those registries is essential, enabling edge nodes to download container images very fast, for example, if workloads must be scaled, offloaded, or moved to achieve the edge-only model. Since latency reduction is a core characteristic of edge computing, this should also be reflected in placing container registries at appropriate locations. Only one publication [33] considered a fully replicated solution across *cloud* and *edge* (●). [44] provided a registry only at the edge (●) to enable fast download times. Often, placing strategies are neglected and neither specified nor discussed (✳).

6   Discussion

After the evaluation of the proposed K8s-based solutions, this chapter will provide a detailed discussion. In Sect. 6.1, we present our findings by answering our research questions from Sect. 1. Subsequently, Sect. 6.2 contains the limitations of our study. Finally, we conclude this chapter with a short assessment if the ambitions modifying and extending K8s should be retained (Sect. 6.3).

---

[14] https://kubernetes.io/docs/setup/production-environment/.
[15] https://kubernetes.io/docs/setup/production-environment/tools/kubeadm/ha-topology/.

6.1 Findings

In the first chapters of this work, we analyzed fundamental characteristics of edge computing (Sect. 2.1), edge orchestration (Sect. 2.2), and K8s as container orchestration platform (Sect. 2.3). Furthermore, we presented and analyzed several studies that considered K8s as basis for cloud-edge orchestration (Sect. 4.1) to obtain the general limitations (Sect. 4.2). This procedure allows us to answer RQ1. The essential requirements of cloud-edge orchestration can be separated into resource- and architectural-related requirements. Resource-related requirements are the different *layers*, which are used by the orchestration architecture to operate. Furthermore, considering real-time *resource* utilization and providing *network* awareness in deployments are important requirements, ideally with dynamic consideration. In regards to architectural requirements, it is important to consider the *topology* of all nodes that are managed, the realization of different *provision models*, and most notably, the implementation of *fault-tolerance* even for the architecture-managing components. Some of these requirements are already covered by K8s. In terms of resources, for example, K8s provides basic scheduling using CPU and memory resources and horizontal scaling based on these metrics. Additionally, K8s offers built-in mechanisms building high availability clusters. As mentioned by [19], it is very convenient with K8s to add and remove nodes to a cloud-edge architecture during runtime. This is a typical practice in edge systems to dynamically add and remove nodes from and to the cluster [28]. We did not include this in our analysis in detail because all cloud-edge architecture implementations offer this implicitly by the usage of K8s. In addition, security was not further analyzed because the system-related communications are secured via HTTPS and provide a built-in system for authentication and authorization.[16] However, there are several shortcomings of K8s in orchestration activities. Firstly, in terms of resource-awareness, K8s is primarily built for the cloud and is not supposed for running on a heterogeneous structure [12]. A major problem is dealing with real-time resource demands and supplies that are not regarded during scheduling activities. Especially missing network-related measurements in the default scheduling behavior, as most significant issue, must be solved. Regarding architecture-related issues, the missing topology awareness was frequently mentioned, limiting the orchestration possibilities. This leads to the issue that K8s will be unable to perform other provision models like edge-only deployments. For example, standalone K8s clusters (i.e., single clusters for cloud, edge, and IoT) might offer basic horizontal scaling with acceptable performance. Inherently, K8s offers a centralized way of scheduling and managing the cluster. As outlined, this violates the decentralized notion of edge computing technologies. However, this issue can be relaxed because there are various non-K8s-based solutions for cloud-edge architectures, as shown by the works of [38,46]. Especially for task offloading, centralized management is used very frequently, as analyzed by [43].

In Sect. 4.1 we analyzed the state-of-the-art of K8s-based cloud-edge orchestration. We also outlined the general limitations of K8s for edge orchestra-

---

[16] https://kubernetes.io/docs/concepts/security/controlling-access/.

tions (Sect. 4.2) as well as potential solutions (Sect. 4.3). This contributes to RQ2 that aimed to investigate the benefits and drawbacks of the solutions that used K8s as orchestration platform for cloud-edge architectures. We argue that many solutions provided reasonable and meaningful proposals getting K8s ready for edge computing. The most notable benefits regarding resource-awareness include adding custom schedulers that make dynamic usage of other resources than CPU or memory and realizing network-aware deployments, especially for the scheduling process. Also, architecture-related issues were approached, like implementing topology-aware deployments. However, there is still a considerable lack in implementing different provision models, fault-tolerance of the cluster architecture, and placement of container registries as critical components for cloud-edge orchestrations.

The qualitative analysis of the K8s-based proposals enabled us to identify shortcomings (Sect. 5), according to our work from the previous chapters. As already indicated, the solutions that were part of our study showed several drawbacks. It is crucial solving them in order to run cloud-edge deployments in production. From our perspective, we believe that most of the challenges are solvable with a foreseeable amount of effort (RQ3). There are partial solutions for almost all problems, which can be combined to realize a unified solution.

We believe that all resource-related issues can be solved. Even if several cloud-edge architectures used only the edge layer for deployment, K8s clusters can be distributed over the different layers or deployed by the usage of cluster federation[17]. As already outlined, many components of K8s can be extended or replaced, like the scheduler component to be aware of real-time resources and network measurements. However, implementing native schedulers for the edge is considered a complex process [12]. This might be the reason why there are no native implementations. In addition, K8s allows the replacement of the metrics server to enrich the type of measurements.

We conclude that essential architecture-related requirements, like network topology, offering different types of provision models apart from edge-only deployments, high availability concepts, and the placement of container registries were not a major focus of the implementations. As already indicated, it might be desirable to include, for example, the IoT layer for containerized deployments as well. Issues like implementing fault-tolerance by replicating clusters, master nodes, or geographically distributed container registries, can be provided quickly and without much effort. However, this requires relaxing essential criteria like the decentralized architecture of edge computing in favor of a unified orchestration platform. As discussed above, this might be an acceptable trade-off.

6.2   Limitations

To the best of our knowledge, we aligned the set of evaluation criteria to the most critical general requirements of edge computing and the derived shortcomings of K8s. In consequence, the evaluation catalog might not cover the complete

---

[17] https://github.com/kubernetes-sigs/kubefed.

set of requirements and represents a simplification that should reveal the state-of-the-art in orchestration activities with K8s. Furthermore, it is still not clear if the selected solutions are comparable. They implement centralized, decentralized, and mixed architectures and follow different approaches and objectives, like implementing a cloud-edge topology, minimizing resource usage, optimizing container allocation, or reducing latency in deployments. However, we state that the type of architecture or objective should not constrain the mission-critical challenges in edge computing. In Sect. 2.1, we described different provision models in edge computing that different edge technologies can implement. Nevertheless, it is questionable if all provision models must be supported by one solution because edge-only deployments seem to be the most frequent deployment, according to our survey. More sophisticated solutions increase the complexity and might influence the performance of large-scale deployments.

6.3   Kubernetes as Unified Cloud-Edge Platform

Lastly, it must be evaluated if K8s should be further considered as a cross-layer platform. As already explained in Sect. 4.3, there are many modifications and extensions needed to fulfill the basic requirements of cloud-edge orchestrations. In addition, the platform is rather designed for cloud computing than for the orchestration of complex multi-layer architectures [22]. However, in our perspective, K8s should still be in focus for cloud-edge orchestrations.

There are mainly three reasons for this, which are as follows: K8s is widely spread and can be seen as the state-of-the-art orchestration platform for containerized workloads. Since container virtualization leverages edge computing, a well-established, maintained, tested, and reliable framework is a crucial success factor fostering the penetration of edge computing, enabling better and more reliable real-time services. There are a lot of cloud providers and other platform as a service companies that offer K8s without an advanced configuration to set up hybrid architectures, for example Google Cloud Platform[18] or Jelastic[19]. Further, because edge computing is a relatively new paradigm, developers can benefit from already available expertise. This reduces the initial hurdle deploying those architectures since developers are already familiar with the technology. Secondly, security and high availability is even a significant aspect in implementing cloud-edge architectures. All interactions between the controlling instances, nodes, and containers that collect metrics must be secured. Otherwise, deployment to production is irresponsible. K8s offers built-in mechanisms for authentication, authorization, and user management. Next, support for high availability deployments, not only restricted to the actual deployment but also to the system-related components that are required to operate the architecture, is worth mentioning at this point. In this regard, there are many other custom implementations for edge computing out there, mostly prototypes, without proper security management or option for high availability. As the third and last

---

[18] https://cloud.google.com/.
[19] https://jelastic.com/.

reason to continue working on K8s for cloud-edge architectures is the extensibility of a well-designed ecosystem. Replacing fundamental components, like the scheduler component, adding labels to realize a network topology, and revising the considered metrics make K8s an eligible candidate for a unified platform.

Indeed, the set of possibilities is a major challenge and needs some standardization. As mentioned by [39], there is a strong need for standardization in orchestration-related activities. Architectural and implementation-related proposals with standardized components can be helpful running K8s in different setups for orchestration of complex and large-scale architectures. Specifically, this refers to providing custom native schedulers for edge computing, which can be easily pulled from a public repository and run alongside or in place of the native scheduler. Potential algorithms for orchestrating the cloud or edge layer should be taken from the literature and provided for K8s to enable widespread usage. This could also foster the use of established edge orchestration strategies, algorithms, or policies. Additional components, like custom metrics server, must also be standardized to expand the limited set of built-in supported metrics like the metrics server.

7   Conclusion and Future Work

Edge computing complements the cloud by bringing additional resources closer to end-users to achieve reliable and low-latency quality of service for real-time applications. Providing and distributing applications is mainly performed with container technology, where workloads are executed on a container runtime, usually pulled from a central registry. Cloud-edge orchestration activities comprise the workload distribution on a set of resource-limited nodes. Over time, several approaches emerged that took K8s, a container orchestration platform built for the cloud, for cloud-edge orchestration. Since many authors claimed that K8s is not ready for this kind of orchestration, they proposed several improvements.

In this paper, we evaluated those architectural proposals that tackle several limitations of K8s as a cloud-edge orchestration platform. We have done this based on essential requirements of edge computing, edge orchestration, and capabilities of native K8s that were obtained from a literature survey.

As a result, we identified several benefits and drawbacks of the established architectures. Major issues like real-time resource utilization, network awareness, and network topology were solved quite well. Other aspects, however, were neglected. These aspects comprise especially implementing different provision models, like scaling and offloading between the cloud and edge layer. Furthermore, fault-tolerant cluster architectures for managing cloud-edge architectures are in the early stages. The missing consideration of appropriate container registry placement strategies was also identified as a major challenge.

In addition, we assessed if the shortcomings of K8s for cloud-edge orchestrations could be resolved with an appropriate amount of effort. We conclude that based on the already available partial solutions, K8s-based cloud-edge orchestration should still be in focus for further improvement and research.

For our future work, we still want to consider K8s as a unified orchestration platform, even for the edge. We do believe that a high degree in standardization of the extensions that are necessary to serve cloud-edge architectures can brace the position of K8s as a standard orchestration system. Our following contributions will specify a set of architectural blueprints that help set up production environments. Further, we want to guide how distinguished generic cloud-edge orchestration strategies, algorithms, and policies can be implemented by the usage of natively implemented K8s schedulers. The public availability of those schedulers provided by a public registry can foster the usage and active participation of K8s in edge computing. To examine the feasibility of the proposed architectural blueprints, we plan to provide reference implementations that are evaluated and tested at scale to achieve evidence that K8s can run large and sophisticated cloud-edge architectures in production.

References

1. Aazam, M., Zeadally, S., Harras, K.A.: Offloading in fog computing for IoT: review, enabling technologies, and research opportunities. Futur. Gener. Comput. Syst. **87**, 278–289 (2018)
2. Ahmed, E., Rehmani, M.H.: Mobile edge computing: opportunities, solutions, and challenges. Futur. Gener. Comput. Syst. **70**, 59–63 (2017)
3. Al-Tarawneh, M.A.B.: Mobility-aware container migration in cloudlet-enabled IoT systems using integrated muticriteria decision making. Int. J. Adv. Comput. Sci. Appl. **11**(9), 694–701 (2020)
4. Amaral, M., Polo, J., Carrera, D., Mohomed, I., Unuvar, M., Steinder, M.: Performance evaluation of microservices architectures using containers (2015)
5. Babou, C.S.M., Fall, D., Kashihara, S., Niang, I., Kadobayashi, Y.: Home Edge Computing (HEC): design of a new edge computing technology for achieving ultra-low latency. In: Liu, S., Tekinerdogan, B., Aoyama, M., Zhang, L.-J. (eds.) EDGE 2018. LNCS, vol. 10973, pp. 3–17. Springer, Cham (2018). https://doi.org/10.1007/978-3-319-94340-4_1
6. Bagchi, S., Siddiqui, M.B., Wood, P., Zhang, H.: Dependability in edge computing. Commun. ACM **63**(1), 58–66 (2019)
7. Barika, M., Garg, S., Zomaya, A.Y., Wang, L., Moorsel, A.V., Ranjan, R.: Orchestrating big data analysis workflows in the cloud. ACM Comput. Surv. **52**(5), 1–41 (2019)
8. Bilal, K., Khalid, O., Erbad, A., Khan, S.U.: Potentials, trends, and prospects in edge technologies: fog, cloudlet, mobile edge, and micro data centers. Comput. Netw. **130**, 94–120 (2018)
9. Bonomi, F., Milito, R., Zhu, J., Addepalli, S.: Fog computing and its role in the internet of things. In: Proceedings of the First Edition of the MCC Workshop on Mobile Cloud Computing - MCC 2012. ACM Press (2012)
10. Casalicchio, E.: Autonomic orchestration of containers: problem definition and research challenges. In: Proceedings of the 10th EAI International Conference on Performance Evaluation Methodologies and Tools. ACM (2017)
11. Casquero, O., Armentia, A., Sarachaga, I., Perez, F., Orive, D., Marcos, M.: Distributed scheduling in Kubernetes based on MAS for fog-in-the-loop applications. In: 2019 24th IEEE International Conference on Emerging Technologies and Factory Automation (ETFA). IEEE (2019)

12. Eidenbenz, R., Pignolet, Y.A., Ryser, A.: Latency-aware industrial fog application orchestration with Kubernetes. In: 2020 Fifth International Conference on Fog and Mobile Edge Computing (FMEC). IEEE (2020)
13. ETSI: Mobile-edge computing - introductory technical white paper (2014). https://portal.etsi.org/Portals/0/TBpages/MEC/Docs/Mobile-edge_Computing_-_Introductory_Technical_White_Paper_V118-09-14.pdf
14. Goethals, T., DeTurck, F., Volckaert, B.: Extending Kubernetes clusters to low-resource edge devices using virtual Kubelets. IEEE Trans. Cloud Comput. (2020)
15. Goethals, T., Volckaert, B., de Turck, F.: Adaptive fog service placement for real-time topology changes in Kubernetes clusters. In: Proceedings of the 10th International Conference on Cloud Computing and Services Science. SCITEPRESS - Science and Technology Publications (2020)
16. Haja, D., Szalay, M., Sonkoly, B., Pongracz, G., Toka, L.: Sharpening Kubernetes for the edge. In: Proceedings of the ACM SIGCOMM 2019 Conference Posters and Demos on - SIGCOMM Posters and Demos 2019. ACM Press (2019)
17. Han, Y., Shen, S., Wang, X., Wang, S., Leung, V.C.M.: Tailored learning-based scheduling for Kubernetes-oriented edge-cloud system (2021)
18. Hong, C.H., Varghese, B.: Resource management in fog/edge computing. ACM Comput. Serv. 52(5), 1–37 (2019)
19. Hoque, S., Brito, M.S.D., Willner, A., Keil, O., Magedanz, T.: Towards container orchestration in fog computing infrastructures. In: 2017 IEEE 41st Annual Computer Software and Applications Conference (COMPSAC). IEEE (2017)
20. Javed, A., Heljanko, K., Buda, A., Framling, K.: CEFIoT: a fault-tolerant IoT architecture for edge and cloud. In: 2018 IEEE 4th World Forum on Internet of Things (WF-IoT), pp. 813–818. IEEE (2018)
21. Kaur, K., Garg, S., Kaddoum, G., Ahmed, S.H., Atiquzzaman, M.: KEIDS: Kubernetes-based energy and interference driven scheduler for industrial IoT in edge-cloud ecosystem. IEEE Internet Things J. 7(5), 4228–4237 (2020)
22. Kayal, P.: Kubernetes in fog computing: feasibility demonstration, limitations and improvement scope: invited paper. In: 2020 IEEE 6th World Forum on Internet of Things (WF-IoT), pp. 1–6. IEEE (2020)
23. Klas, G.I.: Fog computing and mobile edge cloud gain momentum. Open Fog Consortium-ETSI MEC-Cloudlets (2015)
24. Morabito, R.: Virtualization on internet of things edge devices with container technologies: a performance evaluation. IEEE Access 5, 8835–8850 (2017)
25. Mouradian, C., Naboulsi, D., Yangui, S., Glitho, R.H., Morrow, M.J., Polakos, P.A.: A comprehensive survey on fog computing: state-of-the-art and research challenges. IEEE Commun. Surv. Tutorials 20(1), 416–464 (2018)
26. Naha, R.K., et al.: Fog computing: survey of trends, architectures, requirements, and research directions. IEEE Access 6, 47980–48009 (2018)
27. Ogbuachi, M.C., Reale, A., Suskovics, P., Kovács, B.: Context-aware Kubernetes scheduler for edge-native applications on 5G. J. Commun. Softw. Syst. 16(1), 85–94 (2020)
28. Pahl, C., Ioini, N.E., Helmer, S., Lee, B.: An architecture pattern for trusted orchestration in IoT edge clouds. In: 2018 Third International Conference on Fog and Mobile Edge Computing (FMEC). IEEE (2018)
29. Pahl, C., Lee, B.: Containers and clusters for edge cloud architectures - a technology review. In: 2015 3rd International Conference on Future Internet of Things and Cloud. IEEE (2015)
30. Premsankar, G., Francesco, M.D., Taleb, T.: Edge computing for the internet of things: a case study. IEEE Internet Things J. 5(2), 1275–1284 (2018)

31. Qiu, Y., Lung, C.H., Ajila, S., Srivastava, P.: LXC container migration in cloudlets under multipath TCP. In: 2017 IEEE 41st Annual Computer Software and Applications Conference (COMPSAC). IEEE (2017)
32. Qiu, Y., Lung, C.H., Ajila, S., Srivastava, P.: Experimental evaluation of LXC container migration for cloudlets using multipath TCP. Comput. Netw. **164**, 106900 (2019)
33. Santos, J., Wauters, T., Volckaert, B., Turck, F.D.: Resource provisioning in fog computing: from theory to practice †. Sensors **19**(10), 2238 (2019)
34. Satyanarayanan, M., Bahl, P., Caceres, R., Davies, N.: The case for VM-based cloudlets in mobile computing. IEEE Pervasive Comput. **8**(4), 14–23 (2009)
35. Satyanarayanan, M.: Edge computing. Computer **50**(10), 36–38 (2017)
36. da Silva, D.M.A., Asaamoning, G., Orrillo, H., Sofia, R.C., Mendes, P.M.: An analysis of fog computing data placement algorithms. In: Proceedings of the 16th EAI International Conference on Mobile and Ubiquitous Systems: Computing, Networking and Services. ACM (2019)
37. Svorobej, S., Bendechache, M., Griesinger, F., Domaschka, J.: Orchestration from the cloud to the edge. In: Lynn, T., Mooney, J.G., Lee, B., Endo, P.T. (eds.) The Cloud-to-Thing Continuum. PSDBET, pp. 61–77. Springer, Cham (2020). https://doi.org/10.1007/978-3-030-41110-7_4
38. Taherizadeh, S., Stankovski, V., Grobelnik, M.: A capillary computing architecture for dynamic internet of things: orchestration of microservices from edge devices to fog and cloud providers. Sensors **18**(9), 2938 (2018)
39. Vaquero, L.M., Cuadrado, F., Elkhatib, Y., Bernal-Bernabe, J., Srirama, S.N., Zhani, M.F.: Research challenges in nextgen service orchestration. Futur. Gener. Comput. Syst. **90**, 20–38 (2019)
40. Vaquero, L.M., Rodero-Merino, L.: Finding your way in the fog: towards a comprehensive definition of fog computing. ACM SIGCOMM Comput. Commun. Rev. **44**(5), 27–32 (2014)
41. Varghese, B., Wang, N., Barbhuiya, S., Kilpatrick, P., Nikolopoulos, D.S.: Challenges and opportunities in edge computing (2016)
42. Velasquez, K., et al.: Fog orchestration for the internet of everything: state-of-the-art and research challenges. J. Internet Serv. Appl. **9**(1) (2018)
43. Wang, J., Pan, J., Esposito, F., Calyam, P., Yang, Z., Mohapatra, P.: Edge cloud offloading algorithms: issues, methods, and perspectives. ACM Comput. Serv. **52**(1), 1–23 (2019)
44. Wöbker, C., Seitz, A., Mueller, H., Bruegge, B.: Fogernetes: deployment and management of fog computing applications. In: NOMS 2018–2018 IEEE/IFIP Network Operations and Management Symposium. IEEE (2018)
45. Yousefpour, A., et al.: All one needs to know about fog computing and related edge computing paradigms: a complete survey. J. Syst. Archit. **98**, 289–330 (2019)
46. Yu, Z., Wang, J., Qi, Q., Liao, J., Xu, J.: Boundless application and resource based on container technology. In: Liu, S., Tekinerdogan, B., Aoyama, M., Zhang, L.-J. (eds.) EDGE 2018. LNCS, vol. 10973, pp. 34–48. Springer, Cham (2018). https://doi.org/10.1007/978-3-319-94340-4_3

Simulated LoRa Sensor Network as Support for Route Planning in Solid Waste Collection

Miguel Angel Montañez Gomez$^{(\boxtimes)}$ ⓘ and Luis Fernando Niño Vasquez ⓘ

Facultad de Ingeniería - Depto. de Ingeniería de Sistemas e Industrial,
Universidad Nacional de Colombia, Bogotá, Colombia
mmontanezg@unal.edu.co

Abstract. Mass production and population growth have produced an increase in the generation of municipal solid waste (MSW) in urban settlements. In consequence, efficient treatment of waste has become a challenge for cleaning entities, possibly because they continue performing collecting operations using fixed periodic routes that exhaustively go across neighbourhood streets in search of every dumpster. Furthermore, in these operations recyclable material is not separated from disposable one, at least in Bogota, thus causing a negative impact on the environment. This work aims to prototype a sensing system that generates routes based on the actual fulfilment level reported by dumpsters. For this purpose, dumpsters were equipped with a level measurement device that uses a proximity ultrasonic sensor. Information was transmitted using a LPWAN (LoRa), and collected data were used to determine which of the dumpsters needs to be collected in the route planned for a specific date, according to the levels reported. Since an operation requires many collecting trucks, a K-means method is used to group dumpsters that are geographically close. A single district of Bogota was selected for demonstration purposes. The collecting sequence was calculated using an open Web service, whose results are shown on an Android mobile application. The mobile app uses the Google Maps routing service. The system shows important reduction of saturation and overflow of containers.

Keywords: IoT · Waste collection · Wireless sensor networks · LoRaWAN · Sensing system · CVRP · Geographic information GIS · Mobile application

1 Introduction

Globalization and industrialization of factories have changed society consumption habits, which increased the amount of products that are sold, used, replaced and discarded in small periods. Additionally, non-biodegradable packaging used to protect products and the fast growth of population induced massive amounts

Universidad Nacional de Colombia, Bogotá.

S. Paiva et al. (Eds.): SmartCity360° 2021, LNICST 442, pp. 231–243, 2022.
https://doi.org/10.1007/978-3-031-06371-8_15

of MSW production. Indeed, North America waste production has duplicated between 2006 and 2010. According to a report of the World Bank [10], 2.01 billion tons of MSW are generated worldwide each year, and at least 1/3 of that waste is not properly managed.

Non treated solid waste is endangering ecosystems, producing greenhouse gases, and contaminating ecosystems. These effects have a negative impact not only on human's health and life style, but also on animal habitats and ocean ecosystems. Then, an efficient treatment of solid waste management has become a critical aspect.

An efficient treatment of MSW encompasses at least 3 aspects: the reduction of waste generation, a structured recycling process and a proper disposition of non-reusable waste. Waste classification and transportation is an important step in the recycling process, and commonly city governments are responsible for collection logistics.

In [6] they reviewed how collecting MSW has been treated with a deterministic approach using periodic routes for more than 40 years. This problem is known as periodic vehicle routing (PVRP). Under this approach, collector trucks travel along fixed routes one or more days per week, repeating same routes every week. This approach was useful until a few years ago, but now it has shown to be inefficient, considering the increase in MWS production in big cities, such as Bogota. In some districts, solid waste overflows the container capacity and ends dispersed on the ground. This produces aesthetic problems of city cleanness that as a consequence of rotten food and their bad smells might attract insects or rats that transmit infections, thus turning the situation into a public health problem [13].

The remainder of this paper is organized as follows. Section 2 presents a brief review of related work. Section 3 describes the system implementation, including hardware integration, data collection and transmission, transmission range distance test, data simulation, route generation and mobile application demonstration. In Sect. 4, we discuss results and system performance. Finally, conclusions and future work are devised in Sect. 5.

2   Related Work

Trying to be sustainable and considering citizen well-being, governments of the cities strive to find an efficient way to collect and manage MSW. To deal with this concern, many approaches have been proposed. For instance, [2] proposed an efficient simulated annealing (SA) applied to MSW collection in Sanandaj, Iran. A two-phase memetic algorithm that uses clustering and sequencing for solving VRP with time-windows [4], swarm optimization [1]. These studies show important results, the first is reducing distances and collection times, and the second is a fast solution convergence, which is important considering VRP is an NP-hard problem.

Routing of vehicles using Geographic information systems GIS and network analytics has also been studied. In [7,9] they used the ArcGIS network analytics tools to define collection zones and streets paths. In these studies, fuel usage, distance, time and number of vehicles were quantified as variables in an efficiency equation to evaluate the solution performance.

These works offer static routes solutions, which underestimates the fact that waste generation is a non-deterministic phenomena. Then, using static routes might reduce distance, time or even the operation cost, but they are not estimating the real necessities of the city. One of the difficulties to do that estimation is the lack of updated information in relation to solid waste generation. This problem was identified by [12], who highlighted the importance of providing elements of collection systems with certain degree of perception, using IoT components like sensors, RFID labels or cameras to get real time information. The use of IoT can lead to an optimized collection based on the information reported by components.

An interesting solution for waste collection proposed under the IoT approach, is sensing system designed by [15], in which the measurement device integrates a load sensor HX711, temperature and humidity sensor DHT11, and GPS module NEO6M and a low cost ultrasonic sensors HC-SR04, the circuit was assembled on an Arduino board. Data is transmitted using a GPSR module SIM900 which operates in 2G cellular technology.

Cellular communications requires a complex infrastructure and considerable amount of energy, this can be overcome using LPWAN (Low Power Wide Area Networks), which is a set of technologies capable of covering wide areas with few devices. A relevant research of LPWAN applied to waste management systems is presented by [15]. In this case, information is transmitted using LoRa modulation, since the authors declare that the LoRa signal can deliver data in a range from 5 to 15 Km, consuming around 0.5 μA.

When data transmission is completed an IoT server receives data, it processes the information in such a way that efficiently computing routes becomes a challenge of high complexity because finding routes in multiple paths is a combinatorial problem. In the case of waste collection, trucks have a limited load capacity, they should go along a set of locations picking up the waste material until their load capacity is completed.

If locations are updated constantly, routing can be carried out with a combinatorial General Variable Neighborhood search as presented in [14]. With this method, containers are organized by insertion according to their characteristics. They are placed near to containers with similar latitude and longitude. Similarity is measured using Euclidean distance, so containers are organized in ascendant order in order to cluster containers spatially close. Once all the selected containers are inserted in the list, they are separated by preserving order and considering truckload capacity. This algorithm was coded in Fortran and validated with the benchmark offered by Heidelberg University in TSPLIB [17]. These approaches change the way we think about planning and logistics of waste collection process in urban areas.

3   Methods and Results

To solve this problem we propose a sensing system that reports update information of filling levels of dumpster located in the streets, then based on that information we calculate collection routes to save resources and avoid saturation and overflow. The proposed general system structure is outlined in Fig. 1.

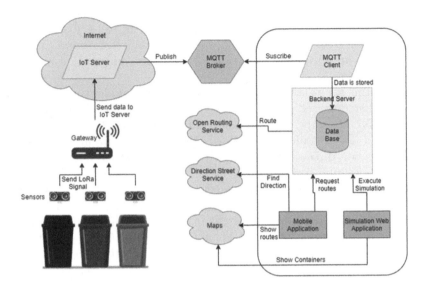

Fig. 1. General configuration and communication of system components

3.1   Hardware Integration

To measure the filling levels we decided to use a distance sensor HC-SR04. The operation principle behind this sensor is to emit an ultrasonic signal that travels through the air until it collides with the closest obstacle, then, the signal is reflected and the sensors receive the signal back. Distance is estimated by measuring the delay between the signal emission and when it is acquired back, as shown in Eq. 1.

$$Distance = \frac{Speed * Delay}{2} \tag{1}$$

To make hardware assembling easier, development boards were used integrating analogical and digital pins. For conceptual reasons, three configurations for measuring units were explored and analyzed. All these configurations are described in the block diagram in Fig. 2.

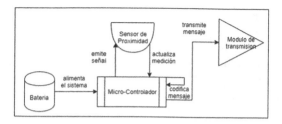

Fig. 2. Block diagram for Measuring unit components

The first configuration was made on the top of an Arduino Mega Board with a LoRa Shield created by Dragino. Both devices were connected according to the pins mapping and digital pins 30 and 31 were used to connect proximity sensors as shown in Fig. 3-B.

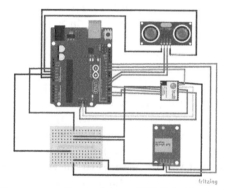

(A)interfacing for Arduino, SX1276, Neo 6M and HC-SR04

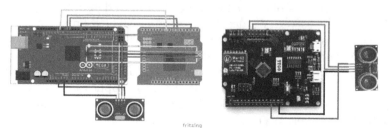

(B) interfacing for Arduino Mega and Dragino. (C) interfacing for TTGO and HC-SR04

Fig. 3. Diagrams of measurement devices connection

The second circuit was set using a board that integrates LoRa transmission module. This simplifies the connection of the component, since the only component that needs to be added to the board was the proximity sensor, as shown in Fig. 3-C.

Finally, the third circuit has a small difference compared with the previous ones, as this one integrates a GPS module (U-blox neo 6-m), so that geographical location is obtained precisely. This can help to be more accurate when planning the route. The circuit was assembled as shown in Fig. 3-A.

The controllers were programmed using a LoRa Library for Arduino written by [11]. The library implements a listener method, which is responsible of establishing a communication session with the IoT server after the joining request is accepted. Then, the distance and location measured by the sensor and GPS can be encoded and transmitted.

3.2 Data Collection and Transmission

Now that data was sensed and transmitted by measure units, it was necessary to configure the gateway, the server and the broker. For the gateway component, we found a commercial solution that can gather data transmitted with Lora modulation in a particular frequency. The selected reference was LG02 from Dragino has two communication channels that allow it to operate in full duplex[1].

For the IoT server, we decided to use the things Network TTN[2] because it supports LoRa authentication methods and simplifies the implementation of decoding and validation rules for the information being reported by the nodes. The first step to use the server is to register the gateway via TTN. We also configured an application that is intended for two purposes. The first is to associate all the measure nodes that will be part of the network. The second is to define general rules and procedures that will be applied to the information reported by the nodes associated to the application, so that information can be managed in a generalized way, e.g., decode functions and integrations.

Then, the integrations phase defines how to process data after it is received and validated in the server. We decided to use an MQTT broker because the server implements a Mosquito[3] instance and creates a topic with the name of the application configured. Therefore, whenever new data reach the server and are successfully evaluated according to the validation and decoding functions, the payload is published in the topic created for the application in the MQTT broker. To extract data from the broker an MQTT client was implemented and ran in the backend server. We used a Java implementation offered by TTN. The Implementation is open and it is available in a public repository [5]. When new information is obtained, we use a backend function that stores it a Postgres data base.

---

[1] Full duplex is a communication mode that allows to emit and receive messages simultaneously.

[2] An IoT server designed for LPWAN available at https://www.thethingsnetwork. org/.

[3] An open source lightweight MQTT broker supported by Eclipse foundation.

3.3   Transmission Results

Once gateway, server and broker configurations were carried out, we ran a trans-mission test. We could see messages passing through the gateway Logread, then those messages were cached by the IoT server, directed to the generated appli-cation, and decoded by the functions that extract measures, latitude, longitude and filling level. Finally, we could see the data being fetch by MQTT client running in the Backend Server. A simple web application interface was built to present the results (see Fig. 4).

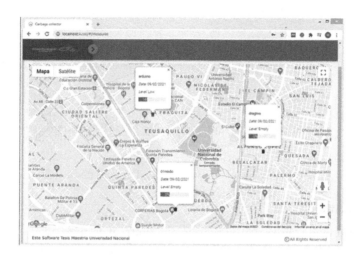

Fig. 4. Web application displaying data reported by measurement units.

The first result to highlight is that information flows along the LoRa network delivering data from measurement units to the backend database, as expected. We carried on the research executing a couple of tests to verify the real distance reached by the selected transmission modules. The gateway was started and placed in a fixed location; then, devices were configured to send a message every minute. These data were stored in the database and represented in a map, and the longest reached distance was measured.

The test results are shown in Fig. 5-A, where the green marker represents the fixed gateway location, while red markers indicate locations retrieved by the GPS in the measure unit. We selected the green marker and the furthest red market locations, after using Google Maps to approximate distance in the first test. The longest distance was about 488 m.

First test evidenced that signal did not reached the gateway when there was an obstacle, e.g., a wall that interrupts the direct line of sight. Thus, we concluded that an effective transmission requires a direct line of sight between both devices. Consequently, for the second test, we decided to find a high-altitude location to place the gateway, then, we started walking away from the gateway in a low-density building area so that the direct line of sight was easier to achieve. The second test showed longer distances than the first one, specifically, 1.39 km (Fig. 5-B).

(A) locations reported by Dragino in transmission test. (B) maximum range reached with Dragino measurement unit.

Fig. 5. Transmission test using Dragino circuit

3.4   Data Simulation

As we only provide three real measurement units, it is hard to generate other significant plans and routes for collecting MSW. Then, it was required to simulate a greater number of units reporting filling levels in order to evaluate route calculation under complex conditions.

The simulation was divided into two phases. The first one was to put representations of empty containers on streets where a truck could reach them and find an even distribution along the study area. The second phase was to update the level of containers using random numbers between 0 and 100 that represented the percentage of filling. These numbers have the same mean and standard deviation found in a dataset of waste collecting routes from Austin Texas, downloaded from Kaggle[4].

When the simulation was completed a heuristic approach was used to prioritize streets reporting container with higher levels of filling, those street were clustered using a K-means method, to avoid over computing finding the number of clusters with a convergence strategy, and we estimate K as the number of trucks required for the operation. That number trucks matches the number of groups. Thus, after grouping, each truck could be assigned exactly to one group, hence, we include a constraint to avoid that the accumulated volume of a group of streets exceeds the volume that one truck can carry. The result of street clustering is shown in Fig. 6.

---

[4] This dataset is offered by Austin government it includes information of Austin waste and diversion 2008–2016 [3].

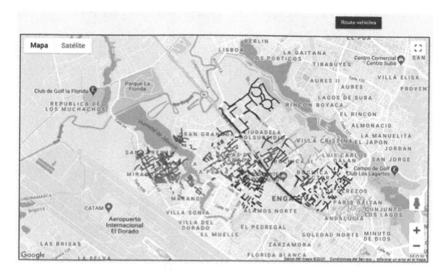

Fig. 6. Prioritized streets clustering with K-means method using K = 9.

3.5   Route Calculation and Delivery

To calculate routes we used a service called ORS, its use is well documented and it is based on an open source project available in a public repository at [8], the API can be tested through a web application[5], K-means lead us to assign exactly one truck to a clustered group of containers; then, we transform each container location to a job to fit the format that the ORS API expects. As a response, the service returns a JSON object containing a list of trucks with an array of container locations with high priority that the truck must visit, in a specific order that reduces the travel distance. Subsequently, the solution is stored in the database to avoid reprocessing. A mobile application was coded in Flutter to show the routes the routing Service delivered; we used a REST architecture simply exposing services to manage the request made by client applications.

A small feature of the mobile app is presented in Fig. 7 A and B, when the start route button is pressed, the application will consume the Google Directions API to find the fastest way to arrive from the driver's current location to the first container in the route using real-time traffic information. When the first container is reached and served, the next container button is enabled to find the path from the last visited location to the next container in the route. This operation is repeated for all containers until all containers in the route are visited, a progress bar indicates the collection progress and it is updated every time a new container is reached.

---

[5] https://openrouteservice.org/dev/#/api-docs/optimization.

(A) Dumpster selected by priority to be collected . (B) Route from location of the driver to the first container.

Fig. 7. Collection route displayed in mobile app

4   Discussion

To evaluate the results, we will analyze them separately by layers. Regarding the data collection process, namely the "physical layer", the measurement units extract precise filling levels and communicate them efficiently to the server, and the MQTT broker acts as a bridge to connect the IoT server with Back-End services. Then, data can be stored in a database where applications can easily access them. Therefore, we consider that although some elements that can be enhanced, the physical part of the system is working properly.

The logical part of the system is an approach to how to profit and manage collected data. There are possibly more precise and efficient ways to treat these data. There are some elements that can significantly be improved in the system. Some of them are:

1. Using LoRa as transmission technology needs some considerations. Since LoRa uses a centered star topology gateway, which is required to find an efficient gateway distribution that maximizes the coverage region by reducing number of gateways.
2. Gateways should be placed in altitude above the building average height, trying to generate a direct line of sight from the gateway to measurement units. Notwithstanding, tuning parameters such as the Spreading Factor might upgrade signal power. It is convenient to review node distribution and configuration, as suggested by [16].

3. Measurement units can perform well even without a GPS sensor, which is not decisive as container locations can be indexed to the data schema when units are installed and identified by a unique ID code. The containers will remain almost in the same locations, so they can be updated few times a year. This reduces the cost of measurement units in 33% approximately, but also reduces energy consumption.

4. To increase profits on collected material, routes should be separated. There must be at least two types of routes: one to collect general disposable waste and another for recyclable material. The last one must be properly classified and managed, avoiding it being contaminated and ending in landfills, where it becomes a source of contamination and damage for the environment.

5 Conclusions

MSW has being constantly increasing in the last years, affecting human health, life style and environments. The city governments made a great effort to treat waste in a responsible and sustainable way. To tackle this situation, an efficient sensing system which allowed cities to plan and take data driven decisions was proposed.

A prototype was implemented using LoRa as transmission technology. Data flow was managed along all the network components until data was stored in a GIS database. Collected data was processed to generate collection routes that prioritize the gathering of containers reporting high levels, thus increasing the collected volume and reducing travel times. Planned routes were displayed in a mobile application in order to assist truck drivers throw the journey, as support for the operation.

The value of these systems is that they target the specific problem of lack of updated information that prevents to plan MSW collection routes in a dynamic way. This is done by selecting the appropriate technologies according to a Bogota single district physical conditions. Then integrating those technologies in an synergistic way along the IoT layers (physical, networking, data processing and Application), Thus, attempting to deliver wellness to collection enterprises and citizens, by bringing benefits such as: clean streets, classification, make the most of recyclable material, producing a circular economy in which production and consumption habits are responsible with the environment and public health.

This research shows why updated data are an important asset and how cities can take advantage of them to better plan typical operations, such as MSW collection. The development of this prototype demonstrates the technical viability of implementing sensing systems enabled by IoT and GIS in real environments.

For a real environment deployment some points need to be consider: i) sensors must be adjusted with a directive angle to acquire accurate measurements; ii) efficiently managing energy on measurement devices; iii) the spreading factor configuration when there are many nodes in a small area and iv) including relevant and detailed terrain characteristics so that routes can be computed more precisely.

References

1. Abdulkader, M.M., Gajpal, Y., Elmekkawy, T.Y.: Hybridized ant colony algorithm for the Multi Compartment Vehicle Routing Problem. Appl. Soft Comput. J. **37**, 196–203 (2015). https://doi.org/10.1016/j.asoc.2015.08.020
2. Babaee Tirkolaee, E., Abbasian, P., Soltani, M., Ghaffarian, S.A.: Developing an applied algorithm for multi-trip vehicle routing problem with time windows in urban waste collection: a case study. Waste Manage. Res. **37**(1_suppl), 4–13 (2019). https://doi.org/10.1177/0734242X18807001
3. Boysen, J.: Austin waste and diversion (2017). https://www.kaggle.com/jboysen/austin-waste
4. Bustos Coral, D., Oliveira Santos, M., Toledo, C., Fernando Niño, L.: Clustering-based search in a memetic algorithm for the vehicle routing problem with time windows. In: 2018 IEEE Congress on Evolutionary Computation, CEC 2018 - Proceedings, p. 8 (2018). https://doi.org/10.1109/CEC.2018.8477710
5. Cambier, R.: TTN Java SDK mosquito integration (2016). https://github.com/TheThingsNetwork/java-app-sdk
6. Campbell, A.M., Wilson, J.H.: Forty years of periodic vehicle routing. Networks **63**(1), 2–15 (2014). https://doi.org/10.1002/net.21527
7. Chaudhary, S., Nidhi, C., Rawal, N.R.: GIS-based model for optimal collection and transportation system for solid waste in Allahabad City. In: Abraham, A., Dutta, P., Mandal, J., Bhattacharya, A., Dutta, S. (eds.) Advances in Intelligent Systems and Computing, vol. 814, pp. 45–65. Springer, Singapore (2019). https://doi.org/10.1007/978-981-13-1501-5_5
8. Coupey, J.: Coupey: Vehicle routing open-source optimization machine. https://github.com/VROOM-Project/vroom
9. Jwad, Z.A., Hasson, S.T.: An optimization approach for waste collection routes based on GIS in Hillah-Iraq. In: ICOASE 2018 - International Conference on Advanced Science and Engineering, pp. 60–63. Institute of Electrical and Electronics Engineers Inc., November 2018. https://doi.org/10.1109/ICOASE.2018.8548889
10. Kaza, S., Yao, L.C., Bhada-Tata, P., Van Woerden, F.: What a Waste 2.0. World Bank (2018)
11. Kooijman, M.: Arduino-LMIC: LoraWAN-in-C library (2015)
12. Medvedev, A., Fedchenkov, P., Zaslavsky, A., Anagnostopoulos, T., Khoruzhnikov, S.: Waste management as an IoT-enabled service in smart cities. In: Balandin, S., Andreev, S., Koucheryavy, Y. (eds.) ruSMART 2015. LNCS, vol. 9247, pp. 104–115. Springer, Cham (2015). https://doi.org/10.1007/978-3-319-23126-6_10
13. Ospina-Pinto, C., Rincón-Pardo, M., Soler-Tovar, D., Hernández-Rodríguez, P.: The role of rodents in the transmission of Leptospira spp. In swine farms. Revista de Salud Publica **19**(4), 555–561 (2017). https://doi.org/10.15446/rsap.v19n4.41626
14. Papalitsas, C., Karakostas, P., Andronikos, T., Sioutas, S., Giannakis, K.: Combinatorial GVNS (General Variable Neighborhood Search) optimization for dynamic garbage collection. Algorithms **11**(4), 38 (2018). https://doi.org/10.3390/a11040038
15. Pardini, K., Rodrigues, J., Kozlov, S., Kumar, N., Furtado, V.: IoT-based solid waste management solutions: a survey. J. Sensor Actuator Netw. **8**(1), 5 (2019). https://doi.org/10.3390/jsan8010005. http://www.mdpi.com/2224-2708/8/1/5

16. Premsankar, G., Ghaddar, B., Slabicki, M., Francesco, M.D.: Optimal configuration of LoRa networks in smart cities. IEEE Trans. Industr. Inf. **16**(12), 7243–7254 (2020). https://doi.org/10.1109/TII.2020.2967123
17. Heidelberg University: TSPLIB (1997). http://elib.zib.de/pub/mp-testdata/tsp/tsplib/tsplib.html

Cognitive Computing and Cyber Physical Systems

Exploring the Effects of Precision Livestock Farming Notification Mechanisms on Canadian Dairy Farmers

Muhammad Muhaiminul Islam[(✉)] and Stacey D. Scott

University of Guelph, Guelph, ON, Canada
{mislam12,stacey.scott}@uoguelph.ca

Abstract. Modern dairy farms are increasingly adopting technologies to monitor animal health and welfare and send notifications to farmers when issues arise. These *precision livestock farming (PLF)* technologies promise increased animal health and farm productivity. Yet, few studies exist on the effects of these technologies on those who use them. Studies from Europe show the 24/7 nature of potential PLF notifications can make farmers feel always "on call", increasing their overall stress levels. An initial online survey of 18 Canadian dairy farmers was conducted to explore their experiences with PLF notifications. Reported benefits of PLF technologies include improved animal health and dairy products, labor benefits, and ease of data collection. The study also uncovered weaknesses of PLF notifications, including information uncertainty and overload, false alerts, inappropriate timing and communication mediums. Design recommendations are presented to improve PLF notification mechanisms.

Keywords: Precision livestock farming (PLF) technology · Notification mechanisms · Impact of PLF on dairy farmers · Farmers' mental workload

1 Introduction

There is a universal trend towards streamlining and enhancing farming practices in both livestock and crop farming by utilizing various state-of-the-art technologies to automate different farm processes. This modern style of farming is commonly called precision agriculture [1] and precision livestock farming (PLF) [2], referring to crop and livestock farming respectively. PLF involves the integration of software and hardware technologies that offer easier animal farm management by monitoring individual animals 24/7 on farms [3]. PLF technologies aim to improve the health and welfare of animals by reporting detected abnormalities to farm staff so they can take appropriate actions [2]. Thus, farmers can manage larger herds with reduced physical workload and labour costs, and allow them to meet increasing global demand [4].

PLF technologies use sensors to monitor animal behaviours and the state of the farm environment, and computer algorithms and applications to process collected sensor data and generate reports or send alerts to the farmer if necessary [5]. However, to be effective,

S. Paiva et al. (Eds.): SmartCity360° 2021, LNICST 442, pp. 247–266, 2022.
https://doi.org/10.1007/978-3-031-06371-8_16

PLF technologies must transform the raw data they collect into meaningful information and communicate this to farmers in a useful manner that facilitates animal care and farm operations [5]. Information from PLF technologies is often automatically sent to farmers in the form of notifications or alerts through various communication mediums (e.g., automated phone call, text message, dashboard application software) to make staff aware of new or ongoing animal or farm environment situations.

Prior research from Europe has shown that these automated communications can be a source of stress and can increase the mental workload for farm staff if the communications are not designed or managed effectively [6, 7]. A recent review [8] of advanced dairy farm technologies concluded:

> *"mental workload (stress) can sometimes be increased [when PLF are used] due to the complexity of the information involved in managing the multiple alarms or alerts and equipment failures...if the tools are not adapted to farmers' needs and skills, PLF can also lead to negative impacts on farmers and animals." (p. 273).*

To our knowledge, no studies have investigated whether automated communications from PLF technologies can be a similar source of stress for Canadian dairy farmers. As farming cultures, practices, and technologies can differ from region to region, it is unclear whether the European studies generalize to the Canadian dairy farming context.

To address this gap, we conducted a survey study to investigate the impact of PLF notification mechanisms on Canadian dairy farmers. Although a larger survey and follow-up were originally planned, the study was scaled back due to complications and additional stresses that dairy farmers faced at the time of data collection related to the onset of the global COVID-19 pandemic and the need for Canadian dairy producers to rapidly pivot operations to meet new health and safety protocols during wide-scale societal lockdowns. So, instead, we report on a pilot study that provides some initial evidence of Canadian dairy farmers' experiences that highlight trends and suggest directions for further research in this area. Note, while various terms are used by PLF technology manufacturers and the farming industry for PLF information automatically sent to farmers (e.g., alerts, alarms, warnings, messages, and communications), herein we collectively refer to these communications as notifications.

The online survey collected data from 18 dairy farmers (owner/operators, herdsmen, and employees) from the province of Ontario, Canada, a large dairy producing region in Canada. Results from this pilot study revealed many positive benefits of the PLF technologies employed on participants' farms, including reduced labour costs, improved appeal of farm work, and reduced difficulty of farm work. The survey also revealed that while the existing PLF notification mechanisms were not perceived as a significant source of stress for survey participants, there were still aspects of their design that sometimes caused stress or anxiety due to factors such as, the timing and medium of communication, false alarms, missed alerts, unclear messages and actions, and unnecessary communications.

To set the context for the study, the paper overviews the literature related to PLF notifications and their impact on farmers, and then details the study methodology. Next, the study results are presented. Finally, we discuss initial insights revealed by the pilot study for the design of PLF notification mechanisms and directions for future studies to better understand how to meet the informational needs of Canadian dairy farmers.

2 Related Literature

The literature review is focused on understanding the challenges with notification mechanisms of available PLF technologies in both academic and commercial literature that communicate with farmers when any abnormality arises. This section also includes how notification management is done from HCI perspectives in other domains.

2.1 Potential Negative Impacts of PLF Notifications on Farmers

While PLF technologies can reduce physical labour of farmers, studies have also shown these technologies can be a source of stress. For instance, a Norwegian study on automated milking systems (AMS) found that farmers reported feeling "always on call" due to information overload from their AMS [7]. A review on the impacts of PLF technologies on farmers found that excessive notifications and complex information from their PLF technologies sometimes increase farmers' mental workload [8]. To address this mental workload issue, Dominiak and Kristensen [39] suggested that PLF systems should prioritize alerts to help farmers understand which alerts require a response and how quickly they should respond.

PLF technologies can reduce physical and mental workload in some situations because farmers do not have to physically monitor their cows [9]. The health issues that are not easily detected by farmers can be measured by PLF technologies, such as vaginal temperature for artificial insemination, body temperature, heart rate, and exact calving time [9]. Yet, even useful PLF notifications may be stressful if not provided in an appropriate manner or at an appropriate time. This study seeks to understand what PLF notification mechanisms are used in the Canadian dairy industry, how effective they are for farmers, and the impacts they have on farmer's lives, both positive and negative.

2.2 Big Data in PLF and Need for Improved Information Interfaces

Many PLF technologies produce and accumulate a large quantity of data, frequently for long intervals of time, and often in real-time [10]. To cope with these large datasets, PLF researchers have started utilizing different big data processing methods for analyzing various process-generated, machine-generated, and human-generated data associated with their farms [11]. Yet, studies have shown that farmers sometimes find the information generated by PLF technologies too complex to use in their decision-making due to either its sheer volume or when no clear action is indicated [10, 12, 13]. This technology complexity can negatively affect farmers' view regarding integration of PLF technologies with their farms [8].

The volume and complexity of PLF data has prompted researchers to explore information visualization techniques to present data to the farmers in a manner that is more easily understood and interpreted to support farm decision-making [14]. The 'Dairy

Brain' system collected data of cows from multiple perspectives, analyzed, and presented these data in a form that facilitated farmers' decision-making [15]. Its approach used one technology to detect all animal and farm issues instead of a suite of technologies designed for a specific purpose to help reduce the complexity of farm management [15]. A recent survey of big data concluded that data science specialists should be involved in the PLF design process to foster creation of appropriate data representations for farmer decision making [11]. The need for improved data representations in PLF technologies was also found in a study of American dairy technologies [13]. However, discussed below, farmers need to be involved in the design process also.

2.3   The Need for a More User-Centred Approach in PLF Technologies

The PLF field is starting to observe and report that integration of these emerging technologies on farms might be hampered by the absence of user-centred (farmers and animals) design since most PLF technology design is technology- and profit-driven [16, 17]. Research has found that some PLF technologies provide limited utility to farmers, partially due to their complex and unfamiliar interfaces, which a 2013 study found to be largely dissimilar to the interfaces of similar traditional technologies [17]. Consequently, these technologies are not as beneficial to farmers in their farm management decision-making as intended [16, 18]. A PLF adoption study in Australia found that dairy farmers believe that involving them more directly in the design process of PLF innovations would help to make PLF technologies easier to learn and use, and would help to better address their farm operation needs [17].

As early as 2005, precision farming researchers identified the need for standard guidelines to guide the structure and incorporation of different precision farming technologies for more effective farmer decision-making [19]. Our pilot study found that while some technologies provide integrated functionalities, many technologies are still operated independently with different notification systems.

2.4   Lessons from the HCI Literature on Notification Management

The topic of automated notifications and how to manage them has been a subject of intense study in the broader human-computer interaction (HCI) field due to the increasing ubiquity of technology in our lives. Indeed, the website *interruptions.net* offers a comprehensive curated bibliography (currently over 900 articles) from the HCI, human factors, and related fields on the topic of interruptions, their affects, and strategies to mitigate them. As PLF notifications often interrupt farmers from other work or life activities, this body of knowledge may offer solutions or inspiration to improve the design of PLF notification mechanisms. Here we overview some relevant findings from the HCI literature but also encourage interested readers to dig further into this broader body of literature.

The timing, content, and medium used for notifying users have all shown to be important for effective notifications [20]. Today, people receive notifications from many different sources, such as text messaging, social media, emails, and mobile applications [21]. Receiving excessive notifications can reduce a person's productivity and can impact negatively on psychological well-being [22]. Notifications can also have negative effects on the user's emotional state [23, 24]. Receiving an irrelevant or non-urgent notification can distract from an important task and lead to task errors and poor decision-making [24, 29, 30]. A notification has two sides, including the utility of the information it provides to the users and the interruption users experience in their ongoing tasks [27–29]. Notification senders usually do not always consider the interruption that users experience upon receiving the notification [30].

HCI researchers have proposed several approaches to mitigate the negative effects of notifications. One approach is to assume some notifications are more important to the user than others and then act accordingly. For instance, a system can time the delivery of a notification based on its automatically classified level of importance [31]. Or, a system could allow users to modify the system settings to determine the timing of receiving a specific type of notification [22]. Our pilot study found that some PLF technologies allowed for this type of filtering, for instance, allowing users to have some types of notifications delivered to their phones and others to a system dashboard.

The importance or urgency of a notification has also been used in the HCI to determine how notifications are displayed to the user. For instance, in the 'Scope' system, notifications from various sources (email, instant messaging, task lists, calendar, etc.) were displayed in different areas of a notification visualization window based on their source and urgency, with more urgent notifications displayed more centrally [32]. A key concept in this system was that notifications from different sources were managed together in one place, which may be relevant for PLF as notifications can come from different devices. An assumption underlying any approach that uses importance or urgency in notification management is that this information is known, or can be discovered, by the system. A starting point is for designers to have a strong understanding of farmer's information needs. Our pilot study provides some insights into this issue.

Another approach to notification management is to try to determine whether it is a good time to interrupt a user, based on their mental or physical context, for instance, their cognitive state (inferred from physiological sensors) [33] or their activity (inferred from various sources, including audio sensors and calendar data) [34]. Kern and Schiele [29] combined the notion of importance and user context in their work to determine when to send notifications to a user, asserting that multiple factors are needed to make appropriate system decisions about notifications.

In summary, the literature shows PLF technologies and their notifications can be stressful and ineffective due to information complexity, information overload, and poor usability. The PLF field has acknowledged the need for a more user-centred approach to improve the utility and usability of PLF technologies and their notification mechanisms. Information overload and interruptions caused by automated notifications is a common problem identified in many domains, and existing solutions from the broader field of HCI may provide some guidance for managing PLF notifications. This will be discussed further during the discussion of the study findings.

3   Research Methodology

The goals of this research were to understand what notification mechanisms are currently used in PLF technologies deployed on Canadian dairy farms, and the positive and negative impacts of these mechanisms on farmers' work and lives. To address these goals, an online survey was conducted of farmers from the province of Ontario, which produces 33% of Canada's milk supply with 3,446 dairy farms [25]. The survey collected both qualitative and quantitative data using the online survey tool Qualtrics®. As afore-mentioned, a large-scale survey, and follow-up interviews, were originally planned, but due to the onset of the COVID-19 pandemic, and the stress and additional workload that ensued for dairy farmers to meet new health and safety measures, data collection was cut short. Here, we report on the initial data collected, which serves as a pilot study that still provides useful insights into industry trends and highlights directions for further study. Yet, it has limits for broad-scale generalizability and should be interpreted as such.

The study protocols were reviewed and approved by the University of Guelph's institutional research ethics office.

3.1 Survey Design

The survey was designed iteratively. The initial survey questions were based on knowl-edge gained from the literature, online research of the dairy and PLF fields, and discus-sion with local dairy experts. The survey was reviewed by HCI experts, academic dairy researchers on our campus, and a dairy industry expert. The survey was revised based on their feedback. The survey consisted of a total of 63 questions, including two questions related to consent and age eligibility. Due to the conditional nature of the question design in some sections, most participants were not asked all questions.

The first block of questions collected demographic information about the participant. The next four blocks related to the notification mechanisms used in four commonly used dairy PLF technologies, including automated milking system (AMS), automated heat detection system (AHDS), automated calving time detection system (ACTDS), and automated activity monitoring system (AAMS).

The questions related to each of the above technologies were displayed only if the participant indicated they used the technology and they received notifications from it. The set of questions in each section were designed to be as similar as possible, to enhance the usability of the survey. Participants were asked how much experience they had with a technology, number of notifications they received in a typical week, medium of receiving those notifications, type of information received, actions they perform after receiving notifications, pros and cons of the current notification mechanism, and overall feedback on the notification mechanism. The final block of questions probed farmers on their perceived level of stress due to PLF notifications and asked for participants' overall thoughts on improving their PLF notification mechanisms.

3.2 Survey Distribution

The survey was advertised through a number of channels, including relevant social media platforms, such as Twitter™ channels of relevant regional farming and agricultural individuals and organizations and regional farming groups on Facebook. Additionally, the research team attended the Southwestern Ontario Dairy Symposium in February 2020 to advertise the online survey in person at a booth at the symposium tradeshow. We provided interested dairy producers with leaflet that included the study advertisement with the study link and QR code they could scan to access the online survey. We have also contacted dairy technology retailers to distribute the survey. The survey data collection period ran from February 6, 2020 to March 31, 2020.

3.3 Data Collection and Analysis

A total of 51 survey records were recorded. The collected survey records were reviewed for validity. First, any "in progress" (i.e. abandoned) surveys were deleted and unusual surveys, such as those completed within 2–3 min or those with IP addresses from outside Ontario, were also deleted. Only survey records that included reasonable, logical response patterns, and topic-relevant free form comments were included in the data analysis. Data culling resulted in a total of 18 complete, valid survey records that were included in the data analysis. There were 3 female and 15 male participants. Twelve participants were owners/managers, three were herdsman, and three were employees. As per the original informed consent letter, five participants were selected from a random draw and provided with $40 gift cards.

The quantitative data were first explored using Qualtrics® built-in analysis tools, which provide simple bar charts showing frequency statistics, and then in Microsoft Excel® when more controlled charts were needed, based on the survey question. Next, correlation analyses were conducted to determine relationships between stress level of the farmers and their demographics. Pearson correlation was used to investigate whether there were any linear relationships between the variables. Finally, the qualitative data in the form of free-form answers were reviewed for themes and insights.

4 Results

The collected pilot study data provided information on what type of PLF technologies participants used, from what technologies they received notifications, and what communication mediums they received these notifications. We also collected information on the perceived benefits, challenges, and stress levels related to these PLF technologies. Note, due to our ethics protocols, participants were free to skip any question in the survey they wished. Thus, when frequency data are reported, the number of respondents for that specific question is always indicated as "of X participants" or "/X" for brevity.

4.1 Sources of PLF Notifications for Study Participants

In total, 11 of 18 participants (61%) reported using one or more automated milking systems (AMS) on their farms. Of those 11 AMS users, 10 participants (91%) reported that they received notification from their AMS. In total, 16 of 17 participants (94%) reported using and receiving notifications from automated heat detection systems (AHDS) on their farms. In total, five of 17 participants (29%) reported using and receiving notifications from automated calving time detection systems (ACTDS). Given the small sample size of ACTDS users, these data were omitted from further data analyses. Thirteen of 17 participants (76%) reported using automated activity monitoring systems (AAMS) on their farms. Of those 13 AAMS users, six participants (46%) reported that they received notification from their AAMS.

4.2 Notification Mediums

Based on our background research, it was anticipated that current PLF technologies used four main communication mediums to convey notifications to farmers: text messages, phone calls, email, and displaying information in the dashboard of the PLF technology's associated computer application for desktop, tablet, or mobile phone. As shown in Fig. 1, the study data confirmed this expectation. The data shows that the application dashboard is used most often across PLF technologies as a communication medium (20 responses in total, across AMS, AHDS, and AAMS), whereas other mediums such as phone calls (7 responses for AMS only), text messages (6 responses across AMS, AHDS, and AAMS), and email (4 responses across AMS, AHDS, and AAMS) are not used as frequently. These data show that, at least among the sampled study population, newer technologies like AAMS and AHDS do not use the phone at all as a communication medium, while this is heavily relied on by AMS.

Some AMS users reported receiving notifications via multiple mediums (e.g., by phone calls and application dashboard). One farmer (P11), who had selected text messages from the survey options for medium, clarified in a free-form response that they meant the AHDS system sends alerts using their native mobile phone alerting system via the AHDS mobile application system. It is possible that other participants who indicated text message notifications meant this as well or may also be receiving notifications via native phone notifications, which was not explicitly captured in the survey.

The study found that some systems, by default, use different mediums to communicate information of different importance or urgency. For instance, one AMS user (P2) reported receiving notifications by phone calls for issues that demanded their attention, while general cow health information was sent to the system dashboard, as illustrated in their comment,

"I consider an alert something that is brought to my attention. In our case this is phone call regarding system operation. Lots of dashboard notifications about cow health, but [I] search reports, don't get a text/phone call about." (P2).

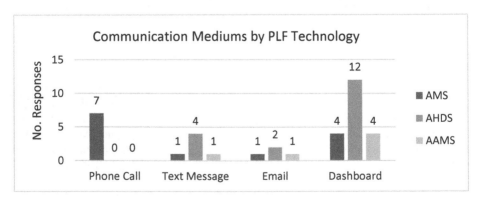

Fig. 1. Reported communication mediums (phone call, text message, email, dashboard) by PLF technology (AMS, AHDS, AAMS)

Some participants reported changing the default factory settings of their AMS to receive different types of information through a preferred medium, for example, changing the settings to receive non-critical notifications through the dashboard instead of through phone calls, as illustrated by the participants' comments, *"Reduced certain non-critical alarms so they don't call but just leave dashboard notice" (P10)*, and *"Send heat detection and distress alerts at night, turned off cleaning alarm phone calls. There is no immediate action anyways." (P16)*.

4.3   Content of PLF Notifications and Farmers' Responses

Most notifications farmers get from AMS are about cow activities such as rumination and lameness (9/11), system failures (7/11), or cows in heat (7/11). They also get notifications about cows overdue for milking (3/11), substances in the milk (3/11), cases of mastitis (3/11), and abnormal cow temperature (2/11). In free-form comments, participants also reported other types of information reported by their AMS not specifically listed in the survey, including cow weight, feeding system issues, and calving distress.

Upon receiving notifications from the AMS, most of the time farmers checked the system (8/11) and reset the system if necessary (3/11). These findings are consistent with the fact that farmers often receive notifications regarding system failures. Participants also reported checking a cow (5/11) as a common action after receiving an AMS notification. In free-form responses, farmers also reported checking the system upon receiving notifications to determine action.

As expected, most notifications farmers reported receiving from their AHDS related to the identity of a cow who is in heat (14/16) and the breeding status of a cow when she is in heat (10/16). Participants (6/16) also reported in free-form text they received notifications about the optimum insemination time. Two participants also reported that their AHDS provided the location of the cow. This is a relatively new feature available in some AHDS systems. One participant (P5) reported in a free-form response that their AHDS notifications only reports a cow is in heat but does not give the identity of the cow. Thus, they had to open the AHDS application to know which cow was in heat. Farmer's responses to the special-purpose PLF technologies AHDS and ACTDS were not collected since actions related to these PLF devices are more predicable (e.g., check the cow and take necessary steps for insemination or calving).

While AAMS systems were primarily reported to provide farmers information about unusual activity timings, such as unusual lying, standing, ruminating, and walking times (11/13), some participants also reported receiving notifications about heat events (4/11) and calving time detection (1/11) from their AAMS. Three commonly reported actions taken by farmers upon receiving these notifications were to check the cow with the reported issue (4/6), provide necessary care to the cow (4/6), and apply medicine if necessary (4/6). Sometimes they contacted their veterinarian (3/6) and separated the cow with issues from other cows, if necessary (2/6).

4.4   Benefits and Challenges of PLF Notification Mechanisms

Participants reported many benefits of PLF notifications, such as improved livestock health (responses: 6 for AMS; 14 for AHDS; 1 for AAMS), labour benefits, including increased appeal of work and flexible and reduced work hours (responses: 12 for AMS; 6 for AHDS; 3 for AAMS), improved milk product (responses: 3 for AMS; 11 for AHDS; 4 for AAMS), ease of data collection for the regulatory board and business operations (responses: 2 for AMS; 11 for AHDS; 6 for AAMS), decreased stress (responses: 2 for AMS; 3 for AHDS), and wanting to keep up with technology and meeting future needs (responses: 7 for AMS; 12 for AHDS; 2 for AAMS). Overall, the study data showed that PLF technologies were highly valued by participants and allowed some to work off-farm–common among small farm operators in Canada who often struggle to turn a profit from farming alone given competition from global and large-scale producers, as illustrated by the following comment related to AMS notifications, *"Can't be there 24/7. Pro, I have an off farm job and the AMS [allows] me to be successful in that role while getting the opportunity to farm as well" (P1).*

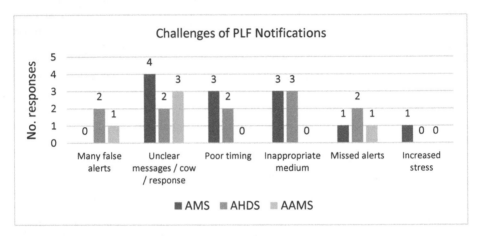

Fig. 2. Challenges of PLF Technologies

Despite these benefits, participants also reported various challenges they experienced with notifications from their PLF technologies, as summarized in Fig. 2. As the data show, the most reported challenge across PLF technologies relates to information uncertainty, for instance, in the form of unclear messages, missing identity of a cow, urgency of the issue being reported, or uncertainty around what, if any, action is needed. One AMS user commented, *"The voice is not always clear and the responsiveness to confirming and resetting the system when you push the appropriate button is not great." (P2).* Some participants reported that notifications are sometimes too generic to be that useful without further investigation. One AHDS user reported that upon receiving notifications from their AHDS they had to go through a *"lengthy process to get into [the] slow app to find out which cow is in heat" (P5).* Thus, sometimes finding the information they required was cumbersome.

Receiving notifications via inappropriate mediums was the next most reported challenge (for AMS and AHDS only). For instance, as discussed in the prior section, farmers preferred non-critical or non-urgent information to be sent to the system dashboard rather than sent via a phone call or text message. The timing of notifications was the next most reported challenge (for AMS and AHDS only). Some farmers reported that the timing of AMS notifications sometimes interrupted more important work or life activities. An AHDS user reported inappropriate notification timing as a challenge, as illustrated by their comment, *"I wish refresh of data would be more current. Mostly 4 h behind, sometimes. [For example] if it is 10am now, the last data point showing is 6 or 8am"* (P2).

A few participants reported they sometimes missed important information because of the timing and/or medium of communication. One AAMS user reported their dissatisfaction with their system's protocol to wait for a period of time before reporting detected abnormal behaviour, as illustrated by their comment, *"Sometimes it does not alert me soon enough. There is a time delay where it waits to see 2 days of decreased inactivity before an alert. Hoping to contact company to make a change on this."* (P11).

A few AHDS and AAMS users reported that their systems sent many false alarms or inaccurate data related to detected heat events or abnormal behaviour, as illustrated by the comment by an AHDS user, *"I feel like there are a lot of bugs because we do receive false alerts all the time and sometimes the readings are incorrect."* (P17). No AMS users reported receiving false alarms from their systems, possibly because AMS technology is a more mature, and potentially more refined, technology. Only one participant, an AMS user, reported increased stress as a challenge experienced by their AMS notifications due to the fact that they could receive a message at any moment.

Overall, AHDS users reported far fewer challenges with notifications from their systems, with 6/16 participants explicitly adding comments like *"no challenges"* and *"no challenges, very happy with alert system"*. This may be due to the very specialized scope of its detection and notification functionality compared to the much broader types of notifications provided by AMS and AAMS systems.

4.5 Perceived Stress Levels Related to PLF Notifications

Participants were asked to rate how stressed they felt during their daily activities because of the notifications they receive from their PLF technologies on a 11-point scale, with the anchors 0 = not at all stressed and 10 = extremely stressed. Most participants rated their stress level very low, with a mean stress rating of 2.006. Some related participants comments included, *"Not many alarms = no stress"* (P15) and *"Don't mind getting alerts. It's always for a good reason. It does not stress me out. It's all about being proactive on the farm instead of being reactive."* (P14).

However, a few participants commented that they felt stressed because of notifications received from their farm technologies. Extracting information from benefit and challenge data explicitly, the result shows that most participants (84%) said that the communications decreased their stress, with only a few participants (16%) reporting the opposite. Some common themes as sources of stress reported by participants included unclear information and required actions, false alerts, inappropriate timing and communication medium, and missed alerts. Although no question asked explicitly about excessive information, one participant reported receiving unnecessary notifications. This reason was also reported as a cause of stress by the participant, as illustrated by their comment, *"I think the alerts should be less and we should only receive alerts if there is a problem. We have done farming for a long time without these systems in place and have done just fine. I think they are good but should just stay in the background." (P17).*

Another reported source of stress was the need to drop what they are currently doing after receiving a notification, as illustrated by the comment, *"Could be away from the farm and receive an urgent alert you may have to leave an event for if there is no one else available to fix the alert" (P5).* Therefore, some farmers feel they cannot travel far from the farm without someone on call. This implies that farmers never feel off duty without someone on call, as illustrated by the participant comment, *"Not leave far from the farm without someone on call. This stress was present to the same degree before installing the alert system." (P5).*

Some participants reported stress due to the fact that notifications can be the source of bad news, such as a system breakdown that is expensive to fix or that causes production loss, as illustrated by the comments, *"Cow time away from robots. Having to fix robot" (P1), "Equipment breaking down and if it breaks down it will be expensive to fix." (P3),* and *"I worry that the alert will be something bad and when I hear it I always stop what I'm doing and look and during that time period I get nervous and increased anxiety" (P17).* Stress can also stem from the timing of a notification, for instance, when it requires the farmer to *"[get] up in the middle of the night" (P16).*

A follow-up question asked participants how they coped with stress experienced from PLF notifications. Farmers reported different strategies to cope with the aforementioned stresses, such as having someone on call when they are away from the farm, involving family members so they can help address problems that arise, not being bothered too much about the notification in the moment, and installing backup technology to help manage system breakdowns. The following sample comments illustrate some of these strategies, *"You just let it go and deal with it when it works best, or the next time you are in the barn" (P10),* and *"Other [second] robot can manage while I am at work. Milking 65 cows on 2 robots" (P1).* Some farmers reported getting better at handling notifications in more effective ways over time as they get used to their devices, as illustrated by the participant comment, *"As I get more used to receiving alerts (we just started less than a year ago) I start to feel less anxious. I also changed the alerts on my device so it just vibrates" (P17).*

Collected data were analyzed to determine possible demographic factors in the stress levels reported by farmers due to PLF notifications. Table 1 represents the correlation matrix between stress level and years of farming experience, age of farmer, and size of farm (number of cows). The correlation coefficient (r) for stress level and years of experience is $r = -0.710$, suggesting a strong negative relationship between stress level and years of experience in dairy farming [1]. Thus, as farming experience increased, the reported stress level decreased. This correlation was significant ($p = .002$). A moderate negative relationship ($r = -0.481$) was found between stress level and age, indicating that older farmers experience less stress, potentially because they have more experience with handling stress. This correlation was marginally significant ($p = .0059$). A weak positive relationship ($r = 0.201$) was found between farm size (numbers of cows) and stress. It might be expected that larger farms would receive more notifications, introducing more

---

[1] Two variables are considered weakly related if the correlation coefficient (r) is $|r| < 0.35$, moderately related if $0.36 < |r| < 0.67$, and strongly related if $|r| > 0.67$ [26].

potential for stress. However, farmers on large farms may have also developed better strategies for notification management, such as adjusting factory settings to minimize alerts. This correlation was not significant (p = .456) .

Table 1. Correlation Matrix Values (r) for the Stress Level against Farm Size, Years of Experience, and Age of the Farmer.

	Years of experience	Age of farmer	Farm size
Stress	−0.710	−0.481	0.201
p-values	0.004*	0.0593+	0.4561

* significant, + marginally significant

5 Discussion

The study revealed several challenges farmers experience related to their PLF notification systems that have implications for the design of future systems. These challenges and related design considerations are discussed below.

5.1 Information Uncertainty

The results show that the information provided by PLF notifications are not always clear or sufficiently meaningful. This uncertainty can cause confusion about what, if any, action they should take upon receiving the notification. This finding is consistent with previous studies on PLF technologies that also found that farmers were sometimes unsure of the content or meaning of PLF notifications [12, 13]. Information uncertainty was reported for all PLF technologies studied in this survey, although the source of uncertainty varied. For AMS users, sometimes the automated voice in notifications received by phone was hard to hear or understand, so the information was not conveyed effectively. For AHDS users, heat event notifications by text messages (or via native mobile notifications) did not contain the identity of the cow associated with the event. For AAMS users, sometimes the content of notifications was too vague to be useful. The study found that farmers would typically have to do further investigation to help clarify the notification's meaning, for instance, by checking a cow or the physical system to determine the issue or by checking the associated software application to determine which cow needs attention and/or what the issue is.

Research from the field of neurobiology shows there is a strong connection between uncertainty and stress and that this type of stress can have negative health impacts [35]. Thus, whenever key information is required for decision-making or action, it should be sent with the notification so that farmers have a clear idea about their required action. Our findings of information uncertainty corroborates previous studies of PLF technologies [7, 8]. Thus, a clear design implication of the study is that PLF notifications should provide key information related to the source of concern, including needed actions and their urgency. For instance, if a notification concerns a specific cow, the identity of the cow should be provided directly. The farmer may have relevant contextual knowledge about that cow that allows them to make informed judgments of needed actions and their urgency.

The study also found the process needed to clarify a notification can sometimes involve cumbersome steps in the associated software application. For instance, as reported in Sect. 4.4, an AHDS user (P5) expressed frustration of the *"lengthy process"* needed to *"get into [the] slow app to find out which cow is in heat"* because the notification did not identify the cow. Thus, another design implication of the study is the need to streamline any system interactions that may be needed to gain more information about system notifications, which can be accomplished through effective user-centred design that ensures interfaces are highly usable by their target user.

5.2 Matching Communication Timing and Medium to Notification Content

The study findings reveal the contents of PLF notifications contain a variety of different kinds of information related to the systems and the cow they are monitoring. They also show that this content has different levels of importance or urgency. For instance, information about a cow being in heat (i.e. ready for impregnation) is considered very important and highly urgent for a dairy farmer because milk production relies on pregnant cows and because heat cycles are relatively short (e.g., two to 48 h depending on the individual cow and their breed). Thus, being aware of this information in a timely manner is crucial for effective farm operations. However, consistent with prior research [36], this study found that notifications are sometimes sent at times and/or through mediums that are ineffective for farmers to make a decision or take an appropriate action.

AMS, AHDS, and AAMS users reported they sometimes received notifications from their systems at inappropriate times. An AHDS user (P2) reported that dashboard notifications in their AHDS application were about four hours behind. Thus, for cows with very short heat cycles, this delay may mean the loss of a breeding opportunity. An AAMS user (P11) reported that their system notifies farmers about certain abnormal behaviours only after two days of anomalous behaviour is detected. Yet, the farmer felt this was too long to wait to hear about a potential *"health issue that needs to be addressed sooner"* *(P11)* and planned to contact the manufacturer to change this feature. Communication timing has been shown to play a vital role in making appropriate, timely decisions [37]. The study results indicate a need for more careful design of PLF notification timing mechanisms.

AMS and AHDS users reported sometimes receiving notifications through an inappropriate medium. Surprisingly, twelve AHDS users (75%) reported that they received notifications of heat events via the system dashboard. The dashboard is something that farmers check as desired, but heat events need immediate checking. Thus, it is surprising that dashboard notifications were, by far, the most reported communication medium used by AHDS users (12/16), with other mediums being reported much less often (text messaging: 4/16, email: 2/16, phone calls: 0/16). AMS users reported receiving "unnecessary" phone call notifications late at night, which was frustrating for them.

The issues of notification timing and medium are closely intertwined. The most effective notification would be received at the right time through the right medium so that a farmer can properly attend to the concern without being distracted by other issues and can easily understand the information being conveyed. Clearly some types of notifications are more urgent than others, for example, a cow in distress or in heat. Thus, using a medium that demands the farmer's attention should be used for urgent concerns, for example, a phone call or text message, as they both typically make sound or vibration to capture attention. A potential reason for AMS notifications to rely heavily on phone calls may be that they are a reasonable medium to use for urgent messages. However, the study found that AMS users received phone notifications for all urgency levels.

Beyond the urgency of the concern, the *content* of the message should also be considered when selecting a notification medium to aid in message comprehension. Different mediums provide different affordances for supporting communication [38], such as how well they support *simultaneity* or *reviewability*. A phone call affords *simultaneity*, which forces the receiver to attend to a message at the same time it is sent. Thus, for urgent messages, this may be an appropriate medium. However, the phone call does not afford *reviewability* (the ability for the receiver to review the message content), which can increase the cognitive workload of understanding and recalling messages sent by phone. Lack of reviewability is especially problematic when the message contains *verbatim* content that must be understood, and recalled later, exactly [38]. For instance, communicating a numeric cow identifier via a text message may be easier to understand and later recall than communicating this information by phone. For extremely urgent issues, use of multiple communication mediums, such as phone call and text message or native mobile phone notification, may help ensure farmers are aware of the issue immediately, and have the correct information ready at hand to understand the concern and take timely action.

The study also found that some AMS farmers adjusted their notification settings to address inappropriate timing and medium issues, for instance, to reduce notifications concerning non-urgent issues or those that did not require actions (e.g., notifications related to system cleaning) and to manage the timing of notifications (e.g., turning certain types of notifications off overnight). However, the fact that an AAMS user mentioned a desire to contact the manufacturer to help adjust the notification timing of some of their system notifications suggests that more user control over notification timing and medium may be needed for some PLF technologies.

As suggested by the HCI literature discussed in Sect. 2, interruptions caused by notifications delivered at inappropriate times may also impact the work or life activities of the farmer, impacting decision-making, productivity, and emotional well-being. An emerging solution to minimize distractions caused by ill-timed notifications is the use of location-based notifications [29]. This approach sends a notification to the user when they are in a certain location based on their GPS coordinates. For instance, a farmer could receive text message notification to check their AMS when they enter the barn. The approach takes advantage of context. When the farmer is in or near the barn, they are more likely to be available to attend to barn-related concerns than if they are in the grocery store. While this approach may not be appropriate for urgent messages that require immediate action, it may be suitable for other types of notifications which are important but less urgent.

5.3 Information Overload

Although this study did not explicitly probe farmers about information overload, several farmers reported they received unnecessary information from their PLF technologies. For example, Participant 17 commented that "the alerts should be less, and we should only receive alerts if there is a problem", and Participant 3 reported that they adjusted their AMS dashboard settings so that only "necessary" information was shown. These findings are consistent with prior research that has reported farmers sometimes receive excessive and unnecessary information from PLF technologies [12, 13], which can be overwhelming and stressful for them [7, 10, 39]. In general, receiving unnecessary information can create information fatigue that can cause users to miss information needed for decision making [40]. A study found that users can experience social media fatigue due to information overload, which leads to intermittent use of social media [41]. Receiving unnecessary information may also hamper effective decision-making and productivity [22]. Therefore, managing notifications to ensure they are not overwhelming for farmers is an important concern for PLF designers. However, ensuring that farmers get sufficient, but not overwhelming amounts of information for them to make proper decisions is difficult.

One approach could be to prioritize notifications where farmers are communicated only relevant issues at appropriate times [29]. For instance, issues such as calving time, insemination time, or severe temperature or lameness, which need immediate attention, could be ranked highest. In contrast, non-urgent matters, such as the slightly reduced amount of milk yield, that could be addressed after a specific period could be ranked lowest. As discussed in Sect. 2.4, using the farmer's context, such as their location (discussed above), or inferred activity (e.g., talking with someone), may help PLF designers determine when (timing) and how (medium) to deliver notifications of different importance and urgency levels to minimize interruptions and also to deliver notifications when the farmer is available and able to attend to the information. Developing effective visualization techniques for PLF applications and their dashboards may also help. For example, the previously discussed 'Scope' system [32], spatially arranged notifications on a screen to indicate their importance level. This contrasts many PLF notification displays that often list system notifications in chronological order. Arranging by order, or distinguishing different types of notifications by colour or intensity may help farmers quickly comprehend the importance or urgency of listed concerns.

5.4 Are PLF Notifications a Source of Stress for Farmers?

While only a few farmers explicitly reported that they experience increased stress from PLF notifications, the study did find many examples of negative user experiences with current PLF notification mechanisms that prior research on notifications and general user interactions with technology, would suggest that cumulatively, these experiences may create stress and anxiety in users over time. For example, participants reported sometimes experiencing frustration, confusion, and uncertainty when receiving and responding to notifications, and experiencing interruptions to other critical work or life activities. As discussed in Sect. 2.4, these types of user experiences can harm productivity and mental wellbeing. This finding is consistent with prior studies [7, 8], which uncovered several reasons for farmers' stress, including unclear information, unclear required actions, false alerts, timing and medium of alerts, and technology breakdowns.

Participant 1 commented their AMS allows them to have an off-farm job while still farming and reported "decreased stress" as a benefit of their AMS. Yet, the same participant also reported their AMS sometimes interrupted more important work or life activities, that sometimes they missed important/urgent messages from their AMS, and that they experienced increased stress because they could receive a message at any moment. Thus, it seems that managing stress related to PLF technologies is complex, as the same technology can both be a source of stress and a means to decrease stress.

Addressing some of the design concerns around information uncertainty, inappropriate notification timing and medium, and information overload discussed in the prior sections will help to reduce the sources of potential stress from PLF notifications. As it is difficult, perhaps impossible, for any designer to completely anticipate what information all farmers consider important or urgent, allowing farmers to customize system settings to receive notifications based on their own preferences may further help address the negative impacts of notifications.

6   Conclusions and Future Work

A pilot survey study investigating the impact of precision livestock farming (PLF) notifications on farmers found that farmers highly valued these systems, but also experienced challenges that reduced the effectiveness of their PLF systems. Some positive effects experienced by farmers were reduced mental and physical workload, improved livestock health, ease of data collection, and improved milk products. Challenges farmers experienced with PLF notifications included information uncertainty, false alerts, missed alerts, inappropriate communication timing and medium, information overload, and increased stress. Improving the technology's performance and accuracy would help to address information uncertainty, false alerts, and missed alerts. Information uncertainty could also be addressed by more clearly conveying the key information related to the topic of concern. Notification systems should also be designed to use appropriate communication timing and mediums suited to the content, importance, and urgency of the notification. Additional information look-up should be extremely easy and effective to do, minimizing unnecessary mental and physical workload. It is strongly recommended that manufacturers adopt user-centric design approaches from the field of HCI to better incorporate farmers' needs and preferences into their PLF notification mechanism designs in the future to develop simple farmer friendly interfaces. HCI techniques such as iterative design and development, and participatory design methods can be followed to design newer technologies engaging with dairy farmers and stakeholders [16].

As a pilot study, this research has limitations. The extent to which the challenges discussed in this study exist across the broader Canadian farming population is unclear. However, their consistency with prior PLF studies of other farming populations provides some support to their generalizability. Nonetheless, a larger study is needed to confirm the scale of the findings. Also, following good user-centred design, other types of user studies are needed to help further understand farmers needs relate d to PLF notifications. For example, observational studies and interviews would help to reveal specific workflows and user challenges related to receiving and acting on notifications.

References

1. Bongiovanni, R., Lowenberg-Deboer, J.: Precision agriculture and sustainability. Precis. Agric. **5**, 359–387 (2004)
2. Berckmans, D.: Precision livestock farming technologies for welfare management in intensive livestock systems. OIE Rev. Sci. Tech. **33**, 189–196 (2014)
3. Wathes, C.M., Kristensen, H.H., Aerts, J.M., Berckmans, D.: Is precision livestock farming an engineer's daydream or nightmare, an animal's friend or foe, and a farmer's panacea or pitfall? Comput. Electron. Agric. **64**, 2–10 (2008)
4. Rutten, C.J., Velthuis, A.G.J., Steeneveld, W., Hogeveen, H.: Invited review: Sensors to support health management on dairy farms. J. Dairy Sci. **96**, 1928–1952 (2013)
5. Halachmi, I., Guarino, M., Bewley, J., Pastell, M.: Smart animal agriculture: Application of real-time sensors to improve animal well-being and production. Annu. Rev. Anim. Biosci. **7**, 403–425 (2019)
6. Désire, C., Hostiou, N.: Mémoire de fin d ' études présenté pour l ' obtention du Diplôme d ' Ingénieur Agronome Option : Elevage en Milieux Difficiles L ' Elevage de Précision : changements dans l ' organisation du travail et la gestion de données dans des exploitations laitière. *Actes des 4e Rencontres Natl. sur le Trav. en élevage* (2015)
7. Hansen, B.G.: Robotic milking-farmer experiences and adoption rate in Jæren. Norway. J. Rural Stud. **41**, 109–117 (2015)
8. Ndour, A., Loison, R., Gourlot, J.-P., Ba, K.S., Clouvel, P.: Biotechnologie, agronomie, société et environnement = Biotechnology, agronomy, society and environment : BASE. Biotechnol. Agron. Soc. Environ. **2017**(21), 22–35 (2017)
9. Allain, C., Chanvallon, A., Courties, R., Billon, D., Bareille, N.: Technical, economic and sociological impacts of an automated estrus detection system for dairy cows. Precis. Dairy Farming, 451–456 (2016)
10. Schewe, R.L., Stuart, D.: Diversity in agricultural technology adoption: How are automatic milking systems used and to what end? Agric. Hum. Values **32**(2), 199–213 (2014). https://doi.org/10.1007/s10460-014-9542-2
11. Wolfert, S., Ge, L., Verdouw, C., Bogaardt, M.J.: Big Data in smart farming – A review. Agric. Syst. **153**, 69–80 (2017)
12. Borchers, M.R., Bewley, J.M.: An assessment of producer precision dairy farming technology use, prepurchase considerations, and usefulness. J. Dairy Sci. **98**, 4198–4205 (2015)
13. Russell, R.A., Bewley, J.M.: Characterization of Kentucky dairy producer decision-making behavior. J. Dairy Sci. **96**, 4751–4758 (2013)
14. Gutiérrez, F., Htun, N.N., Schlenz, F., Kasimati, A., Verbert, K.: A review of visualisations in agricultural decision support systems: An HCI perspective. Comput. Electron. Agric. **163** (2019)
15. Cabrera, V.E., Barrientos-Blanco, J.A., Delgado, H., Fadul-Pacheco, L.: Symposium review: Real-time continuous decision making using big data on dairy farms. J. Dairy Sci. **103**, 3856–3866 (2020)
16. Makinde, A., Islam, M.M., Scott, S.D.: Opportunities for ACI in PLF: Applying animal- And user-centred design to precision livestock farming. ACM Int. Conf. Proceeding Ser. (2019). https://doi.org/10.1145/3371049.3371055

17. Jago, J., Eastwood, C., Kerrisk, K., Yule, I.: Precision dairy farming in Australasia: Adoption, risks and opportunities. Anim. Prod. Sci. **53**, 907–916 (2013)
18. Laberge, B., Rousseau, A.N.: Rethinking environment control strategy of confined animal housing systems through precision livestock farming. Biosyst. Eng. **155**, 96–123 (2017)
19. Dudi, H.: Penentuan Pola Subsidi dan Sistem Distribusi Pupuk di Indonesia. Progr. Pascasarj. Manaj. dan Bisnis IPB **33**, 189–196 (2005)
20. Mehrotra, A., Musolesi, M., Hendley, R., Pejovic, V.: Designing content-driven intelligent notification mechanisms for mobile applications. In: UbiComp 2015 – Proceedings of 2015 ACM International Joint Conference on Pervasive Ubiquitous Computing, pp. 813–824 (2015) https://doi.org/10.1145/2750858.2807544
21. Pielot, M., Church, K., De Oliveira, R.: An in-situ study of mobile phone notifications. In: MobileHCI 2014 - Proceedings of the 18th International Conference on Human-Computer Interaction with Mobile Devices and Services, pp. 233–242 (2014) https://doi.org/10.1145/2628363.2628364
22. Kushlev, K., Proulx, J., Dunn, E.W.: 'Silence your phones': Smartphone notifications increase inattention and hyperactivity symptoms. In: Proceedings of Conference on Human Factors in Computing Systems, pp. 1011–1020 (2016). https://doi.org/10.1145/2858036.2858359
23. Bailey, B.P., Konstan, J.A., Carlis, J.V.: The Effects of interruptions on task performance, annoyance, and anxiety in the user interface. In: Proceedings on INTERACT 2001, pp. 593–601 (2001). https://doi.org/10.1109/ICSMC.2000.885940
24. Zijlstra, F.R.H., Robert A.R., Leonora, A.B., Krediet, I.: Temporal factors in mental work: Effects of interrupted activities. J. Occup. Organ. Psychol.**72**, 163–185 (1999)
25. McFarlane, D.C., Latorella, K.A.: The scope and importance of human interruption in human-computer interaction design. Hum.-Comput. Interact. **17**, 1–61 (2002)
26. Speier, C., Vessey, I., Valacich, J.S.: The Effects of interruptions, task complexity, and information presentation on computer-supported decision-making performance. Decis. Sci. **34**, 771–797 (2003)
27. Bailey, B.P., Konstan, J.A., Carlis, J.V.: Measuring the effects of interruptions on task performance in the user interface. In: Proceedings of IEEE International Conference on Systems, Man and Cybernetics **2**, 757–762 (2000)
28. Czerwinski, M., Cutrell, E., Horvitz, E.: Instant messaging - An instant threat. Comput. Fraud Secur. **2002**, 19–20 (2002)
29. Kern, N., Schiele, B.: Context-aware notification forwearable computing. In: International Symposium on Wearable Computers or ISWC, pp. 223–230 (2003) https://doi.org/10.1109/iswc.2003.1241415
30. Adamczyk, P.D., Bailey, B.P.: If not now, when?: The effects of interruption at different moments within task execution. In: Proceedings Conference on Human Factors in Computing Systems, vol. 6, pp. 271–278 (2004)
31. Dabbish, L.A., Baker, R.S.: Administrative assistants as interruption mediators. In: Proceedings of Conference on Human *Factors* in Computing Systems, pp. 1020–1021 (2003). https://doi.org/10.1145/765891.766127
32. Van Dantzich, M., Robbins, D., Horvitz, E., Czerwinski, M.: Scope: Providing awareness of multiple notifications at a glance. In: Proceedings of Advanced Visual Interfaces AVI, pp. 267–281 (2002). https://doi.org/10.1145/1556262.1556306
33. Afergan, D., Hincks, S.W., Shibata, T., Jacob, R.J.K.: Phylter: A system for modulating notifications in wearables using physiological sensing. Lect. Notes Comput. Sci. (including Subser. Lect. Notes Artif. Intell. Lect. Notes Bioinformatics) **9183**, 167–177 (2015)
34. Begole, J. 'Bo', Matsakis, N.E., Tang, J.C.: Lilsys. 511 (2004). https://doi.org/10.1145/1031607.1031691
35. Peters, A., McEwen, B.S., Friston, K.: Uncertainty and stress: Why it causes diseases and how it is mastered by the brain. Prog. Neurobiol. **156**, 164–188 (2017)

36. Mollenhorst, H., Rijkaart, L.J., Hogeveen, H.: Mastitis alert preferences of farmers milking with automatic milking systems. J. Dairy Sci. **95**, 2523–2530 (2012)
37. Bahir, R.A., Tractinsky, N., Parmet, Y.: Effects of visual enhancements and delivery time on receptivity of mobile push notifications. In: Conference on Human *Factors* in Computing Systems – Proceedings, pp. 5–10 (2019). https://doi.org/10.1145/3290607.3312993
38. Clark, H.H., Brennan, S.E.: Grounding in communication. Perspect. Soc. Shar. Cogn. 127–149 (2004). https://doi.org/10.1037/10096-006
39. Dominiak, K.N., Kristensen, A.R.: Prioritizing alarms from sensor-based detection models in livestock production - A review on model performance and alarm reducing methods. Comput. Electron. Agric. **133**, 46–67 (2017)
40. Buchanan, J., Kock, N.: Information overload: A decision making perspective, pp. 49–58 (2001). https://doi.org/10.1007/978-3-642-56680-6_4
41. Fu, S., Li, H., Liu, Y., Pirkkalainen, H., Salo, M.: Social media overload, exhaustion, and use discontinuance: Examining the effects of information overload, system feature overload, and social overload. Inf. Process. Manag. **57** (2020)
42. Robert, D.M., Douglas, A.L., McAdoo, W.G.: Statistics: An Introduction (Duxbury Pr; Subsequent edition (Oct. 1 1997), 1983). https://doi.org/10.2307/2685790

Concept for Safe Interaction of Driverless Industrial Trucks and Humans in Shared Areas

Christian Drabek[1]([✉]), Anna Kosmalska[1], Gereon Weiss[1], Tasuku Ishigooka[2], Satoshi Otsuka[2], and Mariko Mizuochi[3]

[1] Fraunhofer IKS, Munich, Germany
{christian.drabek,anna.kosmalska,gereon.weiss}@iks.fraunhofer.de
[2] Research and Development Group, Hitachi Ltd., Ibaraki, Japan
{tasuku.ishigoka.kc,satoshi.otsuka.hk}@hitachi.com
[3] Hitachi Europe GmbH, Schwaig, Germany
mariko.mizuochi@hitachi-eu.com

Abstract. Humans still need to access the same area as automated systems, like in warehouses, if full automation is not feasible or economical. In such shared areas, critical interactions are inevitable. The automation of vehicles is usually tied to an argument on improved safety. However, current standards still rely also on the awareness of humans to avoid collisions. Along with this, modern intelligent warehouses are equipped with additional sensors that can help to automate safety. Blind corners, where the view is obscured, are particularly critical and, moreover, their location can change when goods are moved. Therefor, we generalize a concept for safe interactions at known blind corners to movements in the entire warehouse. We propose an architecture that uses infrastructure sensors to prevent human-robot collisions with respect to automated forklifts as instances of driverless industrial trucks. This includes a safety critical function using wireless communication, which sporadically might be unavailable or disturbed. Therefore, the proposed architecture is able to mitigate these faults and gracefully degrades the system's performance if required. Within our extensive evaluation, we simulate varying warehouse settings to verify our approach and to estimate the impact on an automated forklift's performance.

Keywords: Driverless industrial trucks · Human-robot interaction · Infrastructure sensors · Warehouse

1 Introduction

Humans and automated systems work together in shared areas of a warehouse. Thanks to advances in artificial intelligence, robots can already perform many tasks, but some are not yet feasible or economical. Therefore, co-working of humans and machines is an important factor for future competitiveness [28].

S. Paiva et al. (Eds.): SmartCity360° 2021, LNICST 442, pp. 267–283, 2022.
https://doi.org/10.1007/978-3-031-06371-8_17

Efficiency of a warehouse can be greatly improved when the flexibility of human workers and carrying power of automated guided vehicles (AGVs) are available in the same area [30]. Especially autonomous mobile robots (AMRs), which can be considered a subgroup of AGVs with a high degree of autonomous control [7], are used for this purpose. Segregation of automated machines and human workers, e.g., placing robots in dedicated safety cages, cannot be used to ensure safety in shared areas and new safeguards are needed.

This paper explores the safe movement of driverless industrial trucks in the presence of human workers. Within in-house transportation, industrial trucks are a major source of accidents [11] that can harm driver or bystanders. Driverless industrial trucks, such as AGVs, already remove the need for a driver. Further, the safety requirements for driverless industrial trucks [17] provide guidelines to reduce the inherent risk of human-machine-collisions. For some tasks, completely restricting the operation of AGVs and human workers to separate areas can remove the advantages of automation. This necessitates shared areas in which both operate. AGVs are equipped with safe perception capabilities, e.g., lidars or radars, and have to slow down or come to a complete stop, when obstacles in the surrounding are detected [31]. However, a major challenge in warehouses is the limited line of sight, e.g., due to walls, shelves, or storage. In this case, corners become a potential point of risk [13]. Moreover, their location may change when goods are moved. Without an external source of information, constraints need to limit the operation of AGVs in these areas, i.e., no operation or strongly reduced speed [4], as AGVs themselves cannot detect occluded human workers. Human workers also cannot look around the corners and thus, are also in risk of provoking collisions [26]. One solution to mitigate such risks are safety rules for personnel. For example, priority could be given to driving AGVs by persons stopping at each corner and ensuring that there are no AGVs and aided by visual or sound warning signals. However, those measures are likely to be ignored, bypassed or overlooked during work, especially if they are perceived to be rarely useful and reduce efficiency [16]. In this paper, we study how utilizing sensors in the infrastructure can contribute to safer operation of automated forklifts – a specific type of AGV – in the areas where human workers are allowed to enter. As main contributions, we analyze the problem of safe automated movement in a warehouse. Moreover, we present an architecture and novel concept exploiting infrastructure sensors for achieving safe and efficient movements of automated forklifts in shared areas of a warehouse. Our approach is evaluated by thorough simulations of warehouse scenarios and analyzing the adherence to safety goals and operation performance. With the results of this paper, we aim for showing how safety can be achieved, even in the presence of potentially critical blind spots, by dynamically adjusting the forklift's performance with respect to the available perception information.

The remainder of this paper is structured as follows. Section 2 introduces relevant safety standards, related work, and conflict detection at know blind corners. Section 3 describes the used architecture and generalizes conflict detection to the entire warehouse. Section 4 explains the warehouse scenarios, the metrics and the results of our extensive evaluation, before we conclude the paper in Sect. 5.

2   Critical Interactions in Warehouses

Within intra-logistics, industrial trucks are involved in many accidents [11]. Even with extensive guidelines [3,34] and trainings [9] available for forklifts, a more than proportional number of incidents involving them are serious or fatal. Forklift automation already takes the driver out of harm's way. However, full automation of warehouses is not always feasible or economical and humans may still need to access the same area as forklifts. Therefore, automation must be designed carefully to not increase the risk for these humans.

2.1   Safety Standards for Driverless Industrial Trucks

Several safety standards for mobile machinery are being established. Within the European Union, laws such as the Machine Directive and national laws for protection of human safety are complemented by ISO and IEC standards that describe general design principles, cover aspects for a wide range of machinery, or deal with particular machines [24].

For example, ISO 3691-4 [17] defines the requirements for driverless industrial trucks including unmanned forklifts, AGVs and associated systems. It considers four main kinds of access zones. The enclosed space of a **confined zone** does not need personnel detection. However, only authorized personnel may access the zone after all movement was stopped. A **restricted zone**, like a very narrow aisle, may be entered only by authorized persons. In an **operating hazard zone**, a person can be exposed to a hazard. Therefore, audible or visual warnings and a low speed of $0.3 \frac{m}{s}$ are required. Higher speeds like $1.2 \frac{m}{s}$ are only allowed under specific conditions. Only the **operating zone** allows operation at rated speeds and has a minimum clearance (i.e. 0.5 m wide) on both sides of the path and in the direction of travel.

For autonomous machinery, two main problems are currently seen in the standardization of safety requirements [36]: A gap between requirements of these standards and state-of-the-art complicates more gradual paths to develop systems and the safety standards are mainly for machine manufacturers, while the work process and worksite should provide guidance to their implementation.

This research aims for understanding how to ensure safe and efficient operation of AGVs in areas shared with human workers. For AGVs to use up to their rated speed, we target the whole warehouse to be an *operating zone*. Therefore, the initial two requirements for the system were: Gaps between the machine and walls must be at least 0.5 m and active personnel detection mechanisms.

According to the standard, detection of persons is required in the direction of travel only. This is tested using static cylinders [17,18]. However, this ignores possible persons nearby the machine, even when a collision could be caused by the person stepping into the machine's path. Only the requirement of sufficient space around the AGV and the person's awareness of the machine assure safe interactions between AGV and human worker. Thereby, in such systems, human beings still take the responsibility for avoiding collisions. In future however, safety of a technical system is also envisioned to encompass freedom from danger [1]. Therefore, the responsibility of avoiding a collision needs to be moved from humans to the automated forklift.

2.2 Cooperation and Coordination

Safe behavior has been taught to human drivers of forklifts for a long time, e.g., slowing down, sounding the horn, and looking around [9]. While a simple flashing light – even when mounted in a highly visible location – might not always prevent (near) collisions with a robot [15], light spots or symbols projected into the direction of travel or around the forklift can improve awareness similar to beeper alarms for reversing [6].

Different algorithms claiming to provide proven safe motion of autonomous mobile robots have already been explored [2,20]. However, these methods are limited by the information available to the robot. Exchanging messages with robots in the neighborhood helps decentralized coordination [12] and infrastructure-based sensors can provide information on other actors in the warehouse. Real-time locating system (RTLS) based on camera-data [19] or ultra wide band (UWB) technology [30,35] can locate persons with a precision of at least 15 cm in a warehouse and predict the paths of workers [21]. However, the safety integrity of such locating and prediction systems needs to be assessed. For reliable detection, more expensive and less feature rich safety sensors are often used. Spaghetti charts can be created from the recorded movements to further analyze and improve safety [5].

The AGV must receive updates on this changing information continually. Several methods to centrally coordinate vehicles and avoid collisions have been explored already [4,22,23,27,31,33]. Using more resources, e.g. multiple links, the reliability of connections can be improved [32]. However, an always reliable connection cannot be assumed and, if no connection is available, movement of an AGV should only be degraded instead of completely stopped. In the following, we detail how monitors for the infrastructure cooperation performance allow to dynamically adjust the forklift's actions to its available information.

2.3 Conflict Detection at Known Blind Corners

At a blind corner, line of sight to crossing vehicles or humans is limited. Known blind corners in a warehouse are critical locations and have already been examined [4,13]. An intersection can only be passed without slowing down, if all conflicts can be reliably excluded. This situation is illustrated in Fig. 1. An AGV approaching an intersection at position 1 has to start braking at position 2 before it is able to perceive the complete conflict area. Otherwise, the AGV cannot stop at position 3 if there is a hidden conflict. When all potential conflicting crossing objects can be excluded, the AGV can accelerate again. The required braking distance and the point at which the conflict area can be sufficiently viewed by the sensors determines a safe speed limit [37] and recreates the behavior of expert drivers in an automotive use-case [25]. In a warehouse, however, walls and obstacles are often closer and forklifts need to decelerate slower [29,34]. Therefore, the presence of conflicts must be available much earlier to prevent the slowdown [4].

For example, at a speed of 5 $\frac{m}{s}$, a forklift needs to start braking at a distance d_{brake} of 3.5–6.5 m [34]. While processing inputs, the automated forklift travels $d_{process}$ additionally. The forklift needs to detect the intersection and potential conflicts in the *conflict area*. The time the forklift would take to pass the intersection and the passing human's speed define the size of this area:

$$d_{conflict} = v_{other}(d_{process} + d_{brake} + d_{inter} + d_{fl})/v_{fl}. \tag{1}$$

To avoid a potential collision, the forklift must decelerate, if the conflict area including a margin for the detection (d_{detect}) cannot be cleared. Therefore, using only pure line-of-sight [37], the point of decision is close to the intersection and the forklift already almost stops. When using infrastructure sensors to avoid unnecessary slow downs of an approaching forklift, the sensors mounted at the intersection need at least a detection range with radius

$$R > d_{inter} + d_{conflict} + d_{detect}. \tag{2}$$

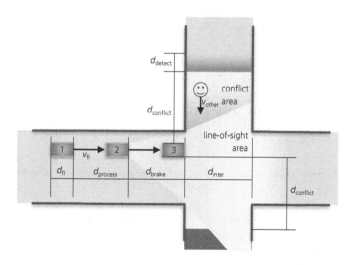

Fig. 1. An automated forklift approaching a blind corner.

Previous work [13] has shown the positive impact on safety and efficiency of automated forklifts at blind corners based on the described conflict detection. Current standards only require personnel detection in the direction of travel. Therefore, industrial trucks may face blind corners at many occurrences. In this work, we examine how this approach can be generalized to reduce risks by automated forklifts for human workers in the entire warehouse, while reducing performance only when necessary.

3   Infrastructure-Cooperative Autonomous Control

In this section, we present our novel approach for safe and efficient automated forklift operation in a warehouse, where human workers might be present. It is based on an architecture [13] that has already been shown to mitigate faults of a safety critical function included using wireless communication, which sporadically might be unavailable or disturbed.

3.1   Infrastructure-Cooperative Autonomous Control Architecture

The infrastructure-cooperative architecture for automated forklifts shown in Fig. 2 covers the core AGV tasks [10] and additional monitoring activities.

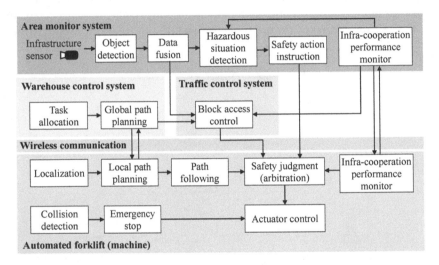

Fig. 2. Infrastructure-Cooperative Autonomous Control Architecture [13]

The **warehouse control system** optimizes the overall operational efficiency by allocating tasks to each forklift and planing necessary routes. The **traffic control system** coordinates the (automated) movement in the warehouse by ensuring that only one machine may enter a certain block at the same time. The **area monitor system** manages the collision risk of machines and workers in the warehouse using available infrastructure sensors. It emits safety actions for safety risks or deviations from rules that are defined as hazardous situation. Safety actions can apply immediately or on a situation detectable by the machine, e.g., an interrupted connection. The **automated forklift** has functions to enable safe and autonomous control, e.g., personnel detection mechanisms using the machine's own sensors required by the ISO 3691-4 [17]. *Safety judgment* ensures safe operation by arbitrating path following, permissions from traffic control, safety action instructions and the system status reported by *infra-cooperation performance monitor*. The monitor detects and mitigates potential hazards introduced by the use of remote information in a safety critical function.

This structure enables collision avoidance in advance and reduces unnecessary deceleration and stoppage of the automated forklift. The operational efficiency can, thus, be expected to be improved. In brief, the proposed architecture ensures safety in three ways:

- block permissions coordinate automated forklifts,
- area monitor safeguards the interaction with humans, and
- emergency stop provides a local backup if remote services are not available.

A key ingredient to ensure safe interaction with human workers is the hazardous situation detection. The following section details how the area monitor can detect such critical situations based on a generalized concept for conflict detection at blind corners.

3.2   Generalized Concept for Conflict Detection

When blind corners are fixed and known, the method described in Sect. 2.3 can detect potential conflicts between a forklift and human workers. However, there are many situations where location of blind corners can rapidly change, e.g., in an area where goods are quickly unloaded from a truck and inspected by humans before they can be moved to a more permanent location. At the same time, interactions between humans and automated forklifts are very likely. Further, as already identified during the discussion of related standards in Sect. 2, any location could be a blind corner for an automated vehicle that only checks for humans in the direction of travel. Therefore, the concept of the conflict area is generalized to assume the occurrence of blind corners anywhere. In the following, we assume that the RTLS has good coverage of the warehouse and its precision is sufficiently considered in d_{detect}.

Conflict detection at known blind corners checks if a forklift can continue at its current speed without interfering with a human at an intersection. This check is performed early enough for the forklift to stop before it enters the intersection and it assumes that this is always safe. A similar check can be performed at any time along the forklifts trajectory. This is shown in Fig. 3. For a constant velocity, (1) can be used to calculate the size of the conflict area. More general, the radius depends on the time ($t_{conflict}$) the forklift needs to reach the checked point and the assumed maximum speed (v_{other}) of human workers:

$$d_{conflict} = t_{conflict} \, v_{other}. \tag{3}$$

For the generalized case, however, stopping might not always be safe and might cause collisions. A trajectory is considered to be safe only, if it ends in a safe position, i.e., if the forklift can stop at its end. Thereby, cases where the forklift can neither stop nor continue safely are avoided. A simple generalized conflict area for a moving forklift is illustrated by Fig. 4. If the area monitor

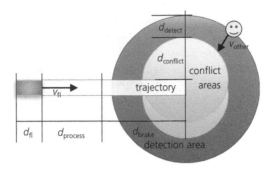

Fig. 3. Generalization of the conflict area.

signals the forklift to brake, the rectangular area denotes the trajectory it needs to safely decelerate. Assuming a maximum speed for human workers, they would only be able to enter the trajectory before the forklift if they are within a conflict area. The conflict areas can be calculated as series of circles along both sides of the trajectory. The resulting conflict areas are marked in Fig. 4. To detect human workers before they enter this area, the detection margin of size d_{detect} is wrapped around the conflict areas. The resulting detection area can be approximated by an isosceles trapezoid and a half circle. Thereby, potential conflicts can be checked quickly. Hazardous situation detection in area monitor will continually check different trajectories for each forklift based on the safety actions it can send to the forklift to avoid conflicts with human workers. Besides stopping and slowing down, maintaining a minimum speed to clear an area before a worker gets closer can also be a possible safety action.

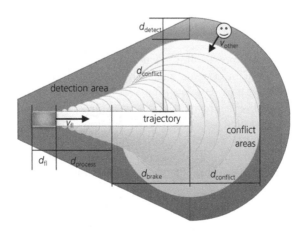

Fig. 4. Conflict and detection area to guarantee the forklift can safely stop.

Forklifts will not only travel in a straight line. For more complex trajectories, waypoints can be placed at turns and other points, e.g. where the forklift's speed will change. Multiple trapezoids with half circles can then be placed along the waypoints, like shown in Fig. 5. For the waypoint marked with the diamond, the time the forklift needs to reach it can be estimated and used to calculate $d_{conflict\_wp}$. The diameter of the half-circle is also used as the length of shorter parallel side of the next trapezoid. Finally, this can be used to avoid checking identical parts of different tested trajectories multiple times.

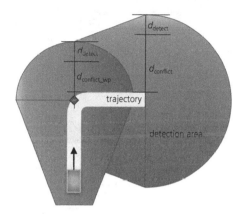

Fig. 5. Detection area for more complex trajectories.

4   Evaluation

4.1   Scenario Description

This section aims for evaluating the effects of the presented concept for safe interaction of industrial trucks and humans on an overall warehouse. For this, simulations including typical warehouse scenes have been created. The evaluation scenario was derived from industrial experiences and existing applications with respect to the warehouse layout as well as tasks of humans and forklifts. Through this, the evaluation scenario leads to various different encounters between automated forklifts and humans. The created warehouse model from bird's eye view is shown in Fig. 6. The warehouse comprises the following main areas: A permanent storage area (blue), two temporary storage areas (grey), and *human-only* areas (green).

Human Workers. In the examined scenario, workers are inspecting goods in the temporary storage areas and, thus, share space with the autonomous forklifts. Within the simulation, human workers' movement is planned along the paths shown by the green and blue lines in Fig. 6. After finishing an inspection cycle, they will directly start the next cycle. In the areas indicated along the paths,

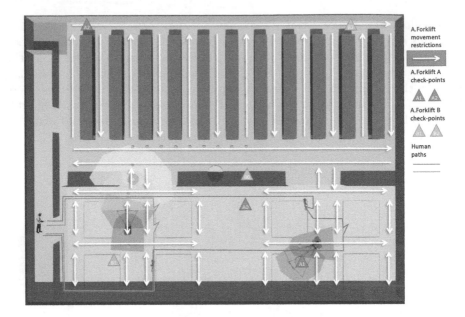

Fig. 6. Webots warehouse model based on the use case derived from common industrial settings (Color figure online)

inspection is simulated by workers performing a small movement cycle. Human workers are moving with constant speed $v_{other} = 1.5\,\frac{m}{s}$, which is slightly higher than average walking speed [8]. To create variations in the scenario, the position where humans start their path has been varied by changing the initial time offset. An offset x indicates that the human worker starts at the position it would have reached after x seconds walking along the path. A range of time offsets from 0 to 120 s have been used to cover a wide range of possible interactions between autonomous forklifts and human workers, resulting in 60 simulation runs for each safety concept and for each scenario.

Human-Driven Forklifts. To test the safety in the presence of faster moving objects, human-driven forklifts have been implemented moving along predefined paths. One human-driven forklift was added to each temporary storage area. The implementation is similar to that of human workers, i.e., collisions with automated forklifts are detected but have no other impact on the simulation. The predefined paths simulate retrieving goods from a nearby truck and placing them in one of the marked areas.

Automated Forklifts. The simulation assumes a rated speed of $5\,\frac{m}{s}$ and a value of $3\,\frac{m}{s^2}$ for brake and acceleration. They are tasked with the transport of goods from the temporary storage area to permanent storage and vice versa. This is simulated by having forklifts move between checkpoints in each area. Navigation options available to automated forklifts are indicated by white arrows. The arrow depicts the direction the forklift may travel. Planning and coordination between forklifts is done using an adapted version of a cloud-based control for cars in a parking area [14]. Therefore, the cloud will plan waypoints for each forklift and provide it with a permission stating how far it may proceed. For permissions, the navigation options, i.e., the shown arrows, have been split into blocks of approximately $9\,m^2$ size. The permissions ensure that only one automated forklift will occupy a block simultaneously, thereby, preventing collisions between automated forklifts.

Safety Concepts. For safe interaction with humans, we evaluated four safety concepts (SC) to compare distinct safety considerations in a warehouse: SC_0 uses the rated speed of the forklift anywhere, unless its local sensors detect a human. SC_1 uses the hazardous zone speed for the temporary storage area and the rated speed otherwise. SC_{slow} and SC_{stop} use the hazardous situation detection as described in Sect. 3.2. The checked areas can also be seen in Fig. 6 around the forklifts. SC_{slow} uses the safety action *slowdown* but will send *stop* for the closest segment. SC_{stop} always uses *stop*. To challenge the robustness of the approach, the algorithm only checks for conflicts every 0.3 s. For any safety concept, local emergency stop of the automated forklift is active and will cause the forklift to stop.

4.2 Metrics

Safety. The primary goal or our introduced safety concepts is to prevent collisions – even though a human worker is violating safety guidelines and not paying attention to his surroundings, e.g., walking into a forklift that is driving according to its safety rules (i.e., follows speed and acceleration constraints, drives along calculated waypoints). Thus, we analyze the number of collisions as main indicator. For implementation reasons, human workers strictly follow their programmed path in the simulation, e.g., they can walk into a slow moving or stopped forklift. Thus, we consider a collision to be safely avoidable in reality, if the forklift reduced its speed to below $1.2\,\frac{m}{s}$ and stopped rotating at least $0.25\,s$ prior to the collision. In these cases, it is assumed that a real human would in general not walk into the forklift. All other collisions are considered unsafe in our evaluation, where we distinct front collisions due to their high severity. In case of front collisions, the tips of the fork make first contact with the human, which is considered to be most severe. Simulation continues without interruption when a collision is logged, i.e., there is no physical impact and collided entities continue their tasks.

Performance. The secondary goal of introducing the novel concepts is to avoid an unnecessary impact on the performance of the system. To compare the performance of the different concepts, the distances which the forklifts traveled have been measured and recorded. For easier comparison, the performance drop is calculated. It is relative to results of SC_0, which is expected to provide the best performance out of all concepts.

4.3 Results

Early Results. An initial, simple approach for hazardous situation detection that checked only the generalized conflict area shown in Fig. 3 enticed with potential but provided unsatisfactory results. Parts of conflict areas were not checked for human presence – especially during turning – which caused many severe collisions. Those experiments, nevertheless, helped to develop the final approach that would minimize the area of detection, while assuring the complete coverage of possible collisions.

Results. Table 1 presents the results for simulations of 2 unmanned forklifts, 2 to 4 human workers (HW) and up to 2 human-operated forklifts (HFL). Collisions listed in the table are considered hazardous, i.e., the speed of an autonomous forklift was higher than the safe speed of 1.2 $\frac{m}{s}$. Without implementing human behavior of avoiding a safely stopped automated forklift, which was out of the scope of this work, all collisions logged when an autonomous forklift was moving at slow speed or slower, are considered as not severe and easily avoidable in real situation. For validation purposes, times of human interacting with completely stopped forklift were still logged.

SC_1 by definition will never cause an unsafe collision because in this scenario, autonomous forklifts are never moving faster than slow speed in the area shared with human workers. SC_{slow} and SC_{stop} also allow to avoid all unsafe collisions. In addition, SC_{stop} allows to completely stop before almost all collisions, i.e., no action of collision avoidance is required from human workers or drivers of manned forklifts. This is a significant improvement compared to SC_0, which shows several or more unsafe collisions, depending on the individual scenario. SC_1 causes almost 7% performance decrease in all scenarios, due to often unnecessary slowing down. SC_{slow} ensures no collisions and decreases performance only by about 1 to 1.6% for scenarios with human workers only. SC_{stop} also ensures no collisions, but reduces performance by 3.2 to 6.4%, depending on the scenario.

When more human workers are introduced, the number of collisions will likely increase and performance drop, because there are more potential interactions between unmanned forklifts and humans. The number of unsafe collisions, increases much more when SC_0 is used, while SC_1, SC_{slow}, and SC_{stop} still avoid all collisions. In the examined scenarios and with the improved conflict detection implemented by the cloud, SC_{slow} and SC_{stop} provide significant improvement of safety compared to SC_0, regardless of the number of human workers in the warehouse. SC_{slow} provides also better performance than SC_1 without compromising safety. On the other hand, SC_{stop} can assure not only severe collisions avoidance, but not collisions at all – the price would be decreased performance. The performance measured as traveled distance decreases with the number of human workers – the more interactions between humans and forklifts, the more time forklifts must perform safety actions and slow down or brake.

The number of collisions significantly increases, when manned forklifts are included in the simulation – but only when SC_0 is used. Again, SC_1, SC_{slow},

Table 1. Simulation results with number unsafe collision, as well as distance in meters traveled by the forklifts summed over all scenarios with the matching amount of human workers (HW) and manned forklifts (HFL). Performance drop is given relative to SC_0.

Scenario			Safety	Performance	
#HW	#HFL	SC	#collisions	Total [m]	Drop [%]
2	0	0	2	31,597	0.0
2	0	1	0	29,522	6.6
2	0	Slow	0	31,275	1.0
2	0	Stop	0	30,583	3.2
3	0	0	2	31,394	0.0
3	0	1	0	29,405	6.3
3	0	Slow	0	30,947	1.4
3	0	Stop	0	30,280	3.5
4	0	0	4	31,085	0.0
4	0	1	0	29,165	6.2
4	0	Slow	0	30,582	1.6
4	0	Stop	0	29,093	6.4
2	1	0	42	31,599	0.0
2	1	1	0	29,522	6.6
2	1	Slow	0	30,596	3.2
2	1	Stop	0	27,851	11.9
2	2	0	67	31,601	0.0
2	2	1	0	29522	6.6
2	2	Slow	0	30,252	4.3
2	2	Stop	0	21,294	32.6

and SC_{stop} provide improved safety in comparison. Costs for the higher safety are lower performance, even lower than for SC_1, in case of SC_{stop}. This is a result of many interactions between unmanned forklifts, manned forklifts, and human workers. However, SC_{slow} allows mitigating these costs.

Discussion. The results show that fast moving manned forklifts might require a different or more refined approach than human workers, who are much slower than vehicles. In turn, movement of vehicles is much more limited by physics, and therefore, some potential interactions could be excluded by reliable predictions. In all executed scenarios, the cloud service checks for conflicts every 0.3 s only. Especially when including fast moving objects like manned forklifts, a higher rate of updates in the cloud could improve this situation. Moreover, depending on the use case, it may be beneficial to limit the maximum speed of manned forklifts to improve the performance of unmanned forklifts. In our experiments, we assumed the same maximum speed for all kinds of forklifts ($5\,\frac{m}{s}$).

As SC_{slow} and SC_1 already avoid all unsafe collisions, the results presented in Table 1 indicate no clear benefit of using SC_{stop}. However, this approach could be beneficial, e.g., to provide safety if untrained personnel can enter shared areas or to help in a transition phase when automated forklifts are firstly introduced. In this case, the systems takes over responsibility that humans cannot collide with a moving forklift. With few humans working in the same area, we observed a performance impact less than or comparable to that of SC_1. Because humans did not avoid collisions in our simulation (even when safely avoidable), we could examine the speed of automated forklifts in these incidents. As expected for SC_{stop}, the automated forklift had already stopped and humans collided with a then static object. Even if just at slow and safe speeds, the forklift was still moving for most incidents of SC_1 and SC_{slow}. Further simulations for cross-validation purposes with additional humans walking between random waypoints in the shared area presented a similar performance drop distribution.

Summary. The results of the simulations clearly show that areas shared by autonomous vehicles and humans or human-driven vehicles require novel approaches to assure safety and to keep the performance on satisfactory level. In this case, safety cannot rely on sensors and systems embedded into vehicles only. Additionally, it is advantageous that modern mobile robots are often already connected to cloud-based systems, e.g., for task planning and navigation purposes. Using infrastructure sensors and sharing information about location of humans makes a system more complex, but it also allows avoiding dangerous collisions while maintaining high system performance.

5   Conclusion and Outlook

This paper examines the interactions of automated forklifts and human workers in shared areas of a warehouse to increase the safety in these areas. Based on an architecture that includes infrastructure sensors, we introduce a novel concept to identify potential conflicts in the movement of automated forklifts and human workers while having minimal impact on performance. The presented results for interactions in the entire warehouse confirm the first observations made for known blind corners [13]. It is clear that relying solely on the forklift's sensors either poses a high risk to human workers if the forklift does not brake as a precaution (SC_0), or suffers a significant drop in performance (SC_1). When the information from infrastructure sensors is added (SC_{slow}), the decision to slowdown can be made dynamically, reducing the impact on performance. Still, a small risk remains if a slowly approaching automated forklift is ignored. However, instructing forklifts to unconditionally stop for nearby humans (SC_{stop}) will lead to unnecessary waiting times.

In the future, the prediction of human workers could be improved when more reliable information is available, for example by recognizing people's intentions and awareness. Switching between the safety concepts can adapt the system to the personnel present in the shared area.

Acknowledgments. The research leading to these results has partially received funding from the Bavarian Ministry of Economic Affairs, Regional Development and Energy as Fraunhofer High Performance Center Secure Intelligent Systems.

References

1. Safety in the future: Whitepaper, International Electrotechnical Commission. (IEC), Geneva, Switzerland, November 2020
2. Alami, R., Krishna, K.M., Siméon, T.: Provably safe motions strategies for mobile robots in dynamic domains. In: Laugier, C., Chatila, R. (eds.) Autonomous Navigation in Dynamic Environments, pp. 85–106. Springer, Heidelberg (2007). https://doi.org/10.1007/978-3-540-73422-2_4
3. Berufsgenossenschaft Holz und Metall: Gabelstapler. DGUV Information 208–004, BGHM, September 2012
4. Boehning, M.: Improving safety and efficiency of AGVs at warehouse black spots. In: IEEE ICCP, pp. 245–249, September 2014. https://doi.org/10.1109/ICCP.2014.6937004
5. Cantini, A., De Carlo, F., Tucci, M.: Towards forklift safety in a warehouse: an approach based on the automatic analysis of resource flows. Sustainability **12**(21), 8949 (2020). https://doi.org/10.3390/su12218949
6. Cao, L., Depner, T., Borstell, H., Richter, K.: Discussions on sensor-based Assistance Systems for Forklifts. In: Smart SysTech, Magedeburg, Germany, pp. 1–8, June 2019
7. Čech, M., et al.: Autonomous mobile robot technology for supplying assembly lines in the automotive industry. AL **7**(2), 103–109 (2020). https://doi.org/10.22306/al.v7i2.164
8. Chandra, S., Bharti, A.K.: Speed distribution curves for pedestrians during walking and crossing. Procedia - Soc. Behav. Sci. **104**, 660–667 (2013). https://doi.org/10.1016/j.sbspro.2013.11.160, https://www.sciencedirect.com/science/article/pii/S1877042813045515. 2nd Conference of Transportation Research Group of India (2nd CTRG)
9. Cohen, H.H., Jensen, R.C.: Measuring the effectiveness of an industrial lift truck safety training program. J. Safety Res. **15**(3), 125–135 (1984). https://doi.org/10.1016/0022-4375(84)90023-9
10. De Ryck, M., Versteyhe, M., Debrouwere, F.: Automated guided vehicle systems, state-of-the-art control algorithms and techniques. J. Manuf. Syst. **54**, 152–173 (2020). https://doi.org/10.1016/j.jmsy.2019.12.002
11. Arbeitsunfallgeschehen 2019. Statistik 21537, DGUV, September 2020. https://publikationen.dguv.de/widgets/pdf/download/article/3893
12. Dini, G., Giurlanda, F.: A new neighborhood monitoring protocol for co-ordination of multi-AGVs. In: The 2010 International Conference on Computer Engineering Systems, pp. 79–84, November 2010. https://doi.org/10.1109/ICCES.2010.5674890
13. Drabek, C., Kosmalska, A., Weiss, G., Ishigooka, T., Otsuka, S., Mizuochi, M.: Safe interaction of automated forklifts and humans at blind corners in a warehouse with infrastructure sensors. In: Habli, I., Sujan, M., Bitsch, F. (eds.) SAFECOMP 2021. LNCS, vol. 12852, pp. 163–177. Springer, Cham (2021). https://doi.org/10.1007/978-3-030-83903-1_11

14. Drabek, C., et al.: Dependable and efficient cloud-based safety-critical applications by example of automated valet parking. In: Martins, A.L., Ferreira, J.C., Kocian, A., Costa, V. (eds.) INTSYS 2020. LNICST, vol. 364, pp. 90–109. Springer, Cham (2021). https://doi.org/10.1007/978-3-030-71454-3_6

15. Everett, H.R., Gage, D.W., Gilbreath, G.A., Laird, R.T., Smurlo, R.P.: Real-world issues in warehouse navigation. In: Mobile Robots IX, vol. 2352, pp. 249–259. SPIE, Boston, January 1995. https://doi.org/10.1117/12.198975

16. Manipulation von Schutzeinrichtungen - Verhindern, Erschweren, Erkennen. Fachbereich AKTUELL FB HM-022, FB HM DGUV, July 2016

17. Industrial trucks — Safety requirements and verification — Part 4: Driverless industrial trucks and their systems. Int. Standard ISO 3691–4:2020(E) (2020)

18. Korte, D.: Sicherheitsbezogenes Sensorsystem für fahrerlose Transportfahrzeuge. Logist. J. **2020**(12) (2020). https://doi.org/10.2195/LJ_PROC_KORTE_DE_202 012_01

19. Košnar, K., Ecorchard, G., Přeučil, L.: Localization of humans in warehouse based on rack detection. In: ECMR, pp. 1–6, September 2019. https://doi.org/10.1109/ECMR.2019.8870913

20. Liu, S.B., Roehm, H., Heinzemann, C., Lütkebohle, I., Oehlerking, J., Althoff, M.: Provably safe motion of mobile robots in human environments. In: 2017 IROS, pp. 1351–1357, September 2017. https://doi.org/10.1109/IROS.2017.8202313

21. Löcklin, A., Ruppert, T., Jakab, L., Libert, R., Jazdi, N., Weyrich, M.: Trajectory prediction of humans in factories and warehouses with real-time locating systems. In: IEEE ETFA, vol. 1, pp. 1317–1320, September 2020. https://doi.org/10.1109/ETFA46521.2020.9211913

22. Lombard, A., Perronnet, F., Abbas-Turki, A., El Moudni, A.: Decentralized management of intersections of automated guided vehicles. IFAC-PapersOnLine **49**(12), 497–502 (2016). https://doi.org/10.1016/j.ifacol.2016.07.669

23. Lopez, F.G.: Predictive and cooperative online motion planning: a contribution to networked mobile robot navigation in industrial applications. Dissertation, Universität Stuttgart, Stuttgart (2019)

24. Markis, A., Papa, M., Kaselautzke, D., Rathmair, M., Sattinger, V., Brandstotter, M.: Safety of mobile robot systems in industrial applications. In: Proceedings of ARW & OAGM Workshop, Steyr, Austria, pp. 26–31 (2019). https://doi.org/10.3217/978-3-85125-663-5-04

25. Morales, Y., Yoshihara, Y., Akai, N., Takeuchi, E., Ninomiya, Y.: Proactive driving modeling in blind intersections based on expert driver data. In: IEEE IV, Los Angeles, CA, USA, pp. 901–907, June 2017. https://doi.org/10.1109/IVS.2017.7995830

26. Okamoto, T., Yamada, Y.: Study of conditions for safe and efficient traffic in an indoor blind corner-based decision model with consideration for tactics and information uncertainty. In: 2012 IEEE RO-MAN, pp. 682–688, September 2012. https://doi.org/10.1109/ROMAN.2012.6343830

27. Pinkam, N., Bonnet, F., Chong, N.Y.: Robot collaboration in warehouse. In: ICCAS, Gyeongju, South Korea, pp. 269–272, October 2016. https://doi.org/10.1109/ICCAS.2016.7832331

28. Platbrood, F., Görnemann, O.: Safe Robotics – die Sicherheit in kollaborativen Robotersystemen. Whitepaper 8020620, SICK AG, June 2018

29. Railsback, B.T., Ziernicki, R.M.: Stand-up forklift acceleration. In: ASME IMECE, pp. 421–424. ASMEDC, Vancouver, November 2010. https://doi.org/10.1115/IMECE2010-38940

30. Rey, R., Corzetto, M., Cobano, J.A., Merino, L., Caballero, F.: Human-robot co-working system for warehouse automation. In: IEEE ETFA, pp. 578–585, September 2019. https://doi.org/10.1109/ETFA.2019.8869178

31. Sabattini, L., et al.: The PAN-robots project: advanced automated guided vehicle systems for industrial logistics. IEEE Robot. Autom. Mag. **25**(1), 55–64 (2018). https://doi.org/10.1109/MRA.2017.2700325

32. Scheuvens, L., Hößler, T., Barreto, A.N., Fettweis, G.P.: Wireless control communications co-design via application-adaptive resource management. In: 2019 IEEE 2nd 5G World Forum (5GWF), pp. 298–303, September 2019. https://doi.org/10.1109/5GWF.2019.8911713

33. Shirazi, M.S., Morris, B.T.: Looking at intersections: a survey of intersection monitoring, behavior and safety analysis of recent studies. IEEE Trans. Intell. Transp. Syst. **18**(1), 4–24 (2017). https://doi.org/10.1109/TITS.2016.2568920

34. Forklift safety - reducing the risks. Technical report, State of Queensland (2019)

35. Sun, E., Ma, R.: The UWB based forklift trucks indoor positioning and safety management system. In: IEEE IAEAC, pp. 86–90, March 2017. https://doi.org/10.1109/IAEAC.2017.8053982

36. Tiusanen, R., Malm, T., Ronkainen, A.: An overview of current safety requirements for autonomous machines – review of standards. Open Eng. **10**(1), 665–673 (2020). https://doi.org/10.1515/eng-2020-0074

37. Yoshihara, Y., Morales, Y., Akai, N., Takeuchi, E., Ninomiya, Y.: Autonomous predictive driving for blind intersections. In: IEEE/RSJ IROS, Vancouver, BC, Canada, pp. 3452–3459, September 2017. https://doi.org/10.1109/IROS.2017.8206185

Feature Fusion in Deep-Learning Semantic Image Segmentation: A Survey

Jie Yuan⊙, Zhaoyi Shi⁽⊠⁾ ⊙, and Shuo Chen⊙

Minzu University of China, Beijing 100000, China
wzzhaoyi@outlook.com

Abstract. Semantic image segmentation is a necessary research and application direction for intelligent systems. Many researchers have tried to design advanced feature fusion to extract beneficial information from different feature maps selectively. However, there is no published review currently that focuses on feature fusion for semantic image segmentation. Therefore, we seek to compile related works and analyze the trends and challenges of feature fusion. In this paper, we introduce feature fusion modules based on different semantic image segmentation models. Then, we analyze typical and state-of-the-art approaches in terms of several effective from fusion. Third, we comprehensively present fusion strategies. Finally, we summarize the challenges as well as the development trend of feature fusion. This survey infers that although significant developments have been obtained, there is still plenty of room for improvement of feature fusion. Interpretability in deep-learning segmentation and the application of novel mechanisms have been important directions for future exploration.

Keywords: Feature fusion · Deep learning · Semantic segmentation

1 Introduction

The main objects of intelligent system research are mathematical models with uncertainty, high nonlinearity, and complex scenes [1]. The neural network is an essential subfield of the intelligent system. Neural network control systems have better intelligence and robustness and can handle high-dimensional, nonlinear, and strongly coupled control problems. Computer vision is one of the most important research directions.

Semantic Image segmentation is a hot branch of computer vision. It tries to understand the class of each pixel in an image semantically (e.g., identifying whether the target is a bicycle, a motorcycle, or some other type). In recent years, semantic segmentation based on deep convolutional neural networks has gained tremendous attention and development, playing an essential role in several visual understanding systems, such as autonomous driving [2].

Accurate classification and fine-grained boundaries rely on both semantic and detailed information [3]. However, it is difficult to obtain them on the same feature map. The shallow layer of the network retains more details, while the deep layer mainly

© ICST Institute for Computer Sciences, Social Informatics and Telecommunications Engineering 2022
Published by Springer Nature Switzerland AG 2022. All Rights Reserved
S. Paiva et al. (Eds.): SmartCity360° 2021, LNICST 442, pp. 284–292, 2022.
https://doi.org/10.1007/978-3-031-06371-8_18

extracts contextual information. Therefore, much work has focused on feature fusion modules for multi-scale features. A part of the work extracts multi-scale features from different levels of the backbone and then fuses them, such as FCN [4], PSPNet [5], Deeplab [6], U-Net [17]. Some work introduces parallel branching to preserve multi-scale features simultaneously during inference and merge them finally, like ICNet [8], BiSeNet [9], Fast-SCNN [10], STDC [11]. Other work applies complex mechanisms to carefully filter and adjust the weight of multi-scale features [12]. For example, Segmenter [13] introduces a transformer-based model for semantic segmentation.

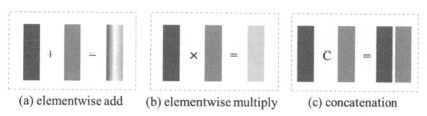

(a) elementwise add   (b) elementwise multiply   (c) concatenation

Fig. 1. Basic fusion operation

This paper reviews the feature fusion for semantic segmentation. Section 2 details typical feature fusion methods for different models and shows common defects and improvements. In Sect. 3, we analyze various fusion mechanisms with different architectures. Section 4 provides a comprehensive account of the feature fusion strategy. Section 5 analyzes the challenges and trends based on the above. Finally, the whole paper is concluded.

2 Feature Fusion in Various Models

In at least seven years, thousands of models have emerged in the field of semantic segmentation. They can be classified into several types according to contributions and structures. One thing is common, a suitable mechanism to merge high-level features with low-level high-resolution feature maps.

FCN [4] first introduces a fully convolutional network for semantic image segmentation for inputting an arbitrary size image and the output of the corresponding resolution segmentation map. The model applies to skip connections to fuse feature maps from shallow layers and uses elementwise add to merge them. It is not fast enough for the real-time task and cannot easily convert to 3D images. For feature fusion, the work does not sufficiently consider global contextual information. ParseNet [14] extracts additional global context by adding global average pooling for the feature map to overcome local confusion and smooth segmentation.

The encoder-decoder structure continuously reduces the feature map size. It increases the number of channels in the first half of the model while upsampling the feature map in the second half to achieve encoding and resolution recovery [15]. Initially, the encoder-decoder architecture serves the primary purpose of image compression and noise removal. The input is a picture encoded by downsampling to obtain a string of features smaller than the original image, corresponding to squeeze, and then a decoder that ideally restores the image to its original state.

SegNet [16] adds a series of novel shortcuts from the encoder to the decoder shown in Fig. 2. The decoder uses pooling indices computed in the max-pooling step of the corresponding encoder to perform nonlinear upsampling. This eliminates the need for learning to upsample.

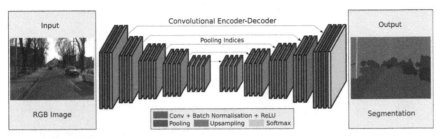

Fig. 2. A Typical Model with Encoder-Decoder Structure from [16]

U-Net [17] achieved excellent performance in medical image segmentation. The architecture consists of a contracting path to capture context and a symmetric expanding path that enables precise localization. The fusion method applies cropping, concatenation, and convolution in turn to achieve size consistency. The complexity of medical images is very high compared to ordinary photos, with an extensive greyscale range and unclear boundaries. U-Net combines low-resolution information in downsampling to provide a basis for object class recognition and high-resolution information in upsampling to provide a basis for accurate segmentation. It also fills in the underlying data with the skip connection to improve segmentation accuracy.

As medical images are relatively difficult to acquire and the amount of data is small, it is easy to over-fit the model if it has too many parameters. In contrast, the U-Net model has fewer parameters, making it more suitable than FCN.

Feature Pyramid Network (FPN) [18] is one of the most notable works using multiscale analysis for object detection and then applied to segmentation. The model uses a pyramid parsing module to harvest different sub-region representations, followed by upsampling and concatenation layers (or other different feature fusing methods) to form the final feature representation [19, 20].

Multiple downsampling or upsampling may lead to the loss of high-resolution representations. Some models contain several branches due to a lack of high-resolution representations. HRNet [21] connect the multi-resolution streams in parallel. The connection fusion unit includes stridden convolution or bilinear upsampling followed by 1 × 1convolution, and elementwise add to merge feature maps finally in Fig. 3.

Li *et al.* [22] study a dynamic routing method to alleviate the scale variance in semantic representation. After the model is trained, the activation of fusion connections is data-dependent, adapting to the scale distribution of each image.

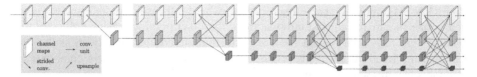

Fig. 3. An example of a high-resolution network [21] with parallel branches

3 Fusion Mechanisms

In this section, we classify feature fusion according to their effectiveness, architecture, and the methods they introduce and present some typical representative work. Table 1 provides the comparison with several representative methods on the Cityscapes test set in terms of frames per second and mIoU class.

3.1 Direct Fusion

For different scales, the direct fusion is to merge the feature maps after unifying the dimensions—no additional connections except for final fusion. Typical merge operations include elementwise add, elementwise multiplication, and concatenation. Channel consistency mainly uses convolution operations, such as 1×1 convolution.

FastSCNN [10] uses bilinear interpolation and convolution to resample feature maps. After that, elementwise add is applied to merge. Although a simple structure is not good enough for a high-accurate segmentation map, it receives a low cost of computing resources.

FasterSeg [23] present an automatically designed semantic segmentation network discovered from a multi-branch search space. The head module aggregates these outputs by direct fusion.

3.2 Multi-level Fusion

Most semantic segmentation backbones output multi-scale feature maps. Some work contains multi-level fusion, where feature maps are merged two by two according to an order. Detailed information can be progressively introduced into deeper features level by level, enabling more delicate boundaries.

FCN [4] chooses three feature maps with different levels and simply merges them sequentially from shallow layer to deep layer by elementwise add. In this way, it generates a segmentation map with the same dimension as the input image.

PSPNet [18] uses the pyramid pooling module to gather context information providing an effective global contextual prior for pixel-level scene parsing. The pyramid pooling module can collect levels of information more representative than global pooling [14].

3.3 Multi-layer Mesh Fusion

Some work tries a more flexible direction of multi-scale feature fusion. The connection between multi-scale branches contains high-level to low-resolution directions and transports high-level features to low-level feature maps.

FRRN [24] employs a two-stream system, where full-resolution information is carried in one stream and context information in the other pooling stream. Full-resolution residual units have both context and detail information through the network with a bidirectional information flow. This results in a network that successively combines and computes features at two resolutions.

DCNAS [25] propose a novel neural architecture search framework. The search space contains cross-level connections. The fusion module can aggregate semantic features from preceding fusion modules and attach transformed semantic features to succeeding ones.

3.4 Weighted Fusion

Different levels of feature maps have different contributions to the generation of fine segmentation maps. Therefore, finding the fusion weights between features is a key direction for improving the semantic image segmentation accuracy. If A and B are the feature maps to be merged, direct fusion and weighted fusion can be following:

$$Direct\,fusion : F_d(A, B) = A + B \tag{1}$$

$$Weighted\,fusion : F_w(A, B) = \alpha * A + \beta * B \tag{2}$$

where α, β represent the weights learned from the feature maps to be fused.

BiSeNet [9] proposes a specific feature fusion module to fuse different levels of the features. It first concatenates the multi-level features of two branches' multi-level features, pools the concatenated feature to a feature vector, and computes a weight vector, like SENet [26]. This weight vector can re-weight the features, which amounts to feature selection and combination by multiplication. With attention mechanism, BPNet [27] introduces a context aggregation module to filter information that learns pixelwise unary attention to emphasize small patterns and pairwise attention for long-range information dependency modeling.

DeepLabv3 [28] propose to augment ASPP with image-level features, similar to [5][14], to incorporate global context information properly. Li *et al.* [12] infer that simply directly combining multi-level features suffers from the semantic gap. And they propose Gated Fully Fusion (GFF) to fuse features selectively.

3.5 Graphical Models

Several methods introduce probabilistic graphical models for more accurate context, such as Conditional Random Fields (CRFs) and Markov Random Field (MRFs).

Chen *et al.* [29] show that responses at the final layer of DCNNs are not sufficiently localized for accurate object segmentation. Due to the very invariance properties, DCNNs are good at high-level tasks. This work combines the responses at the final DCNN layer with CRFs. Liu *et al.* [30] address semantic image segmentation by incorporating rich information into MRFs, including high-order relations and a mixture of label contexts.

Table 1. Performance of segmentation models on the Cityscapes test set

Model	Fusion mechanism	mIoU	FPS
DeepLab-MSc-CRF [29]	Graphical model	61.6	4.9
DPN [30]		66.8	-
Fast-SCNN [10]	Direct fusion	68.0	123.5
FasterSeg [23]		71.5	163.9
FCN [4]	Multi-level fusion	65.3	2.0
PSPNet [5]		78.4	-
FRRN [24]	Multi-layer mesh fusion	71.8	2.1
HRNetV2 [21]		81.6	-
DCNAS [25]		83.6	-
STDC2-50 [11]	Weighted fusion	71.9	**250.4**
BiSeNet-ResNet-18 [9]		74.7	65.5
DeepLabV3 [28]		81.3	-
GFF [12]		82.3	-
HRNet-OCR [33]		**85.1**	-

4   Fusion Strategy

The final stage of feature fusion generally uses one of three essential fusion operations, including element-wise addition, element-wise multiplication, and concatenation shown in Fig. 1. The addition has low computational complexity and is easy to compute. Multiplication increases the training difficulty [28]. Concatenation does not require a consistent number of channels and is more flexible. But it requires post-convolution, such as 1×1 convolution, to merge and filter redundant channels.

Nie *et al.* [27] find that either add or multiplication is not sufficient for feature fusion. They propose a feature fusion block that first adds and multiplies the characteristic graphs separately and then brings these two signals together.

For feature forms, methods usually pre-process the original image and detach the pixel space of the image with poor correlation. Traditional approaches tend to transform an image into a feature vector, while convolutional neural network extract information based on the feature map.

Transformer models have revolutionized Neuro-Linguistic Programming [31]. Recently, there has been some novel work for the usage of transformer structures in semantic image segmentation [32]. They formulate the problem of semantic segmentation as a sequence-to-sequence problem and use a transformer architecture. This work split the image into patches and treated linear patch embedding as input tokens for the transformer encoder, translating the image map to the sequence.

5   Challenges and Opportunities

Learning-based feature fusion modules have achieved excellent performance. However, research needs to investigate their underlying mechanisms further. For example, can the module implement the current functionality in a more compact structure? Can the contribution of multi-scale features be explained in an exact and easy-to-understand form? The interpretability of deep neural networks can help people achieve more efficient designs, approaching truly intelligent systems. A compelling fusion structure can create a more effective flow of semantic information and benefit gradient propagation.

For high availability, the feature fusion module needs low computational complexity, high memory efficiency in some tasks, such as autopilot. The application of neural architecture search helps researchers automatically generate application-competitive modules with the balance of precision and real-time. The boom in the mobile internet has created a massive demand for security, traffic scene awareness, and the need for portable models. Moreover, the design of models with higher energy efficiency contributes to maintaining a low-carbon smart city.

6   Conclusion

Feature fusion as a filtering and merging module for context and detail information plays a massive role in segmentation. Applying the model to specific scenarios and making it more efficient has been a key topic. In this paper, we provide a detailed overview of the feature fusion modules. We introduce representative fusion mechanisms and the essential fusion strategies. Finally, we infer the current challenges and future trends. We hope to provide readers with some helpful, modest guidance.

References

1. Antsaklis, P.J., Passino, K.M.: An Introduction to Intelligent and Autonomous Control. Kluwer Academic Publishers (1993)
2. Forsyth, D., Ponce, J.: Computer Vision: A Modern Approach. Prentice hall (2011)
3. Minaee, S., Boykov, Y.Y., Porikli, F., et al.: Image segmentation using deep learning: A survey. IEEE Trans. Pattern Anal. Mach. Intell. (2021)
4. Long, J., Shelhamer, E., Darrell, T.:: Fully convolutional networks for semantic segmentation. In: Proceedings of the IEEE Conference on Computer Vision and Pattern Recognition, pp. 3431–3440 (2015)
5. Zhao, H., Shi, J., Qi, X., et al.: Pyramid scene parsing network. In: Proceedings of the IEEE Conference on Computer Vision and Pattern Recognition, pp. 2881–2890 (2017)
6. Chen, L.C., Papandreou, G., Kokkinos, I., et al.: Deeplab: Semantic image segmentation with deep convolutional nets, atrous convolution, and fully connected CRFS. IEEE Trans. Pattern Anal. Mach. Intell. **40**(4), 834–848 (2017)
7. Ronneberger, O., Fischer, P., Brox, T.: U-net: Convolutional networks for biomedical image segmentation. In: Navab, N., Hornegger, J., Wells, W.M., Frangi, A.F. (eds.) MICCAI 2015. LNCS, vol. 9351, pp. 234–241. Springer, Cham (2015). https://doi.org/10.1007/978-3-319-24574-4_28

8. Zhao, H., Qi, X., Shen, X., Shi, J., Jia, J.: ICNet for real-time semantic segmentation on high-resolution images. In: Ferrari, V., Hebert, M., Sminchisescu, C., Weiss, Y. (eds.) ECCV 2018. LNCS, vol. 11207, pp. 418–434. Springer, Cham (2018). https://doi.org/10.1007/978-3-030-01219-9_25

9. Yu, C., Wang, J., Peng, C., Gao, C., Yu, G., Sang, N.: BiSeNet: bilateral segmentation network for real-time semantic segmentation. In: Ferrari, V., Hebert, M., Sminchisescu, C., Weiss, Y. (eds.) Computer Vision – ECCV 2018. LNCS, vol. 11217, pp. 334–349. Springer, Cham (2018). https://doi.org/10.1007/978-3-030-01261-8_20

10. Poudel, R.P.K., Liwicki, S., Cipolla, R.: Fast-SCNN: Fast semantic segmentation network. arXiv preprint arXiv:1902.04502 (2019)

11. Fan, M., Lai, S., Huang, J., et al.: Rethinking BiSeNet for real-time semantic segmentation. In: Proceedings of the IEEE/CVF Conference on Computer Vision and Pattern Recognition, pp. 9716–9725 (2021)

12. Li, X., Zhao, H., Han, L., et al.: Gated fully fusion for semantic segmentation. Proc. AAAI Conf. Artif. Intell. **34**(07), 11418–11425 (2020)

13. Strudel, R., Garcia, R., Laptev, I., et al.: Segmenter: Transformer for Semantic Segmentation. arXiv preprint arXiv:2105.05633 (2021)

14. Liu, W., Rabinovich, A., Berg, A.C.: Parsenet: Looking wider to see better. arXiv preprint arXiv:1506.04579 (2015)

15. Noh, H., Hong, S., Han, B.: Learning deconvolution network for semantic segmentation. IN: Proceedings of the IEEE International Conference on Computer Vision, pp.1520–1528 (2015)

16. Badrinarayanan, V., Kendall, A., Cipolla, R.: Segnet: A deep convolutional encoder-decoder architecture for image segmentation. IEEE Trans. Pattern Anal. Mach. Intell. **39**(12), 2481–2495 (2017)

17. Ronneberger, O., Fischer, P., Brox, T.: U-net: Convolutional networks for biomedical image segmentation. In: Proceedings of the International Conference on Medical Image Computing and Computer-assisted Intervention, pp. 234–241. Springer, Cham (2015)

18. Lin, T.Y., Dollár, P., Girshick, R., et al.: Feature pyramid networks for object detection. IN: Proceedings of the IEEE Conference on Computer Vision and Pattern Recognition, pp. 2117–2125 (2017)

19. Zhao H, Shi J, Qi X, et al.: Pyramid scene parsing network. In: Proceedings of the IEEE Conference on Computer Vision and Pattern Recognition, pp. 2881–2890 (2017)

20. He, J., Deng, Z., Zhou, L., Wang, Y., Qiao, Y.: Adaptive pyramid context network for semantic segmentation. In: Proceedings of the Conference on Computer Vision and Pattern Recognition, pp. 7519–7528 (2019)

21. Wang, J., Sun, K., Cheng, T., et al.: Deep high-resolution representation learning for visual recognition. In: Proceedings of the IEEE Transactions on Pattern Analysis and Machine Intelligence, (2020)

22. Li, Y., Song, L., Chen, Y., et al.: Learning dynamic routing for semantic segmentation. In: Proceedings of the IEEE/CVF Conference on Computer Vision and Pattern Recognition, pp. 8553–8562 (2020)

23. Chen, W., Gong, X., Liu, X., et al.: FasterSeg: Searching for faster real-time semantic segmentation. In: Proceedings of the International Conference on Learning Representations, (2019)

24. Pohlen, T., Hermans, A., Mathias, M., et al.: Full-resolution residual networks for semantic segmentation in street scenes. In: Proceedings of the IEEE Conference on Computer Vision and Pattern Recognition, pp. 4151–4160 (2017)

25. Zhang, X., Xu, H., Mo, H., et al.: Dcnas: Densely connected neural architecture search for semantic image segmentation. In: Proceedings of the IEEE/CVF Conference on Computer Vision and Pattern Recognition, pp. 13956–13967 (2021)

26. Hu, J., Shen, L., Sun, G.: Squeeze-and-excitation networks. In: Proceedings of the IEEE Conference on Computer Vision and Pattern Recognition, pp. 7132–7141 (2018)
27. Nie, D., Xue, J., Ren, X.: Bidirectional pyramid networks for semantic segmentation. In: Proceedings of the Asian Conference on Computer Vision (2020)
28. Chen, L.C., Papandreou, G., Schroff, F., et al.: Rethinking atrous convolution for semantic image segmentation. arXiv preprint arXiv:1706.05587 (2017)
29. Liang-Chieh, C., Papandreou, G., Kokkinos, I., et al.: Semantic image segmentation with deep convolutional nets and fully connected CRFs. In: Proceedings of the International Conference on Learning Representations (2015)
30. Liu, Z., Li, X., Luo, P., et al.: Semantic image segmentation via deep parsing network. In: Proceedings of the IEEE International Conference on Computer Vision, pp. 1377–1385 (2015)
31. Dai, Z., Yang, Z., Yang, Y., Carbonell, J., Le, Q.V., Salakhutdinov, R.: Transformer-XL: Attentive language models beyond a fixed-length context. In: Proceedings of the ACL (2019)
32. Zheng, S., Lu, J., Zhao, H., et al.: Rethinking semantic segmentation from a sequence-to-sequence perspective with transformers. Proceedings of the IEEE/CVF Conference on Computer Vision and Pattern Recognition, pp. 6881–6890 (2021)
33. Tao, A., Sapra, K., Catanzaro, B.: Hierarchical multi-scale attention for semantic segmentation. arXiv preprint arXiv:2005.10821 (2020)

MR-Based UAV Route Planning
for the Coverage Task

Jia-Hao Wei[1]([✉]), Jen-Jee Chen[1], and Yu-Chee Tseng[1,2,3]

[1] College of AI, National Yang Ming Chiao Tung University, Taipei, Taiwan
i860510.cai08g@nctu.edu.tw
[2] Academia Sinica, Taipei, Taiwan
[3] Kaohsiung Medical University, Kaohsiung, Taiwan

Abstract. In this work, we define a new problem called coverage task, which is to plan a flying route for a UAV to inspect a structure surface of interest with a certain visual quality ensurance. Users can use the designed MR interface for a coverage task via intuitive head gaze and hand gesture instructions. In particular, we present a spray light interface for easily visualizing the inspection area of a flying route. We also conduct a user study evaluation to verify our framework on HoloLens. The study shows that our spray light interface performs consistently well in subjective usability and improves over other approaches in performance. The results validate that the semi-immersive interface provides a viable alternative to conventional interfaces for UAV route planning.

Keywords: Mixed reality · HoloLens · Unmanned aerial vehicle · Route planning

1 Introduction

Drones are typically used in military surveillance or reconnaissance [3,15]. Recently, drones are more frequently used in industrial applications, such as quality and condition assessment [11,21], post-disaster exploration [1], and agriculture [9,10].

Route planning of drones is an important topic. There are various route planning interfaces for drones nowadays. The conventional interface uses a joystick combined with a 2D interface [19,20]. Recently, more advanced virtual reality and augmented reality interfaces have been proposed [6,14,22].

In this work, we define a new problem called coverage task, which is to plan a flying route for a UAV to inspect a structure surface of interest with a certain visual quality ensurance. To facilitate this task, we design a set of Mixed Reality (MR) interfaces. We consider MR rather than VR because VR will totally block a pilot's vision on the physical environment. Since our main objective is to understand the spatial information of how well the surface under inspection is covered by the current route, existing interfaces that simply focus on

S. Paiva et al. (Eds.): SmartCity360° 2021, LNICST 442, pp. 293–306, 2022.
https://doi.org/10.1007/978-3-031-06371-8_19

virtual route planning does not meet our need. Our goal is to develop interfaces that combine waypoints and drone camera's field of view to help measure the coverage of a specific range. In the meantime, our interfaces have to perform obstacle avoidance and ensure visual quality. To the best of our knowledge, this is the first work addressing these issues for drone route planning.

Our MR interfaces are developed based on Microsoft HoloLens 1. We use the spatial mapping feature from the HoloLens to construct a 3D room model in an indoor environment. Users are asked to use our interfaces to complete a surface inspection task. The entire system provides a semi-immersive and intuitive interaction for route planning mission with a certain visual quality requirement. A spray light interface is provided to help users verify the image quality under the currently planned route. Users can adjust waypoints by hand gestures with head gazes, which is traditionally hard to accomplish on a 2D screen. The overall performance of our interfaces is evaluated by user study analysis. The analysis results and participants' feedbacks consistently indicate that our interfaces have significant improvements in performance and wide applicability in the coverage task.

The rest of this paper is organized as follows. Section 2 reviews some related works. We formally define coverage task and present the whole architecture of our interface in Sect. 3. In Sect. 4, we describe our user study design and procedure. Our user evaluation results are presented in Sect. 5. We make a conclusion and discuss the future work in Sect. 6.

2   Related Work

Traditional human-drone interaction approaches mainly use a joystick controller with a flat-screen to steer drones. Using touch screen devices to manipulate drones are studied in [8,12]. An innovative interface is developed in [8] on an iPad to intuitively steer drones by simple touch gestures and to take videos in an egocentric view. For visualizing 3D spatial data, a toolkit called Rviz is proposed [7]. The work [4] compares the performance of physical or virtual object interaction in Unity, GAZEBO, and Rviz platforms. However, these works are not for interacting with spatial objects.

For spatial interaction tasks, modeling real objects is a key to conveying human intention. The work [18] uses VR interfaces combined with OptiTrack to transform real scenes and objects to VR world. Another direction is to combine VR interfaces with Kinect [6,22], as Kinect can provide more stereoscopic information and gestures for natural interactions.

While VR interfaces only support human-drone interactions in a remote mode, augmented reality (AR) is an option to provide real world scenes of the flying environment and target settings. AR interfaces for displaying virtual drones and targets and piloting by a joystick are proposed in [14,23]. In [13], a 3D scale-down spatial environment is reconstructed by stereo cameras and users can manipulate a drone by using head gazes.

While AR interfaces achieve good performance when a drone is in direct visual range, mixed reality (MR) enables interaction when a drone is in non-light of sight [2]. Through spatial mapping, the work focuses on drone manipulation in egocentric view or exocentric view and makes a comparison on head gazes and joystick for drone steering. The MR interface [5] allows interaction with drones by 3D rendering and voice control. This work renders a grid map of the flight environment with ground tags for drone localization, so drone steering by voice commands in a grid-by-grid manner is possible. Since the grid map is only 4×4 and needs to align with ground tag manually, the flight paths are limited in specific scenarios.

All the above works have achieved immersive rendering. But pure VR lacks of real understanding on physical world, while AR directly overlays graphics on the physical world. Therefore, we choose to build our interface on MR so that users can simultaneously visualize a physical environment and interact with virtual objects.

3   Propose Approach

3.1   Coverage Task

The *coverage task* for UAV is formally defined as follows. A drone needs to be dispatched to an environment to inspect a surface of interest S of a structure with a certain visual quality ensurance. We define quality ensurance by the distance between the drone's camera and the region under inspection. The inspection routing path of the drone is defined as a sequence of waypoints $R = \{ r_1, r_2, \ldots r_n \}$. At any point in R, the camera's field of view (FOV) on S that is within a distance threshold of δ is considered as covered, and the other FOV is considered as uncovered. Two examples are illustrated in Fig. 1. In Fig. 1 (a), since the drone is too far away from the surface, no FOV is considered as covered. In Fig. 1 (b), the central region $[A, B]$ that is within the distance threshold δ is covered, while the other regions $[C, A]$ and $[B, D]$ are uncovered.

Given a routing path R, it is not hard to mark the regions of S that are covered. Depending on the task, one may specify a required coverage ratio p of S that is covered by R. We assume that the environment has been pre-scanned and thus its 3D model is already known. Our goal is to design a MR tool (such as Hololens) and a set of convenient user interfaces to plan a route R to meet the required coverage ratio p. In order to define visual quality ensurance, let us assume that we want to recognize an object (such as a crack) of length L cm by displaying at least M pixels in an image. In order to guarantee this visual quality, we need to compute the minimum distance threshold δ between the drone's camera and the region under inspection. That is, we need to transform to a pixel unit to its actual distance. We apply the *collinearity equations* for the transformation. To relate camera coordinates in a sensor plane (2D) to ground coordinates (3D), let us consider Fig. 2. Let $P = (x, y, y)$ be a point in the ground coordinate, which is projected to point $P' = (x', y', z')$ on the sensor plane through a projection optical centre $C = (x_0, y_0, z_0)$. To relate P and P', since P', projection optical centre C, and P is collinear, we can use proportional function (Eq. 1) to get P'. Let the distance from C to the sensor plane be d, and we can get the following equations (Eq. 2 and Eq. 3):

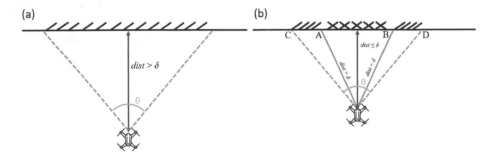

Fig. 1. Examples of covered and uncovered regions (θ = camera view angle).

$$\frac{x' - x_0}{x_0 - x} = \frac{y' - y_0}{y_0 - y} = \frac{-d}{z_0 - z}. \tag{1}$$

$$x' - x_0 = -d\frac{x - x_0}{z - z_0}. \tag{2}$$

$$y' - y_0 = -d\frac{y - y_0}{z - z_0}. \tag{3}$$

Assuming the distance of P and Q is L cm and P, Q are on the same plane, and we can get the pixel distance of the two points by the above equation. With pixel unit, we can derive the minimum distance threshold δ.

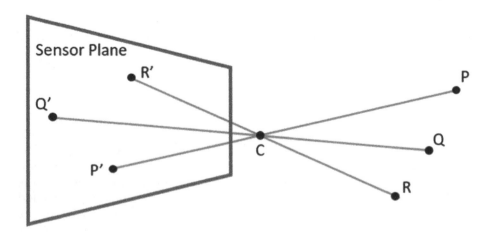

Fig. 2. Point P is (x, y, z), and the relative point P' on the sensor plane is (x', y', z'), projection optical centre is (x_0, y_0, z_0).

3.2   System Architecture

Next, we propose our MR-based model to handle the coverage task. The overall architecture is shown in Fig. 3. We use Microsoft HoloLens 1 in this work. The interface is developed on Unity 2018.4 and Visual Studio Code platform. The task is given as (S, p) and it is for an indoor room environment, of which the 3D spatial model has been pre-scanned by HoloLens.

On the user interface part, there are three components. The spatial information is processed by HoloLens functions to construct the 3D model. HoloLens already provides some head gaze gestures for clicking on the MR world by air tap [17]. We also provide button clicking by head gaze air tap for waypoints selection. The routing path between two adjacent waypoints is connected automatically. There are also interfaces for editing waypoints. As the coverage ratio of the current route is important for a user to understand how well the coverage task is conducted, besides the current routing path, we also provide convenient visualization by rendering the current coverage regions on S based on the distance threshold δ.

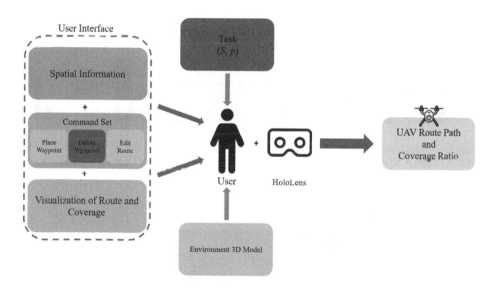

Fig. 3. System architecture.

3.3   Interface Design

Spatial Mapping. First, we scan the space to get its spatial information and construct a 3D space model. This spatial mapping can be done by the visual SLAM algorithm and onboard Lidar of HoloLens [16]. The scanning range is about twenty square meters. It can recognize surface planes, such as table, ceiling, floor, and wall. Detecting and classifying the complicated objects in a messy indoor environment is a challenge. An indoor space is generally surrounded by rectangular ceilings, floors, and walls. Figure 4 (a) shows a real scene in our experiment. After scanning by HoloLens, a triangular mesh model can be constructed by Unity, as illustrated in Fig. 4 (b). Then, ceilings and floors are classified based on their mesh sizes and locations. Further, vertical meshes greater than a certain size (such as three square meters) are classified as wall surfaces. The other meshes are classified as obstacles in the room, which are shown as occlusion objects by HoloLens and should be avoided in route planning. After these processing, we obtain a cleaner room model as shown in Fig. 4 (c).

After the 3D space model is constructed, we designate a region S of wall areas as our inspection targets. That is, users need to plan a route for a drone to inspect the region S. We use translucent gray materials overlaid on the top of large surfaces for visualization. Target surface S is bounded by pink lines. Then users can conduct route planning in the space. We also use spray light of bright color to cover the areas that have been covered by the current route. The uncovered areas, however, remain in translucent gray. So it is hard for users to not observe the uncovered areas. Figure 5 shows our interface.

Fig. 4. Spatial mapping steps: (a) a real room scene, (b) 3D triangular mesh model, and (c) surface model.

Fig. 5. Wall, target inspection surfaces S, and spray light of covered areas.

Waypoint Editing Interfaces. Next, we introduce our interfaces for waypoint editing. We design three buttons, *Place*, *Delete*, and *Edit*, in our mixed reality UI, as shown in Fig. 6. Controlling the cursor, which is on the center of field of vision, is done by head moving. Clicking on any button results in corresponding actions on waypoints. The straight line between two adjacent waypoints is drawn by a white color line. Whenever a new waypoint is added, we render on S the newly covered area by adding more spray light in pink. Also, the current coverage ratio will be shown immediately on screen. The *Place* button is to add a new waypoint at the end of the current route. The new path is shown by white. If there is any physical obstacle exists in the path, the part of the path will be changed to red to remind users. The *Delete* button is to remove a misplaced waypoint. If the deleted waypoint is between two other waypoints, the two waypoints will be connected by a new white line. The *Edit* button is to adjust the position of an existing waypoint. A user can pick the drone and release it at a new position. The new flight route and spray light will be updated automatically. Since this action may change the covered areas, one can visualize the effect by the size of spot light immediately.

Fig. 6. Editing interface: place button, delete button, and edit button.

Visualization of Route and Coverage. In order to visualize the drone route in different circumstances, we use several presentation method. The original route is shown in Fig. 7 (a), where waypoints are connected by white lines. We observe that some users prefer to fine-tune waypoints at the final stage of a task. The original route is obstacle-avoiding before their adjustment. In this case, they should be notified by the color change caused by route change. When obstacles exist in an adjusted part, the part of route will be marked in red to remind users to further revise the part. In Fig. 7 (b), we show a case where an obstacle (whiteboard) exists between two waypoints and the color of the part turns to red. Besides, the size of spray light may change when waypoints are adjusted. This feature is very helpful for users to fine-tune a route to fulfill the target coverage ratio p. In Fig. 7 (c), the size of spray light decreases and then increases because of the middle waypoint changes its position. When a waypoint is too far from S, the corresponding spray light may disappear to warn the users.

Fig. 7. (a) A typical obstacle-free route, (b) a route marked by red when crossing an obstacle, (c) change of spray light when one moves the middle waypoint.

4 User Study

We have conducted experiments to evaluate the efficiency and usability of our interfaces by observing human users to complete a series of coverage tasks. These tasks are meant to represent inspection applications requiring a drone to navigate specific areas and following obstacle avoidance and quality ensurance requirements.

4.1 Participants

We recruited ten participants (one female) from a local university between ages twenty and thirty, and they all had normal or corrected-to-normal vision. Two participants had previous experiences with AR or VR HMDs.

4.2 Study Design

We used a within-subjects design and the distance between the designated surface S and participants is at least one meter. The participants were given tasks of route planning and these tasks are divided into spray light enabled and disabled states (see Fig. 8 for a comparison).

The inspection tasks may involve *large*, *medium*, or *small cracks*, which may lead to different threshold values for δ ($\delta = 30$–50, 50–70, 70–90). To remove the effect of learning effect, the order of δ values is random for every participant. In every state, two shapes of S but of the same size are evaluated (Fig. 8). That is, each participant performed twelve trials (*two states* × *two shapes* × three δ). A participant proceeds to the next trial only when he/she thinks that the current coverage task is finished and we use OpenCV to get the coverage ratio. The average total trial time is about 1 h (Fig. 9).

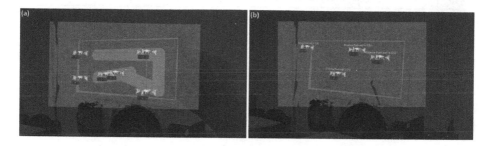

Fig. 8. (a) Spray light enabled state and (b) disabled state.

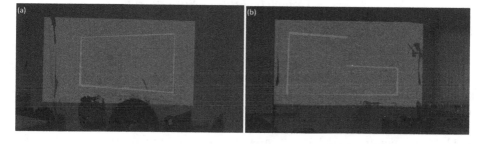

Fig. 9. Two shapes of target surface S.

4.3   Task Execution Procedure

After we explained how to use our interfaces, participants were allowed to practice as much as they felt comfortable. The participants performed two shapes of tasks for each given spray light state and were told to perform each task as fast as possible and try to fill S as much as possible. If needed, they were allowed to take a break between trials. We measured the time, waypoint number, route distances and coverage ratio. Participants then filled out a usability questionnaire (Fig. 10) and we interviewed them after all tasks were completed.

	Question	Score
Q1	I quickly adapted to this interface	1-10
Q2	Controlling the system with this interface came naturally to me.	1-10
Q3	This interface was pleasant to use.	1-10
Q4	This interface was confusing.	1-10
Q5	Without this interface, I cannot finish those task.	1-10

Fig. 10. Usability questionnaire.

4.4   Evaluation Results

Among the ten recruited participants, eight were able to complete the whole procedure. Thus, the analyses are based on these eight participants. To quantify the results, we calculate participants' performance by:

$$Performance = \frac{Coverage\ Rate(\%)}{Complete\ Time + No.Waypoints \times P}. \tag{4}$$

The denominator is considered as penalty. First, the more waypoints there are, the more turning overhead it will incur. Second, we observe that some participants prefer to use more waypoints to cover an area. Therefore, we set $P = 0.5\,s$ as an time overhead. The evaluations of pairwise t-test are shown in Fig. 11 (a). As can be seen, there are significant advantage in using spray light to guide a user. In the small δ case, the enabled state has mean = 73.72 and standard deviation = 15.17, versus the disabled state's mean = 55 and standard deviation = 11.45. In medium and large δ cases, we see the similar trend. In all cases, the p-value is smaller than 0.001. The analysis shows that participants took significantly less time to complete a task when spray light is enabled. We also plot the completion time of pairwise t-test in Fig. 11 (b). In the small δ case, the enabled state has mean = 131 and standard deviation = 28.24, versus the disabled state's mean = 150.67 and standard deviation = 31.67. In medium and large δ cases, we see the similar trend. In all cases, the p-value is smaller than 0.001. The results validate that participants took longer time in disabled state than enabled state in every task.

In Fig. 12, we compare the routing path length as it reflects drones' battery consumption. The enabled state has mean = 38 and standard deviation = 11.84, versus the disabled state's is mean = 62.42 and standard deviation = 18.81. The p-value is also smaller than 0.001. In summary, the analysis reveals that the enabled state is more efficient than to disabled state in all aspects.

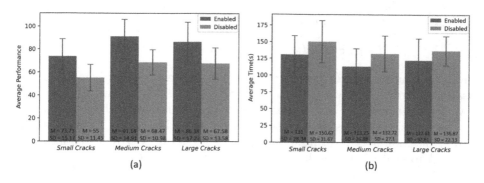

Fig. 11. (a) Performance measurements and (b) Time measurements.

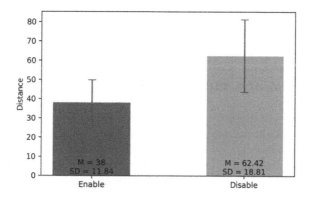

Fig. 12. Distance measurements.

4.5   Interview Comments

In interviews, we receive the similar comments that when the spray light function is enabled, it is much easier to adjust waypoints and visualize the area that are not yet covered. Some participants mentioned that they finished their tasks in the enabled state with less fatigue, as quoted below:

"Comparing to disabled state, I think the interface (enabled state) greatly facilitate manipulation and adjustment." (P2)

"The tasks can be finished in enabled state easily without hesitation and frazzle." (P5)

Additionally, all users can well understand the concept of spray light easily. They did recognize how the coverage areas are reflected by spray light, are quoted below:

"It is hard for me to finish the tasks without spray lighting path." (P1)

"Using enabled one is easy and convenient." (P7)

From the questionnaire results, we conduct post-experiment comparison on usability and flexibility. Note that the fourth question in the questionnaire reverses the valence to test if users are paying attention. In the analysis, this reverse question's scores are inverted to match the other scales. To interpret the survey question as a measuring parameter, we use one-way repeated-measures ANOVA to analyze the results. The spray light enabled state improves an average of 5.35 Likert points over the disabled state (with p-value $= 0.0329 < 0.05$). While this brief survey certainly does not cover all aspects of usability, it does demonstrate a preference for spray light. In addition, we did not observe a significant difference across all metrics when comparing those users with VR experience to those without VR experience. We speculate the reason is that users can still interact with real objects to get spatial information in semi-immersive environment.

5   Conclusions and Future Work

In this paper, we have defined a new coverage task for drone route planning and presented a spray light interface to facilitate users to arrange waypoints while visualizing the covered and yet-to-be-covered areas in a MR environment. A set of design considerations and insights that are unique to the routing planning interaction problem are presented. Our user evaluation results validate the effectiveness and efficiency of our design. In conclusion, the spray light design provides a high degree of freedom and applicability. The interface can be integrated with various interaction techniques and devices in other applications and circumstances. As to future work, we have validated our design for indoor environments, but outdoor environments of larger scales deserve further study. Manipulating multiple drones also deserves further research.

Acknowledgements. This research is co-sponsored by ITRI, Pervasive Artificial Intelligence Research (PAIR) Labs, and Ministry of Science and Technology (MoST). This work is also financially supported by "Center for Open Intelligent Connectivity" of "Higher Education Sprout Project" of NYCU and MOE, Taiwan.

References

1. Aljehani, M., Inoue, M.: Performance evaluation of multi-UAV system in post-disaster application: validated by HITL simulator. IEEE Access **7**, 64386–64400 (2019)
2. Erat, O., Isop, W.A., Kalkofen, D., Schmalstieg, D.: Drone-augmented human vision: exocentric control for drones exploring hidden areas. IEEE Trans. Visual Comput. Graphics **24**(4), 1437–1446 (2018)

3. Giese, S., Carr, D., Chahl, J.: Implications for unmanned systems research of military UAV mishap statistics. In: 2013 IEEE Intelligent Vehicles Symposium (IV), pp. 1191–1196. IEEE (2013)
4. Hoenig, W., Milanes, C., Scaria, L., Phan, T., Bolas, M., Ayanian, N.: Mixed reality for robotics. In: 2015 IEEE/RSJ International Conference on Intelligent Robots and Systems (IROS), pp. 5382–5387. IEEE (2015)
5. Huang, B., Bayazit, D., Ullman, D., Gopalan, N., Tellex, S.: Flight, camera, action! Using natural language and mixed reality to control a drone. In: 2019 International Conference on Robotics and Automation (ICRA), pp. 6949–6956. IEEE (2019)
6. Jie, L., Jian, C., Lei, W.: Design of multi-mode UAV human-computer interaction system. In: 2017 IEEE International Conference on Unmanned Systems (ICUS), pp. 353–357. IEEE (2017)
7. Kam, H.R., Lee, S.H., Park, T., Kim, C.H.: RViz: a toolkit for real domain data visualization. Telecommun. Syst. **60**(2), 337–345 (2015)
8. Kang, H., Li, H., Zhang, J., Lu, X., Benes, B.: FlyCam: multitouch gesture controlled drone gimbal photography. IEEE Robot. Autom. Lett. **3**(4), 3717–3724 (2018)
9. Kellenberger, B., Marcos, D., Lobry, S., Tuia, D.: Half a percent of labels is enough: efficient animal detection in UAV imagery using deep CNNs and active learning. IEEE Trans. Geosci. Remote Sens. **57**(12), 9524–9533 (2019)
10. Kitano, B.T., Mendes, C.C., Geus, A.R., Oliveira, H.C., Souza, J.R.: Corn plant counting using deep learning and UAV images. IEEE Geosci. Remote Sens. Lett. (2019)
11. Kuang, Q., Jin, X., Zhao, Q., Zhou, B.: Deep multimodality learning for UAV video aesthetic quality assessment. IEEE Trans. Multimedia **22**(10), 2623–2634 (2019)
12. Lan, Z., Shridhar, M., Hsu, D., Zhao, S.: XPose: reinventing user interaction with flying cameras. In: Robotics: Science and Systems, pp. 1–9 (2017)
13. Liu, C., Shen, S.: An augmented reality interaction interface for autonomous drone. In: 2020 IEEE/RSJ International Conference on Intelligent Robots and Systems (IROS), pp. 11419–11424. IEEE (2020)
14. Mashood, A., Mohammed, M., Abdulwahab, M., Abdulwahab, S., Noura, H.: A hardware setup for formation flight of UAVs using motion tracking system. In: 2015 10th International Symposium on Mechatronics and its Applications (ISMA), pp. 1–6. IEEE (2015)
15. Ma'Sum, M.A., et al.: Simulation of intelligent unmanned aerial vehicle (UAV) for military surveillance. In: 2013 International Conference on Advanced Computer Science and Information Systems (ICACSIS), pp. 161–166. IEEE (2013)
16. Microsoft: HoloLens 1st hardware-Microsoft docs (2018). https://docs.microsoft.com/zh-tw/hololens/hololens1-hardware
17. Microsoft: Microsoft 2018a. Gestures-mixed reality (2018). https://docs.microsoft.com/en-us/windows/mixed-reality/gestures
18. Paterson, J.R., et al.: Improving usability, efficiency, and safety of UAV path planning through a virtual reality interface. In: Symposium on Spatial User Interaction, pp. 1–2 (2019)
19. Rothwell, C.D., Patzek, M.J.: An interface for verification and validation of unmanned systems mission planning: communicating mission objectives and constraints. IEEE Trans. Hum.-Mach. Syst. **49**(6), 642–651 (2019)
20. Wilde, G.A., Murphy, R.R.: User interface for unmanned surface vehicles used to rescue drowning victims. In: 2018 IEEE International Symposium on Safety, Security, and Rescue Robotics (SSRR), pp. 1–8. IEEE (2018)

21. Wu, W., Qurishee, M.A., Owino, J., Fomunung, I., Onyango, M., Atolagbe, B.: Coupling deep learning and UAV for infrastructure condition assessment automation. In: 2018 IEEE International Smart Cities Conference (ISC2), pp. 1–7. IEEE (2018)
22. Wu, Y., Song, J., Sun, J., Zhu, F., Chen, H.: Aerial grasping based on VR perception and haptic control. In: 2018 IEEE International Conference on Real-time Computing and Robotics (RCAR), pp. 556–562. IEEE (2018)
23. Yu, Y., Wang, X., Zhong, Z., Zhang, Y.: ROS-based UAV control using hand gesture recognition. In: 2017 29th Chinese Control And Decision Conference (CCDC), pp. 6795–6799. IEEE (2017)

Low-cost Real-time IoT-Based Air Quality Monitoring and Forecasting

Hugo Martins[1] , Nishu Gupta[2]([mail]) , M. J. C. S. Reis[3] ,
and P. J. S. G. Ferreira[4]

[1] University of Trás-os-Montes e Alto Douro (UTAD), 5000-801 Vila Real, Portugal
[2] Norwegian University of Science and Technology, Gjøvik, Norway
[3] UTAD/IEETA, Vila Real, Portugal
[4] University of Aveiro/IEETA, Aveiro, Portugal
hugo.m.s.martins@gmail.com, nishugupta@ieee.org,
mcabral@utad.pt, pjf@ua.pt

Abstract. The ultimate goal of a "smart city" is improving the quality of
life of citizens, optimizing city functions and promote economic growth,
through the use of technologies and data analysis. Attention should be
placed in how the technology is used rather than on how much technology
is available. The "smartness" of a city is measured using a set of characteristics, which includes environmental initiatives. Air pollution, in particular, has a great impact on the quality of life. Here, we will present
a low-cost, real-time, compact, lightweight and robust prototype device
(hardware and software) capable of measuring, monitoring and forecasting the indoor (closed spaces) air quality. This device produces an Indoor
Air Quality Index (IAQI), which is calculated based on the CO_2 and
Total Volatile Organic Compounds (TVOC) parameters. The IAQI is
used to activate two RGB LED lights, where people can very intuitively
be aware of the current and predicted air quality: excellent (green); good
(light green); moderate (yellow); poor (orange); and unhealthy (red). The
results achieved by the set of conducted tests proved that the device and
IAQI are reliable.

Keywords: IoT · Real-time · Alert system · Air quality · Low-cost ·
Smart cities · Smart environment

1 Introduction

The ultimate goal of a "smart city" is improving the quality of life of citizens.
This objective is pursued through the use of technologies and data analysis
that aims at optimizing city functions and promote economic growth. Attention should be placed on how the technology is used rather than on how much
technology is available. Environmental initiatives are among the most important characteristics used to measure the "smartness" of a city. Air pollution, in
particular, has a great impact on the quality of life of citizens.

© ICST Institute for Computer Sciences, Social Informatics and Telecommunications Engineering 2022
Published by Springer Nature Switzerland AG 2022. All Rights Reserved
S. Paiva et al. (Eds.): SmartCity360° 2021, LNICST 442, pp. 307–320, 2022.
https://doi.org/10.1007/978-3-031-06371-8_20

Air pollution can be defined as any form of matter or energy with intensity, concentration, time or characteristics that may make the air inappropriate, harmful or offensive to health, inconvenient to public welfare, harmful to materials, fauna and flora or harmful to the safety, use and enjoyment of the property and the quality of life of the community [1].

The effects of poor air quality are generally not as visible as compared to other more easily identifiable factors. Several epidemiological studies have shown strong correlations between exposure to air pollutants and the effects of morbidity and mortality, caused by respiratory (asthma, bronchitis, pulmonary emphysema and lung cancer) and cardiovascular problems, even when the concentrations of pollutants in the atmosphere do not exceed the legally prescribed air quality standards. The most vulnerable populations are children, the elderly and people with respiratory diseases [2,3].

According to the World Health Organization (WHO) "ambient air pollution accounts for an estimated 4.2 million deaths per year due to stroke, heart disease, lung cancer and chronic respiratory diseases" [4]. What is more intriguing is that almost 91% of the world's population lives in places where the bad air quality levels exceed the limits recommended by the WHO.

Air quality management aims to ensure that socio-economic development takes place in a sustainable and environmentally safe manner. Thus, actions to prevent, combat and reduce pollutant emissions and the effects of degradation of the atmospheric environment are essential. Ideally, actions should be developed that allow for a complete and real-time mapping of air quality. Indoor air quality meters are used to prevent, for example, mildew, or monitor CO_2 levels or detect gas leaks. Whether portable or permanent, this air quality monitoring equipment is essential to ensure the health and safety of people, animals and plants.

There are commercially available air quality monitoring devices that meet various industry standards related to personal safety and are used to detect, measure and monitor relative humidity, ambient temperature, carbon dioxide (CO_2) levels, Volatile Organic Compounds (VOC), carbon monoxide (CO), nitrogen dioxide (NO_2), oxygen (O_2), ozone (O_3) and other flammable, hazardous or toxic gases. Some of these air quality measurement devices feature an automatic calibration function that allows for easy calibration of the gas detector. Some of these devices also have the ability to store measurement values, and can later transfer the measurement data to a computer for more detailed analysis. However, these devices are generally of price, weight and dimensions that can be considered high. On the other hand, these systems do not provide any form of sharing the data resulting from the different readings of air quality, being it on a website or any other form.

Here, we will present a low-cost, compact, lightweight and robust device to measure, monitor and forecasting the indoor (closed spaces) air quality in real-time. The forecasting is based on a very low computational cost algorithm to determine the first derivative of discrete band-limited signals.

The solution presented here can be used, for example, by the owner of a restaurant, cafe, or bar, to show their customers that the air quality in their establishment is recommended, and that their customers can be accompanied by their children who are not exposing them to polluted environments. On the other hand, being the device compact, lightweight and of small dimensions, it can be easily transported and/or re-positioned. The way in which the device is powered, by a battery and/or a charger, contributes to this flexibility. Please refer to Figs 3 and 4 below, for an overview of the proposed system. This device can be used to create a "social network" where users share their indoor air quality index data. These data can then be used by local, regional and national level authorities to devise measures for improving citizens' life.

2 Air Quality Index and Measures

An air quality index (AQI) is a descriptive scale used to show how polluted the air is. Unfortunately, there is no standard AQI available, and even the research on the health effects of air pollution in short time frames is something not profoundly studied. This is the main reason why air quality indexes are typically only provided for time periods of an hour or longer. Besides, the different indexes used are more effective when measuring outdoor air quality. The concentrations of some air pollutants in indoor environments can be between two to 10 times higher than in outdoor environments. This justifies the need to notify people living in indoor environments, as soon as possible, when air quality deteriorates. By so doing, people can take immediate and direct action to remedy the situation.

The Total Volatile Organic Compounds (TVOC) concept has been established as a practical time and cost-effective method to assess indoor environments for contamination. Table 1 presents the TVOC exposure recommendations issued by the German Federal Environmental Agency [5,6].

Table 1. Total Volatile Organic Compounds (TVOC) exposure recommendation [5,6] (ppb—parts per billion).

Level	Hygienic rating	Recommendation	Exposure	Limit [ppb]
5—Unhealthy	Not acceptable	Use only if unavoidable. Intense ventilation necessary	hours	2200–5500
4—Poor	Major objections	Intensified ventilation. Airing necessary. Search for sources	< 1 month	660–2200
3—Moderate	Some objections	Intensified ventilation. Airing recommended. Search for sources	< 12 months	220–660
2—Good	No relevant objections	Ventilation. Airing recommended	No limit	65–220
1—Excellent	No objections	Target value	No limit	0–65

It is well known that indoor CO_2 levels have a negative impact on cognitive performance as well as human health. Average indoor CO_2 concentrations range from 600 to 1000 ppm (parts per million), but can exceed 2000 ppm with increased occupancy and poor ventilation. Exposure to a value greater than 1000 ppm can lead to decreased cognitive abilities, while levels greater than 2000 ppm have been linked to kidney calcification, inflammation, oxidative stress, bone demineralization, and endothelial dysfunction [7]. Table 2 shows the CO_2 reference levels used in this study.

Table 2. CO_2 reference levels (ppm—parts per million).

Level	CO_2 [ppm]	Meaning
5—Unhealthy	> 5000	Air quality exceeds maximum workplace concentration values
4—Poor	> 2000	Air quality has reached unacceptable levels
3—Moderate	> 1500	Air quality has reached precarious levels
2—Good	> 1000	Air quality has reached acceptable levels
1—Excellent	< 1000	Air quality remains at harmless levels

We also measure temperature because it is an issue of comfort for indoor environments. High temperatures have been found to increase the concentrations of certain pollutants, this case being particularly studied for outdoor environments. Regulating temperature levels minimize the risk of mould growth indoors, thus helping preventing illnesses like the Sick Building Syndrome.

Based on these facts, here we propose to use a real-time air quality index for indoor applications that looks at the average air quality from the last ten minutes as if it had already been measured in the last full hour. Please recall that this averaging operation acts like a low-pass filter, "smoothing" abrupt transitions in the values. Our indoor air quality index (IAQI) is calculated based on the CO_2 and TVOC parameters, being the final value given based on the worst air quality index rating among them, that is,

$$IAQI = \max\{I_{CO_2}, I_{TVOC}\}, \tag{1}$$

where I_{CO_2} corresponds to the index air quality associated with the CO_2 level and provided by Table 2, and I_{TVOC} corresponds to the index air quality associated with the TOVOC level and provided by Table 1.

This means that the higher the value of IAQI the worst the air quality is. For example, if CO_2 is rated as "Excellent", but TVOC level is "Good", then the overall IAQI rating would be "Good".

3   Predicting Air Quality

We will use the numerical differentiation of the CO_2 and I_{TVOC} levels provided by the device's sensors, as an indicator of the trend of the air quality in a near future. That is, we will use the slope of the first derivative of the signal provided by the sensors as an estimator of how good or how bad the air will be. It is well known, from elementary calculus courses, that we can predict the shape of a function/signal by recalling that its first derivative simply corresponds to the slope of the (original) signal: where a signal slopes up, its derivative is positive; where a signal slopes down, its derivative is negative; and where a signal has zero slope, its derivative is zero.

The first derivative of a time varying signal corresponds to the rate of change of its amplitude (e.g., $x(t)$) with respect to time (e.g., t), that is, $dx(t)/dt$, which is interpreted as the slope of the tangent to the signal at each point, as illustrated in Fig. 1, for the digital case.

Assuming that the time interval between adjacent samples (points) of a digital signal $x[n]$ is constant, a simple algorithm for computing a first derivative is:

$$x'[n] = \frac{x[n+1] - x[n-1]}{2\Delta T_s} \tag{2}$$

for $1 < n < N-1$, where T_s represents the sampling period ($T_s = 1/f_s$, f_s being the sampling frequency) and N the number of samples of the signal. This is called a central-difference method. Its main advantage is that it does not involve a shift in the time (t or x-axis) position of the derivative [8,9].

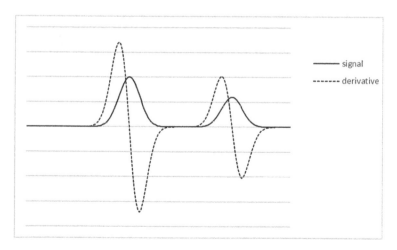

Fig. 1. Plots of a simulated signal $s(t) = e^{-(2(t-4.5))^2} + 0.6e^{-(2(t-8))^2}$, for $t = 1$, $1.05, \cdots, 10$, and its derivative.

Figure 1 shows the plots of the signal given by the samples ($t = 1, 1.05$, $\cdots, 10$) of

$$s(t) = e^{-(2(t-4.5))^2} + 0.6e^{-(2(t-8))^2},$$

consisting of two Gaussian peaks, and its derivative, calculated using Eq. 2. As can be seen, and as expected, the calculation is performed correctly. The method presented here to find the derivative of a signal/function involves only one sub-traction and one multiplication/division and it gives us the precision we need for our application proposes. It should also be noted that, in practice, this method needs a delay of one sample.

However, this (derivative) operation is very sensitive to noise. Consequently, in order to minimize the impact of the noise in the IAQI and in the forecasting, we will use a simple low-pass filter, as discussed in the previous section. The IAQI value will correspond to the average value of the last ten minutes of the IAQI values. This operation introduces a time delay of 10 min in the functioning of the device, but in practice it does only mean that the first IAQI value the user sees is only available 10 min after the start of the device. These effects (delay and low-pass filter) can be clearly seen in Fig. 2. This figure presents the plots of a "noisy signal", that we have created by adding 10% of noise to the signal in Fig. 1, a "low-pass" filtered version of this noisy signal, that was computed by using an average filter of the last 20 samples (corresponding to a time of 10 min of operation of the device), and the "derivative" of this low-pass signal. As can be seen, even in the presence of a strong level of noise our proposal continues to produce a reliable IAQI and forecasting of the air quality.

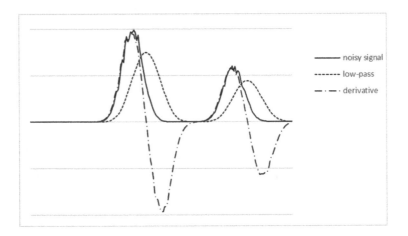

Fig. 2. To the simulated signal in Fig. 1 we have added 10% of noise, resulting in the "noisy signal" plot. Then, we have low-pass filtered this signal, using an average filter of the last 20 samples (corresponding to a time of 10 min of operation of the device), resulting in the "low-pass" plot. Finally, we have calculated the derivative of the low-pass signal, resulting in the "derivative".

Note that both the temperature, CO_2 and TVOC signals resulting from their acquisition/sampling in indoor environments are intrinsically low-pass (it is not expected that these signals have "big changes" within the sampling period of 30 s). Hence, the assumptions that we have made in this section should be correct and proven by the results presented in Sect. 5.

The final predicted IAQI is calculated in the following way. The values of the calculated derivative of the CO_2 and TVOC signals are used with Tables 1 and 2, respectively, to find the air quality indexes given by these derivative signals. To these indexes values we subtract 1, to maintain the current IAQI level as the output of the prediction if the derivative value is low. Then, if the derivative is positive, the index is added to the IAQI level resulting from Sect. 2, and if it is negative, this value is subtracted from the IAQI level resulting from Sect. 2. Finally, if the resulting predicting air quality index value is below 1 it is truncated to 1, and if it is above 5, it is truncated to 5.

It should also be noted that we could use other predicting methods and algorithms like, for example, b-splines or other kernels, both in time or frequency domains [10–13]. However, these other methods will be far more complex and computationally demanding.

4   Description of the Developed Prototype

To fulfill the objectives of monitoring and forecasting the air quality of indoor environments using the principles and methodology described above, we have developed a prototype system consisting of an electronic device and a web/cloud-based server-side application.

The main characteristics of the electronic device are the following ones:

- Compact and lightweight.
- Powered using a USB rechargeable battery, or using a chord charger.
- Measure the temperature, CO_2 and TVOC.
  LED air quality indicator light, with 5 levels: excellent (green); good (light green); moderate (yellow); poor (orange); and unhealthy (red).
- LED air quality forecasting indicator light, with 5 levels: excellent (green); good (light green); moderate (yellow); poor (orange); and unhealthy (red).
- Real-time sending of the measured parameters to a web/cloud-based server application.
- By default, the device is configured to transmit sensor data every 30 s to a web/cloud-based server, but it is re-configurable (time between sensor readings and cloud server address for sending data can be changed).
- The device was developed and implemented in modules, in order to facilitate the incorporation of new sensors in future developments.
- Do not require the installation, calibration and configuration by any type of expert.

Being this device part of a prototype system that aims at monitoring and forecasting the indoor air quality, there is also a web/cloud-based server-side application were a register user can visualize the data, in plot/graph or table form, from any point with Internet access, and access the application using a PC, Tablet or Smartphone. The system is able to generate air quality alerts/alarms (e.g., optionally send SMS), and all the configuration options are carried out based on a web page, with an extremely simple and easy to use interface.

The configuration options currently available are the sampling rate, i.e., the time elapsed between two consecutive acquisition values, and the web address of the server.

In the near future we also want to develop a mobile application (App) where all these functionalities will be available.

The electronic device has the main logical blocks presented in Figs. 3, and 4 presents a photograph of the prototype device implemented. As can be seen in Fig. 3, the device has one temperature sensor, RBG Leds, one Wi-Fi Antenna, one Wi-Fi MCU, and an air quality sensor.

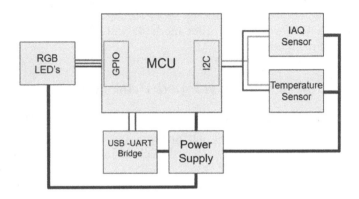

Fig. 3. Main logical blocks of the electronic device to measure the temperature, CO_2 and TVOC values, and produce the measured and forecast IAQI indexes.

To implement the device, we have used the main electronic components listed in Table 3. The main component is an iAQ-Core indoor air quality sensor module, from ams^{TM}, to measure VOC levels and CO_2 equivalent and TVOC equivalent predictions. These data are available via I^2C bus. This sensor module gives reliable evaluation of indoor air quality (output of relative CO_2 equivalents (ppm) and TVOC equivalents (ppb)), has high sensitivity and fast response (sensing range of 450—2000 ppm CO_2 equivalents, and 125—600 ppb TVOC equivalents), is of micro size for convenient installation (MEMS metal oxide sensor technology, SMD type package, reflow capable, and module with automatic baseline correction), and has low power consumption (maximum of 66 mW in continuous mode, and maximum of 9 mW in pulsed mode).

The low-power Wi-Fi module ESP32-DEVKITC-32UE from Espressif Systems^{TM} has 802.11 b/g/n (Wi-Fi, WiFi, WLAN), Bluetooth$^®$ Smart Ready 4.x Dual Mode Evaluation Board capacities. This component targets at a wide variety of applications, including low-power IoT sensor networks. The ESP32-DEVKITC-32UE integrates a vast set of peripherals, including Hall sensors, capacitive touch sensors, SD card interface, Ethernet, high-speed SPI, UART, I^2S, and I^2C. The high-accuracy temperature sensor MCP9800A0T-M/OT, from Microchip Technology^{TM}, has an output type I^2C/SMBus, with a resolution of 11 bit.

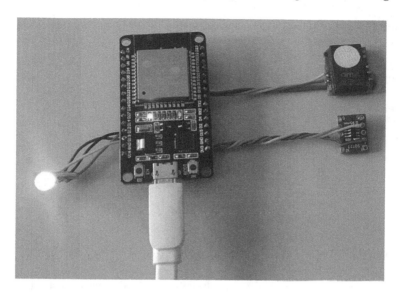

Fig. 4. Photo of the prototype electronic device actually implement.

Table 3. The manufacturers, price, and component's type used in the prototype device presented in Fig. 4. As we can see, the total price is below 35 € (31.01 € to be precise).

Component type	Reference	Manufacturer/Seller	Price (€)
IAQ sensor	IAQ cORE P	ams	20.00
Wi-Fi MCU	ESP32-DEVKITC-32UE	Espressif systems	8.41
Temperature sensor	MCP9800A0T-M/OT	Microchip technology	0.82
Wi-Fi antenna	146153–0150	Molex	1.46
RGB led (x2)	LL-509RGBC2E-006	LUCKYLIGHT	0.32

We have used the values presented in the rightmost column of Table 1 as a reference to control the colors of the RGB LED associated to the current and forecasting air quality: green—Excellent, light green—Good, yellow—Moderate, orange—Poor, and red—Unhealthy.

All the data transferred between the electronic device and the server use the Message Queuing Telemetry Transport (MQTT) protocol. In particular, to upload the temperature, CO_2 and TVOC sampled values to the server and to receive any new configuration parameters, we have used MQTT. Listing 1.1 shows an example of a MQTT message sent from the device to the server.

Listing 1.1. Example of a MQTT message with a JSON object sent by the electronic device to the server to upload the temperature, CO_2 and TVOC sampled values.

```
Topic:
  app/MacAddress/u/uploadSampledValues

Message body:
{
  "uuid":"494c5342-7b17-4eab-a1e1-50fbe796e437",
  "temp": "23.4",
  "co2": "23.6",
  "tvoc": "50"
}
```

5   Results

To assess the developed prototype, we have conducted a set of tests. In the first test, during one day we have installed the electronic device in a room, initially with all doors and windows closed. The test was initiated at 22:34, with the windows opened, with the device placed near a computer. At 12:00 the windows where closed, and at 14:00 they were opened. Next to this room there is a car garage, and a door directly opens to this garage. At 15:48 we started the car's engine, with this door opened. As can be seen the air quality as suffered a great decrease (we can see the peak in the plot). At 16:05 we have closed the windows, at 17:00 the windows where opened and at 22:03 the windows were closed again. The test ended at 22:30. Both the windows and the door were far from the device (more than three meters), but to end the test and disconnect the device we had to move to the vicinity of the device, and thus breathing very close to the sensors (thus increasing the CO_2 levels). As can be seen this influenced the quality of the air. These events are marked with vertical black lines (at the bottom) in the plot in Fig. 5. This figure also shows the values of the temperature, CO_2 and TVOC during the test. The colored horizontal bar shows the colors produced by the light LED, corresponding to the indoor air quality index (green—Excellent, light green—Good, yellow—Moderate, orange—Poor, and red—Unhealthy). The horizontal colored bar at the top of Fig. 6 shows the forecasting air quality values for this test. As can be seen, they are in line with the measured ones, being, as expected, more sever at the moments where the air quality changes abruptly.

In the second test, the device was installed in same room of the first test, near a computer. The test started at 18:45, with all doors and windows closed. At 20:12 we cleaned the computer screens with methanol, and we have not done anything else until the next morning, where we have used some more sprays of methanol close to the device at 09:05, 09:06 and 09:11. At 12:06 we have opened the windows

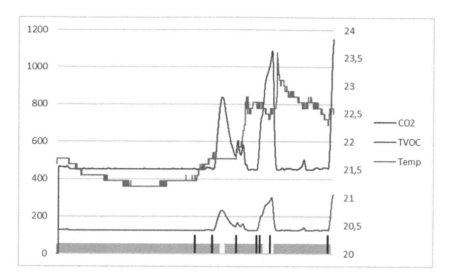

Fig. 5. Plots of the temperature, CO_2 and TVOC values for the first test (please refer to the main text). The vertical black lines (at the bottom) mark the moments where the events have occurred. Also shown by the horizontal colored bar is the color produced by the light LED corresponding to the indoor air quality index (green—Excellent, light green—Good, yellow—Moderate, orange—Poor, and red—Unhealthy). The right vertical axis shows the temperature in Celsius degrees. (Color figure online)

and closed them at 14:02. At 14:50 we used a soldering iron in a PCB board, and cleaned the PCB board at 15:00 using methanol. At 15:44 we have opened the windows and closed the windows at 17:15. At 17:35 we started using heated tobacco (Heets) until 17:36. The windows were then opened again at 19:17, and then the test was ended. These events are marked with vertical black lines (at the bottom) in Fig. 7, along with the registered temperature, CO_2 and TVOC values. Once again, the colored horizontal bar shows the colors produced by the light LED, corresponding to the indoor air quality index (green—Excellent, light green—Good, yellow—Moderate, orange—Poor, and red—Unhealthy). The equivalent horizontal colored bar at the top of Fig. 8 shows the forecasting air quality values for this test. As can be seen, once again, they are in line with the measured ones.

As can be seen, globally, the device and the system correctly follows the changes in the air quality, and it also correctly forecasts the air quality.

Although the device was designed so that it can be battery powered, we have only conducted tests with the device being directly powered through the power-grid. Hence, we did not collect any data concerning battery life, discharging/charging cycles, among other.

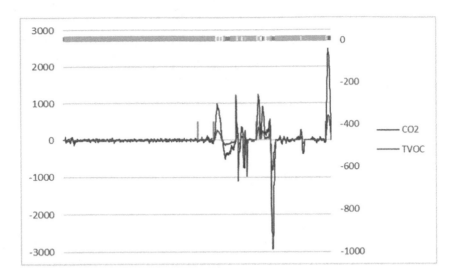

Fig. 6. Plots of the CO_2 and TVOC derivatives values for the first test (please refer to the main text). The vertical black lines (at the bottom) mark the moments where the events have occurred. Also shown by the horizontal colored bar is the color produced by the light LED corresponding to the forecasting of the indoor air quality index (green—Excellent, light green—Good, yellow—Moderate, orange—Poor, and red—Unhealthy). As can be seen, the predicted values are in line with the measured ones (Fig. 5), being, as expected, more sever at the moments where the air quality changes abruptly. (Color figure online)

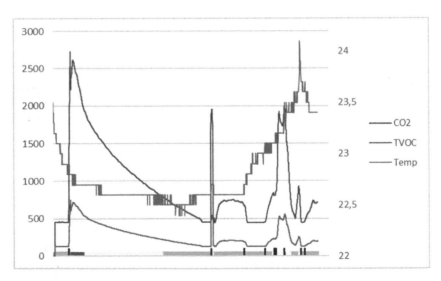

Fig. 7. Plots of the temperature, CO_2 and TVOC values for the second test. The vertical black lines (at the bottom) mark the moments where events have occurred. Also shown by the horizontal colored bar is the color produced by the light LED corresponding to the indoor air quality index (green—Excellent, light green—Good, yellow—Moderate, orange—Poor, and red—Unhealthy). The right vertical axis shows the temperature in Celsius degrees. (Color figure online)

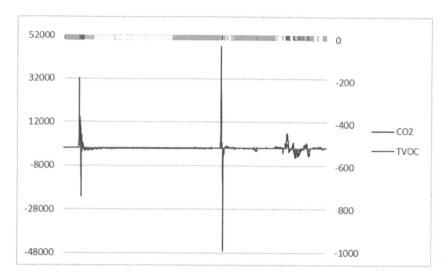

Fig. 8. Plots of the CO_2 and TVOC derivatives values for the second test. The vertical black lines (at the bottom) mark the moments where events have occurred. Also shown by the horizontal colored bar is the color produced by the light LED corresponding to the forecasting of the indoor air quality index (green—Excellent, light green—Good, yellow—Moderate, orange—Poor, and red—Unhealthy). As can be seen, the predicted values are in line with the measured ones (Fig. 7). (Color figure online)

6   Conclusions

We have presented a real-time device (hardware and software) capable of measuring, monitoring and forecasting the indoor air quality. This device is able to measure the temperature, CO_2 and Total Volatile Organic Compounds (TVOC). It produces an Indoor Air Quality Index (IAQI), which is calculated based on the CO_2 and TVOC parameters. Then, the IAQI is used to activate two RGB LED lights, where people can very intuitively be aware of the current and predicted air quality: excellent (green); good (light green); moderate (yellow); poor (orange); and unhealthy (red).

The total price of the device is estimated to be clearly below 35 €. The device is also capable of forecasting the air quality within relative small periods of time.

We believe that this proposal can be used to improve the quality of life of citizens in the context of "smart cities".

The results achieved by the set of tests conducted proved that the device, server-side application and IAQI are reliable. Although not final, the results achieved are highly motivating.

It should also be noted that the IAQI can be used to automatically control the indoor air quality if, for example, connected to an air cleaner.

In a near future, it is also intended to carry out precision tests, preferably with certification by a specialized laboratory. Additionally, and in terms of the future evolution of the device and the complete system, it is also intended to carry out outdoor tests, in order to study the possibility of measuring, monitoring and forecasting the air quality in uncontrolled environments. Concerning forecasting, we want to test the use of other techniques and algorithms, balancing their usage with computational complexity and, ultimately, power consumption.

We believe that this device can be used to create a "social network" where users can share their IAQI data. These data can then be used by local, regional and national level authorities to devise measures for improving the life of citizens.

References

1. Vallero, D.: Introduction. In: Vallero, D. (ed.) Fundamentals of Air Pollution, 5th edn. p. 1. Academic Press, Boston (2014). https://doi.org/10.1016/B978-0-12-401733-7.02001-6, https://www.sciencedirect.com/science/article/pii/B9780124017337020016
2. Chau, T., Wang, K.: An association between air pollution and daily most frequently visits of eighteen outpatient diseases in an industrial city. Sci. Rep. **10**, 2321 (2020). https://doi.org/10.1038/s41598-020-58721-0
3. World Health Organization–Europe: Noncommunicable diseases and air pollution. Tech. rep., World Helth Organization, Denmark (2019)
4. World Health Organization. https://www.who.int/teams/environment-climatechange-and-health/air-quality-and-health/ambient-air-pollution. Accessed 03 July 2021
5. Sensirion: Indoor air quality and volatile organic compounds. Tech. rep., Sensirion The Sensor Company, Staefa, Switzerland (2017)
6. Umweltbundesamt: Beurteilung von innenraumluftkontaminationen mittels referenz- und richtwerten. Bundesgesundheitsbl **50**, 990–1005 (2007). https://doi.org/10.1007/s00103-007-0290-y
7. The Guardian: Indoor carbon dioxide levels could be a health hazard, scientists warn. https://www.theguardian.com/environment/2019/jul/08/indoorcarbon-dioxide-levels-could-be-a-health-hazard-scientists-warn. Accessed 07 July 2021
8. Krishna, B.T., Rao, S.S.: On design and applications of digital differentiators. In: 2012 Fourth International Conference on Advanced Computing, ICoAC, pp. 1–7 (2012). https://doi.org/10.1109/ICoAC.2012.6416802
9. Mitra, S.K., Kuo, Y. (eds.): Digital Signal Processing: A Computer-Based Approach. McGraw-Hill, New York (2006)
10. Ferreira, P.J.: New algorithms for band-limited interpolation and extrapolation: a synthetic view. In: Proceedings of EUSIPCO, Tampere, Finland, 2000. Zenodo, December 2015. https://doi.org/10.5281/zenodo.37308, https://doi.org/10.5281/zenodo.37308
11. Reis, M.J., Ferreira, P.J., Soares, S.F.: Linear combinations of b-splines as generating functions for signal approximation. Digital Signal Process. **15**(3), 226–236 (2005)
12. Unser, M., Aldroubi, A., Eden, M.: B-spline signal processing .i. theory. IEEE Trans. Signal Process. **41**(2), 821–833 (1993). https://doi.org/10.1109/78.193220
13. Unser, M., Aldroubi, A., Eden, M.: B-spline signal processing .ii. efficiency design and applications. IEEE Trans. Signal Process. **41**(2), 834–848 (1993). https://doi.org/10.1109/78.193221

Channel Allocation Mechanism in C-RAN for Smart Transportation

Isha Bharti[1]($\boxtimes$) and Nishu Gupta[2] (iD)

[1] SAP Technology and Innovation, Capgemini, America Inc., Irving 75039, USA
isha.bharti@capgemini.com
[2] College of Engineering and Technology, SRM Institute of Science and Technology,
Kattankulathur 603203, India

Abstract. Recent developments in vehicular communication demands dynamic channel allocation strategies as well as their implementation in an effective way. A cognitive radio ad hoc network (C-RAN) designed specifically to serve the requirements of smart transportation in a smart city scenario is expected to fulfil these demands. Dynamic utilization of available bandwidth can be accomplished through various C-RAN techniques such as spectrum handover. Such mechanism allows a secondary user (non-owner) to exploit the channel utilities when it is not used by the primary user (licensed owner). In this paper, Dynamic Channel Allocation Mechanism (DCAM) is proposed in order to facilitate reduced handovers in C-RANs. With the help of analytical means, the performance of DCAM is evaluated in terms of various metrics and compared with other similar existing techniques. The results are observed to provide significant improvements which strongly lace the proposed scheme ahead of the others in the mentioned performance metrics.

Keywords: Ad hoc network · Cognitive radio · Dynamic Channel Allocation Mechanism (DCAM) · Handover · Smart transportation

1 Introduction

Classical ad hoc networks are poised to meet a dead-end soon as they follow strategies based on fixed channel assignment. On the other hand, significant regions of licensed bands are underused. Cognitive Radio Ad Hoc Networks (CRANs) can overcome this spectrum scarcity problem. A mobile node dynamically accesses the spectrum holes in licensed bands through Dynamic Spectrum Access (DSA) strategy in CRANs. DSA strategy allows to share the licensed bands to the secondary user (SU) along with the primary user (PU) in an opportunistic manner. Cognitive Radio (CR) [1, 2] is an intelligent radio because it can recognize the underused channel in radio environment. On appearance of PU in the same channel, which is already occupied by SU, then SU shift to other unoccupied channel for the consistent communication. This process of channel switching by SU is referred as spectrum handover.

S. Paiva et al. (Eds.): SmartCity360° 2021, LNICST 442, pp. 321–331, 2022.
https://doi.org/10.1007/978-3-031-06371-8_21

Spectrum handover can be classified into proactive, reactive, hybrid spectrum handover. In proactive approach [3, 4], on the basis of PU traffic model, SU approximates PU arrival. After that SU executes spectrum sensing before handover triggering action happens and vacate the channel. In reactive approach [5, 6], once handover triggering action happens, SU executes spectrum sensing to detect a new channel for spectrum handover. In hybrid approach, SU executes spectrum sensing in proactive way and handover action in reactive way. In all the previously explained handover schemes, handover is executed totally in licensed bands. But none of the spectrum handover approach executes handover in the unlicensed bands. Although, number of channels are limited in unlicensed bands, but they may become vacant and hence, in accordance to [7] probability of availability of unlicensed bands for link maintenance can be taken into consideration. In this paper, we examine the issue of reduction in spectrum handover in CRANs using a new spectrum access technique named Dynamic Channel Allocation Mechanism (DCAM). So, CR ad hoc devices can operate in both licensed and unlicensed spectrum bands by using DCAM spectrum access technique. The performance of DCAM is examined by a wide mathematical model. The remaining paper is structured as follows: Section 2, provides related work done in this field. Section 3 provides an overview of DCAM technique. Section 4 provides proposed model for cognitive radio ad hoc networks. Section 5 provides the link maintenance probability. Section 6 provides the spectrum handover survey. Section 6 provides the performance evaluation of DCAM technique. Section 7, the conclusion of the work is provided.

2   Related Work

In [8], an effect of spectrum handover over the link maintenance of an SU is studied. In [9], for reducing spectrum handovers of SUs, spectrum matching algorithms are used. In [10], a three-dimensional Markov chain model has been used to examine the SUs performance, but here spectrum handover of SUs is not involved to examine SUs performance. Figure 1 explains the concept of cognitive channel switching. Whenever a node finds a channel available and it has data to send, it transmits over the channel.

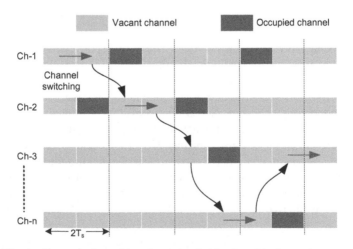

Fig. 1. Concept of cognitive channel switching in vehicular environment

Hence, in all the previous works spectrum handover has not been completely discussed, licensed channels are only used for doing spectrum handovers. The works in [11, 12, 15] are almost relative to our work. In [12] and [15], SUs performance is examined subject to the link maintenance probability and the expected number of spectrum handovers. But in [12] only LCs are used for spectrum handover and in [15] both LCs and UCs are used for spectrum handover. This paper is extension of the work done in [15]. The DCAM technique is explained in the next section.

3 Dynamic Channel Allocation Mechanism (DCAM)

In future, majority of wireless devices will have CR ability and very few wireless devices will be without CR ability. Because licensed bands traverse a large geographic space and considerable parts of the licensed spectrum are underused such as TV bands. So, in CRANs using DCAM technique a SU will use the licensed spectrum as operating spectrum and the unlicensed spectrum as backup spectrum at the instant of PU arrival. At the time of PU arrival, SU should instantly do spectrum handover to unlicensed channels. Here two cases arise: (i) if there are free unlicensed channels available, then SU will shift to a new unlicensed channel and, (ii) if there are no free unlicensed channel available, then SU again do spectrum handover to the licensed channel. For case (ii) again two more sub-cases arise: (a) if there are free licensed channels available, then SU will shift to a new licensed channel and, (b) if there are no free licensed channel available, then SU will halt for a duration with utmost value T_m, So that if any licensed channel becomes free with in duration T_m, then SU will shift to that licensed channel to achieve link maintenance. If no channel becomes free during T_m, then both link maintenance and spectrum handover of SU will fail. In DCAM technique, when channels are available for spectrum handover proactive approach of spectrum handover is used, but for T_m duration reactive approach of spectrum handover is used. Work done in this paper is an addition to the work done in [15].

Different category of users influences the DCAM's performance: (1) primary users (PUs), (2) secondary users (SUs), (3) non-cognitive users (NCUs). NCUs will use only unlicensed bands. The main benefits of utilizing unlicensed bands in DCAM technique are:

- For unlicensed bands all users, whether they are SUs or NCUs, have the identical rights to access them.
- Reduction in spectrum handover count.
- Improvement in link maintenance.

Flowchart of the proposed technique is depicted in Fig. 2.

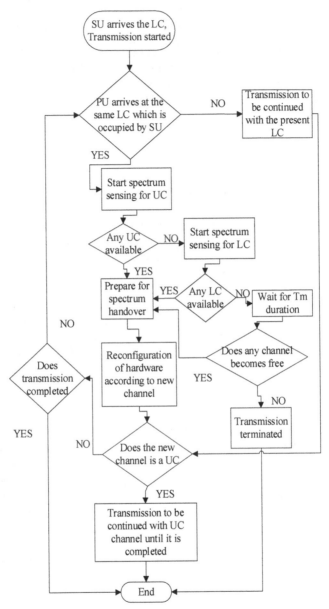

Fig. 2. Flowchart of proposed DCAM technique

NCUs arrivals will affects the SUs link maintenance, so their effects are considered in the next section. DCAM technique is very useful in case when we have to transmit a huge amount of data, i.e., it is better to wait for T_m duration for getting a channel instead of directly terminating the transmission when no free channel is available because if transmission gets terminated than the amount of data which was already transmitted previously has to be retransmitted, which results in wastage of energy as well as time. DCAM technique is very useful for futuristic machine to machine communication.

4 Proposed Model for Cognitive Radio Ad Hoc Networks (CRANs)

This proposed mathematical model discussion by presuming n_1 LCs and n_2 UCs, which are used by nodes of CRANs. The partakers of n_1 LCs will be PUs and SUs, partakers of n_2 UCs will be SUs and NCUs. In case of LCs, SU should leave the channel when licensed user of that channel appears. However, in case of UCs there will be no takeover for any partaker of UCs once it acquires the channel.

4.1 Licensed Users

It is presumed that PU will utilize only licensed channel for its communication motive. It is further presumed that λ_{11} indicates arrival rate of a new PU, whose arrival is a poisson's process. PU inter-arrival time will be denoted by a random variable (RV) $I_{PU_{a'}}$, which will be described as inter-arrival time between $(a' - 1)^{th}$ and a'^{th} PU, with general form I_{PU}. Also, PU inter-arrival time I_{PU} obeys an exponential distribution. Hence probability density function (pdf), $f_{I_{PU}}(t)$, of RV I_{PU} will be expressed as $f_{I_{PU}}(t) = \lambda_{11} e^{-\lambda_{11}t}$. Let PU call holding time will be denoted by RV C_{PU} with expectation $\frac{1}{\mu_{11}}$, pdf $f_{C_{PU}}(t)$, cumulative distribution function (CDF) $F_{C_{PU}}(t) = (1 - \Pr(C_{PU} < t))$. The residual call holding time of a PU will be denoted by a RV $R_{PU,a'}$, which will be described as an interval from an in-between instant to the instant of PU work completion, with general form R_{PU}. Using Residual Life Theorem, pdf of residual call holding time of PU will be expressed as $f_{R_{PU}}(t) = \mu_{11}(1 - F_{C_{PU}}(t))$. Assuming ρ_{11} denotes PU traffic density, i.e., $\rho_{11} = \lambda_{11}/\mu_{11}$. The variable a' which was defined earlier denotes the number of licensed channels currently occupied by PUs, i.e., $0 \leq a' \leq n_1$. Let P_{11} be a RV representing number of PUs owing to steady state probability distribution, which is denoted by $p_{11_{a'}}$ (where, $0 \leq a' \leq n_1$), given as

$$p_{11_{a'}} = \frac{\rho_{11}^{a'}}{a'!} \frac{1}{\sum_{a'=0}^{n_1} \frac{\rho_{11}^{a'}}{a'!}} \tag{1}$$

4.2 Cognitive Users

Cognitive users are also called secondary users (SUs). It is presumed that SUs will utilize at least one channel for their communication motive. It is further presumed that λ_{22} indicates arrival rate of a new SU, whose arrival is also a Poisson process. Let SU call holding time will be denoted by RV C_{SU} with expectation $\frac{1}{\mu_{22}}$, pdf $f_{C_{SU}}(t)$, CDF $F_{C_{SU}}(t) = \Pr[C_{SU} < t]$ and complementary CDF $\overline{F_{C_{SU}}(t)} = \Pr[C_{SU} > t] = 1 - F_{C_{SU}}(t)$.

When PU arrives, it will choose a specific licensed channel with probability $\frac{1}{n_1-a'}$, her a' denotes number of licensed channels currently occupied by PUs. If out of $(n_1 - a')$ licensed channels, arrived PU selects that channel which is occupied by a SU, then SU will perform a spectrum handover. Let P_{sh} denotes SU handover probability, given as

$$P_{sh} = \left(1 - e^{-\lambda_{11}t}\right) \sum_{a'=0}^{n_1} \frac{1}{(n_1 - a')} p_{11a'}$$

Let P_{22} be a RV representing number of SUs engaged available licensed channels owing to steady state conditional probability distribution, which is denoted by $p_{22_{b'|a'}} \left(0 \le a' \le n_1, 0 \le b' \le n_1 - a'\right)$, where variable b' denotes number of licensed channels occupied by SUs. Then probability $p_{22_{b'|a'}} = \Pr[P_{22} = b'|P_{11} = a']$, will be given as

$$p_{22_{b'|a'}} = \frac{\lambda_{22}^{b'}}{b'!(\mu_{22} + P_{sh})^{b'}} p_{22_{0|a'}} \tag{2}$$

where, $(\rho_{22} = \lambda_{22}/\mu_{22})$ and $p_{22_{0|a'}}$ may be provided using standardization condition $\sum_{b'=0}^{n_1-a'} p_{22_{b'|a'}} = 1$.

4.3 Non-cognitive Users

It is presumed that λ_{33} indicates arrival rate of a new NCU, whose arrival is a Poisson process. NCUs call holding time follows exponential distribution with parameters μ_{33}. Let, P_{33} be a RV representing number of NCUs and SUs engaged available unlicensed channels owing to steady state probability distribution, which is denoted by $p_{33_{a'}}$ (where, $0 \le a' \le n_2$), given as

$$p_{33_{a'}} = \frac{\rho_{33}^{a'}}{a'!} \frac{1}{\left(1 + \sum_{a'=0}^{n_2} \frac{\rho_{33}^{a'}}{a'!}\right)} \tag{3}$$

where, $\rho_{33} = \frac{P_{sh}+\lambda_{33}}{\mu_{22}+\mu_{33}}$.

5 Link Maintenance Probability

To prevent service termination in the course of handover, CR users carry out link maintenance operation to resume communication. Let L_s stands for net link maintenance probability. The probability of successful link maintenance of SU when SU departs from the channel is known as link maintenance probability.

- Over UCs the link maintenance is stated as

$$L_u = P_{sh}(1 - p_{33_{n_2}}).$$

If there are no available unlicensed channels, then also link could be preserved successfully, if there is a free LC. If there is no free LC, link could be still preserved successfully if any LC becomes free within T_m time. If no LC becomes free within T_m time, then link maintenance is terminated. T_s denotes actual waiting time for SU, which is equal to least of every PU call holding times, given as

$$T_s = \min(R_{PU,1}, R_{PU,2}, \ldots, R_{PU,n_1-1}, C_{PU,n_1})$$

- Over LCs the link maintenance is stated as

$$L_l = P_{sh}p_{33_{n_2}}((1 - \Omega) + \Omega \Pr(T_s < T_m))$$

where,

$$\Omega = \sum_{a'=1}^{n_1} p_{11_{a'}} p_{22_{n_1-a'|a'}}.$$

On solving, $\Pr(T_s < T_m)$

$$= \Pr(\min(R_{PU,1}, R_{PU,2}, \ldots, R_{PU,n_1-1}, R_{PU,n_1}) < T_m)$$

$$= 1 - ((\Pr(R_{PU} > T_m))^{n_1-1} \Pr(C_{PU} > T_m))$$

$$= 1 - (\Phi^{n_1-1} \Psi)$$

where,

$$\Phi = \Pr(R_{PU} > T_m) = 1 - \lambda_{11} \int_0^{T_m} (1 - F_{C_{PU}}(y))dy$$

$$\Psi = \Pr(C_{PU} > T_m) = 1 - \int_0^{T_m} f_{C_{PU}}(y)dy$$

Then, L_l becomes

$$L_l = P_{sh}p_{33_{n_2}}((1 - \Omega) + \Omega(1 - \Phi^{n_1-1} \Psi))$$

- Net link maintenance probability is stated as

$$L_s = L_u + L_l$$

$$L_s = P_{sh}\left(1 - p_{33_{n_2}} \Omega \Phi^{n_1-1} \Psi\right) \tag{4}$$

6   Performance Evaluation of DCAM Technique

In this part, the performance of DCAM is examined in terms of link maintenance probability and expected number of spectrum handovers. The following operative parameters
are picked: $\lambda_{22} = 0.5^{SU}/_{sec}$, $\mu_{11} = 0.15^{PU}/_{sec}$, $\mu_{22} = 0.5^{SU}/_{sec}$, $T_m = 1sec$, call
holding times of PU and SU follows 2-stage erlang distribution.

The SU link maintenance probability is examined using three distinct scenarios. 6
LCs and 0 UCs are taken in the first scenario. In the second scenario, 6 LCs and 2
UCs are taken, but here T_m is not taken into consideration. In the third scenario (DCAM
scenario), 6 LCs and 2 UCs are taken, but here T_m is taken into consideration. In addition,
low traffic, moderate traffic and high traffic conditions in UCs due to NCUs are also
examined to compare the effect of NCUs on DCAM. Figure 3, 4, 5 shows the link
maintenance probability of SU in terms of λ_{11} for low traffic, moderate traffic and high
traffic conditions in UCs. In all the three traffic conditions DCAM scenario performs
better in comparison to the other two scenarios in terms of link maintenance probability.
This can be elaborated as follows. In DCAM, SUs performs the spectrum handovers to
the UCs along with the LCs, SUs can halt for T_m duration if there is no free channel
available.

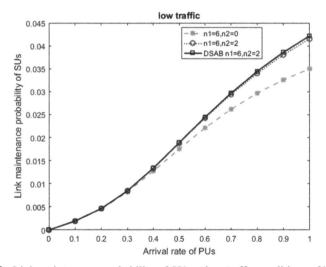

Fig. 3. Link maintenance probability of SUs at low traffic conditions of NCUs

Figure 6 shows the probability for zero spectrum handovers for the DCAM scenario,
i.e., probability for $N = 0$. From Fig. 6, it is clear that, as λ_{11} increases, $P[N = 0]$
decreases. This can be elaborated as follows. As λ_{11} increases, number of PUs in LCs
increases which leads to increase in the chances for spectrum handover for SUs.

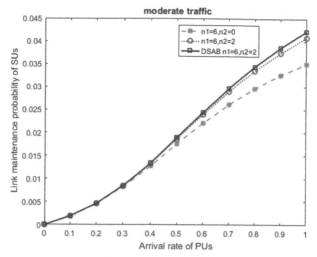

Fig. 4. Link maintenance probability of SUs at moderate traffic conditions of NCUs

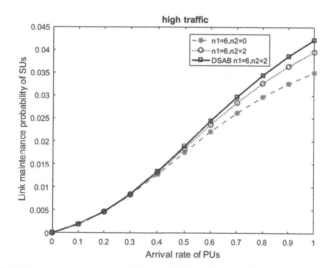

Fig. 5. Link maintenance probability of SUs at high traffic conditions of NCUs

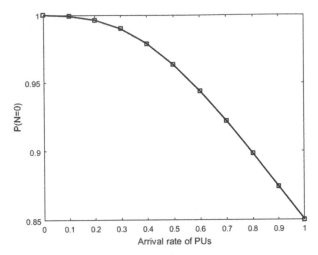

Fig. 6. Probability for zero handovers

7 Conclusion

In this paper, DCAM technique is used for decreasing the number of spectrum handovers in cognitive radio ad hoc networks. The simulation results show an advancement in SUs performance in terms of link maintenance and expected number of spectrum handovers as compared to the previous works. Until now, there have been only a few techniques available for minimizing the spectrum handover, and more studies are needed in these areas.

References

1. Mitola, J., Maguire, G.Q.: Cognitive radio: Making software radios more personal. IEEE Pers. Commun. **6**(4), 13–18 (1999)
2. Wang, P., Chen, C.M., Kumari, S., Shojafar, M., Tafazolli, R., Liu, Y.N.: HDMA: Hybrid D2D message authentication scheme for 5G-enabled VANETs. IEEE Trans. Intell. Transp. Syst. (2020)
3. Tiwari, J., Prakash, A., Tripathi, R.: A novel cooperative MAC protocol for safety applications in cognitive radio enabled vehicular ad-hoc networks. Veh. Commun. **29**, 100336 (2021)
4. Gupta, N., Prakash, A., Tripathi, R.: Medium access control protocols for safety applications in vehicular ad-hoc network: A classification and comprehensive survey. Veh. Commun. **2**(4), 223–237 (2015)
5. Gottapu, S.K., Kapileswar, N., Santhi, P.V., Chenchela, V.K.R.: Maximizing cognitive radio networks throughput using limited historical behavior of primary users. IEEE Access **6**, 12252–12259 (2018). https://doi.org/10.1109/ACCESS.2018.2812743
6. Hu, W., Willkomm, D., Vlantis, G., Gerla, M., Wolisz, A.: Dynamic frequency hopping communities for ecient IEEE 802.22 operation. IEEE Commun. Mag., 80–87 (May 2007)
7. Willkomm, D., Gross, J., Wolisz, A.: Reliable link maintenance in cognitive radio systems. In: Proceedings of the First IEEE International Symposium on New Frontiers in Dynamic Spectrum Access Networks (DySPAN 2005), pp. 371–378 (2005)

8. Akyildiz, I.F., Lee, W.-Y., Vuran, M.C., Mohant, S.: Next generation/dynamic spectrum access/cognitive radio wireless networks: A survey. Comput. Netw. J. (Elsevier) **50**(13), 2127–2159 (2006)
9. Rawat, D.B., Song, M., Shetty, S.: Resource allocation for cognitive radio enabled vehicular network users. In: Dynamic Spectrum Access for Wireless Networks. SECE, pp. 57–65. Springer, Cham (2015). https://doi.org/10.1007/978-3-319-15299-8_5
10. Chiluveru, R., Gupta, N., Teles, A.S.: Distribution of safety messages using mobility-aware multi-hop clustering in vehicular ad hoc network. Future Internet **13**(7), 169 (2021)
11. Bozkaya, E., Canberk, B.: Robust and continuous connectivity maintenance for vehicular dynamic spectrum access networks. Ad Hoc Netw. **25**, 72–83 (2015)
12. Kalil, M.A., Al-Mahdi, H., Mitschele-Thiel, A.: Analysis of opportunistic spectrum access in cognitive ad hoc networks. In: Al-Begain, K., Fiems, D., Horváth, G. (eds.) ASMTA 2009. LNCS, vol. 5513, pp. 16–28. Springer, Heidelberg (2009). https://doi.org/10.1007/978-3-642-02205-0_2
13. Zhang, Y.: Spectrum handover in cognitive radio networks: Opportunistic and negotiated situations. In: Proceedings of the IEEE International Conference on Communications ICC 2009, pp. 1–6, 14–18 Jun 2009
14. Al-Mahdi, H., Kalil, M., Liers, F., Mitschele-Thiel, A.: Increasing spectrum capacity for ad hoc networks using cognitive radios: An analytical model. IEEE Commun. Lett. **13**(9), 676–678 (2009)
15. Gottapu, S.K., Appalaraju,V.: Cognitive radio wireless sensor network localization in an open field. In: Proceedings of the 2018 Conference on Signal Processing and Communication Engineering Systems (SPACES), pp. 45–48 (2018)
16. Kalil, M.A., Al-Mahdi, H., Mitschele-Thiel, A.: Spectrum handover reduction for cognitive radio ad hoc networks. In: Proceedings of the 7th International Symposium on Wireless Communication Systems ISWCS 2010, pp. 1036–1040, 19–22 September 2010

Low Cost ICS Network Scanning for Vulnerability Prevention

Robert Foote[1], Niroop Sugunaraj[2(✉)], and Prakash Ranganathan[2]

[1] Minnkota Power Cooperative, Grand Forks, ND 58201, USA
`rfoote@minnkota.com`
[2] University of North Dakota, Grand Forks, ND 58201, USA
{`niroop.sugunaraj,prakash.ranganathan`}`@und.edu`

Abstract. As newer devices are added to operational technology (OT) networks or remote access to them becomes more prevalent, security best practices are increasingly important to reduce vulnerabilities. This paper goes deeper into the tactical level that is lacking in most other regulatory or strategic literature and references NIST where applicable. Targeted audience is that of personnel in the OT network space, looking for a good low cost starting place to enhance security or mitigate vulnerabilities. Layered security through network segregation, vulnerability scanning methods, and firewall use in these specialized systems are explored. Documenting a baseline of a network is covered as the first step to understanding how to secure the network. Insight into ICS-friendly Nmap settings to assist in the host, port, and service discovery to supplement the baseline is provided. Nmap is shown as a viable open-source intrusion detection testing tool for firewalls to ensure a complete vulnerability assessment of the network. The tests documented in this paper are conducted on a small number of power substation devices, the scans ran through Nmap, and all network traffic monitored via Wireshark. Metrics and simple drawings accompany the ideas and suggestions presented in the text to give readers a place to start their own vulnerability mitigation strategies.

Keywords: Industrial Control Systems (ICS) · Information Technology (IT) · Nmap · Operational Technology (OT) · Vulnerability Assessment (VA)

1 Introduction

The management of SCADA and ICS systems is evolving; no longer are they a set-and-forget type of network where security was considered after reliability. Information technology features are integrated with OT devices, and our younger workforce brings a culture that expects to have networked communication with everything. Therefore, as newer devices and equipment replace the old, these

S. Paiva et al. (Eds.): SmartCity360° 2021, LNICST 442, pp. 332–350, 2022.
https://doi.org/10.1007/978-3-031-06371-8_22

systems become much more capable with routable protocols and remote maintenance access. These actions are fostering the acceptance of merging Internet Protocol (IP) with SCADA/ICS technologies; however, with those actions come IT vulnerabilities, potential attack vectors, and mitigation requirements [12]. These issues are addressed at a high level in the Framework for Improving Critical Infrastructure Cybersecurity (FICIC), published by the National Institute of Standards and Technology (NIST) [24]. NIST sets the benchmark for industry best practices, therefore in this paper we will periodically compare our recommendation with the NIST framework. The first step is to properly document a baseline. This baseline includes a physical inventory of devices and networks to understand how SCADA and/or remote maintenance communication is handled. Next, the logical connections, ports, and services need to be assessed, and this is where OT network managers need to tread lightly. Today, cyber threats are constantly evolving, and so there is pressure to ensure the security of all networks. Unfortunately, older ICS/SCADA networks are being neglected because security audits and penetrations tests are geared more toward modern IT systems [5]. Assets, ports, and services discovery are a critical part of a baseline and vulnerability assessment; however, many IT tools can be too intrusive to be used in the OT environment. Nmap is a free, open-source port scanning tool which has been tested to work, but the right commands are critical and are explained in greater detail within this paper. We wanted to break down the testing and findings in detail, as well as to provide recommended settings based on the results. Adding firewalls in strategic locations within the OT network can provide additional layers of security, but these, too, require periodic vulnerability assessments to verify their effectiveness. Nmap is also a great tool to see what traffic can traverse the firewall, helping to assess vulnerabilities. Security is an investment; and can be costly if an organization becomes a victim of a malicious actor. The recommendations in this paper are very basic in implementation time and cost, and with the right combination of strategies for managing OT networks, vulnerabilities can be mitigated, keeping SCADA/ICS environments safe.

2   OT Security in Simple Terms

The amount of documentation available concerning network security is overwhelming and can frustrate anyone who may be tasked to manage such things. There are many cybersecurity publications addressing OT network management, including ICS/SCADA networks. Many of the recommendations tend to be high level, from program management to how network protocols work. Others are more cautious, warning of issues caused by using IT techniques in OT environments. NIST publishes tools such as guides and frameworks, but those too can be daunting to know where to begin. This paper was written to address the lack of simplistic recommendations with the goal of getting the security "ball" rolling in an organization. Figure 1 shows the Shodan's ICS Radar, which is their own search engine used to crawl the Internet for protocols that provide raw, direct access to ICS [22]. Metrics are provided by Shodan, showing common industrial protocols, and the numbers of exposed devices their search has uncovered. Additionally, a SANS Institute survey found that the percentage of control systems that experiences three or more malicious incidents in the previous 12 months increased from 35.3% in 2017 to 57.7% in 2019 [14]. The Shodan and SANS information proves the need for even the most basic security. Keep in mind that implementing basic security in manageable layers does not need to be complex or costly to be effective, and the sooner an OT network is secured, the safer the systems are that reside within it.

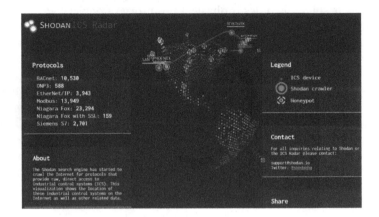

Fig. 1. Shodan ICS Radar

3   Related Work

Security for cyber physical systems (CPSs) such as ICSs and SCADA systems has observed measures that track the infrastructure's cyber health. Peterson [19] recommends using an application called "Quickdraw" funded by the U.S. Department of Homeland Security (DHS). This software was designed to create security event logs of all functional units such as remote terminal units (RTUs) or intelligent electronic devices (IEDs) within an ICS to passively detect any intrusions. This intrusion detection system (IDS) builds upon the open-source and well-known IDS Snort by: (1) augmenting Snort with industry standard protocols such as DNP3 to develop signatures of abnormal behavior for the IDS; and (2) developing a two-packet inspection technique that evaluates response and request packets to create security log events that are sent to authorized personnel for further action.

Graham et al. [7] introduce a security pre-processor for SCADA systems called "SCADA-Guard" to balance and secure both legacy systems which are highly vulnerable, and newer systems. The software-side of the pre-processor has three modules built on the microkernel system seL4: 1) a message authentication module that verifies data from input hardware to grant authentication and 2) a Modbus filter, and 3) DF-1 filter, that implement role-based access control for hardware messages that use the Modbus and DF-1 data communication protocols. Access control is granted or revoked based on on-site policies specified by the system administrator. A control system implemented with this technology demonstrated resistance against buffer overflow and man-in-the-middle attacks among other security issues. This system also performed acceptably in terms of timing delays, exhibiting a maximum delay of 229 ms for a single read/write operation.

Attack-tree based security models proposed in SCADA security are conceptual diagrams that depict how security for a system can be achieved or compromised with the root node of the diagram denoting the goal and several leaf nodes being the means to achieve that goal. Tian et al. [26] propose a multi-faceted approach that enables the SCADA network's analysis and protection. The analysis module utilizes a "preference attack tree (PAT)" architecture which quantifies attacks through frequencies of use, and labeling these frequencies as the attacker's "preferences". This security module recruits three action items from the authors: (1) usage of firewalls to set a bandwidth for network traffic, (2) encrypted communication network and software, and (3) a monitoring system to identify anomalous traffic data. Test results indicate an approximate 100% success rate in preventing DoS, replay, integrity, and data injection attacks.

A three-layered IDS was proposed by the authors in [20] where each layer from the bottom up handles one of three functions: protection of the communication network, authentication for the command-and-control stations, and authentication for field devices. The first layer of this method utilized machine learning algorithms such as random forest (RF) to classify DoS-based attack features. RF exhibited 99.9% accuracy in correctly classifying attacks. The second layer simulates threat scenarios using a high-performance computing environment to test effects and suggest countermeasures. The final layer addresses threats to RTUs and utilizes machine learning algorithms such as AdaBoost/JRipper and Naive Bayes to assist the RTU in identifying and differentiating between a malicious attack and a natural disturbance. The result from the AdaBoost/JRipper model indicates a 94% accuracy in correctly identifying threats.

Chalamasetty et al. [4] use a novel approach in incorporating multiple communication networks such as mobile ad-hoc networks (MANETs), wireless sensor nodes (WSNs), and web-based SCADA. This integration is said to enhance flexibility, scalability, and security. This approach contrasts with traditional SCADA networks which comprise of multiple local area networks (LANs) connected to a single wide area network (WAN). To test the security of this network, the authors propose an intrusion detection and prevention (IDP) system responsible for monitoring, detecting, and rehabilitation (MDR) [1] to prevent DoS attacks. Simulation results indicated that the network's throughput was maintained with the IDP system, while preventing significant delays. The ratio between the packets delivered and packets sent was approximately 100%.

Table 1. A comparison of existing SCADA security tools in research and commercial environments.

Tool	Type	Key feature(s)	Scale	Platform
Quickdraw [19]	Academia	SIEM for SCADA controllers	Limited scaling	Software system
SCADA-Guard [7]		Role-based access control for field devices	Possible Scaling	Hybrid System
PAT-based Model [26]		Network partitioning for SCADA architectures	Possible scaling	Software system
Triple-layer IDS [20]		Data authentication for RTUs using ML	Limited scaling	Software system
MDR-based [4]		IDPS for WSNs	Possible scaling	Hybrid system
Security architecture [23]		Anti-virus solution for SCADA systems	Possible scaling	Software system
QRadar	Commercial	Data recovery & regulatory packages	Possible scaling	Hybrid system
ArcSight		SOAR Integration	Possible scaling	Software system
Exabeam		Compatibility with Multiple vendors	Possible scaling	Software system
LogRhythm		AI-based UEBA	Possible scaling	Software system
InsightIDR (InsightVM)		Deception to detect Malicious behavior	Possible scaling	Software system
Securonix		Open Data, Hadoop based architecture	Possible scaling	Hybrid system

Slay and Miller [23] developed a defense-in-depth security framework to accommodate legacy ICS systems and modern corporate systems. The three main security mechanisms within the framework are implemented at the network gateway at the boundary of the network: (1) a firewall which enforces rules for the passage of network traffic, (2) an IDS to monitor incoming and outgoing traffic between the SCADA and corporate networks, and (3) a network-based antivirus software to prevent virus propagation to the corporate network. A demilitarized zone (DMZ) is implemented within the firewall architecture to create a neutral-resource sharing platform for any unsecured data from sources such as wireless access points (APs). This framework was developed in collaboration with an Australian SCADA integrator and was implemented by PowerSystems Australia to secure its control systems [16].

Table 1 lists and compares research-proposed and commercial tools to identify the current security landscape for SCADA networks and OT systems. 'Scale' is defined as the ability of a tool to augment its capabilities and adapt to different requirements. 'Deployment' refers to the type of components (software, hardware, or a combination) that are required by the tool when deployed to an use-case. All the commercial tools selected for this analysis are offered by leaders in the SIEM space as listed by Gartner in 2020 [13].

4   Baseline Documentation

Before one can implement security in their networks, they need to understand what is contained within and connect to them. Network configurations vary greatly in OT environments, and management methods for these networks will vary based on their device makeup and communication protocols. Knowing where to start in assessing the makeup and current state of devices is a daunting, but necessary task. National Institute of Standards and Technology (NIST) is a great place to look to when first assessing any OT networks. The NIST 800 series of publications relate directly to the topics presented in this paper, albeit at a higher strategic level. NIST recommends forming a team to define, inventory and categorize applications, computer systems and networks in addition to the devices contained therein [24, 25]

Baseline documentation starts with physical assessments and a knowledge of network access needs. Simply looking at devices and physical cabling will allow the creation of a rough network drawing. If network drawings are available, these will be valuable to verify the physical findings against. Drawings are a snapshot in time, so they may not accurately reflect the current state of the network. Assets with specific communication types such as routable, serial or dial-up access need to be documented as such, since protective measures added later will be different for each type. Determine the networks used or needed. Is there a single SCADA network, a remote maintenance network or maybe some other combination? By understanding the accessibility requirements in the organization and determining the needs of both the users and services required for remote connectivity, a balance can be struck between business needs and the appropriate protection methods for critical assets [9]. Once the physical and network baseline is documented, you have completed some of the NIST FICIC functions for IDENTIFY, PROTECT and DETECT; see Fig. 9. Now, the second phase of the baseline can be initiated.

5   Ports and Services Discovery

Knowing what ports and services are running on each device or between networks is key in vulnerability mitigation. There are many IT type network scanning tools which boast asset discovery and network mapping. These tools may require Simple Network Management Protocol (SNMP) to work, and this protocol is not typically utilized in ICS devices. Using IT type tools which have not been tested or properly configured to interact with SCADA networks and their unique devices could cause those devices to become unresponsive [9]. Worse yet, that could alter the actual data being received, transmitted by or stored within the device [6]. That being said, this paper provides a solution to performing the required ports and services scan to obtain critical information about the networked devices.

The overall goal of conducting such a scan is the creation of a list for all active devices and their associated ports, operating and responding within the address block in which the port scanning tool was used [21]. There are a few key security steps to be performed using the new port and service list. First, each device must be accounted for on the scan, and each open port in the device should be validated. If there is not a need for a port or service to be available, it should be disabled within the device if possible. This will reduce exposure risks and may also prevent unneeded communication chatter within the network. Later, the same port and service list can be used when setting up firewalls or other network whitelists. If any of the ports or services were disabled after the scan validation, they will need to be noted as such when documenting the baseline. These actions satisfy some of the NIST FICIC functions for IDENTIFY, PROTECT and DETECT; see Fig. 9.

6   Network Scanning

There is a lot going on within networks that cannot be seen without the right tools. Wireless networks should be assessed to ensure one does not have any unsecured entry points. There are different wireless protocols and tools to sniff them out, however that is beyond the scope of this paper. Just be sure that wireless scanning is not forgotten when any networks are assessed. Many OT devices utilize serial connections since this is typical of older products, as well as basic SCADA requirements. Serial port scanning can only be done by physically connecting to each serial network and running a specific program to capture COM port data. This does not function the same way as a network scanner which can find devices by address connected on the same network. This paper does not discuss scanning serial ports since they do not have the same vulnerabilities as Ethernet.

What is the focus of this paper is Ethernet communication and a no-cost open source scanner which works well within an Ethernet-based environment is Nmap. The official Nmap guide summarizes it best; "Nmap uses raw IP packets in novel ways to determine what hosts are available on the network, what services (application name and version) those hosts are offering, what operating systems (and OS versions) they are running, what type of packet filters/firewalls are in use, and dozens of other characteristics" [18]. While Nmap was designed for use within the IT environment, it has enough flexibility in its commands to be used in the OT networks as well. One goal of performing a network scan is to see what devices are responding and what ports they will respond to. TCP scans require a handshake and these are a bit more accurate. The device and Nmap send brief messages back and forth to know the status of the port. A UDP scan is important to perform because there can be commonly exploitable vulnerabilities in their services as well, but these scans are not as accurate as TCP since there is no handshake. Nmap needs to make an educated guess if the port is closed based on the packet response, or lack thereof. Another goal mentioned in the previous section is to document the discovered ports and services for each device. This information is critical in the quest to reduce vulnerabilities. Many devices come with a multitude of capabilities, however only a few are typically used in most applications. Take measures to "harden" devices by turning off or disabling unused ports and/or features [17]. Nmap can be run initially to see what is active in the network. Once device settings are modified to reduce the open ports and services footprint, the scan can then be run again. The Nmap program has a simple Graphical User Interface (GUI) called ZENmap and it is shown in Fig. 2. This is where the scan commands are entered such as the device or network address, TCP or UDP scan type and other host discovery options. While the laptop performing the test was on the same network as the test lab devices, Nmap allows the user to exclude this from the scan.

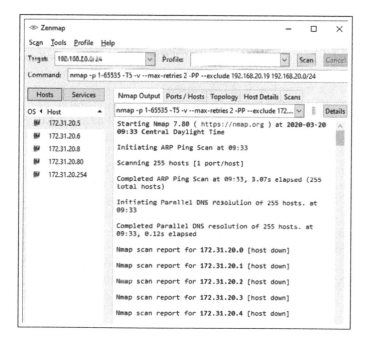

Fig. 2. Nmap/ZENMap GUI.

In Fig. 3 you can see the output report from Nmap. This example shows one device and the ports and services discovered. There are Nmap command options which provide more information such as operating systems and versions; however these were not selected in the sample test shown. The reports can be saved as documentation for each network, or device depending on the target set in the scan. If a device is reconfigured to close an unused port, or a new device is added to a network, a new scan is a great way to validate settings.

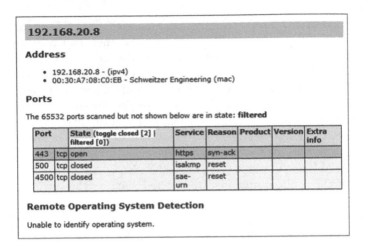

Fig. 3. Nmap output report.

7 Methods

A test lab was set up with a SCADA network and a separate remote access network, both utilizing RJ45 Ethernet connections to a test laptop. The end devices consisted of a NovaTech®Orion LX RTU, NovaTech®Orion LXm RTU, Sierra Wireless®RV50X Cellular Gateway, Schweitzer Engineering Laboratories SEL-3620 Ethernet Security Gateway and a SonicWall®TZ400 firewall. A laptop ran the Nmap program for port scanning, while a separate tool called Wireshark analyzed all network packets. See Fig. 4 for the network diagram. Wireshark is a free open source packet analyzer which allows the user to observe network communication as it happens. This tool was set to focus on dropped packets and other errors that signify disruption to the normal operation of the devices in the test lab. Wireshark observed the SCADA network, and the test was run again with it observing the remote access network. Ultimately we wanted to observe if the Nmap scans caused the devices to become erratic or lose SCADA information or drop polls.

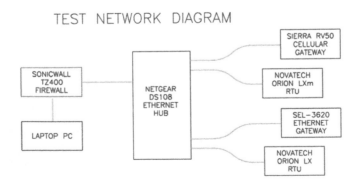

Fig. 4. SCADA test network setup.

Over fifty-five Nmap scans were completed in the test lab using different combinations of commands. Wireshark confirmed if each scan ran cleanly or if there were packet errors. Scan timing speeds were adjusted, the use of a discovery ping was toggled, and many other techniques from the Nmap user guide were explored. We tried using the command to get software and version information, however that introduced packet errors and there was not much data from the OT devices. Many different host discovery commands were tested which mainly consisted of various ping types. The standard Nmap scan uses an initial ping to find devices and that proved to be the most effective. Finally the scan techniques using Null, FIN, XMAS and others only proved to cause packet errors in Wireshark. A few of these scan types also fail to list ports at all. There were far too many combinations to easily present here, so we focused on the significant ones. See Fig. 5 and Fig. 6 for a detailed graphic which shows the focus of tests ran in the lab. The top portion of the chart shows UDP scans and the bottom shows TCP scans. Both scans were done inside the test network by connecting the laptop directly to the Netgear hub via Ethernet and we scanned all 65535 ports on each device and used echo ping for device discovery. Nmap has some prebuilt timing templates which range from T0 (very slow) to T5 (aggressive). These templates include many factors to include number of retries and the time between each host. You can actually specify any of the factors separately which can override that part of the timing template. The graphic focuses on the timing template, number of retries and errors generated in Wireshark. We wanted to understand what scan settings had the best combination of speed, accuracy and gentleness for the OT network. Overall it was noted that timing template T5 was too fast for reliable OT scans. This template leaves a max of only 5 ms of time between ports and some of our OT devices did not react well. While not shown in the graphic, the SEL-3620 seemed to have the most issues with fast T5 UDP scan rates, while the Sierra Wireless®cellular gateway locked up on a T5 TCP scan. Once the timing profile was turned down to T3 where there is 1000 ms maximum delay between ports, the devices seemed happy. Any slower timing profiles can be used, but keep in mind they add considerable time to the scans. The UDP Test graphic shows the T3 scan which is has a green column representing no Wireshark errors. This happens to use zero retries, but you can clearly see when retries are increased, the time the scan requires increases dramatically. This is because of the stateless connection with UDP. Nmap does not know if the port is open so it will retry and use a lot of time for each port to do so. While you may be concerned that there are not any retries, you could still run two of these scans in less time than a single scan using one retry. This would give a good average in case a second scan discovered something the first did not. The TCP Test graphic sows that all T5 through T3 timing profile scans finished in basically the same amount of time. The reason here is because of how TCP reacts. TCP uses a handshake and responds to the scan to state the port status. If the port is definitely open or closed, Nmap knows this right away and therefore there is not any need to retry that port. In effect, this is like using zero retries. We only had a small lab of five devices so the timing profile speed really did not differentiate themselves here.

Had we used a larger network or one that had more filtered ports which sometimes require more reties, the scan times would have been staggered further.

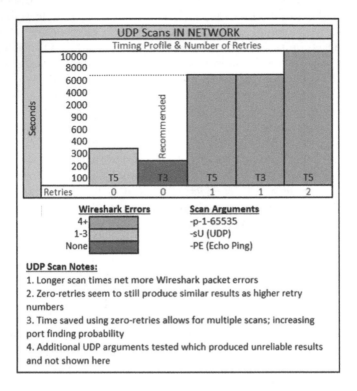

Fig. 5. UDP scans in network.

After thorough testing as noted above, we can recommend specific Nmap commands which are gentle on OT networks while having a good balance of speed and reliability for port and service baselines:

TCP: *nmap -sS -p 1-65535 -v –max-retries 2 –exclude x.x.x 0.0.0/24*
UDP: *nmap -sU -p 1-65535 -v –max-retries 0 –exclude x.x.x 0.0.0/24*

The TCP and UDP scans commands listed above differ slightly and require some explanation. The -sS command specifies a TCP scan, while -sU is the command for UDP. The *-p 1-65535* tells Nmap to scan every single port. If this was not included, Nmap only looks at the top 1000 most common ports and your baseline would be lacking. OT networks typically have less common protocols than IT networks and therefore need the extended port range. The -v allows for a verbose output. This simply gives status updates on the screen every few minutes and keeps you informed during long scans. The -max-retries are another key difference between TCP and UDP scans. As explained above, TCP uses handshakes and UDP scans are stateless which affect scan time. Setting

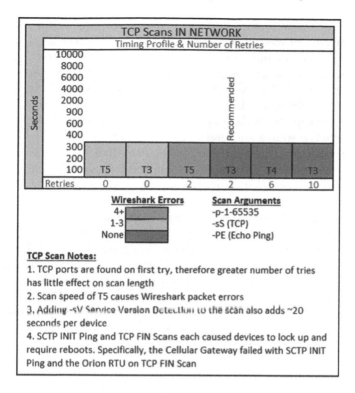

Fig. 6. TCP scans in network.

retries to zero drastically reduces the scan time, though surprisingly the error rate does not increase per our tests. If you are concerned with the potential for errors and have time to conduct lengthy scans, you can set this to 1 or 2 in a UDP scan. The *-exclude x.x.x* portion is how you exclude the computer address you are using for the scan. Substitute the x.x.x with the computer IP address. One would not want to scan the Nmap computer as this adds time and erroneous data to assessing a baseline. Finally, the 0.0.0/24 represents the target network or device being scanned, which should be changed to match the proper IP required for the target. One will notice no timing template is listed in the suggested command. This is because the default is T3 which works best with OT devices. With the steps and ICS-friendly Nmap commands provided, one should be able to quickly start scanning their networks for vulnerabilities.

8   Installing Firewalls

According to the Centre for Internet Security, "Defense in Depth (DiD) refers to an information security approach in which a series of security mechanisms and controls are thoughtfully layered throughout a computer network to protect the confidentiality, integrity, and availability of the network and the data within" [11]. This term applies in the OT environment as well and the utilization of firewalls is an excellent security control layer. To prevent the discovery of ICS/SCADA devices should never be left unprotected connected to Internet or other public-facing network, because search engines such as Shodan, can easily find and track them [3]. Firewalls, Virtual Private Networks (VPNs) and/or Virtual Local Area Networks (VLANs) could all be used to protect these devices, however only firewalls fit in the scope of this paper. A firewall of the "stateful" variety inspects the source and destination IP addresses, as well as port numbers of all incoming or outgoing packets. Rather than using rules to reject or deny packets, use rules to silently drop them instead, as this masks the typical firewall response attackers could use during information gathering. The firewall should be invisible to a malicious hacker and not become a way to map the network based off of its responses [2]. Another benefit to using firewalls is their logs. You can set up logs which can alert when specific rules are challenged, if intrusion detection thresholds are reached or many other triggers. These logs are a great tool to use when troubleshooting communication issues across networks, or as forensics if a malicious event needs to be investigated. Finally, firewalls are a good way to segregate network addresses. Typically a Wide Area Network (WAN) address is set for the main traffic coming from a larger (possibly less secure) network. In the firewall, there is at least one additional network set up with a different network address. This is the Local Area Network (LAN) and using a different network address allows some separating of the end devices in the LAN from your WAN. It is in that "gap" where the firewall uses rules you specify to allow communication through based on addresses or services. Kind of like a bouncer at a club, one must have the right credentials to get in from the WAN to the LAN.

Setting up the firewall to Deny by Default is the only recommended method. This will effectively block everything unless it is something specifically set as allowed within a rule. Nmap scans come in handy here since it is already known what ports, services and device addresses are within the network. Simply use the scan results to then configure firewall rules. Even though the firewall can be used to block unwanted communication, one should still disable unneeded ports and services in their devices as well in case the firewall ever becomes compromised.

In the test lab, the SonicWall®TZ400 firewall was initially used as an end device to be discovered by Nmap. We reconfigured the network to put the SonicWall®between the test laptop and the ICS devices to perform its designed firewall function. Nmap was again used to test different rules and to monitor packets to understand how this device protected the network. Over twenty Nmap scans were completed in the test lab through the firewall and Wireshark was again utilized to observe packets for problems. The Nmap commands were adjusted to understand how the firewall reacted, since we were trying to simulate a malicious actor attempting to perform network reconnaissance. TCP was the only scan type documented here, as all UDP packets were dropped because of the rules we had set up in the firewall.

Scanning through the firewall to the devices behind it tests the firewall rules as well as its alert capabilities. Our test lab was set up as shown in Fig. 4. Nmap has some intrusion detection evasion commands which were tested to see how the firewall logs and alerts would react. Fragmented packets and bad checksum packets were purposely sent and the firewall sent alerts on port scan detection. An IP spoof was launched which allowed the Nmap user to input a fake IP address so the firewall thought the sender was on a different network or on the same one. While these attempts are not captured in Fig. 7, we do show key information. Different timing profiles were used to see if the firewall would react differently. While the scan times do change a small amount, it is negligible for the first nine scans, which only scanned between 1 and 100 ports in each device. The last scan shown in the graphic scanned all 65535 ports and that dramatically increased the time. Another notable finding in the graphic is represented by colors. The green columns had no firewall alerts because those scans did not use Echo Ping (-Pn) to verify the hosts. This is more stealthy yet you can see how it does increase scan times a small amount. All scans using ping raised an IP spoof alert and some scans with higher port numbers generated SYN Flood alerts as well. These alerts will differ depending on firewall settings, however you can use Nmap to tune those settings. The recommended Nmap command for scanning TCP through a firewall would be:

nmap -sS -Pn -p 1-65535 -v –max-retries 2 –exclude x.x.x 0.0.0/24

One of the tests we were most interested in was observing how Nmap reported ports which are blocked by the firewall. If you want to prevent traffic from going to a specific port or service, a rule is set to either deny or discard the attempt. When the rule was set to DENY traffic, Nmap would show the port closed. This is good, but it actually also shows a malicious actor that there is a firewall specifically blocking the traffic. With the firewall rule set to DISCARD traffic, Nmap shows the port as filtered. This would make it harder for a malicious actor to know what is going on in the network. They would not definitively know there is a firewall rule, so it could buy some time and muddy their reconnaissance. Our recommended Nmap commands for scanning through a firewall are the same as the ones used in the network scanning section. One will be able to see how ports show open if a rule allows it, and closed or filtered if the rule denies or discards traffic. The same scan commands generate enough pings and port traffic to easily trigger intrusion detection alerts in the firewall. By utilizing firewalls within your networks, NIST FICIC functions for PROTECT and DETECT are accounted for; see Fig. 9.

9   Separated Networks

Typically, there are two functions for the OT network; to carry SCADA and provide remote access to devices. When the baseline was documented, it should have been noted as to how many and of what function each discovered network served. SCADA traffic should be kept separate from the remote access as much

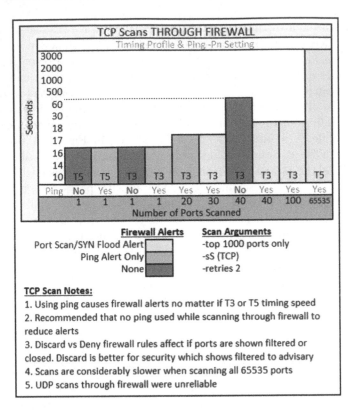

Fig. 7. TCP scans through firewall.

as possible. Large integrated or "flat" networks can easily fall victim to denial of service attacks [15]. Additionally, NIST FICIC and [17] recommends segmenting networks by, where possible, especially separating connected wireless and Internet from the SCADA/ICS devices and remote access networks. If raw SCADA traffic is accessible to anyone trying to remotely log into a device, then this issue should be immediately remedied. Not only could this be a security risk, but network congestion alone could potentially cause missed SCADA polls, lost packets or other anomalies. See Fig. 8 for an example of a separated network. The remote maintenance and SCADA networks are shown as Ethernet with some serial to IP converters, however separation can be accomplished a number of ways.

SCADA network traffic typically only flows in one direction from the device to the receiving master RTU or other collection point, therefore directional protections can be utilized. One such measure is utilizing a data diode which, like diodes used in electronic circuits, only allows one way flow. The diode can be purchased for serial or Ethernet networks and could be installed in specific locations as long as the SCADA network is separate from the remote access network. Ultimately they are cheaper than firewalls and do not introduce as much latency in the communications for time sensitive protocols. The diodes will prevent an

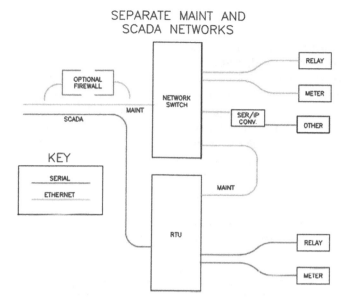

Fig. 8. Separated network.

attack back into a remote SCADA location, but may not be as effective for a man-in-the-middle attempt if the entry point is between the data diode and the SCADA collection point. These diodes require either a full serial connection, or serial to Ethernet conversions at certain points. Having a routable protocol break is actually useful as a way to limit an intruder's ability to move across networks or find specific device addresses.

Some devices allow the user to define the Quality of Service (QoS) settings for each network. If you are using a single radio or multiplexer to pass both networks through, they will typically allow someone to set prioritization rules to favor SCADA traffic, while assigning a lower priority to remote access activity. In the scanning and firewall experiments documented in Sects. 5 and 6, only the remote access network was utilized; not the separate SCADA network. If your network is a not separated and allows both SCADA and remote access, then be sure to test the recommended scans in a controlled environment before working on an operational system. Run Nmap scans against network gateways such as the radios and multiplexers to verify they are not allowing unexpected services. These devices can typically be configured remotely so check the equipment documentation to know what services or port number may be used. The last thing one wants is to configure the end devices and set up firewalls, only to leave their network telecommunication equipment exposed to denial of service attacks or malicious configuration changes.

10 Additional Recommendations

To maintain security, it is wise to try and continually improve one's security posture; after all, cyber vulnerabilities are constantly evolving as well. Keeping devices up to date with virus definitions or security patches is an easy step with minimal cost. Firmware updates or other types of system security patches are essential to improve or sustain device reliability and security [13]. A regular regimen of patching is a good way to ensure vulnerabilities inside the end devices are mitigated in case a malicious actor is able to penetrate current security layers. OT devices are designed to be used for many years longer that typical IT products. With such a long life, one may find that a manufacturer eventually stops supporting firmware updates. In this case, the lack of support should be noted and that risk must be addressed. Either with a plan to replace the device or a verification of the security layers protecting that device. The older the known vulnerabilities are within a device, the more chance that a malicious exploit is out in the wild.

Relevant Section	NIST Cybersecurity Framework		
	FUNCTION/Category	Subcategory	Recommendation
Baseline documentation	IDENTIFY/Asset Mgmt	ID.AM-1	Physical device/Syst. Inventory
	IDENTIFY/Asset Mgmt	ID.AM-3	Org comm and data flows mapped
	DETECT/Anomalies & Events	DE.AE-1	Baseline of data flows
Ports and Services Discovery	IDENTIFY/Risk Assess	ID.RA-1	Asset vulner., discov. and docum.
	DETECT/Continuous Monitor	DE.CM-8	Vulnerability scans
	PROTECT/Protective Tech.	PR.PT-3	Essential only capability
	PROTECT/Info Protection	PR.IP-1	Baseline system config.
Installing Firewalls	PROTECT/Access Control	PR.AC-3	Remote access mgmt
	PROTECT/Maintenance	PR.MA-2	Remote maint access controls
	PROTECT/Protective Tech.	PR.PT-4	Comm networks protected
	DETECT/Continuous Monitor	DE.CM-1	Monitor for cyber events
	DETECT/Continuous Monitor	DE.CM-4	Malicious code detection
Seperated Networks	PROTECT/Access Control	PR.AC-5	Network segmentation

Fig. 9. Mapping research findings to NIST framework.

Another layer of security would be to add in network monitoring software. Idaho National Laboratory conducted a survey of open source and licensed tools that could be extended upon to meet security needs [10]. Finally, another technology that could be utilized that meets security and redundancy needs is Software Defined Networking (SDN). This utilizes a network controller which efficiently determines data flow within the network. SDN is a hybrid of a firewall and network flow manager, where it will make decisions based on user-defined rules and application requirements giving greater control for network administrators [8]. SDN is much more costly than simply adding some firewalls or segregating SCADA and remote access networks, however this would be a technology to consider when performing a holistic network update. Ransomware, denial of service attacks or unauthorized remote access are some cybersecurity challenges that never end well, nor can be prevented with a single solution. A good baseline and system understanding is a great foundation on which to build multi-layer defenses. Showing company leadership they are meeting several functions with the NIST Framework for Improving Critical Infrastructure Cybersecurity is a great way to get buy-in and for future improvements.

11   Conclusion

There is so much recommended reading on cybersecurity out there and it can become overwhelming for anyone looking for a good place to start securing their own OT networks. The motivation behind this paper is providing insight on low cost steps to improve security posture while following NIST's industry best practices. Just like the armed forces will leave no man behind in battle; we too should leave no network behind in the cybersecurity fight. Build a strong foundation by knowing what devices make up the network and documenting that baseline. Scan all devices for that critical map of ports, ensuring any unneeded services are shut down to prevent exploits. We tested Nmap so others do not have to dedicate time doing so, and we found some effective Nmap commands to allow productive scans on OT networks. Keep in mind however, that we only ran Nmap on a remote access network that was not carrying SCADA traffic. This may differ from some environments, so controlled testing is highly suggested. We recommend adding firewalls because they greatly enhance security capabilities. The suggested rule recommendations can help mask the network configuration, and the firewall will also provide some historical logs for troubleshooting and investigations. Remember that network segregation not only allows more flexibility with protections, but it also prevents a single point of failure. If networks are not separated, then be sure to set a goal to work on this in the short term. Finally, maintaining all of one's initial work with the continuous upkeep of security patches or other improvements will bolster their vulnerability mitigation strategy, keeping them on pace with cybersecurity.

Acknowledgment. The authors would like to acknowledge the support from Dr. William Souza, Professor at the University of North Dakota (UND) for his guidance and feedback in improving and revising the manuscript.

References

1. Alsumayt, A., Haggerty, J.: Using trust based method to detect DoS attack in MANETs. The Convergence of Networking, Broadcasting, and Telecommunications, UK, PGNet (2014)
2. Anderson, D., Kipp, N.: Implementing firewalls for modern substation cybersecurity. In: Proceedings of the 12th Annual Western Power Delivery Automation Conference, Spokane, WA (2010)
3. Ceron, J., Chromik, J., Cardoso de Santanna, J., Pras, A.: Online discoverability and vulnerabilities of ICS/SCADA devices in the Netherlands. University of Twente, Netherlands (2019). In opdracht van het Wetenschappelijk Onderzoek en Documentatiecentrum (WODC)

4. Chalamasetty, G.K., Mandal, P., Tseng, T.L.: Secure SCADA communication network for detecting and preventing cyber-attacks on power systems. In: 2016 Clemson University Power Systems Conference (PSC), pp. 1–7. IEEE (2016)
5. Coffey, K., Smith, R., Maglaras, L., Janicke, H.: Vulnerability analysis of network scanning on SCADA systems. Secur. Commun. Netw. (2018)
6. Duggan, D., Berg, M., Dillinger, J., Stamp, J.: Penetration testing of industrial control systems. Sandia National Laboratories (2005)
7. Graham, J., Hieb, J., Naber, J.: Improving cybersecurity for industrial control systems. In: 2016 IEEE 25th International Symposium on Industrial Electronics (ISIE), pp. 618–623. IEEE (2016)
8. Gray, C.: How SDN can improve cybersecurity in OT networks. In: 22nd Conference of the Electric Power Supply Industry, September 2018
9. Department of Homeland Security, C.f.P.o.N.I.: Configuring and managing remote access for industrial control systems, November 2010
10. Hurd, C.M., McCarty, M.V.: A survey of security tools for the industrial control system environment. Technical report, Idaho National Lab. (INL), Idaho Falls, ID, USA (2017)
11. for Internet Security, C.: Cybersecurity spotlight - defense in depth (DiD), January 2021
12. Kalbfleisch, D.J.: SCADA technologies and vulnerabilities, May 2013
13. Kavanagh, K., Bussa, T., Sadowski, G.: Magic quadrant for security information and event management. Technical report, Gartner (2020)
14. Keene, M.: The risks of an it versus OT paradigm. SANS ICS, July 2019
15. Manson, S., Anderson, D.: Practical cybersecurity for protection and control system communications networks. In: 2017 Petroleum and Chemical Industry Technical Conference (PCIC), pp. 195–204. IEEE (2017)
16. Mustard, S.: Security of distributed control systems: the concern increases. Comput. Control Eng. J. **16**(6), 19–25 (2006)
17. Newton, P.: SCADA/ICS dangers & cybersecurity strategies, April 2020. https://www.darkreading.com/endpoint/scada-ics-dangers-and-cybersecurity-strategies/a/d-id/1332278
18. Nmap.org: Nmap reference guide — Nmap network scanning, April 2018
19. Peterson, D.: Quickdraw: generating security log events for legacy SCADA and control system devices. In: 2009 Cybersecurity Applications & Technology Conference for Homeland Security, pp. 227–229. IEEE (2009)
20. Samdarshi, R., Sinha, N., Tripathi, P.: A triple layer intrusion detection system for SCADA security of electric utility. In: 2015 Annual IEEE India Conference (INDICON), pp. 1–5. IEEE (2015)
21. Scarfone, K., Souppaya, M., Cody, A., Orebaugh, A.: Technical Guide to Information Security Testing and Assessment, vol. 800, no. 115, pp. 2–25. NIST Special Publication (2008)
22. Shodhan: Shodhan ICS radar (2020)
23. Slay, J., Miller, M.: A security architecture for SCADA networks. In: ACIS 2006 Proceedings, p. 12 (2006)
24. of Standards, N.I., (NIST), T.: Framework for improving critical infrastructure cybersecurity, ver 1.1. NIST Cybersecurity Framework (2018)
25. Stouffer, K., Falco, J., Scarfone, K.: Guide to Industrial Control Systems (ICS) Security, vol. 800, no. 82. NIST Special Publication (2011)
26. Tian, Z., Wu, W., Li, S., Li, X., Sun, Y., Chen, Z.: A security model of SCADA system based on attack tree. In: 2019 IEEE 3rd Conference on Energy Internet and Energy System Integration (EI2), pp. 2653–2658. IEEE (2019)

Smart Governance for Sustainable Smart Cities

The Development of the Sati Interactive System: A Computer-Based Interactive System that Creates a Sense of Deep Engagement in the User

Renusha Athugala[(✉)] [ID] and Roger Alsop [ID]

Faculty of Fine Arts and Music, Melbourne University, Parkville, VIC, Australia
renusha1@gmail.com, ralsop@unimelb.edu.au

Abstract. In this paper we discuss the development of the Sati Interactive System, including: the interaction design framework, hardware, software, testing, and results. The Sati Interactive System is a computer-based interactive system that creates a sense of deep engagement in the user by integrating colour, sound, and movement. The expression, 'sense of deep engagement' is derived from the Buddhist concept of 'Sati': being aware of and paying attention to the present moment. Experiencing a sense of deep engagement, being relaxed, focused, and not feeling the passing of time may have mental and physical health benefits. An evaluation of the system was based on data collected from 30 participants. 71% of participants provided positive responses to using the system, indicating that the Sati Interactive System was effective in creating a relaxed, focused state, and not feeling the time passing while using the system and afterwards.

Keywords: Computer-based interactive systems · Interaction design

1 Introduction

This paper discusses the development process of a computer-based interactive system that creates a sense deep engagement in the user. Here, a sense of deep engagement is considered as experiencing being relaxed, focused, and not feeling the passing of time, Goodall [1, p. 159] referenced John Cage, describing this as the "vanishing point of time and space". The expression, 'sense of deep engagement' is derived from the Buddhist concept of 'Sati': being aware of and paying attention to the present moment. To create a sense of deep engagement the Sati Interactive system integrates colour, sound, and movement, the main elements of an artwork.

Most computer-based interactive artworks have, as their main goal, entertaining the participants and often creating a sense of excitement, for example, DJ Light created by CinimodStudio [2], Yeosu Spanish Pavilion project created by Zappulla, Toribio [3], and Voice Array created by Lozano-Hemmer [4]. The main goal of computer-based interactive systems such as: Lange et al.'s [5] Interactive game-based rehabilitation using

© ICST Institute for Computer Sciences, Social Informatics and Telecommunications Engineering 2022
Published by Springer Nature Switzerland AG 2022. All Rights Reserved
S. Paiva et al. (Eds.): SmartCity360° 2021, LNICST 442, pp. 353–365, 2022.
https://doi.org/10.1007/978-3-031-06371-8_23

the Microsoft Kinect, Jaume-i-Capó et al.'s [6] Interactive Rehabilitation System for Improvement of Balance Therapies in People With Cerebral Palsy, and the Augmented Chemistry: Interactive Education System by Singhal, Bagga [7], are focused on learning and developing or improving physical characteristics.

The focus of the Sati Interactive System is to create a sense of deep engagement in the user, rather than creating an artwork, or an interactive system towards entertainment, education, training, or healthcare purposes. It does not provide the user with achievements or level-ups, such as in a first-person shooter game, and does not provide options to increase the difficulty; nor does it attempt to educate people.

2   The Sati Interactive System

The Sati Interactive System setup that was used for testing was installed in the Immersive Space 1 at the University of Melbourne (Room 202, Level 3, Arts West–Building 148). This setup was equipped with a computer, a projector, an external webcam, and external speakers. Figure 1 below shows the diagram of the Sati Interactive System setup used for testing.

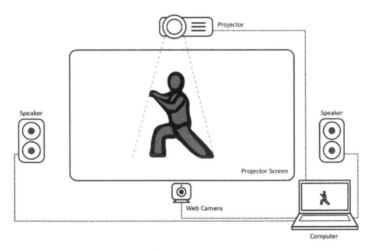

Fig. 1. The Sati Interactive System diagram

2.1   The Interaction

An outline of a person performing Tai Chi movements is displayed through the projector. The user copies the projected movements and moves their body. These body movements trigger various nature sounds. For example, moving the right hand up may trigger sounds of the ocean waves and moving the left hand down may trigger bird sounds from the forest. When the user's movements are accurate with the projected movements, the projected outline is filled with a color. When the user's movements are not accurate, color fades away. This is shown in Fig. 2 below.

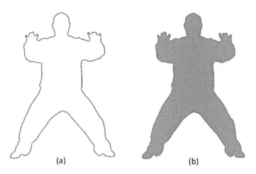

Fig. 2. (a) user movements are not accurate (b) user movements are accurate.

Figure 3 below shows a participant interacting with the Sati Interactive System.

Fig. 3. A participant interacting with the Sati Interactive System.

Sati Interactive System Setup Used at the University of Melbourne. We used an isolated environment to tests the Sati Interactive System with participants because,

- There are no distractions/no external influence–This allows the user to focus on the activity without being distracted, which is an important factor that helps the user achieve a sense of *sati* [8, 9].
- A discrete environment might provide a more immersive experience, easing the process of achieving a sense of deep engagement.

Hardware. The Sati Interactive System setup used at University of Melbourne consists of the laptop that we used to develop the system, an external webcam, a projector, and external speakers. The system was tested in the Immersive Space 1 at the University of Melbourne (Room 202, Level 3, Arts West - Building 148). The laptop specifications are i7 2.8 GHz processor, 16 GB of ram, and a 4 GB dedicated GTX 1050 video card.

Software. Max is used to design the Sati Interactive System. The system is designed to do tasks such as: analyzing the webcam data (body movement), comparing it with the reference video, playing audio clips according to different body movements, and projecting various visual elements according to the analyzed data. The system runs on Windows and MacOS.

2.2 Software Development

Here, I am using Fig. 4 below to describe the development of the Sati Interactive System software.

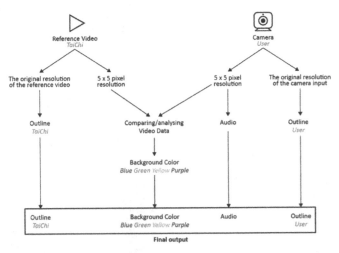

Fig. 4. Diagram of how the Sati Interactive System software works.

As shown in Fig. 4, the Sati Interactive software has two inputs: the reference video[1] (Tai Chi) and the Camera (User). First, the Tai Chi reference video is duplicated to create two outputs. The first output processes the original resolution of the video and creates an outline of the Tai Chi Master. The second output reduces the resolution to 5 by 5 pixels. The same process is done to the input from the camera. The first output uses the original resolution from the camera to create an outline of the user. The second output uses a reduced 5 by 5-pixel resolution. The 5 by 5-pixel is used to ease comparison to the reference video movements (Tai Chi Master's movements) with the user movements and because here we did not attempt to create a 100% accurate comparison. This resolution was enough to detect and compare the user movements and it gave a fast and smooth response. A 100% accurate comparison is not necessary because the purpose of this interactive system is not to make the user move exactly as the projected image. However, if an accurate comparison is needed, it can be accomplished by applying a higher resolution to the second output.

This comparison of the two videos is used to compare the user's movements with the reference video movements to see if the user is in sync with the reference video

---

[1] We have used a Tai Chi video as the reference video here, however, the user can select their own video. In the examples presented here, the ability to add different reference videos have been disabled. The recommended video resolution is 480 p with a frame rate of 30 fps because the application will only output a maximum resolution of 480 p. The resolution is limited to 480 p because it is more likely to work on low-cost computers. The reference videos must have a plain background and the character in the video must be dressed in a colour different from the background colour.

movements. For example, as shown in Fig. 2, when the user movements and the Tai Chi Master's movements are in sync, the Tai Chi Master's outline image will be filled with color (b), when it is not in sync the color will fadeout (a).

The audio changes according to the user movements. Each movement triggers different nature sounds such as: ocean waves, birds, creeks, and waterfalls.

3   Development of the Interaction Design Framework

The development of the framework is based on Forlizzi, Ford, and Battarbee's [11, 12] approaches. This framework is used to develop the Sati Interactive System, its user interface, user-product interactions, backend design program resulting in the product. The framework takes an interaction-centred perspective that includes aspects of user experience.

3.1   Factors that Influence Experience

The first step of designing the framework is to understand what influences experience. Figure 5 shows a summary of the factors that influence user experience, developed using Forlizzi and Ford's influences on experience [12].

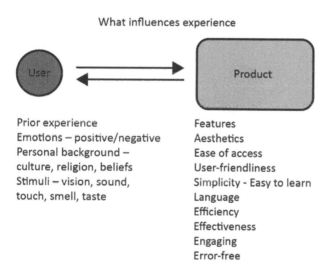

Fig. 5. User and product factors that influence user experience.

Here, we have added additional factors combining aspects specific to HCI usability that affect user experience, such as: efficiency, effectiveness, engaging, error-free, and easy to learn [13]. For example, a product that includes these features has a better chance of creating a positive user experience when competing with similar products. Understanding what influences experience can help develop an interactive system that promotes a positive user experience.

3.2   User-Product Interaction and Experience of the Sati Interactive System

According to the framework of user-product interaction and its relation to user experience presented by Forlizzi and Battarbee [11, p. 263], The Sati Interactive System can be categorized as a product with an expressive interaction that creates an experience with aspects of co-experience.

Expressive interaction–Sati Interactive System consist of functions that enables the user to customize certain aspects of the software to the preference of the user. For example, the user can change the color of the visuals, adjust volume levels, adjust the speed, and adjust the sensitivity of the camera.

An Experience–Using the Sati Interactive System is an activity that provides an experience. This activity has a beginning and end and it influence emotional changes. For example, this activity can be named as 'relaxing' or 'learning tai chi' experience, and the interaction might influence positive or negative emotional changes.

Aspects of Co-Experience–The Sati Interactive System does not inherently allow Co-Experience. However, the Co-Experience is created when individual user experience is verbally shared among others.

3.3   The Interaction Design Framework for Sati Interactive System

The interaction design framework for Sati Interactive System is shown in Fig. 6 below.

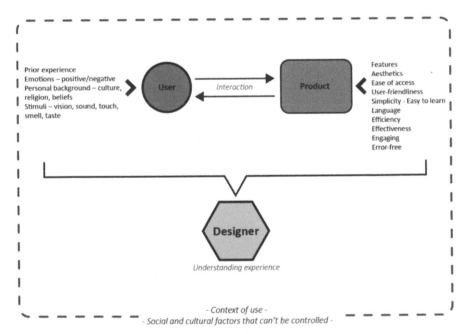

Fig. 6. Interaction design framework for the Sati Interactive System.

The above figure shows the interaction between a user, a product, in this case the Sati Interactive System, and the designers' role of understanding user experience. Here, the designer's role includes understanding both user and product-based aspects that influence user experience. This framework can be used to create any interactive system.

Using the Framework

Initially, according to the framework, the designer does not have control over factors such as social and cultural influences, prior experience of the user, and the personal background of the user. Understanding these limitations is the first step of using the framework.

In Table 1 below, we analyze each component of the Interaction Design Framework and discuss how it is used in the design process of the Sati Interactive System.

Table 1. Using the interaction design framework.

Aspects that influence experience	How it is used in the Sati Interactive System
Emotions–positive emotions	Using variations of color and sound to enhance positive emotions
Stimuli–vision, sound	Positive emotions are stimulated through vision and sound using color, sound, body movement techniques, and real-time interactive motions
Product features	Ability to change the color of the visuals Ability to adjust the speed, camera sensitivity, and volume Ability to plug in various cameras
Aesthetics	Simple graphical interface Interactive smooth visuals Interactive sounds
Ease of access	The Sati Interactive System can be copied to any computer with the required specifications and played Small file size
User-friendliness simplicity	Direct and short instructions Simple user-interface design that includes direct instructions
Efficiency	The software is programmed using simple algorithms and coding techniques to deliver a smooth interaction, using resources efficiently
Effectiveness	The system is designed only focusing on the end goal. The user interface is designed to be user-friendly and simple to be understood by anyone. The system is designed to deliver smooth interactions, quality visuals, and sounds
Engaging	The system is using visuals and sounds to create an attractive environment to engage the user
Error-free	Sati Interactive System is tested in both windows and mac systems

Applying the Principles/Concepts of Computer-Based Interactivity

Here we are focusing on the principles/concepts of computer-based interactivity and how this can be linked to arts-based interactivity. This link is important because we are using an arts-based approach, to develop the Sati Interactive System. An artwork is inherently designed to create a sense of deep engagement/transformative experience; this is what we want the user to experience when they interact with the Sati Interactive System.

Table 2 on the following page gives an explanation of concepts/principles of inter-activity in a computer-based and an arts-based approach and how these two approaches are linked in making of the Sati Interactive System. The first column shows the con-cepts/principles of computer-based interactivity, the second column shows the expla-nation of the concept/principle in computer-based interactivity, the third column shows the explanation of the concept/principle in arts-based interactivity, and the last column shows how these two approaches are linked in making of the Sati Interactive System.

Table 2. The use of the principles/concepts of computer-based interactivity in the Sati Interactive System.

Principles/Concepts	Explanation in computer based (CB) interactivity	Explanation in art based (AB) interactivity	How these two approaches are linked in making of the Sati Interactive System
Directionality	Typically, two-way bi-directional stream of communication–typical for all computer-based interactions	Typically, uni-directional, but this is developing with the advent of computer-based arts and art making	The Sati Interactive System provides 'bi-directionality' as it communicates with the user in real-time by providing feedback. For example, color and sound is generated according to the user movements
Responsiveness	The ability to respond to current and previous communications and the response speed	Typically, non-responsive, but this is developing with the advent of computer-based arts and art making	Sati Interactive responses to the user immediately using visuals and audio
Awareness	Understanding of context and meaning	An artwork is not typically aware or not responsive to its context or meaning. However, this is developing with the computer-based interactive artworks	Sati Interactive is aware of the user's actions such as movements and input via the user interface. However, it does not have an awareness of its context or meaning. The user can understand the context and meaning of the Sati Interactive System

(continued)

Table 2. (*continued*)

Principles/Concepts	Explanation in computer based (CB) interactivity	Explanation in art based (AB) interactivity	How these two approaches are linked in making of the Sati Interactive System
Selectivity	The availability of choices for the user	The creator may have the ability to select the medium used to design the artwork, however the user does not. But the user can select which artwork they engage with	'Selectivity' is achieved by providing choices to the user. Sati Interactive gives the choice to use both color and sound. For example, the user can select different colors, adjust the speed of the interaction, adjust the responsiveness of the interaction, and to adjust the volume. The Sati Interactive user interface consists of a 'help' button that provides information on using the system. Additionally, the user interface also provides clear and detailed information for each available option such as 'play' button, various sliders, 'full screen' button, and audio controllers
Being interchangeable	Communication roles can be interchangeable	Communication rolls cannot be interchangeable. Typically, an artwork does not communicate with the user	'Being interchangeable' is achieved by providing the user with the opportunity to control certain factors of the Sati Interactive System to meet their needs according to the feedback provided by the system. Here, the user communicates with the Sati Interactive System and the communication roles are interchanged by the feedback
Real-time communication	Interactive media should be an instant exchange	An artwork can create real-time communication. For example, an artwork can create a transformative experience in the user at that moment	This is achieved by providing real-time feedback to the user. For example, the user receives feedback from the system in real-time through color and sound. This can also be seen as a way of communication between the user and the system

4   Testing the Sati Interactive System

The testing was conducted in the Immersive Space 1 at the University of Melbourne (Room 202, Level 3, Arts West - Building 148) on four separate days within two weeks. The laptop that was running the Sati Interactive System was connected to the projector and the sound system in the Immersive Space. A Dell XPS 15 9560 laptop was used to run the Sati Interactive application.

Participants. The test consisted of 30 participants who were asked to try the Sati Interactive System, these included: university staff members, students from different universities, and people not related to the university. All participants were above the age of 18. However, age will not be taken into consideration because it is not relevant to the process.

Task and Procedure. The initial plan was to conduct 30 trials of the Sati Interactive System. However, we noticed that three out of the first five participants are only focusing on trying to align them self with the Tai Chi master outline and they try to adjust them self during the movement. We felt like this interferes with what the Sati Interactive System is trying to create, a sense of deep engagement, because the user lost focus, while trying to make adjustments to their pose, rather preventing them from relaxing and enjoying the color and sounds. The participants said that it was hard to keep up with the Tai Chi master's movements.

As a result of this observation, we decided to conduct two types of trials: (1) the user can only see the Tai Chi master (no user image outline) and (2) the user can see their image and the Tai Chi master on the screen (with user image outline). There were 15 participants for each type of trial.

The Fig. 7 below shows the difference between (1) no user image outline and (2) with user image outline.

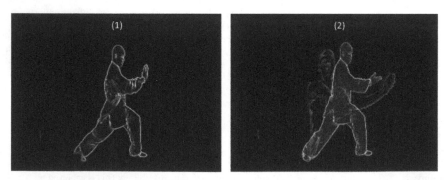

Fig. 7. (1) no user image outline (2) with user image outline

Immediately after engaging with the Sati Interactive System the participants were asked to answer 15 questions, regarding how relaxed and focused they felt, and whether they enjoyed using the system. Each participant engaged with the Sati Interactive System for 5–10 min. All 30 participants completed the questionnaire, and a few provided additional comments on the questionnaire itself.

Measures. The Sati Interactive System is evaluated using the three coding methods used in Grounded Theory: Open coding, Axial coding, and Selective coding [14]. Firstly, the raw data is analyzed using Open code and Axial code, measuring the total amount of positive, negative, and neutral experiences. Later, this data is used to choose the Selective code 'Core category', which will provide the final evaluation.

5 Results and Discussion

According to the results, both trials show an overall positive response, and negative responses are lower than neutral responses. Only two participants showed different results to the trends, these were participant 14 and 27. The highest amount of negative responses, five, is made by participant 14, who also made 8 neutral responses. Participant 27 has six positive responses and nine neutral responses but no negative responses. I consider these responses as anomalies. Twenty-five participants have at least one neutral response and seven participants have more than five neutral responses, which indicates that neutral responses are common among participants.

Overall, there are 71% positive responses, 8% negative responses, and 21% neutral responses. This indicates that the Sati Interactive System is successful in its goals. Most participants providing a positive response suggest that the system helped them become relaxed and focused. However, there was no significant difference in the responses to the questions between the 15 users that saw their outline and the 15 users that did not see their outline when using the Sati Interactive System.

Using the adapted Grounded Theory process, this analysis shows that most participants felt that the Sati Interactive System helped them achieve a sense of relaxation and the ability to focus on that specific moment, a sense of deep engagement. While only one testing process, with a limited number of participants, was carried out, we can surmise that similar responses would occur if we were to do more testing in different environments. The questions were designed to be interpreted by the user.

While the responses to the questionnaires show that the Sati Interactive System is successful in creating a sense of deep engagement in the participants, this success may be argued due to the comparatively small number of respondents. However, this number of respondents, or fewer is not unusual in this field, for example: Castellano, Villalba [15] had only 10 participants when recognizing human emotions from body movement and gesture dynamics, Dow, Mehta [16] had only 12 participants when exploring the impact of immersive technologies on presence and engagement in an interactive drama, and Yang, Bernardo [17] had only 23 respondents when considering the effect of yoga on type 2 diabetes.

6 Conclusion

Here we have discussed the development and the testing process of the Sati Interactive System. The Sati Interactive System is developed using a user-product interaction design framework focusing on the user's prior experience, emotions, and stimuli. We also focused on aspects of the product such as its: features, aesthetics, ease of access, user-friendliness, simplicity, language, efficiency, effectiveness, engaging, and error-free. This process resulted in the Sati Interactive System, which has features developed from the framework that we designed based on Forlizzi, Ford, and Battarbee's approaches as their ideas are flexible and have formed a basis for other interaction designs. These include: features designed to enhance user experience; an application that works on Windows and Mac operating systems; a system that is easy to setup and is of low-cost, and can integrate with a home entertainment system.

The program uses sounds of nature, Tai Chi movement technique, and four types of colors. Nature sounds and colors are used to create positive emotions. Tai Chi movement technique is used as a visual guide to help engage the user in an activity, not for its ability to calm and relax the mind and body.

Results of the Sati Interactive System trials show that it can create an experience of being relaxed, focused, and not feeling the passing of time, a sense of deep engagement. This experience may not be easily expressed in words, similar to how the experiencing of art may not be easily expressed in words. These results also indicate that the interaction design framework can be used to develop similar computer-based interactive systems.

References

1. Goodall, J.: Stage Presence. Routledge (2008)
2. CinimodStudio. DJ Light (2019). http://www.cinimodstudio.com/dj-light
3. Zappulla, C., Toribio, N., Uroz, C.: Yeosu Spanish Pavilion (2019). http://externalreference.com/projects/ysp12
4. Lozano-Hemmer, R.: Voice Array (2019). http://www.lozano-hemmer.com/voice_array.php.
5. Lange, B., et al.: Interactive game-based rehabilitation using the microsoft kinect. In: Proceedings of the 2012 IEEE Virtual Reality Workshops (VRW). IEEE (2012)
6. Jaume-i-Capó, A., et al.: Interactive rehabilitation system for improvement of balance therapies in people with cerebral palsy. IEEE Trans. Neural Syst. Rehabil. Eng. 22(2), 419–427 (2013)
7. Singhal, S., et al.: Augmented chemistry: Interactive education system. Int. J. Comput. Appl. 49(15) (2012)
8. Gunaratana, H.: Mindfulness in plain English (2010). ReadHowYouWant.com
9. Bodhi, B.: What does mindfulness really mean? A canonical perspective. Contemp. Buddhism 12(01), 19–39 (2011)
10. Dede, C.: Immersive interfaces for engagement and learning. Science 323(5910), 66–69 (2009)
11. Forlizzi, J., Battarbee, K.: Understanding experience in interactive systems. In: Proceedings of the 5th Conference on Designing Interactive Systems: Processes, Practices, Methods, and Techniques. ACM (2004)
12. Forlizzi, J., Ford, S.: The building blocks of experience: An early framework for interaction designers. In: Proceedings of the 3rd Conference on Designing Interactive Systems: Processes, Practices, Methods, and Techniques. ACM (2000)
13. ISO, ISO 9241–11:2018(en), Ergonomics of human-system interaction - Part 11: Usability: Definitions and concepts. International Organization for Standardization (2018)
14. Corbin, J., Strauss, A.: Grounded theory research: Procedures, canons and evaluative criteria. Z. Soziol. 19(6), 418–427 (1990)
15. Castellano, G., Villalba, S.D., Camurri, A.: Recognising human emotions from body movement and gesture dynamics. In: Proceedings of the International Conference on Affective Computing and Intelligent Interaction. Springer (2007)

16. Dow, S., et al.: Presence and engagement in an interactive drama. In: Proceedings of the SIGCHI Conference on Human Factors in Computing Systems. ACM (2007)
17. Yang, K., et al.: Utilization of 3-month yoga program for adults at high risk for type 2 diabetes: A pilot study. Evid. Based Complement. Altern. Med. **2011** (2011)

Benefits and Obstacles of Smart Governance in Cities

Katarína Vitálišová$^{(\boxtimes)}$ ⑩, Katarína Sýkorová⑩, Samuel Koróny, and Darina Rojíková

Faculty of Economics, Matej Bel University, Tajovského 10, 975 90 Banská Bystrica, Slovakia
{katarina.vitalisova,katarina.sykorova,samuel.korony,
darina.rojikova}@umb.sk

Abstract. The development of information and communication technologies influences all spheres of our lives and society including the concepts of public sector management and its tools. The aim of the paper is to point out the importance of smart governance and its toolkit in cities as an innovative component of local policy. The success of local development lies right at the heart of the relationships between local municipality and citizens and other stakeholders, including other public administration bodies what smart governance significantly strengths.

The paper presents the findings of the primary research realized by Delphi method among experts in the fields of regional development, strategic planning, public administration from different countries from academia and from practice in second half of 2020. It compares their opinions on the main issues of smart governance in cities (its benefits, obstacles, and tools) with results based on the deep literature and research studies analysis. Subsequently, it identifies the main common features and obstacles of smart governance in local municipalities.

Keywords: Toolkit · Smart governance · Cities · Benefits · Obstacles

1 Introduction

The transformation of public administration at local level is in line with the technological progress, digitalization and "smartness" in decision making and thus has resulted in a new phenomenon smart governance within the smart city ecosystem. This trend is strongly associated with the participation and interactions of local government with all relevant stakeholders on regular and multi-channel communication including the virtual space.

The attribute "smart" in governance of cities enhances the local polycentric system in which a large number of different stakeholders are involved in local policy decision-making processes, based on the knowledge of behavioral economics, traditional tools of local policy in combination with the IT technologies. It is not just about adopting technology but more concerned with obtaining effective governance processes and achieving improved urban outcomes through the innovative use of technologies (Huaxiong 2021).

This approach in cities in Central and European Union had been implemented gradually, but usually not associated with some systematic approach. With ambition to learn

S. Paiva et al. (Eds.): SmartCity360° 2021, LNICST 442, pp. 366–380, 2022.
https://doi.org/10.1007/978-3-031-06371-8_24

from the best, we research among the experts from all over the world, which is the most comprehensive definition of smart governance, what are the benefits and potential obstacles of its implementation, as well as the tools that it uses. However, the treat impact of COVID-19 pandemic is evident also in this issue. In many cities it has speeded up the penetration of smart tools in solving the emerging situation, communication with citizens as well as the negotiations of crisis staffs.

The paper is organized as follows. Section 2 is theoretically oriented and defines the smart governance as a key dimension of smart city. Section 3 details the proposed methodology, including the realized Delhi method among experts in the fields of regional development, strategic planning, and public administration from academia and practice from different countries in second half of 2020. The third section is devoted to presentation of the research results on the main issues of smart governance in cities (its benefits, obstacles, and tools). In the concluding part of the paper, we summarize the main challenges of smart governance development in cities.

2 Smart Governance in Cities and Its Toolkit

Based on the deep literature and research studies analysis, we identified the gradual progress in definition of smart governance. The first group of definitions strongly link the smart governance with the new technology (Gil-Garcia et al. 2014; Scholl and Alawadhi 2016) and the role of e-government (Estevez and Janowski 2013; Janowski et al. 2012). As the theory and its implications in practice developed also more complex definitions were introduced. Firstly, aimed at the smart governance generally (Pereira et al. 2018) and later, specifically in case of cities (Ruhland 2018)[1]. We incline to this definition because it combines all key elements of smart governance as stakeholders, their empowerment (roles and responsibilities), operational framework (structure, legislation, policies, agreements), tools and excepted outputs.

Gil-Garcia and Zhang (2016) declare that the smartness in local governance is based on integration, innovation, evidence-based decisions, citizen orientation, sustainability, creativity, efficiency, effectiveness, equality, entrepreneurship, citizen engagement, openness, resilience and technological capabilities.

However, the key element in building smart governance in cities is a considerable effort from politicians and city management to look for possibilities how to collaborate and empower the residents, entrepreneurs, as well as the various communities in the city and implement these possibilities via relevant tools and methods in local policy decision-making (Vaňová 2021; Lee and Lee 2014; Lombardi et al. 2011). For this process is necessary to create the suitable legislative and organizational framework, technological infrastructure as well as to support activities aimed at strengthening the digital skills of employees but also stakeholders (Nam and Pardo 2011; Mellouli et al. 2014; Maheshwari and Janssen 2014; Nam and Pardo 2014).

---

[1] Ruhlandt (Ruhland 2018, p. 10) defines smart governance in city as "a processual interplay among a diverse set of stakeholders, equipped with different roles and responsibilities, organized in various external and internal structures and organization, driven and facilitated by technology and data, involving certain types of legislation, polices and exchange arrangements, for the purpose of achieving either substantive outputs for cities or procedural changes"

Building smart governance is a long-term transformation process that requires financial and human investment, to which government must commit. That is why a common understanding of the smart governance concept, vision, strategy and sharing of responsibilities is an essential part of success.

The level of smart governance can be then assessed on the basis of transparency in urban management, the involvement of social partners, the level of public services and the implementation of development strategies (Kumar 2017; Zanella et al. 2014; Caragliu et al. 2011).

Smart governance can be seen as a basis for the development of smart administration through the application of new information and communication technologies (ICT) in management of local municipalities (inter alia Pérez-González, Díaz-Díaz, 2015; Pereira et al. 2017; Kleinhans et al. 2015; Castelnovo et al. 2015; Khan et al. 2015; Navarro-Galera et al. 2016). Smart governance with utilization of ICT improves decision-making process by better cooperation of different stakeholders and higher rate of their participation at solving public issues (Vitálišová et al., 2020). Because of the strong independence on the ICT, the great challenge for the cities is to educate and trainee the end-users of the smart governance tools. It assumes to develop tools which are friendly to all groups of stakeholders and moreover to combine the traditional and modern tools of governance to become an equal partner in relationship with local government.

All tools of smart governance can be associated with two main competences of local municipalities - participation in public policy processes (including informing) and involvement in improving services in the city (co-creation of smart city services). Participation of stakeholders increases openness, transparency, accountability of local authority and thus the quality of relations between stakeholders and local governments. Governments use and share data, information and knowledge to support evidence-based decision-making that enables governments to make more informed decisions and improve the effectiveness of public policies and programs. There can be used the traditional tools of participation as well as their innovative forms or new one (Castelnovo et al. 2015; Vitálišová et al. 2021). Co-creation of smart city services can help increase the city's competitiveness and citizens' quality of life, by ICT in city planning and management. Innovative services provide citizens with information, knowledge and actions related to various aspects of their city life (Lee and Lee 2014).

Guimarães et al. 2020 researches the impacts of smart cities on quality of life and clustered them into four areas–(1) transparency (dominant position), (2) cooperation, (3) participation and partnership, (4) communication and (5) responsibility. The smart governance toolkit supports the development of participation. By Smart cities and inclusive growth (2020) it includes several categories: (1) communication (information); (2) consultation; (3) participation; (4) representation in decision-making bodies; (5) partnership; (6) co-production and co-decision.

Based on the in-depth analysis of literature and research studies (inter alia Mackintosh, 2005; Castelnovo, et al. 2015; Estevez and Janowski 2013; Chourabi et al. 2012; Wijnhoven et al. 2015; Gil-Garcia et al. 2015; Johannessen and Berntzen 2018; Simonofski et al. 2019; Guimarães, et al. 2020; Vaňová 2021), we can identify 4 groups of smart governance tools. They overlap and complements each other. The first group includes the tools that strongly support the transparency (e. g. providing information, open data, sharing databases, etc.). The second group includes the tools by which citizens become democratic participants in the city's decision-making process. It contains modern forms of e-participation and e-democracy belong electronic e-voting, e-petition, e- referendum, e-panel, discussion forums and chatting rooms, electronic community, electronic civil boards. Very efficient tools to support the decision-making process are electronic advisory elections, simulation of decision making, quick polls and surveys. These tools overlap partially with last two groups of tools–co-production tools (e. g. participative planning, participative budgeting, surveys, crowdsourcing, crowdfunding, living labs, etc.) and communication tools (websites, social media, PR, blogs, mobile application, etc.).

The implementation of the smart governance concept has been strongly influenced by the COVID-19 pandemic. The crisis has accelerated the need to communicate virtually and well as manage the crisis with the support of IT tools. The pandemic showed that it is never enough to possess the best apps and technologies; and a great need of inclusive policies, ground-up initiatives, and effective leadership (Baharudin 2020; Zhang and Savage 2020; Das and Zhang 2020). A crucial element to predict, detect, and mitigate a pandemic is 'data' retrieved from different sources and the increase of data sources should be pursued by the cities (Costa and G., Peixoto, J. P. J. 2020). The required actions to create smart cities can come from different areas, but governments should play the leading role in this process. Relevant for the future, the local and regional governments stakeholders should identify interventions to be executed in order to build back better after the Covid-19 pandemic and lead towards a more inclusive, safe, and sustainable urban future (Cities for all. Empowering Local Governments on Inclusive Pandemic Response 2020).

3 Material and Methodology

The paper is dedicated to the topic of smart governance, its tools, benefits, and obstacles of its implementation. The paper aims to point out the importance of smart governance in cities as an innovative component of local policy.

The paper presents the findings of the research realized by Delphi method among 33 experts during second half of 2020 mostly from the fields of regional development (39,39%), strategic planning (27,27%), and public administration (15,15%), politics (6,06%) and other (3,03%). They come from academia (85%) and from practice (15%). 49% of experts came from Slovakia, 18% from Poland, 9% from Italy as well as from Czech Republic. Other experts come from Hungary, Belgium, Finland, and Japan.

The experts involved into the research were identified by the authors' analysis of the academic papers and strategical documents of municipalities in Slovakia (the paper is an output of the research project oriented on the exploring smart governance in Slovak cities). In the first round, 278 experts were invited to participate, but we receive responds from 33 experts which were involved in the next steps of research (Fig. 1). That is why we assume that they are perfectly oriented in the topic and their knowledge covers complexly the research issue.

To process the primary data, we used a range of mathematical and statistical methods, especially the descriptive statistics and Kendall correlations.

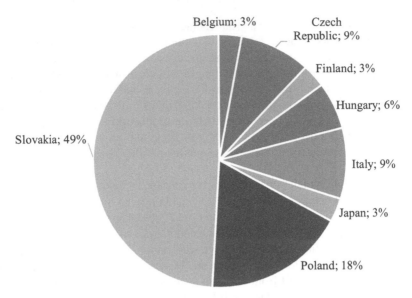

Fig. 1. The structure of research sample according to country

The last part of the paper discusses and summarizes the most important research findings and the main challenges of smart governance development in context of COVID-19 pandemic. All reports were made by Excel and by statistical software IBM SPSS 25.

4   Research Findings and Discussion

Experts involved in our research by Delphi method had the possibility to choose at most two definitions of smart governance in city from definitions stated below:

– Investing in emerging technologies coupled with innovative strategies to achieve more agile and resilient government structures and governance infrastructure in city (Gil-Garcia et al. 2014; Scholl and Alawadhi 2016);
– The application of technology by governments in order to transform themselves, their interactions with customers and the relations with and citizens, businesses, other non-state actors and other arms of government, creating impact on the society in cities (Estevez and Janowski 2013; Janowski et al. 2012);
– Form of governance, allocating decision-making rights to stakeholders and enabling them to participate in effective and efficient decision-making processes to improve the quality of life in cities (Pereira et al. 2018);
– The processual interplay among a diverse set of stakeholders, equipped with different roles and responsibilities, organized in various external and internal structures and organizations, driven and facilitated by technology and data, involving certain types of legislation policies and exchange arrangements, for the purpose of achieving either substantive outputs for cities and procedural changes (Ruhland 2018)

– Other (space for own definition).

46% of respondents marked the definition of smart governance provided by (Ruhland 2018) as the best matching definition. 34% of respondents considered the definition by Pereira et al. (2018) as the most comprehensive and 12% of respondents regarded definition created by Estevez and Janowski (2013); Janowski et al. (2012) as the best matching definition. 6% of respondents chose definitions by Gil-Garcia et al. (2014); Scholl, Alawadhi (2014) and only 3% of respondents noticed own definition of smart governance. For detailed information see Table 1.

Table 1. Best matching definition of smart governance in city according to author(s).

Author(s)	Number of answers	Share (in %)
Ruhland (2018)	23	46%
Pereira et al. (2018)	17	34%
Estevez and Janowski (2013); Janowski et al. (2012)	6	12%
Gil-Garcia et al. (2014); Scholl and Alawadhi (2016)	3	6%
Other (own definition of respondent)	1	2%
Total	50	100%

The definition of Ruhland (2018) is preferred by the regionalists, the definition of Pereira et al. (2018) is preferred by experts in strategical planning. By the answers of respondents there is not clearly selected one best definition what confirms the difficulty to define the term of smart governance. Based on the research results, the definition should combine the approach of both experts. So, the smart governance in cities is a form of governance based on the processual interplay among a diverse set of stake-holders organized in various external and internal structures and organizations, driven and facilitated by technology and data with the appropriate legislation policies, focused on allocating decision-making rights to stakeholders and enabling them to participate in effective and efficient decision-making processes to achieve substantive outputs for cities and procedural changes embodied in the improving of the quality of life in cities.

Benefits of Smart Governance in City
Based on literature research (Savoldelli et al. 2014; Castelnovo et al. 2015; Osella et al. 2016; Navío-Marco and Anand 2018; Guenduez et al. 2018; Pereira et al. 2018; Tomor et al. 2019; Thon and Nhu 2020) and own previous research we set together group of 16 potential benefits of smart governance in the city, that were evaluated by experts involved in the research. Experts marked each potential benefit with grade from 1 (strongly disagree) to 5 (strongly agree). Results are presented in Fig. 2.

As benefits with highest mark (4,27) were selected increasing administrative efficiency and interoperability, promoting social justice together with improving the quality of life in cities. On the second place, but with little difference, there is enabling stakeholders to become more knowledgeable and more skilled (mark 4,21) followed by improving

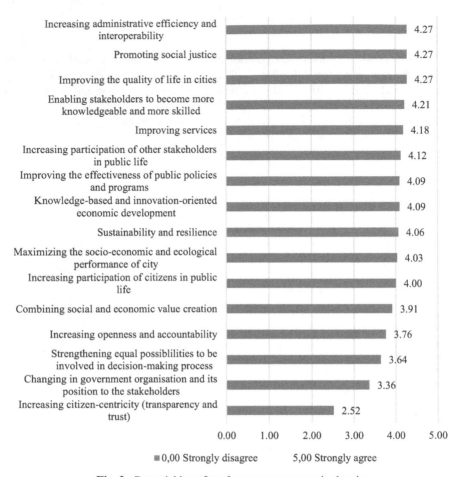

Fig. 2. Potential benefits of smart governance in the city

services (mark 4,18), increasing participation of other stakeholders in public life (mark 4,12), knowledge-based and innovation oriented economic development and improving the effectiveness of public policies and programs (both mark 4,09). According to experts, smart governance in the city increases participation of citizens in public life (mark 4,00), but at the same time increasing citizen-centricity (transparent and trust) is the benefit with the lowest mark (2,52). This is quite surprisingly contradictory.

Based on the research results, the identified benefits of smart governance in cities can be divided into three groups. The first group includes the impacts on the quality of life in the cities (better social and economic conditions, value creation, social justice, performance of the city, sustainability, resilience, etc.). The second group relates to the local municipality and its managing by the local authority (e. g. administrative efficiency, interoperability, effectiveness of public polices, etc.) and the last one is more oriented on stakeholders and its empowerment in local policy (e.g. increasing participation of stakeholders, equality in their role in local policy. However, it is not possible to conclude which of them are dominant because of their overlapping.

Negative Effects of Smart Governance
Other part of our research deals with obstacles and negative effects of smart governance. We defined 7 potential obstacles or negative effects of smart governance (Tomor et al., 2018; Pereira et al. 2018) Experts were asked to evaluate each obstacle/negative effect with grade from 1 (strongly disagree) to 5 (strongly agree). Results are presented in the Fig. 3.

Insufficient learning capacity of local government was marked as the most important obstacle (mark 4). As second critical obstacle experts specified preference of technological innovations instead of the users' needs and expectations (mark 3,73) with little difference followed by exclusion of certain categories of the general population (mark 3,64). On the fourth place with mark 3,36 experts identified higher drop-out rates in participation, especially in e-participation as a potential obstacle of smart governance.

With the use of ICT and collecting necessary data important for improving or development of municipality is closely connected other obstacle citizens transform into operative units for data-collection (mark 3,12). Other examined obstacles scored less than mark 3–negative effects of technology on ecology (e. g. energy consumption and pollution), (mark 2,73) and increasing consumption in the field of nutrition and consumer goods (by other words because of the relatively quick online distribution channels, the customers tent to shop or use more products and services) (mark 2,42).

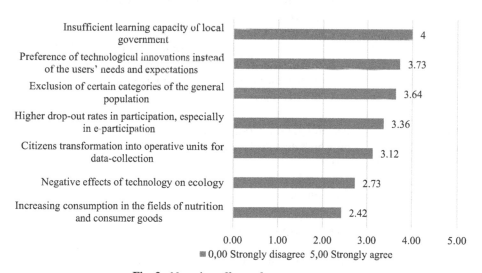

Fig. 3. Negative effects of smart governance

To eliminate these negative effects of smart governance it is necessary to implement smart governance strategically–it means to establish all necessary preconditions in legislative, organizational, procedural as well as technological framework (see more Pereira et al. 2018; Guenduez et al. 2018; Tomor et al. 2019; Thon and Nhu 2020). Moreover, the further research how to prevent them could be helpful for the future development in cities.

Tools of Smart Governance

According to deep literature research and own experience we arranged a list of 28 smart governance tools. We divided tools into four groups–the tools that strongly support the transparency; tools by which citizens become democratic participants in the city's decision-making process; co-production tools and communication tools.

In the Fig. 4 we present the importance of smart governance tools according to expert opinion. Respondents were asked to indicate the importance of each of the 28 smart governance tools using mark from 1 (the least important) to 5 (the most important) for each tool.

We found out, there are very small differences between surveyed tools. According to experts, to the most important smart government tools belong the group of tools supporting transparency, i.e. open data portal on local government issues (mark 4,61), database for sharing information within the municipal office and smart city strategy (mark 4,55). It is followed by tools of co-creation of public services (mark 4,59) and co-production of public services (mark 4,47) and participatory planning (mark 4,47). As the third important group are the tools for active citizenships and the last group are the communication tools. It is important to mention that up to 19 tools scored the mark 4 or more, that means that according to experts the importance of almost all identified tools is relatively high. On the other hand, the successful implementation of most of them requires well developed IT infrastructure, integrated operational system and interoperability of the collected data.

To find the relationships between the smart governance toolkit and benefits we used the Kendall correlations coefficients. We testified the correlations of each evaluated tools with the each indicated benefit (see Fig. 2). The results of tests are presented in Fig. 5. We present just these one, where was the relationship evaluated as statistically important. The tools are again divided into 4 groups:

- red color - the tools that strongly support the transparency;
- yellow color - tools by which citizens become democratic participants in the city's decision-making process;
- blue color - co-production tools and
- green color - communication tools.

The red numbers in the figure presented that the relationships among the tool and benefit is statistically important, the positive number means a positive correlation–as the benefit is evaluated as "more agree", also the tool is more important. The interpretation of the negative correlation has no informative value in this case.

By the tests results, to the increasing openness and accountability contribute public hearings as well as providing information via website (mind positive correlation). Strong positive correlation was indicated also among increasing citizen-centricity and shared architecture of data systems for multi-level governance and cross-city engagement for knowledge. Discussion forums with representatives of stakeholders's groups contribute

Transparency	
Open data portal on local government issues (online and off-line)	4,61
Database for sharing information within the municipal office	4,55
Smart governance strategy/smart city strategy	4,55
Shared architecture of data systems for multi-level go	4,30
Integrated security system	4,15
Electronic identity	3,97
3D map system	3,70
Cloud storage for sharing documents and information	3,48
Tools supporting democracy citizenship	
Electronic tools of e-democracy (electronic voting, petitions, etc.)	4,31
Participation of stakeholders in working group	4,24
Educational activities oriented to stakeholders	4,00
Co-production of public services	
Co-creation of public services	4,59
Co-production of public services	4,47
Participatory planning (online and offline)	4,44
Electronic public services/digital services	4,38
Cross-city engagement for knowledge/experience exchange	4,18
Participatory budgeting (online and offline)	3,90
Communication tools	
Online feed-back system from stakeholders	4,39
Discussion forum with representatives of stakeholders	4,33
Public discussions (hearings)	4,06
Online communication via web applications of the municipality	4,03
Online communication via mobile phone applications of the municipality	4,03
Online communication via social networks	4,00
Website of the city	3,91
Hackathons and competitions for stakeholders	3,73
Organising events	3,59
Questionnaire survey	3,48
Contacting stakeholders by post, e-mail, etc.	2,88

Fig. 4. The importance of smart governance tools

to the changes in government organization and its positions to stakeholders. The positive correlation is also between hackathons and competitions for stakeholders and increasing participation of citizens in public life; databases for sharing information with the municipal office and reducing social justice and improving the quality of life in cities.

The research results on the definition of the smart governance confirm the complexity of the Ruhlandt's definition (2018), as well as our approach to this issue. The smart

Toolkits / Benefits	Increasing administrative efficiency and interoperability	Increasing openness and accountability	Improving the effectiveness of public policies and programs	Changing in government organisation and its position to the stakeholders	Increasing citizen-centricity (transparency and trust)	Increasing participation of citizens in public life	Knowledge-based and innovation-oriented economic development	Combining social and economic value creation	Strengthening equal possibilities to be involved in decision-making process	Promoting social justice	Improving the quality of life in cities
Open data portal on local government issues (online and off-line)	0,086	0,007	-0,498**	-0,135	-0,116	-0,183	0,010	-0,076	0,184	0,018	-0,033
Database for sharing information within the municipal office	0,069	0,076	-0,254	0,183	0,243	0,076	0,038	-0,030	0,318*	0,223	0,344*
Shared architecture of data systems for multi-level governance	0,020	0,173	-0,038	0,191	0,329*	0,241	-0,058	0,219	0,063	0,126	-0,066
Educational activities oriented to stakeholders	-0,111	0,044	-0,333*	0,043	0,072	-0,056	-0,003	-0,023	0,090	0,164	0,032
Participatory budgeting (online and offline)	0,137	0,124	0,049	0,013	0,105	0,005	0,072	-0,065	0,177	0,307*	0,134
Co-creation of public services	-0,363*	-0,027	-0,073	-0,055	-0,043	0,112	-0,159	-0,082	-0,210	0,098	-0,119
Cross-city engagement for knowledge experience exchange	-0,071	0,272	-0,263	0,244	0,428**	0,299	0,056	0,154	0,198	0,238	0,150
Public discussion hearings	0,140	0,444**	-0,089	-0,032	0,165	0,215	-0,052	0,089	0,108	0,046	0,113
Discussion forum with representatives of stakeholders' groups	-0,182	0,016	0,169	0,330*	0,228	0,249	0,020	0,116	0,172	0,182	0,165
Contacting stakeholders by post, e-mail, etc.	-0,254	-0,008	-0,196	0,005	-0,046	-0,046	-0,321*	-0,370*	-0,045	0,107	0,089
Website of the city	-0,128	0,323*	-0,058	0,011	0,107	0,141	0,008	0,014	0,229	0,185	0,039
Online communication via social networks	-0,335*	-0,026	0,075	-0,054	0,150	0,165	-0,185	-0,031	0,163	0,145	0,139
Online communication via web applications of the municipality	-0,417**	0,095	0,028	0,079	0,194	0,231	-0,200	-0,090	0,195	-0,023	-0,027
Hackathons and competitions for stakeholders	0,060	0,101	0,067	0,035	0,140	0,369*	0,165	0,267	0,191	0,023	0,195

* p < 0.05 or ** p < 0.01

Fig. 5. Kendall correlation coefficients between benefits and tools of smart governance in local municipalities

governance approach should be seen as a framework for the various types of interaction and cooperation with the stakeholders in the municipalities realized in the traditional way but also with the support of new IT technologies and collecting data what contribute to design more tailored public services and increase quality of life. These expected outputs were also confirmed as benefits of smart governance implementation.

Moreover, the smart governance can be a suitable way how to increase the administrative efficiency and interoperability, eliminate the paper issues and time wasting. However, it is possible only with the knowledgeable and skilled employees with the will to develop their digital and analytical skills, as a basis of learning capacity of local authority.

The key to successful implementation of smart governance is a tricky balance of implementation of technological and social innovations relevant to the stakeholder's needs and expectation with support of interactive communication tools. The looking for optimal balance in these issues can help eliminate the potential obstacles explored also by our research.

5   Conclusions

The paper reflects very actual topic of smart governance in cities strongly influenced by Covid-19 epidemic. The aim of the paper was to point out the importance of smart governance in cities as an innovative component of local policy with special attention paid to the utilization of smart governance tools in elimination of the effects of the COVID-19 pandemic in cities.

Our findings point out that pandemic situation speeded up the implementation of selected tools of smart governance in cities. Consecutive the utilization of smart governance tool and principles enable municipalities to provide services, created development policy and communicate more effectively with citizens, entrepreneurs, and other stakeholders even in time of pandemics. In this case, the COVID-19 showed that the utilization of the smart governance tools should be a regular part of municipal agenda.

In Slovak municipalities, as a totally new tool that has been used in the time of pandemics, are online–electronic meetings of municipal council/parliament and other municipal bodies According to law, municipal parliament should be in session at least each three months. To ensure meeting of local (municipal) parliaments and avoid infection of the new coronavirus some Slovak cites has started to use online meeting. The municipality has the obligation to create and release a video recording till 48 h after the online meeting and to create and release written record of the meeting till 5 days at the website of the city.

Other example of utilization online tools of smart governance in the city is elaboration of strategic development documents. City Žarnovica has started to prepare its strategic program of economic and social development using ICT and online communication. Working groups built up from representatives of city management, municipal parliament, citizens and representatives of university and other stakeholders had scheduled online meetings via MS Teams application and necessary data were collected from open data portals of Regional government and Statistic office of Slovak republic.

The city Banská Bystrica provides for citizens online reservation form for some public services. Register Office offers the possibility for citizens to register on exact date if they need a specific service for example birth certificate for newborn baby etc.

The pandemic situation has accelerated electronization of public services as well as their real practical utilization in Slovakia. Formally, it was possible to use many electronic services before pandemics, but very little things were really prepared and done.

Our research showed that all tools of smart governance are important and optimal way is to mix them with aim to achieve the multichannel communication with stakeholders which significantly influence the forms of interaction and cooperation in co-creating and co-producing of public services and local policy decision making.

Acknowledgement. The paper presents the partial outputs of project VEGA 1/0213/20 Smart Governance in Local Municipalities and VEGA 1/0380/20 Innovative approaches to the development of small and medium cities.

References

Albino, V., Berardi, U., Dangelico, R.M.: Smart cities: Definitions, dimensions, perfomrance and initiatives. J. Urban Technol. **22**, 3–12 (2015)

Baccarne, B., Mechant, P., Schuurman, D.: Empowered cities? An analysis of the strucutre and generated value of the smart city Ghent. In: Dameri, R.P., Rosenthal-Sabroux, C. (eds.) Smart City– How to Create Public and Economic Value with High Technology in Urban Space, pp. 157–182. Springer, Germany (2014). https://doi.org/10.1007/978-3-319-06160-3_8.

Baharudin, H.: Coronavirus: S'pore Government to make its contact-tracing app freely available to developers worldwide. Straits Time. https://www.straitstimes.com/singapore/corona virus-spore-government-to-make-its-contact-tracing-app-freely-available-to (2020). Accessed 08 Mar 2021

Castelnovo, A., et al.: Smart cities governance: The need for a holistic approach to assessing urban participatory policy making. Soc. Sci. Comput. Rev. **34**(6), 724–739 (2015)

Caragliu, A., Del Bo, C., Nijkamp, P.: Smart Cities in Europe. J. Urban Technol. **18**(2), 65–82 (2011)

Cities for all. Empowering Local Governments on Inclusive Pandemic Response. Cities for All Learning Series "Equity and Access in Times of Pandemic" (2020)

Chourabi, H., Nam, T., Walker, S., Gil-Garcia, J.R., Mellouli, S., Nahon, K., et al.: Understanding smart cities: An integrative framework. In: Proceedings of the Annual Hawaii International Conference on System Science, pp. 2289–2297 (2012)

Costa, D.G., Peixoto, J.P.J.: COVID-19 pandemic: A review of smart cities initiatives to face new outbreaks. J. Inst. Eng. Technol. **2**(2), 64–73 (2020)

Das, D., Zhang, J.J.: Pandemic in a smart city: Singapore's COVID-19 management through technology & society. Urban Geogr. (2020)

De Guimarães, J.C.F. et al.: Governance and quality of life in smart cities: Towards sustainable development goals. J. Cleaner Prod. **253** (2020)

Díaz-Díaz, R., Pérez-González, D.: Implementation of social media concepts for e-government: Case study of a social media tool for value co-creation and citizen participation. J. Organ. End User Comput. **28**(3), 18 (2016)

Estevez, E., Janowski, T.: Electronic governance for sustainable development—conceptual framework and state of research. Gov. Inform. Quart. **30**, 94–109 (2013)

ET al. Eurostat, ESPON 2020 Data and Map Updates, 2017, (2020). https://www.espon.eu/sites/
default/files/attachments/Poster%20Regional%20typology%20of%20eGovernment%20inte
ractions.pdf. Accessed 01 Apr 2021

Gil-Garcia, J.R., Helbing, N., Ojo, A.: Being smart: Emerging technologies and innovation in the
public sector. Gov. Inform. Quart. **31**, 1–9 (2014)

Gil-Garcia, J.R., Pardo, T.A., Nam, T.: What makes a city smart? Identifying core components
and proposing an integrative and comprehensive conceptualization. Inform. Policy **20**, 61–87
(2015)

Gil-Garcia, J.R., Zhang, J., Puron-Cid, G.: Conceptualizing smartness in government: An
integrative and multi-dimensional view. Gov. Inform. Quart. **33**(3), 524–534 (2016)

Guendeuz, A.A., Mettler, T., Schedler, K.: Smart Government-participation and empowerment
of citizens in the era of big data and personalized algorithms. HMD Praxis Der Wirthschaft
Informatik **53**(4), 447–487 (2017)

Guenduez, A.A., Singler, S., Tomaczak, T., Schedler, K., Oberli, M.: Smart governmnet success
factors. Swiss Yearbook of Administrative Sciences **9**(1), 96–110 (2018)

Huaxiong, J.: Smart urban governance in the 'smart' era: Why is it urgently needed? Cities **111**,
6 (2021)

Janowski, T., Prado, T.A., Davies, J.: Government information networks-mapping electronic governance cases through public administration concepts. Gov. Inform. Quat. **29**(supplement 1),
1–10 (2012)

Johannessen, M.R., Berntzen, L.: Smart Technologies for Smart Governments: Transparency,
Efficiency and Organizational Issues. Springer, Heidelberg (2018)

Khan, Z., Anjum, A., Soomro, K., Tahir, M.A.: Towards cloud based big data analytics for smart
future cities. J. Cloud Comput. **4**(1), 1–11 (2015). https://doi.org/10.1186/s13677-015-0026-8

Kleinhans, R., Ham, M., Evans-Cowley, J.: Using social media and mobile technologies to
foster engagement and self-organisation in participatory urban planning and neighbourhood
governance. Plan. Pract. Res. **30**(3), 237–247 (2015)

Kumar, V.T.M.: Smart Economy in Smart Cities (2017)

Lee, J., Lee, H.: Developing and validating a citizen-centric typology for smart city services. Gov.
Inform. Quart. **31**(1), 93–105 (2014)

Lombardi, P., Giordano, S., Farouh, H., Wael, Y.: An analytical network model for smart cities.
In: Proceedings of the 11th International Symposium on the Analytical Hierarchy Process,
Sorrento, Italy (2011)

Macintosh, A., et al.: E-methods for Public Engagement. Bristol City Council, Bristol (2004)

Maheshwari, D., Janssen, M.: Reconceptualizing measuring, benchmarking for improving interoperability in smart ecosystems: The effect of ubiquitous data and crowdsourcing. Gov. Inform.
Quart. **31**, 84–92 (2014)

Mellouli, S., Luna-Reyes, L.F., Zhang, J.: Smart government, citizen participation and open data.
Inform. Polity **19**, 1–4 (2014)

Misuraca, G., Reid, A., Deakin, M.: Exploring emerging ICT-enables governance models in European cities: Analysis of the mapping survey to identify key city governance policy areas most
impacted by ICTs. Serville: European Commission, JRC Technical Notes (2011)

Nam, T., Pardo, T.A.: The changing face of a city government: A case study of Philly31. Gov.
Inform. Quart. **31**, 1–9 (2014)

Nam, T., Pardo, T.A.: Conceptualizing smart city with dimensions of technology, people, and institutions. In: Proceedings of the 12th Annual International Conference on Digital Government
Research, College Park, pp. 282–291. New York, USA (2011)

Navarro-Galera, A., Alcaraz-Quiles, F.J., Ortiz-Rodríguez, D.: Online dissemination of information on sustainability in regional governments. Effects of technological factors. Gov. Inform.
Quart. **33**, 53–66 (2016)

Navío-Marco, J., Anand, P.B.: Governance and economics of smart cities: Opportunities and challenges. Telecommun. policy **42**, 795–799 (2018)

Osella, M., Ferro, E., Pautasso, M.E.: Toward a Methodological Approach to Assess Public Value in Smart Cities. In: Gil-Garcia, J., Pardo, T., Nam, T. (eds.) Smarter as the New Urban Agenda, pp. 129–148. Springer, Schwitzerland (2016)

Pereira, G.V., Parycek, P., Falco, E., Kleinhaus, R.: Smart governance in the context of smart cities: A literature review. Inform. Polity **23**(2), 1–20 (2018)

Pereira, G.V., Cunha, M.A., Lampoltshammer, T.J., Parycek, P., Testa, M.G.: Increasing collaboration and participation in smart city governance: A cross-case analysis of smart city initiatives. Inform. Technol. Dev. **23**(3), 526–553 (2017)

Ruhland, R.W.S.: The governance of smart cities: A systematic literature review. Cities **81**, 1–23 (2018)

Savoldelli, A., Codagnone, C., Misuraca, G.: Understanding the eGovernment paradox: Learning from literature and practice on barriers to adoption. Gov. Inf. Q. **31**, 563–571 (2014)

Scholl, H.J., Alawadhi, S.: Smart governance as key to multi-jurisdictional smart city initiatives: The case of the e-CityGov alliance. Soc. Sci. Inform. **55**(2), 1–23 (2016)

Scholl, H.J., Scholl, M.C.: Smart governance: A roadmap of research and practice. In: Iconeference 2017 Proceedings (2017)

Smart cities and inclusive growth. OECD (2020)

Simonofski, A., Asensio, E.S., Wautelet, Y.: Chapter 4 - Citizen participation in the design of smart cities: Methods and management. In: Visvizi, A., Lytras, M. (eds.) Smart Cities: Issues and Challenges. Elsevier (2019)

Thon, N.Q., Nhu, D.T.: Smart urban governance in smart city. IOP Conf. Ser. Mater. Sci. Eng. **869**, 022021 (2020)

Tomor, Z., Meijer, A., Michles, A., Geertman, S.: Smart governance for sustainable cities: Findings from a systematic literature review. J. Urban Technol. **26**(4), 3–27 (2019)

Vaňová, A.: Trends in the Urban Development (2021)

Vitálišová, K., Vaňová, A., Borseková, K., Nagyová, L., Cagáňová, D.: Tools of smart governance in cities of the slovak republic. In: Santos, H., Pereira, G.V., Budde, M., Lopes, S.F., Nikolic, P. (eds.) SmartCity 360 2019. LNICSSITE, vol. 323, pp. 369–387. Springer, Cham (2020). https://doi.org/10.1007/978-3-030-51005-3_31

Vitálišová, K., Vaňová, A., Borseková, K., Rojíková, D.: Promotion as a tool of smart governance in cities. In: Paiva, S., Lopes, S.I., Zitouni, R., Gupta, N., Lopes, S.F., Yonezawa, T. (eds.) SmartCity360° 2020. LNICSSITE, vol. 372, pp. 497–510. Springer, Cham (2021). https://doi.org/10.1007/978-3-030-76063-2_33

Wijnhoven, F., Ehrenhard, M., Kuhn, J.: Open government objectives and participation motivations. Gov. Inform. Quart. **32**(1), 30–42 (2015)

Zanella, A., Bui, N., Castellani, A., et al.: Internet of things for smart cities. IEEE Internet of Things J. **1**(1), 22–32 (2014)

Zhang, J.J., Savage, V.R.: The geopolitical ramifications of COVID-19: The Taiwanese exception. Eurasian Geogr. Econ. (2020)

New Environmental Indicators for Sustainable Cities of Varying Size Scale: The Use Case of France

Clément Conand(✉), Estelle Randria, and Alexandre Le Borgne

Altran Part of Capgemini, 31700 Blagnac, France
clement.conand@altran.com

Abstract. Nowadays, more and more data about our environment are available. Those data might be of various sources and types such as quality of life, energy consumption or any other domain that may have an impact on people's environment. However, when it comes to evaluating the quality of our environment, a lot of approaches exist which are not easy to use. Hence, this paper introduces a new methodology to calculate an environmental score for cities which takes into account pollution (water and air) indicators, energy consumption, soil uses and artificialization and habitat insulation. This method compares those data with social indicators such as unemployment rate and our purpose is to help city leaders to understand the statement of their city on the environmental topics. Moreover, the methodology that is proposed in this paper can be applied by all French cities, regardless of their size, since it only uses free open source verified data. The calculated scores are available on 31 cities of different size from the Occitanie region in France. As a finding of this paper, we identified that bigger cities have a smaller environmental score while smaller cities get higher scores. Environmental low score for big cities is most often due to low air quality, artificialization of soils and high electrical consumption. With the smaller cities, unemployment and poverty rates are lower, as well as drinkable water quality, mostly due to the chlorine quantity in water.

Keywords: Environment governance · Cities environment indicators · Sustainable smart cities · Air pollution · Water pollution

1 Introduction

Many data are collected nowadays about air quality, energy consumption, quality of life… To address environmental issues, their interpretation and the way they are exploited need to be optimized to obtain proper indicators for citizens and city leaders. Those indicators are useful not only to inform the population but also to provide them clues on which directions they need to improve for city development. Those indicators must be accessible and exhaustive. Our objective is to provide a methodology to produce scores with different indicators related to environmental topics, to improve cities development

© ICST Institute for Computer Sciences, Social Informatics and Telecommunications Engineering 2022
Published by Springer Nature Switzerland AG 2022. All Rights Reserved
S. Paiva et al. (Eds.): SmartCity360° 2021, LNICST 442, pp. 381–391, 2022.
https://doi.org/10.1007/978-3-031-06371-8_25

and increase citizens involvement. Ease of use is the core of this methodology: based only on existing and available governmental data and national goals and laws, it is a low-cost solution, and therefore can be available for any city, regardless its size and its state of development.

In order to get citizens involved in environmental change, it is important to provide them not only with detailed and trustworthy information, but also to make them understand the impact of environmental issues on other aspects of their daily life. In fact, giving indicators may prove to be unsuccessful if citizens can't link them to social dimension. The methodology result should be a final score, which could help cities to focus on the main aspects to improve.

2   State of the Art

This study assumes that global warming must be slow down, and citizens want more ecology in their cities. The Intergovernmental Panel on Climate Change (IPCC) reports on climate change 2021 [1] indicate that GHG (Green House Gases) increased in atmosphere since 1750 and mostly for CO_2 (47%), CH_4 (156%) and NO_2 (23%). This human impact influences global surface temperature (+0.8 °C to + 1.3 °C from 1850–1900 to 2010–201911), land precipitation has likely increased, sea level increased by 3.7 mm/yr between 2006 and 2018. In order to include environment protection int their programs, city leaders have to be familiar with those topics.

Sustainability was defined in the 1987 Brundtland report as "the balance of economic, social and environmental development" [2]. More than 413 indicators already exist to evaluate sustainability [3] and ecological impact [4] of cities. The problem with cities sustainability is the citizens and city leader vision of environmental indicators. They receive wrong information about prices, regulations and controls, and indicators are not sufficiently linked to specific environmental effects [5]. Studies suggested environment indicators on many topics like Impervious surface coverage [6].

These environment indicators must be linked to economical. institutional and social indicators [7]. A detailed method to define social indicators for a sustainable smart city was presented in [8].

In France, standards exist for air and water pollution [9, 10], air pollution [11, 12] and insulation of buildings [13] for example, but standards and thresholds is not always understandable for citizen and city leaders. A method based on North of France already exists, it is a study case to determine an environmental score [11] but it requires data which are difficult to obtain, such as "low level of education" or "no access to car" for the 36 000 French cities. The second point is that this method has been developed for mapping representation and not to determine a distinct score for each city. Therefore, we propose a new approach for measuring different indicators related to different topics linked to environment and make them interpretable for anybody.

3   Methodology

Based on literature recommendations, a new methodology was built using existing open access data. The case study is the Occitanie region of France, where interactions and feedbacks from city leaders are at the core of the elaboration of our smart city study. We started with cities which air pollution data were available, as it is not the case for many cities in Occitanie region.

Data used to develop this methodology come from open databases, and are mostly provided by the French governmental data platform [14]. All data sources are available in the tab "Data sources" of the **Supplementary Materiel 1**, which link is in the Acknowledgement. The key points of the methodology are: (1) Available data: they must be easy to find and free; (2) Indicators built from understandable data measures; (3) Any French city, regardless of its size and number of citizens, can apply this method.

First, we studied raw data to identify trends between environmental data, eco-social data, and size of cities. Second, we proposed various scores for different selected indicators before comparing them. All indicators, data, scores and sources for selected cities are available in the "Cities data and scores" tab of the **Supplementary Materiel 1**.

For environmental score, indicators were selected from different categories: water contamination, air pollution, habitat insulation, electrical consumption, gas consumption and natural and artificial surfaces. Those categories include different indicators. For example, air pollution is composed of 12 indicators on $PM_{2.5}$, O_3, NO_2 and SO_2 concentration in the air.

For eco-social conditions, we selected unemployment rate and poverty rate. Finally, cities were classified in three categories: less than 20 000 people (category "Cities 1"), between 20 000 and 100 000 people (category "Cities 2") and more than 100 000 people (category "Cities 3").

Detailed scores are calculated with different methods. For unemployment and poverty, the score is based on unemployment rates (%) and poverty rate (%). This rate is then normalized to 40% for poverty, meaning that 40% of poverty gives a score of 0/100 and 0% of poverty gives a score of 100/100. The 40% value is defined with the maximum values observed. The same method is used for unemployment but with a normalization of 30%.

For water and air pollution, scores are determined based on comparison between measured concentrations and standard concentrations. Standard values for air pollution [9] are 10 $\mu g/m^3$ (on average per day) for $PM_{2.5}$, 120 $\mu g/m^3$ for O_3, 40 $\mu g/m^3$ for NO_2 and 50 $\mu g/m^3$ for SO_2.

For water pollution, we chose many indicators with standard values for most of them [10] except for taste and look, total chlorine and revivable air bacteria at 22 °C in 68 h. For taste and look, a "no comment" gives a 100/100 score, and any special observation gives 0/100. For total chlorine, 0 mg/l gives 100/100 and > 1 mg/l gives 0/100. The 1 mg/l limit for chlorine is chosen with the maximum concentration observed and is discussed in detail in the discussion part of this publication. For the revivable air bacteria at 22 °C in 68 h, < 1 mg/l gives 100/100 when ≥ 1 mg/l gives 0/100. The other scores (bacteria, pH, ammonium and aluminum) are calculated thanks to the standard values, defining the 0/100 scores.

Scores for the EPD (Energetic Performance Diagnostic of buildings) depend on two criteria for which the insulation of buildings show an estimated consumption (from < 51 $kWhEP/m^2$.yr to > 450). The second criteria is the estimated GHG emissions (from < 5 kg_{eqCO2}/m^2.yr to > 80).

Electrical and gas consumption scores are all calculated from consumptions in different sectors that are Residential (R), Tertiary (T), Industrial (I), Agricultural (A) and Other (X). Final scores for those aspects are composed of two calculated scores which are the Per capita electric average consumption for R area (standardized) and for all sectors (standardized). Normalization is defined with the maximum observed values.

Finally, the Total land score is composed of two scores that are the rate of artificial soils and the rate of natural soils. The natural soil score is calculated by adding Forest and semi-natural soil rate, Wetland rate, Water surfaces rate and Natural soil rate.

4   Results and Environmental Scores

First, we analyzed data which can help cities for environmental transition.

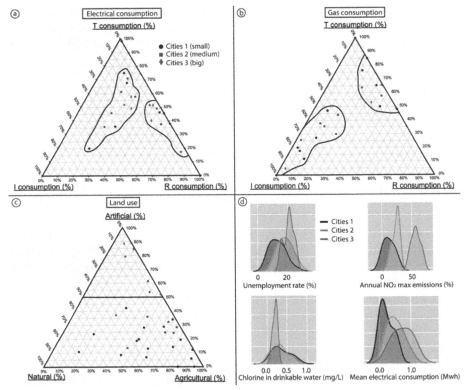

Fig. 1. Available data about **a)** Electrical consumption distribution in the city: rates of Tertiary (T), Industrial (I) and Residential (R) sectors; **b)** Gas consumption distribution in the city: rates of T, I and R sectors; **c)** Land use distribution: rates of artificial, natural, and agricultural lands; **d)** Histogram distribution depending on the cities size are obtain using pandas and seaborn Python libraries. Indicators are unemployment rate (%), annual NO$_2$ emission comparing to the limit standard of emission (%), total chlorine in the drinkable water (mg/L) and mean consumption per citizen for the Residential sector (Mwh).

As energy is a very important aspect in environmental transition, we first studied electrical and gas consumption in cities (Fig. 1a and 1b). Electrical consumption presents two patterns (Fig. 1a): one showing less than 35% of Residential (R) consumption and a distribution of the major component between Industrial (I) and Tertiary (T) consumption. The second one is share between R and T consumption, with a majority of R consumption.

For gas consumption (Fig. 1b), each city shows less than 55% of R contribution, and a majority with less than 30%. Electrical and gas consumption distribution show the major contribution of non-residential activities in the total consumption.

Land use on cities territory (Fig. 1c) is divided into three categories: artificial, agricultural, and natural. This indicator is important for environmental aspect, but also for risk prevention because land use has major impact on it. Flood risks could increase by 255% in 2030 [15] and the reduction of artificial land surfaces could reduce this risk. The distribution of values (Fig. 1c) shows a clear distinction between small cities with a distribution mostly between agricultural and natural land, with a majority on agricultural. For medium and big cities, artificial and agricultural components are the highest with a majority of artificial land. Most of those cities are composed of less than 20% of natural land.

To present the results of social, air pollution, water pollution and electrical consumption, we chose a histogram distribution based on the city size (Fig. 1d). We can observe on those diagrams that unemployment rate, annual NO_2 max emission and mean electrical consumption are growing with the number of citizens in a city. However, chlorine in drinkable water is clearly lower for bigger cities (Cities 3).

The second part of this study is about the calculated scores, their analysis and review, and linkage between them.

Table 1 introduces scores that we calculated for every group of cities. As it is shown, we calculated two main scores that are Unemployment-Poverty and Environmental scores. Those scores are calculated as the average of their sub-scores which have not been weighted for our approach. All scores are calculated on a scale of 0 to 100.

Unemployment-Poverty score is calculated from both unemployment and poverty sub-scores and a higher score indicates good social conditions and a lower one poverty and unemployment.

Environmental score is calculated on a scale of 0 to 100, and a good score means low pollution, consumption, and natural land. This environmental final score is the average of six intermediate scores which are as follows:

- Water quality score evaluates quality of water in cities. Big cities have better scores due to lower concentration of chlorine, aluminum and ammonium and higher number of indicators.
- Air pollution score evaluates quality of air in cities. For this score, SO_2 is quite difficult to analyze because of a lack of available data. NO_2 score is the most discriminating and is often exceeding thresholds as it is the case for $PM_{2.5}$.
- EPD (Energetical Performance Diagnostic) score evaluates energy performance of people housing. This indicator doesn't present any trend at first sight.
- Electrical consumption score shows clearly lower scores for bigger cities, and mostly for the Residential sector.

Table 1. Scores average, median and standard deviation (SD) for the 3 city groups. EPD (Energetical Performance Diagnostic); GHG (Green House Gases); consumption R (Residential); consumption AS (All Sectors)

City size (1, 2, 3)	Cities 1 (small)			Cities 2 (medium)			Cities 3 (big)		
Statistical indicators	Average	Median	SD	Average	Median	SD	Average	Median	SD
Unemployment score	55.6	59.3	17.5	38.9	40.3	16.5	30.9	30.0	12.2
Poverty score	65.5	67.5	14.3	46.5	50.0	15.6	31.3	28.8	13.9
Total Poverty-unemployment score	*59.7*	*59.3*	*15.3*	*42.7*	*45.2*	*15.1*	*31.1*	*29.4*	*13.0*
Bacteria in water score	100.0	100.0	0.0	100.0	100.0	0.0	100.0	100.0	0.0
Water taste and look score	100.0	100.0	0.0	100.0	100.0	0.0	100.0	100.0	0.0
Chlorine in water score	63.5	72.0	22.0	68.2	66.5	20.5	79.0	77.5	5.9
Water pH score	67.9	70.0	17.7	55.0	55.0	13.5	63.8	62.5	10.3
Water ammonium score	100.0	100.0	0.0	100.0	100.0	0.0	100.0	100.0	0.0
Water aluminum score	78.1	79.5	17.2	75.2	72.5	16.9	82.8	82.8	11.0
Water Revive 22 °C bacteria score	68.8	100.0	47.9	70.0	100.0	48.3	75.0	100.0	50.0
Number of water indicator score	86.6	85.7	17.1	94.3	100.0	10.0	92.9	92.9	8.2
Total water quality score	**82.2**	**84.0**	**9.2**	**83.3**	**86.6**	**8.0**	**86.7**	**89.2**	**7.5**
PM$_{2.5}$ air pollution score	41.5	40.2	7.7	34.4	24.6	19.1	32.3	33.7	4.8
O$_3$ air pollution score	70.2	70.1	3.2	70.0	69.3	4.6	71.9	71.4	1.3
NO$_2$ air pollution score	91.6	93.1	7.5	82.3	80.3	4.6	53.9	53.6	9.3
SO$_2$ air pollution score	89.9	89.9	12.5						
Total air pollution score	**70.3**	**69.6**	**13.1**	**71.1**	**75.7**	**10.4**	**52.7**	**53.7**	**4.7**
EPD GHG score	58.0	74.7	28.9	49.1	45.6	13.7	58.5	58.7	4.2
EPD consumption score	42.8	56.6	27.6	34.6	33.1	13.9	45.6	46.4	5.9
Total EPD Score	**50.4**	**66.7**	**28.0**	**41.8**	**38.8**	**13.3**	**52.1**	**52.4**	**4.5**
Electrical consumption R score	78.1	83.7	18.7	51.7	54.7	23.5	31.4	30.3	28.1
Electrical consumption AS score	72.4	79.7	27.3	56.6	63.9	22.5	45.3	53.8	25.3

(*continued*)

Table 1. (*continued*)

City size (1, 2, 3)	Cities 1 (small)			Cities 2 (medium)			Cities 3 (big)		
Statistical indicators	Average	Median	SD	Average	Median	SD	Average	Median	SD
Total electrical consumption score	**75.2**	**78.1**	**19.2**	**54.1**	**58.0**	**19.0**	**38.3**	**43.2**	**25.5**
Artificial land score	83.2	85.8	11.7	55.9	66.0	25.3	34.5	31.7	24.9
Natural land score	23.8	23.0	20.3	10.2	6.5	11.7	10.5	2.9	17.0
Total land use score	**53.5**	**52.9**	**11.8**	**33.0**	**36.9**	**16.5**	**22.5**	**16.2**	**19.4**
Gas consumption R score	62.6	93.9	47.6	90.8	95.1	12.6	98.1	98.1	2.4
Gas consumption AS score	66.4	97.3	45.3	97.5	97.3	2.3	99.3	99.3	0.4
Total gas consumption score	**64.5**	**95.6**	**46.3**	**94.2**	**96.2**	**7.4**	**98.7**	**98.7**	**1.4**
Total environmental score	*66.4*	*67.2*	*5.9*	*62.4*	*63.1*	*4.9*	*54.7*	*54.1*	*7.0*

- Gas consumption score is difficult to interpret since gas is less used in big cities than in rural cities.
- Land use score evaluates the usage of land especially by analyzing how much natural land is available for population. The biggest cities present more artificial lands and thus, lower scores.

After those observations on the different topics, we decided to study correlations between our different scores (Fig. 2) to highlight noticeable relationships between them.

As data were originally collected by hand and stored in a datasheet, performing statistics calculation was not possible because of heterogeneity of the original datasheet. We first separated all data by topics or subtopics in different datasheets and ensured homogeneity concerning names and format conventions. Only raw data were extracted, and scores calculation has been automatized with Python code, and then applied to fill our new datasheets. That way, scores can be calculated automatically whenever new data is added and new cities are interesting by this method. Once this step was realized, it was possible to perform correlations.

Correlation used in this method was the Pearson correlation, used to determine whether a linear relationship exists between two variables. Concerning EPD scores, we noticed that it has a moderate positive correlation with the unemployment-poverty score. A city with low unemployment and poverty tends to have a better EPD score. An unexpected finding is that the correlation between EPD and electric scores is very low, even though we could expect electric consumption to be strongly related to EPD. A focus on $PM_{2.5}$ score highlights two interesting correlations: a moderate positive correlation with water quality and a strong positive correlation with the land use score. The first correlation proves that $PM_{2.5}$ and water quality scores increase in parallel, which means air quality and water quality hold the same priority for cities leaders.

However, the correlation between chlorine score and $PM_{2.5}$ is moderately negative, indicating that the good quality of drinkable water in small cities is probably due to an important chlorine quantity. The second correlation shows that when more natural land is available, $PM_{2.5}$ score is better, as air is cleaner than in cities. The strongest correlation is between the NO_2 score and the number of inhabitants of a city with a R = −0.84: this very strong negative correlation demonstrates that a rise of the population is linked to a decrease in the NO_2 score. Two other interesting correlations are the ones between population, land use and electricity scores. The negative moderate correlations show that when population increases, the two scores decrease. To sum up, a growing number of inhabitants tends to be incompatible with an improvement of air quality score, land use score and electricity score, which is consistent with the fact that it is difficult to favor city expansion while improving environmental issues: NO_2 production increases, as well as land artificialization and energy consumption.

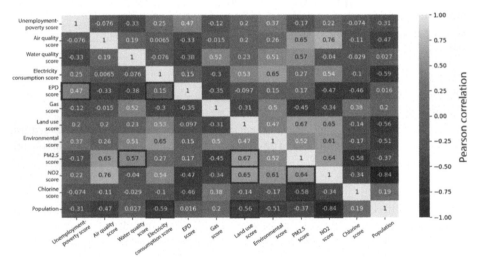

Fig. 2. Pearson correlations between scores. A high absolute value indicates a high correlation when a low absolute value indicates a low correlation. A positive value indicates a positive correlation when a negative value indicates a negative correlation. Green framed values are the most interesting and comment values. (Color figure online)

5   Discussion and Conclusion

In this paper, we proposed a new methodology to calculate an environmental score of cities compared with eco-social score. We built this methodology with the goal to use only open-source accessible data to make it as generic as possible.

Energy consumption analysis of cities shows that tertiary and industrial sectors represent the biggest part of energy, compared with residential consumption. It is an important indicator for cities if they want to reduce consumption. However, scores are even more distant to each other for the residential sector with higher consumption for the bigger cities, showing a clear difference of citizens consumption depending on the size of the city.

Scores computed on 31 cities in the Occitanie region of France show that the increase in citizens number is correlated with an increase in NO_2 and $PM_{2.5}$ air pollution, artificialization of land and electric consumption (Fig. 2). The very low correlation between EPD and electric consumption shows that cities with a good insulation of buildings do not present lower electrical consumption. This is maybe because the higher correlation of unemployment-poverty score is with EPD score, indicating that richer cities have good insulation but high consumption.

Our scores were built considering that each aspect (energy consumption, air pollution, unemployment…) holds an equivalent weight in the final environmental and social scores. But it is possible that each of them may have a different influence and should be weighted differently in our calculation in order to obtain finer-grain results. This solution will be explored in the future.

To discuss standards and limits of pollution and environment, we want to discuss the adherence to current standards and the absence of standards for some of the pollutants. Current standards in air pollution are not met for most pollutants and it is even more true for $PM_{2.5}$ (standard is 10 $\mu g/m^3$) with maximum one-day average of 75.6 $\mu g/m^3$ and NO_2 (standard is 40 $\mu g/m^3$) with maximum one-day average of 105.4 $\mu g/m^3$. The second observation is that the bigger is the city, the higher is the $PM_{2.5}$ and mostly NO_2 pollution. Finally, there are very few stations measuring SO_2 concentration (maximum one-day average of 89 $\mu g/m^3$) and even fewer measuring H_2S concentration (maximum one-day average of 24.6 $\mu g/m^3$) [16]. The number of stations measuring those sulfur gases should increase for a more detailed analysis.

Some pollutants do not have standards in France, and the best example is chlorine in drinkable water. Chlorine used as a disinfectant has impacts on transmission of antibiotic-resistant genes [17]. Standards indicate impact on human health for concentrations of free chlorine >2 mg/l [18–20] but the major part of chlorine studies are old and a more recent study suggests a limit of 0.2 mg/l [21], 10 times lower. A recent detailed study could be interesting to identify potential effects of chlorine on human health in intermediary concentrations (<2 mg/l).

Data in this study reveal concentrations between 0.03 and 0.78 mg/l with clearly lower concentration for Cities 3 (Fig. 1d). This difference is probably due to a difference of water disinfectant method: medium and small cities do not have the same water treatment plants as the big cities and compensate with additional chlorine.

To discuss actual standards, bacterial standard for drinkable water is set to ≤ 0 n/(100mL). The problem is that detection methodologies do not reach this precision, and most measurements indicate <1 n/(100mL) and the standard should be changed.

Now that our methodology is available, we should confront it to more cities from other regions. With more data, we will be able to carry out further studies and confirm whether correlation exists between our scores, because performing correlations now will lead to non-significant results as there are too few data for big cities (Cities 3). Because we need to provide more results for comparison and performance evaluation sake, the future work on this topic will be to collect needed data to calculate those scores on the 36 000 French cities. To assess the relevance of our scores, we will also collect feedback from cities on their usability. To progress further, we are developing an automated solution written in Python language with a web site interface. This tool will allow all citizens and city leaders to see environmental scores on all French cities. The main differences with other existing scores [11] is the reproducibility aspect of our method which can be calculated for all French cities, the easy access of the required data and the understandable scores.

With Covid-19 epidemic, lots of CO_2 sensors are installed everywhere, and many data will soon be available to study evolution of concentrations of gas in closed spaces. Thus, we could complete our study with an indoor air quality score.

Acknowledgment. The authors acknowledge the financial support by the Digital Factory (Altran part of Capgemini) and we greatly appreciated the assistance of Martine Aubret and David Barret. The **Supplementary Materials 1** is shared and made freely available on the open-access repository Mendeley Data (https://doi.org/10.17632/j66797tdw9.2 and link: https://data.mendeley.com/dat asets/j66797tdw9/draft?a=e3608fb5-fe27-4e07-b9e8-afeb90488b11).

References

1. Masson-Delmotte, V., et al. (eds.): Summary for policymakers in Climate Change 2021: The Physical Science Basis. Contribution of Working Group I to the Sixth Assessment Report of the Intergovernmental Panel on Climate Change, Cambridge University Press, août 2021
2. Glossary of summaries - EUR-Lex: https://eur-lex.europa.eu/summary/glossary/sustainable_development.html (consulté le juill. 15, 2021)
3. Mori, K., Christodoulou, A.: Review of sustainability indices and indicators: towards a new City Sustainability Index (CSI). Environ. Impact Assess. Rev. **32**(1), 94–106 (2012)
4. Joss, S., Tomozeiu, D., Cowley, R.: Eco-city indicators: governance challenges. Sustain. City VII Urban Regen. Sustain. **1109** (2012)
5. Button, K.: City management and urban environmental indicators. Ecol. Econ. **40**(2), 217–233 (2002)
6. Arnold, C.L., Jr., Gibbons, C.J.: Impervious surface coverage: the emergence of a key environmental indicator. J. Am. Plann. Assoc. **62**(2), 243–258 (1996)
7. Valentin, A., Spangenberg, J.H.: A guide to community sustainability indicators. Environ. Impact Assess. Rev. **20**(3), 381–392 (2000)
8. Marsal-Llacuna, M.-L.: City indicators on social sustainability as standardization technologies for smarter (citizen-centered) governance of cities. Soc. Indic. Res. **128**(3), 1193–1216 (2016)
9. Article R 221-1 du code de l'environnement, vol. Partie réglementaire, Livre II, Titre II, Chapitre 1er, Section 1 (2007)
10. European Community: Directive 2008/105/CE du Parlement européen et du Conseil du 16 décembre 2008 établissant des normes de qualité environnementale dans le domaine de l'eau, modifiant et abrogeant les directives du Conseil 82/176/CEE, 85/513/CEE, 84/156/CEE, 84/491/CEE, 86/280/CEE et modifiant la directive 2000/60/CE. J. Officiel de l'Union européenne, déc. 16 (2008)
11. Lanier, C., Deram, A., Cuny, M.-A., Cuny, D., Occelli, F.: Spatial analysis of environmental inequalities caused by multiple air pollutants: A cumulative impact screening method, applied to the north of France, Ecol. Indic. **99**, 91–100 (2019)
12. Brousmiche, D., et al.: Data for the assessment of vulnerability and resilience in the field of environmental health in the north of France. Data Brief, p. 107220 (2021)

13. Articles R 126–15 à R 126–29 du code de la construction et de l'habitation (Diagnostique de performance energetique) (2021)
14. Accueil - data.gouv.fr. https://www.data.gouv.fr/fr/ (consulté le juill. 30, 2021)
15. Bubeck, P., Dillenardt, L., Alfieri, L., Feyen, L., Thieken, A.H., Kellermann, P.: Global warming to increase flood risk on European railways. Clim. Change **155**(1), 19–36 (2019). https://doi.org/10.1007/s10584-019-02434-5
16. Atmo Occitanie: https://data-atmo-occitanie.opendata.arcgis.com/datasets/2ab16a5fb61f42c1a689fd9cc466383f/explore?location=43.764492,2.776483,8.00 (consulté le août 17, 2021)
17. Ghernaout, D., Ibn-Elkhattab, R.O.: Is not it time to stop using chlorine for treating water?, Open Access Libr. J. **7**(1), 1 (2020)
18. Hsu, L.H., Hoque, E., Kruse, P., Ravi Selvaganapathy, P.: A carbon nanotube based resettable sensor for measuring free chlorine in drinking water. Appl. Phys. Lett. **106**(6), 063102 (2015)
19. Hoque, E., Hsu, L.H., Aryasomayajula, A., Sclvaganapathy, P.R., Kruse, P.: Pencil-drawn chemiresistive sensor for free chlorine in water, IEEE Sens. Lett. **1**(4), 1–4 (2017)
20. U.S. Environmental Protection Agency: Disinfectant use in water treatment. In: EPA Guidance Manual Alternative Disinfectants and Oxidants, 1st ed., vol. Chap II, Washington, DC, pp. 1–54 (1999)
21. Sikder, M., Daraz, U., Lantagne, D., Saltori, R.: Effectiveness of multilevel risk management emergency response activities to ensure free chlorine residual in household drinking water in Southern Syria. Environ. Sci. Technol. **52**(24), 14402–14410 (2018)

Scalable and Sustainable Community Networks for Inclusive Smart Cities

John Marlo Evangelista[1]([✉]), Karyn Maglalang[1], Lope Beltran II[2],
Colline Estrada[1], Pio Jonel Mijares[1], Ken Abryl Eleazar Salanio[2],
Jhon Aaron Trajano[1,3], John Patrick Zamora[1],
Vladimir Axl Von Carlo Zurbano[1], Isabel Montes-Austria[1],
Cedric Angelo Festin[2], Matthew Podolsky[4], and Roel Ocampo[1]

[1] Electrical and Electronics Engineering Institute, University of the Philippines
Diliman, Quezon City, Philippines
{john.marlo.evangelista,karyn.maglalang}@eee.upd.edu.ph
[2] Department of Computer Science, University of the Philippines Diliman,
Quezon City, Philippines
[3] College of Computer Studies, New Era University, Quezon City, Philippines
[4] University of California Berkeley, Berkeley, USA

Abstract. Community networks can help build smart cities by interconnecting and empowering the underserved and unconnected. However,
communities often face financial and human resource constraints when
building and maintaining such networks. We present a network architecture and some design principles aimed at addressing issues of sustainability and scaling in the face of such resource constraints. With
our proposed approach however, component selection, qualification, and
testing become additional tasks for the community. Programmability and
network function virtualization may instead help address compatibility
issues, promote resource pooling at the edge, and allow dynamic resource
allocation.

Keywords: Community networks · Software-defined networks · IPv6
transition

1 Introduction

Smart cities require an interconnected citizenry. However, in many economies,
the digital divide remains a real and difficult challenge to solve, even in urban
areas. One indicator that the problem still exists in a significant way is the
disproportionate distribution of Internet access, which in turn may be attributed
to several factors: lack of economic incentives for Internet service providers to
invest in areas with potentially low returns, low purchasing power and related
socio-economic factors in targeted areas [14], high infrastructure development
and maintenance costs, difficult terrain and geography, and other factors not
easily addressed by commercial or government-led initiatives [30].

© ICST Institute for Computer Sciences, Social Informatics and Telecommunications Engineering 2022
Published by Springer Nature Switzerland AG 2022. All Rights Reserved
S. Paiva et al. (Eds.): SmartCity360° 2021, LNICST 442, pp. 392–407, 2022.
https://doi.org/10.1007/978-3-031-06371-8_26

It is in this context that community networks continue to be an interesting proposition in addressing the problem of Internet access. There are certainly success stories worth replicating, such as the guifi.net effort [31] and many others [24] from which many lessons continue to be learned. A recurring and common theme is that unlike "top-down" and centrally-driven commercial or government-led efforts, community networks tend to be more grassroots-oriented, with varying models and degrees of organization and management [13]. However, it is precisely the grassroots orientation coupled with the socio-economic context that poses an additional challenge: community networks might indeed be a good solution in economically disadvantaged places, but these are exactly the places where the material resources and specialist skills needed to plan, establish, operate and sustain a community network may be in relatively short supply.

This brings us to two design goals worth considering at an early stage of conceptualization and planning: scalability and sustainability. In the context of this paper, we consider scalability as the ability of a community network to expand either (a) horizontally to accommodate more participants (users and providers), greater usage, or to enhance performance quality, or (b) vertically to be able to provide new and useful services. On the other hand, we define sustainability as the ability to assure continuous operation, management, and growth of a community network through the availability or application of necessary material and human resources as well as policy, social, and organizational frameworks. While there may be a myriad of other worthwhile design objectives and considerations, especially as may be gleaned from the rich experiences of relatively mature community networks [13], we focus on these two objectives that motivate our basic technical question: can an open and software-defined approach help build scalable and sustainable community networks, given the context and constraints in which these networks are situated?

This paper describes our modest 'work in progress' effort to address this question. We share the motivation, technical design principles, and initial experiences in deploying an experimental version of our Bayanihanets community network [25], now based on open and software-defined approaches. Our notion of 'open' refers to both hardware and software platforms with publicly available and extensible source code, designs, abstractions, or interfaces. On the other hand, 'software-defined' may somewhat overlap with the 'open' approach and will encompass the wide range of approaches including control plane - data plane logical separation [18], network programmability and standardized interfaces [22], network functions virtualization [15], network slicing [27], and similar technologies.

Specifically, we wish to explore whether an open and software-defined approach would:

- ensure better interoperability among devices, making it relatively easy for new participants, whether permanent or transient, to join;
- enable rapid deployment of either community- or externally-provided services, even 'deep' within the community footprint itself; and

– provide a more uniform view not only of the network but of user- and community-owned and managed devices as well, reducing the effort and expertise required to support and manage highly diverse and physically distributed hardware and software platforms.

This paper is further organized as follows: in Sect. 2, we pose some design challenges to community network deployment approaches vis-à-vis future needs for scalability and sustainability. Section 3 presents our proposed architecture, as well as results from evaluating candidate platforms and functional components. In Sect. 3.3, we briefly share some initial results as we tested these in two new experimental sites for Bayanihanets, our local community network effort. Finally, in Sect. 4, we conclude with further recommendations for current and future community network operators.

2   Designing Scalable and Sustainable Community Networks

2.1   IP Addressing in the Context of Scalability and Sustainability

It is neither scalable nor sustainable to provide Internet-routable IPv4 addresses to household customer premises equipment (CPEs) especially for community networks with limited Internet-routable IPv4 address pool. IPv6 provides not only larger address spaces but also the ability to use Internet-routable prefixes even within the community mesh itself, aside from link-local addresses. To ensure that interconnecting with the community mesh is a 'plug-and-play' experience without the need to configure addresses and routes explicitly, we use BMX6, an open-source distance-vector mesh routing protocol [26] on the mesh backbone and to join new access nodes, including home routers. BMX6 supports address autoconfiguration of participating interfaces by combining a default prefix (fd66:66:66::/64) with the EUI-64 suffix. BMX6 Unicast Host Network Announcements (UHNA) may be used to advertise IP addresses and internal home subnets at the option of the user, allowing community users to share internally-hosted services to the rest of the community. This paves the way for members to collectively host and support community services such as IoT services and public safety IP-based CCTV (closed-circuit television).

Not all end-devices, sites, or services on the Internet fully support native IPv6 yet, so we still need to support IPv4. Furthermore, some home users may prefer to keep whatever RFC 1918 IPv4 addressing scheme they already have. To allow users to join without needing to change their internal addressing schemes and to support IPv4-only devices and sites, we use 464XLAT [21] to allow traversal over the IPv6-only community mesh and provide network address translation services (provider-side address translation, or PLAT) at gateways to Internet uplinks.

The PLAT network address translation service needs a pool of Internet-routable IPv4 addresses. For community networks, having its own allocation of portable IPv4 addresses may be a challenge either because (1) it might be too expensive to secure membership and IP resources from the appropriate Internet registry, or (2) membership may require a legal entity to be in place, which might not immediately apply to a nascent community network. For the time being, it might have to do with relatively fewer routable IPv4 address assignments from providers. This is an excellent motivating factor for setting up a community network: by purchasing transit Internet access in bulk, the community is better positioned to obtain concessions such as non-portable IPv4 assignments. We also believe that as IPv6 adoption increases on both end-devices, sites, and services on the Internet, the need for larger routable IPv4 pools for PLATs will hopefully decrease.

2.2   Open Platforms, Open Access

Open platforms. We believe the use of free and open-source platforms whenever possible is desirable for two reasons. Firstly, it promotes uniformity and interoperability in deployed and managed platforms, consequently allowing the development of a larger pool of collaborators willing and able to help manage the network. Secondly, open platforms promote community participation in design and configuration decisions: configuration settings, applications, and services may be published, reviewed, downloaded, or pushed in the most transparent manner. This is in stark contrast with the opaque, closed, and often secretive way in which many commercial providers manage customer premises equipment (CPEs) deployed for users.

As a specific example, a platform worth consideration is OpenWrt [10]. Community members may reflash commercially available compatible access points. OpenWrt APs and mesh nodes may natively support IPv4/IPv6 dual-stack, the 464XLAT IPv6 transition mechanism, and BMX6 routing for connectivity to the community mesh backbone. Community members may also share experiences selecting and reflashing commercially available access points, mainly because not all commercially available models are guaranteed to work with OpenWrt. Sharing local experiences and information regarding locally available products is invaluable in this regard.

Open Access. Although an orthogonal issue, we believe that open access may be a worthwhile, if not an altruistic design goal for community networks. If access to community services or the Internet is to be provided to transient or visiting users and capacity might be a concern, lower-than-best (LBE) effort QoS may be provided [25]. In turn, mechanisms like these may be deployed and supported more uniformly and transparently through the use of standardized yet free and open platforms. With Linux-based platforms, it is relatively straightforward to access and configure appropriate queue disciplines to provide LBE QoS to visiting users.

Aside from promoting shared learning experiences and knowledge pools, we believe that free and open-source platforms democratize access and participation in community networks by lowering the barrier to entry that might be posed by, say, standardizing to a single proprietary platform. Open platforms therefore may not only promote open access (basic usage) of the network and its services, but also open up access to operations, management, and decision-making, which in turn encourages better community participation in the management of the pooled resource [28].

2.3   Programmability and Virtualization from Access to Core

The use of programmable and virtualizable hardware, not only at the core but also towards the access edge, may also help with several aspects of scalability and sustainability. Network functions virtualization (NFV) may be used to address issues of compatibility, promote cost-sharing and resource pooling even at localized scales, and allow dynamic resource allocation. It may also help address the human resource challenges of running a network by reducing the need to master diverse and proprietary platforms, and by promoting service orchestration and network manageability at a greater scale. ISPs are potentially able to reduce annual operational expenses compared to legacy IPv4-based networks, thus providing sustainability and affordability for the community [16]. Moreover, the use of cheaper cost-effective commodity WiFi hardware makes SDN-based networks more flexible in their network architecture [29].

3   An Open and Software-Defined Bayanihanets

In this section, we discuss our application of the design principles and goals previously outlined to an evolved version of Bayanihanets, our approach to building community-based networks based on bayanihan, a local traditional and cultural concept of cooperation typically used within the context of community-based volunteer work [25]. The word "bayanihan" in turn is rooted in "bayani," which in the 1600s translated to "common labor or work" [23].

Our earlier work on Bayanihanets focused on the technical mechanisms needed to incentivize individual participation in community-based sharing of network resources by implementing a cooperative networking system using bandwidth aggregation, where owners enjoy the sum of their own bandwidth and whatever bandwidth they could borrow from other contributors. It was designed to make sharing more tangible by providing tools for managing, tracking, and measuring the network resources being shared, and the network resources being consumed while showing the impact of each user's activity on the overall network.

Our current work however evolves Bayanihanets further by incorporating the design principles and goals into its new architecture, presented in the next section. By software-defined Bayanihanets, we do not necessarily refer to the conventional use of frameworks such as OpenFlow, but instead we take the broader view of using programmable and dynamically-instantiated components and services within the network [19].

While other community networks focus on OpenFlow-based SDN approaches [12], our goal is to introduce an "open-access" architecture that will provide interoperability and programmability among the accessible devices in the market, making it relatively easier for community members to join the network. This will further help scale the community network to a wider set of cooperators. This is also made possible by transforming services into virtual network functions, allowing them to be installed in commodity hardware and used as virtualized customer premises equipment [17].

3.1 Architecture

Figure 1 illustrates the evolved architecture. We maintain the original features and functionalities of Bayanihanets, such as allowing users with personal Internet subscriptions to share their uplink capacity on a less-than-best effort (LBE) basis [25]. One of the new features is using a purely IPv6 backbone mesh. To support IPv4 on both the access side and the Internet, we used 464XLAT [21] through the Jool [6] network address translation package for stateless IPv4-to-IPv6 translation on the customer side translator (CLAT) and stateful IPv6-to-IPv4 translation on the provider side translator (PLAT) functions. Routing on the mesh backbone uses BMX6 for 'plug-and-play' functionality. To ensure support for both Jool and BMX6, we require CLAT user gateway devices and BMX6 meshing nodes to support Openwrt [10].

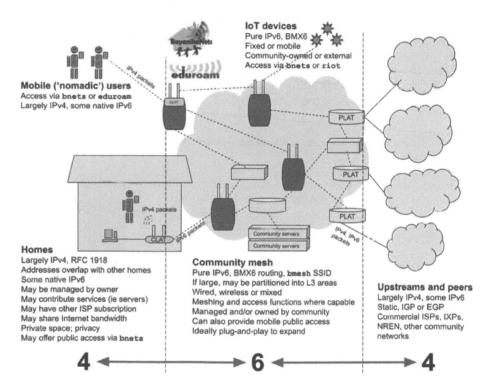

Fig. 1. Bayanihanets community network architecture

Prior to deployment, we went through a component selection process where candidate brands and models were tested. This is discussed in the next section.

3.2   Component Qualification and Selection

While it was relatively straightforward to draw up an architecture based on our design goals and objectives, mapping these to compatible, locally available, and crucially, relatively affordable components was another matter. There were inevitable conflicts between price, platform resources such as memory and processing ability (which would be crucial for programmability), support for open firmware and add-on software components, and performance. These are discussed in the following sections.

User Access and Backbone Mesh Devices. Since OpenWrt support was an important requirement, we searched for prospective user access and backbone mesh devices by first considering the cheapest and locally available Openwrt-compatible devices. We initially settled for a device marketed as an outdoor WiFi meshing platform with the following published specifications [1]. Some of the technical specifications of this platform, called 'Platform A' in the rest of this document, are listed in Table 1.

After installing Openwrt as its main firmware and installing Jool and BMX6 modules, Platform A was positioned as the device under test (DUT) in a simple *traffic source* → *DUT* → *traffic sink* logical configuration.

Table 1. Technical specifications of Platform A, targeted for user access and backbone mesh use.

Hardware resources	CPU 650 MHz, single core, 16 MB flash, 128 MB RAM Qualcomm Atheros QCA9531 SoC Qualcomm Atheros QCA9886
Wireless	300 Mbps 2.4 GHz 802.11b/g/n 867 Mbps 5 GHz 802.11a/n/ac 500 mW (27 dBm) max TX; −96 dBm RX sensitivity Dual external 5 dBi omnidirectional antennas
Wired interfaces	2 × 10/100 Mbps Ethernet

User Access Device Performance. We wanted to see what users of "Platform A" might expect with respect to performance, particularly as a user access device performing CLAT functionality. We generated synthetic TCP traffic using the iPerf3 tool, mostly with default TCP settings (MSS = 1448), letting it seek a steady-state throughput based on the bottleneck bandwidth on the line.

From a macro perspective, the observed steady-state aggregate TCP throughputs across all flows were around 99.5 Mbps, 92.8 Mbps, and 52.2 Mbps for the no-CLAT-device, no-translation-required (i.e. IPv6-only flows), and translation-required (i.e. IPv4-only flows) cases, respectively. Figures 2a and b provide micro views on the impact on each flow as the number of concurrent flows increases. In Fig. 2a, we see that insertion of the CLAT device along the path results in

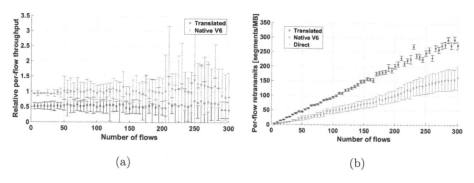

(a)   (b)

Fig. 2. *(a)* Per-flow TCP throughputs, CLAT on "Platform A" relative to the 'no-CLAT' baseline case. This compares throughput performance for pure IPv6 (orange, no translation) and pure IPv4 (blue, with translation) flows through 100 Mbps network interfaces. All values are relative to the 'no-CLAT' average per-flow throughput performance. Error bars extending below the '0' y-axis value are no longer shown here. *(b)* Mean TCP segment retransmissions per unit volume of data transmitted, per-flow, as the number of concurrent flows increase. Points in yellow are for the control setup with no DUT in the path. Insertion of the CLAT device clearly results in increasing TCP retransmissions as concurrent flows increase, but to a larger extent when IPv4 translation needs to be performed. (Color figure online)

an insignificant drop in per-flow throughput when pure IPv6 flows, which do not require any address translation, traverse the "Platform A" CLAT function. However, when IPv4 flows are presented for translation, per-flow throughputs drop to around 50% of the no-translation-required (i.e. pure IPv6 flows) case. In Fig. 2b, we see that mean TCP retransmissions within flows increase linearly as the number of flows increase, indicating worsening packet loss or timeouts. Although this is expected as more flows contend for their share of the bottleneck bandwidth and as each flow exercises bandwidth-probing behavior, we observe worst-case behavior when the CLAT is burdened with address translation work on IPv4 flows.

What do all these mean in practical terms for users? Applications that tend to establish a large number of connections (such as BitTorrent) will degrade per-flow performance beyond the diminishing fair share of the bottleneck bandwidth. It will worsen with IPv4 flows. Users will therefore benefit if they favor IPv6 connections to servers and peers. It would also be advantageous if the community network provisions its local services and sites on IPv6 addresses.

'Platform A' as a Mesh Device. "Platform A" had also been initially positioned as a future wireless mesh backbone device, so a few preliminary tests were made on its performance, shown in Table 2.

These were by no means intensive tests and were just intended to quickly see if reflashing 'Platform A' to Openwrt would significantly impact performance as a meshing node. There was indeed some penalty, which suggests that further intensive testing and qualification would be needed for similar platforms

Table 2. "Platform A" comparative throughputs (in Mbps), stock firmware vs. Open-Wrt. All tests were done with two nodes having line-of-sight over a 2.4 GHz wireless connection. No CLAT translation functionality was used in these tests.

Configuration	TCP		UDP	
	5 m	10 m	5 m	10 m
Stock firmware, bridged	92.5	93.1	96.1	96.0
OpenWrt, adhoc mode + BMX6	84.4	80.1	84.3	82.1

under consideration, perhaps using test environments that better replicate or approximate the intended deployment conditions.

Raspberry Pi as a User Access Device. We briefly tested the popular Raspberry Pi 4 device, equipped with a 1.5 GHz quad-core Cortex-A72 (ARM v8) and 4 GB of RAM. Such a device could function both as a CLAT+BMX6 gateway and as an application end-host as well. We inserted it into the same testbed previously used for 'Platform A' using a USB 3.0-to-Gigabit Ethernet adapter and its built-in Gigabit Ethernet port for connectivity and obtained 319.0 Mbps, and 276.1 Mbps average steady-state TCP throughputs for IPv4 (translated) and IPv6 (no-translation) flows, respectively. We have not evaluated it yet as a combined wireless access point and CLAT gateway. Nonetheless, it can quickly get users connected to use high-bandwidth services. For example, it could rapidly enable students to participate in videoconferencing and other remote learning activities.

Clearly, there are price-performance tradeoffs when selecting user access platforms. Table 3 provides a comparison of the two user access devices evaluated thus far. Community users may benefit from published comparisons not only to ensure interoperability with the local network but also to make informed decisions on platform selection, especially when cost is an important consideration.

Table 3. Price-performance comparisons, 'Platform A' and Raspberry Pi 4. Comparisons like these will help users make informed decisions on platform selection, especially when costs, no matter how relatively low, are an important consideration.

Platform	Local price [A]	TCP throughput		[C]/[A]	Remarks
		IPv6 [B]	IPv4 [C]		
Platform A	USD 37	92.8 Mbps	52.2 Mbps	1.41	Choose if providing wireless access is priority
Raspberry Pi	USD 88	319.0 Mbps	276.1 Mbps	3.14	Clear advantage in throughput and use for applications

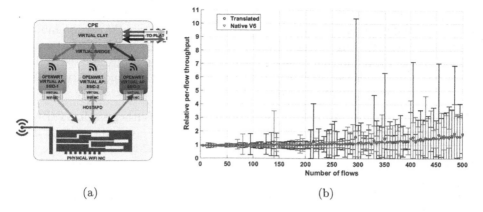

(a)   (b)

Fig. 3. *(a)* Virtual routers and access points as virtual network functions (VNFs) within host hardware shared by a number of users. *(b)* Wired throughput performance of a prototype VNF providing CLAT and BMX6 functionality. Note that these are for a 1 GbE network interface.

Localized Resource Pooling: Virtualized APs and CLATs. Community networks represent a form of network resource pooling that has been part of Internet tradition and architecture but on a reasonably localized scale. Our results from the previous tests of two potential low-cost client access and mesh platforms led us to the question: *would it be cost-effective to pool resources even at the access level?* That is, instead of a handful of households each having to search for an affordable yet compatible access device, would it make sense to deploy a more robust platform for shared use?

To test this approach, we prepared a KVM QEMU version 4.2.1 host on an Ubuntu 20.04.2 LTS (Focal Fossa) server with an Intel Core i7-3612QE 2.10 GHz 4-core/8-thread processor and 16 GB RAM installed. As shown in Fig. 3a, hostapd v2.9 [4] was used to manage the wireless network interface card and provide basic access point functionality. Virtual machines host OpenWrt-based virtual router and access point instances as virtual network functions (VNFs) servicing individual users. Setting aside the need for a prudent resource allocation scheme for the time being, we wanted to know whether the ability to statistically multiplex and occasionally overcommit resources in a flexible environment such as this may bring performance benefits. Figure 3b shows the relative TCP throughput performance of a CLAT router VNF provisioned with 8 vCPUs and 8 GB RAM. There seemed to be no significant performance penalty when the router VNF performs address translation for purely IPv4 flows compared to pure IPv6 flows that needed no translation. This shows that virtualizable, programmable hardware at the access edge has tremendous potential for resource sharing and dynamic resource allocation and provisioning.

VNFs need not exclusively offer OpenWrt-based virtual access point and router functionality, but may be used to flexibly and dynamically provision other functions and services at the edge as well. Platforms like these may also be used to support third-party service delivery and infrastructure reuse, similar to the mobile virtual network operator (MVNO) model in the mobile telecommunications industry. Allowing the entry of multiple competing commercial operators offers potential revenue that may be used to sustain operations and expand the infrastructure. It also eases some of the burdens on the community itself to source and provide needed services.

Jumbo Frame Support. As a final note, devices to be used either as CLAT/BMX6 user gateways connecting to the mesh network or as mesh nodes themselves, must support jumbo frames with maximum transmission unit (MTU) sizes above 1500 bytes. We observed that many IPv4 sites on the Internet send IPv4 datagrams with 1500-byte MTUs and with Don't Fragment (DF) bit set. As these inbound 1500-byte datagrams were translated from IPv4 to IPv6, the larger IPv6 header size yielded a larger inbound packet which could not be accommodated on internal IPv6-only meshing links with the default 1500-byte MTU. Therefore, all IPv6-only links within the community mesh and all interfaces connected to these links should support MTUs above 1500 bytes. We found that in some cases, such as the Raspberry Pi 4, the Raspbian GNU/Linux 10 (Buster) operating system had to be recompiled to support jumbo frames. In other cases, the underlying hardware did not seem to support jumbo frames despite Openwrt compatibility.

Common Core Services. The core of the community network will host typical service provider functions such as shared routing gateways to transit or peering links, domain name servers, Web hosting services, authentication services, and others. We continue to advocate the use of virtualization and software-defined approaches to provision and manage these services.

An essential if not critical architectural component at the core of our community network design is the provider-side address translator (PLAT) that statefully translates N:1 IPv6 addresses to Internet-routable IPv4 addresses and vice versa [21]. As the network and its usage grow, the number and rate at which IPv6 addresses are presented for translation by the PLAT will necessarily grow as well. The consequential growth in the size of the translation tables coupled with the stateful nature of PLAT translation raises reasonable concern in the scalability of this function.

We wanted to determine the impact of an increasing number of flows on a candidate PLAT platform with a 1.70 GHz Intel Xeon 3104 CPU (6 cores) and 8 GB RAM. For this test, we used an iPerf generator machine equipped with 2 × 64-core CPUs running at 2.25 GHz nominal, 256 GB installed RAM, and two Intel x710 10 GbE network adapter cards. To minimize the possibility of the traffic generator itself becoming the bottleneck as the experiments progressed, we ran iPerf with the −zerocopy method of sending data [5], increased buffer sizes [8], and an increased number of RX/TX descriptors [7].

Figure 4 shows the median TCP throughputs for flows undergoing stateful translation by the PLAT, relative to 'no-PLAT' baseline conditions, for 500 concurrent flows and higher. It should be noted that these results are not directly comparable with results in Fig. 2a and Fig. 3b because the interface bitrates in

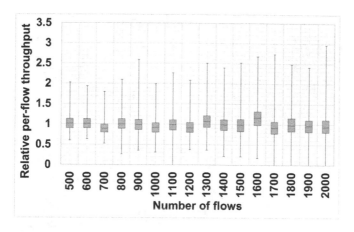

Fig. 4. Per-flow TCP throughput performance of candidate PLAT platform.

those cases were 100 Mbps and 1 Gbps, respectively. On the other hand, results in Fig. 4 are based on 10 Gbps interface bitrates. Steady-state TCP through puts aggregated over all concurrent flows hovered around 3.43 Gbps with PLAT stateful translation. While it may be tempting to naively deduce that this PLAT platform might be able to handle translations from around 65 'Platform A' CLAT devices (equivalently: 65 households), with each presenting roughly 52.2 Mbps maximum worth of TCP IPv6 traffic for translation to IPv4 and vice-versa, clearly this should be validated by equivalently scaling the number of concurrent flows during testing. This might require testing with up to 20,000 concurrent flows and even beyond, which we have not yet been able to perform so far.

As a final note on testing: aside from scaling the number of concurrent flows, it is also important to note that packet processing rates rather than bitrate-based throughputs should be the metric to use. We have chosen to present results here in terms of bitrates simply to present the results in a more intuitive and relatable fashion to a broader and possibly even less technical audience. Finally, tests such as these are best performed using a mix of packet sizes that might better model actual Internet traffic [20].

3.3   Experimental Deployment

We applied the design principles and architecture described in the preceding discussion to pilot deployments in two residential housing clusters near our university's campus. We provided several 'Platform A' devices to some residents so that these could be further tested against real-world usage.

Figure 5 shows a few scenes from one of the two deployment sites. Aside from a local community-specific WiFi SSID, the network also supports the eduroam international WiFi roaming service to support students, teachers and researchers currently studying or working from home [3]. Figure 5 also shows results from the popular Ookla Speedtest online broadband testing service shared by one of the

Fig. 5. Scenes from a pilot deployment. *(a)* Satellite photo of one of two deployment sites. *(b)* Installation and termination of fiber-optic uplink for community network. *(c)* Screenshot showing the local community WiFI SSID as well as the eduroam SSID. *(d)* Speedtest result shared by one of the residents.

residents – note how closely the 51.4 Mbps upload figure tracks the 52.2 Mbps laboratory test result for 'Platform' A in Table 3.

4 Conclusion and Future Work

Community networks can help accelerate the vision of building smart cities by interconnecting and empowering the underserved and unconnected. However, communities often face financial and human resource constraints that obstruct the scalability and sustainability of these networks. To address this problem, we presented a network architecture for community networks that stands on three design principles: (1) scalable, sustainable, and routable addressing, (2) open platforms and access, and (3) programmability and virtualization from access to core. There are well-defined Internet standards and mechanisms that can help with some of the technical aspects of community network sustainability, such as IPv6 and associated transition mechanisms. Additionally, there are free and open-source frameworks and other software components that allow the implementation of these technologies, but the commercial availability of compatible yet affordable hardware may be limited in some areas. This makes platform search, qualification, and testing a new challenging task for community networks. Even so, such an activity will be useful towards achieving technical scaling and sustainability and promoting cost transparency and informed platform choice among users. While not addressed in our current work, it will also be essential to include a security assessment of candidate devices and platforms.

Virtualization and programmable software-defined technologies at the edge may also address certain economic aspects of sustainability by enabling the entry of third-party commercial entities not only as bulk Internet transit providers, but also as virtual network operators deep within the community itself. Towards this end, we hope to see better affordability and availability of platforms that support vCPE (virtual customer premises equipment) and uCPE (universal customer premises equipment) architectures [17], as well as the OpenWiFi initiative [9].

Finally, as resource-constrained communities strive to squeeze out more 'bang for the buck', that is, aim to achieve greater value for money from affordable commodity components, developing skill and expertise in platform tuning, optimization, low-cost acceleration, and similar techniques that used to be associated with high-capacity networks will become a necessity. Topics such as network interface card (NIC) tuning [8] and kernel bypass [2,11] may well become a staple of future training programs for future community-based network engineers, alongside more fundamental ones such as TCP/IP networking, wired and wireless network design and operation, and management of physical media and infrastructure.

Acknowledgement. The work described here is an extension of earlier work done in the Bayanihanoto program funded by the Department of Science and Technology. The ongoing efforts are supported by the PCARI Scalable Community Access Networks (PCARI SCAN) and PCARI PRIME programs funded by the Commission on Higher Education, and the Asi@Connect CONNECT program funded by the European Commission through TEIN*CC. Pilot site deployment is done in collaboration with the University Computer Center of the University of the Philippines. Experimental resource support has been provided by Samsung R&D Institute Philippines. We are grateful to Eric Brewer of the University of California Berkeley for the valuable inputs and suggestions at the early stages of this work. Finally, we thank the APNIC Foundation for its support in disseminating our results.

References

1. Comfast EW72 1200mbps outdoor WiFi router repeater (2021). https://comfastwifi.us/comfast-cf-ew72-1200m-360degree-dual-band-5g-high-power-outdoor-ap
2. Data plane development kit (DPDK) (2021). https://www.dpdk.org/
3. eduroam for students, researchers, and educators (2021). https://eduroam.org/about/connect-yourself/
4. hostapd: IEEE 802.11 AP, IEEE 802.1X/WPA/WPA2/EAP/RADIUS authenticator (2021). https://w1.fi/hostapd/
5. iperf2/iperf3 (2021). https://fasterdata.es.net/performance-testing/network-troubleshooting-tools/iperf/
6. Jool: SIIT and NAT64 (2021). https://www.jool.mx/en/about.html
7. Linux tuning (2021). https://fasterdata.es.net/host-tuning/linux/
8. NIC tuning - Intel 1GE and 10GE NICs (2021). https://fasterdata.es.net/host-tuning/linux/nic-tuning/
9. OpenWiFi: an industry movement for accelerating Wi-Fi infrastructure innovation (2021). https://telecominfraproject.com/openwifi/
10. OpenWrt/LEDE project (2021). https://openwrt.org/about
11. The vector packet processor (VPP) (2021). https://fd.io/vppproject/vpptech/

12. Abujoda, A., Dietrich, D., Papadimitriou, P., Sathiaseelan, A.: Software-defined wireless mesh networks for internet access sharing. Comput. Netw. **93**, 359–372 (2015)
13. Antoniadis, P., et al.: Best practices guide for community networks. Technical report, Network Infrastructure as Commons (2019). https://www.netcommons. eu/index.html%3Fq=content%252Fbest-practices-guide-cns.html
14. Barela, M.C., et al.: Towards building a community cellular network in the Philippines. In: Proceedings of the 8th International Conference on Information and Communication Technologies and Development. ACM (June 2016). https://doi. org/10.1145/2909609.2909639
15. Chiosi, M., et al.: Network Functions Virtualisation: An Introduction, Benefits, Enablers. Challenges & Call for Action. Technical report, European Telecommunications Standards Institute (October 2012)
16. Dawadi, B.R., Rawat, D.B., Joshi, S.R., Keitsch, M.M.: Towards energy efficiency and green network infrastructure deployment in Nepal using software defined IPv6 network paradigm. Electron. J. Inf. Syst. Dev. Ctries. **86**(1), e12114 (2020)
17. Goemaere, P.: The evolution of network virtualization in the home. Technical report, Technicolor (2019). https://www.nctatechnicalpapers.com/Paper/2019/ 2019-the-evolution-of-network-virtualization-in-the-home/
18. Kim, H., Feamster, N.: Improving network management with software defined networking. IEEE Commun. Mag. **51**(2), 114–119 (2013). https://doi.org/10.1109/ MCOM.2013.6461195
19. Kreutz, D., Ramos, F.M.V., Veríssimo, P.E., Rothenberg, C.E., Azodolmolky, S., Uhlig, S.: Software-defined networking: a comprehensive survey. Proc. IEEE **103**(1), 14–76 (2015). https://doi.org/10.1109/JPROC.2014.2371999
20. Lencse, G.: Benchmarking stateless NAT64 implementations with a standard tester. Telecommun. Syst. **75**(3), 245–257 (2020)
21. Mawatari, M., Kawashima, M., Byrne, C.: 464XLAT: Combination of Stateful and Stateless Translation. Technical report 6877, Internet Engineering Task Force (April 2013). https://doi.org/10.17487/RFC6877
22. McKeown, N., et al.: OpenFlow: enabling innovation in campus networks. SIGCOMM Comput. Commun. Rev. **38**(2), 69–74 (2008)
23. Medina, I.R.: A reconstruction of Philippine social history from tagalog dictionaries and vocabularies, 1600–1914. Asian Stud. **21** (2013). https://www.asj.upd.edu.ph/ index.php/archive/104-vol-21-april-august-december-1983
24. Micholia, P., et al.: Community networks and sustainability: a survey of perceptions, practices, and proposed solutions. IEEE Commun. Surv. Tut. **20**(4), 3581–3606 (2018). https://doi.org/10.1109/comst.2018.2817686
25. Montes, I., et al.: Tangible sharing, invisible mechanisms. In: Proceedings of the 2016 Workshop on Global Access to the Internet for All, GAIA 2016. ACM Press (2016). https://doi.org/10.1145/2940157.2940161
26. Neumann, A., Lopez, E., Navarro, L.: An evaluation of BMX6 for community wireless networks. In: 2012 IEEE 8th International Conference on Wireless and Mobile Computing, Networking and Communications (WiMob). IEEE (October 2012). https://doi.org/10.1109/wimob.2012.6379145
27. Ordonez-Lucena, J., Ameigeiras, P., Lopez, D., Ramos-Munoz, J.J., Lorca, J., Folgueira, J.: Network slicing for 5G with SDN/NFV: concepts, architectures, and challenges. IEEE Commun. Mag. **55**(5), 80–87 (2017). https://doi.org/10.1109/ MCOM.2017.1600935
28. Ostrom, E.: Governing the Commons: The Evolution of Institutions for Collective Action. Cambridge University Press (1990)

29. Qureshi, K.I., Wang, L., Sun, L., Zhu, C., Shu, L.: A review on design and implementation of software-defined WLANs. IEEE Syst. J. **14**(2), 2601–2614 (2020). https://doi.org/10.1109/JSYST.2019.2960400

30. Surana, S., et al.: Beyond pilots: keeping rural wireless networks alive. In: 5th USENIX Symposium on Networked Systems Design and Implementation, NSDI 2008, San Francisco, CA. USENIX Association (April 2008). https://www.usenix.org/conference/nsdi-08/beyond-pilots-keeping-rural-wireless-networks-alive

31. Vega, D., Baig, R., Cerdà-Alabern, L., Medina, E., Meseguer, R., Navarro, L.: A technological overview of the guifi.net community network. Comput. Netw. **93**, 260–278 (2015). https://doi.org/10.1016/j.comnet.2015.09.023

Security in V2X Communications: A Comparative Analysis of Simulation/Emulation Tools

João Silva[1]([✉]), Luís Barreto[1,2], and Sérgio Ivan Lopes[1,2]

[1] ADiT-LAB, Instituto Politécnico de Viana do Castelo, Rua Escola Industrial
e Comercial Nun'Álvares, 4900-347 Viana do Castelo, Portugal
`jemanuelsilva@ipvc.pt, lbarreto@esce.ipvc.pt, sil@estg.ipvc.pt`
[2] IT - Instituto de Telecomunicações, Campus de Santiago, 3810-193 Aveiro, Portugal

Abstract. Autonomous driving is becoming a reality and cars are getting connected with everything (traffic lights, roads, bicycles, other cars, people, infrastructure, etc.) being Vehicle-to-Everything (V2X) communications a critical factor in the success of autonomous cars. It is, thus, important to understand and study the main security vulnerabilities of V2X communication standards in the specific application context concerning future Intelligent Transportation Systems (ITS) and contribute with a comparison between existent simulation/emulation tools for security analysis in V2X communications with a focus on the ITS application domain. In that sense, this paper presents ta baseline study of different simulation/emulation tools that can be used to study those vulnerabilities. This study has shown that VENTOS is the simulator more suited for the truck platoon application scenario, and the Eclipse Mosaic is the best choice for simulation in the Cooperative Collision Avoidance application case.

Keywords: Security · V2X communication · ITS · Truck platoon · Intersection collision avoidance · Simulation · Emulation

1 Introduction

In recent years, there has been a significant growth and a rapid expansion of Intelligent Transportation Systems (ITS), mainly in metropolitan areas, and consequently an increase in cars circulating in the interior of those areas and on motorways. Due to this increase, the different types of transportation systems face several problems, such as a general growth in traffic and, as a consequence, a rise in accidents and environmental pollution, impacting the overall sustainable development of the urban ecosystem. These factors impose serious socio-economical problems, thus motivating countless efforts to improve the entire transportation process to become more secure and sustainable. Having this into consideration, policymakers have been joining forces to put forward initiatives such as the "CAR 2 CAR Communication Consortium" [1]—composed of some

© ICST Institute for Computer Sciences, Social Informatics and Telecommunications Engineering 2022
Published by Springer Nature Switzerland AG 2022. All Rights Reserved
S. Paiva et al. (Eds.): SmartCity360° 2021, LNICST 442, pp. 408–421, 2022.
https://doi.org/10.1007/978-3-031-06371-8_27

of the largest car manufacturers—which is becoming a hot topic, not only due to standardization but also in research and academia.

The idea of autonomous vehicles has also boosted the implementation of Intelligent Transportation Systems (ITS), especially within the industry. Typically, ITS present a set of characteristics, such as the measuring of distances between vehicles, the computing capacity of these data, and the ability to communicate with different subjects, that allow vehicles to have some or total independence or just support to driving.

There are several benefits of having autonomous vehicles, such as an improvement in road safety since 94% of serious accidents are due to human error. An autonomous vehicle has the potential to remove this factor, helping to protect passengers from vehicles, bicycles, or pedestrians [2]. Autonomous vehicles can also bring economical and social benefits, given that high amounts of financial resources are annually spent due to high accident rates—and everything that they involve—such as the expenses directly related to the accidents, the reduction in productivity, the loss of lives, and consequently, the loss of quality of life and the increase of government expenditure in the health service. Efficiency and convenience will also improve because ITS is beneficial in the sense of smoothing and making traffic constant, thus reducing the number of hours people spent on mobility-related tasks, directly enhancing their quality of life. On the other hand, reducing fuel consumption and reducing gas emissions present a major goal towards environmental sustainability. Another important benefit is related to the type of vehicles that provide mobility improvements to more people in society, such as older people with limitations to perform safe driving, thus raising its level of independence and improving its social inclusion.

According to [3], vehicle automation can be classified into four different categories: i) Systems that assist driving (driving support systems), which calculate better routes taking into account traffic and distance, fuel/energy consumption, and gas emissions; or ii) Systems that inform the driver of hazards, having no autonomous aspect, e.g., forward-collision warning, blind-spot warning or pedestrian detection and warning; iii) Systems that have partial control of the vehicle, both for driver support and emergency interventions, such as during driver monitoring if it is found that the driver is not in a position to drive or is showing unstable behavior, the system takes control of the vehicle to take it to a safe state; iv) Systems that include total vehicle control such as speed and trajectory, which have the resources, intelligence, and means of communication necessary to be autonomous.

In [4], a quantitative scale maps the systems previously introduced in a 5 level scale:

- Level 0: when there is no automation;
- Level 1: when just driver assistance is considered;
- Level 2: when it uses partial automation;
- Level 3: when there is enough automation and the driver is not necessary to monitor the environment;

- Level 4: includes high automation but still allows the driver to control the vehicle;
- Level 5: for full automation, no need for human intervention.

These systems are dependent on factors that directly relate to other subsystems, such as computing power and decision making, communications between the different network elements. Moreover, all decisions rely on shared information, which is more effective if the reliability and speed of communication are guaranteed. Due to this, several improvements in all types of communication technologies—such as DSRC, C- V2X (LTE/5G), WI-FI, Bluetooth, among others—have been put forward due to the demand of several ITS application domains.

Recently, several V2X communications simulators for different environments have emerged, becoming accessible to more people and without the need to spend high resources, allowing a wider community to focus on its study, i.e. academia and industry. This work will also present an analysis of different V2X communications simulators that are the most suitable for Truck Platoon and Cooperative Collision Avoidance application domains.

The remainder of this document is organized as follows: Sect. 2 introduces the ITS domains under the scope of this work; Sect. 3 presents the general architecture of V2X systems in the ITS application domain; Sect. 4 presents an overview of existent simulation/emulation tools for V2X communications in the ITS application domain and puts forward a discussion regarding the main findings; and in Sect. 6 the conclusions are presented.

2 Related Work/ITS Domains

The ITS application domains can be classified into four general categories: 1) Mobility, 2) Safety, 3) Environmental, and 4) Comfort.

These systems, when applied to mobility, are responsible for traffic management, thus supporting users with information on where the most traffic or hazards are. This results in different actions such as calculating the route, making it shorter or faster, taking into account different factors (distance, energy, traffic, time, weather, etc.), speed management, or cooperative navigation [5]. This information is collected by vehicles or RSU's (Road Side Units) and transmitted to vehicles directly or indirectly. When applied to the context of public transport, Advanced Traveler Information Systems (ATIS), provide users the detailed transport information allowing them to plan their trip, being able to understand the transport schedule, the duration of the trip and the distance the transport is at the location. Traffic Demand Estimation/Traffic Management are applications of ITS with a focus on mobility that aim to manage traffic both in urban centers and on highways, avoiding congestion that can increase accidents, increase pollution and make users spend unnecessary time on the road. Traffic Accurate Position Estimation, which can be applied to the vehicle itself, provides important information about the route and possible changes to the driver and public transport allowing greater ease when the user prepares the trip and the service provider to show the real position of your vehicle. Roadside Service Finder, provides information about nearby petrol stations or hotels, for example, and Cooperative Adaptive Cruise Control (CACC) allows vehicles to be driven in a platoon [6].

Regarding the safety domain, ITS plays a fundamental role contributing to the reduction of traffic accidents, as a consequence of the increase in information and alerts that it presents to the driver about potential hazards that are not yet visible to him, such as speed reduction warning when approaching a tight curve or road in poor conditions. This domain includes different applications such as the "Vehicle Safety Application", which consists of vehicle and driver monitoring, and "Emergency Trajectory Alignment" [7,8]. Collision Warning and Obstacle Warning [9] are capable of informing the driver in advance about the possibility of collision or objects on the route, based on the information shared between the different vehicles and the infrastructure, the same applies to autonomous vehicles. Intelligent Speed Adaptation/Speed Limit informs about the appropriate speed or can adapt it according to the limit indicated on that road, while Incident Detection [10]/Pedestrian Crossing informs drivers/vehicles about accidents or pedestrians crossing the road, in routes where they circulate, respectively. Traffic Lights and Approaching of Emergency Vehicles are also some examples of ITS other applications.

ITS systems also bring environmental benefits, allowing the reduction of harmful gases emissions and fuel consumption. The information shared by the different surroundings in a given location regarding the state of the traffic (congested, free, accident) allows the driver to change its route, reschedule it and even change the trajectory habit, allowing a significant reduction in daily fuel consumption. CACC or Vehicle Platooning are other ITS applications with a great impact on the environment, consisting of one vehicle guiding remaining vehicles and thus controlling different factors of the trip such as (speed, braking, trajectory, etc.), then reducing consumption and consequently the emission of harmful gases. Since this applies mainly to business fleets, it also allows the reduction of the number of drivers. Calculating the route taking into account different factors, or the possibility of route recalculation when there is traffic or an accident also has a high impact on fuel reduction and gas emissions.

The fourth and final domain of ITS is related to "Comfort and Infotainment Applications" and its main objective is to increase the comfort and convenience that the vehicle provides to users, such as providing different applications that users can take advantage of such as VoIP, video, GPS [11], thus allowing you to search for a gas station, the nearest restaurant or hotel, and their prices, to provide internet so that passengers can continue their work, receive and send messages or play an online game.

2.1   Trucks Platoon

Platooning is an application of ITS that allows a group of vehicles to travel together, to define the speed and distance at which they travel among themselves, thus avoiding unexpected behavior by the different autonomous driving vehicles in the group [7]. The platoon is composed of a Platoon Leader (PL) who controls the platoon in distinct aspects—speed, distance, number of vehicles and which vehicles are allowed to enter or leave the platoon—and the Platoon Members (PMs) that follow these guidelines and report their status to the PL. Platooning integrates several technologies, such as Adaptive Cruise Control (ACC) systems, Vehicle-to-Vehicle (V2V) and Vehicle-to-Infrastructure (V2I) communication systems, different sensing technologies such as Radio Detection and Ranging (RADAR) or Light Detection and Ranging (LIDAR), and visible light cameras which can measure the distance between vehicles and inform the ACC system through the vehicle's internal network. In turn, the ACC System sends control messages to the engine and brake modules and steering to control the vehicle's speed and direction. CACC is the most used concept in platooning and consists of adding V2V communications to ACC, either through cellular networks, WiFi, or Bluetooth, allowing vehicles not only to depend on sensor data, but also to exchange information between vehicles or RSU's [12]. The data reaches the ACC system through the in-vehicle network protocols such as Controller Area Network (CAN) and Local Interconnected Network (LIN), which typically do not use encryption, thus being a security breach that can be exploited [13]. CACC allows vehicles to quickly share information, resulting in considerable accuracy and safety improvement when traveling, particularly when braking or accelerating synchronously and cooperatively. Trucks Platooning makes it possible to improve traffic management and road performance as vehicles travel with a reduced distance from each other, as well as safety since the speed variation at which they travel is small reducing the impact speed in the event of a collision [14]. Fuel consumption and consequent pollutant gas emissions [15], can also be reduced as the air resistance to which vehicles are subject [2], decreases. This approach also applies to autonomous or partially autonomous driving vehicles, allowing the reduction of the number of effective drivers [7], thus decreasing operational costs.

2.2   Cooperative Collision Avoidance

Due to the increasing number of vehicles and consequently, traffic accidents, particularly on intersections, there is a need to improve collision avoidance systems. There has been an increase in research in academia and car manufacturing companies, leading to the current state in which the vehicle contains several sensors and cameras that cooperate with each other to reduce risks. However, these sensors have limitations, such as the need for line-of-sight (LoS), crucial for object detection [17]. In urban conditions, LoS is difficult to guarantee since vehicles may be behind buildings until the last moment, i.e. close to the intersection. One way to overcome this limitation can be the inclusion of isotropic wireless communications that cover all the vehicle environment, allowing it to communicate with neighboring vehicles and with RSUs [18]. The communication between vehicles and between vehicle and infrastructure elements improves the performance of these collision avoidance systems since it allows predicting the accident and informing the driver, or in the case of autonomous vehicles, allowing preventive measures to be considered [19]. Communication on these systems is based mainly on IEEE 802.11p, known in Europe as European Telecommunication Standards Institute's (ETSI ITS-G5) or in the USA as Dedicated Short Range Communications (DSRC). In this way, vehicles communicate with the RSUs and exchange important information such as speed, intersection status, and vehicle position, using the GPS signal, and these, in turn, inform other vehicles. Whenever possible, vehicles communicate directly with each other since these types of communication suffer from decreased performance in urban environments with buildings as an obstacle to communication and with when a high density of vehicles occurs. To overcome these difficulties, there are already numerous advances in the application of C-V2X (LTE/5G) technology [20].

When compared to the previously mentioned protocols, the LTE protocol presents as main advantages easy implementation and low cost, since LTE cellular network infrastructure already exists, unlike IEEE802.11p which demands higher investment. LTE-V presents even better coverage, capacity and is a better choice for high mobility environments, using the same frequency spectrum of 3G and 4G. The major disadvantage of LTE-V is related to the transmission bite rate, which is considerably lower when compared with 3G and 4G [57].

Regarding the 5G communication protocol, this is the most promising one since it intends to eliminate most of the existing limitations in the current standards (3G, 4G/LTE), such as dynamic mobility and high relative velocities, extremely low-latency, ultra-high rate, high capacity for high message volume and high availability and reliability. There are still several challenges to guarantee the mentioned topics and make 5G the standard for communication in ITS [58].

3   Network Architecture

Both application cases mentioned in the previous sections share the same network architecture that can be divided into five communication types, as it is possible to observe in Fig. 1. The first type is related to the V2I communication since vehicles have to communicate directly with the RSU units. The second type refers to V2V, where the On Board Unit (OBU) of each vehicle communicates directly with neighboring vehicles. The third type concerns to Vehicle-to-Network (V2N) communications where vehicles communicate with the network, in this communication is normally used by cellular networks C-V2X (LTE, 5G) and they can provide services with support for wide-area coverage being beneficial to applications like traffic management and for infotainment applications [36,37]. The fourth type consists of Vehicle-to-People (V2P) communications which consist of communication between vehicles and pedestrians and should be taken into consideration when studying the cooperative Collision Avoidance context. Lastly, the fifth type concerns in In-Vehicle (IV) communications, the vehicle's internal network that allows communication between its functional components such as ECUs, AUs, Sensors (Radar/Lidar, Camera and Global Positioning System (GPS)) [21].

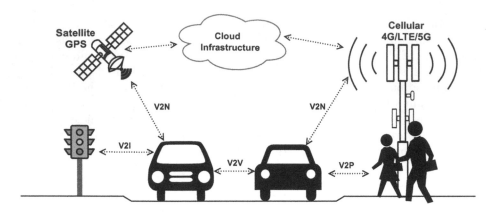

Fig. 1. V2X Network Architecture.

Existing communication technologies for V2I and V2V are supported by wire-less technology and available in the 5.9 GHz band (5.85–5.925 GHz) [16]. This communication is based on the DSRC Protocol (Dedicated Short Range Communications), which evolved from IEEE 802.11p protocol, and was developed from IEEE802.11 to meet all V2X communications requirements. It is through this DSRC protocol that vehicles are able to communicate with their neighboring vehicles, share relevant information—such as speed, location, or acceleration several times per second, with a communication range of a few hundred meters—with the RSUs allowing to inform the state of the signs or the existence of hazards, e.g. the approach of an intersection, or the proximity to an emergency vehicle. At the In-Vehicle domain level, communications between the ACC system and the different ECUs are made using the CAN and LIN protocols, with the disadvantages being the fact that they do not encrypt communications, which is an important threat because it is possible to take complete control of the vehicle since an ECU with outward-facing interfaces can be compromised. These and all the other vulnerabilities related to communication between vehicles which may refer to communication protocols like DSRC, LTE, or 5G need to be avoided to autonomous driving vehicles become reliable for users. Bearing in mind that a failure in the communication between these autonomous or semi-autonomous transport systems can lead, in the best case, to a warning to a driver, which is not effective and an advantage, and, in the worse case, to a catastrophic loss of human lives. Therefore, it is necessary to develop safe and stable systems that are more reliable and trusted by the users. The exchange of information in these systems takes place mainly between V2I, V2V and IV, as for example the data of the different sensors to help autonomous driving or exchange data with other vehicles [22]. The entities used in V2I and V2V communications are vulnerable to attacks from wireless networks, and when an attack is successful a vehicle can be compromised and can trigger false warnings that in turn also impact the vehicles that are connected to each other in the communications stream. Likewise, attackers can create messages with the intention of deceiving other vehicles on the network [59]. These examples show the importance of creating and implementing security requirements in V2X communications that guarantee the needs of users with regard to security, privacy, reliability, and integrity. Below, are presented the critical requirements that have been defined for these type of systems:

1. Authentication - Guarantees the recipient that the sender is trustworthy [23].
2. System and Communications Integrity - ensures that the content of messages is not modified during transmission and reliability and accuracy of message communication can be guaranteed at the destination [24, 25].
3. Access Control - serves for granting access to specific services for the various network entities. The property of access control authorizes a node for performing allowed actions in the network, e.g., the network protocols that the node can execute [26].
4. System and Communications Confidentiality - guarantees non-disclosure of certain resources to unauthorized users without access rights.
5. Availability - services and protocols should remain functional even if faults occur. Therefore, the availability requirement guarantees secure, fault-tolerant and protocols that are able to re-stabilize themselves after the exclusion of the fault [27].
6. Privacy and Anonymity - systems should ensure for protecting the privacy of network users. Therefore, in the context of a broader area, privacy refers to information/data hiding, while anonymity is considered as a subset of privacy in vehicular networks.
7. Non-repudiation - Ensures that when a recipient identifies the source of message, the source takes complete responsibility and cannot deny later of its role [28].

4   Simulation/Emulation Tools

With the need to evaluate the problems identified in the previous section, design new solutions, or validate research studies, several simulators/emulators have been developed in recent years. The use of simulators allows to digitally replicate several real-world scenarios easier, without the need for having costly equipment, such as vehicles or infrastructure. There are several scenarios where these tools prove to be an advantage because they were developed according to the requirements and characteristics of VANET's, allowing to simulate distinct scenarios and network architectures in the ITS application domain, e.g. intersections or traffic jams, where the density of vehicles is high and can overload the network [29]. Moreover, they enable the simulation of the characteristics of high mobility vehicles with rapidly changing network topologies [30], which brings great difficulties for data transmission and routing [31], and requires low latency and high reliability for the V2X communications [32]. Another important aspect is related to the study of security aspects related to the communication between the different actors. The use of simulation tools allows more people to study vulnerabilities in the C-ITS communication protocols and therefore to improve the progress of these technologies.

4.1 Comparative Analysis

There are two different types of simulators, traffic simulators and network simulators. It is possible to integrate different traffic simulators with network simulators to replicate situations with different vehicles such as intersections and communication between vehicles and/or infrastructure elements. This study only considers simulators that already contain both traffic and network simulators integrated. However, to understand which is the best and most appropriate we will study the characteristics of the used traffic and network simulators.

With regard to traffic simulators, the main criteria that will be evaluated are: 1) type of communications it supports, 2) language/interface in which it is developed, 3) if it allows modeling obstacles, and 4) if it allows speed control and Multi-lane. On the other hand, in network protocols, the main criteria that will be used in evaluation will be: 1) type of communication it supports and 2) scalability.

Table 1. V2X simulators/emulators comparison.

Simulators	Traffic software	Network software	License	References
VENTOS	SUMO	OMNet++	Public, OpenSource	[35,47]
ITETRIS	SUMO	Proprietary software	Public	[48,53]
Tectos	SUMO	NetSim	Private	[41,49]
Artery	SUMO	OMNeT++	Public, OpenSource	[33,38,50]
VEINS	SUMO	OMNeT++	Public, OpenSource	[51,52]
Eclipse Mosaic	Eclipse SUMO	OMNeT++/NS-3 /SNS/Cell	Public/Private	[46,54]
VNS	Divert 2.0	NS-3/OMNeT++	Public	[56]
EstiNet11	Proprietary software	Proprietary software	Private	[55]

Most of the simulators in Table 1 are based on Sumo traffic simulator software [3,35]—developed in C++—because it is one of the most used and complete in the ITS application domain, as it allows V2X communications, allows speed control, multi-line simulation, and presents as a major drawback, not having obstacle modeling. However, obstacle modeling can be added using external tools. Moreover, it also allows the integration of other important tools to study different scenarios such as platooning [34], among others. There are other possibilities using proprietary software and Divert 2.0 solutions, but there is little information available about their characteristics and functionalities. In [33], El-Rewini et al. present a detailed assessment of several simulators.

Regarding network simulators, we noticed that the most used ones are OMNet++, which allows only V2V communications and supports graphical interface and high scalability, and NS-3 which allows V2X communications but does not support graphical interface and has reduced scalability (approx. 500 nodes). There are still others like NETSIM [41,42] which is a commercial software, and SNS and Cell [46] with a focus on cellular networks.

5   Discussion

In general, we can see that most of the simulators presented in Table 1 are based on the SUMO software [34] and that it allows the integration with different external tools, which makes it possible to eliminate any limitation that it has when compared to other traffic simulators, thus making it a good choice for the study of any scenario. Regarding network simulators, we noticed that there are significant differences in the two most used, i.e. the chosen simulators and the community adoption. OMNeT++ is presented as a software that allows high scalability but is exclusively dedicated to V2V communications [33,38–40] and NS3 as software whose greatest advantage is to allow the study of V2X communications, however, with less scalability [43–45]. In this way, it is already possible to recognize that the best choice is a public domain solution since they are based on the previously mentioned software. Considering the simulators comparison in the context of studying security vulnerabilities in two distinct application contexts, such as truck platoon and cooperative collision avoidance, VENTOS [35] and Eclipse Mosaic [46], are the simulators that better fill the requirements previously introduced. Besides, the iTETRIS [48] simulator is also a good option for the study of these application domains because it uses SUMO, i.e. its network simulator allows V2X communications, and the main advantage is that iTETRIS's modules are standard compliant with European Telecommunication Standards Institute's (ETSI's)) architecture for ITS Communication, which allows this simulation platform to produce realistic and large-scale ITS system modeling, however, a more detailed comparison is planned as future research. In the case of the Truck Platoon application context, the simulator that best fits the requirements is VENTOS, which is a simulator focused on collaborative driving, such as ACC, CACC, platoon management protocol, and also due to the fact that its stack is developed to study security attacks in collaborative driving situations [35]. In the specific case of the CACC application scenario, the simulator most suitable is the Eclipse Mosaic, since it also uses SUMO as traffic software and allows users to choose between different network simulators, such as OMNet ++ NS3 and the simulator of cellular networks called "Cell".

6   Conclusion

Vehicle-to-Everything (V2X) communication technologies are a critical success factor in autonomous driving, as cars are becoming more and more connected with everything (traffic lights, roads, bicycles, other cars, people, infrastructure, etc.). This work introduced two relevant ITS application domains, i.e. Trucks Platoon and Cooperative Collision Avoidance, and referred its main security vulnerabilities. The main contribution of this work is the presented comparison between existent simulation/emulation tools for the security analysis in V2X communications. The evaluation performed allows to understand which are best adapted to the study of security related problems in the introduced application domains, with focus on important criteria, such as traffic and networking software, licence type and other core technical characteristics. Based on this study, we concluded that VENTOS is the simulator more suited for the truck platoon application domain, and the Eclipse Mosaic is the best choice for simulation in the Cooperative Collision Avoidance application domain.

Future work involves assessing vulnerabilities in the previously mentioned contexts, using the simulators/emulators that proved to be the most suitable.

Acknowledgment. This contribution is a result of ongoing research, in the scope of a dissertation work of the M.Sc. in Cybersecurity, in collaboration with the Applied Digital Transformation Laboratory (ADiT-Lab), and funded by the Polytechnic Institute of Viana do Castelo.

References

1. Kiela, K., et al.: Review of V2X–IoT standards and frameworks for ITS applications. Appl. Sci. **10**(12), 4314 (2020). https://doi.org/10.3390/app10124314
2. Automated Vehicles for Safety (February 2018). https://www.nhtsa.gov/technology-innovation/automated-vehicles-safety
3. Bishop, R.: Intelligent vehicle applications worldwide. IEEE Intell. Syst. Appl. **15**, 78–81 (2000)
4. NHTSA. https://www.nhtsa.gov/technology-innovation/automated-vehicles-safety
5. Karagiannis, G., et al.: Vehicular networking: a survey and tutorial on requirements, architectures, challenges, standards and solutions. IEEE Commun. Surv. Tut. **13**(4), 584–616 (2011)
6. Singh, P.K., Nandi, S.K., Nandi, S.: A tutorial survey on vehicular communication state of the art, and future research directions. Veh. Commun. **18**, 100164 (2019)
7. Bian, K., Zhang, G., Song, L.: Security in use cases of vehicle-to-everything communications. In: IEEE Vehicular Technology Conference, September 2017, pp. 1–5 (2018)
8. Chowdhury, M., Apon, A., Dey, K.: Data Analytics for Intelligent Transportation Systems, pp. 1–316 (2017)
9. Nkoro, A.B., Vershinin, Y.A.: Current and future trends in applications of Intelligent Transport Systems on cars and infrastructure. In: 17th IEEE International Conference on Intelligent Transportation Systems, ITSC 2014, October 2014, pp. 514–519 (2014)
10. Al-Sultan, S., Al-Doori, M.M., Al-Bayatti, A.H., Zedan, H.: A comprehensive survey on vehicular Ad Hoc network. J. Netw. Comput. Appl. **37**, 380–392 (2014)
11. Araniti, G., Campolo, C., Condoluci, M., Iera, A., Molinaro, A.: LTE for vehicular networking: a survey. IEEE Commun. Mag. **51**(5), 148–157 (2013)

12. Singh, P.K., Tabjul, G.S., Imran, M., Nandi, S.K., Nandi, S.: Impact of security attacks on cooperative driving. In: 2018 IEEE Region 10 Conference, TENCON 2018, October 2018, pp. 138–143 (2018)
13. Valasek, C., Miller, C.: "Adventures in Automotive Networks and Control Units," Technical White Paper, p. 99 (2013)
14. Amoozadeh, M., Deng, H., Chuah, C.N., Zhang, H.M., Ghosal, D.: Platoon management with cooperative adaptive cruise control enabled by VANET. Veh. Commun. **2**, 110–123 (2015)
15. Veldhuizen, R., Van Raemdonck, G.M.R., van der Krieke, J.P.: Fuel economy improvement by means of two European tractor semi-trailer combinations in a platooning formation. J. Wind Eng. Ind. Aerodyn. **188**, 217–234 (2019)
16. Dadras, S.: Security of Vehicular Platooning (2019)
17. Rashdan, I., Schmidhammer, M., De Ponte Müller, F., Sand, S.: Performance evaluation of vehicle-to-vehicle communication for cooperative collision avoidance at urban intersections. In: IEEE Vehicular Technology Conference, pp. 1–5 (2018)
18. Thomas, L., Panicker, S.T., Jerry Daniel, J., Tony, T.: DSRC based collision warning for vehicles at intersections. In: 3rd International Conference on Advanced Computing and Communication Systems: Bringing to the Table, Futuristic Technologies from Around the Globe, ICACCS 2016 (2016)
19. Rawashdeh, Z.Y., Mahmud, S.M.: Intersection collision avoidance system architecture. In: 2008 5th IEEE Consumer Communications and Networking Conference, CCNC 2008, pp. 493–494 (2008)
20. Gharba, M., et al.: 5G enabled cooperative collision avoidance: system design and field test. In: 18th IEEE International Symposium on a World of Wireless, Mobile and Multimedia Networks, WoWMoM 2017 - Conference (2017)
21. Hamida, E., Noura, H., Znaidi, W.: Security of cooperative intelligent transport systems: standards, threats analysis and cryptographic countermeasures. Electronics **4**(384), 380–423 (2015)
22. Ghosal, A., Conti, M.: Security issues and challenges in V2X: a survey. Comput. Netw. **160**, 107093 (2020)
23. Heijden, R.V.D.: Security architectures in V2V and V2I communication. In: Proceedings of the 20th Student Conference on IT, University of Twente, Netherlands, pp. 1–10 (2010)
24. Dak, A.Y., Yahya, S., Kassim, M.: A literature survey on security challenges in VANETs. Int. J. Comput. Theor. Eng. **4**, 1007–1010 (2012)
25. Samara, G., Al-Salihy, W.A., Sures, R.: Security analysis of vehicular ad hoc networks (VANET). In: Proceedings of the International Conference on Network Applications Protocols and Services, pp. 55–60. IEEE (2010)
26. Sakib, R.K.: Security issues in VANET, Department of Electronics and Communication Engineering, BRAC University, Ph.D. thesis (2010)
27. Mejri, M.N., Ben-Othman, J., Hamdi, M.: Survey on VANET security challenges and possible cryptographic solutions. Veh. Commun. **1**(2), 53–66 (2014)
28. Hasrouny, H., Samhat, A.E., Bassil, C., Laouiti, A.: VANET security challenges and solutions: a survey. Veh. Commun. **7**, 7–20 (2017)
29. Wang, J., Shao, Y., Ge, Y., Yu, R.: A survey of vehicle to everything (V2X) testing. Sensors **19**(2), 334 (2019)
30. Oluoch, J.: VANETs: security challenges and future directions. World. Acad. Sci. Eng. Technol. Int. J. Comput. Electr. Autom. Control Inf. Eng. **10**, 1033–1037 (2016)

31. Alotaibi, M.M., Mouftah, H.: High speed multi-hop data dissemination for heterogeneous transmission ranges in VANETs. In: IEEE International Conference on Ubiquitous Wireless Broadband (ICUWB), pp. 1–7 (2015)
32. Bai, F., Krishnan, H.: Reliability analysis of DSRC wireless communication for vehicle safety applications. In: 2006 IEEE Intelligent Transportation Systems Conference, pp. 355–362 (2006)
33. El-Rewini, Z.: Cybersecurity challenges in vehicular communications. Veh. Commun. **23**, 100214 (2020)
34. Mena-Oreja, J., Gozalvez, J.: PERMIT - a SUMO simulator for platooning maneuvers in mixed traffic scenarios. In: 2018 21st International Conference on Intelligent Transportation Systems (ITSC), pp. 3445–3450 (2018)
35. Cassou-Mounat, J., Labiod, H., Khatoun, R.: Simulation of cyberattacks in ITS-G5 systems. In: Krief, F., Aniss, H., Mendiboure, L., Chaumette, S., Berbineau, M. (eds.) Communication Technologies for Vehicles: 15th International Workshop, Nets4Cars/Nets4Trains/Nets4Aircraft 2020, Bordeaux, France, November 16–17, 2020, Proceedings, pp. 3–14. Springer, Cham (2020). https://doi.org/10.1007/978-3-030-66030-7_1
36. Sheikh, M.U., Hämäläinen, J., David Gonzalez, G., Jäntti, R., Gonsa, O.: Usability benefits and challenges in mmWave V2V communications: a case study. In: 2019 International Conference on Wireless and Mobile Computing, Networking and Communications (WiMob), Barcelona, Spain (2019)
37. Báguena, M., Tornell, S.M., Torres, Á., Calafate, C.T., Cano, J., Manzoni, P.: VACaMobil: VANET car mobility manager for OMNeT++. In: 2013 IEEE International Conference on Communications Workshops (ICC), Budapest, Hungary, pp. 1057–1061 (2013)
38. De Rango, F., Tropea, M., Raimondo, P., Santamaria, A.F., Fazio, P.: Bio inspired strategy for improving platoon management in the future autonomous electrical VANET environment. In: 2019 28th International Conference on Computer Communication and Networks (ICCCN), Valencia, Spain, pp. 1–7 (2019). https://doi.org/10.1109/ICCCN.2019.8847088
39. Renzler, T., Stolz, M., Watzenig, D.: Decentralized dynamic platooning architecture with V2V communication tested in Omnet++. In: 2019 IEEE International Conference on Connected Vehicles and Expo (ICCVE), Graz, Austria, pp. 1–6 (2019). https://doi.org/10.1109/ICCVE45908.2019.8965224
40. Avino, G.: Poster: a simulation-based testbed for vehicular collision detection. In: IEEE Vehicular Networking Conference (VNC), 2017, Torino, pp. 39–40 (2017). https://doi.org/10.1109/VNC.2017.8275655
41. Malik, S., Sahu, P.K.: Study on wireless communication aspect of VANETs. In: IEEE MTT-S International Microwave and RF Conference (IMaRC), Kolkata, India, 2018, pp. 1–4 (2018). https://doi.org/10.1109/IMaRC.2018.8877354
42. Jat, S., Tomar, R.S., Sharma, M.S.P.: Traffic congestion and accident prevention analysis for connectivity in vehicular ad-hoc network. In: 2019 5th International Conference on Signal Processing, Computing and Control (ISPCC), Solan, India, 2019, pp. 185–190 (2019). https://doi.org/10.1109/ISPCC48220.2019.8988463
43. Liu, W., Wang, X., Zhang, W., Yang, L., Peng, C.: Coordinative simulation with SUMO and NS3 for vehicular ad hoc networks. In: 2016 22nd Asia-Pacific Conference on Communications (APCC), Yogyakarta, Indonesia, 2016, pp. 337–341 (2016). https://doi.org/10.1109/APCC.2016.7581471
44. Days, W., Shagdar, O., Nashashibi, F., Tohme, S.: Performance study of CAM over IEEE 802.11p for cooperative adaptive cruise control. In: 2017 Wireless Days, Porto, 2017, pp. 70–76 (2017). https://doi.org/10.1109/WD.2017.7918118

45. Anadu, D., Mushagalusa, C., Alsbou, N., Abuabed, A.S.A.: Internet of Things: vehicle collision detection and avoidance in a VANET environment. In: IEEE International Instrumentation and Measurement Technology Conference (I2MTC), Houston, TX, USA, 2018, pp. 1–6 (2018). https://doi.org/10.1109/I2MTC.2018.8409861

46. Hilt, B., Berbineau, M., Vinel, A., Pirovano, A.: Simulation of convergent networks for intelligent transport systems with VSimRTI. In: Networking Simulation for Intelligent Transportation Systems: High Mobile Wireless Nodes, 2017, pp. 1–28. Wiley (2017). https://doi.org/10.1002/9781119407447.ch1

47. VENTOS - VEhicular NeTwork Open Simulator. https://maniam.github.io/VENTOS/. Accessed 1 Mar 2021

48. iTETRIS Platform. http://www.ict-itetris.eu. Accessed 1 Mar 2021

49. NetSim-Network Simulator & Emulator. https://www.tetcos.com. Accessed 3 Mar 2021

50. Artery. https://github.com/riebl/artery. Accessed 7 Mar 2021

51. Veins. https://veins.car2x.org/. Accessed 7 Mar 2021

52. Haidari, M.J., Yetgin, Z.: Veins based studies for vehicular ad hoc networks. In: International Artificial Intelligence and Data Processing Symposium (IDAP), Malatya, Turkey, 2019, pp. 1–7 (2019). https://doi.org/10.1109/IDAP.2019.8875954

53. Soua, A., Shagdar, O., Lasgouttes, J.: Toward efficient simulation platform for platoon communication in large scale C-ITS scenarios. In: International Symposium on Networks, Computers and Communications (ISNCC), Rome, 2018, pp. 1–6 (2018). https://doi.org/10.1109/ISNCC.2018.8530962

54. Fraunhofer Fokus, Eclipse MOSAIC - A Multi-Domain and Multi-Scale Simulation Framework for Connected and Automated Mobility. https://www.eclipse.org/mosaic/. Accessed 11 Mar 2021

55. EstiNet - Simulator. https://www.estinet.com/ns/. Accessed 11 Mar 2021

56. VNS - Simulator. https://github.com/enriquefynn/libvns. Accessed 11 Mar 2021

57. Ivanov, I.V., Maple, C., Watson, T., Lee, S.: Cyber security standards and issues in V2X communications for Internet of Vehicles. In: Living in the Internet of Things: Cybersecurity of the IoT - 2018, IET London, Savoy Place, 28–29 March 2018 (2018). ISBN 9781785618437. https://doi.org/10.1049/cp.2018.0046

58. Abdel Hakeem, S.A., Hady, A.A., Kim, H.W.: 5G-V2X: standardization, architecture, use cases, network-slicing, and edge-computing. Wirel. Netw. 26(8), 6015–6041 (2020)

59. Alnasser, A., Sun, H., Jiang, J.: Cyber security challenges and solutions for V2X communications: a survey. Comput. Netw. 151, 52–67 (2019)

Implementation and Comparison of Four Algorithms on Transportation Problem

Eghbal Hosseini[1], Line Reinhardt[1], Kayhan Zrar Ghafoor[2(✉)], and Danda B. Rawat[3]

[1] Department of People and Technology, Roskilde University, Roskilde, Denmark
hosseini@ruc.dk
[2] Department of Software Engineering, Salahaddin University-Erbil, Erbil 44002, Kurdistan Region, Iraq
mrkayhanz@gmail.com
[3] Department of Electrical Engineering and Computer Science, Howard University, Washington, DC, USA

Abstract. The transportation problem is a very applicable and relevant logistic problem. In this paper, to test meta-heuristics on the transportation problem and also improve initial feasible solutions in few number of iterations, four recent and effective meta-heuristic algorithms are used to solve transportation problems. Laying Chicken Algorithm (LCA), Volcano Eruption Algorithm (VEA), COVID-19 Optimizer Algorithm (CVA), and Multiverse Algorithm (MVA) are implemented to solve different sizes of the transportation problem. Computational results show that CVA is the most efficient optimizer for large size cases and LCA is the best algorithm for the others. Finally, convergence of algorithms will be discussed and rate of convergence will be compared. The advantage of these heuristics are that they can be easily adapted to more challenging versions of the transportation problem which are not solveable by the Simplex method.

Keywords: Transportation problems · Meta-heuristic algorithm

1 Introduction

One of the significant linear programming problems is the transportation problem which is used for inventory, assignment and traffic [1,8,10,11]. In the transportation problem a product is transported from a set of sources to a set of destinations minimizing the transportation cost while satisfying the demand, the mathematical formulation has been shown in (1)–(4).

$$\min \sum_{i=1}^{m} \sum_{j=1}^{n} c_{ij} x_{ij} \tag{1}$$

$$Subject\ to\ \sum_{j=1}^{n} x_{ij} \le S_i, i = 1, 2..., m \tag{2}$$

S. Paiva et al. (Eds.): SmartCity360° 2021, LNICST 442, pp. 422–433, 2022.
https://doi.org/10.1007/978-3-031-06371-8_28

$$\sum_{i=1}^{m} x_{ij} = D_j, j = 1, 2..., n \qquad (3)$$

$$x_{ij} \geq 0 \qquad (4)$$

Proposing optimal solution needs to start from a feasible solution as Initial Feasible Solution (IFS). Although several meta-heuristic approaches have been proposed to solve optimization problems, but there just few methods in references which can find IFS for the problem [8]. The existing methods to achieve the minimal total cost do not propose a suitable feasible solution to reduce the number of iterations [2,3]. Thus, it is still a challenge to present a better method of IFS. Our heuristic algorithms have been designed to fit the aforementioned challenges of the transportation problem.

In this paper, Laying Chicken Algorithm (LCA), Volcano Eruption Algorithm (VEA), COVID-19 Optimizer Algorithm (CVA), and Multiverse Algorithm (MVA) [4–7]are used to find IFS of different transportation problems. Feasibility, efficiency and convergence of these algorithms are discussed and finally algorithms with best results are compared with Vogel and ZSM [8,9].

2   LCA, VEA, MVA and CVA Algorithms

2.1   Laying Chicken Algorithm (LCA)

Laying Chicken Algorithm focuses on behavior of laying hens and finding an answer to how does the hen convert the egg to the chicken? LCA converts the feasible solutions to the optimal solution, same as eggs to the chicken. In fact, each feasible solution of a continuous programming problem displays an egg and the optimal solution of the problem is a chicken. Here hens try to warm their eggs; this concept is used to change and improve the solutions in LCA. As the temperature is increased the solutions to the problem are improved. Rotation of eggs is the next concept which will be simulated by a little mutation in the solutions. There are the following steps to formulate of the behavior the hen in the LCA optimizer [4]:

1. The first egg which displays initial solution.
2. More eggs displays initial population close to the initial solution.
3. Improve solutions of population inspiring from warming eggs.
4. Little mutation of solutions inspiring of rotation of eggs.

2.2   Volcano Eruption Algorithm (VEA)

The Volcano Eruption Algorithm, inspired by the nature of a volcano eruption. VEA optimizer imitates the process of volcano eruption, which is a hole on the earth's surface. This phenomenon acts as a vent for release of pressurized gases, molten rock or magma deep beneath the surface of earth. Magma

Algorithm 1. LCA Procedure for Transportation Problem

1: n: Number of solutions
2: N: Number of Iterations
3: α: A given positive number (less than size of the problem)
4: Generate a random initial feasible solution X0
5: Generate initial population near initial solution
6: **for** $i \leftarrow 1$ to N **do**
7:    **for** $k \leftarrow 1$ to n **do**
8:       **if** Xk is not better than X0 **then**
9: $Xk = X0 + \alpha * \left(\frac{Xk}{||Xk||}\right)$
10:      **end if**
11: $Xk = Xk + \frac{Xk}{||Xk||}$
12:    **end for**
13: **end for**

---

is passed through a channel from deep underground called the volcanic pipe. Magma erupts out of the earth's surface when it reaches the hole on the surface. There are the following steps leading to formation of a volcano to VEA optimizer [5]:

1. Rise of magma through the volcanic pipe.
2. Volcanic eruption by rising of magma to the surface of the earth.
3. Lava's cooling down and therefore formation of a crust.
4. Repetition of this process over time leading to several layers of rock that builds up over time resulting in a volcano.

Algorithms 1–4 show the pseudocodes of LCA, VEA, CVA, and MVA algorithms respectively.

2.3 COVID-19 Optimizer Algorithm (CVA)

The Covid-19 Optimizer Algorithm, inspired by the coronavirus, inspired by the coronavirus in nature which has started spreading rapidly due to its high transmission behavior. CVA has two significant parts: outbreaks and export. These outbreaks and export processes have given inspiration to the proposed CVA algorithm to generate its initial solutions and population mimicking COVID-19 spreading behavior. Some of the solutions are removed from the population because of the fact that those cases have recovered or already passed away. So the algorithm will carry on exploring the remaining best solutions. The following steps formulate COVID-19 to create the CVA optimizer [6]:

1. Initial place to start the virus which displays initial solution for CVA.
2. Outbreaks in the initial area displays initial population close to the initial solution.
3. Export processes displays solutions far from initial area.
4. Selection of the best solutions inspiring from the recovery process.

Algorithm 2. VEA Procedure for Transportation Problem

1: n: Number of solutions
2: s: Size of the problem
3: Rand: Random integer number between 1 and s
4: λ: A given integer positive number
5: Generate initial population
6: **for** $t \leftarrow 1$ to λ **do**
7:     **for** $k \leftarrow 1$ to n **do**
8: $Xk = Xk + Rand * \frac{Xk}{||Xk||}$ (Distribution of solutions in feasible region)
9:     **end for**
10: Find best solution
11: Let $Xt = xbest$
12: **end for**
13: **for** $t \leftarrow 1$ to λ **do**
14:     **for** $i \leftarrow 1$ to n **do**
15: $Xi = Xt + Rand * \frac{Xk}{||Xk||}$ (Distribution of best solutions)
16:     **end for**
17: Find best solution
18: Let $Yt = xbest$
19: **end for**

Algorithm 3. CVA Procedure for Transportation Problem

1: n: Number of solutions
2: N: Number of Iterations
3: s: Size of the problem
4: Rand: Random integer number between 1 and s
5: β: percentage of export
6: Generate a random initial solution X0
7: Generate initial population inccluding $(1 - \beta n)$ solutions near initial solution
8: Export $\beta n)$ solutions to other regions
9: **for** $k \leftarrow 1$ to N **do**
10:     **for** $k \leftarrow 1$ to $(1 - \beta)n$ **do**
11: $Xk = X0 + (\frac{Xk}{||Xk||})$
12:     **end for**
13:     **for** $k \leftarrow (1 - \beta)n + 1$ to n **do**
14: $Xk = X0 + Rand * (\frac{Xk}{||Xk||})$
15:     **end for**
16: **end for**

2.4   Multiverse Algorithm (MVA)

Multiverse Algorithm has been inspired from multiverse theory which states that there are several universes, not one, in the world. More particularly, multiverse theory states there are more than one big bangs besides to the big bang of our universe. So MVA algorithm comes from the existence of several worlds and big bangs. Therefore, MVA algorithm starts with a several solutions as initial population. Each universe is built from a very small and dense particle based on multiverse theory. This is the main idea to create the next population very close to the solutions of initial population in the simulated MVA. Finally, all solutions are distributed in the feasible region same as big bangs. Following steps have been used to formulate multiverse theory to MVA optimizer [7]:

1. Several universes which displays initial population including several solutions.
2. Very dense particles display many solutions very close to initial solutions.
3. Distribution of solutions in the feasible region inspiring from big bangs.
4. Rotation of solutions inspiring from the rotation of particles in multiverse theory.

Algorithm 4. MVA Procedure for Transportation Problem

1: n: Number of solutions
2: N: Number of Iterations
3: m: A given integer positive number
4: s: Size of the problem
5: Rand: Random integer number between 1 and s
6: Generate initial population including n solutions
7: **for** $t \leftarrow 1$ to N **do**
8:     **for** $k \leftarrow 1$ to n **do**
9:         **for** $i \leftarrow 1$ to m **do**
10: $Xi = Xk + Rand * \frac{Xk}{||Xk||}$ (Explosion of initial population)
11:         **end for**
12: Find the best solution and let $Xk = xbest$
13:     **end for**
14:     **for** $j \leftarrow 1$ to m **do**
15: $Xj = Xk + Rand * \frac{Xk}{||Xk||}$ (Explosion of the best solutions)
16: Find the best solution and let $XtF = xbest$
17:     **end for**
18: **end for**

The behavior of the algorithms when finding of the optimal solution during the five iterations for an optimization problem with two global optima is shown in Fig. 2.

Figure 2-a shows initial population of LCA algorithm, and Fig. 2-b shows that optimal solutions, large red points, have been surrounded by best solution of LCA after five iterations. Figure 2-c shows initial population of VEA algorithm, and Fig. 2-d shows that one of optimal solutions has been completely surrounded by best solution of VEA. Figure 2-e and Fig. 2-f show the process of MVA to solve the problem. Finally, Fig. 2-g and Fig. 2-h show the behavior of CVA for solving the problem which the optimal solution is the blue point.

Problem 1:
Consider the following non-linear problem:

$$\max e^{-(x-4)^2-(y-4)^2} + e^{-(x+4)^2-(y-4)^2} + 2(e^{-x^2-y^2} + e^{-x^2-(y+4)^2}) \qquad (5)$$

Figure 1 shows optimal solutions, contours and diagram of problem 1.

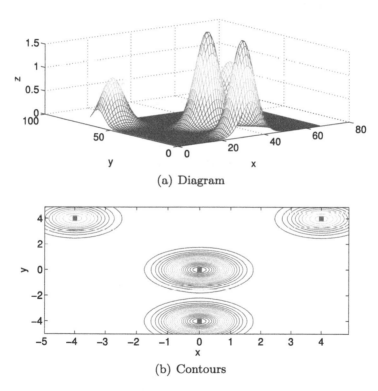

(a) Diagram

(b) Contours

Fig. 1. Contours and diagram of Problem 1

3   Computational Results

To show the numerical efficiency of the algorithms, several transportation problems are solved. CVA is the best for very large size problems and LCA is the best algorithm for others. Convergence rate of algorithms for a given problem has been shown in Fig. 3.

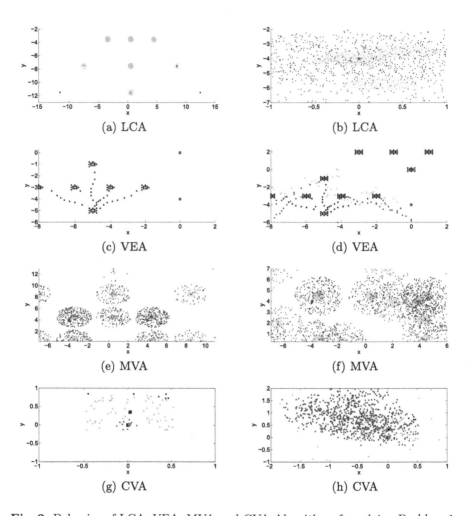

Fig. 2. Behavior of LCA, VEA, MVA and CVA Algorithms for solving Problem 1

Table 1. Results by the first iteration for different sizes of the problem up to four decimal places.

Size of problem	LCA	VEA	MVA	CVA
20 * 10	126.9417	**123.2145**	154.2567	138.6532
80 * 50	889.8801	1004.2255	**821.5467**	1010.3287
200 * 100	**1.3808e+03**	1.4511e+03	1.4321e+03	1.4124e+03
300 * 200	**2.8508e+03**	3.1256e+03	3.0345e+03	2.8621e+03
800 * 500	**7.7524e+03**	7.8865e+03	7.8724e+03	7.7843e+03
2000 * 1000	1.4991e+04	1.6324e+04	1.7843e+04	**1.4985e+04**
5000 * 2000	3.0816e+04	3.2567e+04	3.3587e+04	**3.0003e+04**
7000 * 3000	4.6838e+04	4.8456e+04	4.8632e+04	**4.4802e+04**
10000 * 5000	7.5023e+04	7.7834e+04	7.8246e+04	**7.3543e+04**

Table 2. Results with five iterations for different sizes of the transportation problem

Size of problem	LCA	VEA	MVA	CVA
20 * 10	108.5360	**101.6532**	142.1287	112.4765
80 * 50	826.2148	885.1265	**815.8721**	1000.1263
200 * 100	**1.3635e+03**	1.4167e+03	1.4214e+03	1.4014e+03
300 * 200	**2.8487e+03**	3.003e+03	3.002e+03	2.8523e+03
800 * 500	**7.7487e+03**	7.8860e+03	7.8521e+03	7.7753e+03
2000 * 1000	1.4976e+04	1.6301e+04	1.7821e+04	**1.4821e+04**
5000 * 2000	3.0814e+04	3.2521e+04	3.3501e+04	**2.9831e+04**
7000 * 3000	4.6814e+04	4.8412e+04	4.8600e+04	**4.4786e+04**
10000 * 5000	7.5017e+04	7.7821e+04	7.8213e+04	**7.3521e+04**

Tables 1, 2 and 3 show the results of all four algorithms to find IFS for nine transportation problems with different sizes. Table 1 shows the results at the first iteration, it is clear that CVA is very efficient for very large size problems and LCA is the best for other sizes. Tables 2 and 3 show the results after 5 and 20 iterations respectively. Table 4 shows comparison of LCA, CVA with Min-Cost and Vogel algorithms. Based on the results of this table, proposed algorithm is much better than Vogel algorithm which is the best method to find IFS. Finally, Table 5 shows the improvement of solution rather than Vogel by LCA and CVA.

Figure 2 shows the rate of convergence for LCA, CVA, VEA, and MVA algorithms to find IBFS of a given transportation problem which it's optimal solution is 87.

Table 3. Best results after 20 iterations up to four decimal places.

Size of problem	LCA	VEA	MVA	CVA
20 * 10	101.6923	**87.1245**	132.0327	110.173
80 * 50	820.2360	864.8234	**785.1241**	974.0217
200 * 100	**1.3601e+03**	1.4032e+03	1.4014e+03	1.3846e+03
300 * 200	**2.8300e+03**	2.991e+03	2.972e+03	2.8421e+03
800 * 500	**7.7457e+03**	7.8743e+03	7.8500e+03	7.7658e+03
2000 * 1000	1.4903e+04	1.6281e+04	1.7543e+04	**1.4748e+04**
5000 * 2000	3.0811e+04	3.2503e+04	3.2846e+04	**2.9785e+04**
7000 * 3000	4.6753e+04	4.8401e+04	4.85450e+04	**4.4700e+04**
10000 * 5000	7.5004e+04	7.7811e+04	7.8005e+04	**7.3456e+04**

Table 4. Comparison of LCA and CVA with previous approaches.

Size of problem	Min-Cost	Vogel	LCA	CVA
200 * 50	843.1786	637.5617	**324.9941**	543.7385
400 * 80	1.5780e+03	902.3972	**502.6537**	743.1247
1000 * 800	1.4670e+05	1.4583e+04	**7.0897e+03**	7.1247e+03
3000 * 2000	3.8145e+05	4.6366e+04	2.2907e+04	**2.2901e+04**
8000 * 5000	4.1862e+06	1.2149e+05	7.5494e+04	**7.5356e+04**
12000 * 10000	1.8853e+06	1.8551e+05	1.2971e+05	**1.2886e+05**

Table 5. Improvement rate of LCA and CVA Rather Vogel.

Size of problem	Laying Chicken Algorithm (LCA)	COVID-19 Optimizer Algorithm (CVA)
200 * 50	**49%**	15%
400 * 80	**44%**	18%
1000 * 800	**51%**	50%
3000 * 2000	**50%**	50%
8000 * 5000	37%	**38%**
12000 * 10000	30%	**31%**

All four algorithms have been run for 300 times with 50 agents. Based on the results of this figure, LCA achieves 100 after 90 iterations and CVA obtains 100 after 140 iterations. Best solution by VEA is 365 after 80 iterations and MVA gets 400 after 110 iterations. Tables 6 shows the detail of test problems by [2] and Tables 7 shows the results and comparison of LCA and CVA with ZSM. results after 5 and 20 iterations respectively

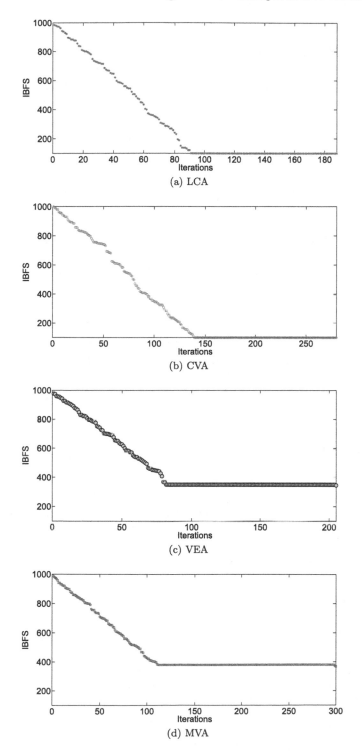

Fig. 3. Convergent Rate of LCA, CVA, VEA and MVA Algorithms with 300 Iterations for Finding IFS

Table 6. Data of proposed problems by [2]

Problems	Data
Problem 2	$C = [6, 8, 10; 7, 11, 11; 4, 5, 12], S = [150, 175, 275], D = [200, 100, 300]$
Problem 3	$C = [20, 22, 17, 4; 24, 37, 9, 7; 32, 37, 20, 15], S = [120, 70, 50], D = [60, 40, 30, 110]$
Problem 4	$C = [4, 6, 8, 8; 6, 8, 6, 7; 5, 7, 6, 8], S = [40, 60, 50], D = [20, 30, 50, 50]$
Problem 5	$C = [19, 30, 50, 12; 70, 30, 40, 60; 40, 10, 60, 20], S = [7, 10, 18], D = [5, 7, 8, 15]$
Problem 6	$C = [13, 18, 30, 8; 55, 20, 25, 40; 30, 6, 50, 10], S = [8, 10, 11], D = [4, 6, 7, 12]$
Problem 7	$C = [25, 14, 34, 46, 45; 10, 47, 14, 20, 41; 22, 42, 38, 21, 46; 36, 20, 41, 38, 44],$
	$S = [27, 35, 37, 45], D = [22, 27, 28, 33, 34]$
Problem 8	$C = [9, 12, 9, 6, 9, 10; 7, 3, 7, 7, 5, 5; 6, 5, 9, 11, 3, 11; 6, 8, 11, 2, 2, 10], S = [2, 5, 6, 9]$
	$D = [2, 2, 4, 4, 4, 6]$

Table 7. Comparison of LCA and CVA with ZSM [2]

Prob. no	ZSM	LCA	CVA	Improvement by LCA	Improvement by CVA
2	4525	4525	**4525**	0%	**0%**
3	3460	**2960**	3220	**14%**	7%
4	920	1030	1010	−11%	−9%
5	864	**664**	764	**23%**	11%
6	476	**380**	402	**20%**	15%
7	3598	4221	3820	−17%	−6%
8	136	210	**130**	−54%	**4%**

4   Conclusion

This paper used four recent efficient meta-heuristic algorithms for finding Initial Feasible Solution (IFS) of transportation problems. The computational results show that not only the algorithms are feasible but also they are very efficient. So, using these algorithms for other practical problems of optimization such as: routing problems, emergency logistics, green supply chain, and stowage planning could be a suitable idea for future works.

References

1. Aizemberg, L., Kramer, H.H., Pessoa, A.A., Uchoa, E.: Formulations for a problem of petroleum transportation. Eur. J. Oper. Res. **237**(1), 82–90 (2014). https://doi.org/10.1016/j.ejor.2014.01.036
2. Amaliah, B., Fatichah, C., Suryani, E.: A new heuristic method of finding the initial basic feasible solution to solve the transportation problem. J. King Saud Univ. Comput. Inf. Sci. **22** (2020)
3. Cosma, O., Pop, P.C., Dănciulescu, D.: A novel matheuristic approach for a two-stage transportation problem with fixed costs associated to the routes. Comput. Oper. Res. **118**, 104906 (2020). https://doi.org/10.1016/j.cor.2020.104906

4. Hosseini, E.: Laying chicken algorithm: a new meta-heuristic approach to solve continuous programming problems. J. Appl. Comput. Math. **6**(1), 1–8 (2017)

5. Hosseini, E., Sadiq, A.S., Ghafoor, K.Z., Rawat, D.B., Saif, M., Yang, X.: Volcano eruption algorithm for solving optimization problems. Neural Comput. Appl. **33**(7), 2321–37 (2021)

6. Hosseini, E., Ghafoor, K.Z., Sadiq, A.S., Guizani, M., Emrouznejad, A.: Covid-19 optimizer algorithm, modeling and controlling of coronavirus distribution process. IEEE J. Biomed. Health Inf. **24**(10), 2765–2775 (2020)

7. Hosseini, E., Ghafoor, K.Z., Emrouznejad, A., Sadiq, A.S., Rawat, D.B.: Novel metaheuristic based on multiverse theory for optimization problems in emerging systems. Appl. Intell. **11**, 1–8 (2020)

8. Juman, Z.A., Hoque, M.A.: An efficient heuristic to obtain a better initial feasible solution to the transportation problem. Appl. Soft Comput. **1**(34), 813–26 (2015)

9. Juman, Z.A.M.S., Hoque, M.A., Buhari, M.I.: A sensitivity analysis and an implementation of the Wellknown Vogel's approximation method for solving unbalanced transportation problem. Malays. J. Sci. **32**(1), 66–72 (2013)

10. Ramadan, S.Z., Ramadan, I.Z.: Hybrid two-stage algorithm for solving transportation problem. Mod. Appl. Sci. **6**(4), 12 (2012)

11. Soriano, A., Vidal, T., Gansterer, M., Doerner, K.: The vehicle routing problem with arrival time diversification on a multigraph. Eur. J. Oper. Res. **280**(2), 504–575 (2020)

Critical Review of Citizens' Participation in Achieving Smart Sustainable Cities: The Case of Saudi Arabia

Abood Khaled Alamoudi[(⊠)] [ID], Rotimi Boluwatife Abidoye [ID], and Terence Y M Lam [ID]

The University of New South Wales, Sydney, Australia
a.alamoudi@student.unsw.edu.au

Abstract. The concept of citizens' participation (CP) has been widely adopted by scholars, professionals and governments around the world. Many frameworks have been developed that include CP as a core domain. Although government agencies admit the usefulness of adopting CP, there is little written about the application of CP in the context of smart cities. The aim of this study is to critically review the literature focussed on engaging, empowering and enabling citizens to participate in achieving smart cities in relation to decision-making, digital communication and socio-cultural pillars, and to develop a conceptual framework that helps in demonstrating the interconnection of the identified fields. The data were retrieved from online search engines. Google trends, annual publications, CP in relation to other domains, authors' affiliations and active authors were reviewed. Since 1985, there has been a considerable number of articles published annually relating to CP, yet there has been a fluctuation in the number of annual publications. Authors have contributed significantly to the topic of smart cities. However, there is little in the literature that contributes to achieving smart sustainable cities through CP. Moreover, recent publications have increased dramatically compared to past years. Universities are the top contributors in terms of authors' affiliations. Subject to validation by empirical evidence, the citizens' participation framework developed can be adopted to achieve smart, sustainable urbanisation in Saudi Arabia. The framework focuses on the empowerment of CP in making decisions, the application of ICT to facilitate CP and effective stakeholder communication between citizens and government.

Keywords: Smart cities · Citizens' participation · Digital communication · Socio-cultural · Decision making

1 Introduction

Since 1968, Citizens' Participation (CP) has been adopted widely, yet to date, there is no clear definition of the role and level of CP in decision making in the built environment. Many measurable models, such as Leadership in Energy and Environmental Design (LEED), the Building Research Establishment Environmental Assessment

© ICST Institute for Computer Sciences, Social Informatics and Telecommunications Engineering 2022
Published by Springer Nature Switzerland AG 2022. All Rights Reserved
S. Paiva et al. (Eds.): SmartCity360° 2021, LNICST 442, pp. 434–454, 2022.
https://doi.org/10.1007/978-3-031-06371-8_29

Method (BREEAM), the Comprehensive Assessment System for Built Environment Efficiency (CASBEE) and the smart city wheel were developed in response to rapid urbanisation challenges (Kuster 2019). These green rating systems are primarily focused on measuring sustainable project outcomes for individual projects and community development. There is no indication of how to engage citizens as the main stakeholders and users who contribute to the development of smart sustainable cities. Many governments have adopted various urban sustainable systems for decades. Urban areas are incredibly sophisticated and complicated, and a holistic system, such as the smart cities concept (SCC), is necessary to cope with their complexity (Girardi and Temporelli 2016; Neirotti et al. 2014). However, smart sustainable cities (SCC) still face challenges in delivering smart sustainable outcomes. These imply heavy techno-centricity, practice complexity and ad-hoc conceptualisation of smart cities (Yigitcanlar et al. 2018b). Smart cities, as reviewed from academia's point of view, are complex ecosystems supported by technological, infrastructural transformation of citizens' engagement, learning and participation (Andone et al. 2014). SCC has been acknowledged as a techno-centric concept because of the leverage of information communication technology (ICT). However, scholars argue that social, cultural, economic and environmental aspects are essential pillars in successfully implementing smart sustainable cities (Aina 2017).

Saudi Arabia has been judged as one of the fastest-growing countries globally (UN-Habitat 2018). Based on the best of the authors' knowledge and a review of the literature over the last 20 years, there is very limited research focusing on CP in relation to achieving smart sustainable cities in Saudi Arabia. Therefore, this paper is an attempt to examine the current state of CP in achieving smart cities in Saudi Arabia. The objectives to be pursued are (1) to identify the most reported CP in relation to decision making, digital communication and socio-cultural areas, and (2) to develop a conceptual framework that helps in demonstrating the gaps of the identified felds. Apart from this introduction section, the remainder of this paper is structured into four sections. The following section will present the background of smart cities and citizens' participation. The third section will present the research methodology adopted in this research. The fourth section will present the results and discussion. The last section will present the conclusions of the study.

2 Literature Review

2.1 Smart Sustainable Cities

The initial emergence of the smart cities concept was in the context of communicating with residents in the neighbourhood and their local businesses for leisure and convenience (Bashynska and Dyskina 2018). Since 1993, the concept of smart cities has evolved and combined more responsibilities to serve society better (see Fig. 1). It is evident that the smart cities concept attracts decision-makers all over the world. The Smart City 3.0 framework comprises six characteristics that are often considered an essential part of the smart city concept. These six characteristics are smart living, smart environment, smart people, smart economy, smart mobility and smart governance (Bashynska and Dyskina 2018).

1993 • Smart Growth, UN Conference, Rio

1997 • Smart Community, Silicon Valley, USA

2007 • The European Union Vision, Smart City Wheel, Vienna University

2010 • Smart City 1.0, Instrumented tools, IBM

2011 • Smart Society for Innovative and Sustainable Cities, Barcelona

2014 • Smart City 2.0, Solve Social Problems, European Parliament

2017 • The Limits To Growth, Volkswagen Foundation

2018 • Smart City 3.0, Cities of the Future, "Smart Sustainable Cities"

Fig. 1. The development of the smart city concept. **Adapted from:** Bencardino and Greco (2014), Shields (2014)

The idea of SCC has attracted many researchers in a wide range of disciplines. However, this concept has been used as a 'label', and its meaning and objective are inconsistent (Bibri and Krogstie 2017a, b). The phrase 'smart city' is interchangeably used in a variety of disciplines under various names: smart city, creative city, resilient city, smart community, knowledgeable city, intelligent city, information city and sustainable city (Yigitcanlar et al. 2018b). For example, the Ministry of Municipal and Rural Affairs (MOMRA) in Saudi Arabia announced that they have successfully implemented the smart city concept, which turned out to be smart parking (Alsitre 2019). Although smart parking is a minor aspect of the concept as a whole, it does not represent the holistic idea of smart cities as it was advertised. Because of the variety of interpretations of smart sustainable cities and the tremendous number of existing performance and measurement systems of smart cities and urban sustainability, pragmatism in measuring the smartness and sustainability of cities is even more challenging and complicated (Ahvenniemi et al. 2017). Researchers argue that to date, the meaning of smart cities is not clear and is inconsistently understood (Ahvenniemi et al. 2017; Yigitcanlar et al. 2018b).

Scholars have been developing frameworks and models around this concept, most of which have not included citizens' participation. For example, the smart city wheel (Lekamge and Marasinghe 2013), European Smart Cities Ranking (Fusero et al. 2013), Smart Benchmarking in China (Lu et al. 2015), Triple-helix Network Model for Smart Cities Performance (Lombardi et al. 2011), Smart City Profiles (Storch 2018), City Protocol (City Protocol 2018) and Citykeys (Airaksinen et al. 2017) are frameworks and models acknowledged in academia, yet participative approaches are less likely to be found in authoritarian states. Likewise, the discussion on 'smart' cities is rather uncritical. There have been a range of researchers that pointed at the risks of smart city concepts, such as its inherent lack of data security and socio-spatial connectedness (Colding and

Barthel 2017), a lack of face-to-face governance, and the tendency to embrace corporate control, which may turn a city into a profit-driven living laboratory (Duffield 2016).

2.2 The Role of Citizens' Participation in Promoting Decision Making

Arnstein (2019) argued that CP is a pillar of policies and governance focused around developing a real sustainable city. Stakeholder Management Theory (SMT) is an approach that involves humans in the development and management of a city and avoids centralised policies and decision making (Garba 2004; Wu and Kang 2013). Freeman and Reed (1983) believe that strategic management is an essential part of any development. However, some countries still do not involve their citizens in development (Bouzguenda et al. 2019; Granier and Kudo 2016). In implementing smart cities, it is crucial to gain insightful datasets by supporting citizens' participation, which could be done quickly and save cost. Yang and Pandey (2011) define citizens' participation as decision-making and management processes that use a bottom-up approach for decision making. The rationale of CP is to design and build services tailored to citizens' real needs. Scholars such as Bouzguenda et al. (2019) see the hierarchy of citizens' participation in three nodes: (1) digital citizens' participation, (2) community engagement and (3) social-cultural sustainability. Other scholars, such as Arnstein (2019), proposed a typology for CP called the ladder of CP that consists of eight levels. The steps of the ladder from bottom to top are as follows: 1- Manipulation, 2- Therapy, 3- Information, 4-Consultation, 5- Placation, 6- Partnership, 7- Delegated Power, 8- Citizen Control. Burke (1968) believes that CP depends on certain conditions and assumptions; thus, not all strategies are effective for all organisations. Best practices are an essential component when learning from others' experiences of successes and failures. For example, the Indian 100 smart mission experienced major challenges that affected the previous implementation and made it difficult for the Smart Cities Mission (SCM) to be accepted in the Indian built environment. Moreover, the European experience was notable and noteworthy for understanding how the government that involves citizens' participation helped their cities to solve many urban issues. Singapore Missions, on the other hand, recorded a tremendous achievement in terms of adopting ICT. Finally, Masdar City witnesses that technicality and technology are not everything in achieving urban sustainability, as humans are one of the pillars of urban development.

3 Research Methodology

This study aims to comprehensively review the existing body of knowledge on CP in achieving smart sustainable cities. Literature reviews are widely used among scholars to determine existing studies (Liberati et al. 2009). Therefore, the method used in this paper is a systematic review of the literature that proposes to support and understand the essential aspects and dimensions related to citizens' participation and smart cities. This study adopts the Preferred Reporting Item for Systematic Reviews and Meta-analysis (PRISMA) framework to identify, screen and assess its literature review (Liberati et al. 2009). The study follows a three-stage procedure via the methodological approach shown in Fig. 2. In Stage 1, keywords are identified based on the literature search. A Google search trend is investigated for the formulated keywords. Stage 2 applies the inclusion and exclusion criteria. Accordingly, yearly publications, authors' affiliations and focus study areas are analysed and synthesised. Stage 3 involves developing a conceptual framework for citizens' participation in relation to decision making, digital communication and socio-cultural factors.

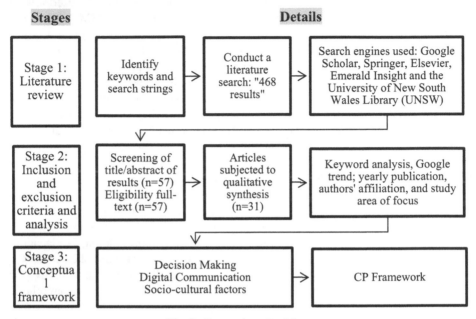

Fig. 2. Research methodology

Stage 1 focusses on addressing the research gap of adopting CP in decision making and examines the extent to which it supports the implementation of smart sustainable cities. Searches were conducted through five databases, namely Google Scholar, Springer, Elsevier, Taylor Francis and the University of New South Wales Library (UNSW). This step required searching for valuable and reliable sources for the collected data. Articles published in journals, conference proceedings and government documents were reviewed. Theses, dissertations, and unpublished articles were not selected for this study because such data may not be publicly available. Moreover, academic journals between 1980 and 2021 were selected for this study were the first published paper was in 1980 (Whitaker 1980) and the most recent studies were published in 2020. Several thematic searches were performed, which consisted of multiple words (Yigitcanlar et al. 2018b). The keywords used in all thematic searches were 'smart cities', 'citizens' participation', 'socio-cultural sustainability', 'policies and governance' and 'Saudi Arabia'. As suggested by Jabareen (2008), there are three steps to determining keywords for a literature search: 1- recognition of similarities, 2- synthesis action of general themes and 3- formation of a multidimensional framework. By applying these steps, three general themes were retrieved: digital communication, decision making and socio-cultural sustainability.

The initial thematic search was conducted using the keywords: ((TitleCombined:(smart cities)) AND ((TitleCombined:(Policies)) OR ((TitleCombined:(Citizens' Participation))). The search resulted in 71 articles, 45 conference proceedings and three government reports. The second thematic was conducted by using the following keywords: ((TitleCombined:('socio-cultural sustainability')) AND ((TitleCombined:(Policies)) OR ((TitleCombined:(Citizens' Participation))). The search resulted in 130 articles, 69 conference proceedings and 25 government reports. The third thematic was: ((TitleCombined:('smart cities')) AND ((TitleCombined:(socio-cultural sustainability)) OR ((TitleCombined:(Policies))). The search resulted in 30 articles, 55 conference proceedings and 40 government reports (see Table 1).

Table 1. Distribution of research thematic

Thematic search	Publisher			Conference proceeding	Government report and websites
	Elsevier	Taylor Francis	Springer		
Smart cities and policies and governance or citizens' participation	45	8	18	45	3
Socio-cultural sustainability and policies and governance or citizens' participation	67	45	18	69	25
Smart cities and socio-cultural sustainability or policies	20	7	3	55	40
Total number	132	60	39	169	68
Percentage	49%			36%	15%

Stage 2, inclusion and exclusion criteria, is an essential step in this study because it applies further visual examination to exclude papers that are not related to the study area but might have been included due to a keyword search. Tijani et al. (2020) adopted a comprehensive scan of abstracts, which exclude the papers that do not fit within the study area. Table 2 shows only that 57 (30 articles, 22 conference proceedings and five government documents) out of 468 articles met the selection criteria for this study and were subjected to further analysis. Table 2 show that 57 papers were initially read to retrieve the most relevant papers. A further reduction was made after reading the full texts and excluding unrelated articles that did not discuss CP in relation to smart cities. The selection of qualified papers was ultimately limited to 31. The 31 selected papers were read, reviewed and then analysed using descriptive analysis to explore the trends in keywords, years and geography of publication, author affiliation, focus study area and active authors.

Table 2. Retrieved publications with selected journals

No.	Journals	Number of previous searches	Number of final searches
1	Journal of the American Planning Association	10	3
2	Sustainable Cities and Society	8	5
3	International Journal of Urban Policy and Planning	12	4
4	Journal of Social Sciences and Humanities		3
5	Malaysian Journal of Society and Space	1	1
6	Advances in Economics, Business and Management Research	3	1
7	Resources Conservation and Recycling	4	1
8	Journal of E-Learning and Knowledge Society	3	2
9	Government Information Quarterly	2	1
10	Socio-Economic Planning Sciences	2	2
11	Journal of Advanced Science and Technology	1	1
12	Cities	4	3
13	The Electronic Journal of Information Systems in Developing Countries	3	2
14	Social Indicators Research	2	1
15	Journal of Information Systems and Operations Management	2	1
	Total	57	31

Table 2 shows the journals in which the selected 31 papers were published. This number is a reason to conduct a critical review on smart cities in relation to CP when compared with previous studies. For example, Yigitcanlar and Kamruzzaman (2015) conducted a literature review with 35 papers focused on smart cities being sustainable, Marrone and Hammerle (2018) conducted a review with 25 papers in the area of stakeholder management and Tijani et al. (2020) performed a review with 38 papers on mental stress in construction.

Stage 3 involves developing a framework related to smart cities and urban sustainability that takes into consideration the CP concept. The framework consists of three main pillars: decision making, digital communication and socio-cultural pillars. Each pillar of the framework was studied and addressed.

4 Results and Discussion

4.1 Global Smart Cities Trends

Figure 3 shows a world map for the top contributing countries based on the keywords used in this study. The results show the top five countries where the studies originated. In terms of geographical distribution, it is clear that the literature review did not fill in the gaps in the Saudi Arabia region. Asian and European countries have intensely adopted the smart cities concept. In Asia, developed and developing countries such as Japan (Granier and Kudo 2016), Korea (Lee and Hancock 2012) and China (Shah et al. 2017) analyse smart cities through digital communication tools, while India (Praharaja et al. 2016; Rajput and Sharma 2017) considers the smart cities concept through policy tourism (Praharaja 2018). The smart cities concept in Asian countries is considered a promising urban planning and management framework and an answer to their urbanisation and environmental challenges (González 2011). The growing interest in smart cities to solve urban issues has attracted governments, institutions, companies and even individuals. In 2012, there were 143 ongoing funded projects, of which 55 were based in Asia, 47 in Europe, 30 in the United States and fewer than 10 in the Middle East and Africa (Ahvenniemi et al. 2017; Albino et al. 2015). On the other hand, the concept of smart cities in European Union countries supports the idea of urban sustainability by promoting the reduction of greenhouse gas emissions through the deployment of technology (Ahvenniemi et al. 2017; Caragliu et al. 2009). The European Union adopts smart cities through six dimensions, which were invented by Boyd Cohen[1] and are commonly known as the European smart cities wheel (Andone et al. 2014; Soe 2017). The dimensions are smart people, smart economy, smart mobility, smart living, smart governance and smart environments (Andone et al. 2014). Although technology has played a key role in smart cities in both East and West, the applications and focus differ (Praharaja 2018). The role of human capital and social capital in urban development based on the availability and quality of ICT may define smart cities (Caragliu et al. 2009).

---

[1] Boyd Cohen is a scholar at the university of Victoria, Canada, who invented the smart cities wheel for the European Union.

Fig. 3. Compared breakdown by region using Google Trends for global search.

Figure 4 shows the world publication's trends from 2004 to 2021 based on decision making, socio-cultural factors and digital communication pillars. Although this study explores publications since 1980, the topic is relatively new, and no record is presented in Google Trend. Figure 4 shows that there is a gap between these keywords. In addition, there was an abrupt increase between 2012 and 2016 in smart city publications. Also, Fig. 4 shows a flat trend for socio-cultural factors in relation to other keywords. This is followed by digital communication. Decision making is the publication since 2004 that has received the most focus. This is probably because it could be embedded with any research topic, in contrast with socio-cultural factors and digital communication, where very few publications were recorded.

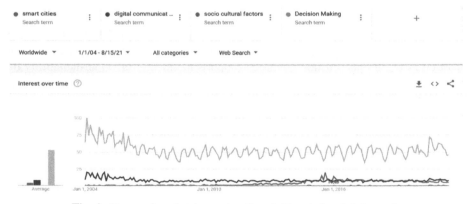

Fig. 4. Keywords and strings using Google Trends for global search.

4.2 Annual Publication of Studies on CP

CP was not given attention among scholars in the past. Figure 5 shows that the degree of interest in the context of smart cities has increased dramatically in the past few years.

Whitaker (1980) published the first article that demonstrates CP in service delivery. The number of publications on CP increased steadily, from one paper to two between 2007 and 2015, then to three papers in 2016. The reason behind the low number of publications per year is related to the unavailability of data between 1980 and 2007, and also the appearance of the smart cities topic, which increased in 2013/2014 when ICT gained huge attention among scholars (Neirotti et al. 2014). Thus, it can be assumed that the increasing number of studies on smart cities and urban sustainability contributes to the increasing number of studies on CP. In addition, the number of publications recorded in 2020 was the highest, and this is because CP has become a global trend among government bodies and the private sector through various initiatives and programs (Kapoor and Singh 2020).

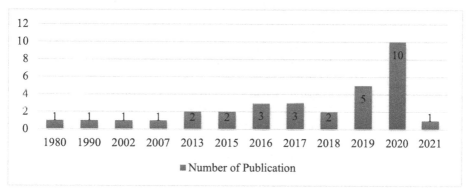

Fig. 5. Number of publications per year. **Source:** Authors' compilation

4.3 Citizens' Participation Publications in Relation to Smart Cities

As mentioned earlier, finding articles that address the role of CP in achieving smart cities was one of the research objectives. Therefore, Table 3 shows information about the authors, findings and domain of each paper. It also demonstrates that CP is interconnected heavily with both urban sustainability and smart cities. Papers published prior to 2016 were mostly focused on considering citizens as a part of stakeholder management. However, recent articles demonstrate that CP is not only a shared opinion but is also bridging the gaps between technology and human needs (Bouzguenda et al. 2019). The only article that addressed governance and CP was conducted by Aina et al. (2019). Therefore, there is a need to discover the relationship between decision making, socio-cultural factors and digital communication with relation to citizen participation. Table 3 shows evidence that developing a framework is necessary to bridge the gap between decision making, digital communication and socio-cultural factors to support CP in achieving smart sustainable cities.

Table 3. Studies on the relationship between smart sustainable cities and citizens' participation

Author	Findings	Domain
Bouzguenda et al. (2019)	The study proposes that the move toward smart sustainable cities requires bridging the gaps between sustainability, social sustainability, community engagement and digital public participation through the application of ICT	Smart sustainable cities
Aina et al. (2019)	Posits a need for a framework of legislation and administration procedures for a top-down approach initiated by those in the top echelon of society who can have a significant influence on the move towards sustainability	Governance, Citizens' Participation
Arnstein (2019)	Proposes a typology of citizens' participation. It is presented in the form of a ladder pattern	Citizens' Participation
Aina (2017)	Developing a smart city by leveraging ICT is necessary but not sufficient; it requires citizens' participation	Smart cities, Citizens' Participation
Gupta and Hall (2017)	This research explores the concept of a smart city and focuses on how Indian cities are defining smart cities as part of the SCM	Smart cities, Citizens' Participation
Granier and Kudo (2016)	The level of citizens' participation in Japan goes beyond involving citizens in city governance and examines both the roles they are assigned and their actual practices	Smart Cities, ICT, Citizens' Participation
Vrabie and Tirziu (2016)	Present a framework on how e-participation can be inclusive and how it might bring citizens closer to the idea of living in a smart city	Smart Cities, ICT E-participation

(*continued*)

Table 3. (*continued*)

Author	Findings	Domain
Marsal-Llacuna 2015	Studies city indicators of social and cultural sustainability as standardisation technologies for smarter (citizen-centred) governance of cities. It shows that citizens, private stakeholders and city councils represent the inclusion of governance of cities	Urban Sustainability, Citizens' Participation

Table 2 summarises the literature review in the areas of smart sustainable cities, smart cities, governance, citizens' participation and urban sustainability. Furthermore, it outlines the most recent body of knowledge in the area of smart sustainable cities, and it informs the research from a global perspective. Scholars such as Bouzguenda et al. (2019), Yigitcanlar et al. (2018b), and Ahvennicmi et al. (2017) have discussed the definition of smart sustainable cities. However, these studies demonstrate the complexity of adopting the concept and discuss how to bridge the gaps between sustainability, social sustainability, community engagement and digital public participation. Other studies consider the smart cities concept as an outcome of a particular aspect in smart cities, such as citizens' participation (Gupta and Hall 2017), smart and human-centred communities (Granier and Kudo 2016; Vrabie and Tirziu 2016), governance (Chourabi et al. 2012; Lazaroiu and Roscia 2012) and urban sustainability (Marsal-Llacuna 2015). The studies mentioned show how scholars view smart cities and their implications for serving the built environment.

As a result, there is very little or nothing in the literature that contributes to the knowledge of smart sustainable cities in the Saudi Arabian context. Researchers have been studying the area of urban planning, including urban sustainability and urban governance (Garba 2004; Senior 2016). Scholars such as Aina et al. (2019) see smart GeoICT as an influence on the development of smart cities. Other scholars see ICT as a tool to serve E-commerce (Al-Hudhaif and Alkubeyyer 2011), e-government (Alassim et al. 2017) and academia (Alkhasawneh and Alanazy 2015). The only study that supports leveraging ICT was conducted by Aina (2017). On the other hand, UN Habitat (2018) focused on promoting urban sustainability in three primary aspects: quality of life, economic competitiveness and environmental protection. However, ICT and citizens' participation are not considered in their report.

4.4 Authors' Affiliations

This study shows that most authors are affiliated with universities, which represent 90.4% of publications, while governmental bodies and the private sector represent 9.6% together. Table 4 shows each author's affiliation, department, country, type of organisation, number of authors and number of publications, showing that university scholars are

the main contributors to smart city research. It is also notable that governmental engagement is present since their contribution is significantly important to this topic. However,
there is not much contribution from and engagement with university scholars. It is worth
mentioning that the smart cities concept and CP are not limited to Built Environment
departments, but also, as seen in Table 4, that Engineering schools, Industrial Environmental Management, Schools of Politics and Public Administration, and Management
Information Systems Departments are contributing to knowledge in this area.

Additionally, in terms of geographical contributions to this topic, authors from many
countries have published their research findings. It could be concluded that Europe is
leading the contribution in smart cities. Twenty-two out of 52 researchers are from
Europe, six are from Australia, three are from the United States, and eight are from
Saudi Arabia. On Saudi Arabia universities' affiliations, only two out of 13 universities have conducted research on smart cities. Surprisingly, even the two universities are
government entities. Lastly, it is worth mentioning that the total number of authors in
this study, as reported in Table 2, is 52, while the total number of publications is 31.
The plausible reason is that there is a major collaboration between scholars globally. For
example, there is a collaboration between researchers from the Queensland University of
Technology in Australia and The University of Manchester in Spain, as well as the Delft
University of Technology in the Netherlands, Fudan University in China and Soochow
University in China. However, Saudi Arabian universities have not witnessed any international collaboration among scholars to adopt the concept of smart cities while taking
into consideration citizens' participation. The collaboration between scholars and professionals needs to be promoted to a higher level, which could result in effective research
outputs.

Table 4. Authors' affiliations

Affiliation	Department	Country	Type of organization	No. of authors	No. of publications
Queensland University of Technology	School of Civil Engineering and Built Environment	Australia	University	6	5
Norwegian University of Science and Technology	Computer and Information Science and Department of Urban Planning and Design	Norway	University	3	4
The University of Manchester	School of Environment	Spain	University	12	4
Clemson University	City planning and real estate development	USA	University	3	3
King Saudi University	Department of Urban Planning	Saudi Arabia	University	5	3

(continued)

Table 4. (*continued*)

Affiliation	Department	Country	Type of organization	No. of authors	No. of publications
Yanbu Industrial College	Department of Geomatics Engineering Technology	Saudi Arabia	University	3	2
University of Genoa	Department of the Built Environment	Italy	University	1	1
University of Cambridge	Department of Engineering	UK	University	2	1
Nazarbayev University	Department of Civil and Environmental	Kazakhstan	University	3	1
Yarmouk University	MIS Department	Jordan	University	3	1
AR Riyadh Development Authority	N/A	Saudi Arabia	Governmental Body	2	1
Lulea University of Technology,	Industrial Environmental Management,	Sweden	University	1	1
Soochow University	School of Politics and Public Administration,	China	University	2	1
Delft University of Technology	Faculty of Technology, Policy and Management	Netherlands	University	1	1
Leiden University	Institute for Area Studies	Netherlands	University	2	1
The Ural Branch of Russian Academy of Sciences	Department of Informatics, Bioengineering, Robotics, and Systems Engineering	Russia	Governmental Body	2	1
Technical Research Centre of Finland	Research Centre	Finland	Private sector	2	1

4.5 Active Authors

Table 5 shows the most active authors who have contributed to this research topic. It also presents their contributions in the area of smart cities and citizens' participation.

Nevertheless, some of the authors' papers were not considered for this study because they did not meet the selection criteria outlined in the methodology section of this study. Yigitcanlar, T., Bibri, S. Krassimira, P. and John G. have published five, four, three and three articles, respectively, and they have contributed to the smart cities area the most. While John G.'s studies focus on CP, Yusuf A. contributes to the knowledge in terms of understanding the relationship between smart cities in Saudi Arabia. On the other hand, the work of Al-Hathloul S. is oriented toward urban sustainability and legal policies. There is no active author currently in Saudi Arabia who studies smart cities and takes into consideration decision making, socio-cultural factors and digital communication with relation to citizens' participation. Table 5 shows that there are 52 authors who significantly contributed to this research topic from different disciplines.

Table 5. Authors' contributions

Authors	Studies	Affiliation	Number of publications
Yigitcanlar, T	Yigitcanlar and Kamruzzaman (2015, 2018), Yigitcanlar et al. (2018a, b, 2021)	Queensland University of Technology	5
Bibri, S	Bibri (2018a, b), Bibri and Krogstie (2017a, b)	Norwegian University	4
Krassimira, P	Martina et al. (2018)	The University of Manchester	3
John, G	Gaber (2017, 2019), Gaber and Gaber (2010)	Clemson University	3
Yusuf, A	Aina (2017), Aina et al. (2019)	Yanbu Industrial College	2
Al-Hathlou, l S	Al-Hathloul (2017), Al-Hathloul and Anis-ur-Rahmaan (1985)	King Saudi University	3

4.6 Conceptual Framework of the Study

CP is a pillar embedded in various models and frameworks, and in the literature in general. According to Arnstein (2019), understanding users' expectations will improve decision making in government services. Based on the three domains identified in the literature review, a conceptual framework is proposed. Through the literature review, the following gaps were identified. Figure 6 presents a conceptual framework for this study and the relationship between the domains to achieve outcomes linked to smart sustainable cities. These domains are decision making, digital communication and socio-cultural pillars. This model suggests how to answer the research questions about how, where and when CP would be determined and what level of empowering CP governments are willing to promote. This model is designed in accordance with stakeholders management theory and urban system theory, which are based on determining the relationship between power, legitimacy and urgency that suggests a separation of stakeholders from non-stakeholders and the extent to which their contribution can influence decision making. Moreover, urban systems theory is a coherent technological infrastructure that is vital for the advancement of smart cities. The framework, therefore, focuses on the empowerment of CP in making decisions, the application of ICT to facilitate CP and stakeholder communication between citizens and government, which can fill in the gaps between the three domains.

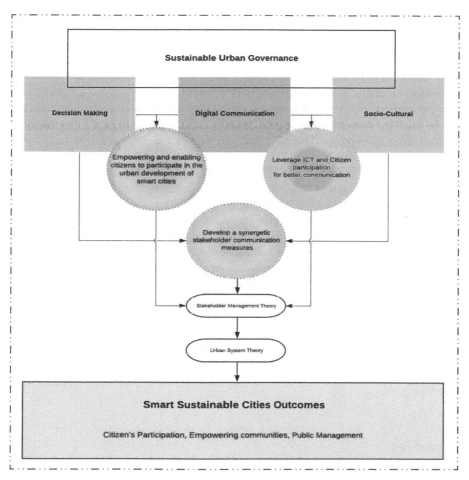

Fig. 6. A conceptual framework for achieving smart sustainable cities that takes CP into consideration

5   Conclusions

This study reviewed the literature on smart sustainable cities from different angles and lenses. This study aims to examine the current body of knowledge of CP in achieving smart cities globally; thus, the objectives are (1) to identify the most reported CP in relation to other domains and (2) to develop a conceptual framework that helps in demonstrating the interconnection of the identified fields. This research adopted a critical review methodology by conducting thematic searches to retrieve the most relevant papers to this study. This resulted in 468 papers overall, and 31 papers were chosen as the best-matched. The findings of this study contribute to the body of knowledge about the involvement of CP globally by investigating Google trends, annual publication, CP in relation to other domains, authors' affiliation and active authors. It could be concluded that Europe is leading the contribution in smart cities, yet a widespread global collaboration between scholars has been observed. In terms of annual publications, the unavailability of data and the appearance of smart city topics were the reasons for the low number of publications in the past years. In addition, the main contributors to this study were scholars affiliated with universities. This study shows that there are gaps that must be filled between the following domains: decision making, digital communication and socio-cultural domains. There is a lack of research focusing on CP as the driver in achieving smart sustainable cities. Therefore, this study presents a conceptual framework that will fill the gaps in these areas. This review study was limited to the online database and scholarly search engines; thus, the articles, conference proceedings, or government documents that are not available online might have been missed out. Regardless of the limitations, the authors ensured that the retrieved documents were available online. In addition, due to the Covid-19 pandemic, this paper was limited to only online papers, whereas offline documents like books and government documents were not available to the public. For future studies, there is a need to examine the level of power to discover if governments are willing to share their decisions with citizens. Moreover, there is a need to explore these challenges and opportunities to provide ideal solutions to achieving the smart cities concept, which will help to successfully achieve sustainable urbanisation.

Acknowledgements. The authors declare that there is no conflict of interest. This study is an integral part of a PhD research project conducted at the UNSW, Sydney, Australia. We are grateful to Imam Abdulrahman Bin Faisal University and the Saudi Arabian government for sponsoring the PhD program.

References

Ahvenniemi, H., Huovila, A., Pinto-Seppä, I., Airaksinen, M.: What are the differences between sustainable and smart cities? Cities **60**, 234–245 (2017). https://doi.org/10.1016/j.cities.2016.09.009

Aina, Y.: Achieving smart sustainable cities with GeoICT support: the Saudi evolving smart cities. Purinergic Signal. (2017). https://doi.org/10.1007/s11302-019-09656-3

Aina, Y., Wafer, A., Ahmed, F., Alshuwaikhat, H.: Top-down sustainable urban development? Urban governance transformation in Saudi Arabia. Cities **90**, 272–281 (2019). https://doi.org/10.1016/j.cities.2019.03.003

Airaksinen, M., Seppa, I., Huovila, A., Neumann, H.-M., Iglár, B., Bosch, P.: Smart city performance measurement framework CITYkeys (2017)

Al-Hathloul, S.: Riyadh development plans in the past fifty years (1967–2016). Curr. Urban Stud. **5**(01), 97 (2017)

Al-Hathloul, S.A., Anis-ur-Rahmaan, S.: The evolution of urban and regional planning in Saudi Arabia. Ekistics **52**, 206–212 (1985)

Al-Hudhaif, S., Alkubeyyer, A.: E-commerce adoption factors in Saudi Arabia. Int. J. Bus. Manage. **6**(9), 122 (2011)

Alassim, M., Alfayad, M., Abbott-Halpin: Understanding factors influencing e-government implementation in Saudi Arabia from an organizational perspective. EF Int. J. Inf. Commun. Eng. **11**(7), 894–999 (2017)

Albino, V., Berardi, U., Dangelico, R.M.: Smart cities: definitions, dimensions, performance, and initiatives. J. Urban Technol. **22**(1), 3–21 (2015). https://doi.org/10.1080/10630732.2014.942092

Alkhasawneh, S., Alanazy, S.: Adopt ICT among academic staff in Aljouf University: using UTAUT model. Mediterr. J. Soc. Sci. **6**(1), 490 (2015)

Alsitre, S.. Mayer of Dammam: launching smart parking. Aljazera (2019). http://www.al-jazirah.com/2019/20190708/ln27.htm

Andone, D., Holotescu, C., Grosseck, G.: Learning communities in smart cities. Case studies. Paper presented at the International Conference on Web and Open Access to Learning (ICWOAL) (2014)

Arnstein, S.R.: A ladder of citizen participation. J. Am. Inst. Plan. **85**(1(4)), 24–34 (2019). https://doi.org/10.1080/01944363.2018.1559388

Bashynska, I., Dyskina, A.: The overview-analytical document of the international experience of building smart city. Bus. Theory Pract. **19**, 228–241 (2018). https://doi.org/10.3846/btp.2018.23

Bencardino, M., Greco, I.: The paradigm of the modern city: SMART and SENSEable cities for smart, inclusive and sustainable growth. In: Murgante, B., et al. (eds.) ICCSA 2014. LNCS, vol. 8580, pp. 579–597. Springer, Cham (2014). https://doi.org/10.1007/978-3-319-09129-7_42

Bibri, S.: A foundational framework for smart sustainable city development: theoretical, disciplinary, and discursive dimensions and their synergies. Sustain. Cities Soc. **38**, 758–794 (2018a). https://doi.org/10.1016/j.scs.2017.12.032

Bibri, S., Krogstie, J.: Smart sustainable cities of the future: an extensive interdisciplinary literature review. Sustain. Cities Soc. **31** (2017a). https://doi.org/10.1016/j.scs.2017a.02.016

Bibri, S.E.: The IoT for smart sustainable cities of the future: an analytical framework for sensor-based big data applications for environmental sustainability. Sustain. Cities Soc. **38**, 230–253 (2018b)

Bibri, S.E., Krogstie, J.: On the social shaping dimensions of smart sustainable cities: a study in science, technology, and society. Sustain. Cities Soc. **29**, 219–246 (2017b)

Bouzguenda, I., Alalouch, C., Nadia, F.: Towards smart sustainable cities: a review of the role digital citizen participation could play in advancing social sustainability. Sustain. Cities Soc. **50**, 101627 (2019). https://doi.org/10.1016/j.scs.2019.101627

Burke, E.M.: Citizen participation strategies. J. Am. Inst. Plann. **34**(5), 287–294 (1968). https://doi.org/10.1080/01944366808977547

Caragliu, A., Del Bo, C., Nijkamp, P.: Smart cities in Europe. VU University Amsterdam, Faculty of Economics, Business Administration and Econometrics, Serie Research Memoranda, vol. 18 (2009). https://doi.org/10.1080/10630732.2011.601117

Chourabi, H., et al.: Understanding smart cities: an integrative framework. Paper presented at the 2012 45th Hawaii International Conference on System Sciences, 4–7 January 2012

City Protocol: Amsterdam smart city (2018). https://amsterdamsmartcity.com/projects/city-pro tocol

Colding, J., Barthel, S.: An urban ecology critique on the 'Smart City' model. J. Clean. Prod. **164**, 95–101 (2017). https://doi.org/10.1016/j.jclepro.2017.06.191

Duffield, M.: The resilience of the ruins: towards a critique of digital humanitarianism. Resilience, 1–19 (2016). https://doi.org/10.1080/21693293.2016.1153772

Freeman, R.E., Reed, D.: Stockholders and stakeholders: a new perspective on corporate governance. Calif. Manage. Rev. **25**(3), 88–106 (1983)

Fusero, P., Massimiano, L., Tedeschi, A., Lepidi, S.: Parametric urbanism: a new frontier for smart cities. Planum J. Urban. **2**(27), 1–13 (2013)

Gaber, J.: Seeing the community's perspective through multiple emic and etic vistas. Health Promot. Int. **32**(6), 1025–1033 (2017)

Gaber, J.: Building 'A Ladder of Citizen Participation': Sherry Arnstein, citizen participation, and model cities. J. Am. Plan. Assoc.: 50 Years since Arnstein's Ladder **85**(3), 188–201 (2019). https://doi.org/10.1080/01944363.2019.1612267

Gaber, J., Gaber, S.L.: Using face validity to recognize empirical community observations. Eval. Program Plan. **33**(2), 138–146 (2010)

Garba, S.B.: Managing urban growth and development in the Riyadh metropolitan area. Saudi Arabia. Habitat Int. **28**(4), 593–608 (2004). https://doi.org/10.1016/j.habitatint.2003.10.008

Girardi, P., Temporelli, A.: Smartainability: a methodology for assessing the sustainability of the smart city, vol. 111 (2016)

González, S.: Bilbao and Barcelona 'In motion'. How urban regeneration 'Models' travel and mutate in the global flows of policy tourism. Urban Stud. **48**(47), 1397–1418 (2011)

Granier, B., Kudo, H.: How are citizens involved in smart cities? Analysing citizen participation in Japanese "Smart Communities." Inf. Polity **21**(1), 61–76 (2016)

Gupta, K., Hall, R.P.: The Indian perspective of smart cities. Paper presented at the 2017 Smart City Symposium Prague (SCSP) (2017)

Jabareen, Y.: A new conceptual framework for sustainable development. Environ. Dev. Sustain. **10**(2), 179–192 (2008). https://doi.org/10.1007/s10668-006-9058-z

Kapoor, A., Singh, E.: Empowering smart cities though community participation a literature review. In: Ahmed, S., Abbas, S.M., Zia, H. (eds.) Smart Cities—Opportunities and Challenges. LNCE, vol. 58, pp. 117–125. Springer, Singapore (2020). https://doi.org/10.1007/978-981-15-2545-2_11

Kuster, C.: A real time urban sustainability assessment framework for the smart city paradigm. Ph.D., Cardiff University (2019)

Lazaroiu, G.C., Roscia, M.: Definition methodology for the smart cities model. Energy **47**, 326–332 (2012). https://doi.org/10.1016/j.energy.2012.09.028

Lee, J.-H., Hancock, M.: Toward a framework for smart cities: a comparison of Seoul. Research Paper, Yonsei University and Stanford University, San Francisco and Amsterdam (2012)

Lekamge, S., Marasinghe, A.: Developing a smart city model that ensures the optimum utilization of existing resources in cities of all sizes. Paper presented at the Biometrics and Kansei Engineering (ICBAKE) (2013)

Liberati, A., et al.: The PRISMA statement for reporting systematic reviews and meta-analyses of studies that evaluate healthcare interventions: explanation and elaboration. BMJ **339**, b2700 (2009). https://doi.org/10.1136/bmj.b2700

Lombardi, P., et al.: An advanced Triple-Helix network model for smart cities performance. In: Green and Ecological Technologies for Urban Planning: Creating Smart Cities (2011)

Lu, D., Tian, Y., Liu, V., Zhang, Y.: The performance of the smart cities in China—a comparative study by means of self-organizing maps and social networks analysis. Sustainability **7**, 7604–7621 (2015). https://doi.org/10.3390/su7067604

Marrone, M., Hammerle, M.: Smart cities: a review and analysis of stakeholders' literature. Bus. Inf. Syst. Eng. **60**(3), 197–213 (2018). https://doi.org/10.1007/s12599-018-0535-3

Marsal-Llacuna, M.-L.: City indicators on social sustainability as standardization technologies for smarter (citizen-centered) governance of cities. Soc. Indic. Res. Int. Interdisc. J. Qual. Life Meas. **128**(3), 1193–1216 (2015). https://doi.org/10.1007/s11205-015-1075-6

Martina, C., Evansa, J., Karvonenb, A., Paskalevac, K., Yangd, D., Linjordete, T.: Smart-sustainability: a new urban fix? Sustain. Cities Soc. (2018). https://doi.org/10.1016/j.scs.2018.11.028

Neirotti, P., Marco, A.D., Cagliano, A.C., Mangano, G., Scorrano, F.: Current trends in Smart City initiatives: some stylised facts. Cities **38**, 25–36 (2014)

Praharaja, S.: A comprehensive analysis of the challenges and opportunities of the 100 smart cities mission in India. Ph.D., The University of New South Wales (2018)

Praharaja, S., Hanb, J.H., Hawkenc, S.: Innovative civic engagement and digital urban infrastructure: lessons from 100 smart cities mission in India. Procedia Engineering **180**, 1423–1432 (2016)

Rajput, S., Sharma, P.: Sustainable Smart Cities in India: Challenges and Future Perspectives. Springer, Cham (2017). https://doi.org/10.1007/978-3-319-47145-7

Senior, A.F.-H.: Actionable recommendations for legislative and institutional reforms: towards the new urban planning act of Saudi Arabia. Paper presented at the Habitat III Conference (2016). https://www.futuresaudicities.org/wp-content/uploads/2017/09/Saudi-Arabia-Presentation.pdf

Shah, M.N., Nagargoje, S., Shah, C.: Assessment of Ahmedabad (India) and Shanghai (China) on smart city parameters applying the Boyd Cohen smart city wheel. In: Wu, Y., Zheng, S., Luo, J., Wang, W., Mo, Z., Shan, L. (eds.) Proceedings of the 20th International Symposium on Advancement of Construction Management and Real Estate, pp. 111–127. Springer, Singapore (2017). https://doi.org/10.1007/978-981-10-0855-9_10

Shields, R.: Smart Cities Timeline (2014). http://www.spaceandculture.com/2014/12/22/smart-cities-timeline/

Soc, R.-M.: FINEST twins: platform for cross-border smart city solutions (2017)

Storch, D.A.: Smart city profiles (2018). https://smartcities.at/activities/smart-city-profiles-en-us/

Tijani, B., Jin, X., Osei-kyei, R.: A systematic review of mental stressors in the construction industry. Int. J. Build. Pathol. Adapt. **39**(2), 433–460 (2020)

UN-Habitat: Country Profile Saudi Arabia: Future Saudi Cities Program (2018). https://unhabitat.org/saudi-arabia/saudi-arabia-documents/

Vrabie, C., Tirziu, A.: E-participation–a key factor in developing smart cities. In: EIRP Proceedings (2016)

Whitaker, G.: Coproduction: citizen participation in service delivery. Public Adm. Rev. **40**, 240–246 (1980)

Wu, W., Kang, X.: The design and realization of digital urban management system. Appl. Mech. Mater. **256–259**(1), 2354–2358 (2013). https://doi.org/10.4028/www.scientific.net/AMM.256-259.2354

Yang, K., Pandey, S.K.: Further dissecting the black box of citizen participation: when does citizen involvement lead to good outcomes? Public Adm. Rev. **71**(6), 880–892 (2011)

Yigitcanlar, T., Kamruzzaman, M.: Planning, development and management of sustainable cities: a commentary from the guest editors. Sustainability **7**, 14677–14688 (2015). https://doi.org/10.3390/su71114677

Yigitcanlar, T., Kamruzzaman, M.: Does smart city policy lead to sustainability of cities? Land Use Policy **73**, 49–58 (2018)

Yigitcanlar, T., et al.: Understanding 'smart cities': intertwining development drivers with desired outcomes in a multidimensional framework. Cities **81**, 145–160 (2018a)

Yigitcanlar, T., et al.: Can cities become smart without being sustainable? A systematic review of the literature. Sustain. Cities Soc. **45** (2018b). https://doi.org/10.1016/j.scs.2018b.11.033

Yigitcanlar, T., Kankanamge, N., Vella, K.: How are smart city concepts and technologies perceived and utilized? A systematic geo-Twitter analysis of smart cities in Australia. J. Urban Technol. **28**(1–2), 135–154 (2021)

Privacy and Forensics in Smart Mobility

An Overview of the Status of DNS and HTTP Security Services in Higher Education Institutions in Portugal

Nuno Felgueiras[1] and Pedro Pinto[1,2]

[1] Instituto Politécnico de Viana do Castelo, 4900-347 Viana do Castelo, Portugal
nunofelgueiras@ipvc.pt
[2] ISMAI, 4475-690 Maia, and INESC TEC, 4200-465 Porto, Portugal
pedropinto@estg.ipvc.pt

Abstract. Currently, there are several security-related standards and recommendations concerning Domain Name System (DNS) and Hypertext Transfer Protocol (HTTP) services, that are highly valuable for governments and their services, and other public or private organizations. This is also the case of Higher Education Institutions (HEIs). However, since these institutions have administrative autonomy, they present different statuses and paces in the adoption of these web-related security services.

This paper presents an overview regarding the implementation of security standards and recommendations by the Portuguese HEIs. In order to collect these results, a set of scripts were developed and executed. Data were collected concerning the security of the DNS and HTTP protocols, namely, the support of Domain Name System Security Extensions (DNSSEC), HTTP main configurations and redirection, digital certificates, key size, algorithms and Secure Socket Layer (SSL)/Transport Layer Security (TLS) versions used.

The results obtained allow to conclude that there are different progresses between HEIs. In particular, only 11.7% of HEIs support DNSSEC, 14.4% do not use any SSL certificates, 74.8% use a 2048 bits encryption key, and 81.1% use the Rivest-Shamir-Adleman (RSA) algorithm. Also, 6.3% of HEIs still negotiate with the vulnerable SSLv3 version.

Keywords: DNSSEC · HTTP · Higher education · Academic · Institutions · SSL · Security

1 Introduction

Currently, there are several security-related standards and recommendations concerning Domain Name System (DNS) and Hypertext Transfer Protocol (HTTP) services. A subset of these standards and recommendations intend to secure the DNS service, i.e. the Domain Name System Security Extensions (DNSSEC) [16–18], and others intended to secure HTTP service. The later, includes Hyper Text Transfer Protocol Secure (HTTPS) [15], Secure Socket

© ICST Institute for Computer Sciences, Social Informatics and Telecommunications Engineering 2022
Published by Springer Nature Switzerland AG 2022. All Rights Reserved
S. Paiva et al. (Eds.): SmartCity360° 2021, LNICST 442, pp. 457–469, 2022.
https://doi.org/10.1007/978-3-031-06371-8_30

Layer (SSL) certificates and SSL/Transport Layer Security (TLS) protocols [7,12,23].

The implementation of these current security standards and recommendations is highly valuable and strongly encouraged for governments and their services, and other public or private organizations [9]. Recent efforts such as the ones described in [5,19,22] had been carried out to analyse, check, evaluate, and report the evolution and adoption of these services in multiple countries, domains and institution.

Educational institutions should also follow these security standards and recommendations. However, since in Portugal [11] and in Europe [2], the Higher Education Institutions (HEIs) have administrative autonomy, this implies different statuses and paces in the adoption of these web-related security services, both in the public and private institutions.

This paper provides an overview of the security status regarding the adoption of DNS and HTTP security services on the Portuguese HEIs. A set of scripts were developed to collect and analyze each of these main protocols (DNS and HTTP) security implementations. Specific data was collected and analyzed regarding the adoption of DNSSEC, the HTTP redirection, and the information regarding SSL certificates (in particular the Certificate Authority (CA), Key Size and Signature types used).

The remainder of this document is organized as follows: Sect. 2 presents the related work. Section 3 introduces the methodology used to obtain the results; Sect. 4 presents the results; Lastly, Sect. 5 presents the conclusions.

2   Related Work

Given that DNS protocol does not implement security mechanisms in its initial versions, there are a set of standards intended to enhance the security of this protocol. The secure version of DNS, including DNSSEC, have been available since 2005 in [16–18]. By mirroring the DNS hierarchy, DNSSEC authenticates the DNS responses and prevents modified or forged DNS records.

A set of efforts have been made to implement DNS Security. Authors in [21] present an analysis regarding the misconfigurations for DNS domains and state that, although progress has been made in the implementation of DNSSEC, over 4% of evaluated domains show misconfigurations. In [10] the authors study the security of DNSSEC deployment at scale, particularly in Top Level Domains (TLDs) that offer economic incentives. They find that DNSSEC implementations in the wild poorly reflects standard recommendations, and, on average, large operators deploy weak DNSSEC security more frequently than small operators. In [19] the authors present a research of the evolution and adoption of top Level Domains and DNSSEC in New Zealand. The study highlights that, the rapid increase in the number of gTLDs give registrants a wider choice of domain names, but it also offers malicious actors more opportunities to attack. It is concluded that DNSSEC deployment at New Zealand national level to be improving but still weaker than global averages. Efforts need to be made to ensure correct

Delegation Signed records are uploaded to the registry to complete the DNSSEC chain of trust.

Standards have been proposed to provide HTTP Security. The SSLv1 was never publicly released. In 1995, SSLv2 [7] has been released but, since its release, it presented security weaknesses and has been replaced in 1996 by the SSLv3 [8]. In 1999, the TLSv1.0 [4] was released and was based on the deprecated SSL Protocol, which was followed in 2006 by the TLSv1.1 [6], in 2008 by TLSv1.2 [14] and, in 2018, the latest was released, the TLSv1.3 [13].

A set of research works are focused on the progress of the implementation of HTTP security. In [22] the authors survey the usage of RC4 stream cipher in online web portals of Sri Lankan Banking and Non-Banking Financial Sector, as well as the awareness level of the Network Security Administrating staff of some of the selected banks which are geographically based in Sri Lanka, regarding the usage of RC4 in SSL. This study revealed that 75% of the Banking and Non-Banking Financial Institutes in Sri Lanka have been upgraded to TLS1.2 from SSL and TLS older versions and hence they have mitigated the RC4 vulnerabilities. In [5], there were measures taken to prevent eavesdropping and tampering a set of Internet protocols that rely on TLS, the authors quantify the adoption of TLS using passive traffic traces captured on a backbone and edge academic network in Japan, monitoring the evolution of five common protocols and their TLS-variants over ten years of traffic data. They found that the adoption of TLS for HTTP only started being significantly used around 2012, while IMAP traffic is mostly encrypted for the last ten years. The deployment of HTTPS is mainly driven by large content providers and migrating the remaining HTTP traffic to HTTPS might require significant efforts as it concerns numerous smaller services who may face compatibility concerns. In [20] the research author, provided a status survey of SSL/TLS sites in 2018 after "search form" issues have been raised. From 2014, several researchers conducted monitored SSL/TLS sites using the top level domain ".jp" based on a URL list extracted from Alexa Top Sites [3], and investigated the usage rate of SSL/TLS versions and Export-grade encryption algorithms. They also pointed out that online login sites belonging to associations of Japanese banks were well-controlled in SSL/TLS server configurations and content management, however ordinary sites had "search form" issues.

3   Methodology

In the initial step of this analysis, a list of all HEIs was collected from the information on the Direção-Geral de Estatísticas da Educação e Ciência (DGEEC) website in [1] and resulted in a list with a total of 320 results. Using two scripts, the 320 were collected and filtered to obtain only the main office or university center. The first script was intended to collect all the links to access detailed information for each HEI and, the second, to access the links previously collected to obtain the information. The scripts were made in PHP using the *file_get_contents* function in order to obtain the HTTP code of the pages and the data obtained by them filtered with *regex*. After filtering the data, a total of 111 HEIs were obtained distributed across the 18 districts and 2 autonomous regions of Portugal. For the collected HEIs, the following set of items were analysed in their implementation or configuration:

- DNS
    - DNSSEC
- HTTP
    - Configuration and Redirection
    - SSL Certificate
        * Certificate Authority
        * Key Size
        * Algorithm
    - SSL/TLS Versions
        * SSLv2, v3
        * TLSv1.0, v1.1, v1.2, v1.3

Three scripts were developed with the following functions:

- Script 1 - Collect the state of DNSSEC
  To capture the state of DNSSEC, the *php-dnssec-validator* library was used in order to know if the institution's domain had DNSSEC and if so, the script would save the Key, KeyTag and Algorithm Values in the database.
- Script 2 - Collect SSL Certificates Information
  To collect information from SSL certificates, the *stream_socket_client* function was used along with openssl in order to obtain information such as CA, Key size and Signature Types.
- Script 3 - Test the negotiation of SSL/TLS protocols
  To test the SSL/TLS negotiations, the script's job was to try to establish a communication for each of the protocols, that is, SSLv2, SSLv3, TLSv1.0, TLSv1.1, TLSv1.2 and the most recent TLSv1.3. To accomplish this, we used the PHP function *stream_socket_client*, with the exception of TLSv1.3 which required the use of *curl* due to compatibility issues.

With the Location data, two more types of information were obtained. Using *regex* it was possible to know if the forwarding was to the same domain or not and if it was already forwarded to a secure connection (HTTPS). The process of developing the scripts and executing them to collect data and was carried out in full during the month of April 2021.

4 Results and Analysis

Table 1 it is possible to see the distribution of HEIs by districts of Portugal, as well as by environment of institution (public or private). The Fig. 1 draws the results of the Table 1.

The district of Lisboa has the highest number of HEIs, followed by Porto and Coimbra. The districts of Beja, Bragança, Évora, Guarda, Ponta Delgada and Viseu only have one HEI, and the district of Porto has a higher count of private

Table 1. Districts with public and private institutions

District	Global		Public		Private	
	#	%	#	%	#	%
Aveiro	5	4,5%	1	20,0%	4	80,0%
Beja	1	0,9%	1	100,0%	0	0,0%
Braga	4	3,6%	2	50,0%	2	50,0%
Bragança	1	0,9%	1	100,0%	0	0,0%
Castelo Branco	2	1,8%	2	100,0%	0	0,0%
Coimbra	10	9,0%	8	80,0%	2	20,0%
Évora	1	0,9%	1	100,0%	0	0,0%
Faro	2	1,8%	1	50,0%	1	50,0%
Funchal	3	2,7%	1	33,3%	2	66,7%
Guarda	1	0,9%	1	100,0%	0	0,0%
Leiria	3	2,7%	1	33,3%	2	66,7%
Lisboa	35	31,5%	15	42,9%	20	57,1%
Ponta Delgada	1	0,9%	1	100,0%	0	0,0%
Portalegre	5	4,5%	5	100,0%	0	0,0%
Porto	25	22,5%	4	16,0%	21	84,0%
Santarém	4	3,6%	3	75,0%	1	25,0%
Setúbal	3	2,7%	2	66,7%	1	33,3%
Viana do Castelo	2	1,8%	1	50,0%	1	50,0%
Vila Real	2	1,8%	1	50,0%	1	50,0%
Viseu	1	0,9%	1	100,0%	0	0,0%
Total:	**111**	**100%**	**53**	**47,7%**	**58**	**52,3%**

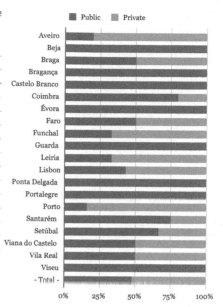

Fig. 1. Districts public/private

institutions. The districts of Beja, Bragança, Castelo Branco, Évora, Guarda, Ponta Delgada, Portalegre and Viseu only have public institutions.

Table 2 presents the results regarding the implementation of DNSSEC on public and private HEIs. Figure 2 draws the results of the Table 2. From these results it can be verified that more than 80% of HEIs do not implement DNSSEC. Less than 75% of HEIs in the districts of Coimbra and Lisboa have DNSSEC implemented. In the districts of Braga, Faro, Santarém and Vila Real only 50% of HEIs have implemented DNSSEC. In the district of Évora the only exising HEIs implements DNSSEC. In the district of Lisboa there is only one private institution that implemented DNSSEC, representing only 0.9% from the total. On public institutions, 10.8% implemented DNSSEC.

Table 3 presents the status on HTTP and HTTPS, namely described using the following conditions:

- HTTP Only: Websites with only HTTP protocol enabled, who do not provide any sort of security
- HTTP & HTTPS: Websites that have both HTTP and HTTPS active. They can be accessed by both protocols, given that they do not have any type of redirects to force HTTPS to be used;
- Invalid SSL Config: Websites that have implemented HTTPS/SSL but misconfigured it. These are websites that may be reachable and look like they are functional, but upon analysis, we found that the certificate information is

Table 2. DNSSEC public/private per districts

District	Total	Without DNSSEC		DNSSEC public		DNSSEC private	
	#	#	%	#	%	#	%
Évora	1	0	0,0%	1	100,0%	0	0,0%
Braga	4	2	50,0%	2	50,0%	0	0,0%
Faro	2	1	50,0%	1	50,0%	0	0,0%
Santarém	4	2	50,0%	2	50,0%	0	0,0%
Vila Real	2	1	50,0%	1	50,0%	0	0,0%
Coimbra	10	8	80,0%	2	20,0%	0	0,0%
Lisboa	35	31	88,6%	3	8,6%	1	2,9%
Aveiro	5	5	100,0%	0	0,0%	0	0,0%
Beja	1	1	100,0%	0	0,0%	0	0,0%
Bragança	1	1	100,0%	0	0,0%	0	0,0%
Castelo Branco	2	2	100,0%	0	0,0%	0	0,0%
Funchal	3	3	100,0%	0	0,0%	0	0,0%
Guarda	1	1	100,0%	0	0,0%	0	0,0%
Leiria	3	3	100,0%	0	0,0%	0	0,0%
Ponta Delgada	1	1	100,0%	0	0,0%	0	0,0%
Portalegre	5	5	100,0%	0	0,0%	0	0,0%
Porto	25	25	100,0%	0	0,0%	0	0,0%
Setúbal	3	3	100,0%	0	0,0%	0	0,0%
Viana do Castelo	2	2	100,0%	0	0,0%	0	0,0%
Viseu	1	1	100,0%	0	0,0%	0	0,0%
Total:	**111**	**98**	**88,3%**	**12**	**10,8%**	**1**	**0,9%**

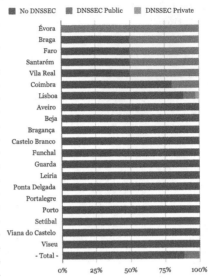

Fig. 2. Differences public/private institutions using DNSSEC

incomplete due to lack of an Intermediate Chain. Example: If a visitor who has never accessed a particular website which its certificate was issued by "Let's Encrypt", and that particular site does not have an intermediate chain, the browser will say that the website has an invalid certificate because it can not verify whether or not the intermediate certificate is valid; However, if that visitor has previously visited another website that had its certificate issued by "Let's Encrypt" as well and, in this case, the website has a valid intermediate certificate, the browser will remember and trust that chain, which results in that particular chain (Let's Encrypt) not being checked by the browser again;

– HTTP to HTTPS (Other): Websites that forward the visitor to a secure page outside of the main domain.
– HTTP to HTTPS (Same): Websites that forward the visitor to a secure page within the main domain.

Figure 3 draws the results of the Table 3. From the results obtained it can be verified that the districts of Beja, Évora, Faro, Ponta Delgada, Viana do Castelo, Vila Real and Viseu HEIs redirect visitors to HTTPS in the same domain. Districts of Lisboa, Porto and Santarém HEIs also redirect the visitors to HTTPS but using others domains. Also, the districts of Lisboa, Coimbra and Porto HEIs also have websites with invalid SSL configuration (without chain). Regarding the districts of Aveiro, Funchal, Lisboa, Coimbra, Porto, Castelo Branco,

Table 3. Web security in the academic institutions per district

Districts	Total	HTTP only		HTTP & HTTPS		Invalid SSL config		HTTP to HTTPS (other)		HTTP to HTTPS (same)	
	#	#	%	#	%	#	%	#	%	#	%
Beja	1	0	0,0%	0	0,0%	0	0,0%	0	0,0%	1	100,0%
Évora	1	0	0,0%	0	0,0%	0	0,0%	0	0,0%	1	100,0%
Faro	2	0	0,0%	0	0,0%	0	0,0%	0	0,0%	2	100,0%
Ponta Delgada	1	0	0,0%	0	0,0%	0	0,0%	0	0,0%	1	100,0%
Viana do Castelo	2	0	0,0%	0	0,0%	0	0,0%	0	0,0%	2	100,0%
Vila Real	2	0	0,0%	0	0,0%	0	0,0%	0	0,0%	2	100,0%
Viseu	1	0	0,0%	0	0,0%	0	0,0%	0	0,0%	1	100,0%
Aveiro	5	0	0,0%	1	20,0%	0	0,0%	0	0,0%	4	80,0%
Funchal	3	0	0,0%	1	33,3%	0	0,0%	0	0,0%	2	66,7%
Leiria	3	1	33,3%	0	0,0%	0	0,0%	0	0,0%	2	66,7%
Lisboa	35	7	20,0%	3	8,6%	1	2,9%	3	8,6%	21	60,0%
Coimbra	10	2	20,0%	1	10,0%	1	10,0%	0	0,0%	6	60,0%
Porto	25	3	12,0%	5	20,0%	2	8,0%	1	4,0%	14	56,0%
Castelo Branco	2	0	0,0%	1	50,0%	0	0,0%	0	0,0%	1	50,0%
Santarém	4	1	25,0%	0	0,0%	0	0,0%	1	25,0%	2	50,0%
Braga	4	1	25,0%	1	25,0%	0	0,0%	0	0,0%	2	50,0%
Setúbal	3	0	0,0%	2	66,7%	0	0,0%	0	0,0%	1	33,3%
Bragança	1	0	0,0%	1	100,0%	0	0,0%	0	0,0%	0	0,0%
Portalegre	5	0	0,0%	5	100,0%	0	0,0%	0	0,0%	0	0,0%
Guarda	1	1	100,0%	0	0,0%	0	0,0%	0	0,0%	0	0,0%
Total:	111	16	14,4%	21	18,9%	4	3,6%	5	4,5%	65	58,6%

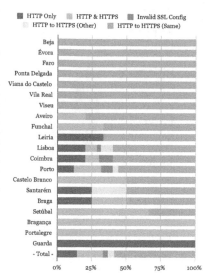

Fig. 3. HTTPS per district

Braga, Setúbal, Bragança and Portalegre, their HEIs have websites with SSL certificates but do not force their usage. The districts of Leiria, Lisboa, Coimbra, Porto, Samtarém, Braga and Guarda have websites without any SSL certificates.

Table 4 presents the CAs used by all the HEIs on public and private HEIs. Figure 4 draws the results of the Table 4. From the results obtained regarding public institutions, 41.5% use *GEANT* and 18.9% use *TERENA*. 13.2% of these institutions use free certificates provided by *Let's Encrypt*, and 15.1% do not use any SSL certificates at all. Regarding the private institutions, 22.4% use free certificates provided by *Let's Encrypt*, 17.2% use *GEANT*, and 8.6% use *Sectigo* as their CA; 20.7% do not use any SSL certificate at all.

Table 4. CAs used by HEIs

CA	Global		Public		Private	
	#	%	#	%	#	%
GEANT Vereniging	32	28,8%	22	19,8%	10	9,0%
No Certificate	20	18,0%	8	7,2%	12	10,8%
Let's Encrypt/R3	20	18,0%	7	6,3%	13	11,7%
TERENA	14	12,6%	10	9,0%	4	3,6%
Sectigo Limited	9	8,1%	4	3,6%	5	4,5%
GlobalSign nv-sa	5	4,5%	0	0,0%	5	4,5%
DigiCert Inc	3	2,7%	0	0,0%	3	2,7%
Cloudflare, Inc.	2	1,8%	1	0,9%	1	0,9%
cPanel, Inc.	2	1,8%	0	0,0%	2	1,8%
GoDaddy.com, Inc.	2	1,8%	0	0,0%	2	1,8%
GoGetSSL	1	0,9%	0	0,0%	1	0,9%
MULTICERT	1	0,9%	1	0,9%	0	0,0%
Total:	**111**	**100,0%**	**53**	**47,7%**	**58**	**52,3%**

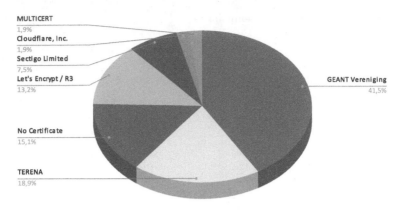

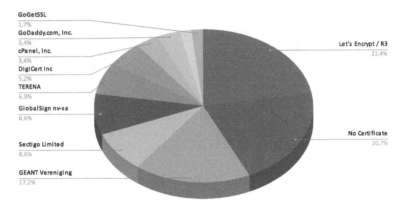

Fig. 4. CAs of public HEIs (above), and private HEIs (below)

Table 5 presents the size of the SSL keys used by the HEIs. Figure 5 draws the results of the Table 5. In regards to the key lenght of Rivest-Shamir-Adleman (RSA) keys used, 50% of HEI websites of the district of Castelo Branco district use 4096 bits RSA keys, 25% of websites on the district of Braga use 4096 bits RSA keys, only one HEIs in the district of Porto uses a 256 bits Elliptic Curve Cryptography (ECC) key. HEIs in the districts of Beja, Évora, Ponta Delgada, Viana do Castelo, Vila Real, Aveiro, Faro, Funchal, Viseu, Setúbal, Bragança and Portalegre use 2048 bits RSA keys.

Table 5. SSL key lenght by district

Districts	Total	Without SSL		2048 (RSA)		4096 (RSA)		256 (ECC)	
	#	#	%	#	%	#	%	#	%
Castelo Branco	2	0	0,0%	1	50,0%	1	50,0%	0	0,0%
Braga	4	1	25,0%	2	50,0%	1	25,0%	0	0,0%
Porto	25	5	20,0%	16	64,0%	3	12,0%	1	4,0%
Coimbra	10	3	30,0%	6	60,0%	1	10,0%	0	0,0%
Lisboa	35	8	22,9%	26	74,3%	1	2,9%	0	0,0%
Beja	1	0	0,0%	1	100,0%	0	0,0%	0	0,0%
Évora	1	0	0,0%	1	100,0%	0	0,0%	0	0,0%
Ponta Delgada	1	0	0,0%	1	100,0%	0	0,0%	0	0,0%
Viana do Castelo	2	0	0,0%	2	100,0%	0	0,0%	0	0,0%
Vila Real	2	0	0,0%	2	100,0%	0	0,0%	0	0,0%
Aveiro	5	0	0,0%	5	100,0%	0	0,0%	0	0,0%
Faro	2	0	0,0%	2	100,0%	0	0,0%	0	0,0%
Funchal	3	0	0,0%	3	100,0%	0	0,0%	0	0,0%
Viseu	1	0	0,0%	1	100,0%	0	0,0%	0	0,0%
Setúbal	3	0	0,0%	3	100,0%	0	0,0%	0	0,0%
Bragança	1	0	0,0%	1	100,0%	0	0,0%	0	0,0%
Portalegre	5	0	0,0%	5	100,0%	0	0,0%	0	0,0%
Santarém	4	1	25,0%	3	75,0%	0	0,0%	0	0,0%
Leiria	3	1	33,3%	2	66,7%	0	0,0%	0	0,0%
Guarda	1	1	100,0%	0	0,0%	0	0,0%	0	0,0%
Total	111	20	18,0%	83	74,8%	7	6,3%	1	0,9%

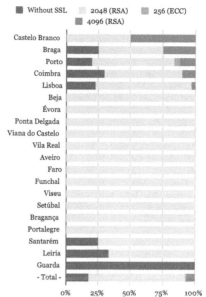

Fig. 5. SSL Key lenght

Table 6 presents the algorithms used by the HEIs per district. Figure 6 draws the results of the Table 6. From the results obtained it can be verified that only one HEI in the district of Porto uses the ECC algorithm, 13 districts use the algorithm RSA, and in the districts of Lisboa, Porto, Braga, Santarém, Coimbra, Leiria and Guarda, the HEIs do not use any algorithm.

Table 7 presents the results on the SSL/TLS versions used by HEIs in their websites. These results are presented in a decreasing order from top (better) to bottom (worst). Figure 7 draws the results of the Table 7. The results show that more than 25% of HEIs in the districts of Porto, Lisboa, Leiria, Funchal and Setúbal already negotiate on the most recent TLSv1.3 version. 25% of HEIs in Santarém negotiate on TLSv1.1 version and, in the remaining HEIs, the best negotiation method is accomplished with the TLSv1.2 version. No data is presented regarding SSLv3 and TLS1.0 since better versions are supported by the HEIs. No data is presented regarding SSLv2 since none of the websites have negotiated with this protocol.

Table 8 presents the results for the worse options offered by the HEIs regarding the negotiation mechanisms. These results are presented in a decreasing order from top (better) to bottom (worst). Figure 8 draws the results of the Table 8. In regards to the TLS ciphers used by the HEIs analyzed, more than 25% of the districts of Portalegre, Viana do Castelo, Castelo Branco, Lisboa, Aveiro, Porto and Setúbal HEIs do not negotiate under TLSv1.2. The districts of Setúbal, Coimbra and Leiria also have HEIs that do not negotiate below TLSv1.1. All HEIs from the districts of Beja, Évora, Ponta Delgada, Vila Real, Faro and Viseu

Table 6. SSL Algorithms by district

Districts	Total	Without SSL		RSA		ECC	
	#	#	%	#	%	#	%
Castelo Branco	2	0	0,0%	2	100,0%	0	0,0%
Beja	1	0	0,0%	1	100,0%	0	0,0%
Évora	1	0	0,0%	1	100,0%	0	0,0%
Ponta Delgada	1	0	0,0%	1	100,0%	0	0,0%
Viana do Castelo	2	0	0,0%	2	100,0%	0	0,0%
Vila Real	2	0	0,0%	2	100,0%	0	0,0%
Aveiro	5	0	0,0%	5	100,0%	0	0,0%
Faro	2	0	0,0%	2	100,0%	0	0,0%
Funchal	3	0	0,0%	3	100,0%	0	0,0%
Viseu	1	0	0,0%	1	100,0%	0	0,0%
Setúbal	3	0	0,0%	3	100,0%	0	0,0%
Bragança	1	0	0,0%	1	100,0%	0	0,0%
Portalegre	5	0	0,0%	5	100,0%	0	0,0%
Lisboa	35	8	22,9%	27	77,1%	0	0,0%
Porto	25	5	20,0%	19	76,0%	1	4,0%
Braga	4	1	25,0%	3	75,0%	0	0,0%
Santarém	4	1	25,0%	3	75,0%	0	0,0%
Coimbra	10	3	30,0%	7	70,0%	0	0,0%
Leiria	3	1	33,3%	2	66,7%	0	0,0%
Guarda	1	1	100,0%	0	0,0%	0	0,0%
Total	111	20	18,0%	90	81,1%	1	0,9%

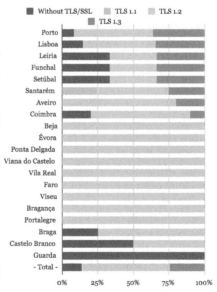

Fig. 6. SSL algorithms

Table 7. Best supported SSL/TLS versions

Districts	Total	Without TLS/SSL		TLSv1.1		TLSv1.2		TLSv1.3	
	#	#	%	#	%	#	%	#	%
Porto	25	2	8,0%	0	0,0%	14	56,0%	9	36,0%
Lisboa	35	5	14,3%	0	0,0%	18	51,4%	12	34,3%
Leiria	3	1	33,3%	0	0,0%	1	33,3%	1	33,3%
Funchal	3	1	33,3%	0	0,0%	1	33,3%	1	33,3%
Setúbal	3	1	33,3%	0	0,0%	1	33,3%	1	33,3%
Santarém	4	0	0,0%	1	25,0%	2	50,0%	1	25,0%
Aveiro	5	0	0,0%	0	0,0%	4	80,0%	1	20,0%
Coimbra	10	2	20,0%	0	0,0%	7	70,0%	1	10,0%
Beja	1	0	0,0%	0	0,0%	1	100,0%	0	0,0%
Évora	1	0	0,0%	0	0,0%	1	100,0%	0	0,0%
Ponta Delgada	1	0	0,0%	0	0,0%	1	100,0%	0	0,0%
Viana do Castelo	2	0	0,0%	0	0,0%	2	100,0%	0	0,0%
Vila Real	2	0	0,0%	0	0,0%	2	100,0%	0	0,0%
Faro	2	0	0,0%	0	0,0%	2	100,0%	0	0,0%
Viseu	1	0	0,0%	0	0,0%	1	100,0%	0	0,0%
Bragança	1	0	0,0%	0	0,0%	1	100,0%	0	0,0%
Portalegre	5	0	0,0%	0	0,0%	5	100,0%	0	0,0%
Braga	4	1	25,0%	0	0,0%	3	75,0%	0	0,0%
Castelo Branco	2	1	50,0%	0	0,0%	1	50,0%	0	0,0%
Guarda	1	1	100,0%	0	0,0%	0	0,0%	0	0,0%
Total:	**111**	**15**	**13,5%**	**1**	**0,9%**	**68**	**61,3%**	**27**	**24,3%**

Fig. 7. Best supported SSL/TLS Versions

Table 8. Worst supported SSL/TLS versions

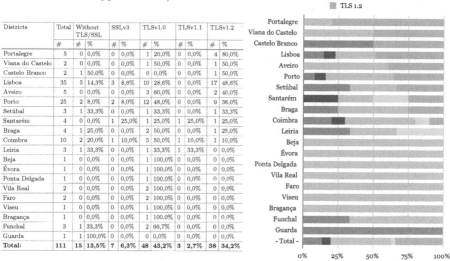

Districts	Total	Without TLS/SSL		SSLv3		TLSv1.0		TLSv1.1		TLSv1.2	
	#	#	%	#	%	#	%	#	%	#	%
Portalegre	5	0	0,0%	0	0,0%	1	20,0%	0	0,0%	4	80,0%
Viana do Castelo	2	0	0,0%	0	0,0%	1	50,0%	0	0,0%	1	50,0%
Castelo Branco	2	1	50,0%	0	0,0%	0	0,0%	0	0,0%	1	50,0%
Lisboa	35	5	14,3%	3	8,6%	10	28,6%	0	0,0%	17	48,6%
Aveiro	5	0	0,0%	0	0,0%	3	60,0%	0	0,0%	2	40,0%
Porto	25	2	8,0%	2	8,0%	12	48,0%	0	0,0%	9	36,0%
Setúbal	3	1	33,3%	0	0,0%	1	33,3%	0	0,0%	1	33,3%
Santarém	4	0	0,0%	1	25,0%	1	25,0%	1	25,0%	1	25,0%
Braga	4	1	25,0%	0	0,0%	2	50,0%	0	0,0%	1	25,0%
Coimbra	10	2	20,0%	1	10,0%	5	50,0%	1	10,0%	1	10,0%
Leiria	3	1	33,3%	0	0,0%	1	33,3%	1	33,3%	0	0,0%
Beja	1	0	0,0%	0	0,0%	1	100,0%	0	0,0%	0	0,0%
Évora	1	0	0,0%	0	0,0%	1	100,0%	0	0,0%	0	0,0%
Ponta Delgada	1	0	0,0%	0	0,0%	1	100,0%	0	0,0%	0	0,0%
Vila Real	2	0	0,0%	0	0,0%	2	100,0%	0	0,0%	0	0,0%
Faro	2	0	0,0%	0	0,0%	2	100,0%	0	0,0%	0	0,0%
Viseu	1	0	0,0%	0	0,0%	1	100,0%	0	0,0%	0	0,0%
Bragança	1	0	0,0%	0	0,0%	1	100,0%	0	0,0%	0	0,0%
Funchal	3	1	33,3%	0	0,0%	2	66,7%	0	0,0%	0	0,0%
Guarda	1	1	100,0%	0	0,0%	0	0,0%	0	0,0%	0	0,0%
Total:	111	15	13,5%	7	6,3%	48	43,2%	3	2,7%	38	34,2%

Fig. 8. Worst supported SSL/TLS Versions

negotiate at least on version TLSv1.0. Lastly, the districts of Lisboa, Porto, Santarém and Coimbra also have HEIs that negotiate on the SSLv3, representing 6.3% at a national level.

5 Conclusions

There are several security-related standards and recommendations concerning DNS and HTTP services. These standards and recommendations are relevant to enhance the security of public and private institutions. HEIs should also comply and be updated regarding these efforts to improve the security of their services and information, however, they present different statuses and paces in the adoption of these web-related security services.

This article presented an overview of the HEIs national panorama regarding the implementation of security-related standards and recommendations regarding DNS and HTTP services. A set of scripts were developed and data was collected namely regarding the support of DNSSEC, SSL certificates (including the respective CA), key size and algorithms used and SSL/TLS negotiations cyphers.

From the results obtained, it was verified that only 11.7% of HEIs support DNSSEC, in which 10% are public. Roughly 14.4% do not use any SSL certificates and those who support it, 18.9% do not force the usage. In regards to the CA used, the guidance is as follows: 28.8% of HEIs use *GEANT* as their CA, on private HEIs the most used CA is *Let's Encrypt*, totalling 11.7%, In regards to the SSL ciphers and algorithms, 74.8% of HEIs use a 2048 bits encryption key and 81.1% use the RSA algorithm. When it comes to SSL/TLS negotiations, 24.3% of HEIs already negotiate with the latest TLS version: TLSv1.3, while 6.3% of HEIs still negotiate with the vulnerable SSL version: SSLv3.

Future efforts of these HEIs should focus on (1) the adoption of DNSSEC, to add an extra layer of protection against DNS attacks and (2) implement correctly the HTTP redirection mechanisms and assure the support of the updated versions of SSL certificates to secure data communication between systems. In particular regarding SSL/TLS negotiation, the institutions that use SSLv3 are strongly encouraged to disable this protocol due to its vulnerability to man-in-the-middle attacks, and they should apply TLSv1.2 and TLSv1.3.

Acknowledgments. This work was developed in the context of a project in the Computer Networks and Systems Engineering graduation at the Instituto Politécnico de Viana do Castelo, Portugal, and it was partially supported by the Norte Portugal Regional Operational Programme (NORTE 2020), under the PORTUGAL 2020 Partnership Agreement, through the European Regional Development Fund (ERDF), within project "Cybers SeC IP" (NORTE-01-0145-FEDER-000044).

References

1. Direção Geral de Estatísticas de Educação e Ciência - Rede atual de Estabelecimentos do Ensino Superior. https://www.dgeec.mec.pt/np4/38/. Accessed 12 Apr 2021
2. EURYDICE - National Education Systems. https://eacea.ec.europa.eu/national-policies/eurydice/national-description_en. Accessed 1 July 2021
3. The top 500 sites on the web the sites in the top sites lists. https://www.alexa.com/topsites. Accessed 5 July 2021
4. Allen, C., Dierks, T.: The TLS Protocol Version 1.0. RFC 2246, January 1999. 10.17487/RFC2246. https://rfc-editor.org/rfc/rfc2246.txt
5. Chan, C.l., Fontugne, R., Cho, K., Goto, S.: Monitoring TLS adoption using backbone and edge traffic. In: IEEE INFOCOM 2018 - IEEE Conference on Computer Communications Workshops (INFOCOM WKSHPS), pp. 208–213 (2018). https://doi.org/10.1109/INFOCOMW.2018.8406957
6. Dierks, T., Rescorla, E.: The Transport Layer Security (TLS) Protocol Version 1.1. RFC 4346, April 2006. 10.17487/RFC4346. https://rfc-editor.org/rfc/rfc4346.txt
7. Elgamal, D.T., Hickman, K.E.: The SSL Protocol. Internet-Draft draft-hickman-netscape-ssl-00, Internet Engineering Task Force, April 1995. https://datatracker.ietf.org/doc/html/draft-hickman-netscape-ssl-00. Work in Progress
8. Freier, A.O., Karlton, P., Kocher, P.C.: The Secure Sockets Layer (SSL) Protocol Version 3.0. RFC 6101, August 2011. 10.17487/RFC6101. https://rfc-editor.org/rfc/rfc6101.txt
9. Incm: Resolução do conselho de ministros 92/2019 (2019). https://dre.pt/home/-/dre/122498962/details/maximized
10. Le, T., van Rijswijk-Deij, R., Allodi, L., Zannone, N.: Economic incentives on dnssec deployment: time to move from quantity to quality. In: NOMS 2018–2018 IEEE/IFIP Network Operations and Management Symposium, pp. 1–9 (2018). https://doi.org/10.1109/NOMS.2018.8406223

11. da República, A.: Lei 62/2007 (2007). https://dre.pt/web/guest/pesquisa/-/search/640339/details/normal?q=Lei. n. º 62/2007
12. Rescorla, E.: HTTP Over TLS. RFC 2818, May 2000. 10.17487/RFC2818. https://rfc-editor.org/rfc/rfc2818.txt
13. Rescorla, E.: The Transport Layer Security (TLS) Protocol Version 1.3. RFC 8446, August 2018. 10.17487/RFC8446. https://rfc-editor.org/rfc/rfc8446.txt
14. Rescorla, E., Dierks, T.: The Transport Layer Security (TLS) Protocol Version 1.2. RFC 5246, August 2008. 10.17487/RFC5246. https://rfc-editor.org/rfc/rfc5246.txt
15. Rescorla, E., Schiffman, A.M.: The Secure HyperText Transfer Protocol. RFC 2660, August 1999. 10.17487/RFC2660. https://rfc-editor.org/rfc/rfc2660.txt
16. Rose, S., Larson, M., Massey, D., Austein, R., Arends, R.: DNS Security Introduction and Requirements. RFC 4033, March 2005. 10.17487/RFC4033. https://rfc-editor.org/rfc/rfc4033.txt
17. Rose, S., Larson, M., Massey, D., Austein, R., Arends, R.: Protocol Modifications for the DNS Security Extensions. RFC 4035, March 2005. 10.17487/RFC4035. https://rfc-editor.org/rfc/rfc4035.txt
18. Rose, S., Larson, M., Massey, D., Austein, R., Arends, R.: Resource Records for the DNS Security Extensions. RFC 4034, March 2005. 10.17487/RFC4034. https://rfc-editor.org/rfc/rfc4034.txt
19. Song, Y.D., Mahanti, A., Ravichandran, S.C.: Understanding evolution and adoption of top level domains and DNSSEC. In: 2019 IEEE International Symposium on Measurements Networking (M N), pp. 1–6 (2019). https://doi.org/10.1109/IWMN.2019.8805011
20. Suga, Y.: Status survey of SSL/TLS sites in 2018 after pointing out about "search form" issues. In: 2018 Sixth International Symposium on Computing and Networking Workshops (CANDARW), pp. 483–485 (2018). https://doi.org/10.1109/CANDARW.2018.00093
21. Van Adrichem, N.L.M., Lua, A.R., Wang, X., Wasif, M., Fatturrahman, F., Kuipers, F.A.: DNSSEC misconfigurations: how incorrectly configured security leads to unreachability. In: 2014 IEEE Joint Intelligence and Security Informatics Conference, pp. 9–16 (2014). https://doi.org/10.1109/JISIC.2014.12
22. Weerasinghe, T., Disanayake, C.: Usage of RC4 cipher in SSL configurations in web portals of Sri Lankan banking/non-banking financial institutes and awareness levels of relevant staff about it. In: 2018 National Information Technology Conference (NITC), pp. 1–6 (2018). https://doi.org/10.1109/NITC.2018.8550064
23. Yee, P.E.: Updates to the Internet X.509 Public Key Infrastructure Certificate and Certificate Revocation List (CRL) Profile. RFC 6818, January 2013. 10.17487/RFC6818. https://rfc-editor.org/rfc/rfc6818.txt

Prevention of IoT-Enabled Crime Using Home Routers (PITCHR)

Mary Asante$^{(\boxtimes)}$ ⓘ, Carsten Maple ⓘ, and Gregory Epiphaniou ⓘ

Secure Cyber Systems Research Group, WMG, University of Warwick, Coventry CV4 7AL, UK
`mary.asante.1@warwick.ac.uk`

Abstract. The home router has traditionally been the access point for home users to access email and web services through a desktop computer but has now become the entry point for a myriad of Internet-connected devices. With nearly all households in Europe having high-speed broadband connection, home routers have become targets for most cyber-attacks. This paper presents the findings of a study on the Prevention of IoT-enabled Crime using Home Routers (PITCHR). The study aims to understand the perspectives of the major stakeholders of the home router network in PITCHR, their respective roles and responsibilities, and make recommendations for future research directions. To achieve this, we conducted a review of state of the art, which informed a series of focus group discussions, with 26 participants from the respective stakeholder groups – Service Providers including Internet Service Providers, Hardware Manufacturers, Citizens, Citizen and Industry Groups, Government and Academics. Ten (10) themes emerged from the thematic coding of the focus group discussions. The findings of the study were presented in a combined stakeholder workshop. The study made recommendations for consideration.

Keywords: Home routers · IoT-enabled crime · Consumer IoT · Internet Service Providers · Home network

1 Introduction

Home-based routers are becoming increasingly integral parts of our way of life, with homes becoming smarter and devices connecting to each other [1]. Having traditionally been the access point for home users to access email and web services through a desktop computer, they are now becoming the entry point for a myriad of Internet-connected devices. These include smart assistants (e.g. Amazon Echo and Google Home), smart wearables (e.g. Fitbit), smart security (e.g. Ring and baby monitors), smart appliances (e.g. smart kettles, fridges and washing machines), smart energy (e.g. Nest and smart plugs) and many more. As such, the router becomes a gateway to a significant number of devices, considerable computing power and a variety of personal information, present challenges [2], which can be exploited with minimal effort [3].

© ICST Institute for Computer Sciences, Social Informatics and Telecommunications Engineering 2022
Published by Springer Nature Switzerland AG 2022. All Rights Reserved
S. Paiva et al. (Eds.): SmartCity360° 2021, LNICST 442, pp. 470–481, 2022.
https://doi.org/10.1007/978-3-031-06371-8_31

Eurostat reported that in 2020, nearly all households in Europe had been switched to high-speed broadband connection, an estimated 91% of households in the EU 27 and 97% in the UK [4]. However, as highlighted by the German Federation Office for Information Security in their requirements for secure broadband routers, "At the same time the number of devices per household that uses or even requires Internet access to be fully functional increases. This trend is predicted to continue and leads to more and more everyday things being equipped with networking and Internet capabilities" [5]. As a result, the nature of the threats that the home router network faces are constantly changing as new risks are being introduced all the time at a very fast pace.

Additionally, a study conducted by Germany's Fraunhofer Institute for Communication (FKIE) analysed over 127 home routers manufactured by top brands, including ASUS, Netgear, D-Link, TP-Link and Linksys, and found that all the home routers have security flaws. Also, 46 home routers had not been updated once within the previous 12 months and had weak passwords which could easily be cracked that users could not change. They also found that 22 home routers were from top vendors had not been updated in two years, and dozens had not received any security update in the past year [6]. These flaws leave home users widely opened and vulnerable to existing and emerging cyber security threats. Moreover, end users are not receiving sufficient information about their devices' security features from manufacturers [7].

The remainder of the paper is structured as follows: Sect. 2 presents the methodology used to collect and analyse the focus groups responses. Section 3 presents the critical analysis of the results. Section 4 presents the key findings and Sect. 5 makes recommendations. Finally, Sect. 6 concludes this paper.

2 Methodology

2.1 Background of This Study

Three key stakeholder focus group discussions were undertaken with industry and security experts to understand the roles that Service Providers, Hardware and Hardware Manufactures and Citizens and Citizen groups play in PITCHR. The focus group discussions offered insights into the various stakeholders' perspectives and the challenges faced by each of these stakeholders in the prevention of IoT-enabled crime using home routers. These include each stakeholder's role in PITCHR, how technology can reduce the impact of future crime and whom the responsibility and the financial burden lies with. A follow-on combined stakeholder workshop was conducted with participants from all stakeholder groups to discuss the findings of the study.

2.2 Participants

Each session had representatives from leading organisations and industry experts such as Cisco, Vonage, BT, and representation from government agencies such as the UK Home Office and National Cyber Security Centre (NCSC). There was an average of 12 participants per session. The sessions were very interactive and provided opportunities for in-depth discussions on the role of:

- Service Providers (Internet Service Providers (ISPs) eg BT, Virgin, TalkTalk etc. and other Service Providers such as Google, Amazon, Microsoft, and payment providers eg Mastercard).
- Hardware and hardware manufacturers such as Linksys and D-Link and IoT device manufacturers.
- Citizens and citizen groups such as Which and Consumer International. In this session, we also explored the roles of organisations such as IoTSF (Internet of Things Security Foundation) and Messaging Anti Abuse Working Group (MAAWG).
- Government, legislation, and standards.

2.3 Procedure

Each focus group discussion lasted 90 min. A sample of the questions used is presented in Table 1. The recordings for each of the sessions were transcribed. The researchers read and re-read through the transcripts to identify potential themes. The researchers used thematic analysis to identify initial codes, which were reviewed and refined to determine the main themes and sub-themes. The themes were shaped by the research topic, Prevention of IoT-enabled Crime using Home Routers (PITCHR) and the literature review conducted as part of the study. Ten main themes were identified as presented in Table 2.

Table 1. Sample Questions for the Focus Group Discussions.

Session 1	Session 2	Session 3
1. How have you seen home router technology evolve over the past decade; how has the role of Service Providers evolved in terms of providing home router security?	How have you seen home router technology evolve over the past decade; how has the role of hardware manufacturers evolved in terms of providing home router security?	To what extent are you aware of the scale of security threats to home router security?
2. Which tools and techniques are you are of that Service Providers are currently using to ensure security of home routers?	Which tools and techniques are you are of that hardware manufacturers are currently using to ensure the security of home routers?	How much responsibility is placed on the individuals in ensuring the security of their home router?
3. In your opinion, how much does it cost Service Providers to currently provide home router defence systems?	Which Tools and techniques can hardware manufacturers deploy and/or enhance to improve home router security?	How sensitive are consumers to paying more for their services for use towards home router security enhancement/improvement?

Table 2. Emergent Themes.

Code	Theme
1	Evolution of Home Router Technology
2	Future of Router Technology
3	The Role of Service Providers
4	The Role of Hardware and Hardware Manufacturers
5	The Role of Citizen and Industry Groups
6	Cost of Providing Home Router Security
7	Regulatory Role and Impact
8	Who is / should be Responsible for Home Router Security
9	User Awareness and Education
10	Changing Nature of Home Router Cyber Security Landscape

3 Results

3.1 Evolution of Home Router Technology

Routers were created as a result of technological research and development in compliance with IEEE802.11, allowing for the wireless transfer of data between devices. They were subsequently made available to home users in 1999, coincidentally, the same year that Kevin Ashton coined the term 'Internet of Things' [8]. Home routers provide internet access for devices on the home network such as wearable devices, smart assistants, gaming systems, mobile devices and smart appliances, as illustrated in Fig. 1. Most homes use wireless routers, although some homes, still use wired routers, using Ethernet cables to connect devices to the routers.

Home routers were very simple and basic, without many features on them. However, all the participants agreed that they have since become a lot more sophisticated over the years, offering many more capabilities, faster speeds, and generally have become more powerful. For example, they incorporate firewall technologies that filter the inflow and set up guest networks in the home, allowing for segregation of traffic on the home network.

New Customer Premise Equipment (CPE) operate pretty much like computers with powerful cores and processors and improved performance [9]. Moreover, in most cases, software capability allowing customisation on the CPE may not be enabled upon delivery to the end-user, thus limiting the CPE's capability. Some of the significant security posture changes are better wireless encryption technology, mandatory password requirements on devices, and enforcing specific initial set up rules for devices.

Routers can automate updates of firmware and software, execute security patches, and block out bad sites to the extent that the end-users are not even aware of what happens in their routers. Home users can configure their home router network to suit their needs. For example, they can set a downtime for the router when it goes to sleep for a set period. Home users can isolate devices off their network and can see the list of devices connected to their network. Home routers can be configured through apps, making it easier for home users to control their network.

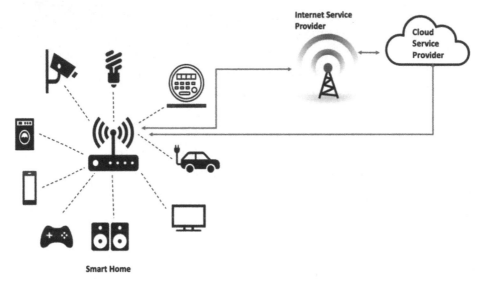

Fig. 1. Smart home router network

3.2 Future of Home Router Technology

The next generation of home routers may be able to provide enhanced connectivity through mobile networks, in addition to the fixed broadband connection, allowing the home router to tap into mobile networks when the fixed broadband does not provide adequate service.

In addition to the service network and guest network, the home router could have more channels opened up, with different security levels to facilitate the different services and numerous devices on the network (For example, a utility network, entertainment network, access network and so on). This will allow users and/or Service Providers to lockdown certain channels whilst relaxing the rule for some of the others.

3.3 The Role of Service Providers

In the UK, the ISPs mostly control the home router hardware the home user ends up within their home. The home user rarely has a say in the router hardware they are provided with. Security implications of this supply of home router hardware are that home users may end up with less secure and cheaper routers in their homes than the most secure and up-to-date technology available on the market. This is mostly because ISPs will provide hardware-based on what is most cost-effective and will give them better margins in what is a competitive market. The home user is rarely aware of the manufacturer of the hardware, 'the box', through which the ISP provide them broadband services.

The participants' general perception was that ISPs could do more than there were currently doing to make home routers more secure. However, the impact of low margins on home routers raises the question of whether ISPs have enough buying power and are in a good position to influence the design, functionality and features of home routers. The ISP has a relationship with the user and the manufacturer. The ISP is, therefore, key to the manufacturer understanding what the user really needs.

Cloud Service Providers
Some participants argued that Cloud Service Providers had better capability and are more equipped to protect home users from malware, virus and phishing attacks than ISPs. Cloud Service Providers like Amazon and Google have been able to harness a relationship with end-users in a way that traditional ISPs have not been able to do. They have managed to get end-users to become more accustomed to them and let them into their everyday lives – Google Home Assistant and Amazon Alexa and Echo, by offering the end-user what they want – a simple and easy lifestyle; thus, overcoming the main barrier that ISPs such as BT, Virgin, TalkTalk and Sky have had for a long time.

They have also demonstrated to the end-users that they can handle massive amounts of data securely. ISPs have not been able to get end-users to change their mindset about sharing their information freely with them.

3.4   The Role of Hardware and Hardware Manufacturers

Hardware manufacturers mostly focus on the design and production of hardware. They put primary hardware functionality ahead of security. This applies to both manufacturers of home routers and IoT devices. Security features may well slow down the performance of hardware, causing frustrations for end users. A gamer may be slowed down by the home router's security functionality, which may seek to block the gaming website or limit access, slowing down their performance.

Hardware manufacturers may contribute to the security of their devices by ensuring that their operating systems are from a secure, reputable source. Rather than go with the cheapest option all the time, they can carefully source and select their providers.

Most IoT devices usually seek to communicate with cloud endpoints and a few more sites and maybe other devices on the home network [10]. This was identified as a new threat to the home router network by one of the participants. They highlighted that manufacturers are gathering information about users and transferring them to the cloud without understanding how to protect that data. For example, a dishwasher manufacturer may not understand or know how to protect and manage the telemetry data their device collected about its user once that data is uploaded to the cloud.

Software
It was also highlighted that software, specifically, open-source software plays an important role in adding value to hardware. Most hardware manufacturers do not develop the software operating on their systems. Therefore, companies supplying this value-added software are also key stakeholders who must also provide home router security.

3.5 The Role of Citizen and Industry Groups

All the participants agreed that their levels of awareness were due to the fact that they are actively engaged and work within the security industry or citizen groups proactively doing work in the area. All the participants agreed that the general populations knowledge and awareness of security risks associated with their home router networks and devices were very limited and, in some cases, non-existent. The ratio in the general population is 80/20 rule.

There are several groups actively trying to raise user awareness around home router cyber security threats. These include Which, Smart Homes and Building Associations, Messaging Anti Abuse Working Group (MAAWG), Consumers International and IoTSF. Some groups will do specific targeted campaigns relevant to the specific groups that they support. It was highlighted that some of the bigger charities such as Victim Support, Citizens Advice and Neighbourhood Watch could help raise user awareness.

3.6 Cost of Providing Home Router Security

On average, businesses spend 4–10% of their IT budget on security. Whilst Service Providers may be spending huge amounts of money on protecting their own networks. There is no evidence to support the fact that Service Providers are spending anywhere near that amount on home router security. Security is being done on the cheap, but that needs to change as the future is online.

From a user's point of view, a home router may cost between £25 and £350 to buy. The cheaper ones are still quite basic, and the more expensive ones have inbuilt capabilities in their operating systems, offering better functionality and security.

The Covid 19 pandemic has seriously highlighted how important the Internet is to our everyday lives. With everything from education, healthcare, work, and social interactions being carried out remotely via the Internet's services. Accessibility to the Internet and technology has become even more critical than they were before. There are increasing concerns over a section of society who cannot afford to pay for the technology or service to benefit from using them. This adds an added layer of complication to the debate around who should pay for security.

3.7 Regulatory Role and Impact

Some participants argued that home router security should be considered a national issue as impacts of attacks due to IoT-enabled crime using home routers such as Distributed Denial of Service (DDoS) attacks are more likely to have major national infrastructure implications than for individuals. That makes it a more compelling issue for the government to get more involved to ensure that routers are secure.

All the participants agreed that regulations have and can play an important role in securing home routers and PITCHR. They also agreed that there is a clear lack of standards, frameworks and regulations in the IoT Space [11].

3.8   Who is/Should be Responsible for Home Router Security

Which of the home router network stakeholders is or should be responsible for home routers' security – the Service Provider, Hardware Manufacturer or the end-user?

Arguably, most end users are not in the best position to have the knowledge or technical know to decide how best to secure their network. Hardware manufacturers may have a role in determining the level of access that devices may need to function appropriately. They can help the end-user understand the right levels of settings users need to use with their devices by stipulating these in the user manuscripts of the devices. This could be difficult as hardware manufacturers may not necessarily know this information. They do not have a direct relationship with the end-user.

Therefore, most participants argued that the ISP is central to providing and ensuring home router security. If the trust levels between the end-user and the ISP are high, the ISP will warn the end-user of any potential threats and provide them with guidance on keeping themselves and their networks secure. The ISP could also forge an even closer relationship with the hardware manufacturer to understand how end-users use their hardware and the end-users' security issues.

3.9   User Awareness and Education

All participants agreed that one of the critical components to achieving home router security is user awareness.

They argued that most users are not aware of any issues associated with their IoT devices or home routers. As a result, they are not demanding that their Service Providers provide secure routers, nor are they factoring in security when purchasing IoT devices.

Most users are also unaware of IoT devices' complexity and connectivity to cloud services add to their home network. They may not be aware that devices are already communicating with each other in a way that requires little human intervention.

Privacy

Do users care about their privacy? Some participants shared the view that users only care about their privacy after they lose it. Users may lose money, financial details, personal details and/or may be victims of fraud and blackmail.

3.10   The Changing Nature of Home Router Cyber Security Landscape

Major aspects of understanding how the home router cyber security landscape is changing are to explore how the threats have evolved over the period of time (see Fig. 2); how they have influenced how technology has changed over the period of time; and, how security has kept up with the threats from criminal actors and whether or not those threats are driving and dictating the change in security. What is considered important to secure and what not to share with organisations and third parties, which could put the home user at risk.

Threats to the home network can be grouped into two: internal threats from inside the home and external threats from outside the home. IoT devices certainly change the nature of security threats from inside the home perimeter. In most cases, Service Providers may

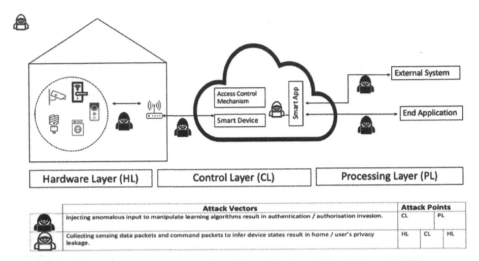

Fig. 2. Attack Vectors in the Home Network, adapted from Mao et al. [12]

be able to detect and manage external threats but not so easily or effectively internal threats that may be introduced by the end users themselves.

As machine to machine communication improves through ML, AI, and other technologies, chances of attacks similar to the Mirai botnets become increasingly likely. Criminals may also be able to use analytics from the home router network and associated IoT devices to inform their decisions on when to attack homes for example, the best time to burgle a home.

Most of the participants agreed that, ultimately, third party services might emerge, which may provide value-added services, in addition to what the service providers are already offering to make the home router network more secure.

4 Key Findings

The key findings of the study are presented as follows:

- The Prevention of IoT-enabled Crime using Home Routers requires a combined effort from all stakeholders.
- legislation – there are currently no specific regulations in the IoT space, although there may be discussions on-going in governments around the world.
- Stringent standards and frameworks are required for establishing baselines for home router security.
- There are no requirements on manufacturers to incorporate security into home routers and IoT devices by design and by default.
- Service Providers invest significantly into protecting their networks but the investment does not necessarily trickle down to the home router network, particularly inside the home environment.

- Service Providers do not collaborate sufficiently with each other, and sharing intelligence on threat landscape is limited, if at all. This makes it easy for cyber criminals to deploy the same techniques to several networks successfully.
- Automation of home router network security may be vital to the Prevention of IoT-enabled Crime using Home Routers.
- It is unclear who should be responsible for providing home router security.
- It is unclear who should pay for home router security
- the average end user of the home router does not have the knowledge and the capability to configure and secure their home router and devices.
- user awareness and education is vital in the Prevention of IoT-enabled Crime using Home Routers

All the combined stakeholder workshop participants agreed that the findings were an accurate representation of the focus group discussions.

5 Recommendations

The researchers would like to make the following recommendations based on the findings of the study:

1. Home router security must be available to all users by default and at an affordable cost.
2. ISPs must be responsible for ensuring that the routers they supply to home users have security capabilities that are enabled for the end-user.
3. ISPs must collaborate with Cloud Service Providers such as Microsoft, Amazon, and Google and other third-party providers to share intelligence on network traffic and device behaviours to effectively prevent IoT-enabled crime using home routers.
4. Service Providers must ensure that their service networks are secure to minimise security risks to connected devices.
5. It will be beneficial for IoT devices to be registered so that each device's activity on the network can be detected and traced to the device. This will help with the isolation of the device when malicious activities or traffic is detected from that behaviour.
6. Security on IoT devices must be improved by ensuring that manufacturers design and build devices with security by design and default.
7. Government must legislate for home router security and ensure that hardware manufacturers and Service Providers comply with security legislation.
8. Government must bring together all stakeholders to ensure that their perspectives inform its decisions.
9. Citizen groups could provide awareness to citizens about the threats of the home router network.
10. End users should be made aware of the nature of the risks associated with their home router network and the devices they use.

6 Conclusion

Smart homes are exponentially exposed to security vulnerabilities, with increasing numbers of smart devices being added to the home network. Most of the home network traffic into and out of the home is driven through the home router, which has minimal or no security built-in. Home router security is an afterthought, and none of the stakeholders, ISPs, hardware manufacturers, consumers, and government bodies is clearly responsible for implementing or enforcing home router security.

The absence of standards, frameworks and regulations in the IoT space and the lack of clarity around who is responsible for providing secure home defence systems continuous to cause significant challenges, exposing the home user to potential attacks, financial loss and loss of personal data.

It is anticipated that as users become more aware of the vulnerabilities and risks associated with their home router network, they may demand better security from their service providers and make informed choices when selecting providers or buying devices. They will implement basic security hygiene and best practice such as changing default passwords, regularly updating their device software, locking down devices and network where appropriate and proactively reporting suspected malicious activities on their network.

The cost of securing the home router environment should be spread out to make it more affordable to all end users. Service providers must be encouraged to dedicate part of their security budgets towards providing home router security and awareness training for the end-user.

Security of home routers must be by default and by design and automated wherever possible to reduce the burden on the end-user and improve the chances of securing the network without end-user intervention. Government regulations will play a critical part in ensuring that responsibility is placed in the Service Providers and hardware manufacturers' hands, not on the end-user who may not know or capability to secure their home network.

Acknowledgements. The study was funded by The Dawes Centre for Future Crime (DCFC) at UCL.

References

1. Ray, A.K., Bagwari, A.: IoT based smart home: security aspects and security architecture. In: IEEE 9th International Conference on Communication Systems and Network Technologies (CSNT), pp. 218–222 (2020)
2. Maple, C.: Security and privacy in the Internet of things. J. Cyber Policy **2**, 155–184 (2017)
3. Stellios, I., Kotzanikolaou, P., Psarakis, M., Alcaraz, C., Lopez, J.: A survey of IoT-enabled cyberattacks: assessing attack paths to critical infrastructures and services. IEEE Commun. Surveys Tutorials **20**, 3453–3495 (2018)
4. Eurostat - Digital economy and society statistics - households and individuals https://ec.eur opa.eu/eurostat/databrowser/view/isoc_ci_in_h/default/bar?lang=en Accessed 5 Feb 2021
5. German Federal Office for Information Security: BSI TR-03148 Secure Broadband Router, BSI TR-03148:Secure Broadband Router (bund.de), Accessed Feb 2021

6. Teiss: All home routers sold by top European vendors feature security flaws https://www.teiss.co.uk/all-home-routers-vulnerable-threats/ Accessed 5 Feb 2021
7. Blythe, J., Sombatruang, N., Johnson, S.: What security features and crime prevention advice is communicated in consumer IoT device manuals and support pages? Journal of Cybersecurity **5**, 1–10 (2019)
8. Kebande, V.R., Karie, N.M., Michael, A., Malapane, S.M.G., Venter, H.S.: How an IoT-enabled "smart refrigerator" can play a clandestine role in perpetuating cyber-crime. In: IST-Africa Week Conference (IST-Africa), Windhoek, pp. 1–10 (2017)
9. Qorvo 'The WiFi Evolution', White Paper https://www.qorvo.com/-/media/files/qorvopublic/white-papers/qorvo-the-wi-fi-evolution-white-paper.pdf Accessed 30 Jan 2021
10. Mocrii, D., Chen, Y., Musilek, P.: 'IoT-based smart homes: a review of system architecture, software, communications, privacy and security. Internet of Things' **1**(2), 81–98 (2018)
11. Department for Digital, Culture, Media & Sports and National Cyber Security Centre https://www.gov.uk/government/news/government-to-strengthen-security-of-internet-connected-products#:~:text=These%20are%3A,on%20in%20a%20timely%20manner Accessed 20 Oct 2020
12. Mao, J., Lin, Q., Bia, J.: Application of learning algorithms in smart home IoT system security, Math. Found. Comput. 2–27 (2018)

Blockchain Technology in Supply Chain Management – A Discussion of Current and Future Research Topics

Tan Gürpinar[1]([⊠]) [iD], Nick Große[1] [iD], Max Schwarzer[2] [iD], Eugen Burov[3], Roman Stammes[4] [iD], Philipp Asterios Ioannidis[1], Larissa Krämer[5] [iD], Rico Ahlbäumer[5] [iD], and Michael Henke[1] [iD]

[1] TU Dortmund University, Leonhard-Euler-Str. 5, 44227 Dortmund, Germany
{tan.guerpinar,nick.grosse}@tu-dortmund.de
[2] Dachser SE, Thomas-Dachser-Str. 2, 87439 Kempten, Germany
[3] Fraunhofer IML, Joseph-von-Fraunhofer-Straße 2-4, 44227 Dortmund, Germany
[4] Brutana-Metrona Group, Max-Planck-Str. 2, 50354 Hürth, Germany
[5] TU Dortmund University, Joseph-von-Fraunhofer-Str. 2-4, 44227 Dortmund, Germany

Abstract. Purpose: Today's supply chain management faces complex and globally distributed networks of customers and suppliers. Blockchain solutions serve as underlying IT infrastructures to connect the network participants and enable multiple applications. This paper aims at bringing together and discussing current and future research topics in the field of blockchain in supply chain management. Methodology: In the paper, seven central research topics of the field - strategic realignment of enterprises, governance and profitability considerations, as well as blockchain-based pay-per-use models, additive manufacturing, decentralized markets and cyber-physical production systems - are presented with a state of the art and a research discussion to stimulate prospective blockchain research. Findings: As an outcome, the research topics are consolidated in a research framework and categorized in strategic or application oriented approaches, as well as assigned to blockchain scientific layers.

Keywords: Blockchain technology · Supply chain management · Distributed ledger technology · Field review · Research agenda

1 Introduction

With the increase in digitalization and globalization enterprises around the world have to rethink the way they deal with challenges along their supply chains. Especially enforced by recent crises, e.g. global pandemics, supply chains need to be kept resilient and sustainable, while complexity increases with the amount of stakeholders involved. In times of competitive ramp-up management, there is also an urgent need for concepts proposing transparency and visibility throughout the supply chains [1, 2]. Against that backdrop, IT infrastructures such as distributed ledger technologies (DLT), and especially blockchain

S. Paiva et al. (Eds.): SmartCity360° 2021, LNICST 442, pp. 482–503, 2022.
https://doi.org/10.1007/978-3-031-06371-8_32

technologies, are getting more attention due to their inherent characteristics and functionalities to address the stated challenges while reducing information asymmetries [3]. Throughout this article we are using the prominent term of blockchain technology but imply and cover also the use of other DLT [4]. The term blockchain hereby is described as a "distributed database that is practically immutable by being maintained by a decentralized P2P network using a consensus mechanism, cryptography and back-referencing blocks to order and validate transactions" [5].

Even though there are multiple successful industry blockchain projects and initiatives that combine research and application like e.g. Blockchain Europe, current analyses show that efforts to implement blockchains along supply chains often remain at an early stage [2, 6] and enterprises struggle in successfully completing implementation projects [7–9]. To bring blockchain projects one step further, the strategic realignment of companies (Setc. 2.1) needs to be examined considering concepts to utilize decentralized business models. It also has to be clarified to what extent, business models need to be transformed in order to adopt new cooperation and coopetition concepts. Additionally, there is a research need on how to design effective governance mechanisms for blockchain based ecosystems to enable confidence in cooperation and to ensure long-term business success (Sect. 3.1). Enterprise blockchain applications are often used within inter-organizational settings and therefore they do not only require an increased governance effort, but also profitability analyses become more complex and research is needed to quantify the occurring network effects (Sect. 3.2). Subsequently, research questions about the potential of blockchain for building trust and achieving consensus in accounting models can be addressed (Sect. 4.1), and in-depth transferred to different application areas like blockchain-based additive manufacturing platforms (Sect. 4.2). Finally, investigations are needed on the use of blockchain in decentralized markets (Sect. 5.1), especially if both machines and humans, are interacting in such ecosystems (Sect. 5.2).

This paper reveals a state of the art overview and research discussion of the stated research topics as well as future research needs. Finally a research framework is presented to consolidate the findings and invite researchers to participate in advancing blockchain and supply chain management research.

2 Field Review

2.1 Scope and Overview

In each chapter of the following field review, first strategic topics that enable the use of blockchain in supply chain management are discussed. Then, more application oriented topics follow up that are characterized by the respective blockchain implementation (Fig. 1).

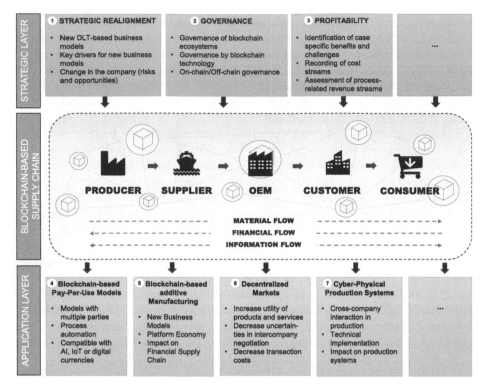

Fig. 1. Research map for blockchain technology in supply chain management

3   Strategic Realignment of Enterprises Through Blockchain

3.1   State of the Art

Academic literature describes constant changes in organizations due to new technology solutions, however, blockchain itself is still a very young field of research. Most distributed ledger technology-based studies are related to blockchain in combination with supply chain management, cryptocurrencies, identities, process architectures, tokenization, energy market, finance, and smart contracts. The combination of blockchain and strategic reorientation of companies has been an underrepresented publication topic so far. A literature review by Klinger and Bodendorf reveals that starting points can be found just on a theoretical foundation with the described topic, but business processes that lead to a strategic realignment through blockchain have not been dealt with more a more practical approach [10]. Current examples of blockchain solutions, development goals for sustainability and new business models are analyzed by [11]. The synergies between blockchain as well as other disruptive technologies are analyzed by Herian, who elaborates on the principle of trust through blockchain technology. Herian explains the change on a strategic shift from the secure assignment of digital property and the associated of new business models [12]. In a systematic literature review, Casino et al. describe the current state of research on blockchain-enabled applications in various fields, such as supply chain, business, healthcare, IoT, privacy, and data management. Trends and emerging research areas are also described, a research gap for strategic reorientation of companies remains open and needs to be investigated [13]. For this reason, it is of interest to investigate the following groups of topics as a research topic: "strategic management, economic theories for blockchain, change management, digital transformation and business models" [14].

3.2 Research Discussion

In view of the growing trend of digitalization, the technical innovation of blockchain is becoming increasingly important. Therefore, the existing research gap with regard to the strategic reorientation of companies is to be closed. It is important to examine what the most important drivers for the strategic realignment through blockchain in the company will be. Furthermore, it is also important to find out what the opportunities and risks of the introduction of new business processes through blockchain will be for the companies. There are a number of research questions that still need to be answered in this area. First of all, it is necessary to clarify what the most important drivers are for the strategic realignment through blockchain in the company. Furthermore, it is necessary to find out what needs in a company require to be changed in order to take advantage of the opportunities offered by blockchain and where the risks lie. Moreover, it is important to clarify how the emerging blockchain technologies can be organized in a way that makes sense for a company and what impact this will have on new business models. Also, the significance of the strategic realignment in the company through the blockchain and what results can be expected are still open questions that need to be clarified.

By closing the research gap of strategic realignment of companies, there are further research gaps that can be investigated. However, the results of the research gaps must be continuously reviewed, as the emerging technologies and thus the market are constantly evolving. It is important to constantly monitor future changes in the framework conditions, technological progress and new scientific findings. Firstly, it is important to find out the most efficient ways to implement blockchain in the enterprises and secondly how the realignment should be implemented in the company. In this way, companies can assess not only the strategic but also the monetary impact when deciding to introduce blockchain solutions. This provides a basis for decision-making with regard to the company's own future design for the use of blockchain.

4 Governance for Enterprise Blockchain Applications

4.1 State of the Art

A few years before blockchain became a subject of discussion, a series of research projects from Weill et al. revealed that a proper (IT-) governance design with a clear assignment of respective roles, decision rights and accountability is indispensable to ensure long-term business success [15]. Enterprise blockchain applications are usually applied to inter-organizational settings, where multiple and diverse participants interact with each other. It becomes apparent that defining a governance model for a distributed cross-organization approach is not as easy as it is for a system managed by a single entity, not least due to several specialties the technology comes along with. A survey from 2019 on global companies in the transportation and logistics industry by the management consulting group 'Boston Consulting Group (BCG)' confirms governance to be a key factor for a successful creation of collaborative blockchain ecosystems [16]. When trying to find suitable recommendations for practitioners and researchers, it might help to first have a look at platform literature. Although this type of literature does not explicitly examine governance questions from the perspective of a blockchain platform or ecosystem, lessons learned are interesting for blockchain governance models, as well [17]. Parker and Van Alstyne, for instance, developed a sequential innovation model to provide practitioners with guidance on the decision about the openness of a platform [18]. They address strategical questions related to the orchestration of external parties from a platform providers' point of view. However, since there are various new features, components and roles that blockchain technologies are endowed with (e.g., on-chain governance mechanisms, token, validators and forks), it is clear that 'classical' platform literature has several shortcomings with regard to the question of blockchain governance.

A second possibility is to seek advice from literature on governance at the protocol level for public permissionless systems, such as Ethereum and Bitcoin. Gasser et al. describe the process by which Bitcoin revised its core code to implement' multi-signature transactions' [19]. Using forum posts as primary data, Andersen and Bogusz develop a framework for assessing the potential consequences of specific forking events [20]. By referring to past Bitcoin forks and the social contexts influencing these forks, their framework tries to help practitioners with the question around what to consider when developing a governance model for blockchain infrastructures. Of course, public permissionless systems clearly differ to private or public permissioned systems designed for consortial / enterprise applications, when it comes to anonymity of participants and legal or jurisdictional questions. Same applies to hybrid approaches, a combination of both, where public permissionless systems can be used for anchoring purposes, meaning that hash values are being stored periodically on these systems for verifiability reasons [21].

4.2 Research Discussion

This indicates a research gap for the design of governance models for enterprise blockchain applications, as researchers focus on non-blockchain platform governance or governance related to cryptocurrencies, such as Bitcoin or Ethereum, so far. Additionally, several industry or politically funded projects highlight the importance to extend academic research to governance of enterprise blockchain applications and networks. The German Federal Ministry for Economic Affairs and Energy, for instance, explicitly states research and development of effective governance structures for using distributed ledger technologies in the logistics sector within their 'Blockchain Strategy' paper [22]. Beck et al. propose an extensive research agenda on blockchain governance, as well [23]. Regardless of the various possible blockchain architectures (private permissioned, hybrid, etc.) for enterprise blockchain applications, it is of interest which components have to be considered for the setup of a respective governance models and how a systematic approach could look like. Conversely, it is of interest how governance models from already existing enterprise blockchain applications can be assessed. Considering a situation where an organization has to evaluate whether a blockchain solution initiated by another industry player meets the own strategic needs (i.e. when it comes to the question whether to join an already existing initiative), the evaluation of the respective governance model could reflect an assessment from a strategic point of view.

Another interesting field of research is the interplay of the two fields governance 'by' blockchain and governance 'of' blockchain. In contrast to the latter, which has been described above, governance by blockchain investigates how blockchain technologies can help to simplify governance referring to the process of governing eventual principal agent problems between investors or share-holders and managers, for instance. Yermack evaluates how blockchain could improve corporate governance decision making processes by providing greater transparency [24]. Pelizza and Kuhlmann argue that blockchain cannot only be seen as information infrastructure that has to be governed ('governance of blockchain'), but also offer the possibility to function as governance actor ('governance by blockchain'), providing a basis for algorithmic decision making [25]. Hence, governance by blockchain tries to identify fields of applications where the technology itself is supposed to help enforcing rules, e.g. voting rights, value distribution, but also simplifying traceability of decision paths on a corporate level [26]. Respective research on the interplay of 'governance by blockchain' and 'governance of blockchain' could investigate to what extend smart contracts can be used for verification purposes regarding the question whether the involved parties adhere to previously defined governance rules.

5 Profitability of Enterprise Blockchain Solutions

5.1 State of the Art

In literature explicitly on blockchain and distributed ledger technologies guidelines can be found that have been developed to decide whether the technology is a good fit for intended use cases. Recently, these guidelines were developed further and extended to more comprehensive process models that cover benefits and challenges. Nevertheless, concrete monetary factors or any further profitability considerations are not included in most approaches [8, 27, 28]. Exceptions are made e.g. by [29] who analyze the benefit factors of blockchain solutions more precise and develop predicted scenarios for the future. In contrast to that, literature dealing with the evaluation of information systems already developed concrete methods and models for profitability analysis. Mainly, the approaches utilize static or dynamic evaluation procedures [30]. Particularly among the dynamic procedures are methods such as the utility analysis that takes qualitative, multidimensional factors into account, which are of relevance when it comes to the evaluation of systems that generate intangible benefits [31]. Even though these methods can be transferred to the blockchain research field, blockchain solutions vary significantly from traditional information systems and therefore certain criteria remain unconsidered.

In the literature field of innovation management and emerging technologies, a number of new approaches exist that provide suggestions to consider profitability. The scholars identify concrete criteria to be evaluated with regard to potential economic evaluations and develop checklists that serve as a first evaluation step [32]. In addition to that, recent approaches utilize methods like the interpretive structural modeling (ISM) to concretize the benefit factors of nascent technologies, like cloud computing or artificial intelligence [33–35].

On the one hand, the state of the art shows that there are no approaches yet to evaluate the profitability of blockchain or distributed ledger technologies. On the other hand, it becomes clear that other research fields do provide methods and models for other objects of investigation that might have the potential to be transferred and analyzed regarding their utilization for the blockchain field.

5.2 Research Discussion

The stated research gap is also supported by various authors. As early as 2014, Platzer pointed out that there is a need for economic investigations of emerging technologies [36]. Following up Platzer, Kesten et al. point out that the factors influencing economic value are often not known to or determined by the practice. As a result, the influencing factors that are critical to the success of an investment are often not taken into account [37]. Klischewski tranfers the problem situation to the topic of blockchain technology in 2018 and points out that the financial benefits and actual costs for companies are a relevant research gap [38]. Andrian follows up on that statement and relates it in particular to the use of blockchain technology in a corporate context. As an example, he refers to a lack of readiness to use the technology unless corporates elaborate the benefits more concretely [39]. Queiroz et al. and Cole et al. also explain that the potential of blockchain technology still needs to be explored in more detail - respectively, that there is a lack of studies on the topic so far [40, 41]. Last but not least, Mika and Goudz point out that a holistic economic assessment of the technology should be made possible in order to scale blockchain implementations [42].

Based on the previously described research gaps, the need of a blockchain-specific model for profitability evaluation emerges. To develop such a model, it can be necessary to first understand what opportunities and challenges arise from the use of blockchain technology when used in enterprises and particularly in enterprise networks. Based on those outcomes more concrete cost and benefit factors can be derived and associated to business processes. If the factors are measurable, as a next step the type of the evaluation situation and types of factors influencing profitability can be analyzed in more detail. This way, the exact requirements of evaluating blockchain solutions in enterprise networks can be derived and compared to existing methods for profitability evaluation. Finally, the design of a particular profitability evaluation model can be determined and validated to ensure it meets all requirements.

6 Blockchain-Based Pay-Per-Use Models

6.1 State of the Art

With the rise of blockchain technology, a variety of new business models emerged. However, the technology also has the potential to reengineer existing processes and models and to expand their functionality and usability [43]. Blockchain-based pay-per-use models are one example. In contrast to the traditional purchase of products or services, pay-per-use is a usage-based pricing model, since products are no longer purchased but are billed according to their respective use, so that neither acquisition costs nor capital commitment are incurred [44]. Manufacturers might no longer act as sellers but rather as service providers. General Electric or Rolls Royce, for example, offer airlines the use of their engines according to operating hours. As a result, their customers pay only for the service they use, the necessary engine thrust, rather than for the product itself [45].

For a successful and sustainable implementation of pay-per-use models, consensus on the consumption data is of decisive importance. In the case of aircraft engines, as explained above, it still seems possible to consult a trustworthy data basis, for example on international flight schedules. In the case of a production machine, such as a 3D printer, which is located on the customer's premises and is also operated by the customer, this is a far greater challenge. Information asymmetries naturally arise, especially on the sales side, and the parties involved must trust the integrity of the available consumption data. While such factors may represent a manageable risk for direct customer-supplier relationships, the degree of complexity increases as corporate networks increase in size. If, for example, additional suppliers, insurance companies or financial service providers are also present in the system, the requirements for data integrity increase. By using connected sensors and measurement tools, and thus IoT devices, trustworthy and transparent data can already be collected in the first step. However, in order to be able to store and use this data in a tamper-proof and traceable manner, the use of blockchain technology is an advisable option.

Recent efforts from industry and practice show the interest in combining blockchain technology and the pricing model of usage-based systems. A prominent example from the financial sector is the "CR Pay per Use" project of the German Commerzbank, which is one of the first major banks to offer a digital, usage-based leasing product, which records and transmits the usage intensity of the object on site via a machine-to-machine (M2M) gateway [46]. Thereby, blockchain is being considered as a trusted data foundation between the bank and the customer [47]. In addition to developments from the financial sector, companies from the manufacturing sector also offer direct usage-based pay-per-use solutions, for example machine manufacturer J.G. Weisser Söhne GmbH & Co, Gebr. Heller Maschinenfabrik GmbH and C-parts specialist Würth Industrie Service GmbH & Co. KG. While existing solutions take advantage of the benefits in terms of increased connectivity through IoT-devices, they do not explore the benefits of integrating blockchain technology. Comparably, the scientific literature is currently investigating the use of IoT devices in usage-based pricing models and addresses the potentials of corresponding business models, the way they can be mapped and how such pricing models can be introduced [48, 49]. However, the benefits of blockchain in such models has not been scientifically studied. Besides initial considerations, such as the representation of pay-per-use models with the support of Blockchain-based smart contracts [50], the topic still needs to be researched further.

6.2 Research Discussion

The characteristics of blockchain generate trust and transparency while ensuring the integrity and tamper-resistance of consumption data. This demonstrates the technology's utility for pay-per-use models. Especially in systems where multiple parties interact, for example along national and especially international supply chains, the integration of blockchain for the realization of pay-per-use models appears reasonable. Blockchain has the potential to address restrictions and problems of pay-per-use models, for example on data confidentiality or tamper-proof traceability of transactions, a scientific analysis is. [50, 51]. Nevertheless, a scientific analysis on the effects of such models for businesses is still lacking. For both, suppliers and customers, the use of blockchain-based pay-per-use models would require adjustments in the area of supply chain management. Adaptions along the financial and information flow need to be made and the material flow may change entirely. Whether these adaptations can be described as disruptive and will lead to a large-scale change in customer-supplier relationships in future still needs to be investigated in more detail.

To engage with this problem, an overview of potential benefits and risks is an important first step. On this basis it will then be possible to question and challenge how corresponding models can be successfully integrated into existing and new processes. When exploring related research questions, one should consider some adjacent developments to ensure a preferably holistic view of the topic. Political regulations for the digital space, such as the introduction and use of digital currencies, can be cited as one example. The combination and functionality in interaction with technologies that are also useful for pay-per-use models, such as IoT, cloud or AI, should also be constantly kept in mind. Ultimately, the goal should be to develop a beneficial process that generates the desired added value independently of blockchain as a technology.

7 Blockchain and Additive Manufacturing

7.1 State of the Art

Blockchain technology appears to be particularly promising in combination with additive manufacturing (AM), as it has the potential to eliminate challenges associated with AM [52]. At the moment, additive manufacturing is largely taking place at the companies themselves. For the time being, this will continue to apply. A survey from Ernst & Young revealed that 56% of the companies surveyed want to continue producing their own products in the future, while 32% of the companies are also considering external manufacturers [53]. Besides a possible future change in the supply chain the worldwide increase in additive manufacturing is also having an impact on global trade. According to an analysis by the Dutch financial institution ING, global trade will decline approximately 23% by 2060, assuming the projected numbers of investments in 3D printers materialize [54].

In practice, the first companies are already recognizing the relevance of blockchain and AM in combination. Established companies as well as start-ups are therefore founding new companies or joining together to form large consortia in order to further research the combination of both technologies. The aim of the Genesis of Things (GoT) project, for example, is to develop a blockchain-based AM exchange platform that connects many independent printing facilities and enables participants to securely store and transfer AM design data on the blockchain. The platform enables companies to select the most suitable print provider for their production needs, place orders and process payments automatically [55]. Thyssenkrupp has developed the "Digital TechCenter for Additive Manufacturing" platform. In addition to consulting and construction services, the platform also offers 3D prints. The underlying concept is based on the International Data Spaces (IDS) and the Hyperledger Fabric as blockchain technology. This should ensure secure data transfer as well as traceability and immutability [56].

Scientific literature mainly deals with the question what changes result from the usage of AM and blockchain for physical supply chain processes, where blockchain is used for secure exchange of construction data and as an enabler of data sovereignty. Guo et al. describe blockchain technology as a promising solution for authentic transmission and protection of copyright for additive manufacturing processes, where blockchain acts as a secure interface between customer and manufacturer of digital twin data [57]. Kloeckner et al. deal with opportunities for business model innovation through blockchain and 3D printing. They show existing problems of business models for decentralized 3D printing with regard to intellectual property and secure data management and analyze which solutions blockchain offers. Additionally, they investigate platform solutions that dynamically exchange printing capacities between several players as required [58].

7.2 Research Discussion

Current industrial projects and related research exclusively deal with the usage of blockchain and its impact on the physical supply chain, where payment transactions play a subordinate role. The focus is primarily on data sovereignty and secure communication. Occasionally, publications on the effects on the financial sector can also be found. Plewnia and Köbernick highlight the importance of AM for the financial sector and the role of the bank [59]. There, however, the impact on the finance side of blockchain and AM is investigated to a limited extend. This indicates a gap for further research on how new AM business models affect the financial supply chain and how finance products will change. With the help of smart contracts, companies could synchronize their automated payments with regard to the transactions of construction plans and specifications. Should peer-to-peer payments become possible in a cross-organizational AM situation, blockchain-based smart contracts would make intermediaries such as banks superfluous. [60]. Therefore, it is of interest, what opportunities and challenges arise from the combined use of additive manufacturing processes and blockchain technology in the financial supply chain. These changes in the financial supply chain are leading to new potential business models for manufacturing companies and financial institutions within platform economies that needs to be researched more closely. Furthermore, it is of interest to determine the effects in pay-per-use approaches, but also for payment terms, financing and risk management.

Based on the previously mentioned problem statements, further questions arise in other areas that could be of interest as well. In case of new business models, current legal regulations need to be reviewed regarding how these may have to be adapted to enable such digital business models. In addition, blockchain offers the possibility of peer-to-peer payments and therefore it requires the development of a token economy in which automated payments are sent via M2M communication. This raises the question of how such a token economy is structured and how it can be used. The overriding question is to what extent such an implementation of blockchain solutions is economically viable. Therefore, economic viability has to be examined for enterprise AM solutions.

8 Decentralized Markets - Trust and Transaction Costs

8.1 State of the Art

Maintenance and production are competing domains in terms of the utilization of production resources such as maintenance capacity [62]. Past research is focusing on appropriate coordination structures to balance the utilization of machine capacity [61, 62]. Since the management of networks is an essential planning layer in the production planning, it is also conceivable that it can be adapted in the fields of maintenance [63]. Interorganizational networks allow industrial companies to cope with uncertainties by spreading the risk evoked by unexpected over- and undercapacities via a market-like capacity stock exchange [64]. Market-driven flexibility and willingness of its participants are determining the potentials of intercompany networks [65].

Uncertainties evoked by information asymmetries between the contractors lead to both, an increase of coordination effort as well as transaction costs and a reduction of trust [66, 67]. To avoid scenarios of instability, such as adverse selection [68], measures to reduce information asymmetries are needed. Trust can reduce social complexity [69] and leads to a reduction of transaction costs [67, 70]. The emergence of trust persist a long time, but its simplicity of breaking leads to a need in functionalities supporting the emergence and maintenance of trust in intercompany networks [71]. To encourage practitioners in the production, maintenance and adjacent domains in the fields of supply chain management to participate within a market-like intercompany network for negotiating capacity, the transaction costs resulting from subcontracting should be lower than the production costs [72, 73]. For that reason, trust becomes an important resource which determines the occurrence of such cooperations [74]. Trust can occur in different layer or levels, such as on an (inter-)personal and (inter-)organizational trust [75–77] whereas in the fields of sharing economy, trust can be differed between trust in peers, platform and trust in the product [78, 79].

To cope with challenges of information asymmetry, emerging technologies such as blockchain technology receives closer consideration, especially in the fields of decentralized markets [80–83]. The data stored within the Blockchain serves as a basis for reducing information asymmetries *"after the transaction and provides a solid basis for performance evaluation, benchmarking and auditing"* and thus contributes in the decrease of behavioral uncertainties [3, p. 6]. However, transparency in the information shared can be both a source for trust and also a source of exploitation [84]. In accordance with SCHMID & WAGNER, an important research question is the influence of blockchain in terms of outsourcing decisions [3]. Apart from supply chains, a transition to adjacent domains in the industrial domains such as the production and maintenance needs to receive closer consideration.

8.2 Research Discussion

It can be stated that a plethora of contributions address the role of trust in the industrial value creation domain, however without concretizing it in detail in conjunction with the capacity exchange. Domain-related contributions indicates that concepts such as intercompany capacity exchange rely on trust and thus requires further investigations about how to ensure it [64]. Recent literature investigated the potential contributions of Blockchain to increase trust in the sharing economy, decentralized markets or intercompany networks [80, 82, 85, 86]. However, the lack of research of blockchain adoption in the fields of maintenance [87] drives research of information asymmetries in the field of capacity exchange of technical services. Preliminary suggestions aligning the Blockchain within the procurement of technical services have been taken up in [88].

Against this backdrop, a research of interest lies within the clarification of the extent in which blockchain ensures trust in outsourcing tasks in the industrial domains and how does a specific blockchain solution has to look like?

To measure the impact of blockchain based solutions in terms of utility, more profound investigations is required with a special emphasis on building and evaluating concrete blockchain based artifacts. Subsequent research allows the derivation of reliable statements in terms of the extend Blockchain can contribute in the emergence or rather maintenance of trust in interorganizational negotiation. A motivation made by the paradigm of Design Science is to extent or rather re-use the existent knowledge base instead of deriving already existing artifacts to known solutions with low degree of maturity [89–91]. The herein proposed state of the art proofs the relevance of DLT-concepts such as Blockchain [92], deserves more attention. It provides a starting point for improving or extending preliminary thoughts of designing blockchain-based artifacts in conjunction with decentralized market from a sociotechnical point of view. This entails the realization and ex-post evaluation of concrete solutions in both artificial and naturalistic environment [93], which herein are Blockchain-based artifacts with a focus on measuring the utility in terms of efficiency due its information-asymmetry reducing characteristics [3, 86] and its impacts on increase the efficiency in outsourcing tasks.

Further investigations could take place in the fields of CPPS, which is partly addressed in recent investigations [94] but is taken up more profoundly in the following chapter.

9   Blockchain-Based Cyber-Physical Production Systems

9.1   State of the Art

In supply chains suppliers, producers and customers are tightly interwoven and dependent on each other. In the course of increasing production variety and decreasing lot size, cyber-physical production systems (CPPS) have emerged that enable flexible, automated and self-configuring production [95]. Even though such systems have gained a lot of recent attention [95–98], several challenges such as trustworthy cross-company interactions, data security, robustness against failures or transparent and reliably documented processes remain unsolved [99]. Blockchain technology as a distributed ledger presents a potential solution to these issues, due to its irreversible, redundant and distributed data storage [100]. The potential of combining cyber-physical systems (CPS) with blockchain technology has been recognized in the literature [101, 102], even though there is little literature on blockchain technology in CPPS [100, 103, 104]. Most authors focus either on robot transactions [105, 106], technical features of blockchain in CPS

[102] or on single use cases such as pay-per-use [107, 108], but do not provide a holistic and practically driven overview of blockchain in CPPS.

For blockchain-based robot transactions, blockchain is used to strengthen the robot coalition algorithm [105]. In the proposed theoretical solution, smart contracts in a publish/subscribe network allow robots in a CPS obtain the overall view and reconfigure on the fly. The contracts are used for task distribution between robots, resource allocation and monitoring of task execution. Pacheco et al. propose a blockchain based robot interaction experiment with a byzantine fault tolerance (BFT) consensus mechanism [106]. In this experiment robots should detect black tiles in an arena. To compute this, robots have to deposit currency to perform an action and receive payment from a smart contract for a successful operation. If a robot does not receive payment for a few times, it will run out of gas and be declared faulty. The communication between robots is realized in a decentralized ad-hoc network. In the setting of CPS the literature presents common challenges of blockchain technology and proposes solutions such as traceability, scalability, security, inaccurate sensor data, lack of granularity or lack of automation, but is not going into detail about the implementation [101]. Barenji et al. present an implementation of a peer-to-peer blockchain network for geographically distributed 3D printing companies [102]. To prevent saving different data structures onto a blockchain, they use an intermediate communication layer, which translates machine-specific language into a common language. This adapter also guarantees security, as it only allows access to specific sets of commands. To improve trust, every order information is stored and processed on a blockchain via smart contracts. In a case study they compare the overall performance as well as two different consensus mechanisms.

Blockchain can also be used as a decentralized marketplace and can improve the pay-per-use method. In a proof-of-concept based on Ethereum smart contracts Ranganthan et al. present a solution to common issues of fees for listing and selling [107]. They also improve the privacy for user data by using tokens instead of clear data. This solution is compared to well-known platforms like eBay and it turns out that selling using a blockchain-based solution is cheaper. Gong et al. also consider the trading aspect and provide a case study on machine-to-machine (M2M) autonomous trading [108]. They carry out a proof-of-concept of such trading via smart contracts and propose a layered architecture for the combination of IoT and blockchain, which they call an 'IoT-Blockchain fusion model'. Privacy issues are not considered and the proof-of-concept is provided by an implementation with Raspberry Pi's. With regard to the use of blockchain technology in CPPS, Afanasev et al. propose a blockchain architecture for CPPS based on the blockchain framework Ethereum [103]. They test the Ethereum network as a backbone for the CPPS and point out several open issues regarding performance and security. Based on this research, a use case for manufacturing including M2M communication is developed [100]. A physical prototype of M2M communication or a blockchain-based CPPS is not implemented. Lee et al. propose a three-layered blockchain architecture for manufacturing systems and carry out a case study in manufacturing machines [99]. Additionally, they present several challenges in blockchain implementation such as realtime implementation, storage capacity and lack of knowledge and infrastructure. Bayhan et al. empathize the theoretical potential of a blockchain-based CPPS and propose the implementation in a physical test field at their university [104].

9.2 Research Discussion

The literature reveals that current research on blockchain-based CPPS either remains on a theoretical level or studies only the implementation of individual components of such a system. This raises several questions regarding the actual impact of blockchain technology on a CPPS and the implementation process. Even though the theoretical potential of blockchain in a CPPS has been revealed, an extensive use case combining the feasible potential has not yet been developed. Thus, it is not evident if the actual impact of blockchain on the CPPS matches its theoretical potential in terms of transparency, automation and security. Additionally, the implementation process and its challenges regarding the combination of an existing CPPS and blockchain technology remain unclear. This includes the design of a suitable blockchain architecture for a CPPS taking into consideration features such as performance, scalability, security and the connection and interaction of heterogeneous IoT devices to and with blockchain. Related research fields such as pay-per-use for robots for performance-based billing or negotiation on decentralized markets relating to free production or storage capacity are also of interest.

10 Consolidation and Assignment to Scientific Layers

To consolidate and structure the prior presented research topics, Fig. 2 assigns them to scientific layers that are prominently used in blockchain research. The presented framework is adopted from Hawlitschek et al. [82] and builds up on a previous work of Notheisen et al. [109]. It consists of a six layered structure, starting with an environment or rather macro layer, in which the constraints and general conditions are clarified. This is followed by the infrastructure layer consisting of soft- and hardware- as well as IT security-related topics. Finally, an application layer is dealing with interactions between actors and the blockchain platform and an agent layer mapping these interactions [109, 110].

Attached to the four layers, the extended framework includes an additional behavioral layer and a so-called trust frontier, which separates the real intentions of the agents from the interactions deposited inside the blockchain platform and allows a more detailed analysis on behavioral aspects [82]. Referring to the seven research topics of this paper, an assignment has been made by highlighted circles on the left side of the graphic. As the figure reveals, no research topic solely entails all layers. However, all layers are at least considered by one research topic. The strategic topics mainly focus on the environmental layer with socio-economic and legal impact, but also have a distribution over most of the other layers. The application-oriented topics mainly deal with interactions among agents and also cover the infrastructure layer partly. Least consideration is found in the trust frontier, followed by the behavioral and infrastructure layers.

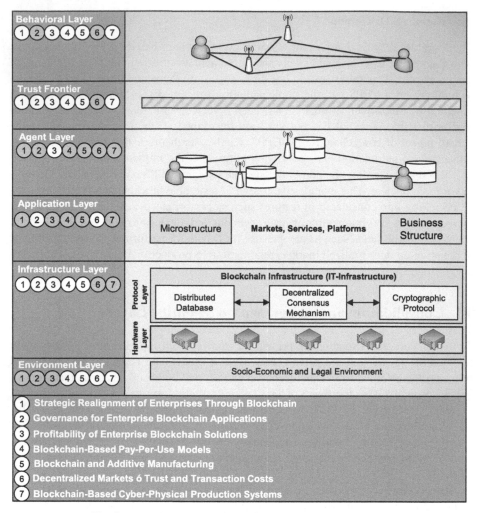

Fig. 2. Scientific layers of blockchain research, based on [82]

11   Conclusion

The paper reveals an overview of central research topics in the field of blockchain and supply chain management and offers a detailed state of the art and a research discussion for each topic as well as future research directions. In order to identify thematic intersections between different research topics, Fig. 1 can be used to classify topics as strategic or application oriented and Fig. 2 to find a common ground within several scientific layers of blockchain research. To give an outlook and sum up the research needs for blockchain in supply chain management, it will be necessary to not only have a strategic realignment to more decentralization, but also to go through comprehensive change management cycles that need to be observed from different perspectives. Moreover, the interplay of 'governance by blockchain' and 'governance of blockchain' needs further investigation, and therefore especially to what extend smart contracts can be used on different utilization degrees and for different verification purposes. Again, at this point different perspectives (technical, organizational, compliance and regulatory) are needed for a comprehensive observation and assessment. Especially on the technical side privacy-preserving techniques to maintain data sovereignty need to be analyzed more intensely. Further research is required in profitability considerations that have to cover the value of the exchanged data and thereby consider network effects over multiple stakeholders. These stakeholders need to be identified, classified and analyzed with respect to their position in the supply chain. When it comes to business models, pay-per-use-models need further investigation especially when considering applications for specific use cases like 3D-printing or other Blockchain-powered platforms. Here again, profitability statements need to be developed in order to demonstrate best practices. Finally, the concepts to bring together supply chain partners in commerce via decentralized markets or in the production field via blockchain-powered cyber-physical production systems need more consideration, especially when it comes to measuring information-asymmetry or enabling performance-based billing and negotiation processes.

Acknowledgements. The work was funded by the Ministry of Economic Affairs, Innovation, Digitalization and Energy of the State of North Rhine-Westphalia.

References

1. Klink, P.: FAST RAMP-UP: Anlaufmanagement nach disruptiven pandemischen Ereignissen. Whitepaper im Rahmen des Forschungsprojekts "Fast Ramp-Up". Fraunhofer-Gesellschaft (2020)
2. Guerpinar, T., Guadiana, G., Ioannidis, P. et al.: The current state of blockchain applications in supply chain management. In: International Conference on Blockchain Technology, Shanghai, China (2021). https://doi.org/10.1145/3460537.3460568
3. Schmidt, C.G., Wagner, S.M.: Blockchain and supply chain relations: a transaction cost theory perspective. J. Purch. Supply Manage. **25**, 100552 (2019). https://doi.org/10.1016/j.pursup.2019.100552
4. Treleaven, P., Gendal Brown, R., Yang, D.: Blockchain technology in finance. Computer **50**, 14–17 (2017). https://doi.org/10.1109/MC.2017.3571047
5. DIN SPEC 16597 Terminology for blockchains; Text in English. Beuth Verlag, Berlin
6. Pai, S., Buvat, J., Lise, O., et al.: Is blockchain the key to a new age of transparency and trust in the supply chain?: How organizations have moved from blockchain hype to reality (2018)
7. Düdder, B., Fomin, V., Gürpinar, T., et al.: Interdisciplinary blockchain education: utilizing blockchain technology from various perspectives. Front Blockchain 3 (2021) https://doi.org/10.3389/fbloc.2020.578022
8. Gürpinar, T., Harre, S., Henke, M., et al.: Blockchain technology – integration in supply chain processes. TUHH Universitätsbibliothek (2020)
9. Gürpinar, T., Straub, N., Kaczmarek, S., et al.: Blockchain-Technologie im interdisziplinären Umfeld. ZWF **114**, 605–609 (2019) https://doi.org/10.3139/104.112117
10. Klinger, P., Bodendorf, F.: Blockchain-based cross-organizational execution framework for dynamic integration of process collaborations. In: Gronau, N., Heine, M., Poustcchi, K. et al. (eds.) WI2020 Zentrale Tracks. GITO Verlag, pp. 1802–1817 (2020)

11. Kewell, B., Adams, R., Parry, G.: Blockchain for good? Strateg. Chang. **26**, 429–437 (2017). https://doi.org/10.1002/jsc.2143
12. Herian, R.: Blockchain and the (re)imagining of trusts jurisprudence. Strateg. Chang. **26**, 453–460 (2017). https://doi.org/10.1002/jsc.2145
13. Casino, F., Dasaklis, T.K., Patsakis, C.: A systematic literature review of blockchain-based applications: current status, classification and open issues. Telematics Inform. **36**, 55–81 (2019). https://doi.org/10.1016/j.tele.2018.11.006
14. Müller, A., Graumann, M., Weiß, H.-J.: Innovationen für eine digitale Wirtschaft. Springer Fachmedien Wiesbaden, Wiesbaden (2020)
15. Weill, P.D.: Don't just lead, govern: how top-performing firms govern it. MIS Q. Exec. **3**, 1–17 (2004)
16. Schmahl, A., Mohottala, S., Burchardi, K., et al.: Resolving the blockchain paradox in transportation and logistics (2019)
17. de Reuver, M., Sørensen, C., Basole, R.: The digital platform: a research agenda. J. Inf. Technol. **33**, 124–135 (2018)
18. Parker, G., van Alstyne, M.: Innovation, openness, and platform control. Manage. Sci. **64**, 3015–3032 (2018)
19. Gasser, U., Budish, R., West, S.: Multistakeholder as Governance Groups: Observations from Case Studies. Berkman Center Research Publication (2015)
20. Andersen, J.V., Bogusz, C.I.: Self-organizing in blockchain infrastructures: generativity through shifting objectives and forking. J. Assoc. Inf. Syst. **20**, 1242–1273 (2019)
21. Cui, Z., Fei, X.U., Zhang, S., et al.: A hybrid blockchain-based identity authentication scheme for multi-WSN. IEEE Trans. Serv. Comput. **13**, 241–251 (2020)
22. German Federal Ministry for Economic Affairs and Energy: Blockchain strategy of the federal government - we set out the course for the token economy (2019)
23. Beck, R., Müller-Bloch, C., King, J.L.: Governance in the blockchain economy: a framework. J. Assoc. Inf. Syst. **19**, 1020–1034 (2018)
24. Yermack, D.: Corporate governance and blockchains. Rev. Finan. **21**, 7–31 (2017)
25. Pelizza, A., Kuhlmann, S.: Mining governance mechanisms: innovation policy, practice, and theory facing algorithmic. In: Handbook of Cyber-Development, Cyber-Democracy, and Cyber-Defense Decision-Making, pp. 495–517
26. de Filippi, P., McMullen, G.: Governance of blockchain systems: Governance of and by Distributed Infrastructure, Blockchain Research Institute and COALA (2018)
27. Fill, H.-G., Meier, A.: Blockchain: Grundlagen, Anwendungsszenarien und Nutzungspotenziale. Edition HMD (2020)
28. Pedersen, A., Risius, M., Beck, R.: A ten-step decision path to determine when to use blockchain technologies. MISQE **18**, 99–115 (2019). https://doi.org/10.17705/2msqe.00010
29. Schlecht, L., Schneider, S., Buchwald, A.: The prospective value creation potential of Blockchain in business models: a delphi study. Technol. Forecast. Soc. Chang. **166**, 120601 (2021). https://doi.org/10.1016/j.techfore.2021.120601
30. Thommen, J.P., Achleitner, A.K.: Allgemeine Betriebswirtschaftlehre, 6th edn. Gabler Verlage, Wiesbaden (2009)
31. Scholz-Reiter, B., Gorldt, C., Hinrichs, U., et al.: RFID - Einsatzmöglichkeiten und Potentiale in logistischen Prozessen (2007)
32. Peukert, S., Treber, S., Balz, S., Haefner, B., Lanza, G.: Process model for the successful implementation and demonstration of SME-based industry 4.0 showcases in global production networks. Prod. Eng. Res. Devel. **14**(3), 275–288 (2020). https://doi.org/10.1007/s11740-020-00953-0
33. Irfan, M., Wang, M., Zafar, A.U., et al.: Modeling the enablers of supply chain strategies and information technology: improving performance through TISM approach. VJIKMS **51**, 461–491 (2021). https://doi.org/10.1108/VJIKMS-06-2019-0082

34. Raut, R.D., Priyadarshinee, P., Gardas, B.B., et al.: Analyzing the factors influencing cloud computing adoption using three stage hybrid SEM-ANN-ISM (SEANIS) approach. Technol. Forecast. Soc. Chang. **134**, 98–123 (2018). https://doi.org/10.1016/j.techfore.2018.05.020
35. Mishra, A.N., Pani, A.K.: Business value appropriation roadmap for artificial intelligence. VJIKMS **51**, 353–368 (2021). https://doi.org/10.1108/VJIKMS-07-2019-0107
36. Platzer, J.: Bitcoin kurz & gut: Banking ohne Banken, 1st edn. O'Reilly, Köln (2014)
37. Kesten, R., Müller, A., Schröder, H.: IT-Controlling: IT-Strategie, Multiprojektmanagement, Projektcontrolling und Performancekontrolle, 2nd edn. Vahlen, München (2013)
38. Klischewski, R.: Blockchains zwischen Anarchie und Governance: Steuerungsansätze für die öffentliche Verwaltung. In: Multikonferenz Wirtschaftsinformatik, Lüneburg, pp. 609–620 (2018)
39. Andrian, H.R., Kurniawan, N.B.: Blockchain technology and implementation : a systematic literature review. In: 2018 International Conference on Information Technology Systems and Innovation (ICITSI), pp. 370–374 (2018)
40. Queiroz, M.M., Telles, R., Bonilla, S.H.: Blockchain and supply chain management integration: a systematic review of the literature. Supp Chain Mnagmnt **25**, 241–254 (2019). https://doi.org/10.1108/SCM-03-2018-0143
41. Cole, R., Stevenson, M., Aitken, J.: Blockchain technology: implications for operations and supply chain management. Supp Chain Mnagmnt **24**, 469–483 (2019). https://doi.org/10.1108/SCM-09-2018-0309
42. Mika, B., Goudz, A.: Blockchain-Technologie in der Energiewirtschaft: Blockchain als Treiber der Energiewende, 1st ed. 2020 (2020)
43. Schmeiss, J.: Will Blockchain Disrupt Your Business? Zenodo (2018)
44. Ematinger, R.: Von der Industrie 4.0 zum Geschäftsmodell 4.0. Springer Fachmedien Wiesbaden, Wiesbaden (2018)
45. Simon, H.: Preismanagement in digitalen geschäftsmodellen. In: Bruhn, M., Hadwich, K.: (eds) Dienstleistungen 4.0. Springer Fachmedien Wiesbaden, Wiesbaden, pp. 261–274 (2017)
46. Commerzbank, A.G.: Pressemitteilung: commerzbank bietet als erste deutsche Bank neue datenbasierte Kredite für Firmenkunden an (2018) https://www.commerzbank.de/de/hauptnavigation/presse/pressemitteilungen/archiv1/2018/quartal_18_02/presse_archiv_detail_18_02_75466.html Accessed 28 Sep 2021
47. Commerzbank, A.G.: Bank mit dem Blockchain-Blick (2019) https://www.commerzbank.ae/portal/media/corporatebanking/auslandsseiten/oesterreich/news/2020-5/ASPEKTE_012019_6-28-29-Commerzbank2.pdf
48. Kehler, M., Regier, S., Stengel, I.: An innovative IoT based financing model for SMEs. In: Proceedings of the 6th Collaborative European Research Conference (CERC 2020), pp. 361–370 (2020)
49. Sato, K., Nakashima, K.: Optimal pricing problem for a pay-per-use system based on the Internet of Things with intertemporal demand. Int. J. Prod. Econ. **221**, 107477 (2020). https://doi.org/10.1016/j.ijpe.2019.08.012
50. Knapp, M., Greiner, T., Yang, X.: Pay-per-use sensor data exchange between IoT devices by blockchain and smart contract based data and encryption key management. In: 2020 International Conference on Omni-layer Intelligent Systems (COINS). IEEE, pp. 1–5 (2020)
51. Guha, K., Saha, D., Chakrabarti, A.: Blockchain technology enabled pay per use licensing approach for hardware IPs. In: 2020 Design, Automation & Test in Europe Conference & Exhibition (DATE). IEEE, pp. 1618–1621 (2020)
52. Alkhader, W., Alkaabi, N., Salah, K., et al.: Blockchain-based traceability and management for additive manufacturing. IEEE Access **8**, 188363–188377 (2020). https://doi.org/10.1109/ACCESS.2020.3031536

53. Ernst & Young GmbH: EY´s Global 3D Prinitng Report 2019 (2019)
54. ING Bank NV: 3D printing: a threat to global trade: Locally printed goods could cut trade by 40% (2017)
55. Stöcker, C., Blechschmidt, B.: Erfahrungsbericht Genesis of Things Project: Ansätze und Herausforderungen bei der Integration von Blockchain in der additiven Fertigung und Geschäftsmodelle (2018)
56. Marx, K.: Herr der Daten: So sichert die Blockchain smarte Produktionsverfahren ab (2019)
57. Guo, D., Shiquan, L., Hao, L., et al.: A framework for personalized production based on digital twin, blockchain and additive manufacturing in the context of Industry 4.0. Unpublished (2020)
58. Klöckner, M., Kurpjuweit, S., Velu, C., et al.: Does blockchain for 3D printing offer opportunities for business model innovation? Res. Technol. Manag. **63**, 18–27 (2020). https://doi.org/10.1080/08956308.2020.1762444
59. Main Incubator GmbH: Gedruckte Disruption: Additive Fertigung und die Finanzdienstleistungen (2020)
60. Ganne, E.: Can blockchain revolutionize international trade? (2018)
61. Kurz, M.: Koordination zwischen Instandhaltung und Produktion mittels Handelsmechanismus: Coordination between maintenance and production by means of a trading mechanism, 1. Auflage. Schriftenreihe Rationalisierung, Band 152. Apprimus Verlag, Aachen (2018)
62. Schuh, G., Kurz, M., Jussen, P., Defèr, F.: Coordination between maintenance and production by means of auction mechanisms for increased efficiency of production systems. In: Mathew, J., Lim, C.W., Ma, L., Sands, D., Cholette, M.E., Borghesani, P. (eds.) Asset Intelligence through Integration and Interoperability and Contemporary Vibration Engineering Technologies. LNME, pp. 545–554. Springer, Cham (2019). https://doi.org/10.1007/978-3-319-95711-1_54
63. Gassner, S.: Instandhaltungsdienstleistungen in Produktionsnetzwerken. Springer Fachmedien Wiesbaden, Wiesbaden (2013)
64. Uygun, Y.: Integrierte Kapazitätsbörse - Entwicklung eines Instrumentariums für den Handel mit Maschinenkapazitäten in regional-lateralen Unternehmensnetzen. Zugl.: Dortmund, Techn. Univ., Diss., 2012. Fabrikorganisation. Verl. Praxiswissen, Dortmund (2012)
65. Siebert, H.: Ökonomische analyse von unternehmensnetzwerken. In: Sydow, J. (ed.) Management von Netzwerkorganisationen, pp. 7–27. Gabler Verlag, Wiesbaden (2010)
66. Eisenhardt, K.M.: Agency theory: an assessment and review. Acad. Manag. Rev. **14**, 57–74 (1989)
67. Cai, R.: Trust and transaction costs in industrial districts (2004)
68. Akerlof, G.A.: The market for "lemons": quality uncertainty and the market mechanism. In: Uncertainty in economics. Elsevier, pp. 235–251 (1978)
69. Luhmann, N.: Vertrauen: Ein Mechanismus der Reduktion sozialer Komplexität, 5. Aufl. UTB, vol 2185. UVK-Verl.-Ges; UTB, Konstanz, Stuttgart (2014)
70. Lee, J., Kim, J., Moon, J.Y.: What makes Internet users visit cyber stores again? Key design factors for customer loyalty. In: Proceedings of the SIGCHI Conference on Human Factors in Computing Systems, pp. 305–312 (2000)
71. Lewicki, R.J., Bunker, B.B.: Trust in relationships: a model of development and decline. Jossey-Bass (1995)
72. Suematsu: Transaction Cost Management (2014)
73. Bretzke, W.-R.: Die möglichen Kostenvorteile der Fremdvergabe. In: Bretzke, W.-R. (ed.) Logistische Netzwerke. Springer, Heidelberg, pp. 477–493 (2020)https://doi.org/10.1007/978-3-662-59757-6_28
74. Duschek, S., Wetzel, R., Aderhold, J.: Probleme mit dem Netzwerk und Probleme mit dem Management: Ein neu justierter Blick auf relevante Dilemmata und auf Konsequencen für die

Steuerung. In: Aderhold, J., Meyer, M., Wetzel, R. (eds.) Modernes Netzwerkmanagement, pp. 143–164. Gabler Verlag, Wiesbaden (2005)

75. Loose, A., Sydow, J.: Vertrauen und Okonomie in Netzwerkbeziehungen- Strukturations-theoretische Betrachtungen. In: Sydow, J., Windeler, A. (eds.) Management interorgan-isationaler Beziehungen, pp. 160–193. VS Verlag für Sozialwissenschaften, Wiesbaden (1997)

76. Schweer, M.K.W.: Vertrauen als Organisationsprinzip in interorganisationalen Kooperatio-nen. In: Schilcher, C., Will-Zocholl, M., Ziegler, M. (eds.) Vertrauen und Kooperation in der Arbeitswelt, pp. 103–121. VS Verlag für Sozialwissenschaften, Wiesbaden (2012)

77. Zaheer, A., McEvily, B., Perrone, V.: Does trust matter? Exploring the effects of interorga-nizational and interpersonal trust on performance. Organ. Sci. **9**, 141–159 (1998)

78. Hawlitschek, F., Teubner, T., Weinhardt, C.: Trust in the sharing economy. Die Unternehmung **70**, 26–44 (2016). https://doi.org/10.5771/0042-059X-2016-1-26

79. Große, N., Guerpinar, T., Henke, M.: Blockchain-enabled trust in intercompany networks applying the agency theory. In: 3rd Blockchain and Internet of Things Conference (2021). https://doi.org/10.1145/3475992.3475994

80. Notheisen, B.: Engineering Decentralized Markets - A Blockchain Approach (2019)

81. Subramanian, H.: Decentralized blockchain-based electronic marketplaces. Commun ACM **61**, 78–84 (2018). https://doi.org/10.1145/3158333

82. Hawlitschek, F., Notheisen, B., Teubner, T.: The limits of trust-free systems: a literature review on blockchain technology and trust in the sharing economy. Electron. Commer. Res. Appl. **29**, 50–63 (2018). https://doi.org/10.1016/j.elerap.2018.03.005

83. DIN SPEC 3103: Blockchain und Distributed Ledger Technologien in Anwendungsszenar-ien für Industrie 4.0. Beuth Verlag, Berlin (2019)

84. Notheisen, B., Weinhardt, C.: The blockchain, plums, and lemons: information asymme-tries & transparency in decentralized markets. Karlsruhe (2019)

85. Mehrwald, P., Treffers, T., Titze, M., et al.: Application of blockchain technology in the sharing economy: a model of trust and intermediation. In: Proceedings of the 52nd Hawaii International Conference on System Sciences (2019)

86. Wieninger, S.: Vertrauen in Unternehmensnetzwerken durch Blockchain-Technologie. Apprimus Wissenschaftsverlag (2020)

87. Abbas, Y., Martinetti, A., Moerman, J.-J., et al.: Do you have confidence in how your rolling stock has been maintained? A blockchain-led knowledge-sharing platform for building trust between stakeholders. Int. J. Inf. Manage. **55**, 102228 (2020). https://doi.org/10.1016/j.iji nfomgt.2020.102228

88. Große, N.: Einsatz der Blockchain zur Schaffung von Vertrauen im Beschaffungsprozess technischer Dienstleistungen . In: Instandhaltungsforum, InFo 2021 Connected. Tagungs-band. Fraunhofer-Gesellschaft, pp. 7–13 (2021)

89. Iivari, J., Hansen, M.R.P., Haj-Bolouri, A.: A framework for light reusability evaluation of design principles in design science research. In: Proceedings of International Conference on Design Science Research in Information Systems and Technology (DESRIST 2018) (2018)

90. Iivari, J., Rotvit Perlt Hansen, M., Haj-Bolouri, A.: A proposal for minimum reusability evaluation of design principles. Eur. J. Inf. Syst. **30**, 286–303 (2021)

91. Gregor, S., Hevner, A.R.: Positioning and presenting design science research for maximum impact. MIS Q. 337–355 (2013)

92. Kannengießer, N., Lins, S., Dehling, T., et al.: What does not fit can be made to fit! Trade-offs in distributed ledger technology designs. In: Bui, T. (ed.) Proceedings of the 52nd Hawaii International Conference on System Sciences. Hawaii International Conference on System Sciences (2019)

93. Pries-Heje, J., Baskerville, R., et al.: Strategies for design science research evaluation. In: ECIS 2008 Proceedings, vol. 87 (2008)

94. Große, N., Leisen, D., Gürpinar, T., et al.: Evaluation of (De-) centralized IT technologies in the fields of cyber-physical production systems (2020). https://doi.org/10.15488/9640
95. Müller, T., Jazdi, N., Schmidt, J.-P., et al.: Cyber-physical production systems: enhancement with a self-organized reconfiguration management. Procedia CIRP **99**, 549–554 (2021). https://doi.org/10.1016/j.procir.2021.03.075
96. Meissner, H., Aurich, J.C.: Implications of cyber-physical production systems on integrated process planning and scheduling. Procedia Manuf. **28**, 167–173 (2019). https://doi.org/10.1016/j.promfg.2018.12.027
97. Lins, T., Oliveira, R.A.R.: Cyber-physical production systems retrofitting in context of Industry 4.0. Comput. Ind. Eng. **139**, 106193 (2020). https://doi.org/10.1016/j.cie.2019.106193
98. Rojas, R., Rauch, E., Matt, D.T.: Research fields and challenges to implement cyber-physical production systems in SMEs: a literature review. In: CMUJNS 20 (2021). https://doi.org/10.12982/CMUJNS.2021.022
99. Lee, J., Azamfar, M., Singh, J.: A blockchain enabled cyber-physical system architecture for Industry 4.0 manufacturing systems. Manuf. Lett. **20**, 34–39 (2019). https://doi.org/10.1016/j.mfglet.2019.05.003
100. Afanasev, M.Y., Fedosov, Y.V., Krylova, A.A., et al.: An application of blockchain and smart contracts for machine-to-machine communications in cyber-physical production systems. In: Systems IICoIC-P (ed.) Proceedings 2018 IEEE Industrial Cyber-Physical Systems (ICPS): ITMO University, Saint Petersburg, Saint Petersburg, Russia, 15–18 May 2018. IEEE, Piscataway, NJ, pp. 13–19 (2018)
101. Dedeoglu, V., Dorri, A., Jurdak, R., et al.: A Journey in applying blockchain for cyberphysical systems. In: 2020 International Conference on Communication Systems & Networks (COM-SNETS): 2020 International Conference on Communication Systems & Networks (COM-SNETS) took place 7–11 January 2020 in Bangalore, India, Piscataway, NJ, pp. 383–390. IEEE (2020)
102. Barenji, A.V., Li, Z., Wang, W.M., et al.: Blockchain-based ubiquitous manufacturing: a secure and reliable cyber-physical system. Int. J. Prod. Res. **58**, 2200–2221 (2020). https://doi.org/10.1080/00207543.2019.1680899
103. Afanasev, M.Y., Krylova, A.A., Shorokhov, S.A., et al.: A design of cyber-physical production system prototype based on an ethereum private network. In: Balandin, S.I. (ed.) Proceedings of the 22nd Conference of Open Innovations Association FRUCT: Jyväskylä, Finland, 15–18 May 2018. FRUCT Oy, Finland, pp. 3–11 (2018)
104. Bayhan, H., Schulze Forsthövel, R., Kaiser, P., et al.: Blockchainbasierte cyberphysische Produktionssysteme. Logistics J. Proc. (2020). https://doi.org/10.2195/lj_Proc_bayhan_de_202012_01
105. Smirnov, A., Teslya, N.: Robot interaction through smart contract for blockchain-based coalition formation. In: Chiabert, P., Bouras, A., Noël, F., Ríos, J. (eds.) PLM 2018. IAICT, vol. 540, pp. 611–620. Springer, Cham (2018). https://doi.org/10.1007/978-3-030-01614-2_56
106. Pacheco, A., Strobel, V., Dorigo, M.: A blockchain-controlled physical robot swarm communicating via an ad-hoc network. In: Dorigo, M., et al. (eds.) ANTS 2020. LNCS, vol. 12421, pp. 3–15. Springer, Cham (2020). https://doi.org/10.1007/978-3-030-60376-2_1
107. Ranganthan VP, Dantu R, Paul A et al. (2018) A Decentralized Marketplace Application on the Ethereum Blockchain. In: 2018 IEEE 4th International Conference on Collaboration and Internet Computing (CIC). IEEE, [Place of publication not identified], pp 90–97
108. Gong, X., Liu, E., Wang, R.: Blockchain-based IoT application using smart contracts: case study of M2M autonomous trading. In: 2020 5th International Conference on Computer and Communication Systems: ICCCS 2020: Shanghai, China, May 15–18, 2020, pp. 781–785. IEEE Press, Piscataway, NJ (2020)

109. Notheisen, B., Hawlitschek, F., Weinhardt, C.: Breaking down the blockchain hype-towards a blockchain market engineering approach (2017)

110. Gürpinar, T., Austerjost, M., Kamphues, J., Maaßen, J., Yildirim, F., Henke, M.: Blockchain technology as the backbone of the internet of things - A taxonomy of blockchain devices. In: Conference on Production Systems and Logistics, Vancouver, Canada (2022)

Characterizing Blockchain Interoperability Systems from an Architecture Perspective

João Otávio Chervinski[1,2(✉)], Jiangshan Yu[1], and Xiwei Xu[2,3]

[1] Monash University, Melbourne, Australia
`joao.massarichervinski@monash.edu`
[2] CSIRO Data61, Eveleigh, Australia
[3] University of New South Wales, Sydney, Australia

Abstract. Blockchains are designed as closed execution environments that only support operations within their own system for security purposes. However, as the technology became popular, interoperation across different blockchains emerged as one of the most desired features to enable the creation of networks of interconnected blockchains. Towards fulfilling this need, multiple academic proposals and industry projects have been developed, but most of those systems are designed to connect specific platforms and cannot be applied to all blockchains. While there are studies that aim to provide understanding on these solutions, they are mainly focused on the cryptographic formalization and dependability of such systems. Limited attention has been paid to the system architecture and organization of such solutions. This paper aims to bridge this gap by characterizing existing cross-chain communication systems from an architecture perspective. We classify ten existing systems into four categories and develop an evaluation framework with criteria from five different aspects. We then evaluate the selected systems based on the proposed framework and present a comparative analysis between the systems in each category. We aim to provide an holistic view of state-of-practice to help developers and the blockchain community to select suitable solutions for their cross-chain communication needs.

Keywords: Distributed ledgers · Blockchains · Interoperability · Cross-chain communication

1 Introduction

Over the last decade blockchain technologies and their applications underwent rapid growth [10,21,28,32,39] leading the number of existing blockchains to surge. This contributed to an increase in blockchain diversity and led to the creation of a host of chains with distinct objectives such as providing transaction privacy [29,30], bridging fiat money and cryptocurrencies [33] or providing smart contract functionality [7].

© ICST Institute for Computer Sciences, Social Informatics and Telecommunications Engineering 2022
Published by Springer Nature Switzerland AG 2022. All Rights Reserved
S. Paiva et al. (Eds.): SmartCity360° 2021, LNICST 442, pp. 504–520, 2022.
https://doi.org/10.1007/978-3-031-06371-8_33

However, when users want to make use of diverse functionalities they must purchase coins in distinct blockchains or exchange their assets for other cryptocurrencies. One popular solution for exchanging assets is using exchange services. This approach, however, has high trading fees, low transparency and reduced security as those services are often targeted by criminals [34].

Blockchain interoperability systems aim to fill this gap by enabling communication between blockchains. Interoperability has been deemed critical for the advancement of the blockchain technology [4] thus the interest in this area of research is growing. Multiple academic proposals [3,13,15,18,20,38] and industry projects [11,16,22,27,31,35] have been proposed to address this challenge.

However, differences in security mechanisms, protocols and scripting capabilities can all pose challenges for cross-chain communication systems. For that reason, many interoperability solutions are developed for specific pairs of blockchains [6].

While existing research provides comprehensive review on the existing systems [4,6,37], a holistic view from the architecture perspective remains unclear. Such a big picture is important to aid developers in the process of understanding the different characteristics of the existing solutions and selecting the ones which meet their needs. In this paper, we bridge this gap by characterizing blockchain interoperability solutions from an architecture perspective.

The main contributions of this paper are summarized as follows: (a) we classify ten leading blockchain interoperability systems into four categories based on their characteristics; (b) we propose an evaluation framework with criteria from five different architectural aspects; (c) we evaluate ten cross-chain communication systems based on the proposed framework; (d) we compare the cross-chain communication systems in each category by analyzing their strengths and weaknesses.

Our framework provides design guidance to assist developers in selecting interoperability solutions that are suitable to their use-cases. Our analysis provides support in the assessment of the benefits and drawbacks of interoperability system categories and individual systems given developer's specific requirements. Throughout this work we refer to blockchain interoperability and cross-chain communication interchangeably.

This paper is organised as follows. Section 2 characterizes the architectures of cross-chain communication systems. Section 3 presents our proposed evaluation framework and Sect. 4 presents a detailed analysis of the system categories and the ten leading systems. Finally, Sect. 5 presents related work and Sect. 6 presents concluding remarks.

2   Interoperability Categories

In this section we propose four categories to characterize and distinguish blockchain interoperability systems. We define blockchain interoperability as the ability to provably transfer information between two distinct blockchains in a semantically compatible format.

The proposed categories were derived from the analysis and comparison of both the architecture and functionality provided by ten leading cross-chain communication systems. The systems we selected are either from academia [11,13,15,18,20] and known by the research community or well-known industrial projects [8,16,22,27,35]. We have selected those systems as we believe they provide a reasonable overview of the state-of-the-art of cross-chain communications. A detailed analysis of each category and its corresponding systems is provided in Sect. 4. Through our analysis of the selected systems we identified four distinct categories of cross-chain communication systems:

Blockchain ecosystems manage networks of independent blockchains that are interconnected through a central chain or hub that forwards information. Ecosystems enable native cross-chain communication between blockchains inside the network and can also allow communication with external blockchains through bridging systems. Blockchain ecosystems have their own native tokens which can be used for stake-based consensus and for voting in feature proposals. Those systems can be permissioned or permissionless. *Cosmos* [22] and *Polkadot* [5] belong to this category.

Relay-Based systems enable a blockchain (called the destination chain) to fetch and validate data coming from a source blockchain. The destination blockchain needs to implement the consensus verification mechanism of the source chain in order to verify the validity of the information received through the relay. A single relay system allows the destination chain to verify events that took place in a source chain, however the contrary is not necessarily true and may require two relays, one in each chain. This category of system includes *BTC Relay* [8], *ETH Relay* [11] and *Proof-of-Burn (PoB)* [20].

Sidechain-based systems are constructions that connect two blockchains and allow them to transfer assets back and forth between each other via a process called a two-way peg [3]. Sidechain-based systems aim to enable users of a blockchain to transfer their assets to another blockchain, called a sidechain, and use those assets to access features and applications not available in the source blockchain. The systems included in this category are *Liquid Network* [27], *Proof-of-Stake sidechains* [13] and *Proof-of-Work sidechains* [20].

Peer-based Systems enable users to exchange assets across distinct blockchains by participating in deals with other users. Peer-based systems exchange information by leveraging protocols that create agreements based on hashed timelock contracts (HTLCs). The systems that belong to this category are *Atomic Cross-Chain Swaps (ACCSs)* [15] and *Interledger* [16].

3   Evaluation Framework

In this section we propose an evaluation framework composed of five criteria to understand and analyze the architecture of cross-chain communication systems. We selected those five criteria because they are key components in the process of transporting and validating data and are therefore essential for establishing cross-chain communication.

The proposed evaluation framework serves as tool to provide a concise overview of the cross-chain communication capabilities of the selected systems and is composed by the following criteria:

Direction of communication defines in which direction cross-chain communication systems are able to transfer information. It can be either unidirectional or bidirectional. Systems with unidirectional data transfer only allow the destination chain to fetch data from the source chain, whereas systems with bidirectional data transfer enables both destination chain and source chain to send and receive data from each other.

Communication channel refers to the medium used to send the information required to execute the cross-chain operation. We divide a cross-chain operation into four phases: *setup, value transfer, claim transfer* and *settlement.*

The *setup* phase is used to exchange information regarding the structure of the deal such as intention to transfer, amount, addresses, conditions and time constraints. Those details should be analyzed when deciding whether to follow through with the deal or to abort the operation.

If participants agree on the parameters of the deal they move on to the *value transfer* phase. In this phase transactions are released to the counterparties or published in the blockchain. This may occur between multiple pairs of users (or hops) in scenarios where multiple participants route payments between blockchains along the way to a destination address.

After the involved parties execute their part of the deal, they enter the *claim transfer* phase, where a verifiable claim must be relayed to the counterparty in order to prove that an agreed upon action was performed and registered in the blockchain.

Finally, during the *settlement* phase, verifiable claims generated in the previous steps are validated and the final transaction in the cross-chain operation is committed to the blockchain, updating the state of the ledger. This may take from a few seconds to hours, depending on the confirmation latency of the involved blockchains. For each phase, one of the following channels can be used:

- *On-chain:* When a phase of the cross-chain operation takes place inside the blockchain, it is considered an on-chain communication.
- *Off-chain channels:* When a phase of the cross-chain operation takes place in a medium predefined by the protocol but is not recorded on the blockchain, we say it requires off-chain channels.
- *Out-of-bound channels:* When a phase of the cross-chain operation requires a communication channel that is not defined by the protocol (such as messaging apps, email, phone calls or in-person), it is considered an out-of-bound channel.

Type of Exchanged Information defines the type of data that can be sent across chains, including digital tokens and arbitrary data.

- *Digital token:* Digital tokens represent cryptocurrencies and are commonly represented as a key-value pair, where the key is the token address and the value is the amount of token balance (i.e., the number of tokens contained in that address) like in the UTXO model [25] or account model [7].
- *Arbitrary data:* Arbitrary data allows non-token data, such as the blockchain state, to be exchanged across chains. This is particularly useful for non-cryptocurrency blockchains, such as Hyperledger Fabric [2].

Verifiable Claims define how a blockchain system proves to another blockchain that an event, e.g., the acceptance of a transaction, has taken place. Events must be verified before committing operations to the blockchain in order to prevent malicious behavior. The verification of claims, as formally defined in a recent work [1], is a challenge for cross-chain communication mechanisms. A system can prove that data has been added to the chain through the following types of claims:

- *Validator signature:* A validator or set of validators are trusted to provide a proof about the internal state of a (commonly permissioned) blockchain. The proof could be in the form of a threshold number of signatures (or an aggregated signature to reduce the proof size) from the set of validators [1, 23, 36].
- *SPV proof:* Simplified Payment Verification (SPV) enables light clients (such as mobile wallets) to verify that a transaction has been included in the blockchain without downloading the entire blockchain history.
- *Pre-commitment:* A pre-commitment is a cryptographic construction which guarantees that a certain action, such as releasing a transaction, is going to be carried out once a condition is fulfilled. Pre-commitments are used to create agreements which prove that transactions are going to be released when all participants of the cross-chain operation commit to executing the deal.

Validator is the entity or group of entities responsible for verifying the validity of a verifiable claim generated in another blockchain. Validators may have elevated privileges, in which case the security of the system relies on the integrity of the set of validators, or may be selected in a trustless manner, leading consensus to be achieved when a majority of the blockchain users agree with the state changes proposed by the validator.

- *Permissionless validator:* We consider validators to be permissionless if they are (possibly weighted) randomly chosen from the set of blockchain participants. They are permissionless as any blockchain user can join the validation process. Systems that employ permissionless validators [7, 25, 29, 30] incentivize users to take part in the validation process through financial compensation.
- *Permissioned validator:* We consider validators to be permissioned if they are chosen from a fixed and pre-determined subset of blockchain participants. Unlike in permissionless systems, not every blockchain user can be a validator in a permissioned system.

4   Analysis

Distinct cross-chain communication systems achieve their objectives by employing mechanisms that differ in their levels of complexity. For that reason different cross-chain communication systems may present strengths and weakness when compared to each other. In this section we classify ten leading cross-chain communication systems (as presented in Table 1) according to our proposed evaluation framework. We also analyze the advantages and disadvantages of each proposed category of cross-chain communication systems using attributes based on those defined by the ISO/IEC 25010 software quality model [17]. Lastly, we provide a comparative analysis between the systems in each category. Rather than discussing the same set of properties for each analyzed system, we discuss only the unique properties that distinguish the systems apart from each other.

Table 1. Classification of cross-chain communication systems.

System attributes		Blockchain Ecosystems		Relay-based systems			Sidechain-based systems			Peer-based systems	
		Cosmos	Polkadot	BTC Relay	ETH Relay	Proof-of-Burn	Liquid Network	PoS Sidechains	PoW Sidechains	Atomic Swaps	Interledger
Direction of	Unidirectional			X	X	X					
communication	Bidirectional	X	X				X	X	X	X	X
Communication Channel*	Setup	●	●	●	●	●	◐	●	●	○	◐
	Value transfer	●	●	●	●	●	●	●	●	●	○
	Claim transfer	●	●	○	○	○	◐	●	○	○	○
	Settlement	●	●	●	●	●	●	●	●	●	●
Verifiable Claims	Validator signature		X				X	X			
	SPV proof	X		X	X	X			X		
	Pre-commitment									X	X
Validator	Permissionless		X	X	X			X	X		
	Permissioned						X				
	Blockchain dependent	X					X			X	X
Type of exchanged	Digital tokens	X	X	X	X	X	X	X	X	X	X
information	Arbitrary data	X	X					X	X		

* On-Chain: ●; Off-Chain: ◐; Out-of-Bounds: ○

4.1   Blockchain Ecosystems

Blockchain ecosystems (illustrated in Fig. 1) are networks that host independent interconnected blockchains. Ecosystems are organized in a topology in which multiple blockchains are connected to one central blockchain. The central blockchain serves as a connector that forwards information across connected blockchains (a.k.a. internal blockchains). Internal blockchains can also establish communication with external chains, i.e., those not deployed inside the ecosystem.

However, this requires the development of bridging systems to adapt the information coming from external chains in such a way that it can be understood by the internal chains.

- **Strengths:**

    Compatibility (Interoperability): Internal chains can participate in cross-chain operations with other internal chains connected to the central chain without requiring adaptations or additional configuration.

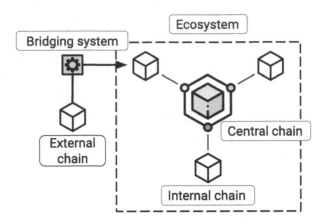

Fig. 1. Architectural overview of blockchain ecosystems.

- **Weaknesses:**

  Portability (Installability): Developing and deploying a blockchain inside an ecosystem is hard and time consuming. Blockchains need to be compatible with the requirements of the ecosystem, e.g., a specific consensus engine. In order to deploy blockchains inside an ecosystem as an internal chain, aspects such as block proposal strategy, validation incentives and feature support might need to reconsidered.

  Portability (Adaptability): Blockchains deployed inside an ecosystem only natively support communication with other internal chains. If communication with an external chain is needed, a bridging system is required.

Cosmos is an ecosystem of interconnected independent blockchains. In Cosmos, there are zones and hubs. Zones are regular blockchains but can also choose to become hubs, which are a special type of blockchains that connects zones together. Zones can communicate with a theoretically unlimited number of other zones as long as they are connected to a common hub. The Cosmos ecosystem is permissionless, allowing anyone to deploy a blockchain in the network. Zones are powered by Tendermint BFT[1]. Cosmos has a native token called ATOM, which is used to secure the Cosmos Hub through a staking-based validator selection process.

Polkadot is a network of interconnected blockchains. In the network there are multiple parachains and one relay-chain. Parachains are independent blockchains that run in parallel and the relay-chain is a central chain that validates blocks proposed by the parachains and coordinates the entire network. The relay-chain provides a shared view of every parachain's state to the ecosystem. Polkadot has a native token that is used for staking, called the DOT. Staking DOTs is

---

[1] https://tendermint.com/core/.

a requirement for being a relay-chain validator and is also required for joining the auction process that leases parachain slots in the network. Polkadot provides a protocol called Cross-Chain Message Passing (XCMP) to enable the transfer of assets and arbitrary data between parachains. Parachains need to open one channel for sending messages and another one for receiving messages for each parachain they want to communicate with. Those channels require funding using DOT tokens, which are returned when the channels are closed[2].

Analysis of Blockchain Ecosystems. The two well-known systems in this category are Cosmos and Polkadot. Both systems aim to reduce the difficulty and time required to develop and deploy blockchains inside their networks by providing frameworks for blockchain development. Cosmos offers the Cosmos SDK and Polkadot offers the Substrate framework. Both are modular frameworks that provide developers with pre-built modules that can be applied to blockchains, eliminating the need for designing basic functionalities such as governance, staking and token distribution.

Polkadot offers a limited number of 100 slots in which parachains can be deployed[3]. Consequently, users are required to participate in an auction process to earn the right to deploy their blockchain inside the ecosystem. This makes it unlikely for small companies and blockchain projects to secure a slot in the network due to the requirement of competing in an auction against well-funded companies and projects. Cosmos in comparison, offers unlimited slots, allowing anyone to create a zone in the network without any barriers to entry.

When it comes to block production, Cosmos zones are responsible for selecting their own set of validators and achieving block finality through Tendermint consensus. Hubs are not responsible for validating transactions issued in the zones connected to it [22]. Parachains, on the other hand, are responsible for determining their own block production strategy, carried out by participants called collators, but cannot validate blocks on their own. Blocks proposed by collators must be approved by a global set of relay-chain validators that are responsible for guaranteeing the security of the entire ecosystem. Relay-chain validators are assigned to parachains in a rotating fashion and perform the validation of proposed blocks before adding them to the ecosystem's relay-chain. As both ecosystems rely on strategies that require a pre-defined set of validators to approve and finalize blocks, they are incompatible with blockchains that employ Proof-of-Work (PoW) based consensus.

Validation is performed locally in Cosmos zones and globally in Polkadot's parachains, therefore their security assumptions differ. The Polkadot network is secured by a large amount of tokens staked by system wide relay-chain validators. In Cosmos, every zone is responsible for maintaining its own state and keeping it secure through their own individual staking process. This means that during cross-chain communication, Cosmos zones need to trust other zones they are interacting with. In Polkadot, parachain's states are shared across the entire

---

[2] https://wiki.polkadot.network/docs/en/learn-crosschain.
[3] https://wiki.polkadot.network/docs/en/learn-auction.

ecosystem through the relay-chain, therefore, trust assumptions are on the relay-chain's validators rather than in the individual parachains. As a consequence of Cosmos' security model, zones with a small amount of staked tokens are more susceptible to attacks when compared to Polkadot's parachains, which are secured by large amounts of staked tokens. If an attacker is able to acquire the majority of the stake in a zone she can influence the outcome of governance proposals and selectively censor transactions.

4.2 Relay-Based Systems

Relay-based systems (illustrated in Fig. 2) enable information about state changes in one source blockchain to be relayed to and validated inside one destination blockchain using a smart contract. This information can be used for asset exchange and asset portability [6]. This process does not require the source chain to have any knowledge of the relay contract. The communication provided by relay systems is unidirectional, if a party needs to fetch information bidirectionally, two independent relay systems must be used.

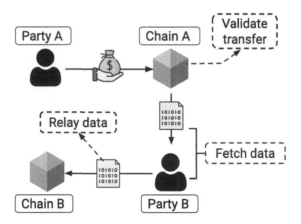

Fig. 2. Overview of asset transfer using a relay-based system.

- **Strengths:**
  Portability (Installability): Relays can be implemented in a destination chain without requiring the source chain to have any knowledge of it.
- **Weaknesses:**
  Performance efficiency (Resource utilization): As smart contracts are leveraged for transaction validation, the cost of verifying data using relay-based systems is proportional to the complexity of the verification algorithm.
  Security (Integrity): Relay-based systems are susceptible to block reorganization attacks. Most relay solutions [8,11,26] only work with source chains that achieve probabilistic block finality and those chains may have their blocks reorganized after suffering an attack, invalidating a previously accepted transaction.

BTC Relay is a system that enables information to be relayed from the Bitcoin to the Ethereum blockchain and allows users to validate this information on Ethereum. BTC Relay receives and stores on the Ethereum blockchain the Bitcoin block information relayed by users. The system charges a fee to validate the received block information according to Bitcoin's consensus algorithm. BTC Relay allows Ethereum to verify and react to the state of Bitcoin's blockchain but not the other way around. No action needs to be taken the Bitcoin blockchain for block information to be relayed neither for it to be verified in Ethereum.

ETH Relay can be deployed in a destination chain to validate block information coming from a source chain in a cost-effective way. This system allows any pair of Ethereum-based blockchains to establish cross-chain communication but only works unidirectionally.

ETH Relay uses an optimistic way of accepting block headers, accepting them without validation at first, but keeping them on a trial period in which users can dispute its validity. ETH Relay also enables efficient transaction verification by storing information about block branches and paths along with block headers, allowing the system to traverse blockchain data in an efficient way.

Proof-of-Burn is a mechanism that allows tokens to be transferred across blockchains by destroying them in a source chain, verifying the operation in a destination chain and then generating a representation of the destroyed assets.

To transfer asset using Proof-of-Burn, digital assets must first be "burned" in the source chain. In order to do that, users need to send the assets to a provably non-spendable wallet address causing them to be lost forever. To verify that the burning transaction has been committed in the source chain, a proof of inclusion has to be relayed to the destination chain. This proof needs to be verified in a smart contract prior to creating new assets. The burning procedure is unidirectional, can only be conducted once and is irreversible once the assets have been transferred to a burn (non-spendable) address.

Analysis of Relay-Based Systems. The relay-based systems category includes BTC Relay, ETH Relay and Proof-of-Burn. Both BTC Relay and ETH Relay serve the same purpose, which is to allow a destination chain to verify state changes in a source chain. In terms of adaptability, however, BTC Relay is limited to verifying Bitcoin state changes inside the Ethereum blockchain, whereas ETH Relay can be applied to any pair of Ethereum-based blockchains. In addition, ETH Relay is more cost-effective than BTC Relay as it employs a block validation strategy that is optimized to consume less computational resources.

Proof-of-Burn on the other hand, was not idealized as a cross-chain communication system, but as a way to burn currency in exchange for participating in the block validation process. Burned assets are lost forever, potentially causing problems such as inflation due to reduction in asset availability if many burning operations are executed. However, while not ideal for simple cross-chain asset transfers, Proof-of-Burn fits niche use-cases such as being used for destroying one type of token in order to transfer value to a different digital asset in a different blockchain [18]. This system should be used cautiously as destroying assets without having a guaranteed way of claiming them in another blockchain may lead to losing them forever. Additionally, if the burn operation is not set up in a secure and verifiable manner, burned assets may be claimed multiple times inside distinct blockchains as the claim remains unknown to other ledgers.

4.3   Sidechain-Based Systems

A sidechain is a blockchain that is connected to another ledger referred to as the main chain through a mechanism that enables assets to be transferred back and forth between both blockchains. The mechanism which allows a sidechain and main chain to communicate bidirectionally is called a two-way peg, thus connected blockchains are also referred to as pegged chains. Sidechain systems must be adapted to a specific pair of blockchains. Figure 3 presents a generalization of the architecture and communication between pegged chains.

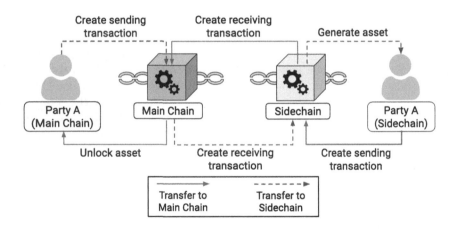

Fig. 3. Transfer of assets between sidechains.

The relationship between a sidechain and a main chain can be either symmetric or asymmetric. When symmetric, both chains are able to operate independently and failure in one of them does not directly affect the other. Nodes in the main chain do not have to be aware of the sidechain and vice-versa, unless they want to actively take part in cross-chain operations [20]. The asymmetric scheme consists of an independent main blockchain and a sidechain that relies on the main chain to operate. All the sidechain nodes are aware of the main chain, however, only main chain nodes who chose to support the sidechain are aware of it. When chains have an asymmetric relationship, failures on the main chain will have an impact on the sidechain, the opposite, however, is not true.

- **Strengths:**
  Maintainability (Modifiability): A benefit of sidechains is the possibility to extend blockchain functionality. Connecting a sidechain to a main chain that is deprived of certain features, e.g., transaction privacy, can enable users of said main chain to have access to additional desirable features without requiring changes in the main chain.
- **Weaknesses:**
  Portability (Installability): Sidechains systems must be developed for a specific pair of blockchains and therefore need to be designed to be compatible with both chains before deployment. Sidechains can also increase the complexity of a system in different levels [3].
  Decentralization: Sidechains are susceptible to centralization of mining when one of the connected chains provides higher mining incentives than the other. This leads miners to work only for the most profitable chain and may slow down block validation in the other chain.

Liquid Network is a federated sidechain that allows assets to be moved from the Bitcoin blockchain and back to it. When assets are moved to the sidechain they fall under custody of a group of participants called functionaries [9]. Bitcoins (BTC) transferred to Liquid are represented as Liquid Bitcoins (L-BTC) inside the sidechain. For every existing amount of L-BTC there has to be a correspondent amount of BTC locked in the Bitcoin blockchain.

Proof-of-Stake Sidechains are sidechain constructions that enable cross-chain communication between Proof-of-Stake (PoS) blockchains. To transfer assets users must diffuse a message signaling their intention to transfer assets to the other chain in the source chain and a recovery message to reclaim its assets on the destination chain. The same operation can then be conducted in the sidechain to transfer the assets back to their source chain. Cross-chain proofs require a signature from a set of validators chosen through a leader election algorithm.

Proof-of-Work Sidechains are sidechain constructions that enable two independent Proof-of-Work based chains to establish cross-chain communication. To prove that an event took place in another chain, the proposed construction uses a cryptographic proof of state called Non-Interactive Proofs of Proof-of-Work (NIPoPoWs) [19]. The use of Proof-of-Work makes this system trustless, as users don't have to trust other peers, but rather validate transactions through a decentralized consensus algorithm. This system has the ability to transfer arbitrary data between chains in addition to transferring digital tokens.

Analysis of Sidechain-Based Systems. The sidechain-based systems category main contains three cross-chain communication systems, namely Liquid Network, Proof-of-Stake sidechains and Proof-of-Work sidechains. Out of all three, the Liquid Network is the most limited in terms of adaptability, being restricted to cross-chain operations between the Bitcoin and the Liquid Network blockchains. Proof-of-Stake and Proof-of-Work sidechains are generic constructions and therefore can be incorporated to any Proof-of-stake and Proof-of-Work based blockchains respectively.

In regards to ease of use, the Liquid Network has an advantage over the other systems in this category. This is due to the fact that Liquid is a sidechain solution that has already been deployed, eliminating the need for development and deployment work. All one needs to start using Liquid is to transfer BTC to a Liquid Network peg-in address to receive an equivalent amount of L-BTC in the sidechain. The Liquid sidechain also provides features not available within the Bitcoin blockchain and makes them accessible via the use of BTC. Those features include fast transaction speed, enhanced transaction privacy and the ability for users to issue their own tokens. On the other hand, Proof-of-Stake and Proof-of-Work sidechains are academic proposals that require considerable effort to be developed into fully functioning sidechains, given that their objective is to provide generic constructions to enable secure cross-chain communication. However, despite not being ready-to-use systems like the Liquid Network, Proof-of-Stake and Proof-of-Work sidechains provide rigorously defined constructions that can be used as a reference for the development of cross-chain communication mechanisms from scratch while enabling developers to design the remaining sidechain components in a way that suits their needs.

In terms of consensus, Proof-of-Stake and Proof-of-Work sidechains were designed to work with blockchains that employ those specific consensus mechanisms and therefore are better tailored for a permissionless setting. The Liquid Network operates under a federated model and relies on a set of pre-defined validators called functionaries to secure the network. When users exchange their BTC for L-BTC, their BTC fall under control of Liquid's functionaries, requiring users to trust that the federation will keep their locked assets secure. The use of federations is a trade-off of decentralization for faster transaction processing speed.

4.4   Peer-Based Systems

Peer-based systems allow users to exchange assets directly with other peers rather than relying on a third party service. Figure 4 presents a generalization of the process of transferring assets using peer-based systems.

User-to-user communication in peer-based systems takes place in communication channels outside of the blockchain environment. To enforce correctness and security during transfers, this category of systems relies on protocols that employ HTLCs and pre-commitments to coordinate the transfer of value across chains. Those systems allow two parties in any two different blockchains to engage in cross-chain asset transfer, as long as both blockchains support the scripting capabilities necessary to set up the exchange contracts.

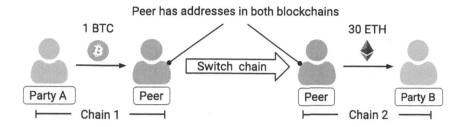

Fig. 4. Process of transferring assets using peer-based systems.

- **Strengths:**
  Portability (Installability): Transfers that leverage peers to forward assets across systems can be executed without the need to deploy complex systems. Setting up the exchange contracts requires less time and effort than deploying other types of cross-chain communication systems such as sidechains and relay contracts.
- **Weaknesses:**
  Performance efficiency (Time behaviour): Settlement of transactions using peer-based systems can have long delays. Those delays are caused by the hashed timelock contracts (HTLCs) and the time required to allow parties to participate in or to abort deals.

Atomic Cross-Chain Swaps (ACCSs) allow users to participate in atomic asset exchanges between blockchains. A swap takes place between parties who hold assets in distinct blockchains, however, users must also have an account or address in the blockchain on which they wish to receive their payment. For example, if Alice wants to exchange BTC for Ether and Bob wants to exchange Ether for BTC, both parties need one address in each participating blockchain to be able to execute a swap.

To set up a deal using ACCSs, the participants must establish an out-of-bounds communication channel to agree on the details of the operation. The asset transfer protocol is coordinated using HTLCs, which carry out actions when the conditions agreed upon by the participants of the deal are met.

Interledger is a protocol suite that allows users in independent blockchains to exchange assets through a payment routing network composed of other users. Interledger is optimized for the transfer of micro payments, making it similar to payment channels. It can be used by anyone without requiring any development or deployment process.

When a user wishes to transfer assets, the Interledger protocol is used to find a route of connected users that can form a path to forward the value packets hop by hop from the sender to the receiver, across different blockchains. Users that connect other peers in the network can earn revenue by taking margins from the transfers they aid in. Whenever a user wishes to forward payments to a different peer, a route of connectors between them must be established before sending value.

Analysis of Peer-Based Systems. The peer-based systems category includes Atomic Cross-chain Swaps and Interledger. Those systems require no development effort in order to be used for cross-chain communication. ACCSs are coordinated using HTLCs and while they require programming knowledge to set up, the effort required is smaller than the effort needed to develop a full-fledged cross-chain communication system. Interledger utilizes the Interledger Protocol to find routes of peers to connect the users that want to exchange payments. All one needs to use Interledger is to use the protocol to find a suitable route of peers through which value packets can be forwarded. Even though fairness issues have been identified in the Atomic Cross-chain Swap protocol and patched [14], in general peer-based systems are secure and enforce correctness of transactions, meaning that users obtain what they expect.

Neither ACCSs or Interledger are tied to specific blockchains, however ACCSs require the ledgers involved in the cross-chain operation to support the creation of HTLCs. Interledger uses hashed timelock agreements (HTLAs), a generalization of HTLCs that can be implemented in any type of blockchain. Additionally, Interledger can also be used to exchange value with fiat money payment networks, a feature that is not supported by ACCSs.

Functional suitability however, is where the two systems differ. ACCSs only allow the execution of one cross-chain deal and need to be set up every time assets need to be transferred across blockchains. Additionally, operations using ACCSs take a long time (can last for 48 h) and users need to stay active throughout the execution of the protocol in order to claim their assets. In contrast, Interledger is optimized for micropayments and allows users to open payments channels with each other and exchange value packets until one of the parties wishes to close the channel and update their balance in the blockchain. This characteristic makes Interledger more suitable for users that need to execute large volumes of small value transactions over a long period of time.

5   Related Work

Since works proposing systems to achieve cross-chain communication in specific scenarios were discussed and analyzed in detail throughout this work, we limit the related work discussion to relevant literature that approaches the problem of cross-chain communication from a broader, more general perspective.

Zamyatin et al. provides a systematic analysis of existing blockchain protocols and formalizes the problem of Cross-Chain Communication [37]. The authors draw a comparison between the process of establishing cross-chain communication and the Fair Exchange problem, arguing that cross-chain communication is impossible without the help of a trusted third party. This work also presents a framework for analyzing blockchain interoperability solutions and uses it to classify existing protocols.

Buterin presents a preliminary view of the blockchain interoperability field, classifies existing solutions into distinct categories and discusses expectations for the future of cross-chain communication [6].

Belchior et al. conducts an extensive literature review on blockchain interoperability [4]. The authors review and classify blockchain interoperability systems and provide up-to-date information on grey literature.

Frauenthaler et al. analyzes the blockchain literature and proposes technical criteria to classify existing work [12]. The authors also define core principles required for achieving interoperability.

Lohachab et al. presents a systematic review of blockchain interoperability and its different aspects, requirements and implementations [24]. The authors propose a taxonomy for blockchain research and a multi-layer architecture to achieve interoperability among heterogeneous blockchains.

6 Conclusion

With the increased interest in blockchain technologies cross-chain communication is more desired than ever. This work provided a study on the architecture of cross-chain communication systems with the aim of expanding the knowledge on the subject and supporting developers and practitioners in the process of selecting cross-chain communication systems suitable for their needs. We hope the community can benefit from our proposed evaluation framework, which provides a concise way of assessing the capabilities of interoperability systems, and our analysis, which provides support in the process of weighing the benefits and drawbacks of existing systems and their respective categories.

References

1. Abebe, E., et al.: Verifiable observation of permissioned ledgers (2020)
2. Androulaki, E., et al.: Hyperledger fabric: a distributed operating system for permissioned blockchains. In: Proceedings of the Thirteenth EuroSys Conference, pp. 1–15 (2018)
3. Back, A., et al.: Enabling blockchain innovations with pegged sidechains (2014)
4. Belchior, R., Vasconcelos, A., Guerreiro, S., Correia, M.: A survey on blockchain interoperability: past, present, and future trends. arXiv preprint (2020)
5. Burdges, J., et al.: Overview of polkadot and its design considerations. arXiv preprint (2020)
6. Buterin, V.: Chain interoperability. R3 Research Paper (2016)
7. Buterin, V.: Ethereum whitepaper (2021). https://ethereum.org/en/whitepaper/
8. Consensys: BTC Relay. https://github.com/ethereum/btcrelay
9. Dilley, J., Poelstra, A., Wilkins, J., Piekarska, M., Gorlick, B., Friedenbach, M.: Strong federations: an interoperable blockchain solution to centralized third-party risks. arXiv (2016)
10. Dujak, D., Sajter, D.: Blockchain applications in supply chain. In: Kawa, A., Maryniak, A. (eds.) SMART Supply Network. E, pp. 21–46. Springer, Cham (2019). https://doi.org/10.1007/978-3-319-91668-2_2
11. Frauenthaler, P., Sigwart, M., Spanring, C., Sober, M., Schulte, S.: Eth relay: a cost-efficient relay for ethereum-based blockchains. In: 2020 IEEE International Conference on Blockchain (Blockchain), pp. 204–213 (2020)

12. Frauenthaler, P., Borkowski, M., Schulte, S.: A framework for blockchain interoperability and runtime selection. arXiv preprint arXiv:1905.07014 (2019)
13. Gazi, P., Kiayias, A., Zindros, D.: Proof-of-stake sidechains. IACR Cryptology ePrint Archive 2018/1239 (2018)
14. Han, R., Lin, H., Yu, J.: On the optionality and fairness of atomic swaps. In: Proceedings of the 1st ACM Conference on Advances in Financial Technologies, AFT 2019, Zurich, Switzerland, 21–23 October 2019, pp. 62–75 (2019)
15. Herlihy, M.: Atomic cross-chain swaps. In: Proceedings of the 2018 ACM Symposium on Principles of Distributed Computing, pp. 245–254 (2018)
16. Interledger Foundation: Interledger protocol v4. https://tinyurl.com/2aj635xm
17. ISO/IEC 25010: System and software quality requirements and evaluation. Technical report, International Organization for Standardization
18. Karantias, K., Kiayias, A., Zindros, D.: Proof-of-burn. IACR Crypto (2019)
19. Kiayias, A., Miller, A., Zindros, D.: Non-interactive proofs of proof-of-work. IACR Crypto **2017**(963), 1–42 (2017)
20. Kiayias, A., Zindros, D.: Proof-of-work sidechains. In: Bracciali, A., Clark, J., Pintore, F., Rønne, P.B., Sala, M. (eds.) FC 2019. LNCS, vol. 11599, pp. 21–34. Springer, Cham (2020). https://doi.org/10.1007/978-3-030-43725-1_3
21. Kuo, T.T., Kim, H.E., Ohno-Machado, L.: Blockchain distributed ledger technologies for biomedical and health care applications. J. Am. Med. Inform. Assoc. **24**(6), 1211–1220 (2017)
22. Kwon, J., Buchman, E.: Cosmos whitepaper (2019)
23. Le, D.P., Yang, G., Ghorbani, A.: A new multisignature scheme with public key aggregation for blockchain. In: 2019 17th PST, pp. 1–7. IEEE (2019)
24. Lohachab, A., et al.: Towards interconnected blockchains: a comprehensive review of the role of interoperability among disparate blockchains. ACM Comput. Surv. (CSUR) **54**(7), 1–39 (2021)
25. Nakamoto, S.: Bitcoin: a peer-to-peer electronic cash system (2008)
26. Network, K.: Peace Relay. https://github.com/KyberNetwork/peace-relay
27. Nick, J., Poelstra, A., Sanders, G.: Liquid: a bitcoin sidechain (2020)
28. Pilkington, M.: Blockchain technology: principles and applications. In: Research Handbook on Digital Transformations. Edward Elgar Publishing (2016)
29. Project, T.M.: About monero (2021). https://www.getmonero.org/resources/about/
30. Sasson, E.B., et al.: Zerocash: decentralized anonymous payments from bitcoin. In: 2014 IEEE Symposium on Security and Privacy, pp. 459–474. IEEE (2014)
31. Sekniqi, K., Laine, D., Buttolph, S., Sirer, E.: Avalanche platform (2020)
32. Tasatanattakool, P., Techapanupreeda, C.: Blockchain: challenges and applications. In: ICOIN 2018, pp. 473–475. IEEE (2018)
33. Tether Operations: Tether cryptocurrency (2021). https://tether.to/
34. Vilner, Y.: New report illustrates the problem with cryptocurrency exchanges, June 2019. https://tinyurl.com/ad9djc6e
35. Wood, G.: Polkadot: vision for a heterogeneous multi-chain framework (2016)
36. Xiao, Y., Zhang, P., Liu, Y.: Secure and efficient multi-signature schemes for fabric: an enterprise blockchain platform. IEEE Trans. Inf. Forensics Secur. **16**, 1782–1794 (2020)
37. Zamyatin, A., et al.: SoK: communication across distributed ledgers (2019)
38. Zamyatin, A., Harz, D., Lind, J., Panayiotou, P., Gervais, A., Knottenbelt, W.: XCLAIM: trustless, interoperable, cryptocurrency-backed assets. In: 2019 IEEE Symposium on Security and Privacy (SP), pp. 193–210. IEEE (2019)
39. Zheng, Z., Xie, S., Dai, H.N., Chen, X., Wang, H.: Blockchain challenges and opportunities: a survey. Int. J. Web Grid Serv. **14**(4), 352–375 (2018)

Micropayments Interoperability with Blockchain and Off-Chain Data Store to Improve Transaction Throughputs

Azmi Amiruddin$^{(\boxtimes)}$

TU Berlin, Berlin, Germany
azmiruddin@tu-berlin.de
https://www.tu-berlin.de

Abstract. Layer2 (L2) techniques have emerged as promising scalability solutions to improve the quality of blockchains services, particularly to increase transaction throughputs. We instantiated a multilayered approach for our L2 scalability solution, composed of a node server, an off-chain data store, smart contracts (for state channel and payment network), and a REST API as an oracle. In the first release of our application, we demonstrated how state channel, payment network, and off-chain data stores allowed us to critically examine how scalability can be achieved by incorporating a state channel, payment network, and off-chain data control. We achieve flexibility and interoperability using proven standards (e.g., ERC-20 and EIP-1474), conducting a multivocal literature review, integrating existing approaches using a payment channel framework, and proposing efficient process execution to reduce on-chain transaction overheads using an off-chain data store mechanism. In return, the proposed solution can reduce on-chain transaction overheads by combining a novel framework that shifts interoperability among blockchains, state channels, payment networks, and off-chain data stores.

Keywords: Blockchain · Layer two · Off-chain · Scalability

1 Background

According to Forbes [7], the six largest financial firms and three technology giants have started to invest in their blockchain ecosystem for widespread adoption. This report is aligned with Gartner's research [2], which predicted that 90% of current blockchain adoptions would require a "technology refresh" to remain competitive and avoid obsolescence. Melanie Swan in [31] placed a fundamental blueprint for the blockchain technology hype. Blockchains' advantages are more than technological innovations and economy; they extend into the political system through digital voting [31]. Blockchain technology offers the opportunity to develop new business and trust models, so the blockchain during the *peak of inflated expectations* is one of the game changers that will necessarily involve new technical foundations and more dynamic ecosystems [26].

© ICST Institute for Computer Sciences, Social Informatics and Telecommunications Engineering 2022
Published by Springer Nature Switzerland AG 2022. All Rights Reserved
S. Paiva et al. (Eds.): SmartCity360° 2021, LNICST 442, pp. 521–549, 2022.
https://doi.org/10.1007/978-3-031-06371-8_34

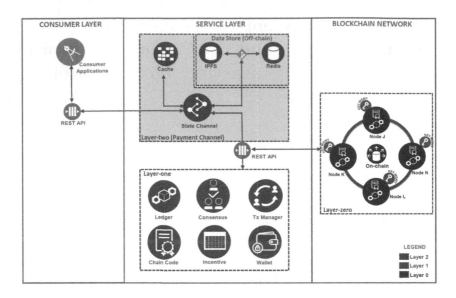

Fig. 1. Blockchain layer

Despite the hype cycle of blockchain implementation in all sectors, the processing time to handle transactions is largely underperformance as compared to that in a legacy system [17]. Research in [17] classified blockchain scaling solutions based on (i) a consensus algorithm, (ii) sharding technique, and (iii) side-chain solutions. In addition, in [17], highlighting the drawbacks of the consensus algorithm indicates modifying one of the core components of a blockchain layer one (L1) while already in use, which creates major unplanned issues, such as lack of backward compatibility, clearly impeding their practical implementation. Changes in L1 might even result in multiple forked systems (e.g., different forked systems are implemented in the blockchain test network, such as Rinkeby using proof of authority (PoA) and Ropsten using proof of work (PoW)). In [17], one promising solution was classified as an L2 scalability solution. L2 components operate independently from L1 components. As a result, some transaction processing within layer 0 (L0) moves outside the blockchain network (off-chain computation).

In this research, we combine state channel framework and payment network protocols, also referred to as an L2 scalability solution. In contrast to the previously mentioned L1 solutions, L2 protocols scale blockchains without affecting the L1 core components. L2 protocols, which are presented in Fig. 1, enable users to save block transactions in the preferred data store technology and then perform off-chain transactions through private and encrypted peer-to-peer (P2P) messages, rather than broadcasting each transaction to the leading blockchain network. This optimization reduces block size and transaction load on the underlying blockchain while remaining completely backward compatible. In [17], the theoretical transaction throughput is only bounded by the data store, network service-level agreements (e.g., bandwidth, density, and latency) of the involved participants. Off-chain transaction confidentiality, integrity, and availability can be guaranteed through collateral allocation, such as in payment channel designs [13, 30] or in providing delayed transaction finality in commit-chains proposal [20].

1.1 Problem Description

Common problems arise when transferring transactions between merchants and buyers. A trusted intermediary is a must in agreements to enforce the terms, but it could be malicious. How is the data transaction managed if the participant is not connected to the system? How to manage when the transaction is partially not submitted to the ledger directly? We devised solutions to mitigate both issues by implementing a state channel and payment network using a data store. We reviewed three significant problems related to scalability issues due to blockchain adoption according to [31, 33].

1. **Throughput.** The public blockchain network has limitations with transaction throughput as it processes only 1 tps, with a theoretical current maximum of 20 tps for the Ethereum network [31, 33]. One method to handle a higher throughput is increasing each block size, but it causes block size and blockchain bloats issues. Comparison metrics in permission and consortium blockchain network are RedBelly (660,000 tps) [10], R3 Corda (1678 tps; 15,000 tps peak) [29] and VISA networks (1,500 tps typical; 7,000 tps peak) [18].
2. **Latency.** Each blockchain transaction block takes 10 min to process and confirm a transaction [31]. Here transaction timeout should be allotted for sufficient security, particularly for large amounts, as the waiting time needs to be longer to override the financial loss of a double-spend threat.
3. **Block size and data placement.** Ethereum blockchain takes 117 GB, and it has grown by 48 GB in the last year[1]. Downloading Ethereum full node takes hours or even days. If 2,000 tps increase the throughput to VISA standards, the result is 1.42 PB/year or 3.9 GB/day [31]. Accordingly, at 150,000 tps, the blockchain would grow by 214 PB per year. The blockchain community refers to the size issue as a "bloat". To scale blockchain to a *plateau of productivity*, it would need to be large and distributed, likely impacting transaction fees like on-chain data costs.

With the issues above confronting the blockchain public network, we identified an opportunity to develop a new application with data store placement to keep the blockchain usable and storable (at much larger future scales) while maintaining its confidentiality, integrity, and availability. Exposing application programming interfaces (APIs) to external consumers, such as those from L2 solutions, which facilitate automated calls to the entire blockchain network, is an

---

[1] Data snapshot as of 30 December 2020, obtained from https://blockchair.com/ethereum.

innovation to address blockchain "bloats" and make data more accessible. Some operations include obtaining address balances, changing balances, and pushing notification service when new transactions state or blocks are created on the network. Other operations are web-based block explorers (e.g. Etherscan[2] or Blockchain explorer[3]), decentralised applications (DApps), mobile digital wallets, middleware software that allow seamless integration and replica placement for off-chain data store (e.g. Chainlink solution [3]). Finally, developing an interoperable framework to address new business requires an understanding of how systems operate to create opportunities that influence blockchains to minimize the challenge on the *plateau of productivity*.

1.2   Research Questions

Blockchain adoption seeks stable guidelines for successful implementation and improvement in systemic qualities during the plateau of productivity stage. Our primary research objective is to achieve scalability in Ethereum blockchains. Moreover, driven by this research objectives in guidance of [1, 15–17, 21], our research questions are as follows:

1. RQ 1: What is state of the art in blockchain scalability models, and how their design patterns look like?
2. RQ 2: How can the architectural approach integrate data store and state channel technique to improve the QoS of the existing blockchain implementation?
3. RQ 3: How can a datastore from [21], state channels [13] and payment network [30] be integrated to improve scalability (increasing transaction throughput) for the current blockchain implementation?

1.3   Contributions

1. An experimental approach is provided by the architecture of incorporating a blockchain into a data store and payment channel solution with off-chain control to improve scalability problems like block size and transaction throughput. A framework to integrate with the baseline work [21] was selected with payment channel technique from [13,30]. Minimizing system quality effect and improvement on the existing payment channel architecture are focused.
2. A practical off-chain technique is built upon a novel multi-tier application based on (i) state channel solution [13,30] and (ii) persistent mechanism, which relies on a distributed data store implemented using Redis and IPFS [21].
3. An application that moves these roles into a layered architecture with a separation of concern for the data layer, business process, resource adapter, and user interface into a separate component-based application is introduced and developed in a method called resource separation (refer to "Single Responsibility Principle").

---

[2] Ethereum blockchain explorer https://etherscan.io/.
[3] Bitcoin blockchain information https://www.blockchain.com/explorer.

Finally, in the future, we will have an architectural goal to expose other L2 scalability solutions (e.g., probabilistic micropayment [6] and incentive mechanism [1]).

1.4   Related Work

Wattenhofer and Decker [11] created an off-chain channel termed blockchain L2 scalability. Some studies define protocols for blockchain L2 scalability and channel networks. The off-chain protocol for the Ethereum network, is covered in (i) Connext [9], (ii) KChannels [19], (iii) Go-Perun [13] and (iv) Raiden [30]. Moreover, in Appendix 1, we provide an overview of current L2 constructions, distinguishing between two-channel techniques: (i) state channels from Go-Perun [13], which support off-chain payment interactions, and (ii) payment networks from Raiden [30], which support off-chain arbitrary interactions.

There are particularly relevant white literature and GL that aim to offer blockchain L2 scalability solutions like the Lightning Network [28]. On the industrial project, a white paper for L2 scalability is presented in Counterfactual [8], and Celer Network [12]. GL related to these projects puts more emphasis on the "engineering-oriented" approach and product information sheet. Thus, it does not discuss the characteristics of the full-state channel procedure. Moreover, most of this work covers all networks in blockchains, including Bitcoin and Ethereum. The most useful literature for this research was described in [13,30], but it did not highlight the solution on the data store approach. Another proposal that works inside the Ethereum network is presented in [23] with release name Sprites, and its extensions Pisa [22] on building multi-party ledger state channels did not discuss the clear data store approach. A group of parties can initiate a multi-party ledger state channel as per [22,23] and a disagreement between the parties is resolved on-chain. Hence, the solutions from [22,23] are not listed by Ethereum community development[4].

Table 1 presents the comparisons of the proposed research work with the existing solutions.

Table 1. Comparison of proposed work with existing solutions

Proposal	Solution
Connext [9]	TypeScript, JavaScript, Extend Hash-Time-locked-Contract, Distributed Balanced Routing
KChannel [19]	TypeScript, Meta-channels, Replaced-by-Incentive
Perun [13]	Go, Replaced-by-Version, Virtual Channel
Pisa [22] and Sprites [23]	Python, Replaced-by-Version, State Channel
Raiden [30]	Python, Hash-Time-locked-Contract, Replaced-by-Revocation, Machine-to-Machine Payment, State Channel
Proposed Work	Java, Datastore, State Channel, Hash-Time-locked-Contract, Replaced-by-Revocation, Replaced-by-Version

---

[4] Ethereum   L2   Scaling   https://ethereum.org/en/developers/docs/scaling/state-channels/.

There are two major distinctions in our work: first, [13,22,23,30] did not support flexible data store mechanisms, and as a result, interacting with the blockchain becomes necessary to establish and close state channels. Second, the solution suggested in this research completely supports the simultaneous execution of multiple contracts within a single channel, whereas [13,22,23,30] focused on the off-chain execution of merely a single contract with additional evaluation on the practical aspects of state channels. We suggest a different channel state solution in this research. Defining a formal data store mechanism is also a primary objective of this research, which was adopted in [21], and our contribution aims at improving the transaction throughput in Ethereum networks, using state channels and a multi-layered architecture that has light components to be plugged in other ecosystems, such as the Internet of Things (IoT).

2 System Design

As an end-to-end solution that can be developed and integrated on existing or future blockchains, our state channel application includes a clean layered architecture that decouples the sophisticated L2 scalability into modular components. The combination of this architecture simplifies the software development life cycle (SDLC), allowing each independent service to evolve inside a continuous integration and delivery pipeline (CI/CD). A well-designed layered architecture should have open interfaces that will allow and encourage different layer implementations as long as they support the same cross-layer interfaces. Moreover, each component only needs to concentrate on its functionality (componentization via services).

One of our architectural goals is to enable state channel techniques, off-chain data control, and object interaction logic that can be used across multiple blockchain networks. Our state channel application aims to create a blockchain-agnostic interoperable platform that can run in the Ethereum networks. Therefore, we adopted a standard off-chain datastore schema, EIP-55 [4], and EIP-1474 [27]. It is also aimed to provide innovative solutions on blockchain L2 and improve scalability for blockchain technology adoption. Our target architecture builds a multi-layer model by adopting a data store engine from [21], state channel technique in [13] and payment network from [30]. Our target multilayered architecture, as shown in Fig. 2, is made up of the layers described below, in bottom-up order.

1. **Data Store.** Fog computing, a novel technology that combines cloud computing resources, allows easy movement of computational infrastructures. Using a prominent data store engine as proven in [21] enables our application to have portability and scalability features simultaneously.
2. **Channel Node.** Our application uses the state channel technique from Go-Perun [13], and Raiden network [30], which allowed us to reduce the scalability challenges that major public blockchain platforms face (e.g., Bitcoin and Ethereum).

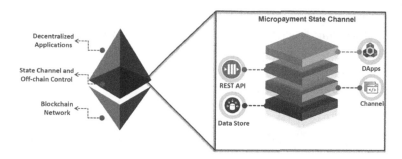

Fig. 2. Target architecture

3. **REST API**. Communicating via lightweight service mechanisms (HTTP resource API) enables the accessibility of consumer applications and semantic interoperability that can be achieved through models of information.
4. **DApps**. The front-end framework, which runs a GUI for off-chain-enabled applications, is accessed directly by the consumer. Our DApp interfaces, namely, React Native framework[5] and JSON server-client component[6], allow us to develop a clear user interface and allow SoC for each component.

The following section will briefly discuss the system functionality based on the layered architecture illustrated in Fig. 2.

2.1 Off-Chain Data Control

We modified the RDF store engine [21] by adding additional logic for saving off-chain transaction data and data portability. Store data come from transaction log where wrapper invokes and returns the standard EIP-1474 message specification [27].

Channel Object. Before the pointer requests a state modification triggered by the consumer application, the response is dispatched to the mediator controller. Next, the *TransactionSave* persists the raw data into the *DataStore* object. This allows the *DataStore* function to record all incoming state channel messages into *RedisBufferLayer* and *IPFSPhysicalLayer*, and all event processes for state channel applications are fully synchronized into Redis and IPFS. The data store process will be executed, as shown in Fig. 3, if the channel participants initiate a state event that is received from an Ethereum transaction. Subsequently, the data input will be parsed into a raw transaction message from the blockchain (JSON data block), and the raw message will be converted into an appropriate plain object that will be parsed into the key-value store.

The data placement feature makes our application different from Go-Perun and Raiden because it allows "on-the-fly" compilation to manage the data store

---

[5] Develop native apps https://facebook.github.io/react-native/docs/getting-started.
[6] JSON DB inside clients browser https://www.npmjs.com/package/json-server.

in case of disputes, crashes, and irregular shutdowns. The shortest path for datastore processing is shown in Fig. 3 and the detailed information flow for channel object creation is presented in Fig. 4.

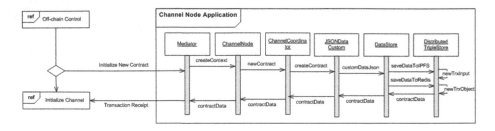

Fig. 3. Data store process

After the data store process starts, the channel object will automatically parse the blockchain log messages (JSON data) and transaction events into our key-value store with the help of *Converter*, *ChannelStatusResponse* and a Web3J wrapper.

1. **Channel Initialise**: initiate to open a channel based on the predefined channel contract address
   a. address: string EIP-55 [4], which encoded the address containing the identifier of the channel[7].
   b. status: response of the contracted event.
   c. transferred: number of assets to be exchanged.
   d. current one: current block transaction count.
   e. synced once: synchronized block transaction with Ethereum.
   f. stateRoot: string containing the EIP-55 encoded condition of the channel represented by a string from the state root. The possible events are as follows: (i) Open: the channel state is created, and tokens are tradeable. (ii) Settlement: the channel has been utilized by a participant and settled. (iii) Closed: the channel has been requested to be destroyed by a participant.
2. **Channel Settlement**: settle the open channel after the successful approval of channel participants deposits
   a. sender: string containing the EIP-55 encoded sender address of the partner with whom we have opened a channel.
   b. receiver: string containing the EIP-55 encoded recipient address of the token network the channel is part of.
   c. auditor: string containing the EIP-55 encoded auditor address to watch the transaction from dishonest behavior.
   d. minActive: minimum number of participants required to open the channel (the possible number is 1).

---

[7] For EIP-55, we implemented *Keccak256* in *ChannelLibrary* contract.

e. maxActive: maximum number of channel participants (implement using *@ConfigurationProperties* with predefined number is 50).

f. deposit: number of assets to be placed during a request to open the channel.

g. closeTimeout: channel automatically closes if the number of participants fails to deposit the token.

h. settleTimeout: string containing the EIP-55 encode blocks time required to be mined from the time the transfer has been locked.

i. auditTimeout: blocks time that is required to be disputed during transaction reversal.

j. closeBlocksCount: block number when the channel requests to close.

k. stateTransition: string containing the EIP-55 encoded transition state. Once the root state has been established, possible state transitions are as follows: (i) Deposit: the channel that has been opened requires to be funded by participants. (ii) Deposit approved: the deposit transfer has been approved. (iii) Active: the channel is open and can accept participants to join the channel. (iv) Dispute: there is a fraudulent transaction where one of the participants automatically changes the state. (v) Transfer lock: the transfer has been locked by the recipients. (vi) Transfer unlock: participants request the asset to be settled in their wallet. (vii) Shutdown: the participant requests to destroy the channel. (viii) Destroy: the channel is automatically closed.

3. **Channel Transfer**: update the open channel with the transaction between participants

a. channelId: string containing the identifier of the channel.

b. transferred: string containing the EIP-55 encoded transfer identifier from Ethereum sends the transaction event (transaction root).

c. value: the amount of transaction to-be transfer (possible value is less than the token value).

d. locked: mix hash key to lock the transfer; the EIP-55 encoded value from Ethereum sends the transaction event (transaction root).

e. signature: transaction hash from channel participants.

The transaction events converted from Ethereum messages are JSON file types and taken care of by the object *TransactionSave*. Then, the results will be saved into a JSON file, handled by the object *TransactionOutputOffchain, ObjectFileTransactionOffChain*. Once the data have the results fixed, the object *SerializeUtils* will serialise and de-serialise the JSON file and insert it into the Redis store with a key. Figure 4 shows the transaction processing on this procedure.

Off-chain Data Lifecycle. Our system starts with the extraction and transformation of raw messages from Ethereum transaction events into our key-value store with the help of plain Java object conversations. The data were used for off-chain computations, such as reading, updating, insert and deleting transaction records. The processing flow of the off-chain data lifecycle presented in Fig. 5 can be briefly explained as follows:

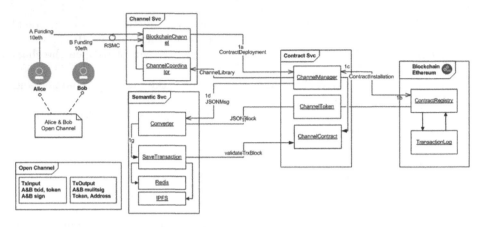

Fig. 4. Information flow (open channel)

- [1a] Channel participants have to deposit tokens into the blockchain and *BlockchainChannel* will handle their request using contract deployment. In this flow, Alice and Bob agreed to deposit 10 ethers to open the channel.
- [1b] A request for contract deployment is received by the *ContractManager* inside the channel service component and then parsed into a specific contract wrapper that will communicate with the Ethereum network (e.g. *Channel-Contract* or *ChannelToken*). Deployment of *ChannelContract* and *Channel-Token* is required in case of off-chain computation.
- [1c] The contract deployment will continue to be installed inside the EVM, the *JSONData* transaction response for this request will be used for our data, and the response will be saved into the key-value store. Inside the data store component, the *Converter* object then converts the data block into our predefined data format.
- [1d] Once the transaction has been saved into Redis and IPFS, and the transaction data block will be validated and returned to the consumer. Once the response has been received, the *ChannelCoordinator* will change to the *run/start* mode to watch the state transition of the channel lifecycle and return the transaction event to the *BlockchainChannel*.
- [1e] After the *ChannelCoordinator* starts in the run mode, and every state change will be processed to get the event. For each of the *StateTransition* events, *OutgoingChannelState* will record the conversation and convert the transaction events and trigger the appropriate data persistent into Redis and IPFS.

During the request to create a channel, the data will be dispatched into the Ethereum network: participant addresses and deposits will be placed in the token network. After deposit approval, the response will be sent back to consumer applications, and the token can be utilised to initiate any off-chain transaction. Before the response message is sent back to the consumer, a state change is dispatched to the *StateTransition* events for processing to write our data into a key-value store called the *TransactionOutputOffchain* and *ObjectFileTransactionOffChain*.

2.2   Channel Design

We built our channel node using Java programming techniques (JDK v1.8)[8] and utilised Web3J[9] to wrap modified contracts from Go-Perun [13] and the Raiden Network [30]. We also utilised the open-source library from Papyrus Network [25], and Blockchain Thunder [24] to build channel-node servers and deploy smart contracts "on-the-fly" when a channel has been established (e.g., in a token reload or channel destroy).

We encapsulated all state channel resources in a layering fashion, as presented in Fig. 2. All the components inside the channel node were deployed using Java Archive (JAR library) and distributed into the application server as the resource library to support DApps. The overall smart contracts design will be briefly presented in the following subsection, and the node server application will be presented further in subsection channel node.

Smart Contracts. Our smart contracts are written using the Ethereum solidity language. Each contract must be deployed before a channel node can be used. However, because this is a complete system development for off-chain computations, we must deploy all of the contracts into the Ethereum test network[10]. Our state channel framework uses interconnected intelligent contracts to define the on-chain logic for channel transitions and off-chain computation for settlements and withdrawals. In our current release[11], we have six smart-contract that will support our application node. Hence, we limited our discussion to highlight the smart-contract that is mandatory to support channel node server to (i) *ChannelManager*; (ii) *ChannelContract*; (iii); and (iv) *ChannelApi*.

1. **Channel Manager**

   The *ChannelManager* is responsible for managing the root state for the channel application. It also needs to ensure that the interface binding for *SCHToken* is in sync with the token contract for each channel that is successfully open. As shown in Rinkeby test network[12], we show that related topics for channel creation also bind to specific token channels and addresses.

2. **Channel Contracts**

   The *ChannelContract* ensures recording of a transition state into the channel-node repository. Because the main part of the communication is off-chain, it will only contact the *ChannelContract* if a transition occurred during the

---

[8] Java documentation https://docs.oracle.com/javase/8/docs/.

[9] Develop on Ethereum with the JVM http://docs.web3j.io/latest/quickstart.

[10] Contract Overview https://rinkeby.etherscan.io/address/0x91db6dce5c2584605d7.

[11] State Channel Application https://github.com/azmiruddin/state-channel.

[12] Contract manager deployment in the Rinkeby network. https://rinkeby.etherscan.io/tx/0x6824.

transaction from channel participants (e.g., open, renew deposit, approved deposit, destroy and close). As we are demonstrating the resiliency of componentisation via services, the *ChannelContract* contract also extends *ChannelLibrary*. It will receive transaction messages (EIP-1474 standard) from the *ChannelLibrary* contract and supply the record to *ChannelContract* with a JSON message. The *ChannelContract* records transaction events related to state transition, which will sync with the channel node via the *ChannelCoordinator*. Client states managed by *ChannelContract* are:

- *ChannelNewBalance* looks after the reload/renew amount of deposit that has been proposed by the channel participants.
- *ChannelCloseRequested* is executed if one of the participants request to gracefully shutdown the channel.
- *ChannelDestroy* is responsible to force-close the channel if the participants cannot transfer the deposit.
- *TransferUpdated* operation updates the transaction.
- *ChannelSettled* operation will cover the operation after the deposit has been transferred and locked inside the token network.
- *ChannelAudited* if there is a dispute transaction, then the reversal will be triggered by the event *ChannelAudited*.
- *ChannelSecretRevealed* will take the responsibility of storing the block height at which the secret was revealed in an off-chain transfer. In collaboration with a watching service *ChannelAudited*, it acts as a integrity measure, allowing all channel to withdraw the transferred tokens. This event also unlocks the transfer.

We also conveyed to fork operations from *ChannelContract* and *ChannelLibrary*, which will improve the processing time and lower gas fees during contract compilation and deployment.

3. **Channel Token**

   SCHToken is a ledger contract that manages channels and deposits on-chain. Each channel will employ a specific address (token network address) that works with a particular ERC-20 token and manages channels between participants. The *SCHToken* deployment manages the deposited tokens and is the main point of contact for any on-chain operations for channel-node applications. Inside *SCHToken*, we also implemented a wallet feature with the capability to hold or receive withdrawal amounts from transactions. The wallet itself is directly associated with the token owner, and it will hold an amount related to the maximum number of deposits submitted during the open channel initiation. We demonstrated the feature of the token network in token test transactions from the Rinkeby test network[13].

4. **Channel API**

   Channel-node applications directly interact with the *ChannelApi* contract, which defines two methods: (i) *applyRuntimeUpdate*, which will be assigned to the channel having state transition, and (ii) *applyAuditorsCheckUpdate* to monitor the off-chain transactions of participants. The *applyAuditorsCheckUpdate* method is also responsible for the dispute and reversal phase during

---

[13] Sample state channel transition https://rinkeby.etherscan.io/address/0x91db6.

off-chain transactions, and it is assumed to revert if any app-specific check fails. The *ChannelApi* will apply state transitions to every new channel that is in a settled state. In our implementation, the communication facilities from the client application (channel participants) with the smart contract were provided by the Web3J library [32]. The operation was used by the *applyRuntimeUpdate* method of the *ChannelApi* contract to forward the operation to the *ChannelManager* contract.

Furthermore, the lifecycle of *applyRuntimeUpdate* and *applyAuditorsCheckUpdate* functions is similar to that described in [17], for the watching service mechanisms. The aim of *ChannelApi* is to demonstrate how a client request into specific contracts can communicate with each other, and it has a watchtower committee (*ChannelApiStub*) for the channel event itself (watching service for the specific transaction state). The detailed execution sequence of the watchtower committee is shown in Appendix 2.

We also deployed two additional contracts to support the main smart-contract deployment: (i) *ChannelApiStub* that will create the interface stub to other contract and (ii) *ChannelLibrary* that will support the *ChannelContract*. In our implementation, the interface call facilities provided by Web3J for the client node application with the node server and gRPC[14] for server-to-server communication were used by the *loadPredeployedContract* method of the *ChannelManager* contract to forward the state operation to the *ChannelApi* and *SCHToken* contracts. Intuitively, the function calls the *loadPredeployedContract* to instantaneously load the token and *channel_api* functions of the *ChannelManager* contract. The following sections will examine the integration procedure between the channel node and channel contract.

Channel Node. The channel node serves as a container server for all channel objects used in our state channel application. Our channel-node server has a hybrid implementation, such that it can be deployed using an open-source application server, e.g., Apache Tomcat[15] or JBoss WildFly[16]. The channel-node server can also stand alone, for example, using the legacy Java archive application runtime or implementing the Spring Boot framework[17].

Our application demo, as shown in Fig. 5, proceeds as follows: If the *Node-Server* is started, then the channel client application can begin transactions. The channel request will be directly routed to the OutgoingChannelCoordinator and *IncomingChannelManagers* within the node server, allowing the client to open channels with other participants within the same channel address and close channels, transaction inquiries, and make deposits or withdrawals. Additionally, *ChannelJoinImpl* enables channel composability for new participants to join the channel, transfer deposit and close off-chain over the state-channel

---

[14] gRPC and protocol buffers https://grpc.io/docs/.

[15] Apache Tomcat v8 https://tomcat.apache.org/index.html.

[16] JBoss managed application runtime https://docs.wildfly.org/.

[17] Spring boot execution runtime https://spring.io/projects/spring-boot.

network intermediaries using *OutgoingChannelCoordinator, IncomingChannel-Managers, BlockchainChannel* (the sequence process is depicted in Appendix 3). When the node server is starting, the detailed execution sequence in Fig. 5 will proceed as follows: the node client application will request *getEndpointUrl*, and once the endpoint is established, the subsequent event *checkAddress* will determine whether the contract has been deployed with a valid return address from *ChannelApiStub, ChannelLibrary, ChannelManager, EndpointRegistryContract,* and *SCHToken*. If one of the check addresses does not match the address of an Ethereum pre-deployed contract, the node server will throw an exception during the startup process.

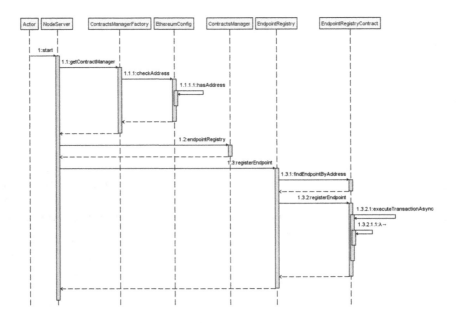

Fig. 5. Channel node start process

- *NodeServer* assumes that the participants are ready to start off-chain transaction.
- *ContractManagerFactory* validates and checks the addresses deployed into the blockchain.
- *EthereumConfig* checks if the address value in the properties is equal to the pre-deployed contract in the blockchain.
- *ContractsManager* assigns the node server to a specific client and then *EndpointRegistry* returns the binding address to the node server.

Once the execution sequence in Fig. 5 is successfully processed, the next *OutgoingChannelState* and *BlockchainChannel* will handle all state modifications and transfer the process execution to the *makeTransitions* operation that is demonstrated in Fig. 6. If the state is opened, then the channel participants

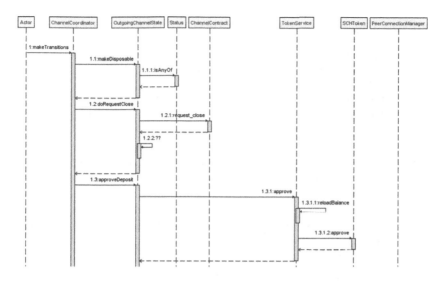

Fig. 6. *ChannelCoordinator* object starts to initiate the state transition

are directly updated off-chain between the two connected end-users, or other participants are allowed to join the channel with a predefined token address encapsulated inside the *ChannelManager*.

Once the execution sequence in Fig. 5 is successfully processed, the next *OutgoingChannelState* and *BlockchainChannel* will handle all state modifications and transfer the process execution to the *makeTransitions* operation that is demonstrated in Fig. 6. If the state is opened, the channel participants are directly updated off-chain between the two connected end-users, or other participants can join the channel with a predefined token address.

– In (1) sequence flow, the *ChannelCoordinator* assumes that channel participants are ready to start the procedure for off-chain transactions. Once the start event is the trigger, the *makeTransitions* will enable the sequencing process for state channel transitions.
– In (1.1.1) activities and subsequent process, the *OutgoingChannelState* validates and checks the address deployed on the blockchain network. The contract has any value of the following states: open, shutdown, destroyed and settled.
– In (1.2) process and subsequent activity demonstrated that the channel would be destroyed automatically if the deposit amount agreed to transfer is not accepted by one of the channel participants.

In our smart contract design, we briefed *ChannelContract* and *ChannelManager* objects that will have the main responsibility of logging the event for state transitions. The two smart contracts will be leveraged in our node server application and during the open state. Our transition states are valid for events: transfer deposit, reload deposit, approved deposit, and destroy channel. The details of the sequence diagram executed by *SCHToken* are presented in Appendix 4. The state interaction execution in Appendix 4 was assumed successful. Here the life-cycle of a state channel is divided into three stages, as shown in Appendix 4: open, update and close.

1. **Open.** If participants want to open the channel, they can transfer some deposits to form the channel. If the other participants cooperate, this process can be done quickly in a single transaction. Suppose the other participants are not available or disagree to cooperate. In that case, the tokens can be reverted through an unlock settlement which is slower and incurs higher gas fees though guaranteed to succeed in a short time. As we presented in Appendix 4, the following sequence will be executed during the channel opening:

   - (1) *deposit* assumes that participants already transferred deposit to form the off-chain transaction.
   - (1.1) *checkStatus*, enum for object *Status* represents a group of constants with the following values: open, deposit, settle, destroy, closed and unlock transfer.
   - (1.2) *renew deposit*, if one of the opened channel participants has insufficient balance, then the state channel application will allow the participants to renew their deposits or reload their ethers into the token network.

   The initial state, after the publication, is successfully settled during the channel opening. Locking and unlocking the number of deposits from all involved parties are performed using an on-chain operation on the Ethereum network. This will lead to further off-chain transactions. Appendix 1 describes the process for the channel opening in detail.

2. **Settlement.** This state also refers to updating the state after the channel has been established and participants exchange assets in the root state. In this phase, the parties will transact by directly exchanging states between them using *OutgoingChannelState* and *BlockchainChannel*. We demonstrated the object channel node implementation in Appendix 2 and Appendix 3. The *OutgoingChannelState* transactions will modify the initial state and distribute the blocked assets among the participants. All parties must approve the agreement to a new state by signing it and sending it to the other participants. The state's order is maintained by a version counter and *transfer_id*. The final state is published by default until the expiry of the challenge period. Each participant can then withdraw the amount corresponding to them in the channel. In the settlement process, the following code with 1.2.1.1:λ will be executed, and the asynchronous transaction process will be directly communicated with the smart contract wrapper.

   The *OutgoingChannelState* will manage state transitions after channel opening. Subsequently, the channel status traverses from the following: (i) settled state, indicating that the deposit has been approved; (ii) closed state, indicating that the channel is destroyed; and (iii) request closed state, where the channel can be shut down. Once the participants are in the settlement state, all parties can do off-chain transactions.

We examine the execution in Fig. 5.15 with preconditions for the channel opening.

- (1) *registerTransfer*: We assume that the participants have sufficient assets for exchange and initiated to form off-chain transactions by registering the transfer.
- (1.3) *getChannelAddress*: The transaction will be registered as per channel address, where the parties subscribe to the channel topic.
- (1.3) *getValue*: The transfer amount is verified, and it checks the sufficiency of participants' funds.
- (1.4) *verifyTransfer*: The channel participants verify the transfer if the deposit amount is sufficient.
- (1.4.2) *getClientAddress*: If the transfer has been verified, then the channel node will check the recipient address.
- (1.5) *getTransferId*: If beneficiary address is valid, the transaction that has been executed will return the *transfer_id*.
- (1.6) *isLocked*: The node locks the transfer until the beneficiary claims the assets that have been transferred. The unlocked process is according to the block hash and signature key.
- (1.7) *getValueWei*: If the block hash and signature key are valid, then the beneficiary can transfer the token into their wallet.
- (1.8) *stateChanged*: Once the transfer is unlocked, the iteration process for the state change will take place. Thus, all the channel parties can have more off-chain transactions and invite new participants to join their channel.

After channel establishment, other participants can renew their deposits by transferring some assets into the *SCHToken* object as detailed in Appendix 5. The number of channel participants per channel address is set at 10 per connection.

3. **Closing**. After completing transactions and achieving a final state, parties may submit the final state to the ledger contract. The *ChannelContract* object validates the published state by matching the signatures with the initial state, settles the channel balances, and pays out to each participant.

We examine the execution in for the channel closing and checking the settlement process.

- (1) *isCloseRequested*: We assume that participants have sufficient channels to close, and the token asset has been settled into their online wallet.
- (1.3) *getCloseRequested*: The node server will receive a message to close the channel, and the *ChannelContract* wrapper object will verify the address. If a block transaction is <= 0, the channel will be shut down gracefully.
- (1.3) *getPendingStatus*: Any pending transaction in the channel that is being closed will be checked, and then the channel node will wait until that pending transaction is settled. The asset is transferred to the recipient's address.

If other participants find the registered state identical to the final state, then no action is required from them. After the challenge duration expires, the state will be finalized on-chain. If a participant discovers that the state is not the most recent, then he can refute it by submitting the most recent state. A sample state channel transition is shown in Rinkeby Test Network[18] that contains the open and close. For example, in the column **Before** is represented the opened state and the channel participants shown in the left column **address**. The close state is shown in the column **After** and the **State Difference** column indicate the block nonce already updated outside the test network. In this case, the settled transaction state is not broadcasted on the Rinkeby test network and affects the block size collected for each transaction settled via the blockchain network.

The implementations of the closing transaction according to the process above can be found in Appendix 4 and Appendix 7.

3   Experimental Set-up

In this research, channel node components were deployed on multiple virtual machines, running RHEL v8 x86 64 (development license) built on Google Cloud Platform (GCP). To fulfill the most minor hardware requirements, 4 virtual CPU cores, 16 GB memory, and 20 GB persistent storage space are provided to every VM. The Redis data store saved off-chain data-related transactions, and Apache Tomcat v8 served as an application server. Inter-region type deployment is performed in this study, where the channel node server datastore is deployed in the Asia-southeast2-a zone Europe-west3-c zone, respectively. According to GCP documentation[19], the implementation of the internal IP address is suggested over external IP in order to get maximum throughput.

The evaluation performed for off-chain transaction is represented by *Signed-Transaction* object whereas on-chain operation is demonstrated by *SignedTransferUnlock*. According to [5], the maximum transactions per second (tps) are calculated using:

$$tps_{on-chain} = \frac{\text{Gas}_{Limit}}{T_{xGas} * \text{Block}_{Time}} \tag{1}$$

where Gas_{Limit} is the block gas limit, Tx_{Gas} is the gas needed to compute the simplest transaction and $Block_{\text{Time}}$ is the blockchain block time. In our channel node server, all the above tps parameters can be configured under application properties (*application.yaml*). The result for on-chain transaction throughput, which we have observed, is presented in Fig. 7. The tps time across 10 transactions was measured for each of the two processes. The results of these measurements are presented as a cumulative transaction in Fig. 7 which will significantly be decreased by pushing new inter- block times. Therefore, for each inter-block times request, the gas price was increased along with the block gas limit. As a result, the throughput for the on-chain transaction was 180 s for six on-chain processing, respectively, and inter-block times were appended after 60 s (we incrementally increased the transaction fees to avoid network timeouts). Contrary

---

[18] Sample state channel transition https://rinkeby.etherscan.io/tx/0x6824.

[19] Network throughput information https://cloud.google.com/compute/docs/network-bandwidth.

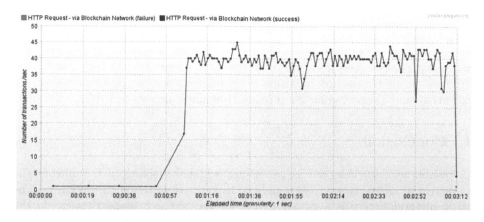

Fig. 7. On-chain transaction via Rinkeby network and gas price 99 GWEI

to on-chain transaction processing for the observed period throughput, the off-chain transaction can be achieved earlier than twice the median from on-chain computation, which is about 1.4 ms for 7 transactions. The observed result for off-chain transaction throughput is depicted in Fig. 8. In this context, transaction throughput refers to the number of requests processed by the server per time unit (seconds, minutes, or hours). The transaction processing times will be faster if the system generates a higher throughput and a more stable transaction success rate. In the off-chain computation that we simulated, we could achieve higher throughput by 1,395,877 in 120 s (around 96 tps). Additionally, all off-chain transfers were guaranteed to be received by other channel participants if the channel closed successfully (Fig. 7).

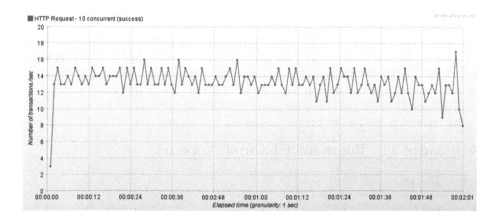

Fig. 8. Off-chain transaction throughput

The throughput report provided in this test is limited to serve the number of tps which can be achieved by off-chain computation. Hence the comprehensive benchmark report will be conducted in the next release. Furthermore, it is planned in the next test iteration to evaluate the overall system benchmark that will include the transaction inclusion time, inter-block time, and smart-contract execution time (in-particular *SCHToken* that implements the ERC-20 library).

4   Conclusion

L2 techniques have emerged as promising scalability solutions to improve the quality of blockchains services, mainly to increase transaction throughputs. The MLR methodology was adopted to design the research steps that guide the achievement of the research objectives and answer the related research questions. For example, the MLR process, awareness of problems and suggestions, was used to gain theoretical knowledge and understand the problem domain. The existing L2 scalability platforms were examined and compared to visualise their functionalities. Only a few of the L2 scalability proposals are currently viable. The main objective of this research is to review solutions that can help achieve scalability solutions in Ethereum blockchains. Based on this work, we planned to have RDF store technology in our solution, so a full-pledge feature from the RDF store engine was not yet implemented. The token network is the first functionality we can incorporate in our channel state application. In particular, we can allow channel participants to deposit their assets using the object and as long as there is another participant who will approve their token deposits. The second functionality is the channel-node application, a multi-user node server intended to facilitate users to open, transact on and settle state channels. Finally, our primary development goal was to demonstrate that our channel protocols, business processes, and underlying intelligent contracts work by the initial MLR. We work on the L2 techniques in the proposed research work to improve the scalability.

This extension of research area will provide instant payments without any intermediaries and the core engine that is backed up by nanopayments with the full-feature RDF store, as well as dimension of Machine-to-Machine Payment similar to μRaiden[20], and will analyze the impact of our proposed solution on the systems security and users privacy.

Appendix 1   Payment Channel Network

1.1   Go-Perun

A concept termed "virtual channels" was introduced by Go-Perun [13], which is used to resolve again the shortcoming mentioned previously. Here, for example, we assume that Bob and Alice are both linked through a blockchain channel

---

[20] https://raiden.network/micro.html.

provided by Ingrid, an intermediate payment hub. A direct linkage can be set up between Bob and Alice through a virtual channel using these ledger channels. Here, the involvement of intermediary Ingrid is not required in every payment. Owing to this, latency and costs are reduced, and privacy is protected. The process for the state channel, as detailed in [13], can be visualised in Fig. 9, which works on-chain only when the participants open and close the channel. Once the channel is established, the transaction will be moved outside the leading network, proceeding with an off-chain computation.

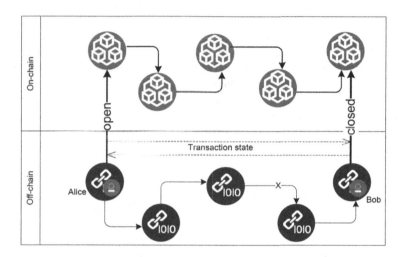

Fig. 9. On-chain and off-chain transactions.

The Go-Perun framework begins with an explanation of ledger payment channels. These channels are formed by interacting with the blockchain, where instant mutual payments are allowed between two parties. In an opening operation, a ledger payment channel β is formed between Bob and Alice, where xA coins and xB coins are deposited by Alice and Bob, respectively. As a result, the channel's balance is represented using [Alice 7! xA; Bob 7! xB]. It shows that Alice has xA and Bob has xB coins. Thus, the value of the channel is xA + xB. These coins will be kept blocked as long as the channel β is closed and cannot be used by the parties. Bob and Alice can modify the division of funds in the channel upon finishing the setup. Payments between Bob and Alice are made through the updated methodology.

Virtual channels are based on the concept of repeatedly applying the channel technique by creating a virtual payment channel, which is on top of the ledger channels. Assume two ledger channels among Bob, Alice, and Ingrid: βA between Alice and Ingrid and βB between Ingrid and Bob. In [13,14].

1.2   Raiden Network

The Ethereum community has approved the Raiden protocol as the first prominent off-chain computation for the L2 scalability solution. The Raiden Network
has published all the sources in this section in [30] as grey literature. Hence, in
this research, we have formalized the literature as white literature that academics
have also cited for a mature solution implemented in L2 scalability inside the
Ethereum network. An off-chain scaling solution, which enables token transfers
that are quick, low cost, and scalable, is termed the Raiden network. It works
with any token compliant with ERC-20 and supports the Ethereum blockchain.
The Ethereum blockchain implements the balance proof for channel participants
in the Raiden network. A Raiden balance proof binds like an on-chain transaction as only two involved parties can approach the tokens transferred to the
smart contract of the payment channel. In this agreement, several others are
shifted to the token contract as a pledge.

The Raiden network offers two core components: (i) when participants open
the channel, the **token network** is used to deposit ethers, and (ii) with considerably enough space between the sender and receiver, the way of payment
channels is **routing network**.

a. **Token Network**

To complete a token transfer, asset transfers employ numerous payment channels. They allow users to make transactions to other users with whom they
do not have a routing network. Alice uses the channels among herself, Bob,
Charlie, and Dave to transfer a payment to Dave, as shown in Fig. 10. A secret
key is needed to claim this amount for tokens until it stays locked as a pending transfer. Dave asks Alice for the secret key after he receives the transfer.
Dave receives the secret key from Alice and uses it for unlocking the pending
transfer. This secret key is then sent to Charlie, and he signs a balance proof.
Afterward, the secret key is sent back to Dave. Then, the process is reversed
until everyone in the mediated transfer channel knows about the secret key.

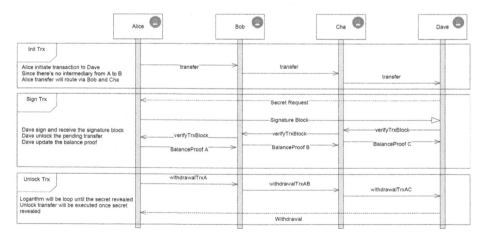

Fig. 10. Raiden token network transaction.

b. Payment Routing

A route of payment network with adequate capacity channels is required between the sender and receiver for a mediated transfer. Capacity refers to the sufficiency of tokens available in the payment channels for establishing pending transactions. In Fig. 11, we present payment routing in the following mechanisms:

- The capacity is adequate as Bob and Alice have five tokens.
- Payment is allowed to be continued because there are four tokens in the custody of Bob.
- This route is not viable as Charlie and Dave have two and eight tokens, respectively.
- A refund transfer is generated by Charlie, which Bob will claim.

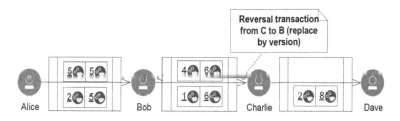

Fig. 11. Payment routing using the Raiden protocol.

A route of a linked network having a channel capacity of three in the mediating payment channel is required by Alice to pay three tokens to Dave. The complete view of the network is contained in the Raiden network protocol [31], and simplified flow is in Fig. 10. Assume that each user has deposited five tokens and performed several transactions. With the discovery of a path with sufficient capacity, the Raiden network will find a different path.

To make sure that the token liability will be paid by the involved participants in a smart contract, tokens must be locked up as a deposit for the complete lifecycle of the PCN. Until the final closing by any of both participants, this deposit guarantees that tokens may only be used to send to the channel partner and receive tokens from an adequate peer. This is how the double spending of tokens to other peers is prevented for both participants.

The involved parties are free to send certified checks back and forth after establishing a channel. However, every peer maintains a copy of the most recent check rather than monitoring all checks. The balance proof is a document signed by the sender digitally that details the final total of all Raiden transfers, which are delivered to a participant up to a specific point. A channel always keeps both of the participants involved in it, and they act as a bar tab of the channel. Various alternating credits are traded, altering the overall amount due between the channel members and perhaps re-balancing the payment route several times.

In our state channel application, we have a modified token network integrated into our system. The *TokenService* object will directly communicate with the state channel token (*SCHToken*) that we have deployed inside the Ethereum network. Figure 12 shows how the *TokenService* works with *SCHToken*, and the following process will be executed during the state channel life cycle.

- (1) First, the actor will initiate token funding. This process will be taken care of by the *TokenService* apart from the payment channel object. The remote function call will go to the *SCHToken* inside the blockchain network, and it will take the responsibility and approve the amount of ether that will be saved inside the token network (1).
- (2, 3, 4) Next, the response message will be saved into the Redis data store via the modified RDF4LED engine [21].
- (5, 6) After saving the transaction record into the data store, off-chain computations (e.g., transfer, withdrawal, and reversal) will directly be controlled between the payment channel and Redis data store.

During the simultaneous opening of the channels, every network participant will have more than one transaction. Due to this reason, the renewal of the deposits in the payment channel is expected in every transaction. Hence, *TokenService* makes it comfortable to reload new deposits into the existing open channel over the network of channels.

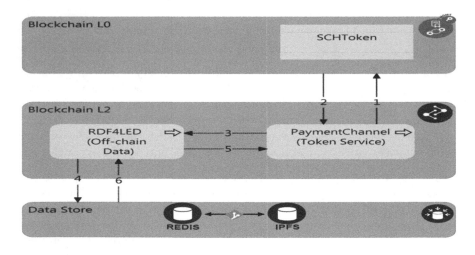

Fig. 12. Off-chain transaction service

Appendix 2   Watchtower Committee

Watchtower committee in Fig. 13 proceed as follow:

- (1) The *OutgoingChannelCoordinator* object will start the watchtower if the open state has been established,
- (1.1) If the channel already in open state, in this context the deposit has been approve by both participants, then

- (1.1.1) The *ChannelCoordinator* will assigned the watcher name to monitor the channel lifecycle,
- Each of watchtower committee object will be deputed to monitor specific channel process, hence, in the sequence flow it will return valid channel address properties.
- This monitoring service will continue until the channel is shutdown.

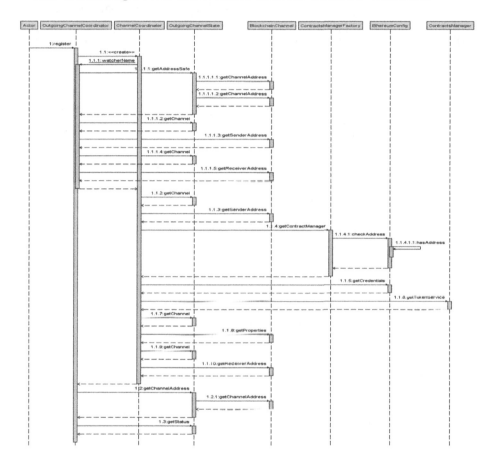

Fig. 13. Watchtower committee.

Appendix 3   Channel composability

One of a feature that we offer inside channel node application is to enable new participants join on the existing channel that has been established. This process in Fig. 14, refer as "Channel Composability" that will be execute as follow.

- (1) If there is new channel participant join the network, the *ChannelJoinImpl* object will start the process execution, by sending new member participant properties into the *ChannelPoolProperties*

- (1.1.1) property values will be check accordingly by *OutgoingChannelPolicy*, if the properties satisfied then in sequence (1.1.10) the new member will added in the existing *OutgoingChannelPoolManager*.
- (1.1.3) once the channel properties updated, the new network configuration will be add into *ChannelPoolProperties*. Those new configuration include the sub-sequence (1.3) *getSettleTimeOut* and (1.7) *getDeposit*.
- (1.10.2.2.λ) the process will loop if there is any new channel participant would like to join the existing network, in this case the looping process will break if the channel capacity is reach n < 10. The node server allow to override existing channel capacity via *application.yaml*.

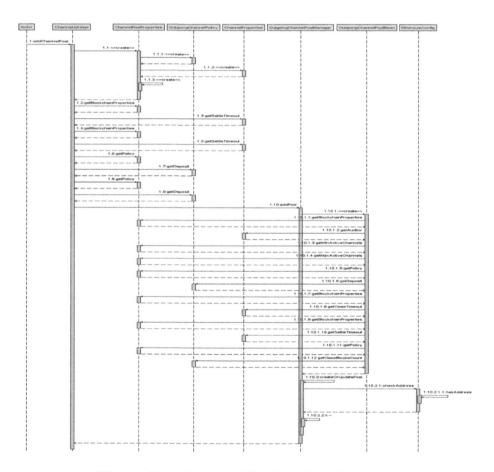

Fig. 14. Channel composability (join channel process).

Appendix 4   Close Channel Sequence Diagram

See Fig. 15.

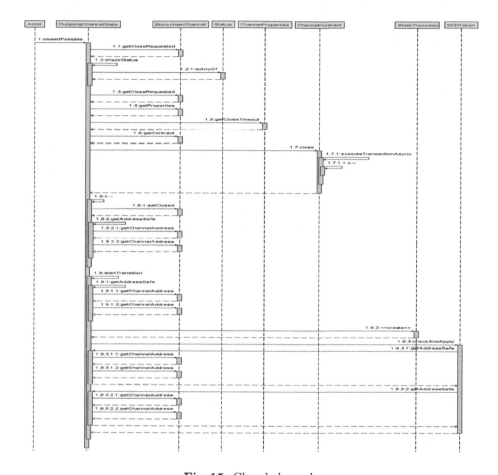

Fig. 15. Closed channel.

References

1. Abadi, D., Arden, O., Nawab, F., Shadmon, M.: Anylog: a grand unification of the internet of things. Cryptography (2018)
2. Adrian, L.: Gartner predicts 90 implementations will require replacement by 2021. https://www.gartner.com/en/newsroom/press-releases/2019-07-03-gartner-predicts-90-of-current-enterprise-blockchain
3. Breidenbach, L., et al.: Chainlink 2.0: next steps in the evolution of decentralized oracle networks (2021)
4. Buterin, V., Van de Sande, A.: Eip-55: mixed-case checksum address encodin (2016). https://eips.ethereum.org/EIPS/eip-55

5. Caccia, F.: On ethereum performance evaluation using PoA (2019). https://blog. coinfabrik.com/on-ethereum-performance-evaluation-using-poa/. Accessed 21 July 2021
6. Cannell, J.S., et al.: Orchid: a decentralized network routing market (2019)
7. del Castillo, M.: The 10 largest companies in the world are now exploring blockchain. https://www.forbes.com/sites/michaeldelcastillo/2018/06/06/the-10-largest-companies-exploring-blockchain/#fc1e3f61343d
8. Coleman, J., Horne, L., Xuanji, L.: Counterfactual: generalized state channels (2018). Accessed 4 Nov 2019
9. Connext: Crosschain liquidity network for ethereum. https://docs.connext. network/. Accessed 10 Apr 2020
10. Crain, T., Natoli, C., Gramoli, V.: Evaluating the red belly blockchain. arXiv preprint arXiv:1812.11747 (2018)
11. Decker, C., Wattenhofer, R.: A fast and scalable payment network with bitcoin duplex micropayment channels. In: Pelc, A., Schwarzmann, A.A. (eds.) SSS 2015. LNCS, vol. 9212, pp. 3–18. Springer, Cham (2015). https://doi.org/10.1007/978-3-319-21741-3_1
12. Dong, M., Liang, Q., Li, X., Liu, J.: Celer network: bring internet scale to every blockchain. arXiv preprint arXiv:1810.00037 (2018)
13. Dziembowski, S., Eckey, L., Faust, S., Malinowski, D.: Perun: virtual payment hubs over cryptocurrencies. In: 2019 IEEE Symposium on Security and Privacy (SP), pp. 106–123. IEEE (2019)
14. Dziembowski, S., Faust, S., Hostáková, K.: General state channel networks. In: Proceedings of the 2018 ACM SIGSAC Conference on Computer and Communications Security, pp. 949–966 (2018)
15. Galal, H., Elsheikh, M., Youssef, A.: An efficient micropayment channel on ethereum, pp. 211–218 (2019)
16. Grubenmann, T., Bernstein, A., Moor, D., Seuken, S.: Financing the web of data with delayed-answer auctions. In: Proceedings of the 2018 World Wide Web Conference, pp. 1033–1042 (2018)
17. Gudgeon, L., Moreno-Sanchez, P., Roos, S., McCorry, P., Gervais, A.: SoK off the chain transactions. IACR Cryptology ePrint Archive **2019**, 360 (2019)
18. Hafid, A., Hafid, A.S., Samih, M.: Scaling blockchains: a comprehensive survey. IEEE Access **8**, 125244–125262 (2020)
19. KChannel: Kchannels is a new payment channel platform for ethereum. https:// docs.kchannels.io/docs. Accessed 10 Apr 2020
20. Khalil, R., Zamyatin, A., Felley, G., Moreno-Sanchez, P., Gervais, A.: Commit-chains: secure, scalable off-chain payments. Cryptology ePrint Archive, p. 642 (2018)
21. Le-Tuan, A., Hingu, D., Hauswirth, M., Le-Phuoc, D.: Incorporating blockchain into RDF store at the lightweight edge devices. In: Acosta, M., Cudré-Mauroux, P., Maleshkova, M., Pellegrini, T., Sack, H., Sure-Vetter, Y. (eds.) SEMANTiCS 2019. LNCS, vol. 11702, pp. 369–375. Springer, Cham (2019). https://doi.org/10. 1007/978-3-030-33220-4_27
22. McCorry, P., Bakshi, S., Bentov, I., Meiklejohn, S., Miller, A.: Pisa: arbitration outsourcing for state channels. In: Proceedings of the 1st ACM Conference on Advances in Financial Technologies, pp. 16–30 (2019)
23. Miller, A., Bentov, I., Bakshi, S., Kumaresan, R., McCorry, P.: Sprites and state channels: payment networks that go faster than lightning. In: Goldberg, I., Moore, T. (eds.) FC 2019. LNCS, vol. 11598, pp. 508–526. Springer, Cham (2019). https:// doi.org/10.1007/978-3-030-32101-7_30

24. Network, P.: Blockchain thunder. https://github.com/blockchain/thunder/. Accessed 10 Aug 2020
25. Network, P.: Papyrus network. https://github.com/papyrusglobal/papyrus/. Accessed 10 Aug 2020
26. Panetta, K.: Trends emerge in the gartner hype cycle for emerging technologies (2018). Accessed 5, 6 June 2019
27. Paul, B., Erik, M.: Eip-1474: remote procedure call specification [draft] (2018). https://eips.ethereum.org/EIPS/eip-1474
28. Poon, J., Dryja, T.: The bitcoin lightning network: scalable off-chain instant payments (2016)
29. R3: R3 corda transactions per second (TPS). https://www.corda.net/blog/transactions-per-second-tps/
30. Raiden: Off-chain scaling solution, enabling near-instant, low-fee and scalable payments. https://raiden-network.readthedocs.io/. Accessed 10 Apr 2020
31. Swan, M.: Blockchain: Blueprint for a new economy, vol. 26. O'Reilly Media, Inc. (2018). Published 24 Jan 2015
32. Web3Labs: Develop on ethereum with the JVM. http://docs.web3j.io/latest/quickstart//. Accessed 10 Aug 2020
33. Xu, X., Weber, I., Staples, M.: Architecture for Blockchain Applications. Springer, Cham (2019). https://doi.org/10.1007/978-3-030-03035-3

A State-of-the-Art Blockchain Approach to the ETSI Implementation for Long-Term Preservation Solutions

Sorin Țeican[1](✉) and Andreea-Elena Drăgnoiu[2](✉)

[1] certSIGN SA, Bucharest, Romania
`sorin.teican@certsign.ro`
[2] Department of Computer Science, University of Bucharest, Bucharest, Romania
`andreea-elena.panait@drd.unibuc.ro`

Abstract. Lately, blockchain technology has been used in various use case scenarios. Our research focuses on whether long-term preservation of digital signatures/seals (for which we introduce the abbreviation LTP-DS) solutions could benefit from using this technology. In this paper, we give an outline on the stateof-the-art blockchain-based LTP-DS-related solutions, while considering the ETSI standards for LTP-DS, and offer directions on how such systems could be implemented.

Keywords: Long-term preservation · Blockchain · Notarization

1 Introduction

The European Commission plans to define a pan-European regulatory sandbox for use cases such as data portability, B2B data spaces, smart contracts, and digital identity (Self-Sovereign Identity), we address what parts of the PKI ecosystem implemented by qualified LTP-DS (long-term preservation of digital signatures) systems can be replaced by blockchain mechanisms. Most Qualified Trusted Service Providers have conventional PKIs with digital certificates issued by certification authorities. A blockchain component has to offer clear advantages, both technical and from the business point of view, to replace or to be added in a qualified setup. An LTP-DS would have to inherit suitability with blockchain mechanisms due to the operations involved essentially providing digital transactions recording and easily (publicly) accessible proof of preservation over time to clients.

The remainder of our paper is structured as follows: Sect. 2 defines the background and related academic work, Sect. 3 describes the ETSI standard for an LTP-DS system, Sect. 4 defines blockchain basic knowledge and blockchain notarization, Sect. 5 gives an overview of the state-of-the-art blockchain LTP-DS-related solutions, Sect. 6 presents characteristics of how LTP-DS blockchain systems should be implemented, propose an SSI implementation, and finally, we conclude.

© ICST Institute for Computer Sciences, Social Informatics and Telecommunications Engineering 2022
Published by Springer Nature Switzerland AG 2022. All Rights Reserved
S. Paiva et al. (Eds.): SmartCity360° 2021, LNICST 442, pp. 550–562, 2022.
https://doi.org/10.1007/978-3-031-06371-8_35

2 Background and Related Work

To our knowledge, most of the blockchain research done in the field of long-term preservation omits the qualified digital signatures/seals which require the availability of information needed to check the validation status of the digital signature/seal that would not be publicly available until the end of the preservation period.

Otto et al. provides an overview of the corresponding standards for long-term preservation of qualified electronic signatures, which are currently developed within ETSI Technical Committee (TC) Electronic Signatures and Infrastructures (ESI), and outline the design of a corresponding reference implementation [1].

Bralić et al. investigate the challenges of the expiration of digital signatures in the context of digital archiving by identifying requirements for the long-term preservation of digitally signed records and comparing them with the existing approaches. The TrustChain 2.0 model is based on previous research conducted as part of the Inter-PARES Trust project. It builds on TrustChain 1.0 by including digital signature certificate chain validity information in a blockchain thus avoiding the issues concerning records confidentiality and privacy information disclosure [2].

Hyla and Pejaś propose a scheme that would allow maintaining signature validity without the necessity to use timestamps from trusted third parties is proposed. The Round-based Blockchain Time-stamping Scheme is proposed to be scalable, i.e., it requires embedding a constant number of bytes into a blockchain independent from several input documents. The scheme allows proving that a document existed not only before a certain date but after a certain date as well. Moreover, the purpose of the scheme is to meet non-repudiation requirements for digitally signed documents. The scheme allows verifying signature validity using a chain model and a modified shell model [3].

Thompson explores whether blockchain technology is a suitable platform for the preservation of digital signatures and public/private key pairs. This paper suggests that the blockchain's hash functions offer a better strategy for signature preservation than digital certificates [4].

3 Standards for Long-Term Preservation of Digital Signatures

3.1 ETSI

ETSI technical specifications [5, 6] define long-term preservation for qualified electronic signatures as the extension of the validity status of a digital signature over long periods and/or of provision of proofs of the existence of data over time, despite obsolescence of cryptographic technology such as crypto algorithms, key sizes or hash functions, key compromises or of the loss of the ability to check the validity status of public-key certificates. [5] identifies three main security risks involved with preserving qualified cryptographic material for long periods:

Risks Based on Collision Attacks of One-Way Hash Functions used within a Digital Signature. In case the preservation service has access to the signed data it can compute a new digital signature or time assertion based on a new hash value of the signed data, cal-culated with a suitable hash algorithm and suitable parameters, to guarantee the integrity and proof of the existence of the signed data before the original hash algorithm becomes weak. In case the preservation submitter only submitted the hash of the digitally signed data to the preservation service, e.g., because it is very large or due to privacy reasons, the preservation service cannot recompute on its own a new hash of the signed data. The client may submit two hash values computed by two different hash algorithms, based on different mathematical principles, to reduce the risk of possible collision attacks. In any case, the preservation service cannot know if the hash value(s) corresponds to the signed data, and can treat them only as arbitrary data related to the signature.

Risks Based on the Digital Signature Algorithm and Key Length. It might be pos-sible that at some moment in time it cannot be guaranteed anymore that the private key by which a specific signature was created, is still private and secret. This problem can be avoided if the digital signature including the certificate is covered by a time asser-tion that proves that it already existed before a specific time from which such an attack became possible. However, some time assertions rely upon mechanisms that will be subject to the same problems. To counter this problem, time assertions are protected by obtaining a new time-stamp that covers the original data, its time-stamps, and the corresponding validation data before the compromise of mechanisms used to generate the time assertions;

Risks Based on the Revocation of a Signing Key. To be able to trust that a digital signa-ture was created by the signer, the certificate needs to be checked that it was not revoked at the signing moment or before. This can be done by using revocation information, like certificate revocation lists (CRLs) or online certificate status protocol (OCSP) responses of the certificate. The preservation service captures and protects revocation information in the preservation evidence, using proof of existence over it, to avoid problems because revocation information is not available anymore.

There are three main variants for a preservation service whether it uses long-term storage, temporary storage, or no storage. When it uses storage, the preservation service may use internal or external storage under its control for preservation. A preservation service can pursue different preservation goals, which influences the supported opera-tional tasks. [6] specifies the following three goals which may be used separately or in combination: *preservation of general data* provides proof of existence over long periods of the submission data object submitted to the preservation service, *preservation of dig-ital signatures* extends over time the ability to validate a digital signature, to maintain its validity status and to get a proof of the existence of the associated signed data, and *aug-mentation* which indicates that the preservation service supports the augmentation of submitted preservation evidence.

According to [6], a preservation service may support different preservation schemes. A preservation scheme supports at least one preservation goal and is operating in exactly one storage model. A qualified preservation service for qualified electronic signa-tures may only be provided by a qualified trust service provider. The preservation service shall preserve all information needed to check the qualification status of the electronic signature or seal that would not be publicly available until the end of the preservation period. Time-stamps used within the preservation evidence should be provided by a qualified TSA (Time Stamping Authority).

As stated in the EIDAS Trusted Service Provider (TSP)-Map [7], 15 countries across the European Union have implemented qualified LTP-DS systems, with the most notable countries by the number of implementations being Hungary, Spain, and Slovakia each with 3 qualified LTP-DS systems.

3.2 ISO

ISO 14641. Describes a reference framework for digital archiving of digital documents (also ones originating from physical) in a manner that covers aspects such as long-term preservation, integrity, ease of access, and use. Storage options considered being physical/logical WORM (write once read many) and rewritable. In the case of digital documents kept on rewritable storage the specification details integrity maintenance procedures such as encryption-like techniques, in particular with checksum calculation or hash function, date and time stamp, or digital signatures [8].

ISO 14721 OAIS. Open Archival Information Systems defines the OAIS model for preserving archival information on a channel accessible to the public. In the OAIS model, there are four types of Preservation Description information: prove-nance, context, reference, and fixity [9, 10]. The OAIS reference model describes concepts, responsibilities, detailed models, preservation perspectives, and archive interoperability. OAIS It takes into account the impacts of changing technologies, including support for new media and data formats, or with a changing user community, stating that the long-term may extend indefinitely. Standards developers are expected to use this model as a basis for further standardization.

ISO 16363. Provides an overview of audit and certification criteria for organizational infrastructure, digital object management, and infrastructure and security risks [11]. [12] provides general requirements for storage with preservation of evidence including legal framework conditions, a middle-ware architecture composed of the following components: ArchiSafe, ArchiSig, Upload & Download module, and a cryptographic module. To validate the implementation conformity and interoperability tests are specified for the architecture.

4 Blockchain and LTP-DS-Related Systems

4.1 Key Blockchain Concepts

A blockchain peer-to-peer network (formed of a "chain of blocks") allows creating a decentralized and distributed environment, where transaction data is cryptographically validated and recorded on a publicly accessible ledger, with no third party in control of the network.

Blockchain blocks are interconnected using hash functions and those generated hash values will be preserved on the blockchain as long as the network continues to operate.

In the blockchain environment, hash values are used to authenticate block data as well as transaction data, and can be stored separately from the application that generated the hash values [13]. Hash values can be grouped to form a single hash, called a root hash, and the structure is called a Merkel tree.

A blockchain network is formed of nodes and recording new information on the blockchain implies that the nodes reach a consensus. The consensus mechanism is based on cryptogr validation methods and ensures the right sequence of blockchain transactions. There are various consensus algorithms among them we mention Proof of Work, Proof of Stake, Proof of Authority, etc. Blockchains make use of signature schemes to sign (authenticate) the transactions and the most common ones are the Elliptic Curve Digital Signature Algorithm (ECDSA) and the Schnorr signatures. Another key concept is that the blocks are timestamped before being recorded in the ledger and do not require intermediaries such as Time Stamping Authoritaphicies (TSA).

4.2   Blockchain Technology and Notarization Standards

Blockchain can be used for document management processes: for version tracking of documents, tracing, change verification, document content, and structure. Each time a new document is created, it can be registered on the blockchain, together with a block timestamp to date the document in time. In this way, the initial document version becomes clear, as well as future document versions, which can be traced back and verified accordingly, if desired. Moreover, document registration on the blockchain represents proof that it was not tampered with, useful when sending document evidence to other parties. The hash values, which are independent of the file format and are used in the blockchain technology allows this technology to be compliant with the preservation standard ISO 18492:2005 (a guide on long-term preservation of electronic document-based information).

The ISO 14721 OAIS can be applied to the blockchain technology. Any document change results in a new document hash value, with a corresponding identifier, so that the digital transitions maintain the history of the document provenance. Blockchain technology is not interested in the context of document creation. The hash value identifies (references) the document version at a certain time, whereas the fixity information for blockchain concerns its immutability property.

For the management and control of records and the associated metadata, the set of rules is defined by ISO 15489-1:2016 standard. The fact that the document is separated from the metadata (usually the document remains on the archive's database, whereas its metadata is recorded on the blockchain platform) enables the blockchain technology to easily comply with this standard, by using metadata formats that are not conditioned by a document type.

Other standards, such as RFC 3161 and ANSI X9.95, describe how digital notaries and trusted third parties (known as TTP) should govern timestamps. While RFC 3161 describes the timestamp request and response format [14], the ANSI X9.95 standard is more focused on the security of financial transactions [15]. The timestamping service, defined in RFC 3161 as a proof mechanism for demonstrating the existence of data at a particular time, can be mapped with the blockchain technology.

5   Comparison Between LTP-DS Blockchain-Relat Solutions

In this section, we introduce several solutions that use blockchain technology in imimplementingedTP-DS related systems. We distinguish between qualified and non-qualified LTP-DS-related solutions. We consider a qualified solution one that makes use of a certified authority (an entity that issues digital certificates) in its implementation. We note that none of them comply with the ETSI standard for LTP-DS systems and that they are mainly notarization solutions. To the best of our knowledge, at the moment, we are not aware of ETSI compliant LTP-DS qualified blockchain solutions. For our research, we considered all the blockchain solutions that were available or mentioned in the literature, at the moment of writing. For this paper, we were only interested in presenting the qualified solutions in more detail. In Table 1, we summarize the gathered information for the qualified solutions into the following properties: the used blockchain platform, timestamp type, type of solution (private or public subscriptions), type of service offered (web or mobile applications), usage of certified authority, and available documentation.

The qualified blockchain LTP-DS-related solutions we found use either their blockchain solution (Guardtime KSI solution [16]), the Bitcoin platform (Enigio [17] solution), or multiple blockchain platforms (Proofstack [18] and Bernstein [19] solutions). All qualified solutions offer private subscription plans, as well as publicly available solution demos, and all of them are accessible via web applications. We remark that the Proofstack solution seems to offer more features than the rest of the solutions from Table 1.

Guardtime KSI [16] uses Keyless Signature Infrastructure (KSI) that allows the verification to be based only on the security of the used hash functions and the public ledger. This permissioned blockchain solution is a "mirror" system, i.e., a solution where the blockchain is used as a repository for digital fingerprints, which are the hash values used, whereas the original records could be in a digital or paper form. It can be considered that Guardtime differs from other blockchain providers by the industrial capacity of their solution. Moreover, Guardtime benefits from the NIST Crypto Algorithm Validation Program, Common Criteria, and NIAP Accreditation, as well as participation in cybersecurity programs.

The Enigio [17] solution, called Enigio time:stamp, uses a timestamp part and a blockchain one. The solution is compliant with the ISO/IEC 18014-3 principles, which are augmented with the company's patents. The company created their blockchain where they aggregate references to other blockchains, such as Bitcoin, and use their time:beat patent, for introducing real references into their blockchain. By using a blockchain aggregator as a service, the solution allows access to an easy-to-use API, which abstracts the processes. Among advantages, Enigio claims that their solution enables easy access and a lower cost, strong traceability, continuous monitoring, speed, and better model performance (compared to proof of work or mining-based models).

Proofstack [18], which was formally known as Copyrobo, claims to be the world's online notary and is the first blockchain startup that uses both qualified authorities and blockchain protocols in a single platform, to create legal global and local proofs via multiple platforms. Their website provides the user with the necessary steps to verify proof, which is called Proof.Link. The Proof.Link unique identifier allows securing, organizing, and distribution of proofs. The company offers different timestamping methods and file options: proof options (blockchain, qualified authority), integration and device options (computer, mobile, Google Drive), backup (email, Google Drive, FTP), and maximum file size.

Bernstein [19] offers a web application in which users can create a digital track of their processes, by using the Bitcoin platform, as well as timestamping national authorities. For using the solution, the user should only upload the chosen document in the application and Bernstein will create a blockchain transaction that contains the cryptographic fingerprint of the documents that were uploaded based on IP, together with the document proof. The digital assets can be secured both with Bitcoin certificates, as well as digital timestamps from trusted timestamping authorities from the EU and China. The registration protocol is completely blockchain agnostic and aalthoughthe solution is implemented on the Bitcoin platform, it can be ported on any type of private or public blockchain.

Table 1. LLTP-DS-relatedblockchain solutions.

Name	Blockchain platform	Timestamp type	Type of solution	Type of service offered	Usage of certified authority	Resources
Guardtime KSI [16]	KSI Blockchain	Qualified Timestamp, eIDAS compliant	Private plan Public demo solution	KSI command-line tool Web app	Yes	GitHub and website
Enigio [17]	Bitcoin	eIDAS compliant	Private plan Public demo solution	Web app	Yes	Website
Proofstack [18]	Bitcoin, Ethereum, Litecoin, EOS, NEO, Stellar	Qualified Timestamp	Free trial Enterprise version	Web app Android iOS	Yes, multiple	Website
Bernstein [19]	Bitcoin, Agnostic Blockchain protocol	Qualified Timestamp	Free plan Subscriptions Payment on using	Web app	Yes, qualified national authority	Website

Similarly, in our research, we have also analyzed the non-qualified solutions. The majority of the solutions use the Bitcoin blockchain for timestamping (OriginStamp [20], NotBot [21], Blocksign [22], Bitcoin.com Notary [23], The Stampd [24], Stampery.com [25], Proof of Existence [26], ProveBit [27], Bitnotar [28]). Only Acronis Notary [29] and CTIE Solution – NotarChain [30] use the Ethereum blockchain. The solutions are either open-source (NotarChain, Proof of Existence, ProveBit, Bitnotar), or available online for usage (NotBot, Bitcoin.com Notary, The Stampd). For the solutions which are not open-source, there are different subscription plans from which the user can choose. The documentation for the solutions is either on Github (Proof of Existence, ProveBit, Bitnotar) or the company website (The Stampd, Stampery.com, Bitcoin.com Notary, OriginStamp, Acronis Notary). The solutions provided are mainly web applications, but some are only Github resources (Proof of Existence, ProveBit, Bitnotar).

As a general remark, we note that there are more non-qualified than qualified LTP-DS-related blockchain solutions available and that the qualified ones seem to be more mature and used in practice by users. There are other systems for the long-term preservation of digitally signed documents that use blockchain technology, such as the ones that are proposed in [1, 31].

6 Discussion

Digital archives can store data either centralized or in a distributed manner. For centralized data storage, data recovery can be difficult at times, but if there are disturbances, there are chances of solving them. On the other hand, in a distributed system, the archive is spread among different geographical locations, and any disturbance in one location, will not affect the other locations.

6.1 LTP-DS Properties that Apply in Blockchain Technology

According to [32], to be able to deliver trustworthy records, blockchain-based systems aiming at long-term preservation should satisfy some properties: the records should be accurate, reliable, and authentic. Accuracy concerns the truth-value of the record's content. To be able to achieve reliability, records should have three characteristics: completeness at the point of creation, consistency with formal rules of creation, and impartiality [32]. Last, but not least, a record is considered authentic, if its origin is genuine if it is authorized, or entitled to acceptance. The digital signatures could serve as a test for authenticity because it does not only identify the creator but also provides a connection between the record and the creator. Moreover, to establish the authenticity of the record, the record should satisfy the identity and integrity properties.

Concerning the accuracy and reliability properties, it is possible that unauthorized, erroneous, or faulty information that has entered into the transactional operational system, to be recorded on the blockchain. For information that is recorded automatically using smart contract code, reliability relies on the developed code of the smart contract creators. Due to interoperability uncertainty between various components of a decentralized system, there is a higher possibility that the above-mentioned properties would be rather negatively influenced, than positively [32]. Accuracy in block-chain can also be affected by the inconsistencies between nodes, or from the different components of the decentralized system. Moreover, network timestamp is important to be accurate, and possible network time attacks should be mitigated. Another inconsistency in the transactional record flow could result from deficient communication among the various system components. Once inaccuracies are introduced in the blockchain system, there should be means of alleviating them. For authenticity purposes, mechanisms to connect the blockchain hashed records with their context should be implemented with care (e.g., link records with unique IDs, use a meta-document with multiple document hashes, use of transaction metadata, use ontologies, etc.).

Thus, when adopting blockchain technology for long-term preservation (and in our case, for notarization), one should be aware of the possible problems that could arise from the previously mentioned properties, i.e., accuracy, reliability, authenticity, integrity Furthermore, it is important to state other notarization problems to be considered, namely persistence, uniqueness, undemocratic operation, anonymity, use of resources, and legal certainty [33].

When using blockchain technology for the long-term preservation of digital signatures/seals, one should carefully balance the pros and cons of using such technology. On one hand, some consider that blockchain technology should not be considered as a panacea for all records management problems [33]. On the other, there are advantages of using blockchain timestamping over TSA timestamping [34]: long-term preservation could be achieved without the costs of maintaining TSA-issued certificates and signature verification of the document signature and the public key is more convenient because the digital signature is not guarded on a central server.

6.2   Designing a Blockchain-Based LTP-DS System

Regulated implementations assure users that their data is acted upon and secured according to strict procedures validated by entities that conform to open and legally defined specifications. Such specifications and procedures currently apply only to PKI implementations of an LTP-DS system. Qualified LTP-DS (QLTP-DS) systems require that components such as signing services, signature validation services, and timestamping services should also be qualified. One place where these services can be integrated into a blockchain implementation is the consensus algorithm. Mining nodes can interface with qualified services for constructing preservation data, such as signing the preservation data object that contains validity reports of user signatures and timestamps attesting that the data existed at a certain point in time.

Irrespective of the nature of the LTP-DS system in question, whether qualified or not, blockchain technology must demonstrate irrefutable advantages over the actual PKI implementation. A key aspect such as the identity of the signatory, which must be vouched for by an entity trusted by the clients that consume preservation evidence seems to take away from the decentralized characteristic of blockchain.

Consensus algorithms can be classified based on the reward mechanism that participating nodes receive, resulting in two classes of consensus, incentivized and non-incentivized. Incentivized consensus algorithms are exclusively used in public blockchain systems to motivate participating nodes to behave accordingly. In the absence of a reward mechanism, the nodes participating in a non-incentivized consensus algorithm are considered trusted and only authorized nodes can help in the block creation process. In [35], the authors define four major groups of properties for consensus algorithms: structural, block & reward, security, and performance. Based on these classifications, properties, and the architecture required to implement an LTP-DS system, non-incentivized consensus algorithms seem to be the most appropriate to be used in LTP-DS systems.

Given the architecture components required by an LTP-DS system (Signing Application, Signature Validation Application, and Time-Stamping Authorities), we consider analyzing the possibility of using the YAC consensus algorithm which is provided by the Hyperledger IROHA [36] open-source blockchain framework because of the mapping of the aforementioned components to the authorized nodes (client, ordering service, peer). An important part that must be considered if the chosen block-chain implementation must store the preservation evidence records inside the block structure, is that said framework must allow custom block structure.

Given that an LTP-DS system should mitigate cryptographic obsolescence, we note that the hash algorithms used for linking blocks that constitute the blockchain should be updated during the preservation duration. If hash values for obsolete algorithms can be reproduced from any input, it remains an open question whether linking the newest block to the chain that used such algorithms with a secure one can maintain the immutability of the previous records.

Maintaining validity status by storing data preservation objects which contain PKI validation responses implies additional storage logic to be implemented by the QLTP-DS system, or the client in case the QLTP-DS system does not support storage. This aspect can be mitigated by implementing the LTP-DS procedure using Self-Sovereign Identity (SSI) if the LTP-DS system can be registered as a service provider using an SSI ecosystem. This is because an SSI architecture can remove the need for storing validation material due to the way user identity claims are stored on a blockchain. If the claims become cryptographically compromised, they will be updated by the SSI provider. The storage transaction containing the data to be preserved can be append-ed on the SSI blockchain, effectively linking the data to the user identity (Fig. 1).

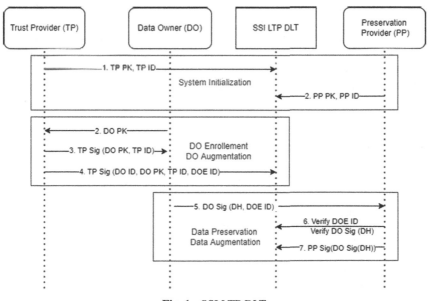

Fig. 1. SSI LTP DLT.

In the context of the proposed permissioned blockchain SSI scheme for long-term preservation which removes the need for augmentation data of the X.509 certificate that contains the public key linked to the key that was used to compute the digital signature, the entity that requires evidence of data ownership may obtain and validate it by querying the distributed ledger for preservation transactions that are executed by long-term preservation service providers that implement cryptographic augmentation logic and requests the owner pprovidea hash of data computed using algorithms accepted as secure.

To obtain verifiable credentials that prove his identity stored on a personal digital wallet, the data owner must first register with an SSI trust provider. After registration, the trusted provider logs the generated SSI credential on the permissioned blockchain using an identifier, the verifiable credential is then sent to the user which stores it in his digital wallet. The process of enrolment between the SSI trusted provider and the user may require the user to generate an RSA, or elliptic curve key pair protected by his digital wallet, sharing the public key through authenticated and secure channels, allowing the trust provider to link it to his identity.

Another aspect of the blockchain SSI implementation requires the trust and service providers to register the cryptographic material (RSA public key, or elliptic curve public key) proving their identity in the genesis blocks. If the cryptographic material becomes obsolete due to new computation techniques or attack vectors, they can update their identities with the SSI blockchain consortium administrators.

Revocation information is one of the most important augmentation data that the qualified preservation implementation used to prove link-ability between cryptographic material and user identity, the new SSI blockchain implementation will allow the trust and preservation providers to invalidate verifiable credentials that prove identity and data ownership in the augmentation process by appending revocation transactions to the SSI blockchain. The data ownership augmentation process requires the preservation provider to notify the user in case of cryptographic material obsolescence, or periodic update of cryptographic algorithms used to compute data hash. In case of augmenting identity cryptographic material, the trust providers can periodically, or in case of urgency (attack vectors, or computational advances) append revocation transactions on the SSI blockchain.

7   Conclusion

In conclusion, this paper aims at presenting state-of-the-art LTP-DS-related blockchain solutions, focusing on the qualified ones. We give directions on how LTP-DS (qualified) blockchain solutions could be implemented, like integration of qualified services into the blockchain consensus algorithm, possibility of using a self-sovereign identity ecosystem. As future work, we plan to continue this research and build such an architecture.

Acknowledgments. This research was financed by European Regional Development Fund, Competitiveness Operational Program 2014–2020 under the project LTPS (code SMIS 2014+: 123423).

References

1. Otto, F., Wich, T., Hühnlein, T., Prechtl, M., Hühnlein, D.: Towards a standardised preservation service for qualified electronic signatures and qualified electronic seals, Open Identity Summit 2019 (2019)
2. Bralić, V., Stančić, H., Stengård, M.: A blockchain approach to digital archiving: digital signature certification chain preservation, Records Management Journal (2020)
3. Hyla, T., Pejaś, J.: Long-term verification of signatures based on a blockchain. Comput. Electr. Eng. **81**, 106523 (2020)
4. Thompson, S.: The preservation of digital signatures on the blockchain, the University of British Columbia iSchool Student J. **3** (2017)
5. ETSI TS 119 511: Electronic Signatures and Infrastructures (ESI); Policy and security requirements for trust service providers providing long-term preservation of digital signatures or unsigned data using signature techniques (2018)
6. ETSI TS 119 512: Electronic Signatures and Infrastructures (ESI); Protocols for trust service providers providing long-term data preservation services (2018)
7. eIDAS TSP map, Accessed 3 June 2021
8. ISO 14641: Electronic document management - Design and operation of an information system for the preservation of electronic documents - Specifications (2018)
9. ISO 14721: Space data and information transfer systems - Open archival information system (OAIS) - Reference model (2012)
10. OCLC/RLG Working Group: Preservation metadata and the OAIS Information Model: A metadata framework to support the preservation of digital objects, http://www.oclc.org/content/dam/research/activities/pmwg/pm_framework.pdf Accessed 3 June 2021
11. ISO 16363: Space data and information transfer systems - Audit and certification of trustworthy digital repositories (2012)
12. BSI TR-ESOR-03125: Preservation of Evidence of Cryptographically Signed Documents (2019)
13. Pedro, F.: Understanding Bitcoin: Cryptography, Engineering and EConomics. John Wiley & Sons Ltd, Chichester (2015)
14. RFC 3161: Internet X.509 Public Key Infrastructure Time-Stamp Protocol (TSP). https://doi.org/10.17487/RFC3161. Accessed 3 June 2021
15. ANSI X9.95-2012: Trusted Time Stamp Management and Security, https://www.sec.gov/rules/proposed/s72703/iac120105.pdf Accessed 3 June 2021
16. Guardtime: KSI Blockchain Timestamping, https://guardtime.com/timestamping Accessed 3 June 2021
17. Enigio, time:beat Proving Data Integrity, https://www.enigio.com/timebeat Accessed 3 June 2021
18. Proofstack, Legal Proof, https://proofstack.io Accessed 3 June 2021
19. Bernstein Technologies GmbH: Own what you make, https://www.bernstein.io Accessed 3 June 2021
20. OriginStamp AG: https://originstamp.com Accessed 3 June 2021
21. e-Genèse France, NotBot, https://notbot.me Accessed 3 June 2021
22. Blocksign, https://blocksign.com Accessed 3 June 2021
23. Saint Bitts LLC Bitcoin.com, https://notary.bitcoin.com Accessed 3 June 2021
24. Stampd, https://stampd.io Accessed 3 June 2021
25. Stampery, https://stampery.com Accessed 3 June 2021
26. Proof of Existence, https://proofofexistence.com Accessed 3 June 2021
27. ProveBit Github Contributors, ProveBit, https://github.com/thereal1024/ProveBit Accessed 3 June 2021

28. Bitnotar, https://github.com/bitcoinaustria/bitnotar Accessed 3 June 2021
29. Acronis International GmbH, Acronis Technology Notary, https://www.acronis.com/en-us/technology/blockchain-notary Accessed 3 June 2021
30. Pinto, A., Silva, J.: Revisiting Blockhain use in notary services: an european perspective. In: Prieto, J., Pinto, A., Das, A.K., Ferretti, S. (eds.) BLOCKCHAIN 2020. AISC, vol. 1238, pp. 101–110. Springer, Cham (2020). https://doi.org/10.1007/978-3-030-52535-4_11
31. Collomosse, J., et al.: Archangel: trusted archives of digital public documents. arXiv preprint arXiv:1804.08342 (2018)
32. Lemieux, V.L.: Blockchain and Distributed Ledgers as Trusted Recordkeeping Systems An Archival Theoretic Evaluation Framework (2018)
33. Van Garderen, P.: Decentralized Autonomous Collections, Medium On Archivy, https://medium.com/on-archivy/decentralized-autonomous-collections-ff256267cbd6 Accessed 26 Apr 2021
34. Amati, F.: Using the blockchain as a digital signature scheme, Medium Signatura, https://blog.signatura.co/using-the-blockchain-as-a-digital-signature-scheme-f584278ae826 Accessed 26 Apr 2021
35. Sadek V., Mohammad J.M.C., Mohammed A.H., Alan W.C.: Blockchain Consensus Algorithms: A Survey, ResearchGate (2020)
36. The Linux Foundation: Hyperledger IROHA, https://www.hyperledger.org/use/iroha, Accessed 3 June 2021

A Review of Crime Scene Investigations Through Augmented Reality

Meshal Albeedan[1], Hoshang Kolivand[1](✉), and Edmond S. L. Ho[2]

[1] Department of Computer Science, Faculty of Engineering and Technology, Liverpool John Moores University (LJMU), Liverpool L3 3AF, UK
H.Kolivand@ljmu.ac.uk
[2] Computer and Information Sciences, Northumbria University, Newcastle upon Tyne, UK

Abstract. This paper discussed the background of crime scene investigations and reviewed a novel Augmented Reality Learning Environment for using HoloLens in crime scene investigation. It clarified the concepts of augmented reality (AR), and virtual reality (VR). With the advancement of technology, forensic investigation is compelled to adapt to corresponding changes and use them to its benefit. In addition, it reviews the extant literature on the use of HoloLens in crime scene investigation. Through this review, the research questions are being formulated for future perspectives of crime scene investigations through Augmented Reality.

Keywords: Crime scene · Forensics · Augmented Reality

1 Introduction

This paper is focused on investigating a novel Augmented Reality Learning Environment for the utilization of HoloLens to aid in crime scene investigation. Traditional forensic investigation commonly involves a considerable amount of time at the scene. However, inadequate time or resources, particularly limitation of time and geographical variations of colleagues, are often the case (Robey et al. 2000). The use of modern techniques to store, visualize, and manipulate evidence is necessary for the efficient utilization of investigative resources. This is specifically true since forensic investigation units tend to be highly-technological to enable small teams to obtain and record various types of data quickly. Considering this need to analyse and classify a range of data, virtual environment (VE) technology provides a user interface (Robey et al. 2000).

At present, law enforcement has broadly developed in solving crimes through the adoption of forensic techniques and processes. Currently, crimes can be solved by thoroughly examining the crime scene and analysing forensic evidence. Forensic scientists contribute largely not only to criminal investigation and prosecution but also to civil litigations, disasters, and global crimes (Inman and Rudin 2001). The success of crime scene investigation is based on a system of teamwork, investigative tools like GPS positioning, video imaging, mobile phones, data mining, and the like. Crime scene investigations have successfully utilised a tri-dimensional (3D) representation of objects. It is also

S. Paiva et al. (Eds.): SmartCity360° 2021, LNICST 442, pp. 563–582, 2022.
https://doi.org/10.1007/978-3-031-06371-8_36

based on the capabilities to appropriately process a crime scene through the recognition, collection, and preservation of all significant physical evidence defined as any evidence that can give useful information for crime investigation (Gaensslen et al. 2008; Lee and Pagliaro 2013). If such physical evidence is not recognized, its forensic value might be lost forever. Despite the availability of current forensic technologies, the efficient use of physical evidence in solving a crime is only limited to the knowledge and integrity of the forensic personnel and the unbiased legal system supporting those functions. The successful outcome of the case relies on the physical evidence obtained from the crime scene. Yet, since some cases lack physical evidence, they remain unsolved. Conversely, some innocent individuals are made to answer for the crime which they did not commit because of witness misidentification or misused forensic evidence (Gianelli 2007; Lee and Pagliaro 2013).

2   The Features of Augmented/Mixed Reality

As this study deals with the use of HoloLens in crime scene investigation, reviewing some works that deal with its use would be of worthy attention. Mixed reality (MR) remote guidance, which combines reality with augmented reality, virtual reality, and augmented virtuality, can help in transitioning between these stages. Reality being enhanced with artificial images enables an easier performance of tasks, such as when individuals in different locations collaborate with each other. Assembly tasks can be carried out remotely, even if the people involved do not meet each other face-to-face (Ladwig and Geiger 2018). Similarly, Teo et al. (2019) described MR as a practical solution that can allow people to collaborate remotely through nonverbal communication. Their study focused on the integration of different forms of MR remote collaboration approaches, allowing a new assortment of remote collaboration to expand MR's features and user experience. Teo et al. presented a MR system that utilised 360 panorama images within 3D restructured scenes. A new technique was also introduced to interact with numerous 360 panorama fields within such restructured scenes. Through this, a remote user is able to switch between numerous 360 scenes, such as live, past, present, and so on, promoting improved understanding of space and interactivity. In Lehr (2018), the use of AR and MR as up-and-coming tools to fight criminality and terrorism was discussed. They even stressed the use of 'smart glasses' that can enable police officers to identify suspects by merely looking at them.

Similarly, a novel MR analysis device providing 3D reproductions of multiple users in a collaborative setting was introduced (Prilla and Ruhmann 2018). This analysis noted the importance of information on individuals' movements and behaviour, as well as how they interact with digital objects. The authors, recognizing the insufficiency of other means of analysis for this purpose, developed and applied a novel device showing users wearing head-mounted devices. Prilla and Ruhmann added that to their knowledge, the features of the MR device cannot be found in other tools, including the means for analysis.

Moreover, virtual environments (VE), VR, AR, and simulations can now be used widely because of recent advances in technology that made them become affordable and accessible to users, practitioners, and researchers alike. In Spain et al. (2018), identifying the manner in which these applications can be developed and applied to enhance human lives across a range of contexts was identified as the main goal of human factors research. Brown and Prilla (2019) affirmed the availability and accessibility of AR devices, which Spain et al. (noted), wherein remote experts support people wearing these devices. 2D peripherals are usually worn by these experts in accessing video feeds of 3D head-mounted tools and augmenting them with verbal or digital information. Whether devices applied for these scenarios can also be applied for remote consultations is a relevant concern; hence, Brown and Prilla carried out a study aiming to re-evaluate this device, leading to findings that showed that despite the evenness of usability scores, participants noted clear preferences for certain settings.

2.1 Collaboration Through Technology

Speicher et al. (2018) cited recent studies' pursuit to explore the potential of 360 videos for the collaboration of several users in remote settings. They furthered that these studies were able to identify some challenges with regard to 360 live streams, including out-of-sync views, amongst others. These challenges were dealt with by creating 360 anywhere, a video framework for multi-user collaboration, in which along with enabling users to view a 360 live stream, projected annotations in the 360 stream were supported. This allows a variety of collaborative AR applications which existing devices do not support.

Just like Speicher et al. (2018) who explored how multi-user collaboration in a remote setting may be undertaken through 360 videos, Kolkmeier et al. (2018) examined remote MR collaborative systems, which enable experts' real-time support., Kolkmeier et al. identified core design areas, such as the remote expert's independent viewpoint on the visitee's position and perception; the presentation technology's immersiveness; and the extent of having the visitor's body represented in the environment of the visitee.

In Ruhmann and Prilla's (2018) work, they emphasised that most studies had been allotted to AR glasses to finish tasks, with technology being recognised as having great potential for cooperative tasks. The authors presented a visual search experiment which was carried out in the context of a cooperative MR environment with Microsoft HoloLens tools. In their study of Microsoft's HoloLens AR head-mounted device, Heinonen (2018) presented a discussion of AR and described HoloLens as having two resolution screens and a 360-degree view field and twelve sensors that used for interacting with the environment. In addition, the device's performance can be compared to a sophisticated mobile device.

Similarly, Ruhmann et al. (2018) focused their study on mixed reality (MR) which can be used for cooperation support. They stated that most work conducted in this context has been focused on individuals. As the authors worked on collaboration support situations in MR, they came to recognise the need for insights into how technology may be used for working together. To examine this, they came up with a computer-generated 3D analysis tool for MR, which embodied interactive and collaborative support and was conducted with Microsoft HoloLens, demonstrating how hard-to-discover interaction can be carried out. The same scenario on the use of MR was examined in Poelman et al. (2012), this time presenting a new MR system developed for the collaboration of crime scene investigators with the remote support of expert colleagues. The head-mounted display can carry out map-making on a real-time basis in order for the investigators to collaborate spatially. This is similar to the direction of Ruhmann et al. (2018) on their use of 3D analysis tool with interactive and collaborative support. In Poelman et al. (2012), a crime scene experiment was conducted to investigate the resulting system, whereby lay investigators collaborated to resolve a spatial problem with experts participating remotely. The findings revealed that the investigation of the physical scene through spatial collaboration with remote experts allowed current issues to be tackled at a distance.

Similar to Ruhmann et al. (2018) who focused on 3D animation for MR, Ma et al. (2010) also carried out 3D animation, this time, for accurate crime visualization, both for the audience and courtrooms. Using actual data as a basis, the scene was reproduced through forensic animations, showing the activity at various points in time. Computer techniques were used to reconstruct crime scenes, thereby replacing the traditional techniques in forensic investigation. The study explored the link between major types of crime in parallel forensic animations and acknowledged that animation with high levels of details and human characters is suitable for many types of crime and crime investigations although it can be used only on a limited basis in the courtroom.

2.2 The Use of Augmented Reality in Crime Scene Investigation

Lukosch et al. (2015a, b) described AR as a technology that enables viewing and interacting in real-time with superimposed virtual images over the real world. AR technology can enable the creation of unique collaborative experiences in such a way that co-located users can both interact with 3D virtual objects and see them. A live video can be annotated so that a remote user can collaborate with another user at a distance to enhance the face-to-face collaborative experience. Using AR technology to investigate crime scenes has been emphasised by many studies (e.g. Rice 2012; Sandvik and Waade 2008; Streefkerk et al. 2013). Recent studies revealed that augmented reality (AR) technology is capable of supporting distributed teams in an investigation of crime scenes (Datcu et al. 2016b; Poelman et al. 2012; Ruhmann et al. 2018). Crime scene investigation is a cautiously planned systematic process that aims to acquire physical evidence to illuminate the physical reality of the crime and ultimately discover the identity of the criminal (Bostanci 2015). Sandvik (2010) particularly described the term crime scene as a model for understanding and augmenting places. It is a place that undergoes a specific state of transformation at a specific moment in time, where the place embodies the scene for some kind of criminal activity. Akman and Jonker (2012) specified that a crime scene investigation can position virtual objects such as found evidence in the scene, where two or more parties and their environment interact and collaborate through a head-mounted AR system. Such a system provides tools, direction, and information to users - on and off the site - to undertake their tasks autonomously and with each other.

It is important to capture the images and videos of the crime scene to analyze deeply the digital evidence for potential clues. Bostanci (2015) brought this idea further in order to utilise the obtained footage to draw the crime scene's 3D model. The results demonstrated that realistic reconstruction can be acquired through advanced computer vision techniques. This same purpose was embodied in the study of Streefkerk et al. (2013) who explored the use of AR annotation tools, whose relevance was grounded on the imperative for forensic professionals to gather crime evidence quickly and contamination-free. This tool enables forensic professionals to practically tag evidence clues at crime scenes and review and shares this evidence. Using a qualitative method, Streefkerk et al. (2013) found that annotation could lead to enhanced crime scene orientation, rapid collection process, and reduced administrative pressures. Whilst existing annotation prototypes are technically limited because of time-consuming feature tracking, AR annotation is more promising, useful, and valuable in investigating crime scenes. This is affirmed by Rice (2012) who stressed the increased value and efficiency of forensic simulations and crime scene investigation in virtual environments using augmented reality tools. Through AR technology, along with useful tools and fast access to major databases, law enforcement, and investigation personnel can enable marking and highlighting evidence and running real-time tests.

On a similar scale, Sandvik and Waade (2008) examined how places are augmented through mediatisation, describing AR as something that represents processes of mediatisation that broaden and boost spatial experiences. These processes are embodied in users' active participation and forming of artificial operational environments which are entrenched in a variety of physical and virtual places. Thus, in another study, Sandvik (2010) used the concept of AR to examine the augmentation of places in different ways through various mediatisation strategies. AR denotes enhanced emotional character of places, including a crime scene, which is an encoded place embedded with certain actions and events that leave various traces to be interpreted and examined. For example, blood, nails, and hair are DNA-coded, in the same way, that gun powder and gun wounds are readable and traceable codes. As AR, the crime scene brings a narrative that is initially hidden and must be disclosed. The investigative process and the detective's ability to rationalise and construe enable the crime scene to be reconstructed from being a place into being a virtual space where the course of events is retold to solve the crime.

Similar to Sandvik (2010) and Sandvik and Waade (2008) who focused on mediatisation in AR, Lukosch et al. (2015a, b) described an interface-based mediated reality system that supports remote collaboration. In particular, the authors introduced a gesture-specific interface to investigate crime scenes, where through interviews and interactive sessions, such interface was shown to be effective, easy to use, and to learn. Datcu and Lukosch (2013) offered an even more innovative AR tool for crime scene investigation, and this is by using free-hand gestures for mobile AR applications. Proposing a computer vision-engineered model for hands-free interaction in AR, the authors emphasised that the project's novelty was the adoption of a hands-free interaction model, with a particular emphasis on the accuracy of a hand-specific pointing system for item selection. The results revealed high pointing accuracy and high viability of hands-free AR interaction. This same efficiency in AR has been earlier emphasised in Bostanci (2015), Rice (2012), and Streefkerk et al. (2013).

Just like other authors in this review, Lukosch et al. (2015a, b) recognised the usefulness of AR technology for operational teams in the field of security, given the capacity of this technology for quick and adequate exchange of context-related information. Information exchange allows the development of distributed situational awareness and collaboration facilitation. At present, operational teams rely on oral communication for information exchange, which can be ambiguous. Using both quantitative and qualitative assessment, Lukosch et al. (2015a, b) revealed that a team's distributed situation awareness can be improved through AR. This result was also the same as that of Datcu et al. (2014a, b) where they compared situational awareness, amongst others, in AR and real-world environments in collaborative complex problem solving, such as a crime scene investigation. Whilst Datcu et al. (2016a) stressed the growth of AR into a mature field, the domains of situational awareness and presence of AR remained to be lacking in research topics. In order to examine various perceptions of situational awareness and presence in real-world and AR scenarios, a collaborative game was introduced in their study. The game was adopted in order to model collaborative complex problem solutions and was proved to be feasible, along with questionnaire design, in examining the various perceptions of situational awareness and presence in real-world and AR scenarios.

Alternatively, Gee et al. (2010) described an AR system designed for 3D annotation of physical environments and included an integration of absolute positioning technology and real-time computer image to produce a virtual 'incident' map. The map was collaboratively developed through the participation of operatives and a remote control hub. The study showed how the system may be utilised to aid forensic investigators in collecting and processing evidence in a crime scene, which was similar to Poelman et al. (2012) and Ruhmann et al. (2018).

Conversely, aiming to report on the development of handheld AR technology in situational attentiveness and collaborative investigation between teams and remote forensic investigators, Datcu et al. (2016b) examined the AR system by focusing on its stability and impact on situational attentiveness and quality of collaboration. It was found that the head-mounted AR system which Poelman et al. (2012) discussed in their study has certain limitations that are tackled by handheld AR technology. However, the divided attention between smartphone AR technology and the real environment affects situational attentiveness.

In another study, Buck et al. (2013) described a tool called GOMATOS, an optical 3D digital technique that is suitable for wound and whole body documentation for identifying injury-inflicting devices and reconstructing the event. These 3D data were integrated into the dead person's whole body model. Besides the findings of the body, a 3D documentation of the injury-inflicting devices and the incident was carried out. With this work, Buck et al. (2013) showed how 3D documentation and data integration helped address reconstructive issues concerning the development of patterned injuries and how this resulted in a real data-based crime scene reconstruction.

Congruent with the direction of Buck et al. (2011), Adamczyk et al. (2017a) presented a new 3D generation calculation approach for forensic documentation, whose purpose was to prepare a more insightful and objective forensic documentation. After conducting a series of interviews with technicians, their study suggested that the developed 3D calculation system had considerable potential for becoming a useful device for forensic technicians. In their other study, Adamczyk et al. (2017b) mentioned that 3D measurements are becoming a standard forensic process. Through the adoption of 3D measurement approaches, a more insightful investigation can be carried out, helping to demonstrate traces in the entire crime scene-setting. In their article, Adamczyk et al. (2017b) presented a hierarchical, 3D measurement system for the forensic documentation process. This system mirrored the particular standards in the forensic documentation process, as it was developed to conduct measurements in two documentation phases. The first phase involved the use of a low-resolution scanner with a large measuring volume, which was used to document the whole scene. The second phase involved a more detailed but high-resolution scanner which was intended for areas requiring a more detailed approach. A software platform called CrimeView3D was used to supervise the documentation process.

3 Environmental Aspects of the Use of HoloLens

Rajeev et al. (2019) mentioned that the quality of the AR environment is based on high accuracy localisation and user positioning tracking. Developers are confronted with the challenge of localising the user based on visible environments. Currently, Global Positioning System (GPS) is largely used for tracking and orientations but its accuracy is only about 10 to 30 m. This is not accurate enough for AR as the precision required by AR should be in millimeters or smaller. Cyrus et al. (2019) noted that the HoloLens is highly accurate in terms of location information. In their study, Rajeev et al. (2019) proposed an AR-based vision indoor navigation system that can give accurate localisation and mapping in an environment where GPS is declined. By contrast, Cirulis (2019) stressed that a major disadvantage of a GPS-based AR system is inadequate accuracy in a virtual object.

Likewise, Cyrus et al. (2019) stressed that location information is typically used to precisely position holograms within the real environment in relation to the user. Since the information is accurate enough, it can be used to report the position. A range of experiments has been conducted to determine possible errors as a result of vibrations or other effects when the HoloLens is moved. An advantage of the HoloLens is that it can be readily positioned indoor without a need for additional infrastructure whilst its main disadvantage is its cost (Cyrus et al. 2019).

Moreover, Cirulis (2019) emphasised that changing from smartphone displays to HMD is important in AR, as this will enhance the immersion level of the environment. Although AR will increasingly become significant in the future, there are still factors that limit its use in various areas and industries. Some related problems arise, for which solutions are being developed. For example, it is inconvenient to use AR in outdoor conditions, but there are available solutions to address this, such as Pokemon Go and Sight Space. However, their inaccuracy is very high, preventing the user from moving freely in the augmented environment. Another example is the short-range in which AR systems can operationally reach. This is resolved by replacing marker-based solutions with depth cameras and spatial mapping (Cirulis 2019).

Cirulis furthered that the functionality for indoor and outdoor environments should be achieved for HoloLens, regardless of weather conditions and lighting. By calculating GDP coordinates, some AR solutions are available for outdoor use. However, in actuality, they have very high accuracy, which prevents the user from moving freely. Further projection can be calculated by putting a target 3D model in a fixed position and using data for internal sensors. Similar to Cirulis, Gee et al. (2010) performed a study of AR in a crime scene, in which a virtual map is made through the collaboration of many operatives and a remote control center. This system covered both indoor and outdoor environments and explained how forensic investigators may be helped by such a system in gathering and processing evidence at a crime scene.

Moreover, Blom (2018) conducted a series of experiments to examine the effects of various light levels on the functionality of a 3D holographic application that operates in HoloLens. He found that such functionality was not considerably affected, except when the surroundings are very dark. In contrast, the visibility of the hologram is affected by bright and muddled backgrounds. Therefore, the virtual content's visibility is reliant on the absence of bright light sources in the environment. This is specifically so in outdoor conditions where the weather conditions largely affect the application experience. However, the HoloLens system could decrease poor visibility in fairly dark environments since it has virtual content that gives its own light (Blom 2018). This is similar to the claims of other authors regarding the use of AR in both indoor and outdoor environments (e.g. Cirulis 2019; Gee et al. 2010).

Cirulis furthered that the functionality for indoor and outdoor environments should be achieved for HoloLens, regardless of weather conditions and lighting. By calculating GDP coordinates, some AR solutions are available for outdoor use. However, in actuality, they have very high accuracy, which prevents the user from moving freely. Further projection can be calculated by putting a target 3D model in a fixed position and using data for internal sensors. Similar to Cirulis, Gee et al. (2010) performed a study of AR in a crime scene, in which a virtual map is made through the collaboration of many operatives and a remote control center. This system covered both indoor and outdoor environments and explained how forensic investigators may be helped by such a system in gathering and processing evidence at a crime scene.

Comparing the Google Tango tablet and the Microsoft HoloLens together, Riedlinger et al. (2019) found that in terms of collaboration, users preferred the Google Tango tablet over Microsoft HoloLens because it felt more natural to interact using the tablet rather than the HoloLens, although the operation in HoloLens is hands-free and its tracking is stable. In addition, getting an overall impression is easier when the Tango tablet is used than the HoloLens. Riedlinger et al. also observed that users using Microsoft HoloLens found it difficult to position objects in similar surroundings with almost similar features. Since the position of the holographic model depends completely on the ability of the HoloLens to trace the position of pixels identified by cameras, changes in the environment would result in drift in the position of the holographic model. The causes of this error are people's movements, materials on site, and other elements that stop variations in lighting conditions (Jahn et al. 2019). These are similar to the results in Blom's (2018) study which described how a muddled and very bright environment affects the visibility of a hologram and how a very dark surrounding affects its functionality.

Alternatively, the study of Cyrus et al. (2019) found that the HoloLens' light detection and ranging (LIDAR) is typically used as a component of autonomous simultaneous localisation and mapping (SLAM). However, with the use of the LIDAR, the device's scanning of the surroundings usually involves just one plane and can be problematic with glass obstructions, such as a glass door. Along with the correct use of suitable software, the information that the LIDAR provides is accurate, given its high accuracy.

4 Blood Spatter Analysis

Analysing the patterns of bloodstains is important in reconstructing the events of a crime scene and has become a domain of specialisation in Forensic Science (e.g. Albalooshi and Eltabie 2015; Buck et al. 2011; Karger et al. 2008; Osborne et al. 2015). Pokupcic (2017) pointed out that blood is an important biological trace that is often left on the crime scene. It contains valuable information, making it an extremely important forensic tool. By analysing various aspects of bloodstains, the circumstances surrounding some violent crimes can be clarified. This critical information can direct criminal investigation in the proper direction towards solving the crime. It can also be used to legally determine criminal offenses which can result in a more accurate and appropriate judgment. Hence, determining the series of events surrounding a violent crime involving blood is very important.

Stringing - BPA's traditional method - involves appending a piece of string to every stain and allowing the string to stand for an estimation of the stain's flight path (Joris et al. 2015). Albeit stringing is used at length, there are several practical downsides that go with it (Joris et al. 2015). That is why various approaches have been employed to improve BPA. Wang et al. (2019) stated that traditional approaches cannot effectively reconstruct the entire crime scene, which is why they presented a portable system with a low-cost VR headset and other components to spatially collect data of crime scenes using a multi-directional 3D imaging technique. Their study analysed a real case to show the system's practical use and to confirm its feasibility and efficiency. The system can measure accurately and determine the relative location of blood sources and compare tools that can inflict injuries.

Gee et al. (2010) stressed that in the field of crime scene investigation, collecting data largely depends on manual recording, which is time-consuming, especially when many personnel is operating within several teams. Technologies like AR, which can make this process more efficient, would be a useful addition to the developments in crime scene investigation (Gee et al. 2010). Sandvik (2010) suggested that the forensic term crime scene may be used in understanding the concept of AR. The crime scene is an encoded space where readable and interpretable traces of crime are left, such as hair, nails, DNA codes, amongst others. Similar to the traces of gunpowder and bullet holes, these traces can be decrypted and deciphered. By reading and interpreting signs and traces in the crime scene, the crime scene becomes encoded (Sandvik 2009). The emergence of VR makes the work more efficient since it is now used for blood splatter analysis, forensic biology, and crime scene re-enactments, amongst others. An example to demonstrate this was the crash of Delta Flight 191 in 1985, which was recreated through a computer-based simulation, where some of its complex evidence was explained to the jury (Ticknor 2018).

Laan et al. (2015) mentioned that as a forensic discipline, BPA allows the determination of the position of victims on the crime scene with the shedding of blood. In order to find out the blood source, straight-line estimation for the trajectory is used, setting aside the effects of gravity and hence over-approximating the height of the source. Laan et al. (2015) ascertained the extent of accuracy of estimation of the origin's location when gravity and drag are included in the reconstruction of trajectory. Their study, therefore, allowed investigators to identify the victim's position and link the wounds to specific patterns, which is necessary for reconstructing the crime scene.

Osborne et al. (2015) mentioned that criminal investigations can utilise BPA to ascertain the events linked to blood depositions. However, it can also be potentially vulnerable to contextual bias. Thus, when taking into account how to deal with the issue of contextual bias in analysis bloodstain patterns, it is necessary to pay attention to context management instead of context elimination. Similar to Albalooshi and Eltabie (2015), Buck et al. (2011) claimed that the pattern of bloodstains in crime scene investigation at the actual site is very important. The bloodstain pattern's morphology helps to identify the estimated locations of the blood source and the positioning of the victim. Through illustrative cases, the authors showed the advantages of 3D BPA, which includes the ballistic estimation of the trajectories of blood drops. In their study, 3D documentations were used for the crime scenes, creating accurate 3D models for the scenes, including bloodstain patterns and traces. In order to determine the areas in which the bloodstain pattern originated, their study analysed the trajectories in photogrammetry software. The ballistic aspect of the trajectories was determined using ballistic software. Buck et al. (2011) stressed that the crime scene investigation benefits from this method through non-contact calculation of the bloodstains and high accuracy of the analysis, amongst others. They emphasised that the accurate outcomes on the number of bloodstains and the position of their areas of origin should be anticipated with this method.

Below is a figure showing the shape of a well-defined blood spatter. The direction and the length of the axes of the elliptical bloodstain are shown in the figure. It also shows the calculation of the direction of the impact of the blood drop and the vertical flight path (Fig. 1).

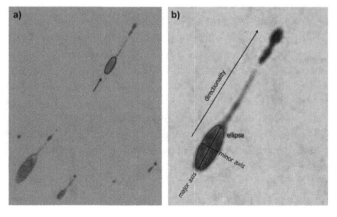

Fig. 1. The shape of a well-defined blood spatter (Source: Buck et al. 2011, p. 25)

Parallel to the study of Buck et al. (2011), Karger et al. (2008) stated that there is important information which the morphology of bloodstain distribution patterns for the reconstruction of the crime brings about. Karger et al. discussed a series of illustrative cases which allowed reconstructing the crime scene through BPA, confirmed by the offender himself. Different types of bloodstains were covered in the cases, such as smear stains, drop stains, splash stains, and arterial blood spatter. Karger et al. (2008) addressed the problems that are commonly encountered in practice, such as adverse environmental situations or mixtures of various bloodstain patterns. They also showed that the morphology of bloodstain analysis can examine bloodstains individually by selecting a certain number of stains from a multifarious pattern for DNA analysis.

On a similar note, Aron and Northfield (2017) looked into how AR goggles can be used in forensic investigation and noted that the AR system helps users to tag objects found in the crime scene, like bullet holes and blood spatter. In addition, a police officer in a remote location can take the first look of the crime by merely watching the user's video stream. Related to this, Yen et al. (2003) stressed that there has been increasing knowledge on bloodstain pattern morphology, owing to a variety of experimental examinations in previous years. Moreover, a scenario in Dath's (2017) study showed how blood pattern analysis could be visualised in a VR environment. It pointed to where the action causing the blood splatter originated. As the visualisation is presented to the user, the user is able to understand how the act leading to the blood spatter trace took place and thus gains a holistic perspective of the crime. Similarly, Joris et al. (2015) recommended an automated and virtual method, in which digital images and fiducial markers were employed. Their findings showed that given the benefits of this proposed method, such as proper operation and other practical functions, it may be a valuable asset for BPA. Joris et al. presented the accompanying software called Hemo Vision to demonstrate its practical use in crime scene investigations.

On the other hand, cognitive robots were used in Acampora et al. (2015) study of BPA. They stressed that BPA is still basically based on manual methods, which lengthens the analysis of a crime scene. Aside from this, crime scene analysis becomes tedious and likely imperfect. Thus, Acampora et al. (2015) proposed a robotic framework for the automation of the BPA. Specifically, the robotic framework has a component that can navigate the crime scene, detect bloodstains, calculate the points of origin, and prepare a technical report that depicts the bloody scenario. Their objective of using the robotic framework is apparently similar to the goal of adopting VR in BPA.

Another attempt to improve BPA in crime scene investigation is Agosto et al.'s (2008) Fully Geomatic Approach. Their study involved the verification of the link between human walk paths and blood patterns, which required pictures taken by first-aid person-nel. In general, crime-scene-related geomatic distortions affect those pictures. A range of GIS functionalities for the simulation of human walk movements served as the basis of the crime scene analysis.

Similarly, Wassom (2015) mentioned that blood patterns and other sensor-sensitive forensic data may be visualised using AR applications. Advanced imaging systems for visualising traumatic penetrating wounds can likewise contribute to the advancement of forensic pathology. Using a game simulation, Bahamon et al. (2014) noted that a user's main goal is to secure a photographic record of all physical evidence that could be found in a crime scene and preserve its integrity. This evidence includes blood spatter, broken glasses, weapons, bullets, and the like. This is meant to improve the analysis of crime scenes and solve the crime. Thus, both Wasson (2015) and Bahamon et al. (2014) noted the value of physical evidence in forensic investigation.

In Sauter's (2019) aim to reconstruct a crime scene in 3D, they stressed that devel-oping an accurate 3D model was the first step. Photographs of the crime scene serve as image maps, which will be used to create a more realistic scene. The trajectories of blood splatter images can be accurately gauged when these images are used as models and are placed in their precise location. By clicking the mouse on the blood or a strand of hair, a DNA report of the victim will be generated. All information about the case will be available to investigators since the 3D crime scene can be accessed online.

On a similar scale, Shen and Cipolla (2006) carried out comparative experiments regarding blood spatter stains using an image analysis algorithm, which can be used in crime scenes. This approach serves as an alternative to the labour-intensive technique of localising the blood's source in 2D. They concluded that the algorithm matched the accuracy expected from forensic investigation. Likewise, this creates a useful insight for the present study regarding how HoloLens can be used by localising the blood's origin in 3D.

5   The Use of Forensic DNA Databases

Each individual has a unique Deoxyribonucleic Acid (DNA) (except for identical twins) which does not change over time (except mutations), making it a viable tool for identification. DNA analysis is the source of every person's makeup, revolutionised forensic science and developed into becoming an important tool in forensic investigation (Frunkin et al. 2010). Owing to scientific developments, DNA databases have been created to serve different purposes, such as law enforcement. According to Roman-Santos (2010), the creation of DNA databases will enable law enforcers not to rely on subjective judgments in solving a crime and will help clear innocent people from being wrongly convicted. However, DNA databases are also critiqued for the potential that DNA might be used for the omission of materials that have a strong proof of the suspect's innocence. Roman-Santos concluded that whilst DNA is useful in fighting crimes, its potential allows it to be likely abused, which led him to infer that leaders should ensure that all DNA profiles should be used only for the limited purposed for which they were gathered and that they should be already destroyed once generated so that they cannot be used for purposes other than forensic identification. In order to expand DNA databases, several states in the United States have implemented laws that require DNA samples from people involved in murder, felony, burglary, and sex crimes (Roman-Santos 2010).

At present, DNA evidence is used for convicting or exonerating suspects of various types of crime (Frunkin et al. 2010). The tremendous power of DNA technology as a tool that can identify criminals had ushered a remarkable change in criminal justice (Panneerchelvam and Nozarmi 2003). Blood, hair, urine, saliva, and other evidence samples can be obtained in crime scene investigations, yielding DNA profiles. Blood from a suspect may be obtained to produce another DNA profile, which is then compared against crime scene evidence to find out whether a genetic match exists. On a similar scale, Hazel et al. (2018) also affirmed the fact that DNA is a very viable crime-solving tool. They pointed out that Kuwait, Saudi Arabia, and UK, amongst others, have been considering a universal DNA database populated by all people in the world. In their study, they discussed the likelihood for a universal database to be more useful and less discriminatory than what the current system fosters, given a correct implementation.

DNA evidence is important in crime scene investigation, and its relevance is that it can be linked to a suspect or can remove a suspect from suspicion. A comparison between properly collected DNA and known samples can be made to put the suspect at the scene of the crime. In the absence of a suspect, a DNA profile gathered from the crime scene can be recorded into the Combined DNA Index System (CODIS) where a suspect can be identified anywhere in the United States or where serial crimes may be made to connect to each other (OVC 2012). The importance of physical evidence such as DNA codes in the crime scene and how AR may be used to make the process more efficient has been noted in several studies (e.g. Sauter 2019; Ticknor 2018; Werry 2011).

Bohannon et al. (2000) stated that developments in DNA sequencing technology enable inexpensive genetic tests; however, although the genetic information obtained from such tests is often valuable, serious concerns have been raised with regard to the privacy of such information, especially when it is gathered into databases. As they carried out an investigation into access control of forensic DNA databases, Bohannon et al. (2000) mainly observed that a target individual has an evidence sample in the form of blood or tissue obtained from a crime scene. They also demonstrated how forensic DNA databases may be carried out in a way that only legitimate concerns are feasible. For example, an individual with unrestricted access to the database will not be allowed to acquire information about another individual unless there is already known genetic information regarding that individual.

Relating to this, Benschop et al. (2017) discussed a particular software technology called SmartRank, developed to allow only relevant candidate suspects to a crime and rank them accordingly. They noted that a national DNA database with complex profiles commonly generates very huge variety of potential matches present several candidates which the forensic investigator needs to further study. When compared against CODIS, SmartRank was found to complement CODIS with regard to DNA database searches. Adopting the best practice principles, SmartRank also allows investigative leads to be obtained in criminal cases without as suspect.

In their study, Frumkin et al. (2010) showed that the present forensic procedure fails to differentiate between samples of blood, amongst others, with artificial DNA, and equivalent samples with natural DNA. In order to address this matter, Frumkin et al. designed an authentication essay, whose function is to differentiate natural DNA from artificial DNA. Forensic procedure uses an authentication essay to maintain the high credibility of DNA evidence in courts. DNA technology can be forensically applied in identifying potential suspects based on a match between their DNA and crime scene evidence, amongst other uses (Roman-Santos 2010).

Another technology which was developed for forensic DNA analysis was discussed in Liu et al. (2008), a real-time integrated system aimed at analysing short tandem repeat (STR). A mock crime scene using real-time STR investigation was conducted to assess the system's usefulness and compatibility with forensic investigation processes. In this mock crime scene, the suspect's blood samples were collected; his DNA was extracted, and the STR was analysed, as a successful CODIS hit was generated. This demonstration of STR analysis validated the potential of real-time DNA typing in determining the biological evidence at a crime scene. Similar to Benschop et al. (2017) and Liu et al. (2008), Greely et al. (2006) studied the scientific potential of DNA forensic technology by using DNA matches from crime scenes to identify the suspect from a pool of relatives who have DNA profiles in forensic databases.

On a similar fashion, Werry (2011) mentioned that photogrammetry, a forensic technique, is used by forensic scientists to create a VR crime scene. Numerous photographs are saved on a computer and combined into a 3D image, which the scientist can revisit anytime to look at the scene. These photographs can also be cross-checked against the statements of the witness or any new information that may arise. There are also databases of DNA, fingertips, and eye scans which can be readily accessed for crime scene investigation.

Furthermore, the implications and cost-efficiency of DNA evidence in the investigation of property crimes were studied in Roman et al. (2009). Aside from conducting traditional investigations, DNA processing was carried out in the treatment group. Since it is more expensive to conduct DNA-based investigations than non-DNA ones, significant investments will be necessary to increase the capacity of the police, crime laboratories, and prosecutors to effectively utilise this investigative tool. DNA Databases such as Combined DNA Index System (CODIS) speeds up the process (Norrgard 2008). In Claes et al. (2014), it was stressed that DNA left at a crime scene could be tested and used to thin down the collection of potential suspects.

6 Forensic Toxicology Reports

According to Dinovo and Cravey (2007), forensic toxicology is defined as "a highly specialised area of forensic science which requires expertise in analytical chemistry, pharmacology, biochemistry, and forensic investigation. Isolating and identifying drugs and other poisonous chemicals from tissues, as well as interpreting the findings for legal authorities like the medical examiner, are the concerns of a forensic toxicologist. Drug cases may involve a clear and apparent overdose, often validated by a suicide note; or a drug-related pathological progression that results in an overall decline in health. Oftentimes, it is the homicide investigator who initially views the scene, and if given a proper training, he keeps the scene intact for the medical examiner whom he summons. The investigator, who carries the main burden of the investigation, is usually the sole member of the medical examiner's staff to essentially look at the scene and talk to witnesses. The tasks that he must accomplish include collecting all information possible from the first officer on the scene, arranging for photographs of the scene, gathering and preserving all evidence, interviewing witnesses, and obtaining the victim's medical history. On the other hand, the forensic pathologist carries out the autopsy, gathers the specific specimens to be analysed, and submits these to the forensic toxicologist, who serves as a crucial member of the team. As such, the evidence he collected must be taken into account, assessed, and clarified in the final assessment of the cause of death (Dinovo and Cravey 2007). Kilgus et al. (2014) stressed that during autopsy, today's forensic pathologists largely depend on visible signs, tactile indications, and experience to identify the cause of death. Although computed tomography can be used for the corpses under examination, the lack of radiological work stations in the pathological site makes these data not used often. Through the data, the forensic pathologist may be prevented from damaging the evidence by enabling him to link, for example, external lesions to internal injuries. Thus, Kilgus et al. (2014) proposed a multi-modal approach to intuitively visualise forensic data and evaluate their feasibility.

Dinis-Oliveira et al. (2010) specified that forensic toxicology determines the relevance of the findings by the nature and integrity of the specimens. This denotes that selecting and gathering specimens, both for ante-mortem and post-mortem, is confronted by various challenges. Dinis-Oliveira et al. stressed that a potential bias may take place in interpreting toxicological results. Favretto et al. (2013) pointed out that the considerable ineffectiveness of the present approaches of toxicological screening to determine the new compounds that enter the market is one of these concerns. There is therefore an immediate need to enhance the screening capacities of toxicological laboratories. On the same note, Murray (2016) stated that whilst significant innovations in the domains of toxicology and DNA analysis have been emerging, most forensic procedures are still using 19th century techniques. Likewise, in Al-Kandari's (2012) study in Kuwaiti setting, a need for virtual autopsy and early DNA measurement in Kuwait was identified.

In order to produce a 3D documentation of findings which other experts can reassess when needed, the research project Virtopsy was introduced in Bolliger and Thali (2015). In this project, autopsy results and forensic imaging were combined together. This forensic imaging allows the findings to be objectively reassessed by other experts even when the body had been buried or cremated, or the victim healed of injuries. In Ebert et al. (2014), a range of 3D image modalities were used to reconstruct crime scenes but since they were presented in a 2D manner on computer screens and paper, they incurred loss of information. Hence, they applied immersive VR techniques and proposed a system that enables a crime scene to be viewed as though the investigators were there at the scene. Using a low-cost VR headset which was originally designed for computer gaming, Ebert et al. (2014) facilitated a 3D and interactive visualisation of the crime scene. Alternatively, Biwasaka et al. (2005) studied the usability of hologram in the 3D recording of forensic objects and the accuracy of restructured 3D images. The virtual holographic image documents the 3D data of the original object. They pointed out that holography can be a functional 3D recording method of forensic objects and found that it appears to function similarly with the computer graphic system; moreover, combining it with the digital technique would broaden its utility in superimposition.

On the other hand, forensic entomology comprises the study of insects found on a cadaver to approximate the time of death. This technique is the only available one for a huge post-mortem interval. However, relevant system complexities lead experts to give imperfect results. In their study, Veremme et al. (2012) described a decision support system (DSS) which was developed to consider the entire parameters of ecosystems and a considerable number of biological models. Similarly, in their study of virtual forensic entomology, Richards et al. (2012) showed how micro-computed tomography can be an effective means to describe internal and external changes in morphology by sampling pupae. This technique can be useful in estimating a minimum post-mortem interval for suspicious deaths, where pupae are shown to be the oldest stage of insect evidence gathered. Emerging technologies to improve forensic entomology may suggest that advancements like HoloLens can be possibly used in this field in the future.

7   Summary

This paper reviewed the literature on the subject under study. It specifically discussed the features of augmented/mixed reality and how collaboration in forensic investigation can take place through technology. It then tackled the use of AR in crime scene investigation, the environmental aspects of the use of HoloLens, blood splatter analysis, and the use of DNA forensic databases. With its review of the literature, this study was able to validate the usefulness of HoloLens in elevating the level of crime scene investigation.

References

Acampora, G., Vitiello, A., Di Nunzio, C., Saliva, M., Garofano, L.: Towards automatic bloodstain pattern analysis through cognitive robots. In: 2015 IEEE International Conference on Systems, Man, and Cybernetics, Kowloon, China, 9–12 October (2015)

Adamczyk, M., Sienilo, M., Sitnik, R., Wozniak, A.: Hierarchical, three-dimensional measurement system for crime scene scanning. J. Forensic Sci. **62**(4), 889–899 (2017a)

Adamczyk, M., et al.: Three-dimensional measurement system for crime scene documentation. In: Proceedings volume 10441. Counterterrorism: Crime Fighting, Forensics, and Surveillance Technologies, Warsaw, Poland, 5 October (2017b)

Agosto, E., Ajmar, A., Boccardo, P., Tonolo, F.G., Lingua, A.: Crime scene reconstruction using a fully geomatic approach. Sensors **8**(10), 6280–6302 (2008)

Albalooshi, Y., Eltabie, M.A.: The importance of bloodstain pattern analysis in the investigation of road traffic accidents: a case report. Arab J. Forensic Sci. **1** (2), 224–228 (2015)

Al-Kandari, N.: A forensic study of unnatural deaths in Kuwait: Epidemiological, virtual autopsy and DNA investigations (2012). http://clok.uclan.ac.uk/6583/1/Al-Kandari%20Nadia%20Final%20e-Thesis%20%28Master%20Copy%29.pdf. Accessed 22 Feb 2020

Aron, J., Northfield, D.: AR goggles make crime scene investigation a desk job. Sch. Law Polic. Forensics (2017). http://eprints.staffs.ac.uk/3675/. Accessed 4 Feb 2020

Akman, O.: Robust augmented reality (2012). https://repository.tudelft.nl/islandora/object/uuid:3adeccef-19db-4a06-ab26-8636ac03f5c0/. Accessed 26 Dec 2019

Bahamon, J.C., Litvinov, M., Wringht, P., Gayle, R., Lippert, K., Young, M.: IC-CRIME snapshots: training crime scene photographers using procedural content generation in games. In: CHI Play, vol. 14, pp. 19–22 (2014)

Benschop, C.C.G., et al.: Validation of SmartRank: a likelihood ratio software for searching national DNA databases with complex DNA profiles. Forensic Sci. Int. Genet. **29**, 145–153 (2017)

Biwasaka, H., Saigusa, K., Aoki, Y.: The applicability of holography in forensic identification: a fusion of the traditional optical technique and digital technique. J. Forensic Sci. **50**(2), 393–399 (2005)

Blom, L.: Impact of light on augmented reality (2018). http://www.diva-portal.se/smash/get/diva2%3A1272321/FULLTEXT01.pdf. Accessed 4 Feb 2020

Bohannon, P., Jakobsson, M., Srikwan, S.: Cryptographic approaches to privacy in forensic DNA databases. In: Third International Workshop on Practice and Theory in Public Key Cryptography, Melbourne, Australia, 18–20 January (2000)

Bolliger, S.A., Thali, M.J.: Imaging and Virtual Autopsy: Looking Back and Forward. The Royal Society Publishing (2015). https://royalsocietypublishing.org/. https://doi.org/10.1098/rstb.2014.0253. Accessed 23 Feb 2020

Bostanci, E.: 3D reconstruction of crime scenes and design considerations for an interactive investigation tool. Int. J. Inf. Secur. Sci. **4**(2) (2015)

Brown, G., Prilla, M.: Evaluating pointing modes and frames of reference for remotely supporting an augmented reality user in a collaborative (virtual) environment: evaluation within the scope of a remote consultation session. In: MuC 2019 Proceedings of Mensch und Computer, pp. 713–717, September 2019

Buck, U., Kneubuehl, B., Nather, S., Albertini, N., Schmidt, L., Thali, M.: 3D bloodstain pattern analysis: Ballistic reconstruction of the trajectories of blood drops and determination of the centres of origin of the bloodstains. Forensic Sci. Int. **206**(1–3), 2–28 (2011)

Buck, U., Naether, S., Rass, B., Jackowski, C., Thali, M.J.: Accident or homicide – virtual crime scene reconstruction using 3D methods. Forensic Sci. Int. **225**(1–3), 75–84 (2013)

Cirulis, A.: Ultra wideband tracking potential for augmented reality environments. In: De Paolis, L., Bourdot, P. (eds.) AVR 2019. LNCS, vol. 11614, pp. 126–136. Springer, Cham (2019). https://doi.org/10.1007/978-3-030-25999-0_11

Claes, P., et al.: Modeling 3D facial shape from DNA. PLoS Genet. **10**(3), 1–14 (2014)

Cyrus, J., Kremarik, D., Moezzi, R., Koci, J., Petru, M.: HoloLens used for precise position tracking of the third party devices – autonomous vehicles. Communications **21**, 20–27 (2019)

Datcu, D., Lukosch, S.G.: Free-hands interaction in augmented reality. In: Proceedings of the 1st Symposium in Spatial User Interaction, Los Angeles, California, 20–21 July 2013

Datcu, D., Lukosch, S.G., Lukosch, H.K.: Comparing presence, workload and situational aware-ness in a collaborative real worlds and augmented reality scenario. In: IEEE ISMAR Workshop on Collaboration in Merging Realities (CiMeR), Adelaide, Australia, 1 October 2014 (2014a)

Datcu, D., Cidota, M., Lukosch, H., Lukosch, S.: On the usability of augmented reality for infor-mation exchange in teams from the security domain. In: IEEE Joint Intelligence and Security Informatics Conference (JISIC), The Hague, Netherlands, 24–25 September 2014 (2014b)

Datcu, D., Lukosch, S.G., Lukosch, H.K.: A collaborative game to study presence and situational awareness in a physical and an augmented reality environment. J. Univ. Comput. Sci. **22**(2), 247–270 (2016a)

Datcu, D., Lukosch, S.G., Lukosch, H.K.: Handheld augmented reality for distributed collaborative crime scene investigation. In: Proceedings of the 19th International Conference on Supporting Group Work, Florida, USA, 13–16 November (2016b)

Dath, C.: Crime scenes in virtual reality: a user-centered study (2017). https://kth.diva-portal.org/smash/get/diva2:1115566/FULLTEXT01.pdf. Accessed 19 Feb 2020

Dinis-Oliveira, R.J., Duarte, F.C., Marques, F.R.A., Santos, A., Magalhaes, T.: Collection of biological samples in forensic toxicology. Toxicol. Mech. Methods **20**(7), 363–414 (2010)

Dinovo, E.C., Cravey, R.H.: Forensic toxicology in death investigation (2007). https://www.ncjrs.gov/pdffiles1/Digitization/44096NCJRS.pdf. Accessed 23 Feb 2020

Du Plooy, G.M.: Introduction to Communication. Juta & Co., Ltd., Kenwyn (1997)

Ebert, L.C., Nguyen, T., Breitbeck, R.: The forensic holodeck: an immersive display for forensic crime scene reconstructions. Forensic Sci. Med. Pathol. **10**(4), 623–626 (2014)

Frumkin, D., Wasserstrom, A., Budowle, B., Davidson, A.: DNA methylation-based forensic tissue identification. Forensic Sci. Int.: Genet. **5**(5), 517–524 (2011). ISSN 1872-4973. https://doi.org/10.1016/j.fsigen.2010.12.001

Favretto, D., Pascali, J.P., Tagliaro, F.: New challenges and innovation in forensic toxicology: focus on the 'new psychoactive substances. J. Chromatogr. **1287**, 84–95 (2013)

Frumkin, D., Wesserstrom, A., Davidson, A., Grafit, A.: Authentication of forensic DNA samples. Forensic Sci. Int. Genet. **4**(1), 95–103 (2010)

Gaensslen, R.E., Harris, H., Lee, H.C.: Introduction to Forensic Science and Criminalistics. McGraw-Hill, New York (2008)

Gee, A.P., Escamilla-Ambrosio, P.J., Webb, M., Mayol-Cuevas, W., Calway, A.: Augmented crime scenes: Virtual annotation of physical environments for forensic investigation. In: Proceedings of the 2nd ACM Workshop on Multimedia in Forensics, Security and Intelligence, Firenze, Italy, 29 October 2010 (2010)

Gianelli, P.: Wrongful convictions and forensic science: the need to regulate crime labs. North Carol. Law Rev. **86**, 163–187 (2007)

Greely, H.T., Riordan, D.P., Garrison, N.A., Mountain, J.L.: Family ties: The use of DNA offender databases to catch offenders' kin. Law Med. Ethics **34**(2), 248–262 (2006)

Hazel, J.W., Clayton, E.W., Melin, B.A., Slobogin, C.: Is it time for a universal genetic forensic database? Science **362**, 898–900 (2018)

Heinonen, E.: HoloLens research and demo application development. Metropolia University of Applied Sciences (2018)

Inman, K., Rudin, N.: Principles and Practice of Criminalistics: The Profession of Forensic Science. CRC Press, Boca Raton (2001)

Jahn, G., Newnham, C., van den Berg, N., Iraheta, M., Wells, J.: Holographic construction. In: Gengnagel, C., Baverel, O., Burry, J., Ramsgaard Thomsen, M., Weinzierl, S. (eds.) DMSB 2019, pp. 314–324. Springer, Cham (2019). https://doi.org/10.1007/978-3-030-29829-6_25

Joris, P., et al.: Hemo vision: an automated and virtual approach to bloodstain pattern analysis. Forensic Sci. Int. **251**, 116–123 (2015)

Karger, B., Rand, S., Fracasso, T., Pfeiffer, H.: Bloodstain pattern analysis – casework experience. Forensic Sci. Int. **181**(1–3), 15–20 (2008)

Kilgus, T., et al.: Mobile markerless augmented reality and its application in forensic medicine. Int. J. Comput. Assist. Radiol. Surg. **10**(5), 573–586 (2014). https://doi.org/10.1007/s11548-014-1106-9

Kolkmeier, J., Harmsen, E., Glesselink, S., Reidsma, D., Theune, M., Heylen, D.: With a little help from a holographic friend: the open impress mixed reality telepresence toolkit for remote collaboration systems. In: VSRT 2018 proceedings of the 24th ACM Symposium on Virtual Reality Software and Technology, Article no. 26, pp. 1–11 (2018)

Laan, N., de Bruin, K.G., Slenter, D., Wilhelm, J., Jermy, M., Bonn, D.: Bloodstain pattern analysis: implementation of a fluid dynamic model for position determination of victims. Sci. Rep. **5**, 11461 (2015)

Ladwig, P., Geiger, C.: A literature review on collaboration in mixed reality. In: Auer, M., Langmann, R. (eds.) REV 2018. LNNS, vol. 47. Springer, Cham (2019). https://doi.org/10.1007/978-3-319-95678-7_65

Lee, H.C., Pagliaro, E.M.: Forensic evidence and crime scene investigation. J. Forensic Investig. **1**(2), 5–9 (2013)

Lehr, P.: Surveillance and observation: the all-seeing eyes of big brother. In: Lehr, P. (ed.) Counter-Terrorism Technologies. Advanced Sciences and Technologies for Security Applications, pp. 115–129. Springer, Cham (2019). https://doi.org/10.1007/978-3-319-90924-0_8

Liu, P., et al.: Real-time forensic DNA analysis at a crime scene using a portable microchip analyzer. Forensic Sci. Int. Genet. **2**(4), 301–309 (2008)

Lukosch, S., Billinghurst, M., Alem, L., Kiyowa, K.: Collaboration in augmented reality. Comput. Support. Coop. Work (CSCW) **24**, 515–525 (2015a)

Lukosch, S., Lukosch, H., Datcu, D., Cidota, M.: On the spot information in augmented reality for teams in the security domain. In: Proceedings of the 33rd Annual ACM Conference Extended Abstracts on Human Factors in Computing Systems, Seoul, Republic of Korea, 18–23 April 2015 (2015b)

Lukosch, S., Poelman, R., Akman, O., Jonker, P.: A novel gesture-based interface for crime scene investigation in mediated reality (2012). https://repository.tudelft.nl/islandora/object/uuid%3Ab9a2b407-a286-41d9-9781-956cd96b3c4e. Accessed 27 Dec 2019

Ma, M., Zheng, H., Lallie, H.: Virtual reality and 3D animation in forensic visualization. Forensic Sci. **55**(5), 227–231 (2010)

Murray, L.: Virtopsy: the future of forensics. Eng. Technol. **11**(7–8), 50–53 (2016)

Norrgard, K.: Forensics, DNA fingerprinting. Nat. Educ. **1**(1), 35 (2008)

Osborne, N., Taylor, M.C., Zajac, R.: Bloodstain pattern analysis and contextual bias. In: Wiley Encyclopedia of Forensic Science. Wiley, Hoboken (2015)

Panneerchelvam, S., Nozarmi, M.N.: Forensic DNA profiling and database. Malays. J. Med. Sci. **10**(2), 20–26 (2003)

Poelman, R., Akman, O., Lukosch, S., Jonker, P.: As if being there: mediated reality for crime scene investigation. In: Proceedings of the ACM 2012 Conference on Computer Supported Cooperative Work Pages, Washington, USA, 11–15 February 2012

[OVC] Office for Victims of Crime: Understanding DNA evidence: A guide for victim service providers (2012). https://www.ncjrs.gov/pdffiles1/nij/bc000657.pdf. Accessed 4 Feb 2020

Pokupcic, K.: Blood as an important tool in criminal investigation. J. Forensic Sci. 3(2), 1–3 (2017)

Prilla, M., Ruhmann, L.M.: An analysis tool for cooperative mixed reality scenarios. In: IEEE International Symposium on Mixed and Augmented Reality Adjunct (ISMAR-Adjunct), Munich, Germany, 29 April 2018

Rajeev, S., Wan, Q., Yau, K., Panetta, K., Agaian, S.: Augmented reality-based vision-aid indoor navigation system in GPS denied environment. In: Proceedings Vol. 10993: Mobile multimedia/Image Processing, Security, and Applications 2019, Baltimore, Maryland, 13 May 2019

Rice, R.: Augmented reality tools for enhanced forensics simulations and crime scene analysis. In: Kisiel, K.W. (ed.) Working Through Synthetic Worlds. CRC Press, Boca Raton (2012)

Riedlinger, U., Oppermann, L., Prinz, W.: Tango vs. HoloLens: a comparison of collaborative indoor AR visualisation using hand-held and hands-free devices. Multimodal Technol. Interact. 3(23), 1–15 (2019)

Richards, C.S., Simonsen, T.J., Abel, R.L., Hall, M., Schwyn, D.A., Wicklein, M.: Virtual forensic entomology: improving estimates of minimum post-mortem interval with 3D micro-computed tomography. Forensic Sci. Int. 220(1–3), 251–264 (2012)

Robey, D., Palmer, I.J., Chilton, N., Bramble, S.: From crime scene to computer screen: The use of virtual reality in crime scene investigation (2000). https://www.researchgate.net/public ation/246248660_From_Crime_Scene_to_Computer_Screen_The_Use_of_Virtual_Reality_ in_Crime_Scene_Investigation. Accessed 20 Feb 2020

Roman, J.K., Reid, S.E., Chalfin, A.J., Knight, C.R.: The DNA field experiment: a randomized trial of the cost-effectiveness of using DNA to solve property crimes. J. Exp. Criminol. 5, 345 (2009)

Roman-Santos, C.: Concerns associated with expanding DNA databases. Hastings Sci. Technol. Law J. 2(2), 267–300 (2010)

Ruhmann, L., Prilla, M.: Joint search patterns in mixed reality (2018). https://dl.gi.de/handle/20. 500.12116/16637. Accessed 3 Jan 2020

Ruhmann, L.M., Prilla, M., Brown, G.: Cooperative mixed reality: an analysis tool. In: Proceedings of the 2018 ACM Conference on Supporting Groupwork, Florida, USA, 7–10 January 2018

Sandvik, K.: Crime scenes as augmented reality: models for enhancing places emotionally by means of narratives, fictions and virtual reality. In: Knudsen, B.T., Waade, A.M. (eds.) Re-Investing Authenticity: Tourism, Place and Emotion, pp. 138–154. Channel View Publications, Bristol (2010)

Sandvik, K.: The anatomy of the crime scene. In: Conference: Motion and Emotion Within Place (2009). https://www.forskningsdatabasen.dk/en/catalog/2398297568. Accessed 1 Feb 2020

Sandvik, K., Waade, A.M.: Crime scene as augmented reality on screen, online and offline. In: Working Paper No. 5 (2008). http://www.krimiforsk.aau.dk/uk/awpaper/KSAWcrimesceneas. w5letter.pdf. Accessed 26 Dec 2019

Sandvik, K.: Crime scenes as augmented reality. University of Copenhagen (2010) https:// static-curis.ku.dk/portal/files/20472434/sandvik_-_crime_scenes_as_augmented_reality.pdf. Accessed 4 Feb 2020

Sauter, P.M.: Introduction to crime scene reconstruction using real-time interactive 3D technology (2019) https://pmsmicro.com/forensicscienceschapter_4d.pdf. Accessed 3 Feb 2020

Shen, A.R., Cipolla, G.J.: Toward automatic blood spatter analysis in crime scenes. In: 2006 IET Conference on Crime and Security, London, UK, 13–14 July 2006

Spain, R., et al.: Me and my VE, part 5: applications in human factors research and practice. In: Proceedings of the Human Factors and Ergonomics Society Annual Meeting, vol. 62, no. 1, pp. 2051–2055 (2018)

Speicher, M., Cao, J., Yu, A., Zhang, H., Nebeling, M.: 360 anywhere: mobile ad-hoc collaboration in any environment using 360 video and augmented reality. In: Proceedings of the ACM on Human-Computer Interaction, vol. 2, no. 9 (2018)

Streefkerk, J.W., Houben, M., van Amerongen, P., ter Haar, F., Dijk, J.: The ART of CSI: an augmented reality tool (ART) to annotate crime scenes in forensic investigation. In: Shumaker, R. (ed.) VAMR 2013. LNCS, vol. 8022, pp. 330–339. Springer, Heidelberg (2013). https://doi.org/10.1007/978-3-642-39420-1_35

Teo, T., Lee, G.A., Billinghurst, M., Adcock, M.: 360 drops: mixed reality remote collaboration using 360 panoramas within the 3D scene, In: SA 2019 SIGGRAPH Asia 2019 Emerging Technologies (2019). https://doi.org/10.1145/3355049.3360517. Accessed 3 Jan 2020

Ticknor, B.: Virtual Reality and the Criminal Justice System: Exploring the Possibilities for Correctional Rehabilitation. The Rowman and Littlefield Publishing Group Inc., London (2018)

Veremme, A., Lefevre, E., Morvan, G., Dupont, D., Jolly, D.: Evidential calibration process of multi-agent based system: an application to forensic entomology. Expert Syst. Appl. **39**(3), 2361–2374 (2012)

Wang, J., et al.: Virtual reality and in integrated crime scene scanning for immersive and heterogeneous crime scene reconstruction. Forensic Sci. Int. **303**, 109943 (2019)

Wassom, B.: Augmented Reality Law, Privacy, and Ethics: Law, Society, and Emerging AR Technologies. Syngress, Waltham, (2015)

Werry, P.: Who Did It? South Pacific Press, Wellington (2011)

Yen, K., Thali, M.J., Kneubuehl, B., Peschel, O., Zollinger, U., Dirnhofer, R.: Blood spatter patterns: Hands hold clues for the forensic reconstruction of the sequence of events. Am. J. Forensic Med. Pathol. **224**(2), 132–140 (2003)

Forensic Analysis of Microsoft Teams: Investigating Memory, Disk and Network

Zainab Khalid[1](✉), Farkhund Iqbal[2], Khalil Al-Hussaeni[3], Aine MacDermott[4], and Mohammed Hussain[2]

[1] National University of Science and Technology (NUST), SEECS, Islamabad, Pakistan
zkhalid.msis18seecs@seecs.edu.pk
[2] College of Technological Innovation, Zayed University, Dubai, UAE
[3] Department of Computer Science, Rochester Institute of Technology, Dubai, UAE
[4] Liverpool John Moores University, Liverpool, UK

Abstract. Videoconferencing applications have seen a jump in their userbase owing to the COVID-19 pandemic. The security of these applications has certainly been a hot topic since millions of VoIP users' data is involved. However, research pertaining to VoIP forensics is still limited to Skype and Zoom. This paper presents a detailed forensic analysis of Microsoft Teams, one of the top 3 videoconferencing applications, in the areas of memory, disk-space and network forensics. Extracted artifacts include critical user data, such as emails, user account information, profile photos, exchanged (including deleted) messages, exchanged text/media files, timestamps and Advanced Encryption Standard encryption keys. The encrypted network traffic is investigated to reconstruct client-server connections involved in a Microsoft Teams meeting with IP addresses, timestamps and digital certificates. The conducted analysis demonstrates that, with strong security mechanisms in place, user data can still be extracted from a client's desktop. The artifacts also serve as digital evidence in the court of Law, in addition to providing forensic analysts a reference for cases involving Microsoft Teams.

Keywords: Artifacts · Digital forensics · Memory forensics · Microsoft Teams · Network forensics · Videoconferencing · VoIP

1 Introduction

Adaptation of videoconferencing applications in the wake of COVID-19 pandemic has proved to be an efficient alternative as businesses and schools continue to utilize them for meetings and online classes. This technology may be used well past the pandemic is over owing to the convenience, higher productivity levels reported by employees and reduced travel costs among other advantages [1]. The market value of Voice over Internet Protocol (VoIP) applications is estimated at $6.03 billion in 2021 [1]. Most prevalent of these applications include Zoom, Cisco WebEx, Microsoft Teams, Google Hangouts, BlueJeans and Adobe Connect according to a recent G2 report [2].

© ICST Institute for Computer Sciences, Social Informatics and Telecommunications Engineering 2022
Published by Springer Nature Switzerland AG 2022. All Rights Reserved
S. Paiva et al. (Eds.): SmartCity360° 2021, LNICST 442, pp. 583–601, 2022.
https://doi.org/10.1007/978-3-031-06371-8_37

Any application that connects to the internet is at risk. It is therefore important to consider the security and privacy risks posed by videoconferencing applications because they store and transmit data of millions of users. Malicious actors leverage the vulnerabilities present and exploit them to gain access to users' account/data to harass, abuse or bully them. *Zoom-bombing* is an example of intruders exploiting a vulnerability (Zoom's screen sharing feature) to hijack meetings to stream improper content or harass attendees [3]. Such vulnerabilities have since been patched; however, other persistent risks can be categorized into: software development risk, personal information loss, communication interception, unlawful access to confidential data and privacy violation [4]. Andrew Lewis, in his report, discusses how it is important to compare the security of a VoIP application compared to others but it is also important to analyze the risks of videoconferencing in terms of a broader digital platform [4].

WebEx, in 2019, was patched for critical vulnerabilities: CVE-2020-3419, CVE-2020-3441 and CVE-2020-3471, which would have allowed a hacker to obtain private user data without leaving a trace, therefore violating confidentiality and non-repudiation [5]. Houseparty was reported to have questionable privacy policies and collecting end-user information while Google Meet did not offer full encryption initially [6].

Evidently, there is a need to forensically analyze videoconferencing applications to extract artifacts that can *attribute malicious actions to guilty individuals*. These artifacts can therefore serve as digital evidence in criminal investigations. Microsoft Teams has experienced a surge in its userbase, with 145 million daily active users and 100+ million downloads on Google Play Store [7]. It is one of the top 3 videoconferencing applications in the market. This research work forensically analyzes the Microsoft Teams desktop application on a Windows virtual client machine to determine, carve and extract artifacts of potential evidential value from different locations on the client's desktop. These include memory, disk-space and network. To the best of our knowledge, this is the first forensic analysis of the Microsoft Teams desktop application.

1.1 Microsoft Teams Protocol Overview

VoIP applications, with their upward trends of demand and userbase, have been scrutinized for the security services they offer. Zoom initially faced backlash in this regard. However, with time, security practices such as: (1) media encryption, (2) session encryption, and (3) hashing for integrity and authentication etc. have been adopted and implemented in these applications. Microsoft Teams has particularly benefitted from Microsoft's mature security model [4]. Security services provided by Microsoft Teams' communication protocols are discussed below [8]:

- Transport Layer Security (TLS) is used for client-to-server signaling and Mutual Transport Layer Security (MTLS) is used to encrypt server-to-server messages.
- Media traffic is encrypted using Secure Real-time Transport Protocol (SRTP).
- Federal Information Processing Standard (FIPS) compliant algorithms are used for encryption key exchanges.
- Client-to-server authentication is achieved using Modern Authentication (MA) which is Microsoft's implementation of OAUTH 2.0. Multi-Factor Authentication (MFA) and conditional access are implemented using MA.

- User Datagram Protocol (UDP) 3478–3481 and Transmission Control Protocol (TCP) 443 over TLS are used by the client to request for audio visuals.
- Microsoft Teams stores files in *SharePoint* which is primarily a *cloud-based document management and storage system* developed by Microsoft. The files stored in SharePoint servers are protected by SharePoint encryption.

With strict encryption and authentication protocols being used for data in transit and at rest, our main goal in this research is to investigate what artifacts can be extracted from a client's desktop (memory, disk-space and network). The contributions of our research are as follows:

- We perform a detailed memory forensic analysis of Microsoft Teams to extract artifacts that are corroborated with artifacts from disk-space and network.
- We analyze the Windows Registry on disk-space to extract registry keys pertaining to Microsoft Teams.
- We present an in-depth network forensic analysis of Microsoft Teams' (encrypted) traffic.

The rest of this paper is structured as follows. Section 2 discusses research previously done in VoIP applications' forensic analysis and other similar Instant Messaging (IM)/social media applications. Section 3 presents the research methodology adopted and the experimental setup. Sections 4, 5 and 6 present the findings of memory forensics, disk-space forensics and network forensics for Microsoft Teams, respectively. Finally, Sect. 7 provides a summary of the contributions and discusses prospects of further research that can be performed in VoIP forensics.

2   Literature Review

Previous research in the domain of forensic analysis of videoconferencing applications is limited. Some of the most recent works in VoIP application forensics are discussed in this section.

Sgaras et al. [9] presented forensic analyses of some IM and VoIP applications namely WhatsApp, Viber, Skype and Tango on both Android and iOS platforms. They developed a taxonomy of the artifacts that can be extracted using logical and manual analyses.

Yang et al. [10] performed an in-depth forensic analysis of Facebook and Skype on a Windows 8.1 machine. Terrestrial artifacts such as installation information, log-in and log-off information, contact lists, conversations and transferred files were extracted from memory, disk-space and network traffic. The authors also observed that uninstalling the applications removed most artifacts from the file-system, but some installation data still remained on the disk; therefore, anti-forensics attempts by deleting data can be detected.

Tandel and Rughani [11] investigated the client artifacts that can be extracted from an Asterisk server during a (Zoiper) VoIP communication if the server is compromised. The authors used Encase to extract usernames, passwords, call records, access logs and error logs from the server.

Dargahi et al. [12] presented the analysis of forensically valuable remnants of mobile VoIP applications: Viber, Skype and WhatsApp messenger on an Android smartphone. They recovered artifacts such as messages, contact details, phone numbers, images and video files from logical images of a rooted Samsung Galaxy S3 GT-i9300 smartphone.

Mohemmed et al. [13] presented a packet level *forensic analyzer* for VoIP network traffic. The framework can identify and analyze the VoIP-SIP stream (which is the protocol used to initiate a VoIP communication session) and regenerate the VoIP-RTP stream (protocol used for data transfer) in order to trace malicious users involved in a conversation.

Recently, Nicoletti and Bernaschi [14] forensically analyzed Skype for Business with a focus on Skype's communication architecture, protocols and VoIP codec to extract artifacts. They presented case studies that elaborated the relevance of extracted artifacts in different investigative cases. They identified the Windows Registry, Event Viewer, client application folder and log files as sources of potential evidence in the presented case studies.

After the COVID-19 outbreak, the number of VoIP applications and their usage has surged but research regarding forensic analysis of the most recent and prevalent videoconferencing applications is still scarce. Zoom, however, has been analyzed in-depth by Mahr et al. [15]. The authors presented a detailed disk-space forensic analysis of Zoom on Windows and macOS desktops. Their research included an analysis of Android and iOS smartphones as well. Various databases in the Zoom data directory were investigated to extract artifacts that included chats, contacts, caches, video meetings and user/device configurations. Preliminary memory and network forensic analyses were also presented.

The Zoom databases analyzed by Mahr et al. [15] were stored on disk in un-encrypted form at the time of their research. However, from our own forensic analysis of the Zoom data directory, we have observed that the databases are now stored in encrypted form on the disk-space. This adds another layer of complexity for the forensic analyst since a passphrase or key is required for decryption.

Similar works include forensic analysis of Social Media applications such as Instagram [16], Facebook, Twitter, LinkedIn [17], WhatsApp, Hangouts and Line [18] on mobile operating systems such as Android and iOS for digital forensic artifacts.

3   Methodology and Experimental Setup

For the purpose of this research, a controlled test environment created using a Windows 10 Virtual Machine (VM) was used. 4 GB RAM and 60 GB disk-space was allotted to the VM. A Microsoft Teams user account was created and signed-in. A clean test environment facilitates a more precise analysis as unnecessary mixing or over-writing of artifacts of Microsoft Teams with other applications or system files is avoided.

To create test data for the forensic analysis, the Microsoft Teams user account was used emulating typical user actions such as: setting up the user profile ID, searching for people in correspondence using keyword search, adding/deleting contacts, audio/video calls and one-to-one/group meetings etc. Table 1 lists features of Microsoft Teams and some user actions that were performed accordingly in order to create the test data.

Table 1. Key features of Microsoft Teams.

Teams feature	User actions
Account setup	Set-up a username, password and profile photo
Search	Find people using keyword search
Contacts	Add/delete contacts
Teams	Create and join teams
Messaging	Send/delete chat messages, URLs, text files and media files
Meetings	Conduct one-to-one and group meetings (+in-meeting chat messages)
Recording	Record meetings
Screen share	Conduct meetings while using the screen sharing feature

Following test user activities, FTK imager was used to create memory and disk images of the VM. For memory analysis, each memory dump was taken after major user actions were performed such as user login, chat messages, meetings etc. to analyze them separately.

For automated analysis of the forensic images, tools such as Volatility, Bulk Extractor and Photorec were used. Manual forensic analysis was performed using string searching, employing relevant keywords/phrases. The artifacts in focus are categorized into different *profiles* [12]: (1) installation data, (2) traffic data, (3) content data, (4) user profile data, (5) user authentication data, (6) contact database, (7) attachment/files and (8) location data.

To capture and analyze the network traffic, we used Wireshark. Network miner was also used to analyze *.pcap* traffic captured using Wireshark. The research methodology is illustrated in Fig. 1 (Table 2).

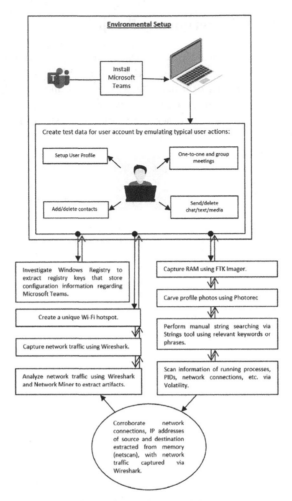

Fig. 1. Research methodology.

Table 2. Tools used for forensic analysis.

Tool	Version	Usage
Windows 10 VM	10	Test OS
Microsoft Teams desktop application	1.4.00.7174	Videoconferencing application under test for forensic artifacts
FTK imager	4.5.0.3	Create forensic image dumps
Volatility	2.6	Forensic analysis of image dumps
Strings	2.53	Manual string searching

(*continued*)

Table 2. (*continued*)

Tool	Version	Usage
Bulk Extractor	1.6.0	Forensic analysis of image dumps
Photorec	7.2	Carve .jpeg images from image dumps
Regedit	10	View the windows registry
Wireshark	3.4.6	Capture/analyze network traffic
Network miner	2.7.1.0	Analyze network traffic

4 Memory Forensics

Random Access Memory (RAM), or memory, stores information about the Operating System's (OS) running processes and applications. Data is often stored in un-encrypted form in the memory which makes it an interesting reserve of information that can serve as digital evidence. Microsoft Teams' artifacts carved from the memory of the VM are presented.

Determining whether Microsoft Teams was running on a device or not was fairly simple; the *pslist*, or *pstree* plug-ins of Volatility showed the *teams.exe* processes running in the memory. The processes were displayed against their Process IDs (PID). The PID's Parent Process Identifier (PPID) can also be traced to make sure that the *teams.exe* originated from the legitimate Teams process and not a foreign/malicious process. The timestamps of the *teams.exe* process also indicated when the application was running. The *pstree* output in Fig. 2(a), shows the Teams processes. Volatility can also be used to investigate the network connections that were listening/established close to when the

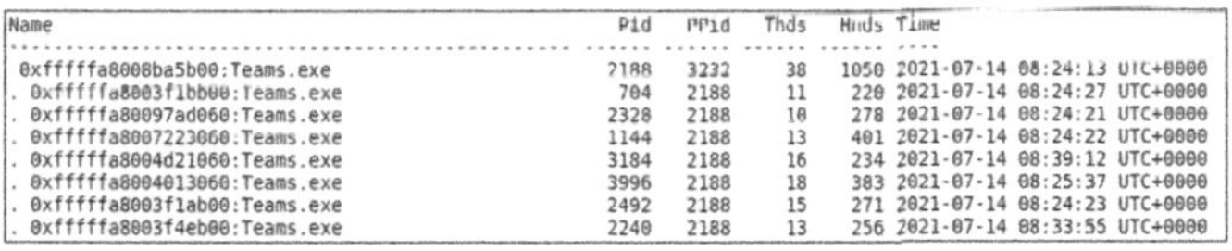

(a)

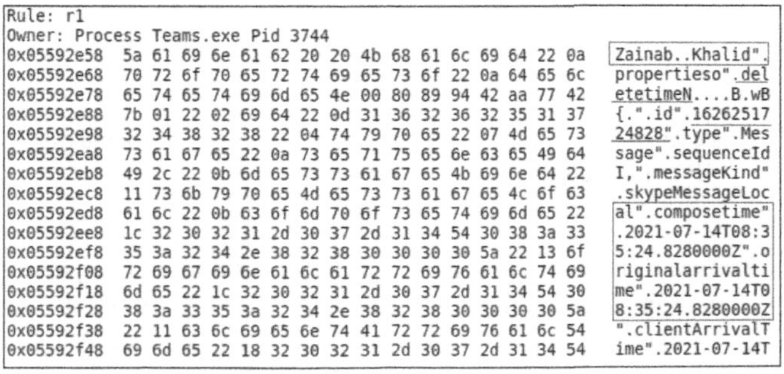

(b)

Fig. 2. (a) Pstree output for Microsoft Teams via Volatility. (b) Yarascan search for PID 3744 via Volatility.

memory image was captured. The output of *netscan* for Microsoft Teams is discussed in Sect. 6.

Yarascan is another Volatility plugin that was used to search artifacts particular to a PID. Figure 2(b) shows information regarding a message deletion related to a Teams process (searched using Teams PID 3744).

As shown, Yarascan searches can reveal useful information about user activity, but it displayed a limited window of information and further analysis required tracing the physical/virtual offsets of the displayed output. The same information was easily extracted using string searching as discussed further.

Another tool, Bulk Extractor was used to carve Advances Encryption Standard (AES) keys, as shown in Fig. 3(a). The email histogram (Fig. 3(b)) showed the user's correspondence in one-to-one and group meetings in an order. It is observed that the user communicated most with user accounts associated with the emails at the top of the histogram.

```
# Feature-Recorder: aes_keys
# Filename: calldump.mem
# Feature-File-Version: 1.1
68887940      1a 6c cd f3 c5 26 3d 06 46 95 30 c5 f8 90    AES128
176251128     48 18 9e 20 04 79 3c 22 c4 6f c3 b1 f3 2c 6c 04 7b 2e 70 2a 17 1f 62 cf 0d d5 ad 6a e7 cd    AES256
176251776     e1 1e 45 71 de f3 fa cc 42 b9 33 4a 3e 8d c1 63 e6 c6 22 32 1c a1 c7 52 52 fb 59 7a 4b 00    AES256
509692536     48 18 9e 20 04 79 3c 22 c4 6f c3 b1 f3 2c 6c 04 7b 2e 70 2a 17 1f 62 cf 0d d5 ad 6a e7 cd    AES256
509693184     e1 1e 45 71 de f3 fa cc 42 b9 33 4a 3e 8d c1 63 e6 c6 22 32 1c a1 c7 52 52 fb 59 7a 4b 00    AES256
1022826464    e1 1e 45 71 de f3 fa cc 42 b9 33 4a 3e 8d c1 63 e6 c6 22 32 1c a1 c7 52 52 fb 59 7a 4b 00    AES256
1145976800    e1 1e 45 71 de f3 fa cc 42 b9 33 4a 3e 8d c1 63 e6 c6 22 32 1c a1 c7 52 52 fb 59 7a 4b 00    AES256
1331799232    cf 33 df a0 8e 3e 74 5b 55 32 5e 5f b5 bd 03 d2 a2 77 20 e4 e6 45 f1 95 00 28 27 2e c1 01    AES256
1384461056    12 b2 79 15 15 00 92 e1 5b 52 19 2b e2 b2    AES128
1860916612    1a 6c cd f3 c5 26 3d 06 46 95 30 c5 f8 90    AES128
2046707016    27 17 6d b4 b8 92 ac 99 fc 75 ea ae cb 80 83 d3 32 1a 0c c4 c2 4e 58 f4 d0 15 15 15 e6 6f    AES256
2046707664    e3 b5 63 aa 3c 58 b8 3c e8 7d 8d da 72 e1 51 d3 a0 a4 f6 2e 17 4e c4 93 c5 1e 89 12 bf dd    AES256
2295347632    48 18 9e 20 04 79 3c 22 c4 6f c3 b1 f3 2c 6c 04 7b 2e 70 2a 17 1f 62 cf 0d d5 ad 6a e7 cd    AES256
2313253472    8b 18 63 cb 13 03 11 5f 8c 02 c4 2c 64 12    AES128
2438508792    48 18 9e 20 04 79 3c 22 c4 6f c3 b1 f3 2c 6c 04 7b 2e 70 2a 17 1f 62 cf 0d d5 ad 6a e7 cd    AES256
2438509440    e1 1e 45 71 de f3 fa cc 42 b9 33 4a 3e 8d c1 63 e6 c6 22 32 1c a1 c7 52 52 fb 59 7a 4b 00    AES256
2712266220    ca b0 c9 13 9d 42 4a 78 51 aa 2e 20 61 66    AES128
2930948584    48 18 9e 20 04 79 3c 22 c4 6f c3 b1 f3 2c 6c 04 7b 2e 70 2a 17 1f 62 cf 0d d5 ad 6a e7 cd    AES256
2930949232    e1 1e 45 71 de f3 fa cc 42 b9 33 4a 3e 8d c1 63 e6 c6 22 32 1c a1 c7 52 52 fb 59 7a 4b 00    AES256
4637786672    33 37 91 70 18 98 85 3e a0 27 86 c4 90 1b 77 34 72 5f d6 8f fe 89 97 f5 33 e7 93 20 26 85    AES256
5031073292    04 21 85 20 00 1b 8e db eb aa 93 28 93 7a    AES128
```

(a)

```
# Feature-Recorder: email
# Filename: calldump.mem
# Histogram-File-Version: 1.1
n=744    zkhalid.msis18seecs@student.nust.edu.pk    (utf16=123)
n=166    haftab.msis17seecs@student.nust.edu.pk     (utf16=19)
n=140    bnoor.msis19seecs@student.nust.edu.pk      (utf16=12)
n=124    bnoor.msis19seecs@nustedupk0.onmicrosoft.com
n=122    meet598@nustedupk0.onmicrosoft.com
n=92     meet598@nust.edu.pk
n=83     info@diginotar.nl
n=49     00@unq.gb        (utf16=49)
n=38     hp@login.microsoftonline.com      (utf16=38)
n=34     premium-server@thawte.com
n=34     sales@ouriginal.com      (utf16=34)
n=30     appro@openssl.org
```

(b)

Fig. 3. (a) AES keys extracted via Bulk Extractor. (b) Email histogram displaying most contacted emails extracted via Bulk Extractor.

Photorec was used to carve photographic images from the memory dumps. We were able to extract critical images, such as: (1) profile photo of the logged-in user account, (2) profile photos of accounts the user interacted with, (3) Microsoft Teams logos and (4) other favicon images related to the application, as shown in Fig. 4. This shows that Microsoft Teams's profile images are processed in un-encrypted form in the memory; a useful artifact in regard to investigations.

User Account Profile Picture   Interacted accounts

Fig. 4. Profile photos carved from memory via Photorec.

Manual forensic analysis was also conducted using string searches against the memory dumps which revealed a plethora of information such as the user's account details (user display name, email address associated with Microsoft Teams and the user ID etc.), as shown in Fig. 5(a). The user password was not found in the memory in plaintext as a result of string search against the memory dump. This was expected since sensitive authentication information is stored in encrypted form.

Figure 5(b) shows details about an audio call that was made. The start time, end time, user ID and display name of the account that made the call and the recipient's user ID were all present in the memory.

The keyword search option in Microsoft Teams enables the user to search for acquaintances and friends. In memory, information regarding searches made using the option were found under the *QueryString* tag as shown in Fig. 5(c).

```
auth_time":1585208534,"family_name":"Khalid","given_name":"Zainab",
"ipaddr":"119.160.64.145","name":"Zainab  Khalid"}
"oid":"b6718102-1033-4ce3-9fed-1834d982ed00",
"tid":"1511ab2e-502b-bd68-f679f549b5a2",
"unique_name":"zkhalid.msis18seecs@student.nust.edu.pk","upn":"zkhalid.msis18seecs@student.nust.edu.pk",
"uti":"VnID4zHLokWt9ROTf-l1AA","ver":"1.0","wids":["b79fbf4d-3ef9-4689-8143-76b194e85509"]},
"userId":"1511ab2e-502b-4e2d-bd68-f679f549b5a2__b6718102-1033-4ce3-9fed-1834d982ed00"
"profileType":"AAD","userName"."zkhalid.msis18seecs@student.nust.edu.pk"}},
"homeUserUpn":"zkhalid.msis18seecs@student.nust.edu.pk"}
```

(a)

```
{"startTime":"2021-05-12T07:52:17.3695395Z","connectTime":"2021-05-12T07:52:30.5273908Z"
"endTime":"2021-05-12T08:01:22.5864977Z","callDirection":"outgoing","callType":"twoParty",
"callState":"accepted","originator":"8:orgid:b6718102-1033-4ce3-9fed-1834d982ed00","target":
"8:orgid:d94d4c0c-ba6b-4813-94ba-db68f7b55389","originatorParticipant":
{"id":"8:orgid:b6718102-1033-4ce3-9fed-1834d982ed00","type":"default",
"displayName":"Zainab  Khalid"},"targetParticipant":
{"id":"8:orgid:d94d4c0c-ba6b-4813-94ba-db68f7b55389"
```

(b)

```
EntityRequests":[{"Query"|{"QueryString":"Hira","DisplayQueryString":"Hira"}
,"EntityType":"People","Provenances":["Mailbox","Directory"],"From":0,"Size":5,
"Filter":{"And":[{"Or":[{"Term":{"PeopleType":"Person"}},{"Term":{"PeopleType":"Other"}}]},
{"Or":[{"Term":{"PeopleSubtype":"OrganizationUser"}},{"Term":{"PeopleSubtype":"Guest"}}]}]},
"Fields":["Id","DisplayName","EmailAddresses","CompanyName","JobTitle","ImAddress",
"UserPrincipalName","ExternalDirectoryObjectId","PeopleType","PeopleSubtype",
"ConcatenatedId","Phones","MRI","Alias"]},{"Query":{"QueryString":"Hira"},"EntityType":"File","Size":3}]
,"LogicalId":"318cbac7-11e2-42f1-90ef-2e1047b82aae","Cvid":"0f77adda-e8f6-4907-9c06-B0dee0c542ff",
"AppName":"Microsoft Teams","Scenario":{"Name":"powerbar"}}
```

(c)

Fig. 5. (a) User account details extracted via manual string search. (b) Call information extracted via manual string search. (c) Keyword search extracted via manual string search.

The *Microsoft Teams Chat Files* tag stores information about the exchanged text files (including deleted text files) as shown in Fig. 6. The user name, email address of the sender, date and time of exchange, user IDs, name and size of the text file were extracted. Under the same (*Microsoft Teams Chat Files*) tag, information about the exchanged and deleted (photo) media files, their sizes and timestamps were also extracted. The SharePoint server addresses, where these files are stored, were extracted under the tag as well.

```
https://nustedupk0-my.sharepoint.com/personal/zkhalid_msis18seecs_student_nust_edu_pk/Documents/Microsoft Teams Chat Files/test.txt"
fileServerRelativeUrl"_/personal/zkhalid_msis18seecs_student_nust_edu_pk/Documents/Microsoft Teams Chat Files/test.txt"
{"from":{"displayName":"Zainab Khalid","email":"zkhalid.msis18seecs@student.nust.edu.pk"},"clientId":"1039047480304289200"}
"draftObjectId":null,"replyChainId":null,"conversationId":
"19:853db850-c649-404f-ab10-4019f1175348_b6718102-1033-4ce3-9fed-1834d982ed00@unq.gbl.spaces",
"subject":"","dateTimeSent":"2021-07-14T08:36:32.501Z","state":null,"isDraft":true,"isNewMessage":true,
"conversationIndex":"1039047480304289200","isPendingSend":true,"body":"","attachments":
[{"objectId":"817b1222-d9af-47c3-94a0-762a8cee734c",
{"id":"973f5f79-7a40-4465-b243-ab92fa1c6518","name":"test.txt","size":19,"viewId":"1039047480304289200",
"progress":5,"state":3,"isNotificationHandled":true,"retentionPolicy":"none","uploadBeginTimestamp":"2021-07-14T08:37:27.336Z",
```

(a)

```
{"id":"20f4ef62-9f4d-4579-9f5e-5380a973abff","name":"del.txt",
"size":6238,"viewId":"626968173333597400","progress":100,"state":2,
"isNotificationHandled":true,"uploadBeginTimestamp":"2021-07-14T08:33:53.433Z"
"sourceProviderMetaData":"{\"code\":null,\"type\":0}","destinationProviderMetaData":"
{\"code\":null,\"type\":0}","sourceOfFile":3,
"siteUrl":"https://nustedupk0-my.sharepoint.com/personal/zkhalid_msis18seecs_student_nust_edu_pk"
```

(b)

```
https://nustedupk0-my.sharepoint.com/personal/zkhalid_msis18seecs_student_nust_edu_pk/Documents/Microsoft Teams Chat Files/books.jpg"
fileServerRelativeUrl"`/personal/zkhalid_msis18seecs_student_nust_edu_pk/Documents/Microsoft Teams Chat Files/books.jpg"
Teams%20Chat%20Files%276@file=%27books.jpg%27
{"id":"2fa24289-006a-4865-98d0-268756f1a11e","name":"books.jpg","size":7537,
"viewId":"5461178093984267000","progress":100,"state":2,"isNotificationHandled":true,
"retentionPolicy":"none","uploadBeginTimestamp":"2021-07-14T08:38:26.208Z",
```

(c)

```
{"id":"bd5db3ba-3fc1-45d8-aa0d-8ee0a601bdf1",
"name":"asdf.jpg","size":10371,"viewId":"626968173333597400",
"progress":66,"state":3,"isNotificationHandled":true,
"retentionPolicy":"none","uploadBeginTimestamp":"2021-07-14T08:33:53.425Z",
"sourceProviderMetaData":"{\"code\":null,\"type\":0}",
"destinationProviderMetaData":"{\"code\":null,\"type\":0}"
```

(d)

Fig. 6. (a) Exchanged text file extracted via manual string search. (b) Deleted text file extracted via manual string search. (c) Exchanged media file extracted via manual string search. (d) Deleted media file extracted via manual string search.

Messages exchanged between the user and other parties were also extracted from the memory under the *skypexspaces-[user ID]* tag, which is the database name of the particular user. This database (stored in *SharePoint*) seemingly stores all the messages of the user including timestamps and other information as shown in Fig. 7. This included deleted messages as well. Microsoft Teams stores messages in the databases even after they are deleted. Using the timestamps, a messaging exchange can be reconstructed in chronological order including the deleted messages. Exchanged Uniform Resource Locators (URLs) were also found under the *skypexspaces-[user ID]* tag (Fig. 7).

Note that some text messages, URLs and media/text files exchanged between users during test activities were deleted. These artifacts were then extracted from the memory dumps using manual string searches as discussed, which shows that deleted information that is *seemingly* deleted and no longer visible on the application's user interface, still resides in the memory and can be recovered using *Microsoft Teams Chat Files* and *skypexspaces-[user ID]* tags. Therefore, anti-forensic attempts like such can be detected using an analysis of the memory.

```
%{"rendererId":"MainRenderer","requestId":"database-142","type":"database",
"payload":{"requestOperationtype":"Put","version":1,
"dbName":"skypexspaces-b6718102-1033-4ce3-9fed-1834d982ed00",
"context":{"storeName":"conversations","
itemOrItems":[{"id":"19:853db850-c649-404f-ab10-4019f1175348_b6718102-1033-4ce3-9fed-1834d982ed00@unq.gbl.spaces",
"type":"Chat","messages":"","properties":{"consumptionhorizon":"1626251363047;1626251372786;361725713246053300",
"consumptionHorizonBookmark":"",
"interopconversationstatus":"None","conversationblockedat":0},"targetLink":"","version":1625478087273,"syncStateUpdatedBy":"
MessageSyncJob_saveSyncState","lastMessage":{"messagetype":"RichText/Html","contenttype":"text",
"content":"<div>Hi how are you doing?</div>","renderContent":"<div>Hi how are you doing?</div>",
"activitytype":"","clientmessageid":"9361982320257786000","amsreferences":[],
"imdisplayname":"Zainab Khalid","properties":{"importance":0,"subject":null},
"id":"1626251376624","type":"Message","messageKind":"skypeMessageLocal","composetime":"2021-07-14T08:29:17.229Z",
"originalarrivaltime":"2021-07-14T08:29:36.624Z"}
"conversationLink":"
blah/19:853db850-c649-404f-ab10-4019f1175348_b6718102-1033-4ce3-9fed-1834d982ed00@unq.gbl.spaces;messageid=1626251376624",
"from":"blah/8:orgid:b6718102-1033-4ce3-9fed-1834d982ed00","idUnion":"9361982320257786000",
```

(a)

```
{"rendererId":"MainRenderer","requestId":"database-162",
"type":"database","payload":{"requestOperationtype":"Put",
"version":1,"dbName":"skypexspaces-b6718102-1033-4ce3-9fed-1834d982ed00",
"context":{"storeName":"replychains",
"itemOrItems":[{"conversationId":
"19:853db850-c649-404f-ab10-4019f1175348_b6718102-1033-4ce3-9fed-1834d982ed00@unq.gbl.spaces",
"parentMessageId":"clientId_6275769237913159000","messages":{"6275769237913159000,8:
orgid:b6718102-1033-4ce3-9fed-1834d982ed00":{"messagetype":"RichText/Html","contenttype":"text",
"content":"<div>Can we schedule a meeting for tomorrow?</div>"
```

(b)

```
{"rendererId":"MainRenderer","requestId":"database-181","type":"database",
"payload":{"requestOperationtype":"Put","version":1,"dbName":
"skypexspaces-b6718102-1033-4ce3-9fed-1834d982ed00",{"storeName":"conversations",
"itemOrItems":[{"id":"19:853db850-c649-404f-ab10-4019f1175348_
b6718102-1033-4ce3-9fed-1834d982ed00@unq.gbl.spaces","type":"Chat","messages":""
"lastMessage":{"messagetype":"RichText/Html","contenttype":"text",
"content":"<div><div><a href=\"https://www.youtube.com/\"
rel=\"noreferrer noopener\" target=\"_blank\"
title=\"https://www.youtube.com/\">https://www.youtube.com/</a><br />\n
```

(c)

```
{"from":{"displayName":"Zainab Khalid","email":"zkhalid.msis18seecs@student.nust.edu.pk"}
"clientId":"4009176384473812000","draftObjectId":null,"replyChainId":null,
"conversationId":"19:853db850-c649-404f-ab10-4019f1175348_
b6718102-1033-4ce3-9fed-1834d982ed00@unq.gbl.spaces",
"subject":"","dateTimeSent":"2021-07-14T08:31:12.678Z","state":null,"isDraft":
true,"isNewMessage":true,
"conversationIndex":"4009176384473812000","isPendingSend":true,"body":
"<div><a href=\"https://www.forensicfocus.com/forums/\"
```

(d)

Fig. 7. (a) Exchanged text message extracted via manual string search. (b) Deleted text message extracted via manual string search. (c) Exchanged URLs extracted via manual string search. (d) Deleted URLs extracted via manual string search.

Information regarding scheduled meetings was also extracted from the memory. Figure 8 shows that a meeting named "Test Meeting" was scheduled for 2 PM Wednesday on July 14, 2021. The organizer's user ID is also extracted along with other information. Chat messages sent (deleted messages included) were also found in the memory (Table 3).

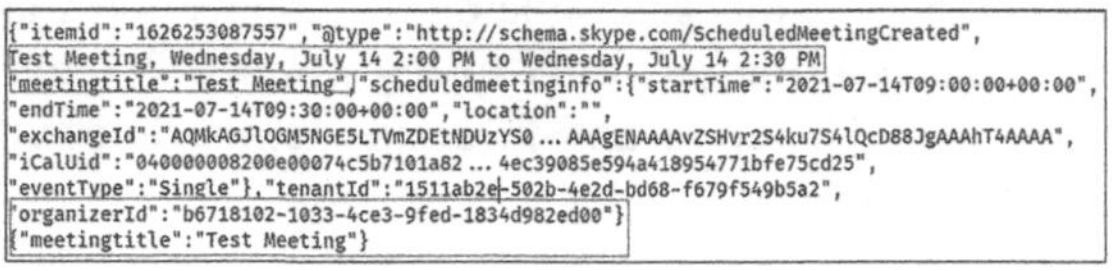

```
{"itemid":"1626253087557","@type":"http://schema.skype.com/ScheduledMeetingCreated",
Test Meeting, Wednesday, July 14 2:00 PM to Wednesday, July 14 2:30 PM
"meetingtitle":"Test Meeting"/"scheduledmeetinginfo":{"startTime":"2021-07-14T09:00:00+00:00",
"endTime":"2021-07-14T09:30:00+00:00","location":"",
"exchangeId":"AQMkAGJlOGM5NGE5LTVmZDEtNDUzYS0...AAAgENAAAAvZSHvr2S4ku7S4lQcD88JgAAAhT4AAAA",
"iCalUid":"040000008200e00074c5b7101a82...4ec39085e594a418954771bfe75cd25",
"eventType":"Single"},"tenantId":"1511ab2e-502b-4e2d-bd68-f679f549b5a2",
"organizerId":"b6718102-1033-4ce3-9fed-1834d982ed00"}
{"meetingtitle":"Test Meeting"}
```

Fig. 8. Scheduled meeting information extracted via manual string search.

Table 3. Summary of memory artifacts of Microsoft Teams.

Artifact	Tool/manual string tag
Running teams processes	(*pslist/pstree*) volatility
Network connections	(*netscan*) volatility
AES keys	Bulk extractor
Profile photos	Image carving against memory dumps via Photorec
User account details (user display name, email address, user ID etc.)	<*unique_name*>/<*userId*> String tag
Keywords searched	<*QueryString*> String tag
Media/text files exchanged (+deleted)	<*Microsoft Teams Chat Files*> String tag
Chat/URLs exchanged (+deleted)	<*skypexspaces-[user ID]*> String tag
Scheduled meetings' details	<*scheduledmeetinginfo*> String tag

5   Disk-Space Forensics

Unlike the memory, disk-space stores information for a relatively longer time. While our analysis of Microsoft Team's client application folder did not reveal information/artifacts of critical value, the Windows Registry is nonetheless a potential source of forensic artifacts. Microsoft Operating System's Windows Registry is a central hierarchal database that stores configuration information about the OS. This includes information about the users, (Microsoft or foreign) applications that are (or were) installed on the device and hardware devices attached to the device. User information can also include credentials and relevant timestamps that can prove useful for an investigation.

We performed an in-depth analysis of the Windows Registry for keys related to Microsoft Teams and it was observed that while basic information about the user account is retrievable from the registry, no credentials/authentication information was found.

The *HKCU\SOFTWARE\RegisteredApplications* key lists Microsoft Teams in registered applications. The *HKCU\SOFTWARE\Microsoft\Office\Teams* key stores basic user account information, as shown in Fig. 9, such as the email address, private meeting settings, the installation source used to install Microsoft Teams, the web account ID and login information etc. The *HKCU\SOFTWARE\Microsoft\Office\Teams\Capabilities\URLAssociations* key stores the URL associations of Microsoft Teams: *sip, sips, im, callto* and *msteams*. The *HKCU\SOFTWARE\Microsoft\Office\Outlook\Addins\TeamsAddin.FastConnect* lists the Microsoft Teams add-in for Outlook. If Microsoft Teams is uninstalled, it is listed in *HKCU\SOFTWARE\Microsoft\UserData\UninstallTimes* key (Table 4).

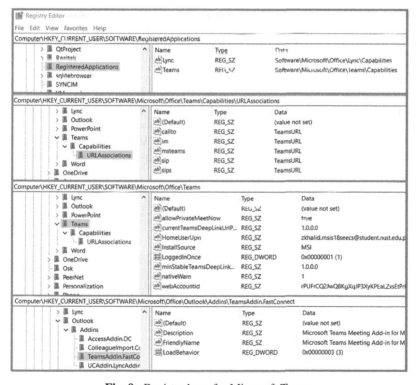

Fig. 9. Registry keys for Microsoft Teams.

Table 4. Registry keys for Microsoft Teams.

Registry key – Value explanation
HKCU\SOFTWARE\RegisteredApplications
List of registered applications in the client desktop (Microsoft Teams inclusive).
HKCU\SOFTWARE\Microsoft\Office\Teams
User account information including email address, private meeting settings, installation source, web account ID and login information etc.
HKCU\SOFTWARE\Microsoft\Office\Teams\Capabilities\URLAssociations
URL associations of Microsoft Teams (e.g., sip, IM, callto etc.).
HKCU\SOFTWARE\Microsoft\Office\Outlook\Addins\TeamsAddin.FastConnect
Microsoft Teams add-in for Outlook.
HKCU\SOFTWARE\Microsoft\UserData\UninstallTimes
Microsoft Teams is listed if it is uninstalled.

6 Network Forensics

The *netscan* output of Microsoft Teams (Fig. 10) shows connections established with Microsoft servers over UDPv4, UDPv6 and TLSv4 while transferring meeting media during a Teams meeting. Volatility seemingly missed some PIDs and IP addresses, which is a recurring problem with the newer versions of Windows (i.e. Windows 10 and its various versions). Nonetheless, the *netscan* output still offers valuable information

Offset(P)	Proto	Local Address	Foreign Address	State	Pid	Owner	Created
0×13a9a8470	TCPv6	:::49152	:::0	LISTENING	528	wininit.exe	
0×13ab3d640	TCPv4	0.0.0.0:49153	0.0.0.0:0	LISTENING	964	svchost.exe	
0×13af83ee0	TCPv4	0.0.0.0:49156	0.0.0.0:0	LISTENING	588	services.exe	
0×13af83ee0	TCPv6	:::49156	:::0	LISTENING	588	services.exe	
0×13a683bd0	TCPv4	192.[ ]:49564	40.77.18.167:443	CLOSED	-1		
0×13a6bdcd0	TCPv4	192.[ ]:49508	20.190.175.23:443	CLOSED	-1		
0×13a9c08f0	TCPv4	192.[ ]:49568	52.114.132.73:443	ESTABLISHED	-1		
0×13addf3d0	TCPv4	192.[ ]:49569	52.114.132.73:443	ESTABLISHED	-1		
0×13b06fcc0	TCPv4	0.0.0.0:49156	0.0.0.0:0	LISTENING	588	services.exe	
0×13c2c3220	UDPv4	192.[ ]:50024	*:*		4076	Teams.exe	2021-07-14 08:58:56 UTC+0000
0×13c2dbec0	UDPv6	fe80[ ]	*:*		3648	svchost.exe	2021-07-14 08:23:40 UTC+0000
0×13c2dfcd0	TCPv4	192.[ ]:49523	52.114.14.235:443	ESTABLISHED	-1		
0×13e77c3a0	UDPv4	192.[ ]:2177	*:*		3648	svchost.exe	2021-07-14 08:46:33 UTC+0000
0×13e6d1450	TCPv4	192.[ ]:49453	52.113.199.100:443	ESTABLISHED	-1		
0×13e6d1cd0	TCPv4	192.[ ]:49546	52.114.36.125:443	ESTABLISHED	-1		
0×13e9ec580	TCPv4	192.[ ]:49553	119.160.63.43:443	ESTABLISHED	-1		
0×13ee6c880	UDPv6	fe80[ ]	*:*		3648	svchost.exe	2021-07-14 08:46:33 UTC+0000
0×13ef0ccb0	UDPv4	0.0.0.0:51209	*:*		4076	Teams.exe	2021-07-14 08:46:02 UTC+0000
0×13ef0ccb0	UDPv6	:::51209	*:*		4076	Teams.exe	2021-07-14 08:46:02 UTC+0000
0×13ef99ec0	UDPv4	0.0.0.0:55228	*:*		3572	Teams.exe	2021-07-14 09:03:23 UTC+0000
0×13ef99ec0	UDPv6	:::55228	*:*		3572	Teams.exe	2021-07-14 09:03:23 UTC+0000
0×13f215240	UDPv4	0.0.0.0:0	*:*		4076	Teams.exe	2021-07-14 08:45:56 UTC+0000
0×13f215240	UDPv6	:::0	*:*		4076	Teams.exe	2021-07-14 08:45:56 UTC+0000
0×13f327900	UDPv4	0.0.0.0:55941	*:*		1212	svchost.exe	2021-07-14 08:57:34 UTC+0000
0×13f55d160	UDPv4	0.0.0.0:60165	*:*		4076	Teams.exe	2021-07-14 08:46:05 UTC+0000
0×13f55d160	UDPv6	:::60165	*:*		4076	Teams.exe	2021-07-14 08:46:05 UTC+0000
0×13ec39790	TCPv4	192.[ ]:49469	52.114.16.76:443	ESTABLISHED	-1		
0×13ee536d0	TCPv4	192.[ ]:49562	52.114.75.149:443	CLOSED	-1		
0×13efe2010	TCPv4	192.[ ]:49520	52.113.194.132:443	ESTABLISHED	-1		
0×13f036820	TCPv4	192.[ ]:49563	20.190.175.23:443	CLOSED	-1		
0×13f1a6bb0	TCPv4	192.[ ]:49547	52.114.36.125:443	CLOSED	-1		
0×13f1e3010	TCPv4	192.[ ]:49567	40.77.18.167:443	CLOSED	-1		
0×13f222a50	TCPv4	192.[ ]:49549	119.160.63.43:443	ESTABLISHED	-1		
0×13f26a700	TCPv4	192.[ ]:49557	52.114.75.149:443	CLOSED	-1		
0×13f2dcac0	TCPv4	192.[ ]:49566	40.77.18.167:443	FIN_WAIT1	-1		
0×13f321470	TCPv4	192.[ ]:49565	40.77.18.167:443	CLOSED	-1		
0×13f329cd0	TCPv4	192.[ ]:49551	119.160.63.43:443	ESTABLISHED	-1		
0×13f7a9330	UDPv4	0.0.0.0:5355	*:*		1212	svchost.exe	2021-07-14 08:23:08 UTC+0000
0×13f7a9330	UDPv6	:::5355	*:*		1212	svchost.exe	2021-07-14 08:23:08 UTC+0000
0×13f7f11c0	UDPv4	0.0.0.0:5355	*:*		1212	svchost.exe	2021-07-14 08:23:08 UTC+0000

Fig. 10. Netscan output via volatility.

including timestamps, and other IP addresses that can be corroborated with the *pslist* output or packets captured using a network protocol analyzer as discussed further. Owing to the volatile nature of memory, it is not always available during an investigation. The disk-space, on the other hand, can be manipulated one way or another. In such a case, the network proves to be a reliable alternative for extracting artifacts because network traffic cannot be tampered with.

To perform network forensic analysis of the Microsoft Teams application, we setup a unique Wi-Fi hotspot to isolate the traffic. This was done to aid the process of analysis. We used the Wireshark network protocol analyzer to both capture and analyze the traffic. Network miner was also used for the analysis of the *.pcap* traffic captured using Wireshark. The IP addresses of servers were investigated using https://ipdata.co/?ref= iplocation.

The traffic was captured intermittently, i.e., the login activity, exchange of messages/URLs/image media and (one-to-one and group) meetings were captured separately to be analyzed individually. From our observations, all the network traffic of Microsoft Teams was encrypted as no credentials, messages, or transferred image or text files were observed in the packet captures in plaintext. The encryption keys were exchanged using the Elliptic Curve Diffie Hellman (ECDH) key agreement protocol, while the application data was transferred using either HTTP over TLSv1.2 or HTTP2, as shown in Fig. 11.

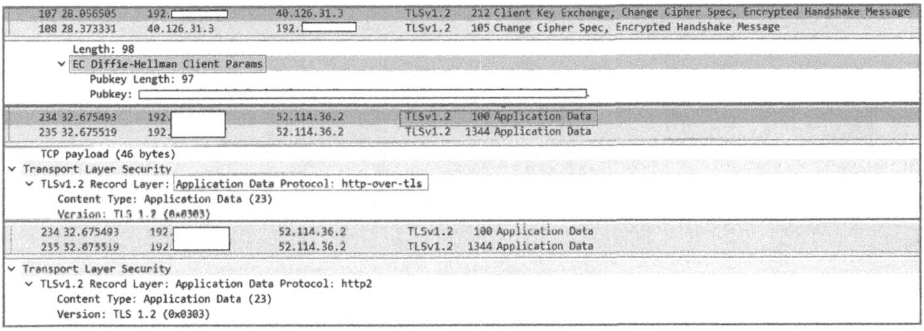

Fig. 11. Communication protocols used by Microsoft Teams as observed via Wireshark.

Sessions between client and Microsoft Teams' servers were encrypted using TLS (Fig. 12). As can be seen, JA3 and JA3S hashing was used to fingerprint the negotiation between client and server.

Analyzing network traffic of Microsoft Teams using Network Miner, we observed that the application makes connections to Microsoft servers mostly (unlike other applications which are likely to use services of other organizations as well). This is expected since Microsoft has an established infrastructure that is capable of all required services. However Akamai Technologies, as observed in the network traffic, is used by Teams as a content distribution system.

Logging into Microsoft Teams, client is first authenticated to the Teams cloud skypedataprdcolneu04.cloudapp.net, login.microsoftonline.com, stamp2.login. microsoftonline on port 443. Another point to note is that Microsoft Teams uses several of Skype's servers as well. Configuration data is fetched from settingsfd-geo.trafficmanager.net, settings-win.data.microsoft.com.

As previously discussed, since network traffic is encrypted, captured frames did not contain any plaintext data. However, digital certificates employed and transferred during the meetings and other activities were extracted. The digital certificates can be used to track whether the communicating hosts were authenticated or not.

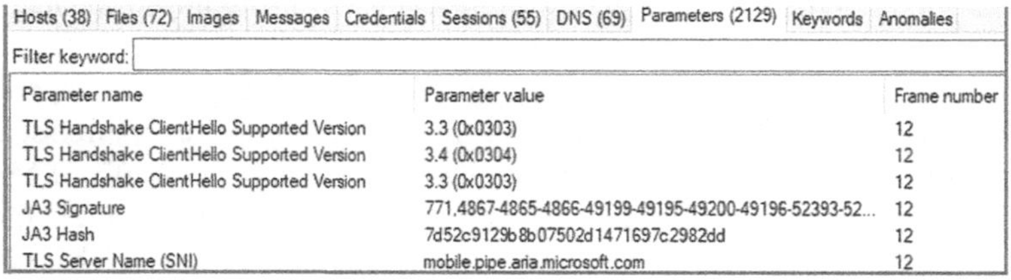

| Hosts (38) | Files (72) | Images | Messages | Credentials | Sessions (55) | DNS (69) | Parameters (2129) | Keywords | Anomalies |

Filter keyword:

Parameter name	Parameter value	Frame number
TLS Handshake ClientHello Supported Version	3.3 (0x0303)	12
TLS Handshake ClientHello Supported Version	3.4 (0x0304)	12
TLS Handshake ClientHello Supported Version	3.3 (0x0303)	12
JA3 Signature	771,4867-4865-4866-49199-49195-49200-49196-52393-52...	12
JA3 Hash	7d52c9129b8b07502d1471697c2982dd	12
TLS Server Name (SNI)	mobile.pipe.aria.microsoft.com	12

(a)

| Hosts (38) | Files (72) | Images | Messages | Credentials | Sessions (55) | DNS (69) | Parameters (2129) | Keywords | Anomalies |

Filter keyword: Case sensitive | ExactPhrase | Any column | Clear | Apply

Frame nr.	Filename	Extension	Size	Source host	S. port	Destination host	D. port	Protocol	Timestamp	Recor
26	events.data.microsoft.com[3].cer	cer	2 534 B	52.114.77.33 [skypedataprdcolneu04.cloudapp.net] [mobil..	TCP 443	192.168.1.100 [HP-PC] (Windows)	TCP 49181	TlsCertificate	2021-06-29 09:45:50 UTC	D:\Sol
26	Microsoft Azure TLS Issuing [3].cer	cer	1 527 B	52.114.77.33 [skypedataprdcolneu04.cloudapp.net] [mobil..	TCP 443	192.168.1.100 [HP-PC] (Windows)	TCP 49181	TlsCertificate	2021-06-29 09:45:50 UTC	D:\Sol
79	teams.microsoft.com[3].cer	cer	1 943 B	52.113.195.132 [s-0005.dc-msedge.net] [teams-office-com..	TCP 443	192.168.1.100 [HP-PC] (Windows)	TCP 49182	TlsCertificate	2021-06-29 09:45:51 UTC	D:\Sol
79	Microsoft RSA TLS CA 01[3].cer	cer	1 374 B	52.113.195.132 [s-0005.dc-msedge.net] [teams-office-com..	TCP 443	192.168.1.100 [HP-PC] (Windows)	TCP 49182	TlsCertificate	2021-06-29 09:45:51 UTC	D:\Sol
101	teams.microsoft.com[4].cer	cer	1 943 B	52.113.195.132 [s-0005.dc-msedge.net] [teams-office-com..	TCP 443	192.168.1.100 [HP-PC] (Windows)	TCP 49183	TlsCertificate	2021-06-29 09:45:51 UTC	D:\Sol
101	Microsoft RSA TLS CA 01[4].cer	cer	1 374 B	52.113.195.132 [s-0005.dc-msedge.net] [teams-office-com..	TCP 443	192.168.1.100 [HP-PC] (Windows)	TCP 49183	TlsCertificate	2021-06-29 09:45:51 UTC	D:\Sol
204	events.data.microsoft.com[4].cer	cer	2 534 B	52.114.77.33 [skypedataprdcolneu04.cloudapp.net] [mobil..	TCP 443	192.168.1.100 [HP-PC] (Windows)	TCP 49184	TlsCertificate	2021-06-29 09:45:53 UTC	D:\Sol
204	Microsoft Azure TLS Issuing [4].cer	cer	1 527 B	52.114.77.33 [skypedataprdcolneu04.cloudapp.net] [mobil..	TCP 443	192.168.1.100 [HP-PC] (Windows)	TCP 49184	TlsCertificate	2021-06-29 09:45:53 UTC	D:\Sol
234	config.officeapps.live.com[2].cer	cer	2 346 B	52.109.112.104 [asia.configsvc1.live.com.akadns.net] [pro..	TCP 443	192.168.1.100 [HP-PC] (Windows)	TCP 49185	TlsCertificate	2021-06-29 09:45:55 UTC	D:\Sol
234	Microsoft RSA TLS CA 02[2].cer	cer	1 374 B	52.109.112.104 [asia.configsvc1.live.com.akadns.net] [pro..	TCP 443	192.168.1.100 [HP-PC] (Windows)	TCP 49185	TlsCertificate	2021-06-29 09:45:55 UTC	D:\Sol
250	config.officeapps.live.com[3].cer	cer	2 346 B	52.109.112.104 [asia.configsvc1.live.com.akadns.net] [pro..	TCP 443	192.168.1.100 [HP-PC] (Windows)	TCP 49186	TlsCertificate	2021-06-29 09:45:55 UTC	D:\Sol
250	Microsoft RSA TLS CA 02[3].cer	cer	1 374 B	52.109.112.104 [asia.configsvc1.live.com.akadns.net] [pro..	TCP 443	192.168.1.100 [HP-PC] (Windows)	TCP 49186	TlsCertificate	2021-06-29 09:45:55 UTC	D:\Sol
290	events.data.microsoft.com[5].cer	cer	2 534 B	52.114.77.33 [skypedataprdcolneu04.cloudapp.net] [mobil..	TCP 443	192.168.1.100 [HP-PC] (Windows)	TCP 49187	TlsCertificate	2021-06-29 09:45:56 UTC	D:\Sol
290	Microsoft Azure TLS Issuing [5].cer	cer	1 527 B	52.114.77.33 [skypedataprdcolneu04.cloudapp.net] [mobil..	TCP 443	192.168.1.100 [HP-PC] (Windows)	TCP 49187	TlsCertificate	2021-06-29 09:45:56 UTC	D:\Sol
304	odc.officeapps.live.com[2].cer	cer	2 269 B	52.109.124.127 [asia.odcsm1.live.com.akadns.net] [prod.o..	TCP 443	192.168.1.100 [HP-PC] (Windows)	TCP 49188	TlsCertificate	2021-06-29 09:45:56 UTC	D:\Sol
304	Microsoft RSA TLS CA 02[2].cer	cer	1 374 B	52.109.124.127 [asia.odcsm1.live.com.akadns.net] [prod.o..	TCP 443	192.168.1.100 [HP-PC] (Windows)	TCP 49188	TlsCertificate	2021-06-29 09:45:56 UTC	D:\Sol
317	odc.officeapps.live.com[3].cer	cer	2 269 B	52.109.124.127 [asia.odcsm1.live.com.akadns.net] [prod.o..	TCP 443	192.168.1.100 [HP-PC] (Windows)	TCP 49189	TlsCertificate	2021-06-29 09:45:57 UTC	D:\Sol
317	Microsoft RSA TLS CA 02[3].cer	cer	1 374 B	52.109.124.127 [asia.odcsm1.live.com.akadns.net] [prod.o..	TCP 443	192.168.1.100 [HP-PC] (Windows)	TCP 49189	TlsCertificate	2021-06-29 09:45:57 UTC	D:\Sol
648	teams.microsoft.com[5].cer	cer	1 943 B	52.113.195.132 [s-0005.dc-msedge.net] [teams-office-com..	TCP 443	192.168.1.100 [HP-PC] (Windows)	TCP 49197	TlsCertificate	2021-06-29 09:46:26 UTC	D:\Sol
648	Microsoft RSA TLS CA 01[5].cer	cer	1 374 B	52.113.195.132 [s-0005.dc-msedge.net] [teams-office-com..	TCP 443	192.168.1.100 [HP-PC] (Windows)	TCP 49197	TlsCertificate	2021-06-29 09:46:26 UTC	D:\Sol
659	events.data.microsoft.com[2].cer	cer	2 534 B	52.114.159.33 [skypedataprdcolnus09.cloudapp.net] [mob..	TCP 443	192.168.1.100 [HP-PC] (Windows)	TCP 49196	TlsCertificate	2021-06-29 09:46:26 UTC	D:\Sol
659	Microsoft Azure TLS Issuing [1].cer	cer	1 527 B	52.114.159.33 [skypedataprdcolnus09.cloudapp.net] [mob..	TCP 443	192.168.1.100 [HP-PC] (Windows)	TCP 49196	TlsCertificate	2021-06-29 09:46:26 UTC	D:\Sol
11555	asyncgw.teams.microsoft.co[10].cer	cer	2 088 B	52.114.14.177 [sa1-api-nonazsc-teams.cloudapp.net] [asm-..	TCP 443	192.168.1.100 [HP-PC] (Windows)	TCP 49200	TlsCertificate	2021-06-29 09:47:30 UTC	D:\Sol
11555	Microsoft RSA TLS CA 01[10].cer	cer	1 374 B	52.114.14.177 [sa1-api-nonazsc-teams.cloudapp.net] [asm-..	TCP 443	192.168.1.100 [HP-PC] (Windows)	TCP 49208	TlsCertificate	2021-06-29 09:47:30 UTC	D:\Sol
11571	msgapi.teams.microsoft.com[2].cer	cer	2 134 B	52.114.36.125 [msgapi-prod-wip-azsc5-1.cloudapp.net] [ap..	TCP 443	192.168.1.100 [HP-PC] (Windows)	TCP 49209	TlsCertificate	2021-06-29 09:47:30 UTC	D:\Sol
11571	Microsoft RSA TLS CA 01[11].cer	cer	1 374 B	52.114.36.125 [msgapi-prod-wip-azsc5-1.cloudapp.net] [ap..	TCP 443	192.168.1.100 [HP-PC] (Windows)	TCP 49209	TlsCertificate	2021-06-29 09:47:30 UTC	D:\Sol
11588	asyncgw.teams.microsoft.co[11].cer	cer	2 088 B	52.114.14.177 [sa1-api-nonazsc-teams.cloudapp.net] [asm-..	TCP 443	192.168.1.100 [HP-PC] (Windows)	TCP 49212	TlsCertificate	2021-06-29 09:47:30 UTC	D:\Sol
11588	Microsoft RSA TLS CA 01[11].cer	cer	1 374 B	52.114.14.177 [sa1-api-nonazsc-teams.cloudapp.net] [asm-..	TCP 443	192.168.1.100 [HP-PC] (Windows)	TCP 49212	TlsCertificate	2021-06-29 09:47:30 UTC	D:\Sol

(b)

Fig. 12. (a) TLS handshake via Network Miner. (b) Digital certificates via Network Miner.

The IP addresses and timestamps from the network traffic were used to reconstruct the history of whom the client device communicated with and when. Table 5 provides details of the captured traffic, IP addresses and servers that the host communicated with. This information can also be used to flag Microsoft Teams' network traffic.

Table 5. Network information.

URLs	IP addresses
Microsoft Corporation.	
skypedataprdcolneu04.cloudapp.net, mobile.events.data.traffic-manager.net, mobile.pip.aria.microsoft.com, teams-office-com.s-0005.s-msedge.net, teams.microsoft.com, asia.configsvc1.live.com.akadns.net, officeclient.microsoft.com, config.officeapps.live.com, asia.odcsm1.live.com.akadns.net, odc.officeapps.live.com, settingsfd-geo.trafficmanager.net, settings-win.data.microsoft.com, sa1-api.nonazsc-teams.cloudapp.net, asm-api-golocal-geo-as-teams.trafficmanager.net, asm.skype.com, as-prod.asyncgw.teams.microsoft.com, apac.ng.msg.teams-msgapi.trafficmanager.net, msgapi.teams.microsoft.com, asm-api-prod-geo-as-skype.trafficmanager.net, as-api.asm.skype.com, teams.events.data.microsoft.com, mobile.pipe.aria.microsoft.com, login.microsoftonline.com, stamp2.login.microsoftonline.	52.114.77.33 52.113.195.132 52.109.112.104 52.109.124.127 52.114.159.33 40.174.108.123 52.114.14.177 52.114.36.126 52.114.15.135 52.114.77.164 138.91.140.216 20.190.175.23 52.114.128.9 52.113.194.132 52.114.16.138 52.114.14.237
Akamai Technologies, Inc.	
e12370.g.akamaiedge.net, cdn.odc.officcapps.live.com.edgekey.net, cdn.odc.officeapps.live.com.	104.120.112.79

7 Conclusion and Future Work

VoIP applications are here to stay. Their tremendous use in business and education raises some security and privacy concerns for users. This paper presented an elaborate forensic analysis of Microsoft Teams in terms of different data localities, namely memory, disk-space and network. Nowadays, companies ensure implementation of security best practices in their applications to build and maintain user trust. Our aim was to analyze Microsoft Teams with its security mechanisms in place and see what critical user information can still be extracted. We presented an in-depth memory forensic analysis of the application, extracting email addresses, profile photos, user account IDs, AES keys, exchanged (including deleted) messages, text/media files, URLs, meeting information and more, in plaintext. Moreover, analysis of Windows Registry keys related to Microsoft Teams revealed some configuration information related to the user account. Network traffic of Teams was encrypted; however, information regarding server domains, their associations, IP addresses and relevant timestamps were investigated. All extracted artifacts can be corroborated holistically to reconstruct events in a forensically sound manner.

Research in the area of forensic analysis of recent VoIP applications is limited; therefore, it would be interesting to extend our research to other videoconferencing applications such as Google Hangouts, BlueJeans and Adobe Connect. Additionally, a comprehensive comparative analysis of the top VoIP applications can be done to highlight the security posture of each application individually as well as VoIP security as a broader communication platform. Secondly, other Operating Systems (such as macOS, Linux, Android and iOS) can be considered for forensic artifact investigation.

Acknowledgment. This study is supported with research funds from Research Incentive Funds (R19044) and Provost Research Fellowship Award (R20093), Zayed University, United Arab Emirates.

References

1. 20 Astonishing Video Conferencing Statistics for 2021. Digital in the Round, 10 May 2021. digitalintheround.com/video-conferencing-statistics/
2. Best Video Conferencing Software in 2020 I G2. *G2*. https://www.g2.com/categories/video-conferencing
3. Lorenz, T.: 'Zoombombing': When Video Conferences Go Wrong. The New York Times, 20 March 2020
4. Andrew Lewis, J.: Video Conferencing Technology and Risk. www.csis.org, 03 December 2020. https://www.csis.org/analysis/video-conferencing-technology-and-risk
5. Zorz, Z.: Cisco WebEx vulnerabilities may enable attackers to covertly join meetings. Help Net Security, 19 November 2020. https://www.helpnetsecurity.com/2020/11/19/cisco-webex-vulnerabilities-attackers-covertly-join-meetings/
6. Gode, S.: Video Conferencing Security Issues and Opportunities. Unify Square. https://www.unifysquare.com/blog/video-conferencing-security-issues-and-opportunities/
7. Warren, T.: Microsoft Teams usage jumps to 145 million daily active users. The Verge, 27 April 2021. https://www.theverge.com/2021/4/27/22406472/microsoft-teams-145-million-daily-active-users-stats
8. Security guide for Microsoft Teams - Microsoft Teams. docs.microsoft.com. https://docs.microsoft.com/en-us/microsoftteams/teams-security-guide#encryption-for-teams
9. Sgaras, C., Kechadi, M.-T., Le-Khac, N.-A.: Forensics Acquisition and Analysis of instant messaging and VoIP applications. In: Computational Forensics, pp. 188–199 (2015)
10. Yang, T.Y., Dehghantanha, A., Choo, K.R., Muda, Z.: Windows instant messaging app forensics: Facebook and Skype as case studies. PLOS ONE **11**(3), e0150300 (2016). https://doi.org/10.1371/journal.pone.0150300
11. Tandel, H., Rughani, P.H.: Forensic analysis of asterisk-FreePBX based VoIP server. Int. J. Emerg. Res. Manage. Technol. **6**, 2278–9359 (2018). https://doi.org/10.23956/ijermt.v6i8.133
12. Dargahi, T., Dehghantanha, A., Conti, M.: Forensics analysis of android mobile VoIP Apps. In: Contemporary Digital Forensic Investigations of Cloud and Mobile Applications, pp. 7–20 (2017). https://doi.org/10.1016/b978-0-12-805303-4.00002-2
13. Sha, M.M., Manesh,T., Abd El-atty, S.M.: VoIP forensic analyzer. Int. J. Adv. Comput. Sci. Appl. **7**(1) (2016). https://doi.org/10.14569/ijacsa.2016.070116
14. Nicoletti, M., Bernaschi, M.: Forensic analysis of Microsoft Skype for Business. Digit. Investig. **29**, 159–179 (2019). https://doi.org/10.1016/j.diin.2019.03.012
15. Mahr, A., Cichon, M., Mateo, S., Grajeda, C., Baggili, I.: Zooming into the pandemic! A forensic analysis of the Zoom Application. Forensic Sci. Int. Digit. Investig. **36**, 301107 (2021). https://doi.org/10.1016/j.fsidi.2021.301107
16. Alisabeth, C., Restu Pramadi, Y.: Forensic analysis of instagram on android. IOP Conf. Ser. Mater. Sci. Eng. **1007**, 012116 (2020). https://doi.org/10.1088/1757-899x/1007/1/012116

17. Awan, F.A.: Forensic examination of social networking applications on smartphones. In: 2015 Conference on Information Assurance and Cyber Security (CIACS), pp. 36–43 (2015). https://doi.org/10.1109/CIACS.2015.7395564

18. Zhang, H., Chen, L., Liu, Q.: Digital forensic analysis of instant messaging applications on android smartphones. In: 2018 International Conference on Computing, Networking and Communications (ICNC), pp. 647–651 (2018). https://doi.org/10.1109/ICCNC.2018.8390330

Machine Learning-Based Predictors for ICU Admission of COVID-19 Patients

Nagham Alhawas[✉] and Serkan Kartal

Department of Computer Engineering, Çukurova University, 0133 Adana, Turkey
nagham_hs@hotmail.com, skartal@cu.edu.tr

Abstract. The burden on the health sector has increased when covid-19 was declared as a critical pandemic, making the decision-taking more crucial. This study aimed mainly to build predictors to aid in making decisions for severe patients to predict whether a patient has to be admitted to the intensive care unit (ICU) based only on the vital records. Statistical techniques were used on the electrical health records (EHR) that were accessible for the covid-19 patients. Samples were processed and then extracted based on criteria that support data imputation. Then, several feature selection techniques were utilized based on the field knowledge, Pearson correlation coefficient, and finally by taking the permutation importance of a hypothetical model to retain features that have the highest relationship with the target variable. Then two versions of data were obtained as stateless and grouped data with and without feature selection which were used to build models with various machine learning algorithms; logistic regression, linear support vector machine SVM, SVM with radial basis function RBF, and artificial neural network ANN. In this respect, the models reached an accuracy of more than 95% in most of the used classifiers and the best one scored is RBF-SVM with accuracy up to 98% and achieve 0.95 areas under curve (AUC) performance. These results indicate that trustworthy models were built to fulfill the high demand for accuracy that is more or less commensurate with the cost of accuracy in the health sector relying only on vital information.

Keywords: Covid-19 · Vital information · EHR · Intensive care unit

1 Introduction

The declaration that happened on March 2020, by the World Health Organization (WHO) that the outbreak of a new corona virus disease (COVID-19), to consider as a pandemic has emerged as a major challenge for the health sector. Given the increase in the number of infections, the variation in symptoms and the patient's health status, there is an obvious burden on the medical staff in determining the optimal condition to follow up on patients. Especially, since the symptoms range from mild that can be treated at home, to intense that requires hospitalization. Without a doubt, due to the tremendous pressure caused by the pandemic, there is an undeniable gap between the number of infections and the ability to deal with them in term of the available resources. Early prediction of acute

S. Paiva et al. (Eds.): SmartCity360° 2021, LNICST 442, pp. 602–616, 2022.
https://doi.org/10.1007/978-3-031-06371-8_38

cases of covid-19 patients may contribute to saving their lives by contributing to the early preparation and management of resources in the ICU. Although there are many studies use machine learning to support decisions in the health sector, there is still a huge demand to work even more in this direction. There are real opportunities for ML to assist in taking the decision in clinics and hospitals during Covid-19 by using the vital and laboratory results from the rapidly growing EHR datasets. There are various healthcare aspects that ML can support. Healthcare generates massive datasets from medical follow-up results of patients that are updated daily or even hourly. ML can be utilized to process all these data to generate valuable information, evidence-based recommendations, or to make augmented tools for taking decisions [1]. One of the important aspects that ML support is the intensive care unit. Recently, and due to the current epidemic period, the interest in researches related to the ICU has increased. We use ML algorithms along with the statistical rules to build models that use the vital information of the covid-19 patients from available dataset to predict the ICU admission of severe cases. For this purpose, python was used as the programming language via Jupyter notebook.

This article has the following scheme, Sect. 2, which contains a literature review that synthesizes a basic view of the relevant works, and reviews the similarities and differences between this study and previous studies. After that, in Sect. 3, the dataset which used in this study is illustrated with a comprehensive description. The approach we used to initialize ML models to assist in predicting the ICU admission with overall structure in addition to the knowledge field discussion is shown in Sect. 4. In Sect. 5, we review and discuss the results in a purely analytical manner. A discussion of the limitations and the probable extensions is shown in Sect. 6. In Sect. 7, we provide the final remark in a brief conclusion.

2 Literature Review

In most of the previous works, researchers have been interested in finding tools to support the decision in clinics and hospitals based on medical records. There is no doubt that the healthcare industry is still struggling as studies are still hampered by the way these industries collect their records. Most of these records are unstructured data. There is an absence in enabling advanced analytics. However, early work has concentrated on training discriminative models according to an obvious target or output. For Instance, S. L. Hyland uses supervised ML techniques along with medical knowledge to predict the circulatory failure for patients in ICU [2]. Other works have focused on the intervention in ICU based on the EHR using unsupervised methods such as the work done by Massachusetts Institute [3]. So, the traction to automate the ICU and its decisions is not a new research field. There are a lot of researches on the topics of mortality prediction in ICU, management of ICU resources by suppressing false alarms in ICU, and prediction of ICU discharge and readmission [4, 5]. However, during the covid-19 period, the research on this matter has increased and several conferences were held to discuss these completed researches [6]. As stated in [7], they detect patients ready to be discharged from ICU by evaluating NLD criteria through machine learning classifiers trained on the MIMIC dataset. By stepping a little bit inside our scope of predicting covid-19 patients' ICU admission, there are also a not insignificant number of projects. In [8], the study focused on the results of laboratory blood tests to develop several analytic methods to predict covid-19 disease severity and mortality outcome with accuracy and precision for predictions that were above 90%. The study used two datasets of corona patients; the former contains samples of 89 covid-19 positive patients, and the latter is the same dataset that we used for this study. At first glance, what caught our attention is that they pointed out that this data set contains samples of 1,945 COVID-19 positive patients; however, this is a stateless consideration as we clarify that this data set contains five records for each 385 which results in 1925 samples. On the other hand, as this dataset -as will be briefly explained- contains a huge number of missing data they eliminated any record that contains at least one missing value. As a result of this elimination, they consider only 545 samples, and they did this kind of elimination after they made it clear that their trails of data imputation for the missing values resulted in poor performance. This is one of the clear differences between their study and ours, as we made it clear that filling in the missing data in the usual way will result in poor performance, but taking into account the points that we will be explained in the next sections will solve this problem. In [9], several classification methods were applied, including robust versions of logistic regression, and support vector machines, as well as random forests and gradient boosted decision trees to predict the following events: (1) hospitalization, (2) mortality, (3) need for ICU and (4) need for a ventilator. Their accuracy for ICU need event reaches, 80% and AUC of 0.54 without prior knowledge about the patient pneumonia and accuracy up to 82% and AUC of 0.63 with prior knowledge about pneumonia condition. Also, their accuracy, for the need of ventilator event inside ICU reached to 83% and the AUC to 0.77. In contrast to much of the works that were cited above, we built various models in an attempt to assist making the decision of admitting the patient to ICU only based on vital information. Taking into account special considerations of the used samples and features as will be explained in the coming sections. Three main factors are distinguishing our work from all works cited here, first: we use only the vital data which measured hourly to predicate the admission of a patient to ICU not the blood test results. The second difference is regarding the way of considering the samples and the way the data imputation was done. Finally, we relied on medical knowledge that was discussed in medical books and researches as illustrated in [10], by D. Silverstein, K. Hoppe that vital information is a strong predictor for the ICU. We aim to prove it through various machine learning techniques, and for each stage analytical explanations and various experiments were carried out to support this hypothesis.

3   Data

To satisfy the purpose of this study, the data of positive covid-19 patients from the Hospital Sírio-Libanês, São Paulo, and Brasilia were acquired from an open-access repository to be used [11]. Three main classes of information can be extracted from this dataset: demographic information, blood test results, and vital information results. It contains anonymous records for patients. There are 1925 samples gathered from 385 4 patients, and each one has 5 records. Along with 231 columns that contain the features, however, there are huge numbers of the missing values that range from 511 to 1140 per column which makes this dataset suffer from sparsity. Unfortunately, some features do not have a description available from the dataset provider. Some of those features are: "disease grouping 1, disease grouping 2, other "etc.

4   Methods

Taking into consideration what we have mentioned in the description of the data in the previous section, our method of processing the missing data and adopting the samples constituted an important stage in the overall process of building the proposed model Fig. 1 shows the overall scheme of the method proposed by us and in the following sub-sections, we will discuss each phase in detail.

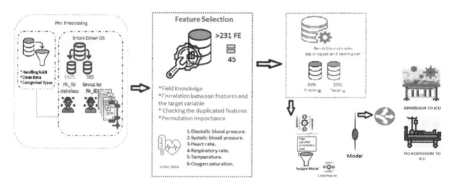

Fig. 1. The overall scheme of the proposed methodology

4.1   Data Pre-processing

In this stage, firstly we deal with the categorical types; hence, one hot encoding is used to put dummy numeric values which result in the binary vector representation of the "age_percentil" and "window columns" which contributed to adding new columns represented these two categorical columns. Then, we cleaned the data by filling in the missing values. In the following section, we will illustrate the consideration we take into account for this purpose.

Data Imputation
Missing data presents a real challenge as it makes the data analysis problematic and implies efficiency reductions, however, imputation is seen as a way to avoid pitfalls involved with these problems [12]. Imputation preserves all cases by filling the missing values with the result of estimation other related available values. In our case, we go into three directions for data imputation. First, we fill the missing value of each column by the mean of all its other values and then through trial and error, we built a hypothetical model, and in any case, even with the features selection, the results of that hypothetical model were not good enough and could not be adopted, so we moved to the second

method of filling in the data which is filling the missing values of each patient from its mean values. This second way which built upon the fact that each patient in the dataset has 5 records so, we just filled in each column with the values of that patient, however, there was no improvement in the accuracy of the model. This prompted us to think about a possible hidden problem in the recorded data and the way that they were recorded. We thought that there might be some data for each patient that was not registered with the correct considerations, which causes noise in the data. In another word, there is no proven explanation of which values in which record of vital information from the five records of each patient led to the ICU admission. For example, assume patient x was admitted in his third record from his hospitalization time, the time of admission may be not accurate and his data in the first or the second record is the one that contributed to his admission not the data of the third record. As we cannot be sure of this information and any problem in the data set might be caused by the data of the people who experienced the ICU in one of their five records. As a consequence, we looked for the data that we considered clean, reliable and of course, those data are for patients who had either never been to intensive care or who had been to intensive care in all of their five records. Thus, the answer to the following question: "Has the patient ever experience the ICU in any of his records?" made us fill in the data with the mean values of each column of those patients' types separately. In other words, we consider only those patients who were never admitted in all of their five records or those who were admitted to ICU in all of their five records then we fill in the missing values by using the mean value of each column separately. Figure 2 shows this process of considering the data of the 190 patients whom never admitted to ICU in all 5 records and the data of 32 patients who were admitted in all of their records.

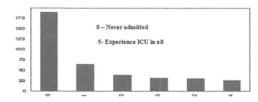

Fig. 2. Patient ICU experience

Data Sampling

Sampling is a process used in statistical analysis in which a predetermined number of observations are taken from a larger population [13]. For our study, sampling is an important consideration whether we will rely on patients' data as being stateless or will we rely on collecting patient data and grouping them. Here we will try the two considerations and compare their results.

Stateless Data

The stateless consideration approach is one way to deal with the samples in the dataset. As discussed in Sect. 3, the dataset contains 1925 samples as a result of five records for each one of the 385 patients specified by unique patient identifier. When considering data as stateless means that these records are independent of each other and save no information of the previous records. Thus, the identifier for each patient is neglected. Each sample is considered as belonging to a different patient. However, only 1110 samples from 222 patients were taken into account based on Sect. 4.1. There are four reasons that encourage us to handle the as a stateless data. First, the main goal for this study is to use the features without adopting the patient's demographic information such as gender, age, or any medical history records. Therefore, we do not intend to study a specific patient's case. Secondly, depending on the literature as in [8], which considers the data as stateless, however, this method was used to increase the number of samples in the dataset. Finally, data imputation which was considered in this study led to consider only the records of patients who never entered the ICU or the data of patients who experienced ICU in all their five records. Thus, there is a state of stability in the values of records, either being normal or abnormal values, and therefore we drop from them the possibility that the previous record affects the current record state, and so on.

Grouped Data
Samples in the dataset can be divided into groups based on the identifier of each patient. Each patient in the dataset has five records; hence, it's possible to calculate the mean of the representative values of each patient to get a single record for each one. For this purpose, the records were grouped by paitent_identifier, and then the mean was calculated for all other values and kept as a new record for that patient in a dataset that we express as grouped data. Unfortunately, the process discussed in Sect. 4.1 to consider only 1110 samples cannot be used to generate the grouped data. Because, after the process of gathering these samples based on the patient's identifier and calculating the mean of the representative values the number of samples in the dataset is 222. However, this dataset can be considered an imbalanced dataset. As shown in Fig. 3 it contains 85.6% of samples for patients who have never been admitted to ICU compared to 14.4% who were admitted to ICU. Obviously, this will cause poor performance in prediction, especially for the class of those who have been admitted to ICU, and therefore it cannot be adopted.

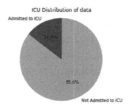

Fig. 3. Distribution when considering 222 samples

As a result of the foregoing, we have increased the samples in an attempt to make the two classes of the target variable as balanced as possible in the dataset, by adopting the data of the 385 patients with some considerations. First: The initial 1925 samples were taken and the missing data were filled by using the mean value of each column of all patients. Then, the samples were gathered by using the paitent_identifier. Subsequently, the mean of all of the representative values of each column of the five records for each patient was calculated for the gathered data to get a single record. Finally, if the patient has experienced the ICU even once in one of his five records, his target value of the ICU column is set to 1. But if he does not experience the ICU in all of his five records, the value of the target variable becomes 0. As a result of this process, the numbers of samples are 385 now. As shown Fig. 4 that 49.3% of patients were not admitted and 50.7% were admitted to ICU and this is a balanced dataset and can be considered.

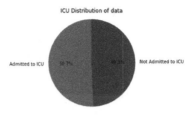

Fig. 4. ICU distribution when considering 385 samples

4.2   Feature Selection

For this dataset, numerous conceivable features can be chosen. Taking into account that we have a large number of algorithms that perform this task, we had to define our primary goal, which is to study the vital signs of patients and their impact on the admission process for ICU, and whether they are already sufficient alone. Therefore, we decided to make two copies of this data, one with the application of feature selection and the other without it, and compare the performance as will be clear in the next parts. To make the feature selection, we relied on the following:

Field Knowledge
As known in the medical field, abnormal vital signs are strong predictors for intensive care unit admission. As pointed in [10, 14], abnormal vital signs are strongly associated with adverse outcomes and significantly associated with ICU admission. This is reinforced by what was stated in the study published in the Journal of Acute Disease. This study shows that the presence of any of the specified trigger vital signs, although representing only a small proportion of the total population, was strongly associated with admission to the ICU [14]. Vital Signs that are available in the dataset that we used are the Body Temperature, Pulse Rate, Respiration Rate, Blood Pressure, and Oxygen Saturation. These signs were extended by calculating the mean, median, min, max, and differences of each sign. Figure 5 shows the results of plotting the variance of each column of vital signs measurements between 222 patients who either have been admitted or not to ICU in all of their five records.

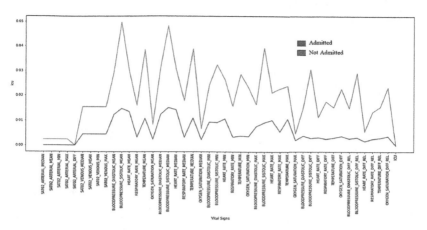

Fig. 5. Vital signs and ICU admission

It shows clearly that there is a clear difference between the vital values for both parties. Obviously, the vital values of the admitted patients vary radically compared to the values of the not admitted patients. Relying on these scientific facts, we can go towards the fact that our assumption of using only vital signs is correct and sufficient, but we will also test this choice for our dataset in the next sections as well to increase our certainty.

Pearson Correlation Coefficient

Pearson correlation coefficient examines the strength and direction of the linear relationship between two continuous variables. The higher the absolute value of the coefficient, the stronger the linear relationship between the variables. The correlation coefficients denote three relationships: positive, negative, and no relationship. For the Pearson correlation, an absolute value of +1 indicates a perfect positive linear relationship. When the coefficients are greater than 0 then this is a positive relationship in which if one variable increases the other will increase as well vice versa [15]. However, it's not worthy for our case as it shows that lactic highly correlated with ICU, but according to the medical knowledge we can say that covid-19 patients suffer from an excessive increase in lactate levels in the blood which means that the disease or condition a person has is causing lactate to accumulate. In general, a super increase in lactate indicates more severity of the condition. As pointed by [16], "When associated with lack of oxygen, an increase in lactate can indicate that organs are not functioning properly". However, this is not a direct or indirect reason for the ICU admission. It's just some of the main abnormalities found in the blood testing results of covid-19 patients. Thus according to this method that is shown in Fig. 6 the relevant features which have higher than 0.5 were the different LACTATE and RESPIRATORY_RATE values. The discussion held before is not enough for this study thus we move to the next method.

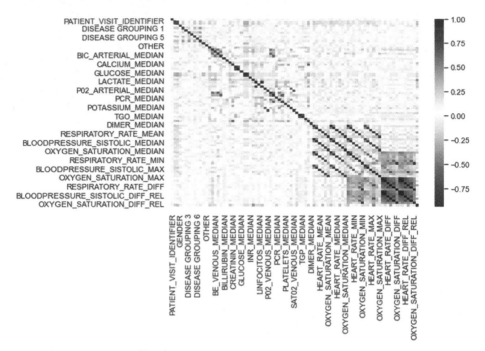

Fig. 6. Heat map shows features correlation

Permutation Importance

In Sect. 4.1 we have illustrated that we have built a hypothetical model, and this was a key decision to compare different models' results with and without the application of feature selection. In this trial and error direction, as we will explain in the next section, we found that one of the ML algorithms, which is the kernelized RBF-SVM, achieved high accuracy. This prompted us to wonder, what are the most influential features on the prediction of this classifier? Feature permutation importance is a model-agnostic global explanation method that provides insights into a machine learning model's behavior [17]. The permutation_importance function calculates the superiority feature of estimators for a given dataset in the training stage of the ML. The n_repeats parameter sets the number of times a feature is randomly shuffled and returns a sample of feature importance. Two results that we reached after obtaining the results of plotting the permutation importance; first of all, a large number of features in the dataset do not contribute to any impact on the prediction. Second: vital signs which are shown in Fig. 5 are the main influence, in addition to lactate values all contribute more than blood tests results.

4.3 Model Selection and Estimation

No doubts that the dataset prosperities are crucial aspect and has a huge impact on the selected models. As each model adjusts its parameters based on the available data that it learns from in the training phase. It was explained in Sect. 3, the dataset is imbalanced and suffers from sparsity. With the methods that were presented in the Sect. 4.1 so and so to improve dataset characteristics, choosing the appropriate model remains important to achieve the purpose of the study. After taking into consideration type of problem, size of the dataset, the number of features, and by considering the studies that have good results in the literature as in [8, 9]; we chose different machine learning algorithms to build the binary classifier which are Logistics regression, SVM with linear and RBF kernels, and ANN. As stated in [9, 7], logistic regression and SVM are very common in health care applications because of the high interpretability of their output and their simplicity. According to many experiments in literature that SVM even without further tuning can provide very accurate prediction in healthcare relevant problems [18, 19, 9, 20]. For ANN a sequential, fully-connected layered architecture are used in which each input neuron is connected to every neuron in the next layer. It consists of one input layer and three hidden layers a long with the output layer. The sigmoid is used as the activation function of the output layer whereas the ReLU (Rectified Linear Activation Unit) is used as the activation function for all hidden layer. The model trained with 0.0001 learning rate in 90 epochs using the Adam optimization function with binary_crossentropy as the lose function.

Training Phase

Taking into account the considerations that we have discussed regarding the samples and the features; we decided to make four comparisons between two partitions of two different considerations of the dataset samples. Firstly, we will consider the dataset as stateless which results in 1110 samples according to the preprocessing that we discussed in Sect. 4.1. Also, to consider it as grouped data with only 385 samples by grouping the data using the patient identifier as illustrated in Sect. 4.2. Secondly, for each part, we will examine them under two more considerations one with feature selection and the other part without feature selection. In all cases, 80% were used for the training and 20% for the testing. This process is held before training any classifiers and is shown in Fig. 7 given below.

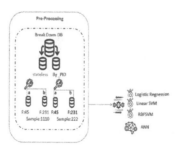

Fig. 7. Preparing dataset

Models Performance and Estimations

As an initial step, we plotted the confusion metric to see how the models perform in predicting each class. In order to measure each model's performance, we have used three main metrics. Firstly, we measure the models testing accuracy to evaluate the percentage of the correct prediction that was made for the testing data. Then, we rely on calculating the True Positive (TP) among TP to False Positive (FP) which defines the precision. The third metric that we define is the recall, as the sensitivity or the True Positive Rat TPR. Actually, the last two matrices are extremely crucial and take the trade-off between precision-recall so, we get an insight of the model relevancy and from the latter, we get a clue of the model competence. As also as an initiative way of judging the model performance is to get AUC interpretation for the classifiers. We plotted the receiver operating characteristic curve ROC and make AUC interpretation for the classifiers that showed better performance compared to the other classifiers under the same pre-training considerations.

$$\text{Accuracy} = \frac{TP + TN}{TP + TN + FP + FN} \tag{1}$$

$$\text{Precision} = \frac{TP}{TP + FP} \tag{2}$$

$$\text{Recall} = \frac{TP}{TP + FN} \tag{3}$$

5   Results and Discussions

After training the models with the different partitions that we have mentioned in Sect. 4.3. We find that we have been effectively able to build a model that predicts the need for intensive care based on vital information. Overall, the trained models' results range from moderate to accurate prediction results. The results imply that there is a strong relationship between the abnormal vital signs results and the ICU admission. The results show that logistic regression and support vector machines generate better models in terms of accuracy. Classification accuracies reached 98% for predicting ICU admission with the RBF-SVM for both pre-training data considerations. The analysis shows that the most important preconditions for making the predictions for the four models derived are: receiving stateless data, perform data imputation based on the patients' ICU experience, and selecting vital information as we explained in Sect. 4, and evaluating samples correctly before making the data imputation. Figure 8 shows the overall accuracy between all of the used classifiers. And from that plot, we can say that all the classifiers achieved performance nearly the same for the stateless data with and without the feature selection due to the way we chose the samples and the way we make the data imputation. One important observation about liner SVM and RBF-SVM is that both share comparable performance when utilized with the stateless consideration of the samples in conjunction with the feature selection as discussed in Sect. 4.2. The best performance is achieved by RBF-SVM with stateless sample consideration and elaborating the feature selection. This is clear as the AUC reaches 95%, hence, it is considered the best model in performance as it shows good generalization capabilities. This model can be deployed in the healthcare decision systems to help in the early prediction of the ICU admission and therefore help in the early allocating of the resource using vital sign results which are very affordable, easy, and inexpensive. Linear SVM showed high performance with stateless data along with the feature selection it scored 95% in accuracy. However, it performs slightly lower with the grouped data with and without feature selection and scored 81% inaccuracy. ANN showed good performance for the stateless data and achieved 97% even without feature selection. Nerveless, it showed poor performance with the grouped data probably due to the limited number of the samples in the trained dataset. As mentioned above, the highest AUC is scored by RBF-SVM and both logistic regression and linear SVM scored 91% and 93% respectively under the same consideration. Whereas the linear SVM and logistic regression imposed poor comparable performance without feature selection as the dataset experienced some non-linearity which makes finding the best hyperplane that best segregate the two classes not visible this this made clear by analyzing their AUC results. Figure 9 shows the AUC graph for those classifiers.

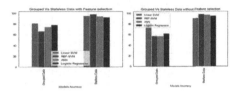

Fig. 8. Overall results of models accuracies with different considerations

We believe that the one who contributed to this result is the method of adopting samples and filling in the missing values. As were mentioned previously, without such consideration, the results of the models were not good enough. The detailed classification report is shown in Table 1 and the precision and recall all are shown for only the ICU admission class. Additionally, we got better precision and recall for the not admitted class but this is quite as expected due the supported number of samples in the dataset. On the other hand, the grouped data achieved unreliable results for both cases with and without feature selection; however, grouped data with feature selection shows slightly better performance.

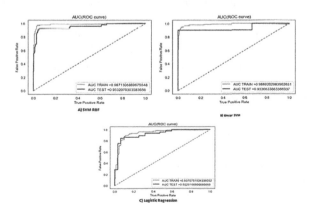

Fig. 9. The AUC for different classifier

Table 1. Overall results

DATA	Feature Selection	Evaluation Matrices	Linear SVM	SVM RBF	Logistic Regression	ANN
Stateless	✓	Accuracy	95%	98%	92%	94%
		AUC	0.93	0.95	0.91	
		Precision	0.93	1.0	0.91	
		Recall	0.74	0.88	0.88	
		F1-Score	0.83	0.93	0.89	
Stateless	✗	Accuracy	91%	98%	95%	97%
		AUC	0.88	0.91	0.87	
		Precision	0.77	0.90	0.94	
		Recall	0.77	0.27	0.77	
		F1-Score	0.77	0.42	0.85	
Grouped	✗	Accuracy	%81	57%	62%	57%
		Precision	0.84	0.56	0.66	
		Recall	0.74	0.80	0.57	
		F1-Score	0.79	0.66	0.61	
Grouped	✓	Accuracy	81%	66%	78%	74%
		AUC	0.84	0.77	0.62	
		Precision	0.74	0.80	0.75	
		Recall	0.91	0.55	0.82	
		F1-Score	0.82	0.65	0.78	

6 Limitation and Potential Extensions

One of the most critical problems that we encountered during our work on this study is the number of samples that are available. Taking into account the fact that this data is actually for 385 patients only, and each patient has 5 records that extend the samples up to 1925. This imposes limitations in dealing with it and that thing what mainly pushes us to consider the data as stateless. Some information we wished the dataset would provide, such as the patient's discharge status and the patient's detailed time record. Such information did not affect our study or its results, but it prevented us from going to another dimension in the study. Actually, there is no information, including whether the patient has yet been released from the intensive care unit, as the data makes it clear that once the patient enters the intensive care unit, he remains in it. Moreover, there is not enough information regarding the time. Since if such information were added (i.e. the patient has been admitted to ICU in the current record, and for example, the same patient in the next record has an improvement and left the ICU). With such information will be able to add other dimensions to our study and search for values that contribute to the improvement of the patient's condition and thus it is possible to predict the patients who may be discharged from ICU. Also predicting the time when something like this is expected to happen. If it is possible to add such information and increase the size of the data samples and add time in a more detailed way, we will be able to go further in building a new and more powerful model.

7 Conclusion

In light of the corona pandemic, the pressure on the intensive care unit has increased. Vital information provides great opportunities to rely on to enhance decision-making in hospitals and clinics, which may relieve pressure, especially at this stage. For this study, we make a critical study of the process of selecting the features and even verifying the correctness of our hypothesis to use only the vital signs. Then, we trained supervised ML algorithms using the patient's vital signs after processing the data under two assumptions as stateless and as grouped data taking into consideration feature selection decisions. Then, we use different evaluation matrices to measure the models performance, completeness, and sensitivity. We have achieved so good results for the stateless data with accuracy up to 98% and the estimated AUC is 0.95 for RBF-SVM. This indicates clearly that we can rely on the vital signs for the covid-19 patients as a strong indicator for ICU admission.

References

1. Debnath, S., et al.: Machine learning to assist clinical decision-making during the COVID-19 pandemic. Bioelectron. Med. **6**(1) (2020). https://doi.org/10.1186/s42234-020-00050-8
2. Hyland, S.L., et al.: Early prediction of circulatory failure in the intensive care unit using machine learning. Nat. Med. **26**(3), 364–373 (2020). https://doi.org/10.1038/s41591-020-0789-4
3. Ghassemi, M., Wu, M., Hughes, M.C., Szolovits, P., Doshi-Velez, F.: Predicting intervention onset in the ICU with switching state space models. AMIA Jt. Summits Transl. Sci. Proc. **2017**, 82–91 (2017). http://www.ncbi.nlm.nih.gov/pubmed/28815112, http://www.pubmedcentral.nih.gov/articlerender.fcgi?artid=PMC5543372
4. Bezzan, V., Rocco, C.D.: Predicting special care during the COVID-19 pandemic: A machine learning approach (2020). http://arxiv.org/abs/2011.03143
5. Syed, M., et al.: Application of machine learning in intensive care unit (ICU) settings using MIMIC dataset: systematic review. Informatics **8**(1), 16 (2021). https://doi.org/10.3390/informatics8010016
6. Machine learning for healthcare (2020). https://www.mlforhc.org/
7. McWilliams, C.J., et al.: Towards a decision support tool for intensive care discharge: machine learning algorithm development using electronic healthcare data from MIMIC-III and Bristol, UK. BMJ Open **9**(3), 1–8 (2019). https://doi.org/10.1136/bmjopen-2018-025925
8. Aktar, S., et al.: Predicting patient COVID-19 disease severity by means of statistical and machine learning analysis of blood cell transcriptome data, November 2020. https://doi.org/10.2196/25884
9. Wollenstein-Betech, S., Cassandras, C.G., Paschalidis, I.Ch.: Personalized predictive models for symptomatic COVID-19 patients using basic preconditions: hospitalizations, mortality, and the need for an ICU or ventilator, no. 1 (2020). International Journal of Medical Informatics
10. Silverstein, D.C.: Critical Care Medicine, 2nd edn. Elsevier, Amsterdam (2015)

11. Sírio-Libanês data for AI and Analytics by Data Intelligence Team, Covid-19 dataset (2020). https://www.kaggle.com/Sírio-Libanes/covid19
12. Kaliamoorthy, S., Saira Bhanu, M.: Multiple imputation inference for missing values in distributed datasets using apache spark. In: Second International Conference, ICACDS 2018, Dehradun, India, 20–21 April 2018, Revised Selected Papers, Part II, pp. 24–33 (2018)
13. Dagar, S.: Instant Notes on Research Methods, 1st edn. The Readers Paradise (2019)
14. Barfod, C., et al.: Abnormal vital signs are strong predictors for intensive care unit admission and in-hospital mortality in adults triaged in the emergency department - a prospective cohort study. Scand. J. Trauma. Resusc. Emerg. Med. **20**, 28 (2012). https://doi.org/10.1186/1757-7241-20-28
15. Abu-Bader, S.H.: Using Statistical Methods in Social Science Research: With a Complete SPSS Guide. Oxford University Press (2011)
16. Labtestso: Lactate (2018). https://labtestsonline.org/tests/lactate. Accessed 28 Apr 2021
17. Gianfagna, L., Di Cecco, A.: Explainable AI with Python. Springer, Cham (2021). https://doi.org/10.1007/978-3-030-68640-6
18. Vijayarani, D.: Liver disease prediction using SVM and Naïve Bayes algorithms. Int. J. Sci. Eng. Technol. Res. **4**(4), 816–820 (2015)
19. Dan, T., et al.: Machine learning to predict ICU admission, ICU mortality and survivors' length of stay among COVID-19 patients: toward optimal allocation of ICU resources. In: Proceedings of the - 2020 IEEE International Conference on Bioinformatics and Biomedicine 2020, pp. 555–561 (2020). https://doi.org/10.1109/BIBM49941.2020.9313292
20. Uddin, S., Khan, A., Hossain, M.E., Moni, M.A.: Comparing different supervised machine learning algorithms for disease prediction. BMC Med. Inform. Decis. Mak. **19**(1), 1–17 (2019). https://doi.org/10.1186/s12911-019-1004-8

A Forensic-Ready Intelligent Transportation System

Abdellah Akilal[1]($\boxtimes$) and M-Tahar Kechadi[2]

[1] Laboratoire d'informatique Medicale Limed, Faculte des Sciences Éxactes,
Université A. Mira Bejaia, Bejaia, Algeria
abdellah.akilal@univ-bejaia.dz
[2] School of Computer Science and Informatics, University College Dublin,
Dublin, Ireland
tahar.kechadi@ucd.ie

Abstract. The Intelligent transportation system (ITS) is a part of a smart city, and will for sure become a reality in the coming decades if not years. Viewed as a pivotal element in an economy, its market size is predicted to grow and governments are already investing in either development or deployment and maintenance. Researchers on the other hand have already investigated its feasibility and provided multiple architectures. Even if the predicted economic venues are interesting, several challenges related to security, privacy, resiliency are still concerning. New attack surfaces are emerging, incidents and cyber attacks are occurring. The omni-connectivity attribute of smart cities is inducing new risks where a digital vulnerability may be exploited to damage physical assets or endanger travellers' safety. If safety is a necessity, the preparedness to conduct a digital forensic investigation is also important. This paper focuses on the ITS Digital Forensic Readiness (DFR). More precisely, we aim to align the Architecture Reference for Cooperative and Intelligent Transportation (ARC-IT) with the digital forensics readiness best practices in particular the ISO/IEC 27043:2015 standard.

Keywords: ITS · DFR · ARC-IT · ISO/IEC/27043/2015 · Cyber crime · Safety

1 Introduction

The Intelligent Transportation System (ITS) global market size is predicted to grow from \$1643.8 million in 2018 to \$8474.2 million by 2026 [13]. Multiple countries are already investing in the deployment and the maintenance of these critical infrastructures. For example, the U.S is already investing more than \$25 billion in deployed ITS. The economic and societal usage of ITS by American travellers is exceeding \$2.3 billion annually [3]. The critical nature of ITS, and the diversity of its ecosystem (components, technologies, stakeholders, etc.) have

S. Paiva et al. (Eds.): SmartCity360° 2021, LNICST 442, pp. 617–630, 2022.
https://doi.org/10.1007/978-3-031-06371-8_39

led several countries to deploy efforts towards the standardization and the development of associated architectures [22]. Therefore, there is abundant work issued from governmental agencies and researchers, such as the ARC-IT (USA) [4], the ITS architecture for Canada [2], and Europe [6,28].

Even if there is a significant advancement in ITS research, there are still several challenges and open questions. In fact, security, privacy, resiliency and safety are among the ITS concerning issues [7,19]. In regards to security, an ITS is exposed to at least three attack vectors (physical, network and wireless) [11]. Moreover, multiple ITS real-world attacks have taken place from 2016 to 2017 ranging from road sign hack [17] to ransomware attacks [11]. More recently, some major Metropolitan Transportation Authority's computer systems were the target of cyber crime [12,31].

Incidents and cyber crimes happen. In this paper, we aim to ensure the ITS due forensic readiness (i.e., enhance the ITS with capabilities that ease the collection of digital evidence with a minimum disruption and less economic impact from a potential investigation). For this purpose, we investigate the opportunities of aligning the ISO/IEC 27043:2015 incident investigation principles and processes standard [15] with the ARC-IT architecture [4].

The rest of this paper is structured as follows: Sect. 2 presents some related works on ITS architectures, digital forensic readiness, forensic-by-design and forensic-ready systems. We then provide details on the ARC-IT and the ISO/IEC 27043:2015 in Sect. 3. In Sect. 4, we investigate the emerging opportunities and challenges from the integration of forensic requirements into an ITS architecture, and we conclude this paper in Sect. 5.

2   Literature Review

The economic impact of transportation is not be demonstrated. In fact, transportation is present in every single aspect of citizens daily life. From travelling to goods and merchandise delivery, the transport sector is a central nerve to a national economy. Thus, it is not astonishing to observe the symbiosis between this sector and the technological evolution in other domains. The ITS takes its origin from the USA in the 20th century [1,22], but it is gaining worldwide attention nowadays. Several projects and architectures have emerged from conjoint efforts of both government bodies and researchers [2,4,6]. The evolution of communication technologies, sensors and computation, in addition to customers needs has led to the emergence of a subset of ITS namely Cooperative Intelligent Transportation Systems (C-ITS) that takes advantage of the communication and cooperation between its participants [1].

Even though ITS benefit from consequent funds and technological advancement from other domains, there are still some challenging issues. In fact, security, privacy and resiliency are among the top concerning problems [7,19]. Moreover, incident and cyber attack are already taking place in ITS [11,12,17,31] and the worst scenario that may happen is the exploitation of a security vulnerability to endanger the travellers' safety [16,23]. Nonetheless, in case of an incident or cyber crime, a forensic investigation is required and initiated. However, the first step in this process focuses on preparedness. The main motive of this study is to enhance the ability of an ITS to collect admissible digital evidence.

Digital Forensic Readiness (DFR) represents the *ability* of an organization or a system to collect admissible digital evidence, whilst minimizing the costs of an investigation. The necessity to enable a system with capabilities to ensure its' forensic readiness was first expressed by [29], later [27] formulated it as a ten step process. There is an abundant literature on DFR; While some researchers focused on the DFR context *(i.e., impact of DFR on domains, such as organization, networks* [5], *and the Cloud computing* [21], *etc.)*, others investigated the standardization aspect such as the work done by [32] that was later included in the ISO/IEC/27043:2015(E) standard [15] *(details on this standard will be provided in* Sect. 3). However, one of the most significant shifts in the DFR perspective is due to [26]. The Forensic-by-design strategy [26] aims towards the integration of forensic requirements during relevant phases of a system' design and development stages. This new vision impulsed the emergence of multiple studies arguing for the application of this new paradigm in several contexts, such as those proposed by [8, 9, 24, 25].

In addition to Forensic-by-design, *"Forensic-ready"* is recently another emerging term. To the best of our knowledge, it was first associated to *"Systems"* by [8] in the context of employing the Forensic-by-design approach to engineer systems that possess the ability to collect admissible digital evidence, and in [24], the author associated this new concept with software systems, and explicitly stated it as the capability of supporting potential digital investigations.

We, in here, consider *"Forensic-ready"* as a system (or software) state that is associated with the system (or software) ability to collect digital evidence whilst minimizing the costs of an investigation and disruption of business, and which is related to a specific period of time along its life cycle. In fact a system (or software) may be engineered (designed and developed) to be forensically ready at the design and development stage by adopting the Forensic-by-design strategy, and continue to be *Forensic-ready* along its life cycle by allocating the required digital forensic readiness capabilities at the production, support and retirement stages. Thus, *"Forensic-ready"* is a temporal state (propriety) of a system (software).

The following section provides details on the selected ITS architecture, and the incident principles and processes standard.

3   Architecture and Standards

In this section, we introduce the ARC-IT architecture, provide details on its different stakeholder, viewpoints, views, and security capabilities, then present the incident investigation principles and processes standard [15].

3.1   Selected Architecture

Among the ITS architectures cited in Sect. 1, the Architecture Reference for Cooperative and Intelligent Transportation (ARC-IT) (USA) [4] is the most advanced and maintained. In fact, the ARC-IT architecture was first initiated in 1996 and is still maintained and updated, even the ITS for Canada [2] is in a re-alignment process with it. Moreover, the U.S. Department of Transportation is licensing all the ARC-IT architecture documents and resources under in the public domain license. For the conjugate of the above arguments, we opted for this architecture.

The methodology behind the ARC-IT is encapsulated in the fact that: *"a system has an architecture, stakeholders have interests and concerns in a system. So, the architecture viewpoints frame the concerns and the architecture views address those concerns"* [4]. The distinction between viewpoints and views is of importance in the ARCT-IT. The group of stakeholders considered in this architecture is composed of: Federal government, state/local government, Non-profit/advisory, private sector and general public. Stakeholders' concerns and interests dictate the architecture viewpoints, therefore, as depicted in Fig. 1, the ARC-IT is composed of four views: (1) Enterprise, (2) Functional, (3) Physical, and (4) Communication.

The Enterprise viewpoint considers the policies, funding, agreements and jurisdictional structure; Provides a basis of ITS understanding for implementers and specifies their roles; Specifies the objectives and goals for the surface transportation system; Provides the policies and process to support transportation planning and project development. Additionally, it answers stakeholders potential concerns on roles and relationships. In fact, ITS involved groups may have roles that vary from installation, maintenance, providing applications or devices, providing transportation-related user services, etc. Therefore, creating an ecosystem of multiple providers and consumers, where relationships must be enumerated in a concise manner. In association with the Enterprise viewpoint, the Enterprise model provides details on concepts, such as Enterprise object, resource, role and relationship.

The Functional viewpoint provides an abstraction of the physical viewpoint to ease the task of potential application, device or service developers'. For this purpose, the Functional view comprises a set of abstract functional elements and their logical interactions, therefore answering potential developer questions on required data format and functionalities for a given service without bothering with the physical details at this layer. On the other hand, the ARC-IT Functional model is developed using a Structural Analysis methodology and use some structural analysis artefacts, such as process, process specification (p-spec), data flows, and terminators. Finally, the ARC-IT [4] specifies that: *"The Functional View defines Processes to control and manage system behaviour, such as monitoring, and other active control elements that are part of describing the functional behaviour of the system"*.

The physical viewpoint is an engineering viewpoint that describes physical elements and enables engineers to answer questions about involved physical elements in a given delivered service, their interfaces, exchanged information, security consideration, etc. Therefore, it defines objects, such as physical objects (P-Object) (Center, Field, Support, Personal, Vehicle), Functional Object, Information flow, Triple, Subsystem, Terminator and Service Package Diagram.

The physical view comprises a set of physical objects (sub-systems and terminators), that are categorized in six different classes. A general ITS class that cover all of ITS, while five more specific classes (Center, Field, Support, Personal, vehicle) as shown in Fig. 2.

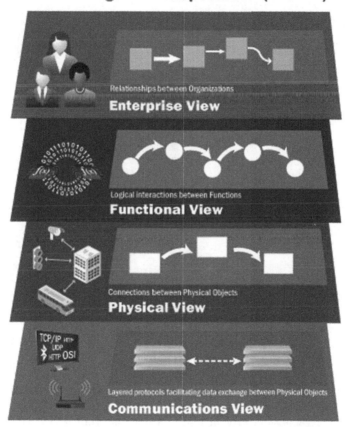

Fig. 1. Architecture reference for cooperative and intelligent transportation (ARC-IT) [4].

The ARC-IT specifies that: *"The general'ITS Object' includes core capabilities common to any class of object"*, thus making it an abstract object from which all the objects of other classes derive. Therefore this object *"include the core capabilities and interfaces that may be included in any ITS system or device"*.

The communication viewpoint provides a set of protocols that enable the communication between physical objects. Thus, this viewpoint specifies a set of requirements, such as performance, interoperability, security, etc. Additionally, it comprises a set of environment and operational challenges associated with existent policies and regulations. Therefore, it aims to provide answers to potential engineers questions. The ARC-IT communication model comprises a set of layers; Access layer, TransNet layer, Facilities Layer, and ITS Application layer. Moreover, it also provides also a mapping with the OSI model, IETF IP Suite, NTCIP model, etc.

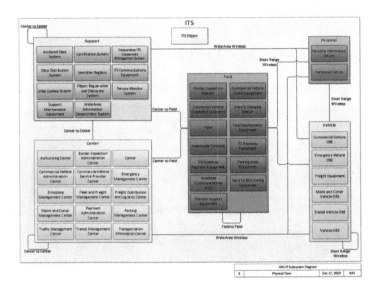

Fig. 2. The ARC-IT [4] physical view.

To prevent the disruption and the alteration of ITS operations, the ARC-IT comprise security measures that address some security aspects, such as information security, ITS personal security, Operational security and security management. The aforementioned security axes are enclosed in the *"Securing ITS"* capabilities, however, the ARC-IT defines eights areas for security appliance; Disaster Response and Evacuation; Freight and Commercial Vehicle Security; HAZWAT Security; ITS Wide Area Alert; Rail Security; Transit Security; Transportation Infrastructure Security; and Travellers Security.

While studying the ARC-IT, it seems that it does not offer any capability to address or support a potential digital forensic investigation. In the following section, we present a standard that aims to empower organization and systems with due capabilities to support potential digital forensic investigation.

3.2   Incident Investigation Principles and Processes

As stated in Sect. 2, incidents and cyber attacks are taking place in ITS. Moreover, some digital vulnerabilities may be exploited to endanger traveller's' safety. Beyond the emergency and the need for a prompt response to accidents, the investigation of incidents'—*physical or digital*—causes, liabilities and responsibilities is of importance. For this purpose, we investigate the emerging opportunities from applying the Incident Investigation principal and Process standard ISO/IEC 27043/2015 [15] to an ITS and more specifically those based on the ARC-IT architecture.

The ISO/IEC/27043/2015 standard [15] include 5 groups of processes; Readiness processes; Initialization processes; Acquisition processes; Investigative processes; and Concurrent processes. In the following, we provide details on the aforementioned processes groups, however, in the context of this study, the main focus will be set on the readiness processes group.

Readiness Processes. This group of processes aims to ensure the due preparedness before the proper investigation and contains 3 processes groups; Planning processes group; Implementation processes group; and Assessment processes group. The first group comprises activities, such as defining scenario where digital evidence is required, identification of potential digital evidence sources, pre-incident gathering, potential digital evidence handling and storage, system architecture definition, etc.

The implementation processes group aims to provide a system with the digital forensic readiness capabilities that were identified by the planning processes group, and which imply the need for the development/acquisition, installation of material, and software, and policies that will enforce the digital readiness across a system.

A continuous assessment of the system' readiness state is required. Thus, the last group aims to evaluate the implementation of the desired preparedness capabilities, in addition to a legal review of all the procedures, controls and architecture in order to ensure the admissibility of the produced digital evidence.

Initialization Processes. This group of processes are triggered at the initialization of an investigation in order to handle the first response to an incident, and to plan and prepare for the remainder of the investigation. Therefore, it comprises processes, such as incident detection, first response, planning and preparation.

Acquisition Processes. Even if an abnormal event is not escalated to a full digital investigation, there may be a requirement for digital evidence either to solidify the due preparedness or to comply with a potential law enforcement request. Therefore, this group comprises processes that ensure the identification, collection/acquisition, transport and storage of digital evidence.

Investigative Processes. In case of an escalation to a full digital forensic investigation, this group contains processes that permit the acquisition, examining, analysis of digital evidence, in addition to capabilities for reports generation and investigation closure.

Concurrent Processes. In addition to the aforementioned processes groups (i.e. readiness, initialisation, acquisition and investigation), this class of processes aims to assist during any phase of a DFI and contains processes, such as obtaining authorization, documentation, managing information flow, preserving chain of custody, preserving digital evidence, and interaction with physical investigation.

The ARC-IT is a reference architecture for building ITS that is system engineering based, and complies with the ISO standard for architecture definition [14]. The conjugate of this architecture and the incident investigation principles and processes is a promising venue for a Forensic-ready ITS. In the following section, we investigate the emerging opportunities from this perspective and potential challenges and issues.

4   Emerging Opportunities and Challenges

To the best of our knowledge, The ARC-IT does not contain any reference to the *"Digital Forensic"*. However, it addresses issues related to incident detection, first response, emergency situation handling, disaster response and recovery, etc. Additionally, it comprises aspects related to traffic management, especially violation enforcement and connection with law enforcement agencies. For the purpose of achieving a Forensic-ready ITS, we plan to adapt the ARC-IT to be aligned with the incident investigation principles and processes.

In the following, we first assess the opportunities to enhance the ARC-IT with capabilities that ensure the due DFR, secondly, we enumerate some of the challenging issues.

4.1   Opportunities

Enhancing an ARC-IT based ITS with the due forensic capabilities imply ultimately the update of the architecture itself. In fact, the ARC-IT is based on the ISO/IEC 42010 [14] architecture description standard.

Methodology. One of the major advantages of the ARC-IT is the fact that it is based on the [14] architecture description standard, which offers the flexibility to start from stakeholders' concerns and interests, establish different viewpoints, and provide associated views. Furthermore, it allows different scales of implementation, going from a local ITS to regional one. Moreover, it is also aligned with the systems and software engineering and adopts the "V" system engineering model [30].

Forensic-by-design. Similar to *"Security-by-Design"*, the *"Forensic-by-design"* [26] paradigm suggests the integrate the forensic requirements at the earliest phases of a system' design and development stages aiming for Forensic-ready system by essence. To the best of our knowledge, among the six key factors of the Forensic-by-design framework *(i.e. Risk management principles and practices, Laws and regulations, Forensic readiness principles and practices, CPCS hardware and software requirements, Industry-specific requirements, Incident handling principles and practices)* only the forensic readiness principles and best practices is missing in the ARC-IT architecture. However, there is an opportunity to integrate this key factor at the design and conception of an ITS by updating the ARC-IT architecture as explained in the following subsections.

Concerns. One of the major key elements in the ARC-IT methodology is the enumeration of stakeholders' *"concerns"*, such as performances, interfaces, security, risks, personal (safety, privacy), deployability, etc. Thus, conciliating the stakeholders' concerns and needs with the forensic requirements is a necessity. This may be achievable through the elevation of awareness about potential real world incidents that may be caused by digital incidents [23]. Once the level of awareness is attained, the integration of forensics requirements into the architecture will be feasible.

Readiness. In the ISO/IEC 27043:2015 standard, the readiness processes group contains indications on the proper methodology to prepare before an incident happens.

The *Scenario definition* process imposes the enumeration of all the scenarios in which digital evidence is required. For ITS scenarios, such as road signalization hack [17], remote car hacking [23], attacks on MTA [12,31], etc. are envisioned. More general scenarios may be derived from the analysis of potential ITS surface attacks. Thus, supposing the compromise of any ITS subsystems, terminator, object (physical, communication, functional) will lead to a scenario worth investigation.

Once the scenario is defined, the enumeration of digital evidence sources is next. For this purpose, the inventory of all potential sources within all the ITS sub-systems is required. In fact, potential evidence may lay inside physical and communication objects, and especially the ITS object which is considered as a template for other objects. Afterwards, the planning of evidence collection and storage will for sure induce changes in the physical, communication and functional objects, in addition to the emergence of new data flows related to evidence handling and storage. Finally the ARC-IT may be updated to contain a sub architecture related to the ITS forensic readiness. Even if there are promising opportunities to add forensic readiness to the ARC-It in order to obtain a Forensic-by-design ITS, there are still some concerning challenges that may undermine the feasibility or the implementation of such type of ITS, in the following some of these challenges.

4.2 Challenges

In the following some of the most important challenges that may impact the feasibility of a Forensic-Ready ITS.

Boundaries. An ITS is delimited by geographic and service boundaries. Therefore, the aggregation of services, data, and resources to investigate a potential incident that may occur outside the ITS borders is problematic. In fact, this challenge is more related to the multi-jurisdiction issues that may emerge. Additionally, the ARC-IT comprises *"Terminators"* (e.g. financial institution, weather service, and enforcement center) that are physical objects but peripheral to the ARC-IT environment and do not contain functional objects. Even if, *"the ARC-IT shows interfaces to and from these supporting or external physical objects but does not define functionality"*. Thus, in case of a cyber crime within the ITS boundaries (e.g. Remote vehicle hack [23] leading to a crash), the ARC-IT contains the capabilities to detect the incident, clear the way for the emergency services, transmit the related incident data to the associated Law Enforcement Agency, but still the conduct of a potential digital investigation on the perpetuated cyber crime is considered outside the scope of the ITS. The hypothesized scenario may become more complex if the remotely hijacked vehicle crash happens outside the geographic ITS' boundaries.

Digital vs Physical. Security is one of the ARC-IT stakeholders' concerns. However, incidents are viewed primarily from the perspective of physical and concrete assets rather than from the information perspective. In fact, incidents monitoring and detection in this architecture are related to traffic management, disaster response and evacuation, alert system, etc. So, securing the physical object and data flow by using devices to detect and monitor "real world" incidents derive from the analysis of scenarios were incidents are caused and initiated by attack on physical assets rather than those where the incident is caused by the exploitation of a digital vulnerability. For example, while investigating a multiple vehicle collision, investigator attention may be centred on conduct misbehaviour, traffic violation. However it may also be caused by light signalization hack. Therefore, the focus on the physical incident may mislead the investigator about the origin of the incident.

Requirements Elicitation. Even if the ARC-IT specifies stakeholders concerns, users needs, sub-systems and services packages requirements, to the best of our knowledge there is no mention of forensic requirements. As stated in potential opportunities, if the forensics concerns are considered then maybe there will be elicitation of its associated requirements.

Scale and Volumes. The implementation of an ITS induces a large scale deployment of sensors and actuators. In fact, the ARC-IT physical view contains

multiple objects (subsystems, terminators), and each system may require a set
of sensors employing different technologies and allocated to different missions.
For example, the Security Monitoring Equipment (class: field), contains a set of
sensors dedicated to tasks, such as providing information on equipments security
and fault indication, environment threats (e.g., chemical agent, toxic, biological,
explosives and radiological), motion and intrusion detection, objects detection
(metal), etc. In addition to sensors, there are also equipment and systems on
vehicles, personal, centers and support physical classes. Therefore the aggregated
data type is heterogeneous (text, images and videos), often in different formats,
and voluminous. In addition to the aforementioned constraints, the nature of the
ITS dictated a real time data processing, at least for traffic incident monitoring.
These difficulties may urge the usage of paradigms such as cloud computing and
fog computing. However, digital forensic readiness and investigation models in
these two domains do not yet gain maturity and are still an ongoing research.

Standards and Practices. While studying the ARC-IT, it appears that there
are no standards associated with multiple physical objects, such as security monitoring equipment, vehicle OBE, emergency telecommunications system, alerting
and advisory system, etc. In addition to the lack of standards, vehicle forensic
investigation is very challenging [18,20] in many aspects, such as vehicle con-
structors obfuscation of technical details, digital evidence collection issues, lack
of vehicle digital evidence acquisition and analysis tools, and the need for a sound
forensic investigation approach. Finally, one most important issue is related to
the first responder and LE training [10], and their ability to recognize the necessity of digital forensic and to properly acquire, collect and handle digital forensic
evidence on-scene, such ability is strongly required in case of a fatal vehicle crash.

5   Conclusion and Future Work

The Intelligent Transportation System (ITS) is part of a smart city and a pivotal
element of an economy. The growth of ITS associated market size, the diversity
of devices providers, government funding either in development, deployment are
clear indicators of the effervescence it generates. Considered as a critical infrastructure, the ITS involves several stakeholders that have interests and concerns.
Even if there are concrete advances in this field, there are still some concerns
related to security, privacy, resiliency and safety. Incidents and cyber crime are
no matter of speculation. In fact, Intelligent Transportation Systems are already
targets of cyber attacks going from ransomware to road sign and remote car
hack.

In this paper we investigate the feasibility of a Forensic-ready ITS, more
precisely, we aim to analyse the opportunities and challenges that may arise
from enhancing an existing ITS architecture with the due forensic readiness
capabilities in order to ensure a designed forensic ready ITS. For this purpose,
we provided details on the ARC-It which is an ITS reference architecture, and
the investigation principle and process standard.

Even if there are some promising opportunities associated to the flexibility of the ARC-IT and the digital forensic readiness processes, there are still some challenges related to the ITS boundaries, the necessity to reconsider the balance between the digital vs physical aspects of an incident, the complexity of an ITS, the generated data volume, and finally the lack of standard and best practices.

Nonetheless, we believe that there are real opportunities to achieve a Forensic-ready ITS if only and only if there is a stakeholders' awareness on the possibility of exploiting a digital vulnerability to endanger traveller's safety.

In future works, we will aim to establish a digital forensic investigation model for ITS, aiming at first to enumerate some scenarios where digital evidence is required and then specify a sound and clear methodology to conduct a forensic investigation within an ITS.

References

1. Alam, M., Ferreira, J., Fonseca, J.: Introduction to intelligent transportation systems. In: Alam, M., Ferreira, J., Fonseca, J. (eds.) Intelligent Transportation Systems. SSDC, vol. 52, pp. 1–17. Springer, Cham (2016). https://doi.org/10.1007/978-3-319-28183-4_1
2. Transport Canada: Its architecture for Canada (2021). https://www.itscanada.ca/about/architecture/index.html. Accessed June 08 2021
3. Chan-Edmiston, S., Fischer, S., Sloan, S., Wong, M.: Intelligent transportation systems (its) joint program office: strategic plan 2020–2025, Technical report, U.S. Department of Transportation (2020). https://www.its.dot.gov/stratplan2020/ITSJPO_StrategicPlan_2020-2025.pdf
4. DoT, U.: Architecture reference for cooperative and intelligent transportation (2021). https://local.iteris.com/arc-it/. Accessed June 08 2021
5. Endicott-Popovsky, B., Frincke, D.A., Taylor, C.A.: A theoretical framework for organizational network forensic readiness (2007). J. Comput. **2**(3), 1–11. https://doi.org/10.4304/jcp.2.3.1-11
6. ETSI: Its Europe (2021). Accessed June 08 2021. https://www.etsi.org/technologies/automotive-intelligent-transport
7. Ganin, A.A., et al.: Resilience in intelligent transportation systems (ITS). Transp. Res. Part C Emerg. Technol. **100**, 318–329 (2019). https://doi.org/10.1016/j.trc.2019.01.014
8. Grispos, G., Garcia-Galan, J., Pasquale, L., Nuseibeh, B.: Are you ready? Towards the engineering of forensic-ready systems. In: 2017 11th International Conference on Research Challenges in Information Science (RCIS). IEEE (2017). https://doi.org/10.1109/rcis.2017.7956555
9. Grispos, G., Glisson, W.B., Choo, K.-K.R.: Medical cyber-physical systems development: a forensics-driven approach. In: 2017 IEEE/ACM International Conference on Connected Health: Applications, Systems and Engineering Technologies (CHASE). IEEE (2017). https://doi.org/10.1109/chase.2017.68
10. Holt, T., Dolliver, D.S.: Exploring digital evidence recognition among front-line law enforcement officers at fatal crash scenes. Forensic Sci. Int. Digit. Invest. **37**, 301167 (2021). https://doi.org/10.1016/j.fsidi.2021.301167
11. Huq, N., Vosseler, R., Swimmer, M.: Cyberattacks against intelligent transportation systems, TrendLabs Research Paper (2017)

12. The Philadelphia Inquirer: Septa was attacked by ransomware, sources say. It's still restoring operations stifled since august (2021). https://www.inquirer.com/transportation/septa-malware-attack-ransomware-fbi-employees-cybersecurity-20201007.html. Accessed 06 June 2021
13. Fortune Business Insights: Intelligent transportation system market size, share and global industry trend forecast till 2025 (2021). https://www.fortunebusinessinsights.com/enquiry/request-sample-pdf/intelligent-transportation-system-market-102065. Accessed 08 June 2021
14. ISO: Systems and software engineering—architecture description, Standard, International Organization for Standardization, Geneva, CH (2011)
15. ISO: Information technology—security techniques—incident investigation principles and processes, Standard, International Organization for Standardization, Geneva, CH (2015)
16. Jafarnejad, S., Codeca, L., Bronzi, W., Frank, R., Engel, T.: A car hacking experiment: when connectivity meets vulnerability. In: 2015 IEEE Globecom Workshops (GC Wkshps). IEEE (2015). https://doi.org/10.1109/glocomw.2015.7413993
17. Kelarestaghi, K.B., Heaslip, K., Khalilikhah, M., Fuentes, A., Fessmann, V.: Intelligent transportation system security: hacked message signs. SAE Int. J. Transp. Cybersecur. Priv. 1(2), 75–90 (2018). https://doi.org/10.4271/11-01-02-0004
18. Kopencova, D., Rak, R.: Issues of vehicle digital forensics In: 2020 XII International Science-Technical Conference Automotive Safety. IEEE (2020). https://doi.org/10.1109/automotivesafety47494.2020.9293516
19. Lamssaggad, A., Benamar, N., Hafid, A.S., Msahli, M.: A survey on the current security landscape of intelligent transportation systems. IEEE Access 9, 9180–9208 (2021). https://doi.org/10.1109/access.2021.3050038
20. Le-Khac, N.-A., Jacobs, D., Nijhoff, J., Bertens, K., Choo, K.-K.R.: Smart vehicle forensics: challenges and case study. Future Gener. Comput. Syst. 109, 500–510 (2020). https://doi.org/10.1016/j.future.2018.05.081
21. De Marco, L., Kechadi, M.-T., Ferrucci, F.: Cloud forensic readiness: foundations. In: Gladyshev, P., Marrington, A., Baggili, I. (eds.) ICDF2C 2013. LNICST, vol. 132, pp. 237–244. Springer, Cham (2014). https://doi.org/10.1007/978-3-319-14289-0_16
22. Meneguette, R.I., De Grande, R.E., Loureiro, A.A.F.: Intelligent transportation systems. In: Intelligent Transport System in Smart Cities. UC, pp. 1–21. Springer, Cham (2018). https://doi.org/10.1007/978-3-319-93332-0_1
23. Miller, C.: Lessons learned from hacking a car. IEEE Des. Test 36(6), 7–9 (2019). https://doi.org/10.1109/mdat.2018.2863106
24. Pasquale, L., Alrajeh, D., Peersman, C., Tun, T., Nuseibeh, B., Rashid, A.: Towards forensic-ready software systems. In: Proceedings of the 40th International Conference on Software Engineering: New Ideas and Emerging Results. ACM (2018). https://doi.org/10.1145/3183399.3183426
25. Rahman, N.H.A., Cahyani, N.D.W., Choo, K.-K.R.: Cloud incident handling and forensic-by-design: cloud storage as a case study. Concurr. Comput. Pract. Exp. 29(14), e3868 (2016). https://doi.org/10.1002/cpe.3868
26. Rahman, N.H.A., Glisson, W.B., Yang, Y., Choo, K.-K.R.: Forensic-by-design framework for cyber-physical cloud systems. IEEE Cloud Comput. 3(1), 50–59 (2016). https://doi.org/10.1109/mcc.2016.5
27. Rowlingson, R.: A ten step process for forensic readiness. Int. J. Digit. Evid. 2(3), 1–28 (2004)

28. Sjoberg, K., Andres, P., Buburuzan, T., Brakemeier, A.: Cooperative intelligent transport systems in Europe: current deployment status and outlook. IEEE Veh. Technol. Mag. **12**(2), 89–97 (2017). https://doi.org/10.1109/mvt.2017.2670018
29. Tan, J.: Forensic readiness, Cambridge, MA:@ Stake, pp. 1–23 (2001)
30. National ITS Architecture Team: System engineering for intelligent transportation systems, Technical report, vol. 2007. Iteris, Inc., USA (2007)
31. The New York Times: The M.T.A. is breached by hackers as cyberattacks surge (2021). Accessed 08 June 2021. https://www.nytimes.com/2021/06/02/nyregion/mta-cyber-attack.html
32. Valjarevic, A., Venter, H.: A harmonized process model for digital forensic investigation readiness. In: Peterson, G., Shenoi, S. (eds.) DigitalForensics 2013. IAICT, vol. 410, pp. 67–82. Springer, Heidelberg (2013). https://doi.org/10.1007/978-3-642-41148-9_5

Sensor Systems and Software

A Multi-sensor Information Fusion Method for Autonomous Vehicle Perception System

Peng Mei[1,2(✉)], Hamid Reza Karimi[2], Fei Ma[3], Shichun Yang[1], and Cong Huang[2,4]

[1] School of Transportation Science and Engineering, Beihang University, Beijing, China
maple@buaa.edu.cn
[2] Department of Mechanical Engineering, Politecnico di Milano, Milan, Italy
[3] Autonomous Driving Center, SAIC Motor Passenger Vehicle Co., Shanghai, China
[4] School of Transportation and Civil Engineering, Nantong University, Nantong, China

Abstract. Within the context of the environmental perception of autonomous vehicles (AVs), this paper establishes a sensor model based on the experimental sensor fusion of lidar and monocular cameras. The sensor fusion algorithm can map three-dimensional space coordinate points to a two-dimensional plane based on both space synchronization and time synchronization. The YOLO target recognition and density clustering algorithms obtain the data fusion containing the obstacles' visual information and depth information. Furthermore, the experimental results show the high accuracy of the proposed sensor data fusion algorithm.

Keywords: Autonomous driving · Sensor data fusion · Lidar and Monocular camera

1 Introduction

Autonomous driving has recently become a hot topic in the automotive field, while low-level autonomous vehicles have gradually entered people's daily lives [1–3]. Based on the driving environment, the vehicle perception system can provide real-time information for the AVs.

As a vital part of AVs, the environment perception system can provide information about the driving environment for the AVs. The driving environment is usually quite complex, and it is hard to be predicted. Thus, AVs need to focus on the changes in the surrounding environment. It is challenging to complete all perception tasks with a specific sensor [4]. Generally, the sensors used in AVs include onboard cameras, lidars, radars, and millimeter-wave radars [5]. Compared to other sensors, lidar has more obstacle detection and tracking advantages. According to the running time of the laser, we can get the relative distance between the AVs and the obstacle. Due to the high energy density and frequency, the laser beams can easily capture the contour details of obstacles in the environment. Compared with lidar, millimeter-wave radar has no advantage in capturing detailed information. However, its anti-interference ability is

S. Paiva et al. (Eds.): SmartCity360° 2021, LNICST 442, pp. 633–646, 2022.
https://doi.org/10.1007/978-3-031-06371-8_40

strong, and it is often used for sensing road conditions. The camera can express the surrounding environment intuitively, but it is hard to obtain accurate depth information. Radar is cheap and has a long service life. Because of the low resolution, radar has significant limitations in acquiring dynamic information [6].

As the sensor combination of lidar and camera can well identify surrounding vehicles and other obstacles, AVs sensing systems have begun to combine lidar and camera in recent years [7]. The lidar receives three-dimensional space coordinate information, while the camera obtains two-dimensional plane coordinate information. The key is to establish a mapping relationship between three-dimensional space points and a two-dimensional plane to fuse these sensors' data.

Some scholars have done related research on the multi-sensor fusion algorithm of AVs. Elhousni et al. [8] believe that the material of the calibration target will affect the reflection intensity of the laser signal, which will affect the final calibration result. Therefore, they use a glass calibration target, and the surface is smooth and has high reflectivity. By fitting the contour of the calibration target, its edge line equation is obtained. Due to the penetrability of the laser beam is not considered, there is a gap between the calibration result and the expected value. Vasconcelos et al. [9] used a single-line lidar instead of a multi-line lidar case to reduce the error. Specifically, a single-line lidar is used to scan the entire calibration target area. With the small number of laser beams, the amount of data is less than that of the multi-line lidar. Therefore, this method can obtain a more accurate checkerboard corner detection. To simplify the calibration process, Zewei et al. [10] achieved the external parameter calibration of the camera by using Zhang's calibration method. However, the obtained rotation matrix ignored the relative distance between the camera and lidar coordinate systems. The experimental approach has shown some limitations; when the radar's relative position and the camera are far, the calibration result's deviation error will be obvious. On this basis, Park et al. [11] optimized the calibration process and obtained a better fusion effect. However, this method only achieves fusion from the data level, which is not optimized for specific goals. Based on the independence of two planes, Li et al. [12] described the corresponding relationship between laser point cloud coordinates and image coordinates. Finally, they obtained the rotation and translation relationship.

In summary, as two indispensable sensors for AVs, camera and lidar have their advantages and disadvantages, respectively. It is necessary for the perception system to fuse these two sensors' data and then obtain environmental information. The experimental results show that the accuracy of the data fusion method reaches up to 98.42%.

2   Sensor Model

2.1   Camera Observation Model

Through the principle of optical imaging, the vehicle camera maps the coordinate information of the three-dimensional space to the two-dimensional plane, thereby realizing the imaging of the object [13]. Typically, the specific position of the camera in space is uncertain, so it is necessary to establish a spatial coordinate reference system to describe this mapping relationship. Thus, this article introduces four coordinate system references, as shown in Fig. 1.

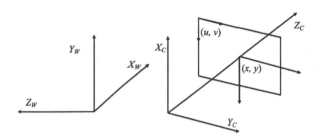

Fig. 1. Coordinate system diagram.

The coordinate points are represented by (X_w, Y_w, Z_w) in the world coordinate system, it can describe the proper object position in three-dimensional space. In the camera coordinate system, the coordinate points are represented by (X_c, Y_c, Z_c). Generally, a specific coordinate axis of the camera coordinate system coincides with the camera's optical axis. The coordinate point in the image coordinate system is represented by (x, y), and the coordinate points in the pixel coordinate system are represented by (u, v).

The target under each coordinate system can be scaled, rotated, and translated to realize the transformation of the research object. The rotation transformation can be achieved by using a rotation vector through a three-dimensional vector, it can be shown as follows,

$$R = [R_1, R_2, R_3] \tag{1}$$

where R means the rotation matrix.

The calculation formula can be shown as follows,

$$t = \left[t_x, t_y, t_z\right]^T \tag{2}$$

where t denotes the translation vector.

Through the rotation matrix R and the translation vector t, the conversion relationship between the world coordinate system and the specific coordinate points in the camera coordinate system can be described as follows [12],

$$\begin{bmatrix} X_c \\ Y_c \\ Z_c \end{bmatrix} = R \begin{bmatrix} X_w \\ Y_w \\ Z_w \end{bmatrix} + t = \begin{bmatrix} R_{11} & R_{12} & R_{13} \\ R_{21} & R_{22} & R_{23} \\ R_{31} & R_{32} & R_{33} \end{bmatrix} \begin{bmatrix} X_w \\ Y_w \\ Z_w \end{bmatrix} + \begin{bmatrix} t_x \\ t_y \\ t_z \end{bmatrix} \tag{3}$$

In order to simplify the correspondence between the camera coordinate system and the image coordinate system, it is assumed that the X_c axis and Y_c axis of the camera coordinate system are corresponding to the x-axis and y-axis of the image coordinate system, respectively. Therefore, the corresponding relationship between the two coordinate systems can be described as follows,

$$\begin{bmatrix} x \\ y \end{bmatrix} = f \begin{bmatrix} \frac{X_c}{Z_c} \\ \frac{Y_c}{Z_c} \end{bmatrix} \tag{4}$$

where f is the focal length of the camera.

The transformation between the pixel coordinate system and the image coordinate system is mainly obtained through the scaling of the corresponding coordinate axis. Assuming that any pixel point coordinates are the corresponding image coordinate point, it is scaled by α times and β times in the x-axis and y-axis respectively. The origin of the pixel coordinate system is located at the top left corner of the image, and the image coordinate system will produce c_x and c_y offsets in the x-axis and y-axis, respectively. Based on the above analysis, the corresponding relationship between the pixel coordinates and the image coordinates can be obtained as follows,

$$u = \alpha x + c_x, v = \beta y + c_y \tag{5}$$

where c_x and c_y are the offsets parameters.

In summary, the coordinate points in a certain world coordinate system can be mapped to the pixel coordinate system by formula (6).

$$
\begin{aligned}
z_c \begin{bmatrix} x \\ y \\ 1 \end{bmatrix} &= K \begin{bmatrix} X_c \\ Y_c \\ Z_c \end{bmatrix} = \begin{bmatrix} f_x & 0 & c_x \\ 0 & f_y & c_x \\ 0 & 0 & 1 \end{bmatrix} \begin{bmatrix} X_c \\ Y_c \\ Z_c \end{bmatrix} \\
&= \begin{bmatrix} f_x & 0 & c_x \\ 0 & f_y & c_x \\ 0 & 0 & 1 \end{bmatrix} \left(\begin{bmatrix} R_{11} & R_{12} & R_{13} \\ R_{21} & R_{22} & R_{23} \\ R_{31} & R_{32} & R_{33} \end{bmatrix} \begin{bmatrix} X_w \\ Y_w \\ Z_w \end{bmatrix} + \begin{bmatrix} t_x \\ t_y \\ t_z \end{bmatrix} \right)
\end{aligned} \tag{6}
$$

There are usually two types of distortion, including barrel distortion and pincushion distortion, as shown in Fig. 2. The characteristic of barrel distortion is that as the distance between the imaging point and the optical axis increases, the image magnification decreases. As the distance between the imaging point and the optical axis increases, the image magnification increases, and it is called pincushion distortion. The processing of imaging distortion is generally achieved by calibrating the camera's internal parameter matrix.

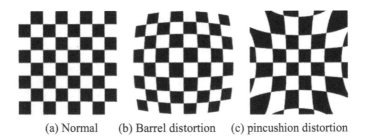

(a) Normal   (b) Barrel distortion   (c) pincushion distortion

Fig. 2. Imaging distortion.

2.2 Lidar Point Cloud Processing

This paper proposes straight-through filtering to preprocess the original point cloud data. The specific method is given as follows. First, define the coordinate system of the point cloud data. As shown in Fig. 3, assume that the laser radar installation position is the origin of the coordinates, the lateral direction of the vehicle is the x-axis, the longitudinal direction of the vehicle is the y-axis, and the vertical direction of the vehicle body is the z-axis. According to the above coordinate system, the straight-through filtering method limits the range of point cloud data. Among them, $x \in [-10,10]$, $y \in [-10,30]$, $z \in [-1,2.5]$. This range can ensure the obstacles are detected in the surrounding environment, and it can also filter out point cloud data that is not related to environmental perception. The point cloud data preprocessing is shown in Fig. 4.

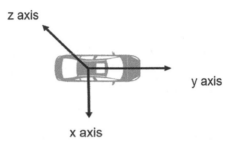

Fig. 3. Point cloud data coordinate system.

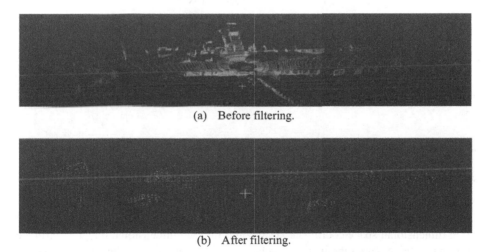

(a) Before filtering.

(b) After filtering.

Fig. 4. Data point cloud preprocessing.

2.3 Sensor Parameters

The sensors used in this article are Beike Tianhui mechanical Lidar and LI-USB30-AR023ZWDRB monocular camera to verify the sensor fusion algorithm. The technical parameters of the sensor are shown in Tables 1 and 2.

Table 1. Lidar technical parameters.

Type	R-Fans 32
Detection distance	200 m
Measurement accuracy	<2 cm
Horizontal angular	<0.1°
Working frequency	15 Hz
Vertical field of view	32°
Vertical angular	1°
Operating voltage	24VDC
Operating temperature	(−20,55)°C
Size	113 mm(D) × 70 mm(H)
Power consumption	<15 W

Table 2. Camera technical parameters.

Type	LI-USB30
Resolution	1920 × 1080
Frame rate	30 fps
Size	30 mm(D) × 30 mm(H)
Operating voltage	5VDC
Operating temperature	(−20,80)°C
Power consumption	<5 W

3   Sensor Data Synchronization Mapping

3.1   Spatial Synchronization

Sensor spatial synchronization is mainly used to realize the unification of lidar coordinates and camera pixel coordinates. Generally, the mapping relationship between the three-dimensional space coordinate system and the two-dimensional image coordinate system is obtained by calibrating the camera's external parameters. The two-dimensional pixel point be expressed as follows,

$$m = [u, v]^T \tag{7}$$

where m means pixel projection point.

Its corresponding three-dimensional space point can be expressed as follows,

$$M = [X, Y, Z]^T \tag{8}$$

where M denotes three-dimensional space point.

Perform homogeneous coordinate transformation of the above two vectors, ones get,

$$\tilde{m} = [u, v, 1]^T \tag{9}$$

$$\tilde{M} = [X, Y, Z, 1]^T \tag{10}$$

According to the imaging principle of the camera, the corresponding relationship between M and m can be shown as follows,

$$\tilde{m} = \frac{1}{s} A[R\,t]^T \tilde{M} \tag{11}$$

where s stands for the scale factor, and A means the internal parameters of the camera. $[R, t]$ is to transform the world coordinate system to the camera coordinate system for rotation matrix and translation vector, which is the external parameters of the camera.

Define A as follows,

$$A = \begin{bmatrix} \alpha & \gamma & u_0 \\ 0 & \beta & v_0 \\ 0 & 0 & 1 \end{bmatrix} \tag{12}$$

where (u_0, v_0) are the principal coordinate points, α and β are scaling factors, which contains the focal length information of the camera, γ is used to describe the skewness of the two image coordinate axes and the pixel coordinate axis.

It is assumed that the plane of the calibration target coincides with the base plane of the world coordinate system, that is $Z = 0$. Denote the i-th column in the rotation matrix R as r_i, which can be obtained by formula (11):

$$s\begin{bmatrix} u \\ v \\ 1 \end{bmatrix} = A\begin{bmatrix} r_1 & r_2 & r_3 & t \end{bmatrix} \begin{bmatrix} X \\ Y \\ 0 \\ 1 \end{bmatrix} = A\begin{bmatrix} r_1 & r_2 & t \end{bmatrix} \begin{bmatrix} X \\ Y \\ 1 \end{bmatrix} \tag{13}$$

Then the relationship between the point M and its corresponding pixel m can be defined by a homography matrix H, we can obtain the following equation,

$$s\tilde{m} = H\tilde{M} \tag{14}$$

$$H = A\begin{bmatrix} r_1 & r_2 & t \end{bmatrix} \tag{15}$$

From the Eq. (13), we can get the following equations,

$$u = \frac{h_{11}X + h_{12}Y + h_{13}}{h_{31}X + h_{32}Y + h_{33}} \tag{16}$$

$$v = \frac{h_{21}X + h_{22}Y + h_{23}}{h_{31}X + h_{32}Y + h_{33}} \tag{17}$$

From the Eq. (15), we can get the following equation,

$$\begin{bmatrix} h_1 & h_2 & h_3 \end{bmatrix} = \lambda A\begin{bmatrix} r_1 & r_2 & t \end{bmatrix} \tag{18}$$

where λ is any non-zero constant. According to the nature of the rotation matrix, r_1 and r_2 are orthogonal vectors, then we can get:

$$h_1^T A^{-T} A^{-1} h_2 = 0 \tag{19}$$

$$h_1^T A^{-T} A^{-1} h_1 = h_2^T A^{-T} A^{-1} h_2 \tag{20}$$

Define the matrix B as follows,

$$B = A^{-T} A^{-1} = [B_{i,j}]_{3*3} \ (i, j = 1, 2, 3) \tag{21}$$

Since B is a symmetric matrix, set the vector b as follows,

$$b = [B_{11}, B_{12}, B_{22}, B_{13}, B_{23}, B_{33}]^T \tag{22}$$

The i-th column of the homography matrix H can be expressed as,

$$h_i = [h_{i1}, h_{i2}, h_{i3}]^T \tag{23}$$

$$h_i^T B h_j = v_{ij}^T b \tag{24}$$

where $v_{ij} = \left[h_{i1}h_{j1}, h_{i1}h_{j2} + h_{i2}h_{j1}, h_{i2}h_{j2}, h_{i3}h_{j1} + h_{i1}h_{j3}, h_{i3}h_{j2} + h_{i2}h_{j3}, h_{i3}h_{j3} \right]$.
From (23) and (24), we can get the following formula,

$$\begin{bmatrix} v_{11}^T \\ (v_{11} - v_{22})^T \end{bmatrix} b = 0 \tag{25}$$

$$vb = 0 \tag{26}$$

Based on the calibration target to collect images at different positions, the matrix B and homography matrix H can be obtained. The homography matrix H contains the camera's internal and external parameters. To achieve spatial synchronization, Cholesky decomposition is adopted to obtain the camera's internal and external parameters.

According to the spatial synchronization method, the lidar and the camera are spatially synchronized. As shown in Fig. 5, the square paper calibration target is used, and it is hung vertically about 3 m in front of the sensor. Figure 6 is a comparison diagram of the sensors used before and after spatial synchronization. The red color represents the contour of the object in the pixel coordinate system. After coordinating conversion, the blue point represents the object contour obtained by the laser radar, and then output to the pixel coordinate system. Among them, Fig. 6(a) indicates the fusion effect without spatial synchronization, Fig. 6(b) shows the effect after synchronization. It can be seen that after space synchronization, the objects in the two coordinate systems can achieve the effect of overlapping.

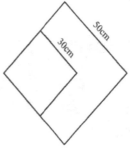

(a) Actual calibration target   (b) The size of calibration target

Fig. 5. Calibration target parameters.

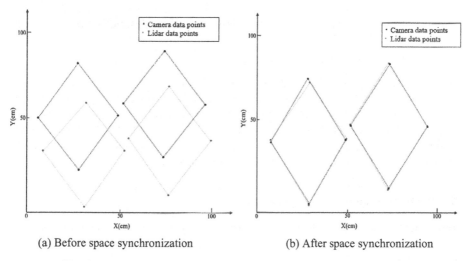

(a) Before space synchronization   (b) After space synchronization

Fig. 6. Spatial synchronization effect comparison. (Color figure online)

3.2 Time Synchronization

Due to the different operating frequencies of lidar and vehicle camera, their respective observation times are also inconsistent. If we use non-synchronized sensor data to perform data fusion directly, it will affect the accuracy of the fusion result. Therefore, time synchronization is a prerequisite for the integration of lidar and camera data. In the environment of the robot operating system, a certain moment is taken as a benchmark. Find the time stamp of the lidar point cloud data and camera image data at this moment, and then keep the data with the same time stamp.

Based on both space synchronization and time synchronization, the synchronous mapping of lidar and camera data can be achieved. The laser radar point cloud data is output to the camera image data, and the processing effect is shown in Fig. 7. It can be seen that the sensor can not only work under a unified time and space reference, but also can identify obstacle information in the surrounding environment.

Fig. 7. Synchronous mapping effect.

4   Target Recognition and Depth Information Association

4.1   Camera Target Detection

Target detection refers to the ability to accurately identify the type and location of an object through a target recognition algorithm. YOLO target detection treats the target detection problem as a regression problem and then directly returns the position and category of the Bounding Box in the output layer [1, 14, 15]. Its advantages are fast recognition speed and high accuracy, which can be used in real-time systems. This article uses the YOLO algorithm to achieve target recognition.

4.2   In-Depth Information Association

Above-mentioned shows that the sensor data was synchronized in time and space to complete the vehicle target recognition. However, the integration of data is not related to each other, so this data fusion needs to be processed.

   To solve this problem, this paper is based on the DBSCAN (Density-based spatial clustering algorithm with noise) algorithm to achieve sensor depth information association [16–19]. This algorithm is a commonly used density clustering algorithm. The main idea is to divide the dense points in the area into the same cluster. It can realize clusters of any shape without inputting category information in advance. Therefore, it can be used for the preliminary fusion data to realize deep information association.

4.3   Experimental Verification

This paper uses the yellow and blue cones, a diameter of 20 cm and a height of 20 cm, to verify the target recognition algorithm and depth information association, as shown in Fig. 8.

   First, a training data set is generated by labeling 1000 pictures containing cones, and the marked feature information is the color of the cones. Then train the Darknet53 neural

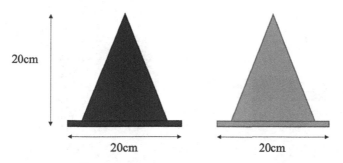

Fig. 8. The size of the cone.

network under the YOLO target recognition framework. The camera can accurately identify the cone information, while mark the shape and color of the cone in the picture. Secondly, the image data and the lidar point cloud data are synchronized in time and space, simultaneously, to obtain preliminary fusion data. Then, we can find a cone point group in the pixel coordinate system. By calculating the sum of the coordinate variances of each point from the remaining points, we can obtain a point with the smallest variance sum. In this process, we regard the coordinates of this point as the cone coordinate reference point. Finally, the integration of data with cone color information and depth information is obtained.

The experiment process is shown in Fig. 9. The two-color cones are arranged as shown in the figure, and the initial position is the observed position 1.

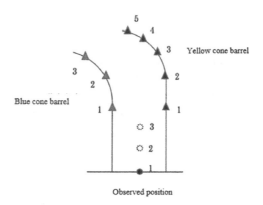

Fig. 9. A schematic diagram of fusion effect verification experiment.

The data fusion of the sensor moving from position 1 to position 3 is recorded, and 100 frames of fusion data of three observation points are respectively taken to obtain 300 sets of data. Visualize one group of data, as shown in Fig. 10.

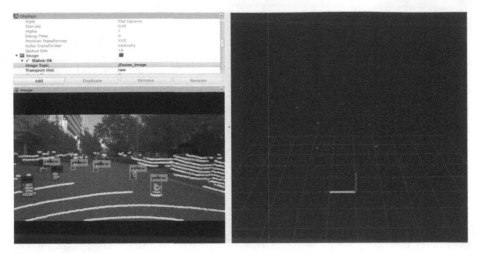

Fig. 10. Verify experiment visualization.

4.4   Results and Discussion

(1) Target recognition error discussion

Above all, each data group contains three blue cones and five yellow cones, with 2400 recognition results. The data obtained from the statistical experiment is shown in Table 3, and the table is called the confusion matrix. The sum of each row represents the true sample size of the category. Each column of the confusion matrix represents an accurate classification of the cones. The result shows its accuracy rate reaches 98.42%.

Table 3. Statistics of experimental results.

$n = 2400$	Recognized as blue	Recognized as yellow	Total
Actually blue	887	13	900
Actually yellow	25	1475	1500
Accuracy	$(887 + 1475)/2400 = 98.42\%$		

(2) Depth information error discussion

Since the depth information in the fusion algorithm used in this paper comes directly from the measurement data of the lidar, the distance error of the fusion data is consistent with the measurement error of the lidar. Moreover, the distance error is less than 2 cm. Therefore, the data fusion method proposed in this paper has high accuracy.

5   Conclusion

Aiming to improve the environment perception of AVs, this paper combines the sensor data of lidar and monocular cameras. This paper proposes a sensor fusion algorithm that combines space synchronization and time synchronization simultaneously to solve the problem of different sensor time and space coordinate systems. For the spatial synchronization of the lidar and the camera, the external parameter matrix of the camera is calibrated through a checkerboard grid, which realizes the mapping of three-dimensional space coordinate points to a two-dimensional plane. Based on YOLO's target recognition algorithm, the recognition of obstacles is completed. In view of the density clustering algorithm, the target depth information association is realized. Finally, the fusion data containing the visual information and depth information of obstacles is obtained. Through the experiment result, we can verify the effect of the sensor data fusion algorithm. In the following work, we will compare the accuracy of different algorithms and apply them to AVs with these two sensors.

References

1. Kiran, B.R., Sobh, I., Talpaert, V., et al.: Deep reinforcement learning for autonomous driving: a survey. IEEE Trans. Intell. Transp. Syst. (2021)
2. Karimi, H.R., Lu, Y.: Guidance and control methodologies for marine vehicles: a survey. Control. Eng. Pract. **111**, 104785 (2021)
3. Mei, P., Karimi, H.R., Yang, S., et al.: An adaptive fuzzy sliding-mode control for regenerative braking system of electric vehicles. Int. J. Adapt. Control Signal Process. **36**(2), 391–410 (2022)
4. Thuruthel, T.G., Shih, B., Laschi, C., et al.: Soft robot perception using embedded soft sensors and recurrent neural networks. Sci. Robot. **4**(26), eaav1488 (2019)
5. Zang, S., Ding, M., Smith, D., et al.: The impact of adverse weather conditions on autonomous vehicles: how rain, snow, fog, and hail affect the performance of a self-driving car. IEEE Veh. Technol. Mag. **14**(2), 103–111 (2019)
6. Bilik, I., Longman, O., Villeval, S., et al.: The rise of radar for autonomous vehicles: signal processing solutions and future research directions. IEEE Signal Process. Mag. **36**(5), 20–31 (2019)
7. Roriz, R., Cabral, J., Gomes, T.: Automotive LiDAR technology: a survey. IEEE Trans. Intell. Transp. Syst. 1–16 (2021)
8. Elhousni, M., Lyu, Y., Zhang, Z., et al.: Automatic building and labeling of HD maps with deep learning. Proc. AAAI Conf. Artif. Intell. **34**(08), 13255–13260 (2020)
9. Vasconcelos, F., Barreto, J.P., Nunes, U.: A minimal solution for the extrinsic calibration of a camera and a laser-rangefinder. IEEE Trans. Pattern Anal. Mach. Intell. **34**(11), 2097–2107 (2012)
10. Liu, Z., Lu, D., Qian, W., et al.: Extrinsic calibration of a single-point laser rangefinder and single camera. Opt. Quantum Electron. **51**(6), 1–13 (2019)
11. Park, S., Chung, M.: Extrinsic calibration between a 3D laser scanner and a camera using PCA method. In: 2012 9th International Conference on Ubiquitous Robots and Ambient Intelligence (URAI), pp. 527–528 (2012)
12. Li, N., Hu, Z., Zhao, B.: Flexible extrinsic calibration of a camera and a two-dimensional laser rangefinder with a folding pattern. Appl. Opt. **55**(9), 2270–2280 (2016)

13. Yu, H., Tseng, H.E., Langari, R.: A human-like game theory-based controller for automatic lane changing. Transp. Res. Part C Emerg. Technol. **88**, 140–158 (2018)
14. Santos, H., Pereira, G.V., Budde, M., Lopes, S.F., Nikolic, P.: Science and Technologies for Smart Cities: 5th EAI International Summit, SmartCity360, Braga, Portugal, 4–6 December 2019, Proceedings. Springer, Cham (2020). https://doi.org/10.1007/978-3-030-51005-3
15. Huang, C., Karimi, H.R.: Non-fragile H∞ control for LPV-based CACC systems subject to denial-of-service attacks. IET Control Theory Appl. **15**(9), 1246–1256 (2021)
16. Guo, F., Hao, K., Xia, M., Zhao, L., Wang, L., Liu, Q.: Detection of insulator defects based on YOLO V3. In: Han, S., Ye, L., Meng, W. (eds.) AICON 2019. LNICSSITE, vol. 287, pp. 291–299. Springer, Cham (2019). https://doi.org/10.1007/978-3-030-22971-9_25
17. Huang, C., Mei, P., Wang, J.: Event-triggering robust fusion estimation for a class of multi-rate systems subject to censored observations. ISA Trans. **110**, 28–38 (2021)
18. Cai, Z., Wang, J., He, K.: Adaptive density-based spatial clustering for massive data analysis. IEEE Access **8**, 23346–23358 (2020)
19. Lu, Y., Karimi, H.R.: Recursive fusion estimation for mobile robot localization under multiple energy harvesting sensors. IET Control Theory Appl. **16**, 20–30 (2021)

Propagation Characteristics of LoRa-Based Wireless Communication in Steel Ship Cabin

Wanli Tu[1,2]([⊠]), Lingchao Meng[1], Qiubo Ye[3]([⊠]), Mingxian Shen[4], and Yiqun Xu[1,2]

[1] Marine Engineering Institute, Jimei University, Xiamen 361021, People's Republic of China
wanlitu@163.com
[2] Fujian Provincial Key Laboratory of Naval Architecture and Marine Engineering,
Xiamen 361021, People's Republic of China
[3] Information Engineering Institute, Jimei University, Xiamen
361021, People's Republic of China
qbye@jmu.edu.cn
[4] Navigation Institute, Jimei University, Xiamen 361021, People's Republic of China

Abstract. The deployment of wireless sensor network in ship application traditionally relies on human experience and lack of theoretical analysis so far. Based on electromagnetic theory calculation (ray-tracing method) and experimental measurement, this paper investigates the propagation of radio signals inside ship cabin for wireless sensor network with LoRa (Long Range) technology. A three-dimensional model of radio wave propagation in typical hull ship cabin with the main diesel engine and central control room is established. The multipath propagation prediction is carried on and the received power of the receiver is calculated. Besides, through comparative analysis with experimental test, the main influence of cabin spatial factors on the characteristics of wireless signal is discussed. The results clearly demonstrate that the wireless network with LoRa band is possible and quite feasible in ship cabin, and the simulated results could give well agreement with experimental data about the rules of influence on wireless signal in different areas of the ship's cabin. Some important guidance is also given for communication link design of actual LoRa network in ship.

Keywords: LoRa technology · Ray-tracing method · Ship cabin · Propagation characteristics

1 Introduction

The main engine room is the power center of a ship. Monitoring the equipment state of the ship cabin during navigation is of great significance to the stability and safety of the ship's operation. With the traditional method, the data transmission in the cabin adopts wired communication using fieldbus technology (such as CAN or Modbus protocol). The cost of marine wired communication cable layout in a ship is relatively high, and it takes very long period for construction. The ship is usually designed as a relatively compact and complex structure. When it is necessary to install new equipment on the

© ICST Institute for Computer Sciences, Social Informatics and Telecommunications Engineering 2022
Published by Springer Nature Switzerland AG 2022. All Rights Reserved
S. Paiva et al. (Eds.): SmartCity360° 2021, LNICST 442, pp. 647–658, 2022.
https://doi.org/10.1007/978-3-031-06371-8_41

ship during its service, the cables need to be rearranged, and new holes may need to be cut on the steel plate, which would affect the strength of the hull structure and was strictly controlled. In addition, broken and aging cable is a major hidden risk of fire. The International Maritime Organization (IMO) requires the installation of fire detection sensors in each cabin and major zone on a ship. Therefore, wireless sensor network (WSN) and internet of things (IoT) solution are adopted for ship application [1, 2].

The WSN consists of low power devices, and its sensor module can move easily due to small size as well as lower cost, which makes it potential alternative for traditional ca-bling networks. Some researches employed the WSN system based on 2.4 GHz Zigbee communication technologies to establish real-time monitoring system on board [3–6]. Furthermore, propagation modeling of such frequency band in ship also have been studied [7]. This work group did some researches on 2.4 GHz wireless channel propagation in the ship cabin of a sand carrier, and the simulated results were agreed well with the experimental results, as can be seen in our previous works [8]. However, despite its significant benefits, using WSN-based Zigbee protocol in the engine room also needs to face some problems such as large battery consumption and interference of transmission sig-nals. For the large-scale ship with more complex environment which contains abundance of reflecting and diffracting elements, it need communication technology with longer transmission distance, longer battery life and better pass-through ability.

Low Power-Wide Area Network (LP-WAN) has received much attention and development due to its significant advantages in long-distance transmission and low endnode's power consumption. LoRa (Long Range) is based on Chirp Spread Spectrum (CSS) modulation, where each chirp encodes 2 m symbol values for spreading factor. And LoRa modulation uses cyclic error correction coding for forward error detection and error correction which can make LoRa more robust against the interference and maintain high acceptance sensitivity and anti-jamming ability even in complex environments [9, 10]. Feasibility of LoRa technique applying for indoor environment of ship has also been verified by researchers. Zhang Qin et al. designed a ship-based temperature measurement system based on LoRa technology and proved its stable working performance [11]. On the other hand, so far researches on applications of LoRa technology on ship were mostly focused on experimental test, and the installation location of the access point was mainly based on the experience of designers, which would greatly lengthen the construction cycle and demand lots of resources. It is critical to design a reliable communication link that collects the data from wireless sensors in the harsh channel environments and conveys them to the center node. Thus further analysis about the impact of ship cabin environment on LoRa-based wireless communication technology is still required.

Establishing accurate indoor path loss model and predicting the propagation characteristics of wireless signal according to the propagation environment would greatly re-duce the cost of network construction and would also be of great significance to maintain communication stability [12]. In this work, a ray-tracing based model is established to calculate and analyze the propagation characteristics of wireless signal at 433 MHz frequency band in typical and complex vessel cabin environment. The influence of reflection, transmission and diffraction on wireless signals caused by large obstacles and other factors is taken into account. In addition, the experimental measurement with LoRa module is also carried out in a real ship cabin. The simulated results are compared with the experimental detection results, which could help to learn the propagation characteristics of wireless communication in cabin and is valuable for better application of LoRa technology in steel ship. The analysis could provide important guidance for the rational deployment of wireless sensing systems.

2 First Section Modeling of Radio Wave 433 MHz Propagation in Ship's Engine Room Based on Ray-Tracing Method

2.1 Ray-Tracing Method

Simulation-based studies of wireless networks require simple path loss models that can capture indoor propagation effects such as attenuation, scattering, diffraction, and reflection with enough accuracy. By ray-tracing method, the electromagnetic wave propagation characteristics could be analyzed based on the principle of geometric optics [13]. Figure 1(a) shows the diagram of wave propagation by ray-tracing method, and Fig. 1(b) is the spherical coordinate system. For the diffraction caused by the obstacle, it emits a ray from the transmitting antenna (Tx) and then tracks the ray to see if it collides with the surface of an obstacle and is received by the receiving antenna (Rx), then calculates the power or electric field associated with the ray to contribute to the receiving point.

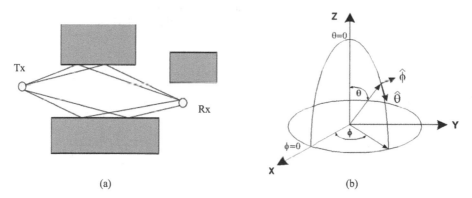

(a)   (b)

Fig. 1. (a) Diagram of wave propagation by ray-tracing method (b) The spherical coordinate system

According to the geometrical position of the incident and the electrical parameter characteristics of the obstacle, the situation of reflection, transmission, diffraction or some combination of these can be determined so that the next path can be tracked until the ray is received or the exit tracking condition is reached. It was validated as an effective method of solving the problem of radio wave transmission planning and prediction in indoor complex environment. When there is no line of sight for propagation path between the transmitter and receiver, the signal fading in transmission is closely to the Rayleigh distribution. The presence of obstructions along the path may cause the signal more distorted or impaired than it would under free space condition [14]. The received power is an important parameter to evaluate the communication system and characterize the received signal strength, which determines whether the receiving end can receive information well. The average received power of total propagation path P_N is defined by the sum of the average received power of the i-th propagation path P_i, as follows [13, 15]:

$$P_N = \sum_{i=1}^{N_P} \left(\frac{\lambda^2 \beta}{8\pi \eta_0} \left| E_{\theta,i} \sqrt{|G_\theta(\theta_i, \phi_i)|} e^{j\psi_\theta} + E_{\phi,i} \sqrt{|G_\phi(\theta_i, \phi_i)|} e^{j\psi_\phi} \right|^2 \right) \quad (1)$$

where N_P: the number of propagation path; λ: signal wave length; β: parameter related to the center frequency and bandwidth of the transmitter and receiver; η_0: impedance of free space; $E_{\theta,i}$ and $E_{\phi,i}$: electric field intensity of the i-th receiving path in θ and ϕ direction, respectively; θ_i and ϕ_i: arrival direction of the i-th ray; G_θ and G_ϕ: antenna gain of receiver in θ and ϕ direction, respectively; ψ_θ and ψ_ϕ: phase in θ and ϕ direction of the far-zone, respectively. All simulations reported here are performed using the Remcom Wireless InSite commercial software package.

2.2 Three-Dimensional Model of Ship's Main-Engine Room

'M/V YU DE', a 64000-ton-class cargo training ship, was chosen for this study. It is the largest training vessel in the world and has been used for seafaring education, training and scientific research as well as carrying bulk cargo. The main engine room is located at the rear of the ship. Figure 2 shows the side view of 'M/V YU DE' and Table 1 shows its specifications [16].

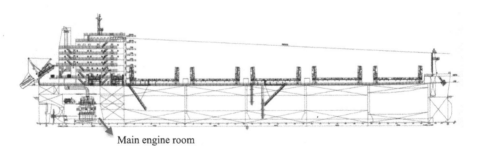

Main engine room

Fig. 2. Side view of 'M/V YU DE'

Table 1. Specifications of 'M/V YU DE'

Length (m)	Width (m)	Height (m)	Tonnage (ton)	Speed (knot)	Main engine
199.90	32.26	18.00	64000	14.0 (max. 15)	MAN-B&W 5S60ME-C8.2(Tier II)

The wireless communication tests and wave propagation investigation are conducted in the main-engine room which houses the vessel's prime mover, diesel engine. The main engine room accommodates lots of equipment such as motor, diesel engine, water pumps, compressors and so on. To examine how the equipment affects the wireless signal propagation, the diesel engine is selected and modeled in this simulation, as it is the largest equipment obstacle for signals. The diesel engine is located in the middle place of the engine room, and there are three platforms with connecting staircase on the side, which can be seen from Fig. 3(a). The established model is shown in Fig. 3(b). The bottom platform has set-wire cabinets at its rear part, the middle platform has auxiliary machine at its rear part and corridor around the diesel engine, and the control room is located in the top platform with a corridor around the engine and pipes. Some detail interior construction is ignored and simplified.

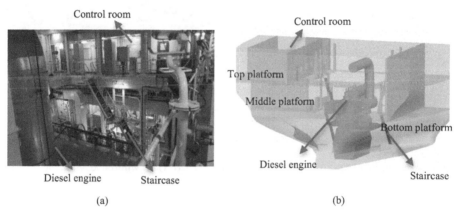

Fig. 3. Layout of main engine room (a) Main engine room of the real ship (b) Three-dimensional model of main engine room

2.3 Simulation Parameter Setting

Arrangement of the initial transmitter (Tx) and the receiver (Rx) is shown in Fig. 4. Figure 4(a) is the wireframe rendering view, and Fig. 4(b) is the solid rendering view, where the roof and surrounding walls are set invisible for observation convenience. Tx is placed at a height of 1.7 m above floor level on the bottom platform of cabin, and Rx is moving away from the Tx and is set at various route around the diesel engine. The transmission of wireless signals is still possible due to the open three-storey structure of the cabin with staircase connection and the glass windows of control room. Vertical polarization mode leads to lower path loss than horizontal polarization mode and has the best coverage in indoor environment. Therefore, an omnidirectional monopole antenna working in vertical polarization mode is chosen in this investigation. The performance is investigated in the center frequency of 433 MHz, with the bandwidth 250 kHz, the transmitting power 17 dBm, the path gains 15 dBi, and the transmitting signal adopts sinusoid wave shape. Set up radio waves to undergo 5 reflections, 2 refractions and 2 diffractions during propagation. Further, in all simulations, the factors such as atmospheric propagation losses, and the non-uniformities of the surface materials are not considered for simplicity. Different from the propagation in traditional building space, the ship cabin structure is mainly made of metal material which would made all energy reflected. Besides, absorption loss of electromagnetic waves propagation in the atmosphere is negligible for the humidity in the ship cabin is not high and is relatively stable, which would hardly affect the spread of narrow band signals [14]. The simulated results of received power is obtained for further analysis.

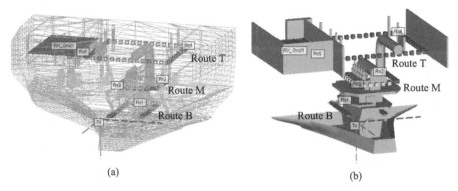

Fig. 4. Arrangement of the transmitter (Tx) and receivers (Rx) (a) wireframe rendering view (b) solid rendering view

3 Experiment Measurement

The experiment measurement is taken at the main engine room of 'M/V YU DE'. The experimental equipment includes LoRa communication nodes, a small computer with Uart Assist serial port program, as well as a tripod used for adjusting measuring receiver. The layout is shown in Fig. 5. The omnidirectional and monopole copper rod antennas working with vertically polarized mode are used as the stationary transmitter and roaming receiver. The overall height is 205 mm with effective length 175 mm, thus the monitoring is done with 433 MHz frequency at the measuring points which are selected alongside the same path in simulation. The average received power over fifty measurement results for each measurement point is adopted to ensure stabilization.

(a)   (b)

Fig. 5. Experimental test for LoRa wireless communication (a) The stationary transmitter antenna (b) The roaming receiver antenna on a tripod

4   Results and Discussion

The influence of large device such as the diesel engine on the signal transmission couldn't be ignored and should be analyzed. As can be seen from Fig. 4, there are three receiver routes for investigating signal transmission characteristics around the diesel engine. R × 1 is set at the bottom platform of engine room which is named Route B here. R × 2 and R × 3 are set at the middle platform which is 5.0 m height distance from the bottom one and it is named Route M. R × 4 is set at the top platform which is 9.8 m height distance from the middle one and it is named Route T. Obviously, due to the irregular structure of diesel engine, there is significant difference between the measurement paths. Thus, the receiver points set at each route are various, where Route B has 25 points, Route M has 22 points and Route T has 50 points. The received power values are measured every 1 m from the starting point to the end point of each route by the receiver.

Figure 6(a) is the comparison of experimental and simulated results of the Route B, where normalization is done in order to facilitate the comparison. The vertical axis represents received power value, and the horizontal axis is the receiver point of the corresponding path. The #8 receiver point which is 7 m distance from #1 receiver point has large received power, both in simulation or in experiment. It is located between the staircase and engine within this environment, where the reflection and the diffraction paths of the transmitter signal are superimposed and make a larger received power. The similar situation also happens on the #21 receiver point. The minimum received power of simulation occurs at #15 receiver point which is 20 dBm less than the adjacent point #16. Figure 6(b) shows their three most strong wave propagation paths obtained by simulation, where the two receiver point are arranged in the diagonal position of the Tx. Here, dBm is an abbreviation for the power ratio in decibel (dB) of the measured power referenced to one milliwatt (mW). Zero dBm equals one milliwatt. Obviously, the received power strength of #16's propagation paths is larger than that of #15's, which subsequently makes the significance difference of their received power. In experiment, the minimum received power of Route B is −25.14 dBm. It should be pointed out that in simulation the receiver point with minimum value is not in the same place with that in experimental test. It is mainly because the model couldn't fully represent the actual complicated ship structure. Even so, the simulation could still provide effective guidance for excluding the bad receiving region ahead, and the best node location can be determined with relatively few experimental test. Compared to the traditional method which is mainly depended on the experience of designers or amount of on-site test, it is better targeted and more efficient for wireless node deployment.

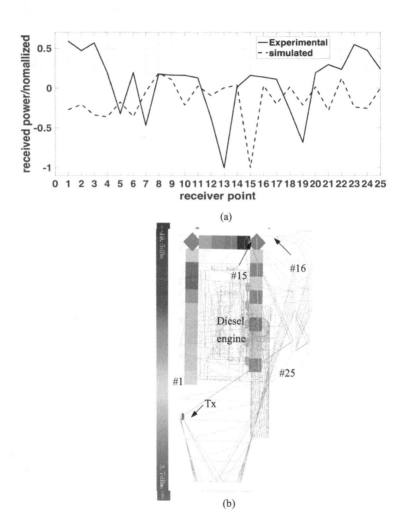

(a)

(b)

Fig. 6. (a) Comparison of experimental and simulated results of the Route B (b) Propagation path of some receiver points

Figure 7(a) is the comparison of experimental and simulated results of the Route M, where place of receiver points is shown in Fig. 7(b). In experiment, the minimum received power of Route M is −48.58 dBm. As can be seen from the results, although the Route M is 5.0 m height distance from the Tx, the receiving situation of this floor is still good. The receiver point #9 has small received power, similar to the #15 point in Route B, because it is arranged in the diagonal position of the Tx. The receiver points #2, #3, #17 and #18 have larger value, similar to #22 point in Route B, mainly because the metal staircase helps to improve the propagation path. Besides, in this floor, the simulated results are well consistent with the experimental measured results, especially the distribution of strengths and weakness of received power. Due to the idealization and simplification of the model, certainly there is difference exist between the simulated results and actual measurement values, but the similar changing trends could provide good reference for node deployment.

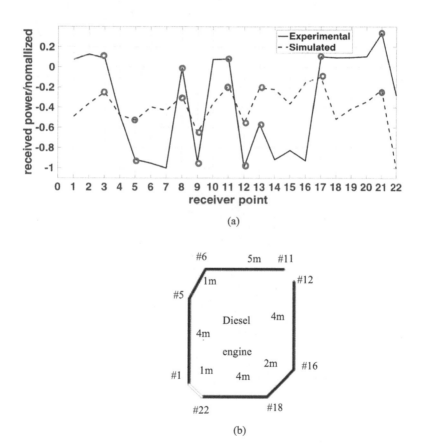

Fig. 7. (a) Comparison of experimental and simulated results of the Route M (b) Distribution of receiver points in the measurement path

Figure 8(a) is the comparison of experimental and simulated results of the Route T. In experiment, the minimum received power of Route T is −51.6 dBm. Figure 8(b) shows a few propagation paths of some receiver points obtained by simulation. As can be seen from the figure, the receiver point #10 has small received power because it is located directly beneath the main chimney of the diesel engine and close to the chimney, where the impact of the multipath Rayleigh fading results in great loss of transmission wave. On the other hand, #31, #31, #40 and #47–#49 receiver points have relatively low value, mostly because of their locations behind the columns.

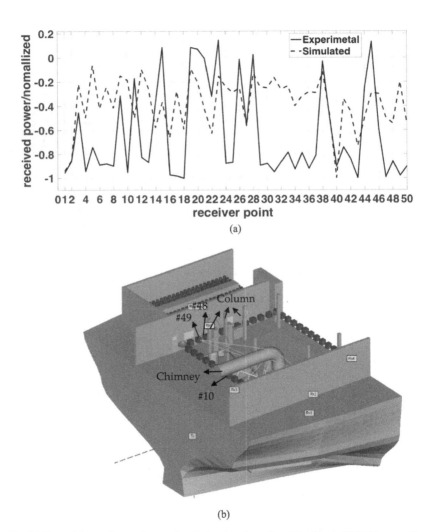

(a)

(b)

Fig. 8. (a) Comparison of experimental and simulated results of the Route T (b) Propagation path of some receiver points

The received power gets stronger change with the increase of the platform height relative to the position of transmitter. And the amplitude variation of experimental test is much bigger than the simulated results. That is mainly because of the complexity of the real cabin environment with a lot of machinery equipment as well as metal racks, pipes and grooves. Nonetheless, it shows similarities in signal transmission trends along the measurement path, given the relative roughness of the ship cabin models. The special cabin environment is much more different from the common building interior space; hence some special phenomenon is appeared in the signal transmission characteristics. It's worth noting that even the Tx is set at the bottom platform when Rx is located at the top platform, the received power could still meet the requirement of the transmission system, which ensures the implementation of wireless transmission network in cabin. The receivers are suggested to located near the staircase which would be helpful for the transmission, but avoid the region beneath the chimney of diesel engine or in the diagonal position of transmitter which would reduce the received power.

5   Conclusions

For the welded steel ship, the cabin environment would cause the wireless signal to fade through complex phenomena such as reflection, transmission and scattering and so on. A three-dimensional (3D) ray-tracing model is developed here to simulate the radio wave propagation in the ship environment and a LoRa band communication system is employed to evaluate the LoRa wireless system effectively. It investigates the influence of large equipment on wireless signal transmission. Either the simulation or experimental analysis indicates that the signal propagation in the steel ship cabin is very different from the propagation in ordinary buildings, which is strongly affected by multipath effect. Although large obstacles exist in cabin environment, the wireless signal transmission system using LoRa technology can still meet the requirements with suitable deployment. Deploying a base station near the glass window and avoiding being near the back of the main switchboard in the control room could help to establish good communication link even from the bottom platform of the diesel engine in cabin. The analysis validated that simulation research based on ray-tracing method could help to provide guidance for designing wireless sensor networks with LoRa band. It could clearly show the areas which are prone to produce impact of multipath fading on signal propagation and need to be avoided, as well as the suitable location which would enhance the signal strength. Therefore, LoRa-based wireless communication could be recommended for ship cabin applications, and using the ray-tracing model combined with few on-site measurements to evaluate the signal propagation will be less time-intensive and less costly.

Acknowledgments. We gratefully acknowledge support from the cargo training ship 'M/V YU DE'.

Funding. This research was funded by the Fujian Provincial Natural Science Foundation (grant numbers 2020J01683), Jimei University National Fund Breeding Program (grant numbers 2P2020012).

Conflicts of Interest. The authors declare no conflict of interest.

References

1. David, P.: Enabling the maritime internet of things: CoAP and 6LoWPAN performance over VHF links. IEEE Internet Things J. **2018**, 1 (2018)
2. Zhang, H., Lu, X.: Vehicle communication network in intelligent transportation system based on internet of things. Comput. Commun. **160**, 799–806 (2020)
3. Al-Zaidi, R., Woods, J.C., Al-Khalidi, M., Hu, H.: Building Novel VHF-based wireless sensor networks for the Internet of marine things. IEEE Sens. J. **18**(5), 2131–2144 (2018)
4. Paik, B.G., Cho, S.R., Park, B.J., Lee, D.K., Bae, B.D.: Development of real-time monitoring system using wired and wireless networks in a full-scale ship. Int. J. Naval Archit. Ocean Eng. **2**(3), 132–138 (2010)
5. Wu, S.B., Chen, X.Q., Chen, H.X., Lu, J.Q.: Intelligent fire early warning and monitoring system for ship bridge based on WSN. Int. J. Sci. **7**(8), 248–255 (2020)
6. Ma, Y., Liu, K., Chen, M., et al.: Deadline-aware adaptive emergency navigation strategy for dynamic hazardous ship evacuation with wireless sensor networks. IEEE Access **99**, 1 (2020)
7. Yan, C., Ge, L.H., Fan, X.P.: Simulation and analysis of radio wave propagation characteristics in ship cabin. J. Shanxi Datong Univ. (Nat. Sci.) **34**(6), 17–20 (2018). (in Chinese)
8. Tu, W.L., Xu, H., Xu, Y.Q., Ye, Q.B., Shen, M.X.: Research on 2.4 GHz wireless channel propagation characteristics in a steel ship cabin. Int. J. Antennas Propag. **6623638**, 1–12 (2021)
9. Muhammad, A.U., Junnaid, I., Arliones, H., Richard, D.S., Hirley, A.: K-Means spreading factor allocation for large-scale LoRa networks. Sensors **19**, 4723 (2019)
10. Ji, Y.H., Yang, H.: Applications of LoRa and NB-IoT in internet of things. Am. J. Inf. Sci. Comput. Eng. **5**(2), 25–28 (2019)
11. Zhang, Q., Yang, S.L., Zhang, H., Chui, X.S.: Design and implementation of marine temperature measurement system based on LoRa. In: 2018 International Symposium in Sensing and Instrumentation in IoT Era, pp.1–4 (2018)
12. Michelson, D.G., Ghassemzadeh, S.S.: Measurement and modeling of wireless channels. In: Tarokh, V. (ed.) New Directions in Wireless Communications Research, pp. 1–27. Springer, Boston (2009). https://doi.org/10.1007/978-1-4419-0673-1_1
13. Shikhantsoy, S.: Industrial indoor massive MIMO human EM-exposure evaluation. In: Proceedings of the Joint Annual Meeting of the Bio Electromagnetics Society and the European Bio Electromagnetics Association, pp. 403–406 (2018)
14. Su, G.C., Mao, H.H., Xing, G.Y., Sui, Y.: Propagation characteristics of 433MHz wireless channel in greenhouse under high humidity. J. Agric. Mech. Res. **41**(11), 204–210 (2019). (in Chinese)
15. REMCOM: Wireless InSite 3.2.0 Reference Manual (2017). http://www.remcom.com/-Wir elessInSite
16. Wang, D.A., Li, J., Can, Y.: General design of JiMei university training ship 'M/V YU DE'. J. Ship Des., 34–38 (2016). Extra edition 2. (in Chinese)

Efficient 2D Processing of 1D Sensor Signals

Ömer Nezih Gerek[(✉)] [iD]

Department of Electrical and Electronics Engineering, Eskisehir Technical University,
26555 Eskisehir, Turkey
ongerek@eskisehir.edu.tr

Abstract. Signal processing had been the flagship technology behind the intelligent systems for applications ranging from multimedia to biomedicine, from renewable energy systems to telecommunications. It is customary to apply processing tools dedicated for the natural sensor output. For instance, audio signals are processed with 1D techniques, whereas captured images are processed via 2D methods. On the other hand, many 1D sensor outputs exhibit an intrinsically cyclic behavior. Solar radiation recordings, captured line voltage values, cardiac potential, electric consumption, etc. are all fine examples to 1D signals which already have the quasi-periodicity. Recent research efforts of the authors have shown that the cyclic behavior of such signals may help a 2D rendition of the same information, provided that the natural period is accurately determined and assigned as the "width" of the 2D matrix. Experimental results indicate improved efficiency of 2D representation in terms of modelling, prediction and error detection. This work aims to provide a mathematical reasoning to the efficiency of such 2D rendition over 1D processing in terms of reduced autocorrelation orders.

Keywords: 2D rendition · Signal modeling · Efficient sensor data processing

1 Signals with Cyclic Behavior

Regular 1D sensors generate continuous time (CT) or discrete time (DT) signals at their output stages for further processing. For simplicity, and for the sake of computer processing capability, let us consider that the sensors generate a DT signal with a sampling period of T_s seconds, for a total duration of T_{Max} seconds, making an eventual array (denoted by the vector, $\mathbf{x}$) of length $N = {T_{Max}}/{T_s}$. In a majority of cases, the vector does not exhibit any form of periodicity (or a quasi-periodicity). Speech waveforms and wind speed data are examples to such. However, for *some* cases, the data tends to have a weak or strong repetitive nature. In the following subsections, we will exemplify some of the useable and almost periodic signals that can be acquired in the form of 1D signals.

1.1 Solar Radiation Signals

Thanks to the precise rotation of planet earth, the solar extra-terrestrial irradiance on a given geo-location of earth surface can be accurately calculated [1, 2]. Assuming the

S. Paiva et al. (Eds.): SmartCity360° 2021, LNICST 442, pp. 659–672, 2022.
https://doi.org/10.1007/978-3-031-06371-8_42

660   Ö. N. Gerek

solar time t_s as a minute count, the hour-angle can be defined as:

$$\omega = \frac{2\pi}{24}\left(\frac{t_s}{60} - 12\right). \tag{1}$$

Let the sensor tilt (from horizontal tangent) be β (can be zero), azimuth angle is γ and the latitude is ϕ. Due to the geo-tilt, the declination angle must be separately calculated as:

$$\delta = 0.41 \times sin\left(2\pi\frac{284 + d}{365}\right) \tag{2}$$

Abstract. For the Northern Hemisphere. Combining the terms, the angle of incidence (a.k.a. zenith angle) satisfies:

$$cos\theta_z = cos\phi cos\delta cos\omega + sin\phi sin\delta, \tag{3}$$

which yields a global extra-terrestrial solar radiation expression of:

$$G_0 = G_{sc}\left(1 + 0.033cos\left(\frac{2\pi d}{365}\right)\right)cos\theta_z \tag{4}$$

for the day, d, with $G_{sc} = 1367$ W/m^2.

Despite the relative complexity of the expression, it is clear that the radiation term is eventually periodic with a period of 1 year. However, things get more interesting if the quasi-period of 1 day is considered. Because then, rendition of an hourly (or minute-wise) solar radiation becomes almost the same for adjacent dates (Fig. 1 and Fig. 2).

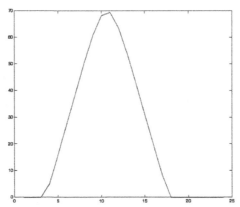

Fig. 1. Extraterrestrial solar radiation in 2005 over location in UK for 26th (solid red) and 27th (blue dash-dot) of July [3]. The curves are almost indistinguishable. (Color figure online)

Since the daily variations are expected to be minimal, the 2D rendition of the solar radiation data is expected to make perfect sense when a period of 24 h is selected as the width of the 2D matrix, where every day makes a row of the 2D matrix. Since the extraterrestrial radiation is a deterministic signal with no random component (due to facts such as cloudiness, rain, dust, environmental reflections, etc., the 2D rendition should, in fact, be applied to the measurement sensor outputs. Consider an hourly observation of fixed panel solar radiation in Eskisehir region is rendered for a complete year of 2005 in Fig. 3 [4, 5].

The congested plot in Fig. 1 merely shows any meaningful information regarding the hourly changes. Nor is it of any help in constructing an hourly prediction model. Now, with the above-mentioned idea, if the data is rendered in 2D (with a width corresponding to 24 h), the new representation becomes as in Fig. 4.

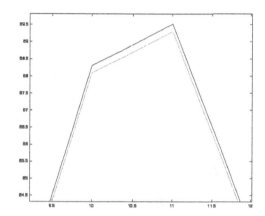

Fig. 2. A zoom-in of Fig. 1 shows the very slight difference in values.

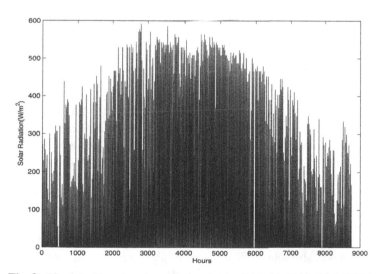

Fig. 3. 1D plot of hourly solar radiation data collected in Eskisehir in 2005.

The new 2D representation of the *same* data instantly provides a new insight and possibilities for modelling and analysis tools. Even the stochastic components of the 2D data due to atmospheric and meteorological phenomena seem to pertain for multiple days, providing a relation to the *vertical* (daily) axis. Therefore, the new axis provides an extra degree of freedom for analysis or representation purposes. The linear and neural models in [4] and spectral models in [6, 7] have already proven to be successful, yet this application constitutes only one example for the possibility of the 2D rendition.

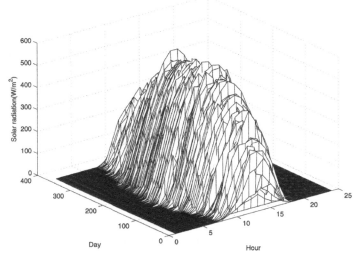

Fig. 4. 2D rendition of the hourly solar radiation data in Fig. 3.

1.2   Line Voltage and Power Quality Signals

An intrinsically periodic signal is the well-known line voltage waveform, which happens to have a frequency of 50 or 60 Hz (correspondingly 110 V or 220 V RMS) according to the regulations of the available country. Therefore, high resolution digitized voltage waveforms constitute a perfect candidate for 2D rendition as illustrated in Fig. 5. Following a power quality experiment in our laboratories and recording the voltage values at 20 kHz sampling rate, the 2D rendered data are shown in mesh plot and in the gray-scale image form in Fig. 6(a) and (b), respectively. It must be noted that the 2D rendition carries valuable information, not only revealing the power quality events, such as sag and arcing faults, but also clearly showing the very slightly lower frequency of the voltage (only a tad slower than 50 Hz, which is almost impossible to accurately detect using 1D methods) [8]. It was also found efficient to use this representation for the compression, transmission and storage of the recording [9, 10].

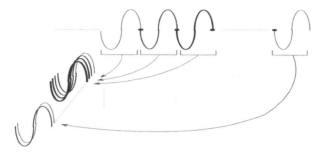

Fig. 5. 2D rendition of the periodic voltage waveform by stacking each period to a row.

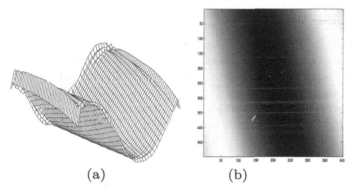

(a)   (b)

Fig. 6. Actual voltage waveform recordings, shown in 2D using (a) mesh plot and (b) gray-scale image.

1.3 Energy Demand and Load Data

Although it is us, humans, who judiciously utilize electricity according to our needs and desires, electric energy demand for a region connected to the same grid busbar naturally exhibits an oscillatory characteristic. The oscillations are in the form of hours of the day, days of the week and weeks through yearly seasons, all due to reasons such as working hours, house utilization hours or seasonal air conditioning. Of course, this particular data waveform has more random variation due to economic or population effects. Normally the load and demand tend to gradually increase together with the population. Figure 7 shows hourly electric consumption from year 2002 to 2005 in Turkey (data courtesy of Turkish Electric Power Company).

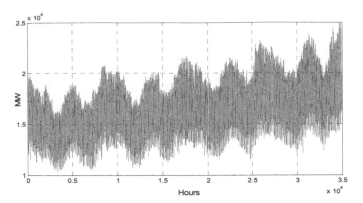

Fig. 7. Hourly electric consumption from 2002 to 2005 in Turkey.

Again, the relatively congested plot in Fig. 7 broadly indicates seasonal changes and an overall inclination to steadily grow. However, the daily and hourly variations (within a day) are not available for detailed analysis. On the other hand, when we render the data in 2D by choosing a row width corresponding to 24 h, the visualization becomes as in Fig. 8(a), which can be easily modelled as a surface in Fig. 8(b) using low order models [11].

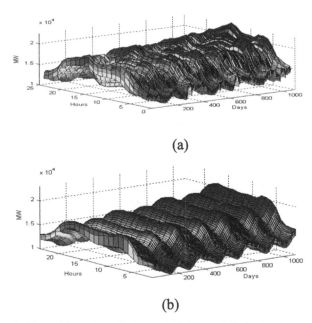

(a)

(b)

Fig. 8. Data in Fig. 7 (a) rendered in 2D and (b) 2D modelled using low order models.

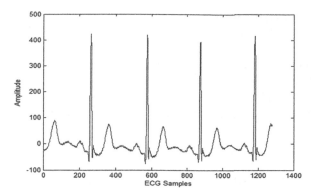

Fig. 9. A typical plot of ECG data.

1.4 ECG Data

Due to its relatively steady periodicity, a further example that enables 2D rendition is the ECG amplitude waveform (Fig. 9). The ECG data has an approximate period which can be set as the width of a 2D rendition (also known as the "waterfall plot" - see Fig. 10), as available in many off-the-shelf ECG analysis tools used by the medical doctors [12].

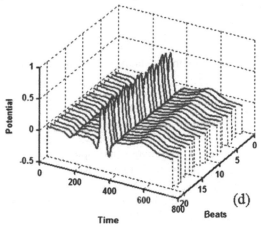

Fig. 10. A 2D rendition of the same ECG data.

2 Strength of 2D: Examples

The 2D rendition of *almost* periodic data is *cool* or visually revealing. In a majority of scholar works that are exemplified above, the 2D representations provide a clear advantage regarding analysis, detection, forecasting or compression. Here, we present a few cases of these advantages. In the later section, a mathematical reasoning of these advantages will be provided by means of autocorrelation order reductions.

2.1 Solar Radiation Models

In two different approaches, the observed solar radiation data could be better modelled in 2D as opposed to their 1D counterparts. In the first approach, simple linear or neural network models were applied for hourly forecasting. A simple 3-tap 2D predictor utilizes 1-hour-before, 1-day-before and 1-day-and-1-hour-before samples for predicting the current radiation sample in the following form:

$x_{i,j}$	$x_{i,j+1}$
$x_{i+1,j}$	$x_{i+1,j+1}$

by the simple linear predictor of:

$$x_{i+1,j+1} = a_1 x_{i,j} + a_2 x_{i,j+1} + a_3 x_{i+1,j} \tag{5}$$

whose coefficients (a's) can be simply obtained a 3-lag correlation information using the 3×3 matrix-vector form of:

$$\mathbf{a} = \mathbf{R}^{-1} \cdot \mathbf{r} \tag{6}$$

In an analogous way, the 3 neighboring samples can be fed to a simple 3-input neural network. It was observed that the 2D versions (as opposed to using 1D 3-past data, i.e. 3 past hours of the same day) reduces the prediction RMSE by 4.5 in the linear predictor (with an RMSE value of 41.09) and by 6 in the 3-input neural network (with an RMSE value of 39.17). What is more striking is that, if linear prediction is to be used, the efficiency of 2D 3-tap linear predictor could be achieved by a massive 62-tap 1D linear predictive filter! Or, if neural networks are compared, the prediction equality could be achieved by the 1D counterpart using 55-input neurons with 55 hidden layer neurons! This clearly shows that the 2D rendition efficiently yields daily relations as well as hourly relations.

Analogously, the 2D rendered information is modelled accurately with a sinusoidal model of only 6 variables using the following curve fit:

$$a(day) = sin(2\pi \times day/720) + 162.1$$

$$c(day) = sin(2\pi \times day/712) + 2.664$$

producing:

$$\text{surface}(day, hour) = a(day) \times e^{-\left(\left(hour - 12.5\right)/c(day)\right)^2} \tag{7}$$

which gives an RMSE of 57.24 (see Fig. 11). For a comparison, the sinusoidal (or a polynomial, thereof) model that uses only 1D form requires 18 parameters to reach to the same RMSE value.

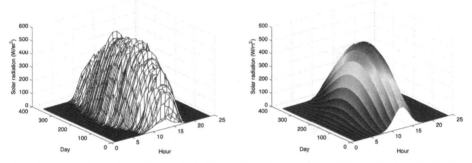

Fig. 11. Recorded solar radiation (a) in Eskisehir region and (b) its 2D model given in Eq. 7.

2.2 Power Quality Data

The strength of the 2D representation in power quality data is obviously different than that of solar radiation data, where a predictive model was necessary. Here, the engineering problem is either the *detection* (and classification) of the power quality event, or the low bandwidth compression of the recording with minimum MSE. The research in [8] provides a methodology to first render the voltage recordings in 2D (see Fig. 6) and then apply a 2D discrete wavelet transform to observe the data in four 2D subspaces: φ_{ll}, ψ_{lh}, ψ_{hl}, ψ_{hh}. These four subspaces are, indeed, horizontal and vertical applications of a low-pass and a high-pass filter. Consider one level application of a discrete wavelet transform and its output subspace images in Fig. 12 and 13.

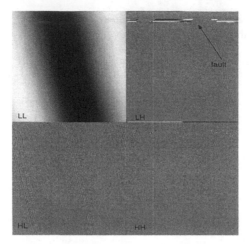

Fig. 12. One-level 2D-DWT decomposition of voltage waveform with arcing fault.

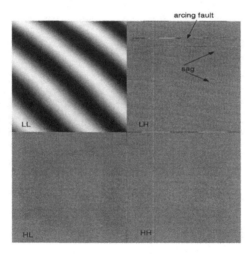

Fig. 13. One-level 2D-DWT decomposition of voltage waveform with two PQ events.

The case in Fig. 12 contains an arcing fault, which becomes clearly identifiable at the LH subband (thanks to the vertical high-pass filtering applied in that subband). The data in Fig. 13 is slightly different, as the 2D rendition was obtained using not one, but two cycles for the width of the matrix form. In that example, there is both an arcing fault and a sag event. Although the arcing faults are usually obvious regardless of the rendition, the sag here is approximately 0.5% in magnitude, and the 1D methods mostly suffer in their detection. Because of the vertical high pass filtering in the LH subband, even the slightest sag could be interpreted as an "edge" of the image, therefore it gets amplified and revealed in the corresponding subband. Consequently, making an "image" out of the PQ data provides an extra vertical dimension to work on and provide an improved efficiency.

Another efficiency of the 2D representation of sampled voltage data arises when the slight tilt in the LL subbands of Fig. 12 and 13 are considered. These tilts appear because the actual period of the voltage waveform is *slightly* greater than the expected 1/50 s. With a sampling frequency of 20 kHz, one period must exactly match to 400 samples (the width of the image). However, in both Fig. 12 and 13, the period was about 400.3 samples, meaning that the actual frequency of the line voltage was not 50 Hz, but it was 49.9625 Hz. Using a 1D Fourier technique, it requires 10.000 point FFT to reach to this precision. In the 2D image, a tilt of only 1° can be measured using the Hough transform [13]. This means that the frequency difference down to 49.9986 or 50.0014 Hz could be measured, which necessitates a 1D FFT of over 100.000 points. The above practical impossibilities of 1D spectral methods render the 2D approach a resourceful methodology in such subtle power quality events.

The final efficiency example of the 2D representation can be given regarding data compression for low bandwidth transmission or storage. Since many image compression methods are deliberately devised for high quality and low bandwidth compression, the 2D representation of the power quality recordings provides a compression efficiency with over 10 dB better MSE (see Fig. 14) for lossy and 9-to-5 compression ratio efficiency using lossless encoders.

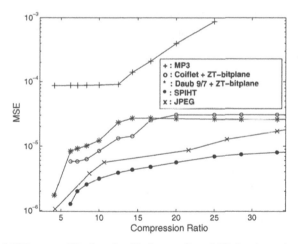

Fig. 14. MSE versus CR plots for 1D (i.e. mp3) and 2D (i.e. image) encoders.

2.3 Energy Load Data

In certain cases, such as the energy demand or load, the cyclo-stationary behavior of the data enables an efficient 2D rendition (see Fig. 7). However, the best modeling approach for these signals is not necessarily the complete 2D analytical model. In fact, splitting the data into increasing and stationary portions provides an even better efficiency. In

[11], the data of Fig. 7 is first modelled according to its increase tendency (see Fig. 15) using a weekly quadratic formula:

$$f^m(w) = 5.118w^2 + 1931w + 2454000 \tag{8}$$

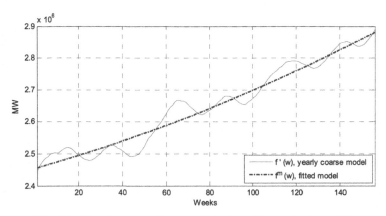

Fig. 15. Weekly averaged curve of Fig. 7 and its quadratic model.

Once the data is normalized with this inclination function, the remaining coarse fluctuations provide another 1D oscillation due to seasonal changes, which can be accurately modelled with four complex Fourier series coefficients and provide the fit as shown in Fig. 16.

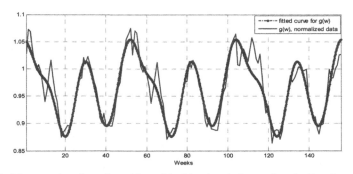

Fig. 16. Model approximation of weekly residual load variations using the Fourier series model.

After the second normalization, the remaining hourly load data can be easily modelled within a week as the 2D rendition model given in Fig. 17.

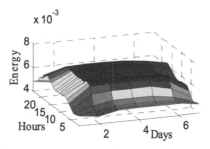

Fig. 17. Normalized hourly variations visualized in 2D within a week.

3   Conclusions and Discussions

The review of the cases described herein provides several examples where 2D rendition of the sensor outputs provide unexpected efficiency improvements even though the original data waveform could be essentially 1D. The examples of solar radiation, line voltage and energy load had been performed by the research group of the authors in different dates, whereas the ECG 2D rendition is another example which gets commonly used by the medical doctors, recently. Although the applications and the engineering problem are different in each case, the shared idea is the conversion of 1D signals into 2D matrix form according to a cyclic pattern that exists inside the data waveform. This natural (yet novel) rendition provides an efficiency, regardless of the mathematical approach or the sought-after result. For example, in solar radiation modeling, as the name indicates, the engineering problem is to find an accurate model and use it for forecasting. The linear models as in Eq. 5 and 6 or the neural network complexities in the 2D case automatically gets reduced as opposed to the overly complex counterparts in 1D. As an illustration, a 1-day before information automatically necessitates the model order to increase 24-tap (corresponding to 24 h) more. Another day information, another 24 more taps for the prediction order. However, for the 2D model, they are nothing more than 1 more addition to the tap order.

As explained herein, the sampled voltage waveforms for power quality analysis are a different animal, where modeling or prediction is not an issue, but detection and classification are the main problems. In that case, the 2D rendition opens completely different doors by revealing the vertical degree of freedom, which easily provides image processing tools for detecting faults such as voltage sag/swell or slight error in the AC period/frequency. In some of such cases, the 1D methods not only require orders of magnitude more complexity in spectral methods, but they sometimes completely lack the possibility of making any reasonable detection, whatsoever.

The last example that was conducted within the authors' research group was the energy load/demand modeling. There, the cyclo-stationary behavior was gradually oscillating with seasons, and also gradually increasing in overall by years. Therefore, a normalization according to these gradual changes were first applied, then the residual periodic structure within one week was modeled as in Fig. 17. Again, the total model orders were orders of magnitude smaller than directly modelling Fig. 7 using a 1D method. In fact, it was found out that the data in Fig. 7 could not be used for long-term (but hourly precision) forecasting with any linear 1D model with a model size below 1000 taps.

We conclude that it is beneficial to render the sensor output data to 2D whenever possible (with a cyclo-stationary behavior). Candidates for such include the induction motor health monitoring, society consumption of agricultural commodities, financial data, genomic data, etc. We further claim that even data that contains no pronounced cyclic behavior can be rendered in 2D (as long as there exists a decisive and natural period), such as the wind speed readings of a wind turbine, where a segment of 24 h is the natural repetition period. Application of this approach to biomedical case of ECG also improves the argument. Further research of such applications remains an open problem.

Acknowledgement. This work was supported by Eskisehir Technical University, Scientific Research Project Funds under contract no: 20ADP181.

References

1. Widen, J., Munkhammar, J.: Solar Radiation Theory. Uppsala University (2019)
2. Kalogirou, S.A.: Environmental Characteristics (Chapter) in Solar Energy Engineering, 2nd edn. Academic Press, Cambridge (2014)
3. Photovoltaic Geographical Information System – web resource (2019, updated). https://re.jrc.ec.europa.eu/pvg_tools/en/tools.html
4. Hocaoglu, F.O., Gerek, O.N., Kurban, M.: Hourly solar radiation forecasting using optimal coefficient 2D linear filters and feed-forward neural networks. Sol. Energy **82**(8), 714–726 (2008)
5. Hocaoglu, F.O., Gerek, O.N., Kurban, M.: A 2 dimensional solar radiation model. In: IEEE 16th Signal Processing, Communication and Applications Conference (2008)
6. Hocaoglu, F.O., Fidan, M., Gerek, O.N.: A novel Fourier based solar radiation model. ICIC Express Lett. **3**, 1101–1106 (2009)
7. Fidan, M., Hocaoglu, F.O., Gerek, O.N.: Harmonic analysis based hourly solar radiation forecasting model. IET Renew. Power Gener. **9**(3), 218–227 (2014)
8. Ece, D.G., Gerek, O.N.: Power quality event detection using joint 2D wavelet subspaces. IEEE Trans. Instrum. Meas. **53**(4), 1040–1046 (2004)
9. Gerek, O.N., Ece, D.G.: 2D analysis and compression of power quality event data. IEEE Trans. Power Deliv. **19**(2), 791–798 (2004)
10. Gerek, O.N., Ece, D.G.: Compression of power quality event data using 2D representation. Electr. Power Syst. Res. **78**(6), 1047–1052 (2008)
11. Filik, Ü.B., Gerek, O.N., Kurban, M.: Hourly forecasting of long-term electric energy demand using a novel modeling approach. ICIC Express Lett. **4**(4), 115–118 (2010)
12. Azuace, F., Clifford, G., McSharry, P.: Advanced Methods and Tools for ECG Data Analysis. Artech, Boston (2006)
13. Shehata, A., et al.: A survey on Hough transform, theory, techniques and applications. IJCSI **12**(1) (2015). arXiv:1502.02160

Clustered WSN for Building Energy Management Applications

Luis Magadán$^{(\boxtimes)}$ iD, Francisco J. Suárez iD, Juan C. Granda iD, and Daniel F. García iD

Department of Computer Science and Engineering, University of Oviedo, Gijón, Asturias, Spain
{magadanluis,fjsuarez,jcgranda,dfgarcia}@uniovi.es

Abstract. Wireless sensor networks are usually deployed in mesh topologies using radio communication links. The mesh selforganizes to route data packets from sensors to the sink. However, if not carefully designed, this may create holes of uncovered areas and energy holes when many networks paths traverse a limited number of sensors. This paper presents the design and performance evaluation of a low-cost clustered wireless sensor network for Building Energy Management (BEM) applications using Bluetooth Low Energy (BLE) and Better Approach to Mobile Ad-hoc Networking (BATMAN). The latter is used to interconnect gateways and cluster headers that have enough power to forward packets and make computations without compromising their battery lifetime, while the former is used to connect sensors to a cluster header. A prototype of a BEM application has been developed and the performance of the network was tested. Results show that the throughput and latency achieved are adequate for BEM applications.

Keywords: Internet of Things (IoT) · Better Approach to Mobile Ad-hoc Networking (BATMAN) · Bluetooth Low Energy (BLE) · Building Energy Management · Wireless Sensor Network (WSN) · Clustered-topology

1 Introduction

The Internet of Things (IoT) has gain tremendous momentum due to the large number of smart devices connected to the Internet. It connects everyday objects (lights, televisions, etc.) as well as more sophisticated objects (motors, agricultural systems, etc.) with the Internet in order to collect data and control cyber-physical objects [1,2]. The application domains of IoT include Smart Cities [3], Health Care [4] and the Industrial Internet of Things (IIoT) [5].

Wireless sensor networks (WSNs) are increasingly used in Building Energy Management (BEM) applications due to the large number of sensors and the distance between them. These sensors are usually powered with batteries that

S. Paiva et al. (Eds.): SmartCity360° 2021, LNICST 442, pp. 673–687, 2022.
https://doi.org/10.1007/978-3-031-06371-8_43

work over long periods of time without recharging or changing [11]. Energy harvesting is also used to power sensors or increase their battery lifetime [33]. The latter can also be achieved using clustering techniques [12], as energy efficiency in devices is improved. IoT applications such as condition monitoring of electric motors [7,8], agricultural IoT services [9] and BEM applications [10] take advantage of these techniques.

One of the main challenges of WSNs are coverage holes, also known as uncovered areas, which are the result of correlated node failures, sensor movements and obstacles that hinder communications [13,14]. This leads to a loss of part of the network nodes and therefore to a loss of quality of service, or even to permanent damage to the network [15].

In WSNs the traffic is sent following a many-to-one pattern, from the nodes to the sink or gateway. Energy holes are created around the sink due to the higher battery consumption of surrounding nodes, which receive and forward large numbers of packets through the network. When this happens, no more packets can be sent to the sink, causing a reduction of the network lifetime [16]. In addition, many IoT applications deal with a large number of devices producing enormous amounts of data that must be filtered, processed and stored in the cloud. In order to cope with the challenges this entails, the fog computing paradigm proposes using edge devices to reduce the use of cloud resources [6]. This further increases the energy consumption of nodes in the WSN.

In this paper, we propose a low-cost dual-layer WSN designed for BEM applications. The WSN avoids uncovered areas by including redundant cluster headers and reduces the number of energy holes as cluster headers are connected to the power grid. It also enables the use of fog computing to reduce cloud costs by applying data processing and filtering on edge devices. The main contribution of this work is the combination of low cost, fog-computing capacity and performance of the proposed WSN in a real BEM scenario. The rest of the paper is organized as follows. Previous work in the research context is outlined in Sect. 2. The dual-layer WSN is presented in Sect. 3.1, while the dimensioning of the WSN and its performance analysis can be seen in Sect. 3.2 and Sect. 3.3 respectively. Section 4.1 shows a case of study in a BEM system. The experiments and results are discussed in Sect. 4.2. Finally, Sect. 5 presents the conclusions.

2   Background

In BEM applications multiple low-power wireless communication protocols are used to communicate multisensor modules and gateways or cluster headers. Bluetooth, Bluetooth Low Energy (BLE), Near Field Connection (NFC), Z-Wave and ZigBee are the most commonly used short-range low-power protocols. Table 1 shows the maximum data rate, coverage range, battery consumption and cost of devices for each of these protocols. As can be seen, NFC offers the shortest range and a maximum data rate of 848 kbps. In the case of Bluetooth, the maximum range is 100 m, offering a maximum data rate of 2 Mbps but a higher battery consumption than the other protocols. Z-Wave and ZigBee also have a coverage area

Table 1. Low-power communication protocols

	Characteristics			
	Maximum bitrate	Coverage area	Battery consumption	Cost
Bluetooth	2 Mbps	100 m	Medium	Low
BLE	1 Mbps	100 m	Very low	Low
NFC	848 kbps	10 cm	Low	Low
Z-Wave	100 kbps	100 m	Low	Medium
ZigBee	250 kbps	100 m	Low	Medium

of 100 m [18], with maximum data rates of 100 kbps and 250 kbps respectively. Finally, the Bluetooth Low Energy protocol has a maximum data rate of 1 Mbps, a theoretical maximum range of 100 m, the lowest battery consumption [35] and is supported by most low-cost devices [17].

In order to build a WSN connecting gateways and cluster headers, there are three types of routing protocols: proactive, which have the route available at all times; reactive, which compute the optimal route on demand; and hybrid, which are a combination of the two and are used in large networks [19]. The main difference between them is that proactive protocols have lower latency than reactive protocols, while reactive protocols have higher throughput [20] and need lower bandwidth and lower energy [21]. Having low latency and high throughput are the most important factors in real-time and time-sensitive IoT applications [22].

In the work by Jornet-Monteverde et al. [23], a heating, ventilation and air conditioning (HVAC) system is developed using a WSN based on the Raspberry Pi computer and the CC3200 device provided by Texas Instruments. It is a low-cost, low-power IoT application that uses WiFi and MQTT protocols to establish communications. A monitoring and ventilation control platform was proposed by Lachhab et al. [24], using a WSN composed of sensors to measure air quality and an Arduino Uno, which communicates using an NRF24 module with a Raspberry Pi 3 acting as a gateway. The use of these devices reduces cost and power consumption. Finally, Nigam et al. [25] developed a structural health monitoring (SHM) system that uses three different types of sensors connected to an Arduino Nano to measure the temperature, humidity, physical strength and electrical charge of an area. It communicates with the corresponding gateway using ZigBee. As in the previous cases, a low-cost, low-power WSN is deployed.

Luca Davoli et al. [31] carried out an analysis of the performance of a Better Approach To Mobile Ad-Hoc Networking (BATMAN) mesh using Raspberry Pi's as nodes. Their results show that communications between the nodes forming the mesh is reliable and throughput, latency and jitter are influenced by the number of hops between nodes. Another performance analysis of the BATMAN protocol is done by Edmundo Chissungo et al. [32] in an indoor mesh potato testbed. They prove that communications between nodes are reliable for VoIP applications.

The main issue of most of these low-cost BEM approaches is the high battery consumption. They commonly use WiFi rather than other low-power communication protocols such as ZigBee or BLE [26]. Also, the use of ZigBee as the main communication protocol leads to a lack of control of the network topology. This make it difficult to implement optimal fog architectures for time-sensitive applications to reduce the resources of storage and communication in the cloud [27]. Most of them do not deal appropriately with uncovered areas and energy holes when many paths traverse a limited number of sensors.

3   Network Architecture

The following subsections present the developed WSN, the dimensioning of the network and the performance analysis carried out.

3.1   Topology

The WSN developed follows a clustered approach in which the first layer is composed of multisensor modules and the second layer is composed of heterogeneous gateways and cluster headers. The first layer follows a star topology, where the central node is a gateway or cluster header, which manages a set of heterogeneous multisensor modules using BLE. The second layer follows a meshed topology using the BATMAN protocol. All nodes in this layer have access to the cloud and use WiFi to improve throughput. Some resilience is achieved by using redundant gateways.

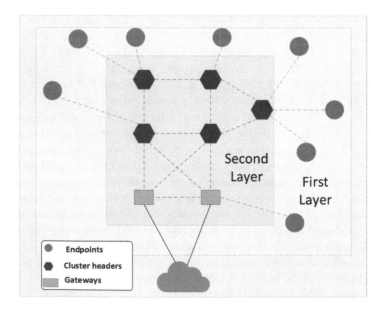

Fig. 1. Dual-layer topology

Figure 1 shows the organization of the entities that compose the WSN:

- Cluster headers: they are connected to other cluster headers and gateways using WiFi. They forward messages through the mesh network until they reach a gateway in order to communicate with the cloud. These devices control a set of endpoints and perform the necessary transformations and operations on the data received, so fog computing approaches can be implemented. Raspberry Pi's 3 Model B+ and Raspberry Pi's 4 are used as cluster headers.
- Gateways: they are connected to the Internet and forward the data collected by sensors and processed at the cluster headers to the cloud. They can also manage a group of endpoints, collecting the data gathered by sensors and processing it before sending it to the cloud. Raspberry Pi's 4 are used as gateways.
- Endpoints: they are heterogeneous multisensor modules collecting data from the environment. These devices are connected to a cluster header or gateway following a star topology. Some low-cost multisensor modules used as endpoints are SensorTag CC2650, SmartBond DA14585 IoT, Sensortile.box and BlueTile.

Due to the low cost of the multisensor modules used, the number of protocols supported for communicating with the cluster headers or gateways is limited. The Sensortag CC2650 supports ZigBee and BLE, but a CC2531 dongle is necessary for using ZigBee. In the case of the Sensortile.box, BlueTile and SmartBond DA14585 IoT, only BLE is supported. BLE has been selected as the low-power communication protocol used to communicate multisensor modules with cluster headers and gateways not only for its compatibility with more manufacturers but also for its higher noise immunity and higher bandwidth [17,34].

In order to connect cluster headers and gateways the protocol selected to build and manage the mesh network is BATMAN. BATMAN is a decentralized, proactive protocol used in multi-hop ad-hoc mesh networks [28]. Knowledge about the best route between two nodes through the network is distributed among all the nodes composing the route: each node only stores information related to its neighbouring nodes. This reduces the overhead on the network and the amount of information stored with other proactive routing protocols [29].

3.2   Dimensioning

Before deploying the WSN, it is necessary to determine the maximum distance between devices. Firstly, the maximum distance between gateways and cluster headers, and secondly, the maximum distance between the multisensor modules and the gateway or cluster header that manage them must be studied.

To determine the maximum distance between gateways and cluster headers, a gateway was positioned at a fixed point and a cluster header was moved to different distances from the gateway with no obstacles, taking the RSSI level between the devices for each position. Table 2 lists the signal strength values, the associated state of the network [30], and a description of the consequences of each RSSI level. As seen in this table, any value greater than −80 dBm can be used in BEM applications.

This experiment was carried out six times per distance. The results are shown in Fig. 2(a). As can be seen, the RSSI values are above −80 dBm up to approximately 17 m, although sometimes at this distance the RSSI is below the threshold value (rounds 5 and 6). Therefore, the maximum distance between gateways and cluster headers has been set at 14 m, a distance at which the average RSSI obtained in this experiment is close to −72 dBm. This is suitable for use in BEM applications.

The process followed to calculate the maximum distance between gateways or cluster headers and multisensor modules was similar. A gateway was positioned at a fixed point and the multisensor modules were moved to different distances. For each of the multisensor modules, the fluctuation of the RSSI as the distance varies was studied by performing six tests and then calculating the average at each of these distances.

Table 2. Received signal strength indicator (RSSI)

RSSI	State	Description
-30 dBm	Excellent	Maximum possible signal
-67 dBm	Very good	Minimum RSSI level for applications that need a reliable delivery and reception of packages
-70 dBm	Good	Minimum RSSI level for reliable package forwarding
-80 dBm	Bad	Minimum RSSI level for basic connectivity Package forwarding is somewhat unreliable
-90 dBm	Inoperable	Unlikely to carry out any functionality

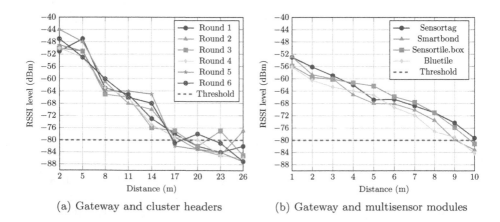

(a) Gateway and cluster headers   (b) Gateway and multisensor modules

Fig. 2. RSSI-distance between gateway, cluster headers and multisensor modules

Fig. 3. Scenario used for the performance analysis

Based on the results, shown in Fig. 2(b), the maximum distance for the Sensortag CC2650 and Sensortile.box was set at 9 m, since at this distance the RSSI is above the established threshold, -74.34 dBm and -75.83 dBm respectively. However, in the case of the Smartbond DA14585 IoT and BlueTile, the mean RSSI is very close to the threshold value at a distance of 9 m (-79.84 dBm and -79 dBm respectively), sometimes dropping below it. Thus, 8 m was selected as the maximum distance for all devices.

3.3   Performance Analysis

After establishing the maximum distance between the devices that compose the WSN, an analysis of the network performance was carried out, studying the throughput, latency and jitter between gateways and cluster headers according to the number of hops between them (single hop, two hops or three hops). For this performance analysis, the tests were performed on the scenario shown in Fig. 3, which consists of a router, a gateway and three cluster headers connected in a chain. The gateway is connected to the router through an Ethernet link and through the BATMAN protocol with cluster header 1. This in turn is connected to cluster header 2 also with BATMAN. Finally, cluster header 3 also uses BATMAN to connect to cluster header 2. All cluster headers are 14 m apart, which was determined as the maximum distance between gateways and cluster headers in Sect. 3.2.

Firstly, a throughput analysis was performed using the **batctl throughputmeter** command, which consists of the transfer of 14 MB of data between two nodes: between gateway and cluster header 1 (single hop), gateway and cluster header 2 (two hops) and gateway and cluster header 3 (three hops). The purpose of this test is to evaluate the throughput obtained according to the number of hops using BATMAN. It was tested 30 times per round, each round separated by a period of 5 min, with a total of 6 rounds. Figure 4(a) shows the average throughput obtained per round. For the one-hop case, the throughput is in the range between 2512.7 kB/s and 3008.33 kB/s, for two hops, between 522.18 kB/s and 620 kB/s, and for three hops, between 76.53 kB/s and 98.55 kB/s.

Secondly, a study of latency and jitter was carried out, using the **batctl ping** command, which executes a layer 2 ping command. The latency was approximated as the round-trip time (RTT) divided by 2. This test was done in the same way as the throughput test, performing 6 rounds separated by 5 min, each round consisting of 30 executions of the command. Figure 4(b) shows the average latency obtained per round. In the case of one hop the latency is between 0.99 ms and 1.34 ms, between 2.7 ms and 3.33 ms for two hops and between 3.07 ms and 3.91 ms when there are three hops. The average jitter for each round is shown in Fig. 4(c). For one hop the jitter ranges from 0.44 ms to 1.77 ms, for two hops between 1.53 ms and 5.30 ms, and for three hops the average jitter varies between 1.54 ms and 4.52 ms.

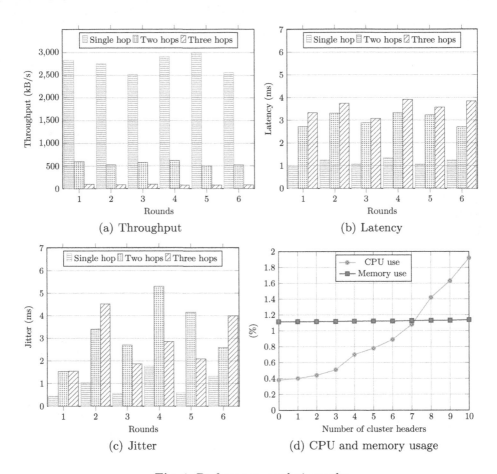

Fig. 4. Performance analysis results

From the results of these tests, it can be seen that an increase in the number of hops leads to a decrease of throughput. Latency increases with the number of hops. However, the results obtained with respect to jitter do not show any pattern: the jitter obtained with three hops is not always higher than with two.

Finally, a analysis of the CPU and memory use on the gateway while using the BATMAN protocol was carried out using the command **sar -u -r 1**, which returns the percentage of both CPU and memory use. Figure 4(d) shows the CPU and memory use as the number of cluster headers in the network increases from 0 to 10, each of them sending 108 bytes/s through the network. The CPU use is extremely low, although it seems to increase exponentially as the number of cluster headers in the mesh increases, reaching 1.92% when there are 10 cluster headers. Memory use increases gradually as the number of cluster headers increases, varying from 1.1137% with no cluster headers to 1.1382% with 10.

4   Case Study: Building Energy Management System

The following subsections present the implementation of a BEM system following the dual-layer WSN previously defined. It also describes the experiments carried out to analyze the communications between the different devices that form the BEM system with the cloud.

4.1   Prototype Deployment

A BEM prototype has been deployed to monitor light level, temperature, humidity and barometric pressure in the Computer Science Department building at the University of Oviedo. This information is displayed to the user using the dashboard shown in Fig. 5. For this prototype 3 Raspberry Pi's 4 were used, one of them acting as a gateway and the other 2 as cluster headers in the mesh network. A Raspberry Pi 3 Model B+ was used as another cluster header. A total of 16 multisensor modules were used: 5 Sensortag CC2650 and 4 Smartbond DA14585 IoT to monitor rooms, and 2 Sensortile.box and 5 BlueTile to monitor building halls and corridors.

The distribution of the devices in the building is shown in Fig. 6. The gateway is located on the ground floor, connected to the router via an Ethernet link and managing 5 multisensor modules. The Raspberry Pi 3 Model B+ is on the first floor acting as a cluster header that manages 3 multisensor modules. On the second floor there is another cluster header with 5 multisensor modules. Finally, another cluster header was installed in the basement, managing other 4 multisensor modules. The ground, first and second floors are connected by an interior courtyard, while the ground floor and the basement are separated by a concrete floor.

There is usually one hop between cluster headers and the gateway, although sometimes there are two between the second floor cluster header and the gateway. This depends on the best route computation based on the network performance. Each of the cluster headers and the gateway collect data from the multisensor modules on the same floor using BLE and perform the necessary operations to send them to the cloud using the MQTT protocol.

4.2   Experiments and Results

On this prototype, a study similar to the one performed in Sect. 3.3 was carried out: first, an analysis of the RSSI level between the cluster headers and the gateway, and then between the multisensor modules and the gateway or the cluster

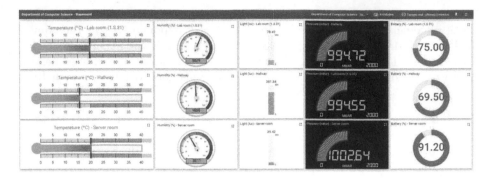

Fig. 5. BEM dashboard application

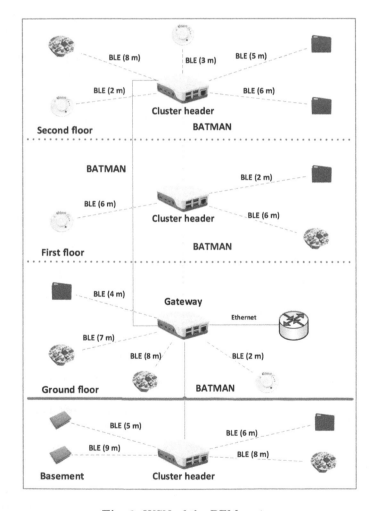

Fig. 6. WSN of the BEM system

headers controlling them. Finally, the throughput, latency and jitter between the cluster headers and the gateway was analysed.

The average RSSI levels between the cluster headers and the gateway are shown in Table 3. As can be seen, in all of the cluster headers the RSSI level is over the threshold of −80 dBm, so their distance is not an issue when forwarding packets.

Table 3. RSSI level between Cluster headers and Gateway

Cluster head	Basement	First floor	Second floor
RSSI level	−76 dBm	−62.5 dBm	−64.67 dBm

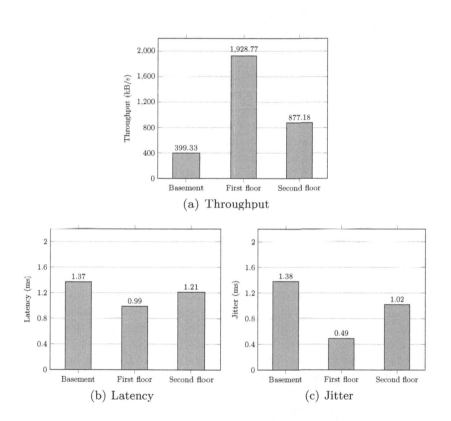

(a) Throughput

(b) Latency   (c) Jitter

Fig. 7. Building energy management prototype analysis

The same occurs with the RSSI level between the multisensor modules and the cluster header or gateway. Depending on the type of multisensor module, the maximum RSSI level obtained may be closer to the threshold. The maximum RSSI level of the Sensortag CC2650 is −74 dBm, −65 dBm for Smartbond

DA14585 IoT, −79 dBm for Sensortile.box, and −79 dBm for BlueTile. All of these are over −80 dBm, so the communication between multisensor modules and the gateway or cluster header is not an issue.

The throughput analysis has been carried out between each of the cluster headers and the gateway. Figure 7(a) shows that the throughput obtained between the cluster header located in the basement and the gateway is 399.33 kB/s. The throughput measured between the cluster header on the first floor and the gateway is 1928.77 kB/s. Finally, the cluster header on the second floor gives a throughput of 877.18 kB/s. Therefore, the throughput obtained for all of the cluster headers is enough to carry out BEM communications.

Figure 7(b) shows the latency measured. The latency obtained is 1.37 ms, 0.99 ms and 1.21 ms for the cluster headers located in the basement, first floor and second floor respectively. These results are similar to those obtained in Sect. 3.3, as the cluster header located in the basement, which is the one with the lowest throughput, has the highest latency. The same happens with the cluster header located on the first floor, which has the highest throughput and the lowest latency.

The analysis of the jitter in this case is conclusive, as it is exactly the same as in the case of latency (see Fig. 7(c)). The cluster header located in the basement has a jitter of 1.38 ms, the one on the first floor has a jitter of 0.49 ms, and the one on the second floor has a jitter of 1.02 ms.

All these analyses show that the cluster header located in the basement has worse results than the rest. This is mainly due to the fact that the ground floor, first floor and second floor are connected by an open inner courtyard, while the basement is separated by a concrete floor. Even so, the results obtained for the three cluster headers indicate that communication can be carried out with no problem.

5   Conclusions

In this paper, a clustered WSN using BLE and BATMAN has been presented. The WSN uses BLE to carry out the communications between low-cost multisensor modules with gateways and cluster headers, using the BATMAN protocol to create a mesh network between gateways and cluster headers. This WSN avoids uncovered areas due to the use of redundant gateways and cluster headers. It also prevents energy holes by taking advantage of cluster headers connected to the power grid. This facilitates the integration of fog architectures in order to reduce cloud costs by applying data processing in cluster headers and edge devices.

The WSN was dimensioned by analyzing the RSSI level between devices. Maximum distances between gateways and cluster headers, and between sensors and the gateway were established.

Once the WSN was deployed, a performance analysis was carried out studying the variation in throughput, latency and jitter as the number of hops between gateways and cluster headers increases. Latency increases and throughput decreases as the number of hops increases. In addition, an analysis of CPU and memory use was performed in the gateway. The results show very low CPU use with a possible exponential increase, while memory use gradually increases as more cluster headers are added to the network. Thus, the number of cluster headers must be thoroughly studied in WSN deployments.

Finally, this WSN was implemented as a case study, creating a BEM application. This application collects data such as light level, temperature, humidity and barometric pressure for cloud storage. A performance analysis was carried out to ensure that communications are performed correctly, studying the RSSI level between devices, latency, throughput and jitter. The results obtained confirm that the communication in the clustered WSN can be performed with no problem even in the presence of concrete floors.

Future work will be focused on using the WSN in more challenging scenarios such as condition monitoring in industrial environments. Applications can take advantages of fog deployments, so vibration or current signals are filtered and processed at the cluster headers to save cloud resources.

Acknowledgment. This research has been partially funded by the Spanish National Plan of Research, Development and Innovation under the project OCAS (RTI2018-094849-B-100) and the University of Oviedo.

References

1. Sethi, P., Sarangi, S.R.: Internet of things: architectures, protocols, and applications. J. Electr. Comput. Eng. **2017**(1), 1–25 (2017)
2. Singh, D., Tripathi, G., Jara, A.J.: A survey of Internet-of-Things: future vision, architecture, challenges and services. In: 2014 IEEE World Forum on Internet of Things, WF-IoT, pp. 287–292. IEEE, March 2014
3. Alavi, A.H., Jiao, P., Buttlar, W.G., Lajnef, N.: Internet of Things-enabled smart cities: state-of-the-art and future trends. Measurement **129**, 589–606 (2018)
4. Dang, L.M., Piran, M., Han, D., Min, K., Moon, H.: A survey on internet of things and cloud computing for healthcare. Electronics **8**(7), 768 (2019)
5. Sisinni, E., Saifullah, A., Han, S., Jennehag, U., Gidlund, M.: Industrial internet of things: challenges, opportunities, and directions. IEEE Trans. Industr. Inf. **14**(11), 4724–4734 (2018)
6. Kamienski, C., et al.: Smart water management platform: IOT-based precision irrigation for agriculture. Sensors **19**(2), 276 (2019)
7. Magadán, L., Suárez, F.J., Granda, J.C., García, D.F.: Low-cost real-time monitoring of electric motors for the Industry 4.0. Procedia Manuf. **42**, 393–398 (2020)
8. Oyekanlu, E.: Predictive edge computing for time series of industrial IoT and large scale critical infrastructure based on open-source software analytic of big data. In: 2017 IEEE International Conference on Big Data, pp. 1663–1669. IEEE, December 2017
9. Chen, R.Y.: An intelligent value stream-based approach to collaboration of food traceability cyber physical system by fog computing. Food Control **71**, 124–136 (2017)
10. Afroz, Z., Urmee, T., Shafiullah, G.M., Higgins, G.: Real-time prediction model for indoor temperature in a commercial building. Appl. Energy **231**, 29–53 (2018)

11. Xu, L., Collier, R., O'Hare, G.M.: A survey of clustering techniques in WSNs and consideration of the challenges of applying such to 5G IoT scenarios. IEEE Internet Things J. **4**(5), 1229–1249 (2017)
12. Patel, J.A., Patel, Y.: The clustering techniques for wireless sensor networks: a review. In: 2018 Second International Conference on Inventive Communication and Computational Technologies, ICICCT, pp. 147–151. IEEE, April 2018
13. El Khamlichi, Y., Mesmoudi, Y., Tahiri, A., Abtoy, A.: A recovery algorithm to detect and repair coverage holes in wireless sensor network systems. J. Commun. **13**(2), 67–74 (2018)
14. Rafiei, A., Abolhasan, M., Franklin, D.R., Safaei, F., Smith, S., Ni, W.: Effect of the number of participating nodes on recovery of WSN coverage holes. In: 2017 27th International Telecommunication Networks and Applications Conference, ITNAC, pp. 1–8. IEEE, November 2017
15. Deng, X., Yang, L.T., Yi, L., Wang, M., Zhu, Z.: Detecting confident information coverage holes in industrial Internet of Things: a energy-efficient perspective. IEEE Commun. Mag. **56**(9), 68–73 (2018)
16. Wu, X., Chen, G., Das, S.K.: Avoiding energy holes in wireless sensor networks with nonuniform node distribution. IEEE Trans. Parallel Distrib. Syst. **19**(5), 710–720 (2008)
17. Oliveira, L., Rodrigues, J.J., Kozlov, S.A., Rabêlo, R.A., Albuquerque, V.H.C.D.: MAC layer protocols for Internet of Things: a survey. Future Internet **11**(1), 16 (2019)
18. Chhaya, L., Sharma, P., Kumar, A., Bhagwatikar, G.: Communication theories and protocols for smart grid hierarchical network. J Electr. Electron. Eng. **10**(1), 43 (2017)
19. Garnepudi, P., Damarla, T., Gaddipati, J., Veeraiah, D.: Proactive, reactive and hybrid multicast routing protocols for wireless mesh networks. In: 2013 IEEE International Conference on Computational Intelligence and Computing Research, pp. 1–7. IEEE, December 2013
20. Reddy, M.C.K., Sujana, A., Sujita, A., Rudroj, K.: Comparing the throughput and delay of proactive and reactive routing protocols in mobile ad-hoc networks. In: 2018 2nd International Conference on Inventive Systems and Control, ICISC, pp. 1278–1283. IEEE, January 2018
21. Er-Rouidi, M., Moudni, H., Mouncif, H., Merbouha, A.: An energy consumption evaluation of reactive and proactive routing protocols in mobile ad-hoc network. In: 2016 13th International Conference on Computer Graphics, Imaging and Visualization, CGiV, pp. 437–441. IEEE, March 2016
22. Verma, S., Kawamoto, Y., Fadlullah, Z.M., Nishiyama, H., Kato, N.: A survey on network methodologies for real-time analytics of massive IoT data and open research issues. IEEE Commun. Surv. Tutorials **19**(3), 1457–1477 (2017)
23. Jornet-Monteverde, J.A., Galiana-Merino, J.J.: Low-cost conversion of single-zone HVAC systems to multi-zone control systems using low-power wireless sensor networks. Sensors **20**(13), 3611 (2020)
24. Lachhab, F., Bakhouya, M., Ouladsine, R., Essaaidi, M.: Monitoring and controlling buildings indoor air quality using WSN-based technologies. In: 2017 4th International Conference on Control, Decision and Information Technologies, CoDIT, pp. 0696–0701. IEEE, April 2017
25. Nigam, H., Karmakar, A., Saini, A.K.: Wireless sensor network based structural health monitoring for multistory building. In: 2020 4th International Conference on Computer, Communication and Signal Processing ICCCSP, pp. 1–5. IEEE, September 2020

26. Abbas, Z., Yoon, W.: A survey on energy conserving mechanisms for the internet of things: wireless networking aspects. Sensors **15**(10), 24818–24847 (2015)
27. Bittencourt, L.F., Diaz-Montes, J., Buyya, R., Rana, O.F., Parashar, M.: Mobility-aware application scheduling in fog computing. IEEE Cloud Comput. **4**(2), 26–35 (2017)
28. Sanchez-Iborra, R., Cano, M.D., Garcia-Haro, J.: Performance evaluation of BATMAN routing protocol for VoIP services: a QoE perspective. IEEE Trans. Wireless Commun. **13**(9), 4947–4958 (2014)
29. Kulla, E., Hiyama, M., Ikeda, M., Barolli, L.: Performance comparison of OLSR and BATMAN routing protocols by a MANET testbed in stairs environment. Comput. Math. Appli. **63**(2), 339–349 (2012)
30. Popleteev, A.: Indoor positioning using FM radio signals (Doctoral dissertation, University of Trento) (2011)
31. Davoli, L., Cilfone, A., Belli, L., Ferrari, G.: Design and experimental performance analysis of a BATMAN-based double Wi-Fi interface mesh network. Futur. Gener. Comput. Syst. **92**, 593–603 (2019)
32. Chissungo, E., Blake, E., Le, H.: Investigation into Batman-adv protocol performance in an indoor mesh potato testbed. In: 2011 Third International Conference on Intelligent Networking and Collaborative Systems, pp. 8–13. IEEE, November 2011
33. Adu-Manu, K., Adam, N., Tapparello, C., Ayatollahi, H., Heinzelman, W.: Energy-harvesting wireless sensor networks (EH-WSNs): a review. ACM Trans. Sens. Netw. **14**(2), 1–50 (2018)
34. Astafiev, A.V., Demidov, A.A., Zhiznyakov, A.L., Kondrushin, I.A.: Development of an algorithm for positioning a mobile device based on sensor networks from ble beacons for building autonomous navigation systems. In: 2021 International Russian Automation Conference, RusAutoCon, pp. 1056–1061. IEEE, September 2021
35. Nair, K., et al.: Optimizing power consumption in IOT based wireless sensor networks using bluetooth low energy. In: 2015 International Conference on Green Computing and Internet of Things, ICGCIoT, pp. 589–593, IEEE, October 2015

Realizing Seamless Integration of Sensors and Actuators into the IoT

Reinhardt Karnapke[1,2]($\boxtimes$) and Karsten Walther[1]

[1] Perinet GmbH, Berlin, Germany
{reinhardt.karnapke,karsten.walther}@perinet.io
[2] Brandenburg University of Technology, Cottbus-Senftenberg, Germany
karnapke@b-tu.de
https://perinet.io

Abstract. Ever since the inception of wireless sensor networks more than twenty years ago, we were promised networks consisting of dozens, hundreds, or even thousands of nodes with sensors and/or actuators that would use self-X properties in order to form a functioning network by themselves. User interaction would not be necessary, or at least be absolutely minimalistic in all cases, including the later addition of more nodes. This promise has been ubiquitous regardless of network type, be it wireless sensor network, home automation, Internet of Things or Industrial Internet of Things.

Even though these self-X properties have long been promised, planning a deployment still offers a lot of obstacles to this day. One of these obstacles manifests in the form of a break in semantics when looking top to bottom at IoT/IIoT deployments. While process management level, operations management level and corporate management level are almost everywhere IT based, sensors and actuators are often still analog, which results in a mixture of systems in between.

In this paper, we describe the problems that arise when trying to close this semantic gap in detail, explain how taking the last mile in IIoT by enabling sensors and actuators with network capabilities removes these problems, and show additional benefits that stem from our solution. Moreover, we describe the inception of the periCORE, the first module which enables the integration of sensors and actuators into Single Pair Ethernet (SPE) worldwide.

Keywords: Internet of Things · Industrial Internet of Things · Seamless integration

1 Introduction

Wireless sensor networks have been envisioned and much researched since the 1990 s. Papers about smart dust (e.g. [1,2,4]) have given rise to the assumption that within a short amount of time it would be possible to deploy hundreds or

S. Paiva et al. (Eds.): SmartCity360° 2021, LNICST 442, pp. 688–701, 2022.
https://doi.org/10.1007/978-3-031-06371-8_44

thousands of nodes within a short interval, possibly even throwing them from planes, without having to configure them manually. Instead, nodes should be organizing themselves automatically, and deliver measured valued to the user via some gateway or similar mechanism.

Even though the number of nodes is usually smaller, the same promise, nodes that can be added almost without any effort from the user, has been made in other areas of IT. Home automation products, from smart light bulbs to automatic blinds, should make the life of the inhabitants more relaxed and should be easy to (re-)configure. Adding an intelligent fridge with internet connection leads to the Internet of Things (IoT). Once more, adding a device should be easy and not involve a lot of configuration effort. However, the opposite is often true. Smart homes need to be built and configured by experts, and intelligent fridges come with a manual the size of a telephone book.

Still, sensors and actuators are being produced, shipped and installed in ever increasing numbers. This does not primarily stem from private use but largely from industrial purposes. They are used in realization of the Industrial Internet of Things (IIoT) to take over numerous tasks that are currently still done manually. However, there are a number of pitfalls that need to be mastered between the acquisition of new sensors/actuators and the existence of a continuously working system:

1. Process management level, operations management level, and corporate management level are almost everywhere IT based nowadays. Yet, they need to interact with the Fieldbus systems below in a non-IT based way, resulting in a semantical break (see Fig. 1). Therefore, the goal should be to be able to attach sensors and actuators directly to IT-based systems in order to close this semantic gap. This leads to a drastic simplification of the whole architecture, enabling a number of further improvements.

2. A large number of sensors and actuators leads to a lot of Data that needs to be transmitted from the sensors, usually to a central decider, where it can be interpreted. Thereafter, a decision must be made whether some things changed, and if such changes require actions, it must be decided which actuators should perform which concrete actions. Finally, these decisions must be transmitted to the actuators.

   Such a centralized approach does not scale well, as all actions described above increase the Data load massively and can lead to overload situations a) in the network due to the transmission of large amounts of raw Data from the sensors to the decider, b) at the centralized decider itself, which has to handle and interpret huge amounts of Data, and c) in the network during the communication of control commands, possibly augmented with Data that originated at the sensors, from the decider to the actuators.

3. For many applications, functional properties like correctness of values are not all. Rather, non-functional properties like runtime, latency, and jitter play a big role. At least the latency increases with the network size, jitter depends on the used medium access control protocol and the network load. A low

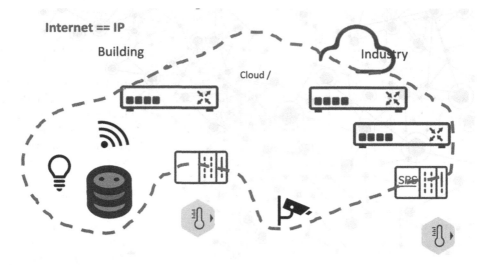

Fig. 1. Current state of connectivity. While upper layers are IT based, sensors and actuators are still analog and often connected through Fieldbusses.

latency despite a large network requires expensive high speed networks and specialized real-time capable medium access control protocols.

4. The fact that a lot of sensors supply only analogous Data or bitfields and can only be addressed by the port of a machine they are attached to leads to a complicated installment procedure and high deployment overhead. Therefore, these installments usually need to be carried out by experts.

In this paper we describe a way to simplify these four points, in order to allow users an easy entry into IoT and IIoT or an easy retrofitting. We started by closing the semantic gap between IT-based and non-IT-based systems with the introduction of network capabilities into the sensors and actuators. This is achieved though the design of the periCORE, the worlds first module for integration of sensors and actuators into Single Pair Ethernet (SPE) However, on one hand this was not enough, on the other hand it opened more possibilities than those we initially aimed for, resulting in quite some follow-up work.

The remainder of this paper is structured as follows: Sect. 2 looks at the problems described above one by one and produces a theoretical solution for each of them. Section 3, in contrast, focuses on the new challenges that arise when trying to apply the theoretical solutions to the real world. In Sect. 4, we show the hard- and software we designed at Perinet, taking into account the insights from both the theoretical as well as the practical challenges, the hardware and software. We finish with a conclusion and future work in Sect. 6.

2   Seamless Integration in Theory

Our main idea was to take the term "Internet of Things" literally. We are talking about networking, meaning the connection of devices where every part of the route, down to the last sensor, is made network-capable. This is a deliberate distancing from traditional, bus based sensors, moving on to network based ones. This results in a role switch for the sensors, as they turn from purely passive devices that get read from time to time using polling into smart communication partners that can decide on their own if and when communication is necessary, and even initiate this communication themselves. This solves a number of the problems mentioned above directly:

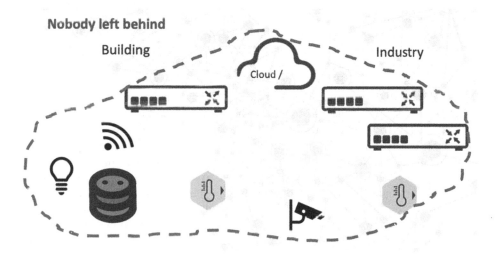

Fig. 2. Envisioned future connectivity: network connectivity down to the last sensor and actuator

1. The network capabilities of the sensors enable a direct communication from process management level, operations management level and corporate management level to them. The semantic gap is removed and no more translations are necessary. Due to the fact that each sensor has its own IP-Address, they can be directly addressed from any level using HTTP (see Fig. 2). It is no longer necessary to know to which port on which machine they have been connected, and to communicate with this machine first. This also enables a rethinking in the design process for future IIoT installments: Instead of starting with the focus on the Fieldbus (bottom up), systems can now be designed top down.
2. As the application does not change, the amount of Data that is produced by the sensors and must be processed does not change. However, this Data no

longer needs to be transmitted through the whole network in their raw, large form. Adding not only network capabilities but also a little processing power to the sensors means that local preprocessing of the Data can be realized directly in the sensors, which not only enables a reduction in size but also local decisions whether the Data needs to be transmitted at all. Instead of periodic polling and data transmission to the central decider, we are now able to realize an alarm functionality, meaning that sensors only transmit their (already preprocessed) Data if changes occurred and, for example, a threshold was exceeded.

This results in an avoidance of the overload situation in the network that stemmed from the communication between sensors and central decider. Also, the local decisions relieve the central decider and remove the danger of overloading it. Moreover, the maintenance overhead is reduced, as there is no need to maintain a (widely) distributed system anymore.

As for the actuators, the same principle can be applied to them, in order to reduce the network load due to communication between decider and actuators, reducing the danger of overloading the network even further. Moreover, the preprocessing and Data reductions prevent the accumulation of expensive Data-Lakes, as only relevant information is transmitted by the sensors. In fact, it is even possible to move the decisions, which actions are necessary, completely to the sensors and actuators, removing the need for a central decider. Of course, for monitoring reasons, it might still be desirable to collect some information about the state of sensors, actuators, and network at a central location from time to time in order to enable easy access for humans. This is, however, no longer required for the general operating of the system.

3. When communication only takes place locally, the latency does not increase with an increase in network size, as most communication will stay within certain boundaries. This means that standard components can be used for the network, and there is no need to install expensive high speed networking hardware. Real-time capable medium access control protocols might still be necessary, but their realization is much easier if they are only necessary on a local basis with only the few necessary participants.

This focus on local communication can be seen in detail in the following: A sensor decides autonomously how its measured values need to be interpreted. Instead of transmitting the values as it was done before, it already evaluates them and decides, whether they merit a reaction. If so, the sensor addresses the corresponding actuator directly. However, this is not a static one-to-one connection where a sensor is assigned an actuator beforehand. Instead, the smart communication partners, in this case the sensor itself, can choose the actuator that is interested in values that lie within a certain range and can react accordingly. This removes the detour via the central decider.

Even more, not only the sensors are equipped with intelligence, so are the actuators. A single measured value, even one that has already been digitalized and boxed within certain boundaries, can have different origins. Often, only the combination of multiple values measured by different sensors can bring clarification. Being able to detect such connections has previously been the advantage of the centralized approach, as the central decider could fuse multiple received values to form its decision. In our approach we also want to be able to perform this fusion, albeit at a different location. This can be realized by coupling multiple sensors, as a sensor might be interested in the measured values of other sensors to finish the evaluation of its own values. Alternatively, it can be realized in actuators. An intelligent actuator can declare that it is interested in the values of multiple sensors and fuse these to decide whether it needs to act.

4. The fact that each device has a unique identity that is independent of the port it is attached to and even the place it is located enables an easy installation and configuration that no longer needs to be carried out by experts. Users that already have experience with the internet are used to opening their browser and configuring new devices there, meaning the users do not need to learn to work with a new configuration tool (even without internet connection the devices can be configured in the browser). As all devices are network capable in our solution, they can be simply connected to the local network. Once they are connected, they announce their presence and can be configured using the browser the user is used to. Also, due to the network capability of the sensors, they can be easily replaced or reconfigured at runtime. Moreover, the fact that all parts of the network arc now IP-based enables a number of improvements for security. Standardized end-to-end encryption protocols like TLS [5] can easily be included, and now also encompass the "last mile", the connection to the sensors.

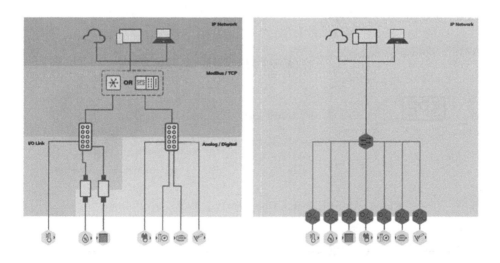

Fig. 3. Example of current setups (l) and future setup (r)

Figure 3 shows a comparison between a typical setup as might have been realized in the past (left) and the setup that we want to achieve with IP-based sensors or analog sensors retro-fitted with network capabilities. Whereas until now a lot of different interfaces and analog/digital converters are needed, a simple switch should suffice in the future when IP-based communication is realized down to the last sensor/actuator.

3 Seamless Integration in Practice

As wonderful, logical and simple as this idea seems, there is one question that you always need to ask when you want to build a new company based on a seemingly simple idea: Why has no one done that before? The answer, in our case, was that there were a number of obstacles that had to be overcome, concerning the technology as well as at the usability.

3.1 Challenges: Hardware

Starting from the bottom, one of the main challenges was the missing availability of standardized cabling and connectors for IP based sensors and actuators. This changed with the appearance of the Single Pair Ethernet (SPE) standard IEC 63171–6 which was proposed to feature the T1 interface from Harting in 2016 and was released on January 23rd, 2020 [3].

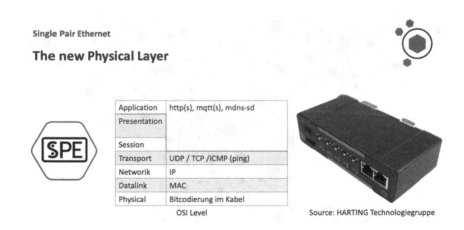

Fig. 4. An SPE switch from Harting Technology Group

Figure 4 shows an SPE switch from Harting Technology Group, which can be used to connect up to five SPE cables with a classic LAN.

Building upon IEC 63171–6, we started the design of our hardware. At the same time, software had to be taken into account and the development started in parallel because, as mentioned before, usability is also a main issue for IoT and IIoT devices.

3.2   Challenges: Software

In the following, we describe a few design decisions and challenges our software needed to be adapted to.

User Interface. Most of the potential users will not be IT experts, therefore they will not want to work with some strange setup program. However, almost everybody is used to use a web browser nowadays. If all configurations and all presentations of results could be done in the browser, user acceptance is expected to be high. Therefore, it was decided to use a browser based approach as described above. Browsers differ, though, and services that run on one browser might not be runable on another, resulting in exhaustive testing for different browsers.

Device Discovery. Even though IPv6 theoretically offers enough IP addresses for all embedded devices worldwide, it is not viable to print the IP of every node on its outside. Partly because the nodes shall be encased, partly because users should be spared the effort of copying long IPv6 addresses from all nodes into their computers manually. Therefore, we need device discovery mechanisms. Whether we can use DHCP is strongly dependent on the local configurations at the deployment site. For routers, there is the default IPv4 127.0.0.1 which can always be used but which default value should be used for sensors and actuators? As it should be only visible within the local network, a link local value would be good. However, for these to work a local name translation is required.

Name Translation. One of the major problems with the name translation we ran into is that it is not limited to local. This results in high delays. In combination with standard browser timeouts, this led to cases where our hardware was correctly connected but the browser did not show it because the discovery time was higher than the default browser timeout.

We also saw that IPv4 is still often preferred to IPv6 in browsers. A simple example which illustrates this can be found when using the Chrome browser. Chrome tries to connect to the internet using IPv6 when starting and if that initial connection fails, it switches to IPv4. While this is of course the correct behavior to enable the connection to the internet that is usually sought by the users, Chrome remains completely in IPv4 mode for the rest of its operation, oblivious to any IPv6 elements that might be connected or try to connect later. If you have only an IPv4 connection to the internet, you can not use IPv6 in your local network. This means that our sensors will not be discovered even though they are connected correctly, as Chrome does not support their link local addresses.

Another interesting observation that can be made here is that there are standards actually solving these problems, but most browsers do not fully implement these standards.

Zeroconf [6] already tried to address and solve all of these problems 20 years ago. However, the IETF working group dedicated to this problem was closed in 2004 due to their inability to reach a consensus.

4 Perinet

All of the ideas, challenges and features above described make for a nice academic thought experiment. However, it is even much more useful when completely realized and ready to roll out. For this reason, the Perinet GmbH was founded in 2018. Building upon the knowledge of the then upcoming Standard IEC 63171–6, Perinet already startet designing additional hardware and software. By now, we have designed a number of different modules with which the final gap in IoT can be closed. These include the periCORE, periNODE, periSWITCH, periSTART periLINE and periMICA.

4.1 The periCORE SPE Communication Module

Fig. 5. The periCORE SPE communication module. Cent coin for scale

The periCORE (Fig. 5) is the central piece of the innovation and the main product of Perinet. It has about the size of a euro cent coin and can be used to make sensors and actuators directly network-capable. However, this would only be possible for the manufacturers of sensors and actuators.

4.2 The periNODE Smart Adapter

Even if sensors and actuators would be manufactured with network-capability in the future, a lot of factories, automated buildings etc. already exist with analogous sensors and actuators. As we know that these would need support for transitioning to completely IP-based solutions without replacing all existing sensors and actuators, the periNODE smart adapter was developed (Fig. 6). It is an adapter that can be attached to bus-based sensors and actuators to make them network-capable. This way, existing deployments can be retrofitted and extended to be completely IT-based. This would lead to a realization as was already depicted in Fig. 3, with IP communication all through the network, down to the periNODE.

Fig. 6. The periNODE smart adapter. Euro coin for scale

4.3   The periSWITCH Multi-port Switch, periSTART Media Converter and periLINE

Now that we have the possibility to retrofit existing sensors and actuators or build new ones with networking capabilities already included, we still need a network that connects them. For this reason, we designed the periSWITCH, periSTART, and periLINE.

As networking needs switches, the periSWITCH (Fig. 7, left side) was designed and is offered by Perinet. It is a multiport SPE switch equipped with either three or eight ports.

Fig. 7. A periSWITCH multi-port switch with three ports (l) and a periSTART media converter (r)

In order to convert between different media, the periSTART (Fig. 7, right side) can be used. It can be attached directly to a periSWITCH or periLINE.

The periLINE (Fig. 8) is a hybrid cable (power and ethernet) that can be used to span distances. The figure shows an example where it is used to connect a periNODE that has been used to retrofit a distance measuring sensor with a periSTART media converter.

Fig. 8. A periLINE connecting a periSTART with a periNODE that has been attached to an analog distance measuring sensor for retrofitting network capabilities

4.4 The periMICA Modular Edge Computer

The periMICA (Modular Industrial Computing Architecture) (Fig. 9) is an extremely compact and robust industrial edge computer with a modular hardware and software design for gathering and preprocessing data locally, close to the source of data, i.e. sensors and actuators. It comes in different variants and two protection classes - IP20 and IP67. Customization options are available both on the hardware as well as on the software side. The figure shows the backsides of two different versions: A minimalistic version with only two interfaces (I/O and PoE) and a version with multiple interfaces, including two times USB.

4.5 Basic Setup

Figure 10 shows a basic setup of the components described above. Two sensors, temperature and distance, are each retrofitted with a periNODE. The periNODEs are connected to a three-port periSWITCH by periLINEs, which in turn is connected to a periMICA. On the periMICA, calculations that are too complex to be performed directly on the sensors or actuators and the periNODEs connected to them can be carried out. Also, the periMICA can store values for later inspection. The periMICA is connected to the local network. As most local networks are not using SPE, this is done with a normal LAN cable.

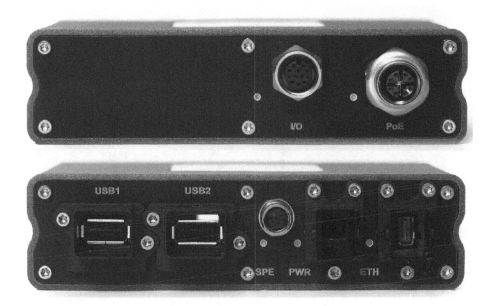

Fig. 9. Two different versions of periMICA: A minimalistic version with only the two interfaces for I/O and PoE (top) and a second version with maximized different interfaces (USB, ETH etc.)

Therefore, Perinet offers all elements needed to switch from bus based systems to network based ones. As far as we know, there is no comparable solution offered by any competitor at the moment.

5   Example Project

While we of course tested our designs ourselves, we also have taken up contacts within the industry and realized a first reference project.

This first reference project is currently being realized in a plant for the electroplating of plug contacts. In this type of finishing, monitoring of the prevailing PH value is necessary for quality assurance purposes. Permanent manual monitoring of the PH value is very expensive, which is why this shall be done fully automated in the future.

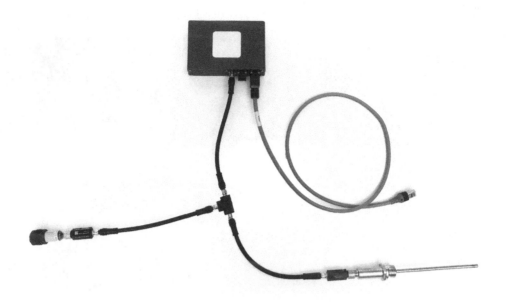

Fig. 10. Complete Setup

In a first step, a PH-value probe, which was not network capable until now, was connected to the network by means of a periNODE. The data from the probe is transferred to a MICA, where it is analyzed and stored. The analyzation/preprocessing also includes the comparison of the measured values with thresholds, and the raising of an alarm if one of them is exceeded. Thus, workers only need to intervene when they receive a notification that there is a deviation from the desired value range.

6   Conclusion and Future Work

In this paper, we have described our vision for the seamless integration of sensors and actuators into the (Industrial) Internet of Things. This vision can only be realized using IP-based technology end-to-end. However, there are a number of snares and pitfalls that need to be avoided in order to have this vision become reality. The new IEC 63171–6 standard is a big step in this direction, and Perinet supplies compatible nodes, switches, and cables.

Realizing the user interface in a browser enables end users to work in a familiar environment. However, the fact that most browsers are still focussed on connections to the Internet leads to problems when trying to realize local networks. Therefore, the fact that most browsers do not completely follow the standards resulted in a lot of extra work for us. For the future, we would wish for browser versions that are more focussed on local networks or at least do not throw any bricks in our way. If browsers completely implemented existing standards, a lot of problems would be solved.

Currently, we use a link local address to assure network connectivity between sensor and the operating system on a user's computer. However, the user might or might not see the device in his/her browser, depending on the browser variant. Typing the sensors address into the browser manually would solve this problem but require, from our point of view, too much work from the user. We are currently investigating how to solve this problem even if browsers remain non-compliant to standards. Moreover, we are looking into approaches to increase the intelligence of sensors and actuators even further.

References

1. Chatzigiannakis, I., Nikoletseas, S., Spirakis, P.: Smart dust protocols for local detection and propagation. In: POMC 2002: Proceedings of the Second ACM International Workshop on Principles of Mobile Computing, pp. 9–16. ACM Press, New York (2002). https://doi.org/10.1145/584490.584493
2. Chatzigiannakis, I., Nikoletseas, S., Spirakis, P.G.: Efficient and robust protocols for local detection and propagation in smart dust networks. Mob. Netw. Appl. **10**(1–2), 133–149 (2005). https://doi.org/10.1145/1046430.1046441
3. https://www.vde-verlag.de/iec-normen/248360/iec-63171-6-2020.html
4. Kahn, J.M., Katz, R.H., Pister, K.S.J.: Next century challenges: mobile networking for "smart dust". In: MobiCom 1999: Proceedings of the 5th annual ACM/IEEE International Conference On Mobile Computing And Networking, pp. 271–278. ACM Press, New York (1999). https://doi.org/10.1145/313451.313558
5. https://tools.ietf.org/html/rfc8446.html
6. https://datatracker.ietf.org/wg/zeroconf/charter/

Detection Against Replay Attack: A Feedback Watermark Approach

Xudong Zhao[1(✉)], Le Liu[1], H. R. Karimi[2], and Wei Xing[1]

[1] The Key Laboratory of Intelligent Control and Optimization for Industrial Equipment, Dalian University of Technology, Ministry of Education, Dalian, China
xdzhaohit@gmail.com, wxing@mail.dlut.edu.cn
[2] Department of Mechanical Engineering, Politecnico di Milano, via La Masa 1, 20156 Milan, Italy
hamidreza.karimi@polimi.it

Abstract. Since malicious cyber attacks are common in modern industry, cyber security has become an important issue. Motivated by this, a novel feedback watermark approach is proposed to defend cyber physical systems against replay attacks in this paper. Specifically, we propose a new secure control framework to defend systems against replay attacks, where a feedback channel and a feedback control function are constructed. We address the problem starting from the problem formulation with a linear quadratic Gaussian (LQG) controller, a Kalman filter and a χ^2 detector. We investigate the LQG performance with replay attacks and study the LQG performance loss after adding feedback watermarks. It is also proved that the detector output will converge to a new steady point with a class of feedback function when an attacker launches replay attacks. It is shown that our approach can increase the probability of detecting replay attacks. Finally, we show the validity of feedback watermarks with a numerical example.

Keywords: Cyber physical system · Physical watermark · Replay attack

1 Introduction

Nowadays, due to the development of hardware equipment and telecommunication, more data has been used to guide industrial processes. Networks are more effective to deal with the explosion of data, and hence are frequently used in cyber physical systems (CPSs). However, the openness of networks has caused many drawbacks in security [6]. For example, Stuxnet Worm [13] destroyed the centrifuges in Iran. Such malicious attacks may even be harmful to people's lives.

This work are supported by the National Natural Science Foundation of China (61722302, 61573069), the Liaoning Revitalization Talents Program (XLYC1907140), National Major Science and Technology Project (J2019-V-0010–0105) and the Fundamental Research Funds for the Central Universities (DUT19ZD218).

S. Paiva et al. (Eds.): SmartCity360° 2021, LNICST 442, pp. 702–715, 2022.
https://doi.org/10.1007/978-3-031-06371-8_45

Therefore, cyber security has become a significant issue in industry and detection of malicious attacks is an urgent problem to be solved.

There are two types of malicious attacks widely concerned in the research community. The first one is denial of service (DoS) attack, which enables attackers to jam communication channels. DoS attacks are simple to launch and hence have been adopted by malicious hackers in many cases (see e.g. [7]). However, DoS attack consumes more energy and is not disguised. Signal to interference plus noise ratio (SINR) is frequently used to construct the energy consumption of DoS attacks and researchers have proposed different strategies to defend CPSs under DoS attacks. For example, based on game theory, Li et al. [8] has developed a framework design the transmission strategy, which can be used to defend remote estimation. De Persis et al. [3] has designed secure control in linear systems under DoS attack by appropriate scheduling of transmission time.

False data injection (FDI) attack, the second type of attack, is more destructive since it has the ability to generate malicious signals. However, it is not easy to launch this type of attack since most of the malicious FDI attacks (e.g. [11]) need full knowledge of the system. Detection of false data injection attacks is hard and many people have proposed different methods to detect this type of attack. For instance, Li et al. [7] separated sensors into benign ones and susceptible ones. They designed a fusion algorithm to distinguish malicious sensors.

Replay attack is one of false data injection attacks, which only needs to record sensor measurements and replay them to a fusion center. In other words, it does not need any knowledge about the system. Because of the simplicity of replay attacks, it could be utilized in many scenarios (e.g., the Stuxnet Worm [13]) and even bypassed detectors. Therefore, we concentrated on detection of replay attacks in this paper. To be more specific, we utilize physical watermarks to detect replay attacks.

In order to detect malicious attacks, physical watermarks are small noises added to the control input, which were originally proposed in [12]. Mo et al. [10] have extended the result to general controllers, and they designed a specific detector to detect replay attacks. Weerakkody et al. [15] have used physical watermarks to detect false data injection attacks when some of the controllers are eavesdropped by the attacker. To reduce the performance loss and increase the detection rate, Miao et al. [9] applied a game theoretic approach in the watermark design to detect replay attacks. They developed an algorithm to calculate a suboptimal solution in a finite time case. Huang et al. [5] applied watermarks to guard remote estimation. Satchidanandan et al. [14] have equipped CPSs with Neyman-Pearson detectors and used watermarks to defend systems. Fang et al. [4] added watermarks with a periodic schedule to reduce performance loss.

In this work, a novel feedback watermark approach is proposed to defend CPSs against replay attacks. First, we formulate the whole system and analyze the effects of replay attacks. Furthermore, the system performance is investigated after adding feedback watermarks. Then we introduce feedback watermarks and propose a formula to design the feedback control function. With the above function, it is proved that feedback watermarks are more efficient. We summarize the main contributions of this paper as follow:

(1) The effects of replay attacks are investigated. To be more specific, we show that the system is stable under replay attack if the system matrix A is Hurwitz.
(2) We propose a novel feedback watermark approach, which can be seen as an extension of the existing works [10]. Moreover, we study the LQG performance loss after adding the watermark. It is shown that the detection rate will increase to a new steady point and our method is more effective than the method in [10].
(3) A design formula is given to design feedback control function, which can be utilized to generate physical watermarks. One can develop specific feedback control function based on our formula.

The rest of this paper is organized as follows: in Sect. II, we formulate a CPS with a Kalman filter, a controller and a χ^2 detector. In Sect. III, we deeply investigate the effects of replay attacks. Section IV proposes the feedback watermark approach and investigates a formula to design feedback control function. In Sect. V gives a numerical example to show the validity and advantages of the proposed methods. Section VI provides some concluding remarks.

Notation: $\mathbb{R}$ represents the set of real numbers. $\mathbb{E}(\cdot)$ is the expectation of a random event. $\mathcal{N}(\mu, \Sigma)$ denotes a Gaussian distribution with mean μ and covariance matrix Σ.

2   Problem Formulation

2.1   System Dynamic and Kalman Filter

Consider the following discrete linear invariant system:

$$x_{k+1} = Ax_k + Bu_k + w_k, \tag{1}$$

$$y_k = Cx_k + v_k, \tag{2}$$

where $x_k \in \mathbb{R}^n$ and $y_k \in \mathbb{R}^m$ is the state and the measurement output. $u_k \in \mathbb{R}^l$ is the control input. w_k and v_k is the Gaussian noise with covariance Q and R. It is assumed that w_k and v_j are independent of each other, w_k is independent of $w_j, \forall j \neq k$ and v_k is independent of $v_j, \forall j \neq k$ i.e., $\mathbb{E}[w_k v_j^T] = 0, \forall k, j, \mathbb{E}[w_k w_j^T] = 0, \forall k \neq j$ and $\mathbb{E}[v_k v_j^T] = 0, \forall k \neq j$.

A Kalman filter is used in this paper to estimate the state, it is well known that a Kalman filter can be expressed in an iteration form:

$$\hat{x}_{k|k-1} = A\hat{x}_{k-1|k-1} + Bu_{k-1}, \tag{3}$$

$$P_{k|k-1} = AP_{k-1|k-1}A^T + Q, \tag{4}$$

$$K_k = P_{k|k-1}C^T(CP_{k|k-1}C^T + R)^{-1}, \tag{5}$$

$$\hat{x}_{k|k} = \hat{x}_{k|k-1} + K_k(y_k - C\hat{x}_{k|k-1}), \tag{6}$$

$$P_{k|k} = (I - K_kC)P_{k|k-1}, \tag{7}$$

where $P_{k|k-1} = \mathbb{E}[(x_k - \hat{x}_{k|k-1})(x_k - \hat{x}_{k|k-1})^T]$ and $P_{k|k} = \mathbb{E}[(x_k - \hat{x}_{k|k})(x_k - \hat{x}_{k|k})^T]$. It should be pointed out that a Kalman filter will enter the steady state exponentially fast. Therefore, it is without loss of generality that we assume the Kalman filter run in the steady state at the beginning, i.e.,

$$P_{0|-1} = \bar{P}, K_k = K, \Pi_0 = (I - KC)\bar{P}, \tag{8}$$

$$\hat{x}_{k|k-1} = A\hat{x}_{k|k} + Bu_{k-1}, \tag{9}$$

$$\hat{x}_{k|k} = \hat{x}_{k|k-1} + K(y_k - C\hat{x}_{k|k-1}), \tag{10}$$

where $\bar{P} \triangleq \lim_{k \to \infty} P_{k|k-1}$, $K \triangleq \bar{P}C^T \left(C\bar{P}C^T + R\right)^{-1}$.

2.2   Linear Quadratic Gaussian (LQG) Optimal Control

The LQG controller in this paper minimizes the infinite time linear quadratic objective function [2] as follows:

$$J = \min \lim_{T \to \infty} \mathbb{E}\{\frac{1}{T} \left[\sum_{k=0}^{T-1} (x_k^T W x_k + u_k^T U u_k)\right]\}, \tag{11}$$

where W and U are semidefinite matrices. Given the state estimate $\hat{x}_{k|k}$, a fixed gain controller will solve the minimization problem, taking the following form:

$$u_k = u_k^* = - \left(B^T SB + U\right)^{-1} B^T SA\hat{x}_{k|k}, \tag{12}$$

where u_k^* is the optimal control input, and S is the solution of the following Riccati equation [2]:

$$S = A^T SA + W - A^T SB \left(B^T SB + U\right)^{-1} B^T SA. \tag{13}$$

Let us define $L \triangleq - \left(B^T SB + U\right)^{-1} B^T SA$, then

$$u_k^* = L\hat{x}_{k|k}. \tag{14}$$

Using the above fixed gain controller, J becomes a constant dependent on system parameters: [2]:

$$J = \text{trace}(SQ) + \text{trace} \left[\left(A^T SA + W - S\right)(P - KCP)\right]. \tag{15}$$

2.3 χ^2 Detector

A χ^2 detector is a very commonly used detector to detect abnormal behavior in a system. Let us define $z_k = y_k - C\hat{x}_{k|k-1}$. Then, a χ^2 detector takes the following form:

$$g_k = \sum_{i=k-\mathscr{T}+1}^{k} z_i^T \mathscr{P}^{-1} z_i \underset{\mathscr{H}_1}{\overset{\mathscr{H}_0}{\lessgtr}} \eta, \tag{16}$$

where $\mathscr{P} = C\bar{P}C^T + R$, $\mathscr{T}$ is the window size and η is the threshold. $\mathscr{H}_0$ denotes that the system is operating normally, and $\mathscr{H}_1$ denotes that an attacker implements an attack strategy $\mathscr{L}$. The probability of detection β_k when the system is under attack and the probability of false alarm α_k are defined respectively as

$$\beta_k \triangleq \Pr\left(g_k > \eta \mid \mathscr{H}_1\right), \quad \alpha_k \triangleq \Pr\left(g_k > \eta \mid \mathscr{H}_0\right). \tag{17}$$

In this paper, the window size $\mathscr{T}$ is set to be 1. However, it is trivial to extend our results to the scenario where $\mathscr{T} > 1$ by vector stack.

2.4 Some Lemmas

Before introducing replay attacks, the following lemmas are recalled here to facilitate the understanding of the paper:

Lemma 1. *[1]*
  (i). z_k is a Gaussian distributed vector with probability distribution function (PDF) $\sim \mathscr{N}(0, \mathscr{P})$.
  (ii). $E[z_k^T z_l] = 0$, $\forall k \neq l$.

Lemma 2. *[10] Define $\mathscr{A} = (A + BL)(I - KC)$. If $\mathscr{A}$ is stable, the detection rate β_k will converge to α_k, i.e.,*

$$\lim_{k \to \infty} \beta_k = \alpha_k. \tag{18}$$

Conversely, if $\mathscr{A}$ is unstable, the detection rate β_k will converge to 1, i.e.,

$$\lim_{k \to \infty} \beta_k = 1. \tag{19}$$

Remark 1. Lemma 1 and Lemma 2 are technical and used in the proof of Theorem 1.

3 Effects of Replay Attacks

In this section, we concentrate on the detector performance provided the attacker is launching a replay attack. Without loss of generality, it is assumed the replay attack begins at time 0. Following [10], we can think of y_k's (the attacker's records) as outputs of the following virtual system:

$$x_{k+1}' = Ax_k' + Bu_k' + w_k', \tag{20}$$
$$y_k' = Cx_k' + v_k', \tag{21}$$
$$\hat{x}_{k+1|k}' = A\hat{x}_{k|k}' + Bu_k', \tag{22}$$
$$\hat{x}_{k+1|k+1}' = \hat{x}_{k+1|k}' + Kz_k', \tag{23}$$
$$u_k' = L\hat{x}_{k|k}' + \Delta u_k', \tag{24}$$

where $\Delta u_k' \sim (0, \mathscr{L}')$. Define $\hat{x}_{0|-1}' - \hat{x}_{0|-1}' = \xi$ and $z_k^a = y_k' - C\hat{x}_{k|k-1}'$. It is worth pointing out that z_k^a is the innovation when a replay attack occurs.

Assumption 1. $\mathscr{A}$ *is stable.*

Assumption 2. x_0 *is independent of* x_0', w_k' *and* v_k'.

Remark 2. Even though the two assumptions seem very harsh at the first sight, it is reasonable since a replay attack will be detected immediately if $\mathscr{A}$ is unstable. Then, we don't need to design a mechanism to detect replay attacks. Moreover, an attacker is more likely to record a long period measurements. And the replay part signal is almost independent to the real time signal (x_0) due to the system is stable. It should be noticed that $z_k' \triangleq y_k' - Cx_{k|k-1}'$ is independent of x_k since Assumption 2 holds.

Theorem 1. *Under the Assumptions 1 and 2, the system will be stable if A is Hurwitz. When A is Hurwitz, the LQG performance under a long period replay attack without being detected is:*

$$J = \mathrm{trace}(\tilde{W}\bar{P}^a), \tag{25}$$

and $\bar{P}^a \in \mathbb{R}^{2n}$ satisfies the following equation,

$$\bar{P}^a = \tilde{A}\bar{P}^a\tilde{A}^T + \tilde{B}\begin{bmatrix} Q & 0 \\ 0 & \mathscr{P} \end{bmatrix}\tilde{B}^T, \tag{26}$$

where $\tilde{W} = \begin{bmatrix} W + L^TUL & L^TUL \\ L^TUL & L^TUL \end{bmatrix}$, $\tilde{A} = \begin{bmatrix} A+BL & BL \\ 0 & A \end{bmatrix}$ *and* $\tilde{B} = \begin{bmatrix} I & 0 \\ -I & K \end{bmatrix}$.

Proof. Rewrite $\hat{x}_{k+1|k}$ as

$$\hat{x}_{k+1|k} = \mathscr{A}\hat{x}_{k|k-1} + (A+BL)Ky_k'. \tag{27}$$

For the virtual system,

$$\hat{x}_{k+1|k}' = \mathscr{A}\hat{x}_{k|k-1}' + (A+BL)Ky_k'. \tag{28}$$

Then it can be shown that

$$\begin{aligned} z_k^a &= y_k' - C\hat{x}_{k|k-1}' + C\hat{x}_{k|k-1}' - C\hat{x}_{k|k-1} \\ &= z_k' + C(\hat{x}_{k|k-1}' - \hat{x}_{k|k-1}) \\ &= z_k' - C\mathscr{A}^k\xi. \end{aligned} \tag{29}$$

Considering $\mathscr{A}$ is stable, this shows the residue under attack will coverage to the normal residue z_k', which means that a replay attack can bypass the χ^2 detector.

$$\begin{aligned} \hat{x}_{k+1|k+1} &= \hat{x}_{k+1|k} + Kz_k \\ &= (A+BL)\hat{x}_{k|k} + Kz_k^a \\ &= (A+BL)\hat{x}_{k|k} + Kz_k' - KC\mathscr{A}^k\xi. \end{aligned} \tag{30}$$

The system dynamic (1) combined with (14) can be rewritten as:

$$x_{k+1} = (A + BL)x_k + BLe_k + w_k. \tag{31}$$

Now Let us define $e_k \triangleq \hat{x}_{k|k} - x_k$, $\theta_k = [x_k^T, e_k^T]^T$ and $P_k^a \triangleq \mathbb{E}(\theta_k \theta_k^T)$. Subtracting the above two equations, it can be obtained

$$e_{k+1} = Ae_k + Kz_k' - w_k - KC\mathscr{A}^k\xi, \tag{32}$$

and

$$\theta_{k+1} = \tilde{A}\theta_k + \tilde{B}\begin{bmatrix} w_k \\ z_k' \end{bmatrix} + \tilde{E}\mathscr{A}^k\xi, \tag{33}$$

where $\tilde{A} = \begin{bmatrix} A + BL & BL \\ 0 & A \end{bmatrix}$, $\tilde{B} = \begin{bmatrix} I & 0 \\ -I & K \end{bmatrix}$ and $\tilde{E} = \begin{bmatrix} 0 \\ -KC \end{bmatrix}$. It can be observed that the estimation error will go to infinity when the system parameter A is not Hurwitz and hence the system will be unstable. When A is Hurwitz, one can obtain $\lim_{k\to\infty} P_k^a = \bar{P}^a$, which satisfies the following condition:

$$\bar{P}^a = \tilde{A}\bar{P}^a\tilde{A}^T + \tilde{B}\begin{bmatrix} Q & 0 \\ 0 & \mathscr{P} \end{bmatrix}\tilde{B}^T. \tag{34}$$

It can be obtained that

$$\begin{aligned}
J &= \lim_{T\to\infty} \mathbb{E}\{\frac{1}{T}\left[\sum_{k=0}^{T-1}(x_k^T W x_k + u_k^T U u_k)\right]\} \\
&= \lim_{T\to\infty} \mathbb{E}\{\frac{1}{T}\left[\sum_{k=0}^{T-1}\left(\theta_k^T\begin{bmatrix} W & 0 \\ 0 & 0 \end{bmatrix}\theta_k + \theta_k^T\begin{bmatrix} L^T U L & L^T U L \\ L^T U L & L^T U L \end{bmatrix}\theta_k\right)\right]\} \\
&= \text{trace}(\tilde{W}\bar{P}^a), \tag{35}
\end{aligned}$$

where $\tilde{W} = \begin{bmatrix} W + L^T U L & L^T U L \\ L^T U L & L^T U L \end{bmatrix}$. This ends the proof.   ∎

Remark 3. Since a replay attack is usually launched for a long time [13] and $\mathscr{A}$ is a Hurwitz matrix, it is reasonable to omit the last term of (30). Moreover, if an attacker has the ability to eavesdrop the sensor measurements, the time to begin replay attacks will be chosen carefully to avoid being detected, meaning that y_0 and y_0' will be chosen to be approximately the same and hence ξ will be small. Therefore, a replay attack cannot be detected easily when $\mathscr{A}$ is stable

4   Detection of Replay Attacks

In order to defend against replay attacks. Mo et al. [12] proposed a physical watermark approach, where physical watermarks denote small noises in the control inputs. To be more specific, the watermark signals are only known to the system and the attacker has no information about it. In order to efficiently

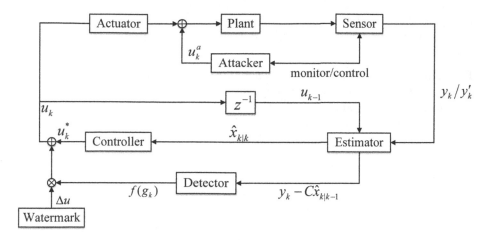

Fig. 1. System architecture

detect malicious attacks, we propose a feedback watermark approach, where we connect the physical watermark with the detector output (See Fig. 4). Let $\Delta u_k^* \sim \mathcal{N}(0, \mathcal{Q})$ denote the ordinary watermark which is independent of x_0, w_k and v_k for all k, our feedback watermark is given by:

$$\Delta u_k = f(g_k)\Delta u_k^*, \tag{36}$$

where $f(\cdot) := \mathbb{R}^+ \to [0, \delta]$ is a measurable function to control the watermark signal. Therefore, we call this function as a feedback control function. The reason why we adopt an upper bound δ here is to avoid an unbearable physical watermark. Otherwise, a small malicious signal may lead a serious consequence in the control system. In other words, we would like to adopt a mechanism to increase the covariance of watermarks with a relatively small impact on the system when the system is under attack. Furthermore, if $f(g_k) = 1$, we may obtain the ordinary watermark as in [10], meaning that our approach is an extension to the existing ones.

In the next part, we want to explore the effects of the feedback control functions $f(\cdot)$. $f(\cdot)$ can be designed according to Theorem 2. First, let us explore the LQG performance loss after adding physical watermarks.

Theorem 2. *When there is no attack, the LQG performance J' after adding feedback physical watermark is given by*

$$J' = J + \Delta J, \tag{37}$$

where $\Delta J = \tilde{h} \operatorname{trace}\left(\left(B^T S B + U\right) \mathcal{Q}\right)$, with $\tilde{h} = \mathbb{E}[f(g_0)^2]$.

Proof. The proof is similar to the proof of Theorem 1 in [12] and hence is omitted here. ∎

The next theorem shows that the covariance of Δu_k is larger when the system is under attack, i.e., $\mathbb{E}[f(g_k)^2] \geq \mathbb{E}[f(g'_k)^2]$. Therefore, our approach can be used to defend systems against replay attacks.

Theorem 3. *Let $h(x) \triangleq f(x)^2$. If $h(x)$ is a monotone increasing truncation function, then the following statements hold:*
(i) $\mathbb{E}[h(g_k)]$ will converge to a steady point $\bar{h}$,
(ii) $\lim_{k \to \infty} \mathbb{E}(g_k) = m + \mathrm{trace}\left(C^T \mathscr{P}^{-1} C \bar{\Sigma}\right)$, where $\bar{\Sigma} = \mathscr{U} + \mathscr{W}$, $\mathscr{U}$ satisfies $\mathscr{U} - \bar{h} B Q B^T = \mathscr{A} \mathscr{U} \mathscr{A}^T$ and $\mathscr{W}$ satisfies $\mathscr{W} - \bar{h} B Q B^T = \mathscr{A} \mathscr{W} \mathscr{A}^T$.

Proof. The system dynamic now becomes:

$$x_{k+1} = A x_k + B u_k + B \Delta u_k + w_k, \tag{38}$$

and thus z_k^a can be recalculated as

$$
\begin{aligned}
z_k^a &= y'_k - C \hat{x}'_{k|k-1} + C \hat{x}'_{k|k-1} - C \hat{x}_{k|k-1} \\
&= z'_k + C \mathscr{A} (\hat{x}'_{k-1|k-2} - \hat{x}_{k-1|k-2}) - C B (\Delta u_{k-1} - \Delta u'_{k-1}) \\
&= z'_k - C \mathscr{A}^k \xi - C \sum_{i=0}^{k-1} \mathscr{A}^{k-i-1} B (\Delta u_i - \Delta u'_i) \\
&= z'_k - C \mathscr{A}^k \xi - C \sum_{i=0}^{k-1} \mathscr{A}^{k-i-1} B (f(g_k^a) \Delta u_i^* - f(g'_k) \Delta u_i^{*\prime}). \tag{39}
\end{aligned}
$$

Then, it can be calculated that

$$
\begin{aligned}
\mathbb{E}(z_k^a z_k^{aT}) &= \mathbb{E}\{ z'_k z_k^{\prime T} + C \mathscr{A}^k \xi \xi^T (\mathscr{A}^k)^T C^T \\
&\quad + C \sum_{i=0}^{k-1} h(g_i^a) \mathscr{A}^{k-i-1} B \Delta u_i \Delta u_i^T B^T (\mathscr{A}^{k-i-1})^T C^T \\
&\quad + C \sum_{i=0}^{k-1} h(g'_i) \mathscr{A}^{k-i-1} B \Delta u_i^* \Delta u_i^{*T} B^T (\mathscr{A}^{k-i-1})^T C^T \} \\
&= \mathscr{P} + C \mathscr{A}^k \xi \xi^T (\mathscr{A}^k)^T C^T + C \sum_{i=0}^{k-1} \mathbb{E}[h(g_i^a)] \mathscr{A}^{k-i-1} B Q B^T (\mathscr{A}^{k-i-1})^T C^T \\
&\quad + C \sum_{i=0}^{k-1} \mathbb{E}[h(g'_i)] \mathscr{A}^{k-i-1} B Q B^T (\mathscr{A}^{k-i-1})^T C^T \}, \tag{40}
\end{aligned}
$$

where the superscript a helps to clarify vectors under attack. Since $C \mathscr{A}^k \xi \xi^T (\mathscr{A}^k)^T C^T$ will be close to zero arbitrarily when k is large enough, this term is omitted in the following proof. Now (40) becomes

$$
\begin{aligned}
\mathbb{E}(z_k^a z_k^{aT}) &= \mathscr{P} + C \sum_{i=0}^{k-1} \mathbb{E}[h(g_i^a)] \mathscr{A}^{k-i-1} B Q B^T (\mathscr{A}^{k-i-1})^T C^T \\
&\quad + C \sum_{i=0}^{k-1} \mathbb{E}[h(g'_i)] \mathscr{A}^{k-i-1} B Q B^T (\mathscr{A}^{k-i-1})^T C^T \}. \tag{41}
\end{aligned}
$$

First, we show that $\mathbb{E}[h(g_1^a)] \geq \mathbb{E}[h(g_0^a)]$. Define $\Sigma_k \triangleq \mathbb{E}(z_k^a z_k^{aT})$, it is trivial to prove $\Sigma_1 \geq \Sigma_0$. Also, let $v_0^a = \mathscr{P}^{\frac{1}{2}} z_0^a \sim \mathscr{N}(0, \mathscr{P}^{\frac{1}{2}} \Sigma_0 \mathscr{P}^{\frac{1}{2}})$ and $v_1^a = \mathscr{P}^{\frac{1}{2}} z_1^a \sim \mathscr{N}(0, \mathscr{P}^{\frac{1}{2}} \Sigma_1 \mathscr{P}^{\frac{1}{2}})$. Suppose z_k^a is a scalar, i.e., $m = 1$, it can be shown that (recall that the window size $\mathscr{T} = 1$)

$$
\begin{aligned}
\mathbb{E}[h(g_1^a)] - \mathbb{E}[h(g_0^a)] &= \mathbb{E}[h\left(z_1^{aT} \mathscr{P}^{-1} z_1^a\right)] - \mathbb{E}[h\left(z_0^{aT} \mathscr{P}^{-1} z_0^a\right)] \\
&= \int_{\mathbb{R}} h(v_1^{a2}) p_1(v_1^a) dv_1^a - \int_{\mathbb{R}} h(v_0^{a2}) p_0(v_0^a) dv_0^a \\
&= \int_{\mathbb{R}} h(v^2)\left(p_1(v) - p_0(v)\right) dv \\
&= \int_{\mathbb{V}} h(v^2)\left(p_1(v) - p_0(v)\right) dv + \int_{\mathbb{R}\backslash\mathbb{V}} h(v^2)\left(p_1(v) - p_0(v)\right) dv \\
&\geq \int_{\mathbb{V}} h(\bar{v}^2)\left(p_1(v) - p_0(v)\right) dv + \int_{\mathbb{R}\backslash\mathbb{V}} h(\bar{v}^2)\left(p_1(v) - p_0(v)\right) dv \\
&= 0,
\end{aligned} \tag{42}
$$

where $\mathbb{V} = \{v | p_1(v) \leq p_0(v)\}$ and $\bar{v}$ satisfies $p_1(\bar{v}) = p_0(\bar{v})$. Since the density function of a Gaussian distribution is symmetrical and h is a monotone increasing function, the inequality holds. When z_k^a is a vector, the additional step in the proof is to diagonalize the covariance matrix first and then the following proof is similar. Hence, we omit the detailed proof for the general case here.

Now, it is trivial to see that $\Sigma_2 \geq \Sigma_1$ and $\mathbb{E}[h(g_2^a)] \geq \mathbb{E}[h(g_1^a)]$. Following the same procedure, it can be shown that $\mathbb{E}[h(g_k + 1^a)] \geq \mathbb{E}[h(g_k^a)]$. Combined this with $\mathbb{E}[h(g_k^a)] \leq \delta^2$, it can be concluded that $\lim_{k\to} \mathbb{E}[h(g_k^a)] = \bar{h}$, which proves (i). To prove (ii), it can be shown from (i) and the last two terms of (41) will converge to the steady state given by the Lyapunov equations that

$$
\lim_{k\to\infty} \Sigma_k = \bar{\Sigma}. \tag{43}
$$

It can be calculated that

$$
\begin{aligned}
\lim_{k\to\infty} \mathbb{E}(g_k) &= \lim_{k\to\infty} \mathbb{E}(z_k^{aT} \mathscr{P}^{-1} z_k^a) \\
&= \lim_{k\to\infty} \operatorname{trace}\left(\mathscr{P}^{-1} \Sigma_k\right) \\
&= \operatorname{trace}\left(\mathscr{P}^{-1}(\mathscr{P} + C\bar{\Sigma}C^T)\right) \\
&= m + \operatorname{trace}\left(C^T \mathscr{P}^{-1} C\bar{\Sigma}\right),
\end{aligned} \tag{44}
$$

which finishes the proof.   ∎

Remark 4. It should be emphasized that h is a monotone increasing function since we would like to generate a larger physical watermark when the system is in anomaly. It is also worth pointing out $\bar{h} \geq \tilde{h}$ by $\mathbb{E}[h(g_k^a)] \geq \mathbb{E}[h(g_0^a)]$, meaning that our approach is more effective when the ΔJ is the same. This shows that our method will have a higher detection rate compared with that in [10] when the performance loss is the same. Furthermore, the detector proposed in [10] can

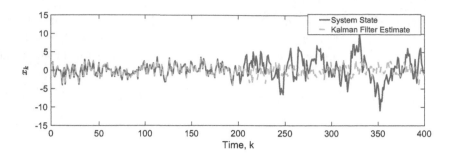

Fig. 2. System state and Kalman Filter estimate under replay attacks.

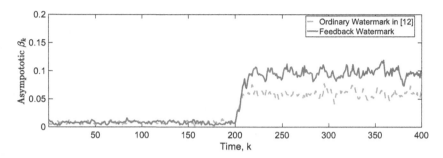

Fig. 3. Comparisons between feedback watermark and ordinary watermark in [10].

also be utilized in this paper. Actually, any detector using statistical properties of the innovation z_ks can be used in this paper. We adopt χ^2 detector in this paper for the brevity of explanations.

5   Numerical Example

In this section, we provide a numerical example to show the effectiveness of our approach. The system parameters are as follow: $A = 0.8$, $B = 1$, $C = 1$, $Q = 1$, $R = 0.1$, $W = 1$, $U = 1$, $\mathscr{T} = 10$ and the feedback function is chosen as $f(x) = \sqrt{x}$, which means that the square root of the output of χ^2 detector is directly multiplied with the ordinary Δu_k^*. The upper bound δ is chosen as 5. Under this condition, $\tilde{h} = m\mathscr{T} = 10$ is the standard expectation of a χ^2 detector. ΔJ with feedback watermarks can be calculated by Theorem 2 as $\Delta J = 23.7\mathcal{Q}$.

It can be seen from Fig. 2, the estimate deviates from the system states when the replay attack begins at time step 201. Therefore, the controller can not have a satisfactory LQG performance.

In order to compare with the existing watermark approach in [10], we make ΔJ the same in the two methods. Thus, we set $\mathcal{Q} = 0.02$ in our method and $\mathcal{Q} = 0.2$ in the ordinary watermark. Moreover, the false alarm rate is set to be 0.001. The attacker records the measurements from time 1 to time 200 and

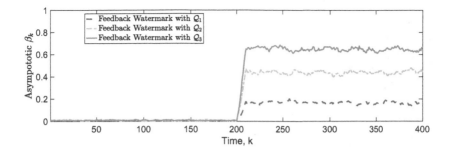

Fig. 4. Comparisons between feedback watermark with different Qs.

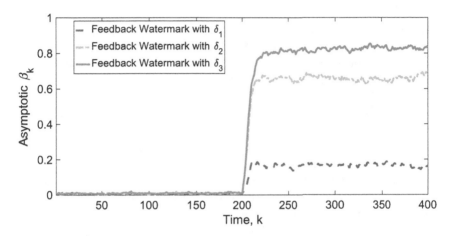

Fig. 5. Comparisons between feedback watermark with different δs.

replay them between time 201 and time 400. The results are the average of 1000 times experiments.

From Fig. 3, one can see that feedback watermark is more effective than the ordinary one. We wish to investigate the detection rates with different Qs. To do this, we set $\delta = 2$ and $Q_1 = 0.1$, $Q_1 = 0.2$, $Q_1 = 0.3$. From Fig. 4, one can find that a larger Q can lead a larger detection rate.

To better illustrate the effect of the upper bound δ, we set $\delta_1 = 2$, $\delta_2 = 4$, $\delta_3 = 6$. In this case, $Q = 0.1$. It is important to recall here that a larger δ means the system can endure a larger noise. It is immediately seen from Fig. 5, a larger δ is beneficial to the detection rates. However, the choice of a larger δ increases the uncertainty of the whole system.

We also give a diagram Fig. 6 demonstrating the detection rates with different parameters. A system designer can choose the feedback control function according to this diagram.

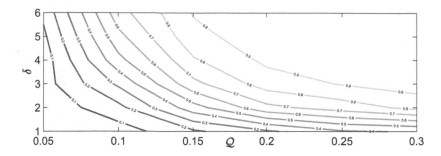

Fig. 6. Detection rates with different Qs and δs.

Finally, it is worth pointing out here that our feedback approach can be utilized to generate dependent watermark in [11]. Moreover, other works mentioned in the introduction mainly focus on other scenarios. Hence, we omit the other comparisons here.

6 Conclusions

In this paper, a feedback watermark approach has been designed to detect malicious replay attacks. First, the effects of replay attacks have been analyzed. Then, we discussed the LQG performance loss after adding feedback watermark. It has been proved that the detector output converge to a steady point when a class of feedback function is utilized, meaning that our approach is more effective than the ordinary watermark. Finally, we have shown the validity of feedback watermarks with a numerical example. However, since the feedback function can be designed in different forms, we will explore more efficient feedback functions in future work.

References

1. Anderson, B., Moore, J.B.: Optimal filtering. Prentice-Hall, Englewood Cliffs (1979)
2. Berstekas, D.P.: Dynamic programming and optimal control. Athena scientific (1995)
3. De Persis, C., Tesi, P.: Input-to-state stabilizing control under denial-of-service. IEEE Trans. Autom. Control **60**(11), 2930–2944 (2015)
4. Fang, C., Qi, Y., Cheng, P., Zheng, W.X.: Optimal periodic watermarking schedule for replay attack detection in cyber-physical systems. Automatica **112**, 108698 (2020). https://doi.org/10.1016/j.automatica.2019.108698
5. Huang, J., Ho, D.W., Li, F., Yang, W., Tang, Y.: Secure remote state estimation against linear man-in-the-middle attacks using watermarking. Automatica **121**, 109182 (2020). https://doi.org/10.1016/j.automatica.2020.109182
6. Lee, E.A.: Cyber physical systems: design challenges. In: 2008 11th IEEE International Symposium on Object and Component-Oriented Real-Time Distributed Computing, ISORC (2008)

7. Li, Y., Shi, L., Chen, T.: Detection against linear deception attacks on multi-sensor remote state estimation. IEEE Trans. Control Network Syst. **5**(3), 846–856 (2018). https://doi.org/10.1109/TCNS.2017.2648508

8. Li, Y., Shi, L., Cheng, P., Chen, J., Quevedo, D.E.: Jamming attacks on remote state estimation in cyber-physical systems: a game-theoretic approach. IEEE Trans. Autom. Control (2015). https://doi.org/10.1109/TAC.2015.2461851

9. Miao, F., Zhu, Q., Pajic, M., Pappas, G.J.: A hybrid stochastic game for secure control of cyber-physical systems. Automatica **93**, 55–63 (2018). https://doi.org/10.1016/j.automatica.2018.03.012, http://www.sciencedirect.com/science/article/pii/S0005109818300992

10. Mo, Y., Chabukswar, R., Sinopoli, B.: Detecting integrity attacks on SCADA systems. IEEE Trans. Control Syst. Technol. **22**(4), 1396–1407 (2014)

11. Mo, Y., Weerakkody, S., Sinopoli, B.: Physical authentication of control systems: designing watermarked control inputs to detect counterfeit sensor outputs. IEEE Control Syst. Mag. **35**(1), 93–109 (2015)

12. Mo, Y., Sinopoli, B.: Secure control against replay attacks. In: Conference on Communication, Control, and Computing (2009)

13. Langner, R.: To kill a centrifuge a technical analysis of what stuxnet 's creators tried to achieve. Technical report, November 2013. www.langner.com/en/wp-content/uploads/2013/11/To-kill-a-centrifuge.pdf

14. Satchidanandan, B., Kumar, P.R.: Dynamic watermarking: active defense of networked cyber-physical systems. Proc. IEEE **105**(2), 219–240 (2017)

15. Weerakkody, S., Ozel, O., Sinopoli, B.: A bernoulli-gaussian physical watermark for detecting integrity attacks in control systems. In: 2017 55th Annual Allerton Conference on Communication, Control, and Computing, Allerton, pp. 966–973 (2017)

Author Index

Printed in the United States
by Baker & Taylor Publisher Services